HEATH ENGLISH

An Integrated Approach to Writing

10

J. A. Senn
Carol Ann Skinner

HEATH
D.C. Heath and Company
Lexington, Massachusetts • Toronto, Ontario

Editorial Barbara Brennan, Christopher Johnson, Kathleen Kennedy Kelley, Peg McNary

Series Design Robin Herr

Book Design Lisa Anne Fowler, Caroline Bowden

Cover Design Len Massiglia

Production Donna Lee Porter

Acknowledgments start on page 857.

Published simultaneously in Canada

Printed in the United States of America

International Standard Book Number: 0-669-37739-2

2 3 4 5 6 7 8 9 10-KP-98 97 96 95

Consultants and Reviewers

Program Consultant

Henry I. Christ
Former Chairman of the English Department
Andrew Jackson High School
St. Albans, New York

Program Reviewers

Arizona
Patricia Nash
North High School
Chandler Unified School District
Chandler, Arizona

Florida
Carol Alves
Apopka High School
Apopka, Florida

Ohio
Linda Fulton
Lincoln High School
Gahanna, Ohio

Oklahoma
Sandra L. Benson
Edison High School
Tulsa, Oklahoma

Pennsylvania
Bernadette Fenning
Cardinal O'Hara High School
Springfield, Pennsylvania

Tennessee
Alan F. Kaplan
Hume-Fogg Academic High School
Nashville, Tennessee

Texas
Victor Valenzuela
South Grand Prairie High School
Grand Prairie, Texas

Jan W. Blount
Berkner High School
Richardson, Texas

Contents

Unit 1
Exploring the Writer's Craft

SAVE THE DOGS

Unit 2
Achieving the Writer's Purpose

Unit 3 Applying Communication and Study Skills

Unit 4 Language Skills Resource

Grammar

Usage

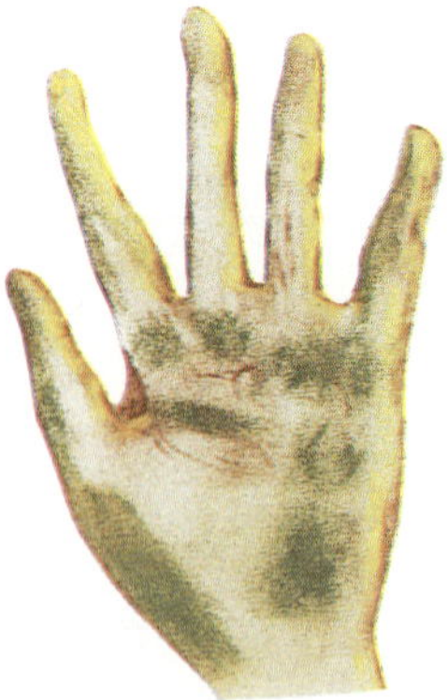

f a 1956
magination of the
ells of receiving a sudden
hours is "about the best you c
d pilot who had had consid
ca. Her bravery handling
our imagination
speaks of
lphabet, nor t
continents: The
an airplane can
night. You are the stre
ecurity of solitud
the win

Unit 1
Exploring the Writer's Craft

Chapter

1 The Writing Process

Part 1 Reading to Write

THEME: *Identity*

A person's identity is like a plant, changing and growing throughout a lifetime. Think of the identity you have right now with your family members, your friends, your teachers, your coaches, and your guidance counselor. Is your identity the same for all these people? How does it differ? Are you pleased with it? Are you interested in changing it?

These are some of the questions about identity that people ask themselves—and often try to answer by writing. For one person the question may take the form of a poem entitled "Who Am I?" For another the answer might emerge in a personal essay exploring the meaning of a childhood incident. Part of the fun and excitement of writing is investigating what your opinions are, what experiences have changed you, and what your goals are.

As you learn about the writing process in this chapter, you will be asked to write about the theme of identity. Before you start writing, though, read the four poems that follow. In them you will find four very different views on this matter of identity. As you read, think about what each poem is saying to *you*.

Identity

Julio Noboa Polanco

Let them be as flowers,
always watered, fed, guarded, admired,
but harnessed to a pot of dirt.

I'd rather be a tall, ugly weed,
clinging on cliffs, like an eagle
wind-wavering above high, jagged rocks.

To have broken through the surface of stone,
to live, to feel exposed to the madness
of the vast, eternal sky.
To be swayed by the breezes of an ancient sea,
carrying my soul, my seed, beyond the mountains of time
or into the abyss of the bizarre.

I'd rather be unseen, and if
then shunned by everyone,
than to be a pleasant-smelling flower,
growing in clusters in the fertile valley,
where they're praised, handled, and plucked
by greedy, human hands.

I'd rather smell of musty, green stench
than of sweet, fragrant lilac.
If I could stand alone, strong and free,
I'd rather be a tall, ugly weed.

Theme for English B

Langston Hughes

The instructor said,

Go home and write
a page tonight.
And let that page come out of you—
Then, it will be true.

I wonder if it's that simple?
I am twenty-two, colored, born in Winston-Salem.
I went to school there, then Durham, then here
to this college on the hill[1] above Harlem.
I am the only colored student in my class.
The steps from the hill lead down into Harlem,
through a park, then I cross St. Nicholas,
Eighth Avenue, Seventh, and I come to the Y,
the Harlem Branch Y, where I take the elevator
up to my room, sit down, and write this page:

It's not easy to know what is true for you or me
at twenty-two, my age. But I guess I'm what
I feel and see and hear, Harlem, I hear you:
hear you, hear me—we two—you, me, talk on this page.
(I hear New York, too.) Me—who?

Well, I like to eat, sleep, drink, and be in love.
I like to work, read, learn, and understand life.
I like a pipe for a Christmas present,
or records—Bessie,[2] bop, or Bach.

I guess being colored doesn't make me *not* like
the same things other folks like who are other races.
So will my page be colored that I write?
Being me, will not be white.
But it will be
a part of you, instructor.
You are white—
yet a part of me, as I am a part of you.
That's American.
Sometimes perhaps you don't want to be a part of me.
Nor do I often want to be a part of you.
But we are, that's true!
As I learn from you,
I guess you learn from me—
although you're older—and white—
and somewhat more free.

This is my page for English B.

1. **college on the hill:** Columbia University in Manhattan.
2. **Bessie** (1893–1937)**:** Bessie Smith, the celebrated jazz and blues singer.

I'm Nobody

Emily Dickinson

I'm nobody! Who are you?
Are you nobody, too?
Then there's a pair of us—don't tell!
They'd banish us, you know.

How dreary to be somebody!
How public, like a frog
To tell your name the livelong day
To an admiring bog.

Mirror

John Updike

When you look
into a mirror
it is not
yourself you see,
but a kind
of apish error
posed in fearful
symmetry.

kool uoy nehW
rorrim a otni
ton si ti
,ees uoy flesruoy
dnik a tub
rorre hsipa fo
lufraef ni desop
.yrtemmys

Responding to the Theme

Identity

Responding in Your Journal For your journal choose a loose-leaf notebook. Then, if some of your entries are too personal to share with your teacher, you can remove them before turning your journal in for review. Start each entry with the date; and, if you are writing about a piece of literature, include the title and author of the selection. (*See page 13 for more about journals.*)

In the second stanza of Langston Hughes's poem "Theme for English B," the student states, "But I guess I'm what I feel and see and hear." For the next several days, use your journal to investigate what you feel and see and hear. Set aside three pages in your journal and write one of these heads on each page: *Feelings, Sights, Sounds.* Today choose one page and write about the feelings, sights, or sounds that you observe within the period of time you are writing. Respond on the other pages on following days.

Speaking and Listening With your teacher's permission, work in a group of five or more. Select readers to read aloud Julio Polanco's poem "Identity" and Emily Dickinson's "I'm Nobody, Who Are You?" Then discuss the poets' positions on personal independence and fame. Have each person in the group explain why he or she agrees or disagrees with the convictions of the poets. Assign a recorder to take notes and present your group's findings to the class.

Critical Thinking: Analyzing Write a paragraph analyzing the generalization from "Theme for English B" that you are ". . . yet a part of me as I am a part of you. That's American."

Extending Your Vocabulary John Updike's poem is a clever representation of what happens when you look in the mirror. One of the startling images he uses to describe this experience is *apish error.* Consult a dictionary for the meaning of *apish.* Then extend your vocabulary by creating a list of verbs and adjectives that use animal names as their roots. You may use a dictionary. Save your list in your journal and use some of these words in a composition.

EXAMPLE	Adjectives	Verbs
	dogmatic	buffalo
	fishy	bear

Mirror and Plastic, Michael de Camp

Part 2 *Writing*

In each of the poems you have read, each person reveals an insight about personal identity. How did Polanco and the other three poets achieve such creative insights about identity? Creativity is always something of a mystery, but it is safe to say that the poets went through a *process*. That is, they started by exploring their ideas and then worked on expressing those ideas in new and interesting ways—until they got their poems just right.

This chapter will help you explore *your* ideas by showing a process for writing—a way to plan, draft, revise, edit, and publish your work. You will not *always* follow these steps in the same order for each composition you are working on. For instance, you may get an inspiration for your introduction and draft it even before you have finished planning the rest of the composition. As you study the needs and progress of your composition, you may even decide to return to the planning stage if you are not pleased with the early drafts. Writers, then, rarely march step-by-step through the writing process as if they were taking part in a military drill. Instead, they recognize the flexibility of the writing process and move in and out of the various stages of the process as needed.

This chapter will also teach some writing strategies that have been successful for many writers. You will have an opportunity to practice these strategies and choose those that work best for you.

The Writing Process

The following diagram illustrates the different stages of the writing process. Notice that the diagram loops back and forth. This looping shows how writers often move back and forth between various stages instead of going step-by-step from beginning to end. They can go back to any stage until they are satisfied with the quality of their writing.

Prewriting includes all the planning steps that you can take before you write the first draft. During prewriting you find a subject, develop it, and organize the details.

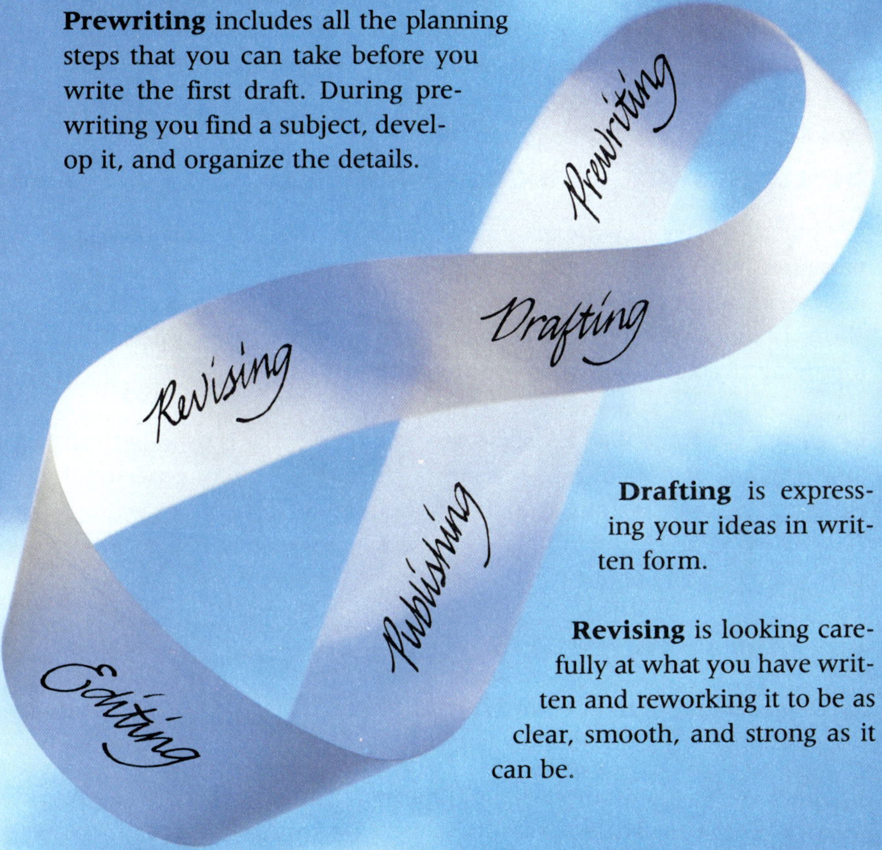

Drafting is expressing your ideas in written form.

Revising is looking carefully at what you have written and reworking it to be as clear, smooth, and strong as it can be.

Editing means checking your final draft for mistakes in grammar, usage, spelling, and mechanics and correcting any errors you may find.

Publishing means presenting your finished work to others in an appropriate way.

Prewriting

Writing Process

The novelist Ernest Hemingway wrote, "My working habits are simple: long periods of thinking, short periods of writing." As Hemingway knew, much of the work in producing a good piece of writing takes place before the writer ever sits down and actually drafts the story, article, or essay.

Prewriting occurs before you write the first draft. During prewriting you plan your work—decide on a subject, think of ideas, gather information, and organize your material. As you plan, it is a good idea to keep a writing folder in which you can store your prewriting notes and any other pieces of writing you wish to save.

Strategies for Thinking of Subjects

Subjects for writing are all around you—in current events, in conversations with friends, in the day-to-day life of your family, in sporting events, and on the television and radio. Finding subjects to write about is simply a matter of keeping your mind and eyes open. The following strategies will help you do both.

Drawing on Personal Experience Good writing is usually fresh and original. If you draw on material from your unique personal experiences, your writing is bound to be convincing and appealing. The following activity will help you discover 15 writing subjects that only *you* can write about well.

WRITING ACTIVITY 1 *Exploring Personal Experience*

Answer each question as completely as you can. Be sure to save your notes in your writing folder for later use.

1. What three people have played the most important roles in my life? What has each done to direct me along my current path?
2. What three national problems (poverty, pollution, racism, for example) seem to have the greatest impact on my life? What is that impact? What can I do about it?
3. What three subjects do I always like to read about? Why?
4. What three talents or skills do I have?
5. What two interests have I had for most of my life? What new interest have I developed in recent years?

Writing Is Thinking

Critical Thinking

Recalling

Your writing can be original and convincing if you enrich it with as many details from your past as possible. If you concentrate, you can **recall** a surprising number of details from half-forgotten scenes from your own life. Just think of your memory as a photographic film. All of your experiences have made an impression on the mind's film; and everything you have ever seen, touched, tasted, smelled, or heard has left an impression, however slight, in your memory.

The challenge is to learn to develop some of the images stored in your mind and to use them to enliven your writing. For instance, concentrate on the last year and recall an experience you have had. Perhaps you visited an underground cave such as Mammoth Cave in Kentucky. Make a chart like the following to help you recall a past experience. Next to each heading, list all the details you can recall.

Recalling a Visit to Mammoth Cave

Sight	huge room, pale light, dark shadows, stalactites, stalagmites, tourists' faces
Sound	echoes/voices, dripping, guide's voice
Touch	cool, clammy, sticky hands, limp clothes
Smell/Taste	musty, odor of sulphur gas (like rotten eggs)
My Reaction	awe, curiosity, uneasiness; fear of large, dark places

Thinking Practice Choose one of the following topics or another from your past and list as many details as you can recall. Make a chart like the one above to help unlock your memories.

1. The first time I ever went swimming
2. My first dance
3. A childhood birthday party

Freewriting Another good way to unlock subject ideas is to use the strategy of *freewriting*—writing as quickly and freely as you can. As you write, do not pause to reflect. Instead, let one idea lead to another.

Student Model: *Freewriting*

> I don't feel that I have much to say, but I'll keep writing so one idea will lead to another. How could anyone not like music? I really love rock music. Right now I wish English class were over and school were out for the day because I can't wait to go to that rock band rehearsal tonight. I get a kick out of seeing Dave and the other guys practice their songs with guitars and other instruments.

By writing whatever was on her mind, this student writer soon found her thoughts focusing on a rehearsal by a rock band. She had the first glimmer of a very promising subject to write about.

Freewriting can also be done on a specified subject. This type of writing, called *focused freewriting,* is another good way to let one idea lead to another—sometimes with surprising results.

WRITING ACTIVITY 2 *Freewriting*

For five minutes practice the strategy of freewriting by writing down everything that passes through your mind. Relax and let your mind run free. If you come to a dead end, write *anything* that comes to mind—even if it is *"I don't know what to write about."* At the end of five minutes, stop writing and place your work in your writing folder for later use.

WRITING ACTIVITY 3 *Focused Freewriting*

This time freewrite for five minutes on the subject of why music is important in your life. Start by focusing on that subject alone but then let your mind take you where it will. Because you may have an idea you could develop further, save your work in your writing folder.

Keeping a Journal Another good way to discover worthwhile writing subjects is to keep a journal. A *journal* is a notebook in which daily entries are made. The types of entries can vary widely, from simple recall of the day's events to more complex analyses of your thoughts, feelings, relationships, hopes, and dreams. Your journal will become a rich resource to mine for writing ideas.

In this textbook you will also use your journal in other ways. The chart below outlines some additional purposes for the journal.

Additional Uses of the Journal

RESPONDING TO LITERATURE

A journal is a good place to write your responses and reactions to books, stories, poems, and other literature. After reading each literature selection in this book, you will have the opportunity to use your journal for this purpose, as you did on page 7. Be sure to begin each entry with the author's name and the title of the selection.

LEARNING LOG

The Learning Log is a special section of your journal where you can write down ideas and information about math, science, history, health, or any other subject that you find particularly interesting to write about.

PERSONALIZED EDITING CHECKLIST

Personalized Editing Checklist is a section of your journal where you can keep a list of errors that recur in your writing. You might include words you frequently misspell, usage mistakes, mechanical errors, and so forth. When you edit a composition, you should refer to this checklist. *(See page 36 for more information about the Personalized Editing Checklist.)*

WRITING ACTIVITY 4 *Writing in Your Journal*

"Most of the basic material a writer works with," wrote Willa Cather, an American novelist, "is acquired before the age of fifteen." Over the next several days, write in your journal about the "basic material" of your life. Remember to date each entry. You may wish to use the questions on the next page as guides.

1. What title would you use in a novel about your life? Why?
2. If you could make a movie about just *one* important time in your life, which time would it be? Why? Tell about the setting, plot, actors, and special effects, if any, in your movie.
3. If you were going to paint a self-portrait, what would it look like? What pose would you place yourself in? What setting? What would you be wearing? What expression would be on your face? What would the portrait reveal about you?

Exploring Literature for Writing Ideas In addition to finding ideas for writing in your interests and experiences, you can also discover excellent subjects for writing in your reading. Here are some strategies for finding writing ideas in literature.

Exploring Literature for Writing Ideas

FICTION, POETRY, AND DRAMA

1. Write about a piece of literature, exploring plot, character, setting, author's style, or some other aspect of the literature. *(See "Writing Essays about Literature" on pages 298–337.)*
2. Write about the theme, or central message, of a story, poem, or play. If the story deals with family relations, for instance, you may be able to write a story or an essay about your family.
3. After reading a story or a play, write about some aspect of one of the characters. For instance, if one of the characters in the story is poor, you may want to write an editorial, a poem, or a story about how a person triumphs over poverty.

NONFICTION

1. Decide whether you agree or disagree with an editorial in a newspaper.
2. Look through newspapers and magazines to find issues or subjects that you could explore and write about.
3. Think about biographies and autobiographies that you have read. Write about the subject of any of them.

WRITING ACTIVITY 5 *Exploring Literature*

Read an article or an editorial in today's newspaper. Then list five subjects that you could write about and save your work.

Choosing and Limiting a Subject

Exploring your interests, freewriting, journal writing, and exploring literature are all ongoing activities that will help you find a suitable writing subject. At any time you can look back over what you have produced and select the most promising subject.

How can you tell, though, which of your subjects is most promising? In general, look for a subject that you would like to write about. The following guidelines for choosing a subject will help you select from among many good ideas the one that is best for each writing occasion.

Guidelines for Choosing a Subject

1. Choose a subject that genuinely interests you.
2. Choose a subject that will most likely capture the interest of your readers.
3. Choose a subject you can cover thoroughly through your own knowledge or through a reasonable amount of research.

WRITING ACTIVITY **6** *Writing on Your Own*

WRITING ABOUT THE THEME

Reread the poems at the beginning of this chapter and review all the prewriting work in your writing folder and journal that you have done so far. Look carefully for promising subjects about the theme of identity and jot down between five and ten such subjects suggested by your prewriting work. For instance, you might want to write about a special interest, talent, or experience. Use numbers to rank each subject according to how well it fulfills the guidelines above. After eliminating all your average and weak ideas, think carefully about each of the strong subjects. Then choose one you would most like to write about. Circle this subject and save the results in your writing folder.

Limiting a Subject Once you have selected your subject, you may have to limit it so that it is more manageable. For example, a very broad subject like "the federal government" or "the Olympic games" cannot be covered in a paragraph or a short essay. To limit such a broad subject, use the strategies suggested in the box on the next page.

Limiting a Subject

1. Limit your subject to one person or one example that represents the subject.
2. Limit your subject to a specific time or place.
3. Limit your subject to a specific event.
4. Limit your subject to a specific condition, purpose, or procedure.

Notice how the student writer automatically limited her subject in her freewriting.

SUBJECT	rock music
LIMITED SUBJECT	after-school, rock band rehearsal in friend's basement

WRITING ACTIVITY 7 *Limiting a Subject*

The following subjects are too broad for a paragraph or an essay. On your paper write three limited subjects for each broad subject, using the strategies from the box above.

EXAMPLE	BROAD SUBJECT	aerobic exercise
	LIMITED SUBJECTS	aerobic classes at town hall (place)
		aerobic walking marathon (event)
		aerobic dancing (example)

1. dieting
2. skiing
3. holidays
4. hobbies
5. pollution
6. literature
7. movies
8. sports
9. crafts
10. architecture

Considering Your Purpose and Audience

Before you begin to develop your limited subject, think about your purpose for writing and your audience. Most writing that you do, of course, will have a built-in *purpose,* or reason for writing. The chart on the following page summarizes some of the main purposes for writing and gives examples of each one.

Writing Purposes

- to explain or inform (an essay on a scientific subject)
- to create (a short story, play, or poem)
- to persuade (an editorial)
- to describe (a poem)
- to express your thoughts and feelings (a personal essay)

Your purpose will affect both the content and the language of your writing. For example, if you were writing to inform your audience about a voyage into space, you would use specific details and formal language. However, if your purpose was to entertain your audience with a science-fiction story about space, you might use funny or imaginary details and less formal language. Keep in mind too that writing purposes often overlap. An informative essay may also entertain and describe, while an entertaining short story may also be very persuasive about a social issue.

In addition to establishing your purpose for writing, you should keep in mind your *audience*—the people who will be reading your finished work. The following questions will help you shape your composition to meet the needs of your audience.

Audience Profile Questions

1. Who will be reading my work?
2. How old are they? Are they adults, teens, or children?
3. What background do they have in my subject?
4. What interests and opinions are they likely to have?
5. Are there any words or terms I should define for them?

Audience, like purpose, also affects the content and language of your writing. If you were writing a letter to your mayor complaining about the lack of public basketball courts, you would use formal language and persuasive details. On the other hand, if you were writing a humorous letter to a relative about the same problem, you would most likely use friendly, informal language and very different, amusing details.

WRITING ACTIVITY 8 *Writing for Different Audiences*

1. Write a paragraph describing the athletic facilities of your high school. Assume your audience is a new member of the school committee who is in charge of the Finance Committee.
2. Write a second paragraph describing the same facilities to a foreign student about to arrive for a six-month stay.
3. Compare the two versions. In what ways are they different? In what ways are they the same?

WRITING ACTIVITY 9 *Writing on Your Own*

WRITING ABOUT THE THEME

Look at the subject related to personal identity that you chose in Writing Activity 6. If necessary, limit your subject by using the strategies on page 16. Then choose a purpose for writing about this subject and an appropriate audience. Save your work in your writing folder for later use.

Strategies for Developing a Subject

After choosing and limiting a subject and establishing your purpose and audience, you can begin to collect information such as facts, examples, incidents, and reasons about your subject. The strategies that follow will help you collect interesting and lively details.

Observing A helpful strategy for collecting details about your subject is to use your own powers of observation. Observing is especially useful if your purpose is to describe a person, place, or object. Observing, though, involves more than merely looking. When you observe, open your senses. The sensory impressions—including sights, sounds, smells, tastes, and feelings—associated with a subject are vital to bringing that subject to life. Following are some techniques that will help you gather details through observation.

Techniques for Observing

1. Be aware of why you are observing. Keep in mind your purpose as you decide what and how to observe.
2. Use all your senses. Look, listen, smell, touch, taste.
3. Use your mind. Think about what your observations mean.
4. Observe from different viewpoints. Look at your subject from all angles: near and far, above and below, inside and out.
5. Sketch your subject. Make a drawing of what you observe.
6. Take notes. Keep a record of your observations.

Hand with Reflecting Sphere
M. C. Escher, 1935

WRITING ACTIVITY 10 *Observing*

Observe a person, place, or object that you will later write about. Follow these steps.

1. Review your journal entries and the prewriting notes in your writing folder. Look for subjects to describe—subjects that you can observe in person. You may want to do some additional focused freewriting, starting with the following: *When I think about observing, I think about . . .*
2. Choose a subject, using the guidelines on page 15.
3. Decide on your writing purpose.
4. Observe your subject, using the techniques for observing. Look for details you never noticed before.
5. Place your notes in your writing folder.

Brainstorming for Details Brainstorming for details is another good way to develop your subject. *Brainstorming* means making a simple list of details that come to mind in the order you think of them.

When you brainstorm, do not worry about form or organization. Just write down *everything*—even details that at first seem incidental. In the process of brainstorming, you will unlock one detail after another until you have called to mind many more details than you might have realized you even knew. Following is part of a brainstorming list on the subject of a rock band rehearsal.

Student Model: *Brainstorming a List*

SUBJECT: rock band rehearsal

—wires going everywhere
—giant speakers
—jumble of sounds as musicians tune instruments
—shiny instruments
—lots of knobs on equipment
—colored light beams bouncing off basement walls
—loud metallic sound
—snapping fingers and tapping feet
—thump in stomach as bass guitar and drums begin to pound
—smell of hot lamps

Group Brainstorming When the entire class is writing on the same subject, you can brainstorm in order to generate details about that subject. Usually your teacher will direct you to form a small group of three to five students. The following guidelines will help you.

Guidelines for Group Brainstorming

1. Set a time limit on the brainstorming session.
2. Write the subject on a piece of paper and assign one group member to be the recorder. If your group meets frequently, take turns recording ideas.
3. Start brainstorming for details—such as facts, reasons, and examples. Since you can eliminate irrelevant ideas later, contribute any and all ideas.
4. Build on others' ideas by adding to them or modifying them to make them better.
5. Avoid criticizing the ideas of other group members.

When you have finished brainstorming, get a copy of all the ideas from the group recorder and select only those ideas and facts that are most appropriate for your own composition.

WRITING ACTIVITY 11 *Group Brainstorming*

With your teacher's permission, form a small group and brainstorm to find a clever title for a new television comedy about a songwriting team—a sophomore from an American high school and a fifteen-year-old from outer space. Think of at least five possible titles. Then brainstorm again to decide how the two characters should meet in the first episode. Using your best ideas, write a simple plot outline for the first episode. Save your work in your writing folder.

Clustering *Clustering*—another form of brainstorming—is an especially good strategy for developing details. Rather than listing ideas, however, when you cluster, you connect them. You begin with a single word or phrase enclosed in a box or circle and then arrange associated ideas around that nucleus, linking the ideas to the original word or phrase. You then go on to link each of the these words or phrases, in turn, to other words as they occur. In the end you have a diagram that provides you not only with details, but groups—or clusters—of related details. Following is a cluster on the subject of observing a rock band rehearsal.

Student Model: *Cluster*

WRITING ACTIVITY 12 *Clustering*

Use the clustering technique to brainstorm on the subject of your achievements at home, at school, and in your community. Write the words *my achievements* in a box in the middle of your paper. Then write whatever comes to mind and circle your ideas. Connect related ideas with lines. Save your work in your writing folder.

Inquiring You can also develop supporting details by using the strategy of *inquiring*, or asking questions. Through inquiring—especially with questions that begin with *who, what, where, why, when,* and *how*—you will find answers that will help you develop your subject. Suppose, for example, you were writing on the subject of how scientists study past cultures that have no written records. You might think of the following questions.

Student Model: *Inquiring to Develop Details*

SUBJECT: scientists and prehistory
Who are some of the scholars learning about prehistory?
What clues did early people leave behind?
Where are these clues found?
Why study early people?
When did scientists first study prehistory?
How are the ages of clues determined?

The answers to these questions would be valuable details to use in your composition.

WRITING ACTIVITY 13 *Inquiring*

Think of ten questions you could ask to help develop details on the subject of how teenagers are portrayed in movies today. Be sure to use each of the six question words listed on the previous page at least once.

WRITING ACTIVITY 14 *Writing on Your Own*

WRITING ABOUT THE THEME

Go back to the subject related to identity that you selected in Writing Activity 9. Think of facts, examples, incidents, reasons, and other specifics by using prewriting strategies that you have just learned. Continue your work until you feel you have thought of all possible details. Save your work in your writing folder for later use.

Strategies for Organizing Your Details

In order to collect ideas and details about your subject, you have let your mind run free through such activities as brainstorming, clustering, and observing. Now it is time to provide a focus, or main idea, and to organize your ideas so that they will make sense to a reader. The following strategies will help you do just that.

Focusing Your Subject Before you can decide how best to organize your details, you need to zero in on an exact focus, or main idea, for your composition. To do so, simply ask yourself what you want to say about your subject. For example, you might think of a meaningful generalization that can be drawn from the specifics you have developed in your prewriting work. This main idea will help you organize your entire composition.

After deciding on a main idea, think once again about your purpose and audience. Is your main idea appropriate for your purpose and audience? If not, refocus and change your main idea to make it more suitable for the purpose you need to accomplish and the readers you need to reach.

The student who brainstormed and clustered her observations of her friends' rock band rehearsal chose as her main idea her impression that rock bands give off feelings of great confusion and power. She established that her writing purpose was to inform and entertain and that her audience was her classmates. Her main idea, then, suited both her purpose and audience.

WRITING ACTIVITY 15 *Writing on Your Own*

WRITING ABOUT THE THEME

Look over your work from Writing Activity 14 on the theme of identity. If you do not already have one in mind, choose a focus, or main idea, from among your prewriting notes. Then write that main idea on a sheet of paper and place it in your writing folder for future use.

Grouping Your Details When you look over the details that will support your main idea, you will probably see that they fall into several groups, or categories. For example, if you were writing about your interests, you might see that your supporting details break down into such large categories as swimming, music, computers, and movies. Some of this grouping automatically occurs in clustering. For example, the sample cluster on page 22 shows three categories of details—sounds, sights, and feelings—for observing the rock band rehearsal. Grouping your supporting details in logical categories will help your reader easily follow your thoughts. You may also see that, because certain details do not fall into any category, they should be eliminated.

Ordering Your Details Finally, after grouping your supporting details in categories, decide on the best order to use. The following chart shows some common ways to order material.

Methods of Ordering Supporting Details

CHRONOLOGICAL	Arranges events according to when they happened
SPATIAL	Arranges details according to their location (near to far, etc.)
ORDER OF IMPORTANCE, SIZE, OR DEGREE	Arranges details according to degrees of importance, size, etc.

After deciding on the best order in which to present your supporting details in your composition, make a simple list or chart showing the details in that order. The following list shows the order in which the student writing about the rock band rehearsal chose to present her details. Because she wanted to give the feeling of the rehearsal from start to finish, she chose chronological order.

Student Model: *Chronological Order of Details*

When I first arrived
- dark basement
- wires going everywhere
- giant speakers
- shiny instruments
- musicians tuning
- lots of knobs on equipment
- jumble of sounds
- colorful, offbeat clothes

Once rehearsal was underway
- colored lights flashing
- loud metallic twang of guitars
- pounding drums
- excited thump in stomach

During intermission
- feelings of confusion
- worry about noise level

After Intermission
- wail of voices
- snapping fingers and tapping feet

When rehearsal ended
- cheering, stamping, and whistling

Four Corrugated Cubes from One
Robert Cumming, 1980

WRITING ACTIVITY 16 *Organizing Details*

For each of the following composition subjects, decide which method of organization would be most appropriate. Indicate your answer by writing *chronological, spatial,* or *order of importance or degree* after the proper number.

1. reasons that people should avoid smoking
2. description of sky theater at the planetarium
3. story about the first time you tried to sew
4. news account of an earthquake
5. the tallest buildings in the United States

WRITING ACTIVITY 17 *Writing on Your Own*

WRITING ABOUT THE THEME

Return to the main idea you chose in Writing Activity 15 and your prewriting notes. Group your supporting details into categories, if appropriate. Then decide on the best possible order in which to present your supporting details and make a simple list of them in that order. Save all your work in your writing folder.

Drafting

During the drafting stage of the writing process, you review all the prewriting work you have done and put your ideas and supporting details into complete sentences. As you write your first draft, you will soon be able to tell whether you have a workable subject or whether you need to go back and rethink your ideas. Follow these strategies to produce your first draft.

Strategies for Drafting

1. Write an introduction that will capture the reader's interest and express your main idea.
2. After you write your introduction, use your organized prewriting notes as a guide but depart from those notes when a good idea occurs to you.
3. Write fairly quickly. Do not worry about spelling or phrasing. You will have the opportunity to go back and fix such problems when you revise.
4. Stop frequently and read what you have written. This practice will help you move logically from one thought to the next as you draft.
5. Try to write a conclusion that drives home to the reader the main point of the composition.

Composing a Title After you have completed your first draft, think of several possible titles for your composition. A good title should interest and inform your audience and also arouse your reader's curiosity. At the same time, a title must give some idea of the subject matter of your paragraph or essay. The student who wrote the sample draft decided on the title "Rock Band at Work."

WRITING ACTIVITY 18 *Writing on Your Own*

WRITING ABOUT THE THEME

Review all the work related to the theme of identity that you have done so far in developing your composition. Using the plan you developed in Writing Activity 17, draft your composition. From time to time, read over what you have written to make sure your ideas are logically organized. Then compose a title. Save your draft in your writing folder.

The sample below shows the first draft of a composition on the subject of a rock band rehearsal. There are, of course, a number of mechanical errors in the draft that will be fixed later.

Student Model: *First Draft*

Rock Band at Work

I am watching the rehearsal of a rock band. It is an interesting experience, to say the least. Your senses get hit from almost every direction, untill you feel almost over powered by the experience.

When you first come into the room you see wirse go everywhere, and giant speakers rising up off the floor like skyscrapers. You also see the musician's shiney instruments and the colorful, offbeat clothes they usualy wear. In the dark basement, you seem to be in another world. Along with the wires going everywhere there are lots of knobs on the fancy electronic equiptment the musicians plays.

When the sounds start coming up, the feeling of confusion are made even stronger. When the musicians tune up, playing little bits and peices of songs all at the same time. The noise sounds like a very strange jumble of sounds.

The overwhelming feeling once the rehearsal actually started was one of loudness, of a piercing metallic sound. The room was soundproofed, sort of, but the lead guitar player's father still complained about the noise. When you're sitting soclose, the music seems to take you over completely. You feel a thump in your stomach with the pounding of the Bass guitar and drums. I felt a need to tap my foot and move my body in rhythm, almost like I could'nt control myself.

By the time the rehearsal was over, I felt I had been transported to a different level of existance. To hear the loud, driving beat, to see the crazy blend of shiny instruments and scruffy clothes, feeling the music take over my body was experiences I will never for get.

Revising

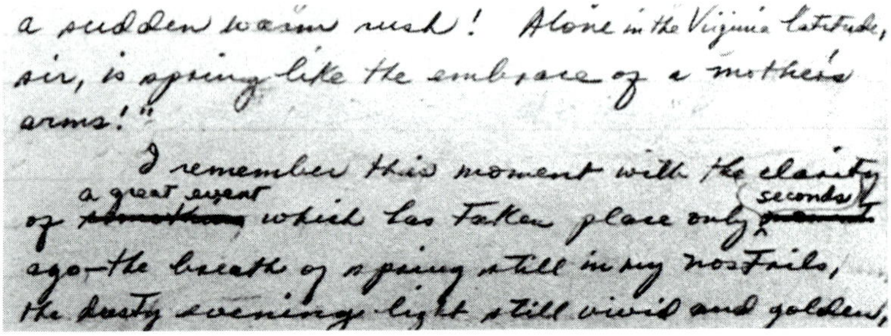
a sudden warm rush! Alone in the Virginia latitude,
sir, is spring like the embrace of a mother's
arms!"
I remember this moment with the clarity
of ~~something~~ a great event which has taken place only ~~moments~~ seconds
ago—the breath of spring still in my nostrils,
the dusty evening light still vivid and golden,

from *Confessions of Nat Turner,* William Styron

The writer Dorothy Canfield Fisher once remarked, "Very young writers often do not revise at all . . . They are hypnotized by what they have written. 'How can it be altered?' they think. 'That's the way it was written.' Well, it has to be altered. You have to learn how. That is chiefly what English classes can teach you."

Revising means "seeing again." When writers revise, they stand back from their work and "see it again" with fresh, new eyes. To do this, you should put your first draft away for a few days. Then you will be able to read it over and evaluate it objectively. Reading the composition aloud will also help you evaluate it, because you can often hear awkward sentence structure and other problems.

Revising on Your Own

Some of the strategies for revising that writers use are described below. You may need to use some of these techniques more than others or vary them according to your writing needs.

Adding Ideas As you look over your draft, ask yourself the following questions. Have you covered every aspect of the subject? Are your ideas fresh and original enough to interest your audience? Have you explored the subject in depth, not just superficially? If not, you may need to think of new ideas. Freewrite about the subject or discuss it with someone more knowledgeable about the subject than you.

Adding Supporting Details Look over your draft again. Have you fully developed your subject? Have you included enough supporting details? Are the supporting details specific enough to make your ideas clear and interesting? Add whatever seems to be lacking.

Rearranging Check the organization of your ideas and details. Are all your details in the proper order? Does one idea lead to another so that the reader can easily follow your train of thought? If not, rearrange your material so that one idea flows logically into another.

Deleting Unnecessary Words or Details Is all the information you have provided necessary? Have you avoided repeating yourself unnecessarily? Are all the details related to the main point? If not, delete any unnecessary words or details.

Substituting Stronger Words and More Varied Sentences Once again read over your draft. If any part seems confusing, think of a clearer way to express the same idea. Replace any dull, boring words and phrases with more original ones. Use vivid adjectives, strong action verbs, and the active voice instead of the passive voice. Vary your sentence structure and length to keep from sounding monotonous.

Using a Revision Checklist Using a revision checklist like the one below is a handy way to see whether your latest draft has all the qualities of a good composition. Throughout the composition chapters in this book, you will find several revision checklists that guide you through the revising stage. Personalize these checklists by adding or modifying items to suit your writing needs.

Revision Checklist

1. Did you clearly state your main idea?
2. Does your composition have a strong introduction, body, and conclusion?
3. Did you include enough interesting details to explore your subject in depth and support your main idea?
4. Did you present your ideas in a logical order?
5. Do any of your sentences stray from the main idea?
6. Are your ideas clearly explained?
7. Are your words specific?
8. Are any words or ideas repeated unnecessarily?
9. Are your sentences varied and smoothly connected?
10. Is the purpose of your composition clear?
11. Is your writing suited to your audience?
12. Is your title effective?

WRITING ACTIVITY 19 *Studying a Revision*

Carefully read the following portion of a revised draft on the rock band rehearsal. (Any remaining errors in spelling, capitalization, and usage will be corrected later.) Then write answers to the following questions.

1. Which detail was deleted?
2. Which idea was out of place?
3. Point out three places where additional information and/or details were added.
4. Point out one example of a strong word that replaced a weaker one.

Student Model: *Revision*

Rock Band at Work

~~I am~~ watching the rehearsal of a rock band. ~~It~~ is an
unforgetable
~~interesting~~ experience, ~~to say the least~~. Your senses get
bombarded.
~~hit~~ from ~~almost~~ every direction, untill you feel almost
over powered by the experience.

When you first come into the room you see wirse go
everywhere, and giant speakers rising up off the floor
Monitors and high-tech equipment crowd the room
like skyscrapers. ~~You also see~~ the musician's shiney
– glossy red guitars and silverey drums – twinkles.
instruments ~~and~~ the colorful, offbeat clothes they usualy
are like uniforms. All wear a Diamond-like earring
wear. ~~In the dark basement, you seem to be in another~~
in one ear, a T-shirt with SAVE THE DOGS across the
~~world. Along with wires going everywhere there are lots of~~
front, and jeans with knees worn out.
~~knobs on the fancy electronic equiptment the musicians~~
~~plays.~~

WRITING ACTIVITY **20** *Using a Revision Checklist*

Using the checklist on page 31 and the strategies suggested on pages 30–31, revise the following paragraph, written for the purpose of informing a tenth-grade audience.

Imaging

More and more people are beginning to appreciate and realize the value of imaging. Imaging is very widely used by people who are in competitive fields. Imaging is a technique by which you use all the mental powers of your brain to visualize yourself in a positive situation. If you are preparing for a hard and difficult test, you concentrate on picturing yourself answering every question with confidence. You picture yourself handing in the test early. Of course nothing beats studying hard as a way to do well on a test. A high jumper will picture himself or herself going over that bar. Top-rated athletes use imaging all the time to help themselves achieve their goals. Some say that about 80 percent of their training time is given to imaging. A field-goal kicker will picture the ball going through the goal posts. The mental picture becomes so strong that failure no longer seems to be a possibility. Anyone can learn the secrets of imaging and use them to advantage in stressful or competitive situations in life.

Revising through Conferencing

Conferencing is another excellent strategy you can use for revising. Conferencing is a meeting for a variety of purposes, such as sharing information, identifying and resolving problems, and evaluating one another's work.

One way to conference is to use a test reader. Ask a friend, family member, or classmate to read your draft and tell you specifically what was good and what could be improved. When your reader responds, do not try to defend your work. Just listen to the comments. Afterward you should decide which suggestions are worth taking.

Peer Conferencing Another way to conference is to form a small group with three or four other students and read one another's drafts. Then take turns discussing each person's draft, offering praise for what each person has done well and providing suggestions to make the drafts better.

Whether you choose to conference with only one other person or in a small group, the following guidelines will help you get the most out of this revising technique.

Guidelines for Conferencing

1. Read your partner's work carefully.
2. Start your comments by saying something positive like "Your introduction made me really curious to read more!"
3. Be specific. Refer to the specific word, sentence, or section of the composition when you make a comment.
4. Phrase your criticisms as questions. For example, if you think the introduction was weak, ask, "What can you say that might better capture your audience's attention?"

WRITING ACTIVITY 21 *Writing on Your Own*

WRITING ABOUT THE THEME

If your teacher permits, exchange with a classmate your first draft from Writing Activity 18 and refer to the guidelines above to assist your peer conferencing. Then, mindful of your partner's remarks, finish revising your draft. Use any of the following revision strategies that your composition requires.

- add ideas
- add more details or information
- rearrange ideas
- delete unnecessary words or ideas
- substitute stronger words and more varied sentences
- use a revision checklist

Editing and Publishing

Writing Process

Once you have drafted your composition and revised it to your satisfaction, you are ready for the final stages of the writing process. These stages involve editing your composition and making a neat final copy, as well as publishing it.

Strategies for Editing

By the time you reach the editing stage, you will have a draft that reflects your best effort. Along the way you probably tried to follow all the rules you know for correct mechanics, but for the most part you concentrated—rightly so—on the *content* of your composition rather than on its form. Now that you are satisfied with your content, however, you need to correct errors in grammar, usage, mechanics, and spelling. Such errors can ruin the good impression you have tried to make in your writing.

Using an Editing Checklist When you edit, you should slowly proofread your work at least three times, concentrating on one kind of error at a time. For example, read each sentence first for errors in usage, such as agreement of subject and verb, consistency of verb tense, agreement of pronoun and antecedent, and comparison of adjectives and adverbs. *(See Usage unit, pages 658–753.)* Then read each sentence a second time, looking for spelling problems. *(See pages 470–479.)* Finally, read over your paper and check for errors in punctuation and capitalization. *(See Mechanics unit, pages 754–829.)* The Editing Checklist below will help you concentrate on particular types of errors.

Editing Checklist

1. Are your sentences completely free of errors in grammar and usage?
2. Did you spell each word correctly?
3. Did you use capital letters where needed?
4. Did you punctuate each sentence correctly?
5. Did you indent your paragraphs as needed and leave proper margins on each side of the paper? *(See page 41.)*

Creating a Personalized Editing Checklist You may also want to reserve an eight-page section at the end of your journal to use as a Personalized Editing Checklist. *(See page 13.)* Write one of the following headings on every other page: *Grammar Problems, Usage Problems, Spelling Problems, Mechanics Problems* (i.e., capitalization and punctuation). You will then have two pages for each type of problem. Throughout the year record on these pages any mistakes that recur in your writing. Look up those problems in the index and next to each error write the page in this textbook that helps you correct it. It is a good idea to include a few examples of the corrected problem.

Using Proofreading Symbols While editing their work, writers use a shorthand method to correct their errors. Some of the most common symbols of this shorthand, called *proofreading symbols,* are shown in the chart below.

Proofreading Symbols

∧	insert	Meet me ∧at three o'clock.
∧,	insert comma	Hello∧, my name is Claire.
⊙	insert period	Dr⊙Chan told me to call.
℘	delete	Where is ~~is~~ that dog?
¶	new paragraph	¶Before dawn the fog had lifted.
....	let it stand	What ~~surprising~~ news!
#	add space	Jack hit a home#run.
⁀‿	close up	I'll do it my self.
∼	transpose	I did'nt hear the phone ring.
≡	capital letter	The party is on saturday.
/	lowercase letter	Where is the highest Mountain?

The following model shows how a student edited with proofreading symbols.

Student Model: *Editing with Proofreading Symbols*

Rock Band at Work

Watching the rehearsal of a rock band is an unforgetable experience. Your senses ~~get~~ bombarded from every direction, untill you feel almost over powered by the experience.

When you first come into the room you see wirse go everywhere and giant speakers rising ~~up off~~ the floor like skyscrapers. monitors and high-tech equiptment crowd the room The musician's shiney instruments--glossy red guitars and silverey drums--twinkles. The colorful, offbeat clothes ~~they~~ usualy wear are like uniforms. All wear a Diamond-like earring in one ear, a T-shirt with SAVE THE DOGS across the front, and jeans with knees worn out.

WRITING ACTIVITY 22 *Using Proofreading Symbols*

Number your paper 1 to 10. Copy the following paragraph and edit it, using proofreading symbols. There are 10 errors.

What's Next?

I still am not sure what I should do after I graduate from High school. While I plan to go to college I am not ready to start immediately since I love to paint, I want to attend artschool for at least one year. Through out school all my art teachers thought I had talent and they told me to spend more time at my easel. I also want to read and study my favorite artist's techniques. My mom and dad, however, say that I should wait to study art until after I finish college. Its a dilemma!

Language Integrating Skills

Grammar in the Writing Process

Editing

"Go home and write a page tonight. And let that page come out of you—then, it will be true." This is the assignment in the poem "Theme for English B" by Langston Hughes. What words come out of you on a first draft may be *true,* but the agreement among them or their punctuation may not be correct. To correct errors like these is always an important part of the writing process.

When you edit, you pull together, or integrate, what you know about a variety of usage and mechanics skills. As you review different skills in each composition chapter, write them in your Personalized Editing Checklist. Then, at the end of the composition section, you will see that you have covered every major language skill in this book.

Sentence Fragments Some writers begin their editing with subjects and verbs, because they are the foundation of every sentence. If a subject or a verb is missing from a group of words, you no longer have a sentence at all. Instead, you have a *sentence fragment,* or only part of a sentence. Because sentence fragments can create misunderstanding, always check your work for any missing subjects and verbs. *(For more information about fragments and practice in correcting them, see pages 647–651.)*

SENTENCE FRAGMENT	Musicians in worn-out jeans and scruffy sneakers. [The verb is missing. You do not know what the musicians are doing.]
SENTENCE	Musicians in worn-out jeans and scruffy sneakers **are practicing their instruments**.

Subject and Verb Agreement The next logical step in editing is to check if the subject and verb in each sentence agree in number. *Number* refers to whether the subject and the verb are singular (one) or plural (more than one). To agree, therefore, both the subject and the verb must be either singular or plural. *(For more information on the singular and plural endings of subjects and verbs and practice in correcting errors in subject and verb agreement, see pages 705–707.)*

In the following examples, the subject is underlined once, and the verb is underlined twice.

SINGULAR SUBJECT AND VERB	The drummer sits in a chair.
PLURAL SUBJECT AND VERB	The guitar players stand in the front.

Words Interrupting a Subject and Verb Checking for subject and verb agreement, of course, is not always as easy as in the examples above. Sometimes, for instance, words separate the subject from the verb. As a result, you can easily make a mistake by having the verb agree with a nearby word—rather than with the subject. *(For information about other subject-verb agreement problems and practice in correcting them, see pages 707–723.)*

AGREEMENT ERROR	That horn by the speakers belong to Jim. [The verb must agree with the subject *horn,* not with the word *speakers*—even though that word is closer to the verb than the subject is.]
CORRECT AGREEMENT	That horn by the speakers belongs to Jim. [The singular verb *belongs* now agrees with the singular subject *horn.*]

If you want your writing not only to be true but also to be clear and easy to understand, never skip the editing stage of the writing process.

Editing Checklist

1. Are there any sentence fragments? *(See pages 647–651.)*
2. Do the subject and verb in each sentence agree—even if words interrupt them? *(See pages 705–723.)*

WRITING ACTIVITY 23 *Writing on Your Own*

WRITING ABOUT THE THEME

Return to the latest draft of your composition about personal identity that you revised in Writing Activity 21 and edit it, covering specifically the problems in the checklist above. Also review the Editing Checklist on page 35 and your own Personalized Editing Checklist in your journal. *(See pages 13 and 36.)* If you find any errors, streamline your work by using the proofreading symbols on page 36 to correct them. Then save your proofread draft in your writing folder.

Publishing Your Work

Publishing is the final stage in the writing process. When you publish your work, you present it in neat final form to an audience. Of course, some writing is not meant for an audience. Diaries, for example, are written for the sake of the writer. Most writing, however, is an act of communication—of sending a message to someone. As such it would be incomplete without an audience at the receiving end. Publishing your work, therefore, is the best way to deliver your message. The following chart has many good suggestions for publishing.

Ways to Publish Your Writing

1. Display your work on a bulletin board.
2. Present your final draft to the class.
3. Create a class library to which you submit your work. This library is a collection of student writing kept in folders. Each folder is devoted to a certain type of writing (stories, for example, or reports).
4. Submit your composition to the school newspaper, the yearbook, or the school's literary magazine.
5. If your topic is about another subject area, submit your writing to a teacher in that discipline.
6. Enter your composition in a contest. For more information on writing contests, write to National Council of Teachers of English, 1111 Kenyon Road, Urbana, Illinois 61801.
7. Make an audiotape of your work and ask for permission to read it over your school's public address system.
8. Start a writing group with classmates or friends. Read and respond to one another's writing.
9. Present the composition to school or community groups, such as the Scouts, a garden club, or a senior-care center.
10. Make a video based on your written work and send the tape to a local cable television station.
11. Send your writing to a professional—such as a politician, business person, or a television producer—who has an interest in the topic.
12. Write and present a speech to use when running for student office.
13. Start a bulletin board in your school or public library. Post final drafts with visuals.
14. Present a radio program with sound effects.

Using Standard Manuscript Form The appearance of your composition can be almost as important as its content. A sloppy paper that has jagged margins and words crossed out or crowded together is difficult to read. To make a positive impression on your reader, use the following guidelines for standard manuscript form to help you prepare a neat and legible final copy of your composition or report. The finished student composition, "Rock Band at Work," appears on pages 42–43 and shows how standard manuscript form is used.

Standard Manuscript Form

1. Use standard-sized, 8 1/2- by 11-inch, white paper. Use one side of the paper only.
2. If handwriting, use black or blue ink. If typing, use a black typewriter ribbon. Double-space the lines if typing or using a word processor.
3. Leave a 1 1/4-inch margin at the left and a 1-inch margin at the right. The left margin must be even. The right margin should be as even as possible, without too many hyphenated words.
4. Put your name, the course title, the name of your teacher, and the date of the composition in the upper right-hand corner of the first page.
5. Center the title about 2 inches from the top of the first page. Do not underline your title or put quotation marks around it.
6. If handwriting, indent the first line of each paragraph 1 inch. If typing, indent 5 spaces.
7. Leave a 1-inch margin at the bottom of all pages.
8. Starting on page 2, number each page in the upper righthand corner. Begin the first line 1 inch from the top of the page. (If using a word processor, the page number and the heading may appear on each page.)

WRITING ACTIVITY 24 *Writing on Your Own*

WRITING ABOUT THE THEME

Using standard manuscript form, make a neat final copy of your composition about the theme of personal identity. Then use the Ways to Publish Your Writing chart on page 40 to find an appropriate way to publish your work.

Student Model: *Final Draft*

½ inch

2 inches

Roberta Yarns

English 10: Mr. White

March 14, 1992

Rock Band at Work

4 lines

5 spaces

Watching the rehearsal of a rock band is an unforgettable experience. Your senses are bombarded from every direction, until you feel almost overpowered by the experience.

When you first come into the room, you see wires going everywhere and giant speakers rising from the floor like skyscrapers. Monitors and high-tech equipment crowd the room. The musicians' shiny instruments--glossy red guitars and silvery drums--twinkle. The colorful, offbeat clothes the musicians usually wear are like uniforms. All wear a diamondlike earring in one ear, a T-shirt with SAVE THE DOGS printed across the front, and jeans with knees worn out.

1 inch

1¼ inches

When the sounds start, the feeling of confusion increases. As the musicians tune up by playing bits and pieces of different songs all at the same time, the noise is a very strange jumble of sounds. Once the band starts rehearsing the same song, the noise turns to a piercing metallic sound and is overwhelming.

1 inch

1 inch

2

Even though the room is soundproof, the lead guitarist's father still complains about the noise.

Because I am sitting so close to the musicians, the music seems to swallow me. I feel a thump in my stomach as the bass guitar and drums pound. I feel a need to tap my foot and move my body in rhythm. I can't seem to control myself.

By the time the rehearsal is over, I feel I have been transported to a different level of existence. To hear the loud, driving beat, to see the crazy blend of shiny instruments and the scruffy clothes, and to feel the music controlling my body are experiences I will never forget.

1¼ inches

1 inch

A Writer Writes

WRITING ABOUT THE THEME

A Composition about a Phase in Your Life

PURPOSE: to narrate and inform
AUDIENCE: your teacher and classmates

Prewriting A phase in your life is a period of time—from several weeks to as long as a year or more that was noticeably different from other times in your life. A phase could be the month you were on a diet, your best year as a basketball player, the semester you made the honor roll, or any other time period that made a lasting impression in your memory.

STEP 1: List as many phases of your past life as you can think of.

STEP 2: Look over your list and choose the phase you would most enjoy writing about.

STEP 3: Use clustering, charting, or other prewriting techniques to recall as much as possible about that phase. List very specific details in your notes, including details of people, places, objects, and feelings.

STEP 4: Look over your notes. Then write freely to answer each of the following questions.

- When and for how long did the phase take place?
- How did I feel during this phase of my life?
- How did the phase change me?
- Why is this phase important in my life?

STEP 5: Look over all your notes, clusters, charts, and freewriting. Making a simple outline or chart, organize some of the key events in this phase in a logical order.

Drafting Use your notes to write a first draft of a composition telling about this phase in your life. Make the beginning catchy and the ending a clear summary of your ideas. Every now and then, pause and read what you have written to be sure your ideas are making sense.

Revising If your teacher permits, exchange papers with a partner. Answer the following questions about each other's work.

- Which parts did you like best?
- Which parts need more work?
- Are the events in order?
- Are there vivid, specific details? Is the writing interesting to read?
- Does the writer show why the phase was different from other times in his or her life?
- Does the writer tell why the phase was important?
- Is the beginning catchy?
- Does the ending clearly summarize your ideas?

Use comments from your partner and your own best judgment to revise your composition. Also, refer to the revision strategies on pages 30–31 for ways to improve your work.

Editing When you are satisfied that your draft is the best you can make it, use the checklist on page 35 to edit it. As you edit, use proofreading symbols.

Publishing Present a neat final copy of your work to a person in your life who was involved in this phase or someone who would most appreciate its importance to you.

WRITING ABOUT THE THEME

Independent Writing

Write a short analysis of yourself as a friend. First form a small group and brainstorm about friendship. What is friendship? What constitutes a good friend? Then think about your identity as a friend. Are you a good friend? Why? Could you be a better friend? How? After the discussion follow the checklist on page 47 for help with your composition.

WRITING ABOUT THE THEME

Creative Writing

Write a radio play about a crucial event in your life. Brainstorm a list of all the details you can remember from that event and list all the people involved in the event. Then use your prewriting notes to write a first draft of a script for a radio play that dramatizes this central event. Use the following form for dialogue:

COACH ROSEN: Ben, you won't make the team with that attitude.
BEN: (resentfully) You'll see. I'll show you.

Finally, using your classmates or friends, cast your play and listen while it is read through, taking notes for yourself about parts that you think need improving. Invite comments from your cast about ways to improve your script. Continue revising until you are satisfied that the dialogue sounds natural and that the event is portrayed well.

WRITING ABOUT THE THEME

Writing about Literature

A *simile* is a figure of speech that compares two essentially different people or things by using the word *like* or *as*. For example, in the poem "Identity," the poet compares people other than himself to flowers when he says, "Let them be as flowers." In a paragraph explain how those people are like flowers.

Writing in Another Subject Area

Biology Choose a living organism to study in close detail. It could be a pet, a houseplant, a tree in your backyard, or any other living thing you can observe for long periods of time. For the next three days, spend at least ten minutes observing your object. Record your observations each day. Note everything you see, including changes. At the end of the period, write a paragraph telling what you learned through your close observation.

Chapter 1 Checklist

The Writing Process

Prewriting

- ✓ Find a subject to write about by exploring your interests, freewriting, keeping a journal, and exploring literature. *(See pages 10–14.)*
- ✓ Choose the subject that you find the most interesting and then limit your subject so that it is more manageable. *(See pages 15–16.)*
- ✓ Consider your purpose for writing and your audience. *(See pages 16–17.)*
- ✓ Develop your subject by observing, brainstorming a list, group brainstorming, clustering, and inquiring. *(See pages 18–23.)*
- ✓ Organize your material by focusing on a main idea, grouping your supporting details into categories, and ordering your details. *(See pages 24–26.)*

Drafting

- ✓ Write a first draft and give it a title. *(See pages 28–29.)*

Revising

- ✓ Use self-evaluation, revision strategies, and the Revision Checklist to rework your composition and finalize your title. *(See pages 30–31.)*
- ✓ Use individual and group peer conferencing to share ideas for improving your composition. *(See pages 33–34.)*

Editing and Publishing

- ✓ Polish your work by correcting any errors in grammar, usage, capitalization, punctuation, and spelling. Use proofreading symbols to edit. *(See pages 35–37.)*
- ✓ Make a neat final copy of your work following standard manuscript form. *(See pages 41–43.)*
- ✓ Publish your composition for interested readers. *(See page 40.)*

Chapter

2 Developing Your Writing Style

Part 1 *Reading to Write*

THEME: *Communication*

A phone rings and rings in an empty, dark house. Across a dinner table, a father and son try to have a conversation, but each misunderstands the other. A friend tries to explain how you hurt her, but her words come out barbed and painful. In all these cases, real communication never takes place—and the people remain lonely, misunderstood, and hurt.

Imagine some different scenes. A phone rings in a busy house; and a voice says, "Sure, come on over if you're lonely—we'd love to see you!" Over dinner a father and son who usually disagree with one another listen as each presents his opinion on the merits of a college education. When a friend tells you—in kind and considered words—just why she felt hurt, you suddenly understand her viewpoint and quickly apologize. In all cases people have communicated well.

In this chapter you will read, think, and write about the theme of communication. As you write, you will be honing your own communication skills to develop your own writing style. By choosing exactly the right words and by shaping clear, smooth sentences, your communications will ring clear and true.

To continue your thinking about communication, read the following literature.

No Problem, but It Needs a Solution

Bill Cosby

When your fifteen-year-old son does speak, he often says one of two things: either "Okay," which, as we know, means "I haven't killed anyone," or "No problem."

"No problem" has been my son's philosophy of life. Two years ago, he was one of the top ten underachievers in our state and whenever you asked him how he was doing in school, he always said, with simple eloquence, "No problem." And, of course, his answer made sense: there *was* no problem, no confusion about how he was doing. He had failed everything; and what he hadn't failed, he hadn't taken yet. (Undoubtedly, F's had even been penciled in for next year.) He had even failed *English*.

His failing his native tongue piqued my curiosity, so I said, "How can you fail English?"

"Yeah," he replied.

Hoping to get an answer that had something to do with the question, I said again, "Please tell me: how can you fail English?"

"I don't know," he said.

"Son, you didn't really fail *English*, did you? You failed handing in reports on time, right? Because you can understand people who speak English, can't you? And when you talk, *they* can understand *you*, can't they? So the teacher *understood* what you had written but just didn't care for the way you put it, right? You just failed *organization*, right? I mean, the teacher who failed you in English also said, 'He can do the work,' right? It's just that you don't *want* to do it yet. And all it'll take is maybe leaving you out in the wilderness with no food or money in the middle of winter. Just a dime to make a collect call saying that you're ready to study."

"No problem," he said. ◆

Primer Lesson

Carl Sandburg

Look out how you use proud words.
When you let proud words go, it is
not easy to call them back.
They wear long boots, hard boots; they
walk off proud; they can't hear you
calling—
Look out how you use proud words.

Responding to the Theme

Communication

Responding in Your Journal In your journal, freewrite responses to the following questions. As you read "No Problem, but It Needs a Solution" by Bill Cosby, did you sympathize or identify with the author's fifteen-year-old son? Why or why not? What, do you think, is the boy communicating when he says, "No problem" and "I don't know"? Do you have any suggestions for the boy about ways he might express himself more clearly to other people? By reading this excerpt, have you learned anything about what you can do to improve the way you communicate? Describe what it is that you have learned.

Speaking and Listening With your teacher's permission, form a group of three to five students. Then plan a skit for the following episodes about communication situations similar to those in "No Problem, but It Needs a Solution."

- The boy tells a friend about his difficulties in school.
- The boy tells his guidance counselor about his difficulties.
- The boy tells his father about his difficulties.
- The boy explains to his teacher how he will improve.
- The boy tells his coach why he was not at practice.

As you plan your skit, concentrate on the communication problems the boy faces in each episode and discuss the specific words and phrases that both parties can use to share their concerns. Then, if time permits, present your skit to the class.

Critical Thinking: Interpreting What, do you think, is the message or lesson at the heart of the poem "Primer Lesson"? How does this lesson apply to your life? Write a short composition answering these questions.

Extending Your Vocabulary In his poem "Primer Lesson," Carl Sandburg speaks of proud words that wear long, hard boots. Brainstorm for ten adjectives that you can think of to describe the kinds of words the poet refers to. The first adjective might be *self-righteous*.

The Scrabble Game, January 1, 1983, photographic collage, 39" × 58" © David Hockney

Part 2 *Writing*

The selections you have recently read and their accompanying activities on page 51 should suggest to you the importance communication has in your daily life. It is fair to say that carefully chosen words and sentences are the tools of skillful communication.

> "When *I* use a word," Humpty Dumpty said, in rather a scornful tone, "it means just what I choose it to mean—neither more nor less."
>
> "The question is," said Alice, "whether you *can* make words mean so many different things."
>
> "The question is," said Humpty Dumpty, "which is to be master—that's all." LEWIS CARROLL, *Alice in Wonderland*

Are you a master of the words and sentences that you use in your writing? Speakers use facial expressions and subtle changes in tone of voice to communicate their meaning. When you write, though, you must choose your words and shape your sentences in such a way that your message is clear. This chapter will help you become a master of the words and sentences you write.

Choosing Vivid Words

Writing Process

Precise, vivid language helps to etch a writer's message in a reader's mind. Using general words is like sketching the outline of a person without adding distinguishing features. Specific words, on the other hand, supply details that convey an image precisely. As a result, specific words leave a deeper impression than do dull, general words.

GENERAL NOUN	noise
SPECIFIC NOUNS	crash, whisper, clang
GENERAL VERB	walked
SPECIFIC VERBS	ambled, strolled, lumbered

The specific words in the following passage create a mood and make the scene from the novel *Ethan Frome* easy to picture.

Model: *Specific Words*

> They walked on in silence through the blackness of the **hemlock-shaded** lane, where Ethan's sawmill **gloomed** through the night, and out again into the comparative clearness of the fields. On the farther side of the hemlock belt the open country **rolled** away before them, grey and lonely under the stars. Sometimes their way led them under the shade of an overhanging bank or through the thin obscurity of a **clump** of leafless trees. Here and there a farmhouse stood far back among the fields, **mute** and **cold** as a gravestone. The night was so still that they heard the frozen snow **crackle** under their feet. The **crash** of a loaded branch falling far off in the woods **reverberated** like a musket shot, and once a fox barked, and Mattie **shrank** closer to Ethan and quickened her steps.
>
> EDITH WHARTON, *Ethan Frome*

WRITING ACTIVITY 1 *Choosing Specific Words*

Number your paper 1 to 20. Then write two specific words for each of the following general words.

1. tree
2. car
3. clothes
4. books
5. airplane
6. nice
7. cute
8. pretty
9. great
10. ran
11. went
12. saw
13. said
14. thought
15. walked
16. excellent
17. wanted
18. looked
19. moved
20. disagreed

Denotation and Connotation

When you search for precise, vivid words, keep in mind that most words have two levels of meaning. Their literal meaning is called *denotation.* On the other hand, most specific words also convey an emotional meaning, or *connotation.*

POSITIVE CONNOTATIONS	silent, hushed
NEGATIVE CONNOTATIONS	mute, tomblike

Good word choice involves choosing not only precise, specific words but also words with the appropriate connotation.

Writing Tip: Use **specific words** with **connotations** appropriate to your meaning.

WRITING ACTIVITY 2 *Choosing Connotations*

Write the word in parentheses that has the connotation given in brackets.

EXAMPLE The snow (buried, blanketed) the mountain town. [positive]
ANSWER blanketed

A Cold Hike

1. After the storm (an adventurous, a foolhardy) boy set off on snowshoes for a hike. [negative]
2. As he climbed higher, he (drew in, gasped) deep breaths of the pure mountain air. [positive]
3. With each step he became more (self-satisfied, confident). [negative]
4. When he reached the top of the ridge, he (bellowed, proclaimed) for all to hear, "This mountain is mine!" [positive]
5. His echoing (boast, claim) was all that was needed to unlodge the new snow above him. [negative]
6. Within seconds a sheet of ice and snow came (moving, charging) down the slope toward him. [negative]
7. On the other side of the ridge, a group of experienced hikers heard the boy's shout and the (loud, thunderous) avalanche. [negative]
8. They trekked (determinedly, defiantly) across the ridge to search for the boy. [positive]
9. At last they found him when they heard a (low sound, moan). [negative]
10. The boy (survived, recovered) with prompt care, but he never again claimed a mountain as his own. [positive]

Figurative Language

Good writers create *figurative language*—words and phrases employed for a highly imaginative rather than a literal meaning. Such figurative language often uses vivid comparisons called *similes* and *metaphors*. Both of these figures of speech express a similarity between two essentially different things. Similes use *like* or *as* to state the comparison. Metaphors, on the other hand, *imply* a comparison without using *like* or *as*. Notice how the use of a simile and a metaphor enlivens the following sentence.

DULL	After her chores Karen quickly ran out of the house.
SIMILE	After her chores Karen exploded out of the house **like a Fourth of July firecracker.**
METAPHOR	**Karen became a Fourth of July firecracker,** exploding out of the house after her chores.

Clichés Overused, worn-out comparisons or figures of speech drain life from your writing. Such worn-out expressions are called *clichés*. Therefore, you should always replace clichés with fresh similes or metaphors or with specific words.

CLICHÉ	One club member spoke for half an hour, **making a mountain out of a molehill.**
FRESH METAPHOR	One club member spoke for half an hour, **making a blaze out of an ember.**
SPECIFIC WORDS	One club member spoke for half an hour, **making a dilemma out of a small problem.**

Writing Tip: Use **similes** and **metaphors** to enliven writing. Avoid **clichés**.

WRITING ACTIVITY 3 *Identifying Similes and Metaphors*

Write *simile* or *metaphor* to indicate which figure of speech is used in each of the following sentences.

1. The afternoon light entered the room like a shy visitor.

2. Dim rivers of light were flowing from horizon to horizon.

ARTHUR C. CLARKE, *2001: A Space Odyssey*

3. Japan is a necklace of islands.
4. The sunset was a treasure chest of gold laid in the meadow.
5. Somewhere at the end of the column a driver sang—the wailing toneless voice rose and fell like a wind through a keyhole.

   GRAHAM GREENE, *The Heart of the Matter*
6. We settle down, like walruses stranded on rocks.

   VIRGINIA WOOLF, *The Waves* (Adapted)
7. The child stood like a lost pup in the street.
8. The drumbeat of her blood was urging her on to the finish line.
9. Catching the sunlight, the raindrops seemed like cat's-eye marbles.
10. She was very old and small and she walked slowly . . . with the balanced heaviness and lightness of a pendulum in a grandfather clock.

    EUDORA WELTY, "A Worn Path"

WRITING ACTIVITY 4 *Revising to Eliminate Clichés*

Replace the underlined clichés in the following sentences with fresh similes or metaphors or with specific words.

1. Mom's smile is as sweet as pie.
2. This book is right up your alley.
3. Losing the straw poll by 30 percentage points took the wind out of the candidate's sails.
4. Sally still saw a ray of hope.
5. The television show was as dull as dishwater.

WRITING ACTIVITY 5 *Writing on Your Own*

WRITING ABOUT THE THEME

Prewriting You undoubtedly have had a number of experiences in the past that have taught you the importance of careful communication. Brainstorm a list of times when you had to deal with a difficult communication. For instance, your teammate may have complained you did not play your best, or your friend told you that you should not gossip so much. Nevertheless, you were impressed with the generous, kind, or helpful way that person communicated. Choose one meaningful experience and freewrite to recall it in detail.

Drafting Write a short composition relating that event, emphasizing the positive, caring way the message was given.

Revising Revise your writing, looking for places to use specific language and figurative language effectively. Also eliminate any clichés. Save your writing for further work.

Writing Is Thinking

Critical Thinking

Comparing

When you *compare,* you find similarities between people, places, things, or even events. When you write a simile or metaphor, however, you compare in a particular way—you show how two unlike subjects are alike. You find qualities that the subjects share. For example, if you compare a baseball glove with a butterfly net, you can find some startling similarities. Both require the use of hand and arm and the skill to catch flying objects, and both are used by someone running to pursue an object.

Effective similes and metaphors, then, use original, thought provoking comparisons that cause people to look at things in new and different ways. The following metaphor compares a person to a panther.

Daniel leapt with the silent, sleek agility of a panther.

Making a chart like the one that follows will help you construct similar comparisons.

Comparison Chart

PERSON, PLACE, THING, ANIMAL, EVENT	SIMILAR QUALITIES	COMPARISON
SUBJECT 1 DANIEL	leaps with silent, sleek agility	DANIEL = PANTHER
SUBJECT 2 PANTHER	leaps with silent, sleek agility	

Thinking Practice Create your own comparison by making a chart like the one above for one of the following phrases. Then write your simile or metaphor.

1. My best friend walks . . .
2. The bus lurched . . .
3. The thunderclouds hovered . . .
4. The wooded path stretched . . .

Writing Concise Sentences

Referring to a truly effective piece of writing, the English writer Katherine Mansfield once remarked, "There mustn't be one single word out of place or one word that can be taken out." Writing that follows this advice is *concise;* it contains no unnecessary words or phrases.

Writing Tip: Express your meaning in as few words as possible.

Redundancy

One way to revise wordiness is to eliminate unnecessary repetition, or *redundancy.* In a redundant sentence, the same idea is repeated without any new shades of meaning.

REDUNDANT	The **slowly moving** train crawled into the station.
CONCISE	The train **crawled** into the station.
REDUNDANT	She grew four **inches in height** in one year.
CONCISE	She grew four **inches** in one year.

WRITING ACTIVITY 6 *Eliminating Redundancy*

Revise each of the following sentences by eliminating the redundant words or phrases.

1. Jonathan scowled angrily when Stephanie insulted him.
2. The strange feeling was very peculiar.
3. Dogs can hear sounds that are inaudible to the human ear and cannot be heard by people.
4. Sharks blink their eyes at strong light by closing a membrane over their eyeballs.
5. We packed the necessary things we needed for our trip.
6. Terry was alone in the damp cave because there was no one else in it.
7. The student was given a medal for his brave heroism.
8. The wave was huge in size and awesome in nature.
9. She set her alarm for 3:00 A.M. in the morning so she could watch the meteor shower.
10. The fog over the city was thick because low clouds hung over the buildings.

Wordiness

When you revise your writing, streamline the sentences by eliminating expressions that add no meaning and by reducing wordy phrases.

Empty Expressions Fillers like those listed in the following chart often take up space in a sentence without adding any meaning. When you revise, eliminate such fillers.

Empty Expressions	
on account of	due to the fact that
what I want is	the reason that
in my opinion	the thing/fact is that
it seems as if	there is/are/was/were
it is/was	what I'm trying to say is that
because of the fact that	I believe/feel/think/that

EMPTY Despite **the fact that there has been** a drought in the food bowl of the Great Plains, most crops are surviving.

CONCISE Despite the drought in the food bowl of the Great Plains, most crops are surviving.

EMPTY **In my opinion** the high-fashion clothes advertised in most magazines are like costumes.

CONCISE The high-fashion clothes advertised in most magazines are like costumes.

EMPTY **What I'm trying to say is that** little lies lead to big lies.

CONCISE Little lies lead to big lies.

WRITING ACTIVITY 7 *Revising to Eliminate Empty Expressions*

Revise the paragraph on the next page by eliminating the empty expressions or by replacing them with more precise language.

EXAMPLE In my opinion Ernest Hemingway's house in Key West, Florida, is part of history.

POSSIBLE REVISION Ernest Hemingway's house in Key West, Florida, is part of history.

A Writer's Home

Key West is an interesting place to visit for the reason that it is the southernmost city in the continental United States. On account of the fact that it has the Atlantic Ocean on one side and the Gulf of Mexico on the other, Key West is a popular boating, fishing, and snorkeling spot. It was Key West's great fishing that was what drew writer Ernest Hemingway to the area in the 1920's. The fact is that Hemingway was the first writer of renown to set up a home in Key West, although the famous naturalist John James Audubon had lived there earlier. The fact of the matter is that Hemingway owned his home in Key West from 1931 to 1961. Because of the fact that Hemingway was very much interested in Spain, his home has many beautiful Spanish objects. It seems as if his wife wanted a swimming pool, so the home also has the first pool built in Key West. On account of the fact that he needed privacy, Hemingway had a studio in the loft above his pool house. It was there that he would work on his writing in the company of some of his 50 cats. Due to the fact that they were so much a part of the home, the cats were allowed to stay, and their offspring now wander contentedly around their famous home.

Wordy Phrases and Clauses Some sentences can be reduced so that the same meaning is expressed in fewer words. Notice how the following wordy examples can be written more concisely.

WORDY	Kristin danced **with a graceful style.** [prepositional phrase]
CONCISE	Kristin danced **gracefully.** [adverb]
WORDY	Ricky wore a jacket **made of suede.** [participial phrase]
CONCISE	Ricky wore a **suede** jacket. [adjective]
WORDY	The tree **that is in my backyard** is older than my grandmother. [adjective clause]
CONCISE	The tree **in my backyard** . . . [prepositional phrase]
WORDY	*Nicholas Nickleby,* **which is a novel by Charles Dickens,** was made into a nine-hour play. [adjective clause]
CONCISE	*Nicholas Nickleby,* **a novel by Charles Dickens** . . . [appositive phrase]

WRITING ACTIVITY 8 *Revising to Delete Unnecessary Words*

Revise the following paragraph, eliminating redundancy, empty expressions, and wordy phrases and clauses.

Robots at Work

Automated robots are not just a fantasy of the future. Today there are already 40,000 robots in the United States that perform repetitive jobs in factories. Robots are also used in other industrialized countries where industry has developed. Nissan Motor Company, which is a Japanese carmaker, uses robots for nearly all its welding. The fact of the matter is that these robots are controlled by computers. Some robots can even distinguish shapes and colors due to the fact that they use TV cameras as eyes. Robot experts who know a lot about these things predict that the use of robots will increase dramatically in the next ten years.

WRITING ACTIVITY 9 *Writing on Your Own*

WRITING ABOUT THE THEME

Revising Read over the composition about communication, which you started in Writing Activity 5. Check it carefully, revising to eliminate unnecessary words. Save your composition.

Creating Sentence Variety

Sentences are the building blocks of paragraphs. If all sentences in a composition were the same length and structure, the composition would undoubtedly be drab and uninteresting. If the sentences are varied, however, the composition will more than likely hold the reader's attention.

Writing Tip: Vary the length, structure, and beginnings of your sentences.

Sentence Combining Strategies

Good writing uses a mixture of short and long sentences to imitate the natural rhythms of speech. Therefore, whenever possible, use the following strategies to combine short and choppy sentences into longer ones.

Combining Sentences with Phrases One way to combine short sentences is to express some of the information in a prepositional phrase, an appositive phrase, or a participial phrase. *(See pages 600, 601–603, and 607 for information about the different types of phrases.)*

A. The Blue Angels perform spectacular stunts. They are part of the United States Navy. They perform aviation stunts at air shows. The shows are held around the world.

The Blue Angels **of the United States Navy** perform spectacular aviation stunts **at air shows around the world.** [prepositional phrases]

B. Blue Angel pilots must have at least 1,500 hours of flying time. They are some of the best-trained pilots.

Blue Angel pilots, **some of the best-trained pilots,** must have at least 1,500 hours of flying time. [appositive phrase]

C. The Blue Angels usually please the audience most. They bring the show to a thrilling finish.

Bringing the show to a thrilling finish, the Blue Angels usually please the audience most. [participial phrase]

WRITING ACTIVITY 10 *Combining Sentences with Phrases*

Combine each of the following sets of short sentences, using the models on page 62. (The letter in brackets indicates which model to use.) Remember to use commas where needed.

Blue Angels

1. The Blue Angels' Skyhawks gain speed quickly. They speed from 0 to 140 miles per hour in 2 seconds. [C]
2. Six Blue Angels perform together. They perform in tight formation. There are only three feet between planes. [A]
3. The seventh Blue Angel does not fly. He is the announcer. [B]
4. These superb flyers carefully watch the weather. They choose either their high show or their low show. [C]
5. High-speed climbs and star bursts require clear skies. High-speed climbs and star bursts are part of the high show. [B]
6. One pilot gives all the orders. He is the leader. [B]
7. The Angels communicate in flight. They use microphones and earphones. [A]
8. The soloists follow orders from the leader. They sometimes take off from the formation. [C]
9. Two soloists sometimes travel at speeds of nearly 1,000 miles per hour. They approach from opposite directions. [C]
10. In upside-down stunts, the Angels are held in the pilot seat. They are held in place by harnesses. [A]

Combining Sentences by Coordinating Another way to combine your sentences is to link items of equal importance with one of the following coordinating conjunctions: *and, but, or, for, yet,* or *so.* The resulting combinations will contain compound elements. *(See pages 531, 585–587, and 588–589 for more information about compound elements.)*

A. John Adams died on July 4, 1826. Thomas Jefferson died on July 4, 1826.

John Adams and Thomas Jefferson died on July 4, 1826. [compound subject]

B. Coincidences often intrigue people. Coincidences often frighten people.

Coincidences often **intrigue or frighten** people. [compound verb]

C. The number *88* was thought unlucky for James II of Scotland. The number *88* was thought unlucky for Mary Stuart, Queen of Scots.

The number *88* was thought unlucky **for James II of Scotland and Mary Stuart, Queen of Scots.** [compound object of the preposition]

D. James II died in battle in 1488. Mary Stuart was beheaded in 1587.

James II died in battle in 1488, **but** Mary Stuart was beheaded in 1587. [compound sentence]

E. Superstitions are foolish. Superstitions can be interesting, though.

Superstitions are **foolish but interesting.** [compound predicate adjective]

F. In superstitious societies the people most feared are magicians. In some superstitious societies, however, the people most feared are witch doctors.

In superstitious societies the people most feared are **either magicians or witch doctors.** [compound predicate nominative]

WRITING ACTIVITY 11 *Combining Sentences by Coordinating*

Combine each of the following pairs of sentences, using the preceding models. Within the brackets are the letter indicating which model to use and the correct conjunction. Use commas where needed.

EXAMPLE The earliest electronic computers were not compact. They were not reliable. [E—*neither/nor*]

ANSWER The earliest electronic computers were neither compact nor reliable.

Leading the Way

1. The first electronic digital computer contained 18,000 vacuum tubes. It filled a room the size of a gymnasium. [B—*and*]
2. This huge machine was invented at the University of Pennsylvania by J. Presper Eckert. It was also invented by John W. Mauchly. [C—*and*]
3. Overheated wires were a constant problem. Burned-out bulbs were a constant problem. [A—*and*]
4. The solution was a large team of technicians. An air-conditioning system powerful enough to cool the Empire State Building also helped. [F—*and*]
5. Today's much smaller computers are more powerful and more reliable than the old giant machines. They use less energy. [B—*yet*]

Combining Sentences by Subordinating When ideas in two short sentences are of unequal importance, you can combine them by *subordinating.* To subordinate, express the less important idea in a dependent adjective clause or adverb clause. *(See pages 627–637 and 786 for more information about subordinating with dependent clauses.)* The words below are often used to introduce dependent clauses; however, for a complete list of subordinating conjunctions, see page 628.

Relative Pronouns		Subordinating Conjunctions	
who	that	after	because
whom	which	until	whenever
whose		unless	although

A. Ludwig van Beethoven began to lose his hearing at the age of twenty-six. Many regard him as the world's greatest composer.

Ludwig van Beethoven, **whom many regard as the world's greatest composer,** began to lose his hearing at the age of twenty-six. [adjective clause]

B. He suffered this misfortune throughout his life. His last words sang of hope: "I shall hear in Heaven."

Although he suffered this misfortune throughout his life, his last words sang of hope: "I shall hear in Heaven." [adverb clause]

WRITING ACTIVITY 12 *Combining by Subordinating*

Revise the following paragraph. Combine each pair of sentences, using the preceding models. The brackets tell which model to use and the correct joining word. Use commas where needed.

Saving the Queen

The Statue of Liberty needed extensive repair work. It was built more than 100 years ago. [A—*which*] The monument was badly corroded. Its uplifted arm has welcomed millions to the United States. [A—*whose*] The statue needed work from head to toe. Pollution had caused it to rust.[B—*because*] Liberty cost only $500,000 to build. It cost millions of dollars to repair. [B—*although*] The improvements should last. The statue celebrates its 200th birthday in the year 2086. [B—*until*]

Varying Sentence Structure

To avoid monotony and keep your reader's interest, strive to use a mixture of sentence structure in your compositions. *(For a review of sentence structure, see pages 638–639.)* Notice the variety in the following passage. To enhance your appreciation of the sentence variety, read the paragraph aloud and notice the various rhythms you hear.

Model: *Paragraph with a Variety of Sentence Structures*

Encounter with Gorillas

SIMPLE	Suddenly the air was shattered by the screams of five male gorillas bulldozing down the foliage toward me.
COMPLEX	Their screams were so deafening that I could not locate the source of the noise.
COMPOUND-COMPLEX	I knew only that the group was charging from above; then the tall vegetation gave way as though an out-of-control tractor were headed directly for me.
SIMPLE	Only on recognizing me did the group's dominant silverback swiftly brake to a stop three feet away, causing a five-gorilla pileup.
SIMPLE	I then sank to the ground submissively.
COMPOUND	The hair on each male's headcrest stood erect; canines were fully exposed.
COMPOUND	The irises of their eyes, ordinarily soft brown, glinted yellow, and an overpowering fear odor filled the air.
COMPLEX	For a good half hour, all five males screamed if I made even the slightest move.
SIMPLE	After a 30-minute period, the group allowed me to pretend to feed meekly on vegetation and then finally moved rigidly out of sight.

DIAN FOSSEY, *Gorillas in the Mist* (Adapted)

WRITING ACTIVITY 13 *Revising to Vary Sentence Structure*

The following paragraphs contain only simple sentences. Using the sentence combining techniques on pages 62–66, revise the paragraphs so that they contain a mixture of simple, compound, complex, and compound-complex sentences. Remember to use commas where needed. When you have finished, read your revisions aloud to check for sentence variety. Then, if your teacher permits, exchange papers with a classmate and compare your revisions.

1. Handwriting Analysis

Experts at handwriting analysis use only their eyes and a microscope as tools. Handwriting analysis is an inexact science. Experts are called on to discover forgery. They compare two documents side by side. They look for telling details about the handwriting. They look for the dots above *i*'s and the crosses through *t*'s. They look for the angle of the pen. They analyze the beginnings and ends of pen strokes. Sometimes experts disagree. Many people doubt the reliability of handwriting analysis. These doubts will not disappear. Courts allow experts to testify. Juries are often persuaded by the testimony of handwriting experts.

2. Today's Armor

Armor of the past was heavy and prone to rusting. Today's armor is, in contrast, lightweight and rustproof. Most bulletproof vests for police officers, for example, are made from a fabric called Kevlar. Kevlar is five times stronger than steel. The fabric has a coating of resins on the surface nearest the body. This coating adds extra strength. Rust on armor of the past had to be cleaned and treated with sand and vinegar. Today's armor is machine-washable. Police officers are not the only people who wear armor today. Goalies on hockey teams suit up in padded armor that protects them from the fast-moving puck. Welders protect their faces from dangerous sparks with a medieval-looking face shield. Fire fighters and construction workers wear helmets. These helmets are tough. They are also lightweight. Probably the most advanced armor of today is the space suit. The space suit protects astronauts from the uninhabitable environment of outer space.

Varying Sentence Beginnings

Sentences that always begin with subjects become tiresome to read or hear. When you revise, begin your sentences in a variety of ways, such as those shown in the following examples.

SUBJECT	The Greek **city-states** of Elis and Pisa were at war in the spring of 776 B.C.
ADVERB	**Finally,** they made peace in the summer.
INFINITIVE PHRASE	**To celebrate the peace,** each city decided to hold athletic games.
PARTICIPIAL PHRASE	**Wishing to honor the gods,** they held their games jointly in Olympia.
PREPOSITIONAL PHRASE	**In this first Olympic match,** the only sport was foot racing.
ADVERB CLAUSE	**Because the Greeks cared only about winning,** no speed records were kept.
INVERTED ORDER	**Out of this match** grew the Olympic Games.

WRITING ACTIVITY 14 *Varying Sentence Beginnings*

Revise the following paragraph. Vary the beginnings of the sentences by using the openers suggested in the brackets.

Basic Signals

There are two basic types of signals in the field of electronics, analog and digital. [*prepositional phrase*] You can observe familiar appliances to understand their difference. [*infinitive phrase*] A car speedometer is an analog device, registering a continuous range of speed. [*participial phrase*] The channel selector on your TV set is digital, because it can work only in certain set positions. [*adverb clause*] Digital clocks give more accurate readouts than analog clocks because they tell you in numbers the hour, minute, and second. [*adverb clause*] You must estimate these details to read the time from an analog clock's hands. [*infinitive phrase*]

WRITING ACTIVITY 15 *Writing on Your Own*

WRITING ABOUT THE THEME

Reread your composition about communicating from Writing Activity 9. Then revise it carefully to create as much sentence variety as possible. Save your work for later use.

Eliminating Sentence Faults

Good writers, like trail guides, blaze clear paths for readers to follow. To help readers through your paths of thought, revise your sentences to eliminate clutter and confusion.

Writing Tip: When you revise, eliminate **faulty coordination, faulty subordination, rambling sentences,** and **faulty parallelism.**

Faulty Coordination and Subordination

When joining ideas of equal importance, use the correct coordinating conjunction because faulty coordination leaves readers confused. In the following example, the conjunction *and* does not clearly express the relationship between the two ideas.

FAULTY COORDINATION — The Boston Marathon was draining, **and** I'm looking forward to next year's run.

PRECISE COORDINATION — The marathon was draining, **but** I'm looking forward to next year's run.

You can also use a semicolon and a transitional word to join ideas of equal importance. *(See pages 816–817.)*

PRECISE COORDINATION — The Boston Marathon was draining; **nevertheless,** I'm looking forward to next year's run.

The following chart shows words that express coordination precisely.

To Show Similarity	To Show Contrast	To Show Result
and	but	so
both/and	yet	thus
not only/but also	or, nor	hence
besides	however	therefore
indeed	instead	consequently
furthermore	still	accordingly
moreover	nevertheless	as a result

Faulty coordination also results if unrelated ideas are joined. When you revise, express the unrelated idea in a separate sentence.

FAULTY COORDINATION	My basset hound had five puppies**, and** we have had her for two years.
IMPROVED	My basset hound had five puppies**. We** have had her for two years.

Sometimes a coordinating conjunction connects ideas that are not of equal importance. When you revise, correct this type of error by changing the less important idea into a phrase or a subordinate clause.

FAULTY COORDINATION	Martin Barrie quickly left the house**, and** he locked the doors.
IMPROVED	**After locking the doors,** Martin Barrie quickly left the house. [gerund phrase]
FAULTY COORDINATION	The acrobat performed his daring act, **and** the audience looked on in amazement.
IMPROVED	**While the audience looked on in amazement,** the acrobat performed his daring act. [subordinate clause]

To avoid faulty subordination, make sure that the more important idea is expressed in the independent clause.

FAULTY SUBORDINATION	Elizabeth was the youngest on the team, **although she competed as well as the oldest players.**
IMPROVED	**Although Elizabeth was the youngest on the team,** she competed as well as the oldest players.

Correcting Faulty Coordination and Subordination

1. Use a connecting word that clearly shows the relationship between your ideas (similarity, contrast, or result).
2. Express unrelated ideas in separate sentences.
3. If the ideas are not of equal importance, express the less important idea in a phrase or a subordinate clause.
4. Express your more important idea in an independent clause.

WRITING ACTIVITY 16 *Choosing the Best Connecting Word*

Number your paper 1 to 5. Then complete each of the following sentences, using the list of words on page 70.

1. Michael has _______ confidence _______ persistence, a combination that often brings him success.
2. They said their good-byes, _______ Sarah boarded the train.
3. I would like to go with you; _______, I must be home by 7:30.
4. Tina had a toothache, _______ she went to the dentist.
5. The movie lacked action; _______, it seemed very long.

WRITING ACTIVITY 17 *Revising to Correct Sentence Faults*

Use the strategies on pages 70–71 to improve the faulty sentences in the following paragraph. Remember to use commas where needed.

Eclipse

The moon glowed orange, and it was hard to believe humans have actually stood on it. Hurrying to set up the telescope, we worried that the eclipse was about to begin. We watched for a long time, and nothing seemed to be happening. Finally, the earth's shadow took a bite out of the moon; consequently, the moon continued to glow. Little by little the shadow covered the moon, yet we watched intently. We understand what causes the eclipse, and to the ancients it must have been very frightening. The telescope magnified the moon so that we could see the craters, and it had been my grandfather's. The eclipse reached totality, and we could still see a faint, copperish, crescent-shaped glow. The moon finally reappeared, and the shadow passed into the darkness. The eclipse took more than three hours, although we enjoyed every minute of it.

Rambling Sentences

Sentences with long strings of phrases and clauses are hard to follow because they often contain excessive coordination and subordination and thus clutter the main point. When you revise, break up any of these long rambling sentences into two or three shorter sentences.

RAMBLING	Computers are used by some major-league baseball teams to help managers make decisions because baseball is a game that depends on statistics to judge a player's worth, and the computer can use these statistics to make suggestions about batting order and which player to send in as a designated hitter or runner under a variety of circumstances, including number of outs, number of men on base, weather conditions, and opposing pitcher.
IMPROVED	Some major-league baseball teams use computers to help their managers make decisions. Since statistics are often used to measure a player's worth, the computer can use these figures to choose the right player for a specific situation. It can recommend batting order and designated hitters or runners. It can also weigh such variables as number of outs, number of men on base, weather conditions, and the opposing pitcher.

WRITING ACTIVITY 18 *Revising a Rambling Sentence*

Revise the following sentence by breaking it into shorter sentences. Remember to capitalize and punctuate the new sentences correctly.

Back to the Future

Your grandparents were probably happy when grocery stores did away with food in barrels and started selling food in small packages on the shelves, but grocery stores are now stocking food in barrels as well as on shelves, and you can choose prepackaged food from the regular shopping aisles, or you can help yourself to foods like flour, rice, dried fruit, and peanut butter from large vats, from which you can scoop up as much or as little as you like, and your grandparents may like being reminded of the good old days.

Faulty Parallelism

Parallelism gives a sentence balance. *Faulty parallelism* occurs when two or more similar ideas are expressed in different grammatical constructions joined by *and, but,* or *or.* The following sentences show several ways to correct faulty parallelism.

FAULTY Rosie's favorite sports are **swimming, water-skiing,** and **to go horseback riding.** [two gerunds and an infinitive phrase]

PARALLEL Rosie's favorite sports are **swimming, water-skiing,** and **horseback riding.** [three gerunds]

FAULTY The athletes were not only **energetic,** but also **they had a great deal of enthusiasm.** [predicate adjective and an independent clause]

PARALLEL The athletes were not only **energetic** but also **enthusiastic.** [two adjectives]

FAULTY **Silent, watchful,** and **having an owlish quality,** the woman slowly turned her head. [two adjectives and a participial phrase]

PARALLEL **Silent, watchful,** and **owlish,** the woman slowly turned her head. [three adjectives]

FAULTY The child demanded **a bottle of juice** or **that his mother buy him a toy car.** [a noun and a noun clause]

PARALLEL The child demanded **a bottle of juice** or a **toy car.** [two nouns].

WRITING ACTIVITY 19 *Correcting Faulty Parallelism*

Revise each of the following sentences to eliminate faulty parallelism. Use the strategies shown in the sentences above.

1. Joanne was determined to find a car with air-conditioning, with an AM/FM radio, and one that had automatic transmission.
2. The student who won the lead in the school play was tall, handsome, and with style.
3. Going to a school dance is much more fun than to go to a movie.
4. Carla walked on stage slowly, confidently, and with pride.

5. The president of the sophomore class is athletic, friendly, and a good student.
6. Chester's guidance counselor recently told him that laughter and to cry are good for the soul.
7. The whisper of leaves, the gurgle of water, and that the birds were chirping made me feel peaceful.
8. Penniless, friendless, and having no home, the man limped toward the open door.
9. Benjamin asked us either to come for a picnic or that we stay for supper.
10. Summer is the smell of mowed grass, the sound of outdoor concerts, and the way grilled hamburgers taste.
11. Succeeding at team sports requires conscientiousness, discipline, and having a cooperative attitude.
12. The next year brought new construction and that our playing in the vacant lot was ended.
13. Jim's job is taking tickets for the games and to run the concession stand.
14. The striking workers demanded higher pay and that the working conditions be made safer.
15. The coach remarked that the young gymnast was powerful yet like a graceful dancer.
16. The bewildered tourists inquired about a restaurant and where to shop for records and souvenirs.
17. Driving safely means obeying all traffic laws and to watch out for the other guy.
18. Tired but with elation, the winner of the cross-country ski marathon spoke to reporters.
19. The piano teacher was a taskmaster, a perfectionist, and inspired his students.
20. The invitation asked that we bring a dish for the main course and to dress very casually.

WRITING ACTIVITY 20 *Writing on Your Own*

WRITING ABOUT THE THEME

Return once again to your composition about communicating from Writing Activity 15. This time check it carefully for sentence faults, including faulty coordination, faulty subordination, rambling sentences, and faulty parallelism. Make any necessary revisions. Save your paper for later use.

Integrating Language Skills

Editing and Publishing

Grammar in the Writing Process

In the poem "Primer Lesson," Carl Sandburg warns you that once you say proud words, you can never call them back. His warning is a good reminder of a big difference between speaking and writing. When you speak, your words come out once and are gone. When you write, however, you have many chances to revise your words. As you revise and edit your writing, keep in mind that your choice of words and your spelling and punctuation of those words are important.

Capitalization of Proper Nouns Previously in this chapter, you learned that specific nouns are better than general nouns. One way to make nouns more specific is to use proper nouns where possible. A *common noun* is any person, place, or thing; but a *proper noun* is a particular person, place, or thing. All proper nouns, as you may recall, begin with a capital letter. *(For examples of words that should be capitalized and for practice in writing them correctly, see pages 756–766.)*

COMMON NOUNS	The **team** is sponsored by a **store** in **town.**
PROPER NOUNS	The **Strikers** is sponsored by **Mullen's Hardware** in **Newington.**

Punctuation with Possessive Nouns A noun that shows possession or ownership is written with an apostrophe. To form the possessive of a singular noun, simply add *'s*. To form the possessive of a plural noun, however, you need to do one of two things: add only an apostrophe to a plural noun that ends in *s* or add *'s* to a plural noun that does not end in *s*. *(For examples and rules concerning possessive nouns and for practice in writing them correctly, see pages 809–811.)*

SINGULAR POSSESSIVE	No one could find the **catcher's** mitt.
PLURAL POSSESSIVE	The **coaches'** friends and the **children's** parents attend most of the at-home games.

Punctuation of a Series Three or more similar items together form a *series*. You will often have the occasion to write a series of nouns. Keep in mind, however, that other words, phrases, and clauses can also be written in a series. Without commas to separate the items in a series, the items would run into one another and cause confusion and misunderstanding. *(For examples of commas separating words in a series and for practice in writing words in a series correctly, see pages 774–776.)*

INCORRECT All new team members need a catcher's mitt a uniform and a book of rules.

CORRECT All new team members need a catcher's mitt**,** a uniform**,** and a book of rules.

Spelling the Plurals of Nouns Most of the time you simply have to add an *s* to make a singular noun plural. In a few cases, however you must change the ending of a noun before adding *s*. For example, if a word ends in a consonant and a *y*, you must change the *y* to *i* and add *es;* therefore, *salary* becomes *salaries*. *(For other spelling rules that affect plural nouns and for practice in writing plural nouns correctly, see pages 473–476.)*

SINGULAR My **family** enjoys softball.

PLURAL Many of the **families** enjoy softball.

Editing Checklist

1. Are all proper nouns capitalized? *(See pages 756–766.)*
2. Is an apostrophe used correctly with possessive nouns? *(See pages 809–811.)*
3. Do commas separate any series of words? *(See pages 774–776.)*
4. Are plural nouns spelled correctly? *(See pages 473–475.)*

WRITING ACTIVITY 21 *Writing on Your Own*

WRITING ABOUT THE THEME

Editing Keep in mind the items in the checklist above as you read through your composition about communicating from Writing Activity 20. Also review the Editing Checklist on page 35 and your own Personalized Editing Checklist.

Publishing When you feel that your composition is the best it can be, write a final copy. Then send a copy of your composition to the person you wrote about. In a letter explain how you admire that person for handling a difficult situation so nicely.

A Writer Writes

A Movie Review

PURPOSE: to evaluate a movie
AUDIENCE: readers of a local newpaper

Prewriting You have been asked to contribute a short movie review to the local newspaper. To prepare for writing the review, recall a recent movie you saw on TV or in a theater. Freewrite about it, expressing your reactions to it.

STEP 1: Cooperative Learning

Put your notes aside temporarily and if your teacher permits, form small discussion groups. Together brainstorm a list of criteria, or standards, for evaluating movies. These criteria might include the quality of the acting and directing, the story line, the photography, and the pacing. After a discussion, come to an agreement about five criteria that seem most important and rank these in order of importance. Take notes so that you remember the ranking system.

STEP 2: Developing and Organizing Ideas

Return to your desk and reread your freewriting about the movie you saw. Then explore—through more freewriting, brainstorming, or clustering—how your movie rates against the criteria your group developed. In your notes, list specific details from the movie to expand on your evaluation of each point. Using this evaluation, decide whether you will recommend the movie or not. Finally, arrange your prewriting notes in a logical order that would make sense to anyone who reads your review.

Drafting Using your prewriting notes, write your movie review. State your overall impression of the movie and include a point-by-point evaluation of it in relation to the criteria you helped develop. Finally, you should recommend whether or not people should see the movie.

Revising If your teacher permits, find another student who reviewed the same movie that you did. Exchange papers and read your partner's review carefully, focusing on the evaluation. Did your partner include all the criteria? Did he or she agree with you? If not, did your partner provide any details that changed your view of the movie?

After reading your partner's review, revise your review to improve it. Then look it over three times. First, perk up your word choice by substituting lively, specific words where needed. Second, if possible, create sentence variety by combining sentences. Third, correct any faulty coordination, faulty subordination, rambling sentences, or faulty parallelism.

Editing and Publishing Refer to the Editing Checklist on page 35 to edit your movie review, using proofreader's symbols for your corrections. *(See page 36.)* Then make a neat copy of your review. If your teacher agrees, create a poster for your review and form a committee to decide where to display your poster and those of your classmates.

WRITING ABOUT THE THEME

Independent Writing

Reread your journal entry about communicating that you wrote in response to the selection "No Problem, but It Needs a Solution" on page 49. Think of recent events that required you to communicate effectively. These may be occasions when you had to communicate with a figure of authority, with someone in need of your help, or with someone who has offended you. Choose one of these events and write a narrative showing what the situation called for and whether or not you succeeded in your efforts to communicate.

Creative Writing

Think of a striking simile or metaphor and develop it into a poem. For ideas, you might try looking for comparisons between the items in Column 1 and the items in Column 2.

Column 1	**Column 2**
a good joke	a giant sequoia tree
success	a thunderstorm
teenagers	a baseball diamond
the future	a jungle gym
sadness	fireworks

WRITING ABOUT THE THEME

Writing about Literature

Tone is the writer's attitude toward the subject. In "No Problem, but it Needs a Solution," the author's tone is humorous—even though his subject is quite serious. Write a paragraph that explains why you think a humorous tone is more effective in this selection than a serious tone would have been.

Writing in Other Subject Areas

World History Write a vivid, accurate description of Hagia Sophia, the Cathedral of Holy Wisdom, in Istanbul, Turkey. Gather information about it from the library or from your world history textbook. Use specific, lively words that appeal to the senses.

Humanities Write a vivid, accurate description of a well-known piece of classical music, such as the first movement of Beethoven's *Fifth Symphony,* or of a painting, or even of a setting for a film or play. Use comparisons—metaphors and similes—where appropriate to express your ideas.

Chapter 2

Checklist

Developing Your Writing Style

Choosing Vivid Words

- ✔ Use specific words with connotations that match your meaning. *(See page 54.)*
- ✔ Use figurative language to enliven writing. *(See page 55.)*
- ✔ Avoid clichés in your writing. *(See page 55.)*

Writing Concise Sentences

- ✔ Eliminate redundancy. *(See page 58.)*
- ✔ Avoid empty expressions. *(See page 59.)*
- ✔ Revise wordy phrases and clauses. *(See page 61.)*

Creating Sentence Variety

- ✔ Vary the length of your sentences by using phrases or by coordination or subordination. *(See pages 62–66.)*
- ✔ Use a mixture of simple, compound, complex, and compound-complex sentences to create sentence variety. *(See page 67.)*
- ✔ Vary the beginnings of your sentences. *(See page 69.)*

Eliminating Faulty Sentences

- ✔ Eliminate faulty coordination and subordination. *(See pages 70–71.)*
- ✔ Eliminate rambling sentences by separating your ideas into a variety of short and long sentences. *(See page 73.)*
- ✔ Use parallel constructions in your sentences. *(See page 74.)*

Chapter

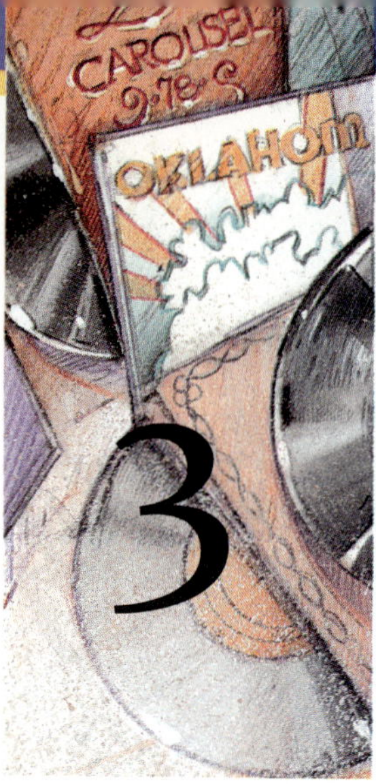

3 Writing Expository Paragraphs

Part 1 *Reading to Write*

THEME: *Music*

> Music hath charms to . . . soften rocks,
> or bend a knotted oak.
>
> WILLIAM CONGREVE, "The Mourning Bride"

Would you agree that music has extraordinary powers? How do you feel, for example, when you hear "The Star-Spangled Banner" or your school song? Throughout history songs have stirred up powerful emotions, such as patriotism, enthusiasm to win, religious fervor, nostalgia, sentimental feelings about loved ones, and a craving for the beautiful. It is not unusual to see how a particular song can make some people instantly light up with a smile, rock in rhythm, shed a tear, or vividly relive a memory.

How does music affect you? For example, have you ever noticed that a song can change your mood? Perhaps you were sad but, after hearing a song, realized that you were suddenly feeling better. Perhaps music affects you in other ways as well. Stop and think for a minute about music's impact on you. Think about it as you read the next selection, "The Sounds of Richard Rodgers." Music affected every aspect of Richard Rodgers's life. He loved it, wrote it, played it, and enjoyed enormous success because of it.

Richard Rodgers (1902–1979) was a famous American composer who collaborated with lyricists Lorenz Hart and Oscar Hammerstein in writing musical comedies.

The Sounds of Richard Rodgers

Ellen Goodman

He came into our house with the first Victrola[1] . . . and stayed. By the time I was ten I knew every song on our boxed and scratched "78" records: songs from *Oklahoma!* and *Carousel* and *South Pacific.* They were, very simply, the earliest tunes in a house that was more alive with the sound of politics than the sound of music.

As I grew older, I knew he was no Beethoven[2] or Verdi[3], or John Lennon[4] for that matter. By then his songs had been orchestrally overkilled into the sort of Muzak that kept you company in elevators or "on hold" at the insurance company line.

1. **Victrola** [vik trō'lə] *n.*: Brand name for a phonograph.
2. **Ludwig van Beethoven** [lüt'vik vän bā'tō vən] (1770–1827): German composer.
3. **Giuseppe Verdi** [jü zep' pe ver'dē] (1813–1901): Italian composer of operatic masterpieces.
4. **John Lennon** (1940–1980): Leader of the Beatles, a British rock music group.

But the fact is that from the time I was a child, to the time I sat with my own child watching the Trapp family[5] escape again over the mountains, there has always been a Richard Rodgers song in the background.

His work has been, very simply, our musical common exchange—as familiar and contagious as the composer ever hoped.

By the time he died, he was that rare man, someone who accomplished what he set out to do: "All I really want to do is to provide a hardworking man in the blouse business with a method of expressing himself. If he likes a tune, he can whistle it and it will make his life happier."

And, at seventy-seven, he was something even rarer, a man who remained centered in his work over six decades.

The numbers were overwhelming: 1,500 songs, 43 stage musical scores, 9 film scores, 4 television scores. He wrote music when he had a heart attack and music when he had cancer and music when he was learning to talk through his esophagus. He wrote music when his plays were huge successes and music when they were not; music when he needed the money and music when he didn't.

5. **Trapp family:** The Austrian Trapp family of musicians who escaped from Hitler during World War II. *The Sound of Music* is a musical about their experiences.

At fourteen, he composed his first song and at sixty-seven he still wrote to a friend: "I have a strong need to write some more music, and I just hope nothing stands in the way."

Yet when he was praised, he said, "I admit with no modesty whatever that not many people can do it. But when they say, 'You're a genius,' I say, 'no, it's my job.'"

Music was his job. It is a curious phrase. Yet it seems to me, looking back over his career, how little attention we've paid recently to the relationship between a life and "a job." For the past several years we've been more intrigued by life styles than by work styles, more curious about how someone sustains a marriage or a health regimen than how someone sustains an interest in his work.

The magazines we read are more focused on how we play than how we produce. We assume now that work is what we do for a living and leisure is how we enjoy living. When we meet people who do not understand this split, we label them "workaholics."

But Richard Rodgers was never seen in *People* magazine wearing his jog-togs. His "job" was writing music and his hobby was listening to it.

Usually we think of creative work as either inspired or tortured. We remember both Handel[6] writing "The Messiah" in three weeks and Michelangelo[7] mounting the scaffolding of the Sistine Chapel[8] year after year. Rodgers for his part once wrote a song in five minutes. But when asked about it, he said, "The song situation has probably been going around in my head for weeks. Sometimes it takes months. I don't believe that a writer does something wonderful spontaneously. I believe it's the result of years of living, or study, reading—his very personality and temperament."

The man knew something about the relationship between creativity and productivity. He knew something about the satisfactions of both, and managed to blend them. He could write music when handed the lyrics and write it before the lyrics. He could and would write a song to fit a scene. If Woody Allen is right in saying that "Eighty percent of life is showing up," well, Richard Rodgers showed up.

6. **George Frederick Handel** [han' dəl] (1685–1759): British composer who was born in Germany.
7. **Michelangelo** [mi kəl an'jə lō] (1475–1564): Italian sculptor, painter, architect, and poet.
8. **Sistine Chapel:** The chapel in the Vatican at Rome whose ceiling was painted by Michelangelo from 1508–1512.

"Some Enchanted Evening" will never go into the annals of great classics. *The King and I* is not *Aida*.[9] Rodgers was a workaday artist and he knew it. But he also knew that for some people there is a fuzzy line between work and play, between what is hard and what is fun.

"I heard a very interesting definition of work from a lawyer. Work, he said, is any activity you'd rather not do . . . I don't find it work to write music, because I enjoy it," said Rodgers. Yet he also said, "It isn't any easier than when I began, and by the same token it isn't any harder."

He was a man who was lucky in his work and lucky in his temperament. In an era when we tend to doubt the satisfactions that can come from work and tend to regard hard workers as a touch flawed in their capacity for pleasure, this composer showed what work can be: how it can sustain rather than drain, heighten rather than diminish, a full life. He leaves us a legacy in the sound of his life as well as his music. ◆

9. ***The King and I . . . Aida:*** Rodgers and his partner Oscar Hammerstein wrote *The King and I.* The Italian opera *Aida* was composed by Verdi.

Responding to the Theme

Music

Responding in Your Journal Richard Rodgers wrote his first song at fourteen. From that moment on, his whole life revolved around music. It was the most important thing in his life. How important is music in your life? Would you agree with the words, "Without music life would be a mistake"? Do you *have* to listen to the radio each day? Would a day without music be a terrible day? What does music do for you? Does it affect your emotions or cause you to daydream? Does it give you energy and ambition? Can you concentrate on homework better if you have music playing in the background? In your journal each day this week, write a response to one of these questions about music—or to any other question about music that you want to explore. Begin now by writing about the kind of music you like best. What is it about that kind of music that you like so much? Do you also like any other kinds of music? Has your favorite kind of music changed over the years?

Speaking and Listening What makes some people like Richard Rodgers live for music? Write a set of questions that try to get to the heart of this matter. For example, you could ask a musician when he or she first became interested in music and what created that initial interest. Then choose someone you know who is deeply involved in music, set up an interview, and ask your questions. During the interview, either tape the answers or jot down notes and reconstruct the answers later. Then, if time permits, your teacher will allow class time for you to compare your answers with those of other students.

Critical Thinking: Evaluating Ellen Goodman, author of "The Sounds of Richard Rodgers," suggests that all kinds of music such as classical, rock, and songs by Richard Rodgers have value, or purpose. Do you agree with the author? Write a paragraph that explains your answer.

Extending Your Vocabulary A selection about music usually includes some musical terms. Write the dictionary definition of the following words. Then use those words and any other musical terms you find interesting in a paragraph of your own.

composition musical score lyrics

Part 2 Writing

Composers use the notes of the musical scale to express their musical ideas in a piece of music. Writers use indented paragraphs to mark off their main ideas. A paragraph is a group of related sentences that develop a main idea.

Writing Term A **paragraph** is a group of related sentences that present and develop one main idea.

What will you write in most of your paragraphs? Richard Rodgers had the answer when he said, "I don't believe that a writer does something wonderful spontaneously. I believe it's the result of years of living, or study, reading." He was, of course, referring to the writing of music, but his words apply equally as well to the writing of words. What you will write about most will be those things which you know through living, working, studying, and reading. Whenever your purpose is to explain or inform, you will be writing *expository* paragraphs.

Writing Term An **expository paragraph** explains or informs.

In this chapter you will learn several strategies that will help you inform and explain effectively.

Paragraph Structure

A well-written paragraph has three basic parts: a topic sentence, supporting sentences, and a concluding sentence. Notice how each part serves a purpose in the following expository paragraph.

Student Model: *Expository Paragraph*

Life in Caves

TOPIC SENTENCE STATES MAIN IDEA

BODY OF SUPPORTING SENTENCES DEVELOPS MAIN IDEA

CONCLUDING SENTENCE ADDS FINISHING TOUCH

Most large caves have three distinct zones, and each zone is home to a different kind of natural life. In the innermost part of the cave, the darkness is complete, and the temperature never varies. Without light, green plants cannot live and animals have no need for eyes. The next zone, although still dark and moist, has a variable temperature. Animals that otherwise live outside inhabit this zone seasonally. The third zone, called the twilight zone, begins wherever light from the cave entrance can first be seen. A few green plants can grow in this zone. Most of the animals in this zone use the cave as shelter from the outdoors. In each zone the plants and animals adapt to the meager resources of their home.

In some paragraphs the main idea is implied rather than stated directly in a topic sentence. In others the main idea may be expressed in two sentences instead of one. Most paragraphs that stand alone, however, have a clearly stated topic sentence, a body of supporting sentences, and a concluding sentence that adds the finishing touch.

Topic Sentence

The *topic sentence* can come at the beginning, middle, or end of a paragraph. Although its placement may vary, its purpose is always the same.

Writing Term A **topic sentence** states the main idea of the paragraph.

The main idea of a paragraph is like a summary statement of its details. The topic sentence is, therefore, more general than the other sentences in the paragraph. It is also specific enough to focus the subject to one main point that can be covered in a paragraph. The topic sentence in the following paragraph is suitably specific.

Model: *Topic Sentence*

TOPIC SENTENCE	On my recent trip to Sea World, I learned a great deal about the amazing dolphin. Dolphins, like other higher animals, show many signs of caring for their fellow creatures.
SUPPORTING SENTENCES	Mother and child are closely attached. Some dolphins become close friends and stay close friends. When a friend or mate dies, a dolphin shows signs of sorrow. It may circle the body, making a whistling noise. It may even refuse to eat.
CONCLUDING SENTENCE	These signs have convinced scientists that dolphins are intelligent, feeling creatures.

PATRICIA LAUBER, *The Friendly Dolphins* (Adapted)

The following topic sentences are too general. The reader would not have known what to expect in the rest of the paragraph.

TOO GENERAL Dolphins are interesting creatures.
TOO GENERAL Dolphins behave in an interesting way.

Use the following guidelines to identify and write good topic sentences.

Topic Sentence

A topic sentence
1. states the main idea.
2. focuses the limited subject to one main point that can be adequately covered in the paragraph.
3. is more general than the sentences that develop it.

WRITING ACTIVITY 1 *Identifying Topic Sentences*

Write the topic sentence of each of the following paragraphs.

1. A Doozie

Have you ever heard someone say, "It's a doozie!" when they were describing an item that was really special or of extra high

quality? This expression is not used much today, but in the 1930's it was quite common. It originated in connection with the fabulous Duesenburg, the finest automobile ever produced in the United States. Something that was considered as good as a Duesenburg was very good indeed. RICHARD L. KNUDSON
Fabulous Cars of the 1920's and 1930's

2. Remnants of Pompeii

Archaeologists working on the ruins of Pompeii have discovered an ingenious way of reconstructing some of their finds. When the lava from the eruption of A.D. 79 cooled, it solidified around all the objects which had been unable to escape. Over the centuries many of these objects decayed, leaving hollows in the solid lava. Archaeologists refill these with liquid plaster. The plaster is allowed to set. The lava can then be chipped away, leaving an accurate plaster cast of whatever was trapped by the lava flow nearly 2,000 years ago. IAN ANDREWS, *Pompeii*

3. Arctic Etymology

Once a large flightless bird called the giant auk lived in the cold Arctic regions. It had strong wings adapted for swimming, a big beak, and a dark brown head with white patches around the eyes. Fishermen from Brittany called it by the ancient Welsh name *pen-gwyn,* meaning "white head." That reminded scholars of the Latin word *pinguis,* meaning "fat." Since the giant auk was plump, they called it pinguin, "fat bird." The Latin *pinguis* blended with the *pen-gwyn* of the fishermen led to our modern word for the auk, *penguin.* ROBERT SILVERBERG
Forgotten by Time (Adapted)

4. Silken Status Symbols

To settlers in early New England, clothes were often a measure of a person's wealth, and people were supposed to dress according to their station in life. The wealthy dressed themselves in expensive clothes imported from London, while poorer people wore clothes made from rough homespun. Dressing above one's station was actually against the law. In 1678, 68 young people were fined for wearing silken clothes. In a strange new world, settlers tried to hold fast to laws and customs that made their society feel orderly. ANN PALMER
Growing Up in Colonial America (Adapted)

Supporting Sentences

A topic sentence on an interesting subject usually raises questions in a reader's mind. The *supporting sentences,* which form the body of a paragraph, answer these questions. They back up the main idea with specific information.

Writing Term **Supporting sentences** explain the topic sentence with specific details, facts, examples, incidents, or reasons.

As you read the following topic sentence about the moon's eclipse, think about the questions you would want answered in the rest of the paragraph.

TOPIC SENTENCE About every 18 months, the moon passes directly between the earth and the sun, and somewhere in the world a brilliant drama unfolds in the sky.

If you are like most readers, you expect the rest of the paragraph to answer questions about the appearance of the earth and the sun when the moon travels between them. The supporting sentences provide specific details that answer those questions.

Model: *Supporting Sentences*

SUPPORTING SENTENCES The silhouetted moon begins to eat into the sun's disk, producing an ever-narrowing solar crescent. At first nothing particularly remarkable occurs on the earth below. Shadows gradually sharpen, colors soften, the landscape and sky darken. Then, as the moon's shadow arrives, racing over the countryside at 1,000 miles an hour, there is a descent into darkness. The sun, giver of warmth and life, is suddenly gone. All that remains is a black hole in the sky, fringed by flamelike tongues and the pearly glow of the corona. It is a sight that has left its mark on mythology, art, and history. In 585 B.C., an eclipse so unnerved a battlefield full of Lydians and Medes that they threw down their weapons on the spot.

DENNIS OVERBYE, *Discover* (Adapted)

WRITING ACTIVITY ◆2 *Writing Supporting Sentences*

For each of the following topic sentences, use brainstorming or clustering to develop a list of specific details, facts, examples, incidents, or reasons to support the topic sentence. Then write three supporting sentences from each list.

1. Our high school offers excellent extracurricular activities.
2. We need to take seriously the threat of drug abuse to our society.
3. Teenagers can benefit from participating in community service.

Concluding Sentence

A televised sporting event usually ends with a wrap-up of the highlights and outcome. In the same way, good paragraphs end with a sentence that wraps up the main idea.

Writing Term A **concluding sentence** adds a strong ending to a paragraph.

Good concluding sentences avoid a dull summary or a repetition of the topic sentence. They offer, instead, a fresh insight that locks the main idea in the reader's mind. These sentences are called *clinchers.* The following paragraph has a weak concluding sentence.

Model: *Supporting Sentences*

Prey and Predator Asleep

Whether a mammal dreams or not depends in part on whether it is a predator or a prey. In a dream state, sleep is very deep, and an animal does not know what is going on around it. The dream state is safer for a predator than for a prey because a predator does not have to worry about sudden attack. A prey, in contrast, needs to be able to make a quick getaway. As you can see, dreams depend on whether a mammal is a predator or a prey.

CONCLUDING SENTENCE

The following concluding sentence is stronger. It clinches the main idea by adding new information.

CLINCHER Experiments show that a predator dreams, but a prey sleeps in a shallow, dreamless state.

WRITING ACTIVITY 3 *Identifying Strong Concluding Sentences*

In the following pairs of concluding sentences, one sentence is better than the other. Write the letter of the clincher from each pair.

EXAMPLE **a.** That is the way some rock bands have made it big.
b. For some, rock music has been a profitable business.

ANSWER **b**

1. **a.** In conclusion, opening the right kind of bank account will allow your money to earn interest.
b. With the right kind of bank account, a penny saved is more than a penny earned.

2. **a.** As you can see, Newton was indeed a great scientist.
b. Newton's inventive work led to a whole new way of seeing the world.

3. **a.** Despite the headaches owning a car is often an adventure in freedom.
b. Owning a car certainly has both a good side and a bad side.

4. **a.** In a nutshell becoming a veterinarian takes hard work.
b. A lasting love for animals sustains many veterinary students through the years of hard work.

5. **a.** To creators of television comedies, the phrase *a laugh a minute* is no joke.
b. As I've said, creators of television comedies plan the laugh lines to come at regular intervals.

Prewriting

Writing Process

A good expository paragraph offers a stimulating idea on a subject of interest. Subjects for expository writing are everywhere—on television, in books, and even in your own experience. In fact, *choosing* a subject from among the many possibilities poses a real challenge.

Discovering Subjects to Write About

The search for subjects calls for a free mind and an active pen. Asking the right questions and jotting down answers through freewriting, brainstorming, clustering, and other prewriting techniques will unlock a storehouse of ideas.

Drawing on Personal Experience One way to find subjects is to think about your interests, hobbies, skills, and special knowledge. Another way is to ask, "What do I know that my classmates probably do not know?" Then jot down answers, which may give you ideas.

Drawing on Outside Sources Books, magazines, television, radio, and conversations with people also provide a wealth of information. Asking questions about what you read or hear is another way to discover interesting subjects for expository writing. Critical readers and listeners question much of what they read or hear by asking *How? Why? What?* and *Do I agree?*

Writing Tip Draw on personal experience and outside sources to find subjects for writing.

WRITING ACTIVITY 4 *Finding Subjects from Personal Experience*

Brainstorm answers to the following questions. Save your work.

1. Of the subjects you take in school, which is your favorite? What are two ideas concerning this subject that you could write about?
2. What are your interests outside school? Name two you could write a paragraph about.
3. Have you ever taken any lessons? If so, what did you learn that you could explain to others?

4. What is your position in the family—youngest child? oldest? only child? only girl? What general truth can you state about people in your position?
5. What careers are you interested in? What kind of personality do you think would be best suited to each of the careers you named?

"Write about dogs!"

WRITING ACTIVITY 5 *Finding Subjects from Reading*

Read the paragraph below. Then write five questions that occur to you as you read it.

Seaweed for Sale

The possibility exists that seaweed algae could have commercial value in this country. Dried, it could be fed to livestock. Collected in quantity and decomposed, it could give off sufficient methane gas to be used as fuel. So far, however, no one has succeeded in producing a crop that is commercially usable. Scientists are testing a system, however, that may produce vast quantities of algae at very low cost. One scientist, Walter Adley, has discovered that algae will grow extremely rapidly under the proper conditions: sunlight, wave action, and harvesting at an early age. In the waters off the West Indies, he has tested a scheme to build platforms covered with a heavy plastic screen. Kept wet by the waves, algae grow rapidly on the screens. Adley has successfully harvested the algae. Adley's technique may make it possible to put algae to many good uses. L. E. TAYLOR

Measuring the Pulse of Life on Maine's Coast (Adapted)

Choosing and Limiting a Subject

After you find several possible subjects, the next step is to choose one subject and refine it until it is suitable for a one-paragraph explanation. Use the following guidelines to choose a good subject for an expository paragraph that clearly introduces and expands on one subject.

Choosing an Expository Subject

1. Choose a subject that interests you.
2. Choose a subject that will interest your chosen audience.
3. Choose a subject you know enough about or can learn enough about to explain accurately.
4. Choose a subject that is limited enough to be adequately explained in one paragraph.

Exploring a Subject One way to decide which subject to choose is to use freewriting or brainstorming to see how much you know about a subject. The following questions will help you assess your knowledge.

Exploratory Questions

1. What do I already know that would help me explain my subject clearly to my audience?
2. What further information do I need to find out?
3. Where can I find this information?

If you can think of only one or two answers to these questions and cannot think of sources for finding more, you probably should choose another subject. If, on the other hand, your paper becomes crowded with scattered ideas, your subject is probably too broad for one paragraph. Of the subjects that are left, choose one, explore it, and limit it by following the Steps in Limiting a Subject on the next page.

Limiting a Subject To limit a broad subject so that it is manageable, ask questions that lead to specific answers. Continue the process until you can express in one phrase what your paragraph will be about.

Steps in Limiting a Subject

	BROAD SUBJECT	careers
1.	Ask yourself	**Which** career?
	MORE LIMITED	computer programming
2.	Ask yourself	**What about** computer programming?
	SUITABLY LIMITED	how to prepare for a career in computer programming

WRITING ACTIVITY 6 *Limiting Expository Subjects*

Choose five of the following subjects. Then, using the Steps in Limiting a Subject as a guide, limit each subject for one paragraph.

1. music
2. sports
3. part-time jobs
4. clothes
5. foreign lands
6. modern heroes
7. food
8. machines
9. space travel
10. fads

WRITING ACTIVITY 7 *Writing on Your Own*

WRITING ABOUT THE THEME

Review the journal entries you wrote about music. Freewrite about any questions or ideas you wish to explore about the world of music. Based on these ideas, think of five subjects for an expository paragraph about music. Limit each subject, writing each limited subject beside the original broad subject. Finally, circle the subject you think has the most promise for development into an expository paragraph. Save your work in your writing folder for later use.

Determining Your Audience

When your purpose is to explain, think carefully about who will be reading your work. To suit your writing to your audience, ask yourself the following questions.

Audience Questions

1. What do my readers already know about my subject? What else might they need to know as background information?
2. What are my readers' attitudes toward my subject? If these attitudes differ substantially from mine, how can I address those differences?
3. Why are my readers reading my writing? How can I address their needs?

WRITING ACTIVITY 8 *Writing on Your Own*

WRITING ABOUT THE THEME

Determine who will be reading the expository paragraph for which you chose a subject in Writing Activity 7. Then ask yourself the Audience Questions above. Brainstorm answers to the questions and write suggestions for tailoring your essay to the background and needs of your audience. Save your work in your writing folder for later use.

Developing Supporting Details

Supporting details include any specific information that will help explain your subject. The following chart shows some of the different types of details you can use to support the main idea in an expository paragraph.

Types of Supporting Details

examples	incidents	facts/statistics
reasons	directions	steps in a process
causes	definitions	comparisons/contrasts
effects	analogies	classifications

When you choose the type of supporting details to use, keep in mind the purpose of the paragraph and the kinds of questions a reader may have about the subject.

Writing Tip List details that suit the main idea of your paragraph and that explain the subject clearly to the reader.

If you are familiar with the subject you are writing about, you may already have many supporting details on hand. More likely, though, you will have to do research by reading and talking to knowledgeable people. *(See pages 350–370 for research techniques.)*

WRITING ACTIVITY 9 *Listing Supporting Details*

For each of the following subjects, list four supporting details that would help you explain it. The following example and the questions on page 97 will help you with this activity.

SUBJECT the value of team athletics

SUPPORTING DETAILS
- staying in shape helps you feel good
- being part of a team builds understanding
- a team is like a family
- the time when the star player had to sacrifice to help the team win in the play-offs

1. the pleasures of listening to music
2. the importance of Martin Luther King, Jr., Day
3. how to be a good student
4. how to lose ten pounds
5. ways that every citizen can help protect the environment
6. the importance of a part-time job
7. making a vegetable garden
8. how to wash a car
9. a winning streak
10. caring for an animal

WRITING ACTIVITY 10 *Writing on Your Own*

WRITING ABOUT THE THEME

Review the Types of Supporting Details on page 99. Determine which ones would be most useful in explaining the subject you chose in Writing Activity 7. Research or brainstorm to develop a list of supporting details. Save your work in your writing folder.

Classifying Supporting Details

After listing details about your subject, classify them to find the best way to develop your paragraph. When you *classify,* you group specific details into general categories. The following examples show different ways to classify supporting details in an expository paragraph. Notice that each way of classifying is appropriate to the main idea. *(For more information about classifying, see page 211.)*

1. MAIN IDEA — Computers can perform certain tasks very fast.
DETAILS — **Classify** details according to facts about the tasks computers perform and examples of how fast they perform the tasks.
METHOD OF DEVELOPMENT — Facts and examples

2. MAIN IDEA — Learning how to use your computer is fun and easy if you follow certain steps.
DETAILS — **Classify** details into a set of directions for using the computer.
METHOD OF DEVELOPMENT — A set of directions

3. MAIN IDEA — After an hour with my friend's computer, I learned the meaning of *user-friendly.*
DETAILS — **Classify** details according to the incidents leading to the understanding of *user-friendly.*
METHOD OF DEVELOPMENT — Incident

4. MAIN IDEA — A program instructs the computer to perform tasks.
DETAILS — **Classify** details according to the characteristics of a program.
METHOD OF DEVELOPMENT — Definition

5. MAIN IDEA — The process of writing a software program involves many steps.
DETAILS — **Classify** details according to the steps in the process of writing a software program.
METHOD OF DEVELOPMENT — Steps in a process

6. MAIN IDEA — To understand the inside of a computer, imagine that the chip is a railroad switch.
DETAILS — **Classify** details according to the similar characteristics of a chip and a railroad switch.
METHOD OF DEVELOPMENT — Analogy

7. MAIN IDEA The typical computer has five basic parts.
DETAILS **Classify** details according to the function each part performs.
METHOD OF DEVELOPMENT Analysis

8. MAIN IDEA The microchip is responsible for the computer revolution.
DETAILS **Classify** details about the microchip (cause) and the computer revolution (effect).
METHOD OF DEVELOPMENT Cause/effect

9. MAIN IDEA Computers and calculators share certain features, but they differ in major ways.
DETAILS **Classify** details according to the similarities and differences between a calculator and a computer.
METHOD OF DEVELOPMENT Comparison/contrast

10. MAIN IDEA There are many different types of computers.
DETAILS **Classify** computers according to their types.
METHOD OF DEVELOPMENT Grouping into types

Two techniques you can use to classify supporting details are charting and outlining. *(See pages 216–217 for information about outlining.)* The following model shows how one student used charting to classify the supporting details from example number 7 above.

Student Model: *Charting to Classify Details*

Basic Parts of the Computer

PARTS	FUNCTION PERFORMED
1. input device (keyboard)	user enters information and instructions by typing
2. storage disk	receives information and permanently stores it
3. monitor	displays information that user is working on
4. central processing unit (CPU)	holds information being used and directs the computer functions
5. printer	prints the processed information on paper

The following model shows the expository paragraph that resulted from the charting on the previous page.

Student Model: *Expository Paragraph*

The Parts of a Computer

Before I attended computer camp, I was very confused about this complicated monster that would rule my life. After a few days, though, I began to understand how it works. Regardless of its size or type, the computer has five basic parts. First, there is a keyboard on which the user types information and instructions. Second, there is a storage disk, usually referred to as a memory, which receives the information and permanently stores it. Third, a monitor, or screen, displays the information the user is working on. Fourth is a central processing unit (CPU) where the computer functions take place. The CPU holds the information while it is being worked on and directs the computer to perform functions. Finally, a printer prints the processed information on paper. This astonishing combination of parts produces a machine that has an enormous impact on our lives.

TOPIC SENTENCE

SUPPORTING DETAILS ANALYZE PARTS OF THE WHOLE

CONCLUDING SENTENCE

WRITING ACTIVITY 11 *Identifying Methods of Development*

Write the method of developing supporting details used in each paragraph. Use the examples on pages 101–102 as a guide.

1. Miller Race Cars

Harry Miller was an automotive genius who dominated American racing for many years. His front-wheel-drive (fwd) cars were well-suited to American oval-track racing because of their superior cornering. Miller's first fwd racer was built in 1924. Two years later 9 out of the first 10 finishers at Indy were driving Miller cars. In the 1929 race, 27 of the 33 cars on the Indy track had Miller engines, and 7 Millers were among the first 10 cars to cross the finish line.

RICHARD L. KNUDSON
Fabulous Cars of the 1920's and 1930's

2. Mining for Gold

Gold set free from rocks and mixed with streambed sand and gravel is called placer gold. Placer mining was the only kind practiced in California in the first two years of the gold rush. It was brutal work. The prospector squatted beside a stream and dipped a washbowl into the water, scooping up a panful of dirt. Then he performed the delicate task of panning for gold by swirling the contents of the washbowl. The trick was to let the surplus sand and gravel spill over the edge of the pan. At the same time, any gold that might have been scooped up had to be kept inside. Since the gold was much heavier than the gravel, it would settle to the bottom of the basin. ROBERT SILVERBERG

Ghost Towns of the American West (ADAPTED)

3. Basic Training

Operant conditioning is often used to train porpoises. In this kind of training, the animal makes something happen. He starts it; he is the operator. When he does something, a reward appears. It is the same sort of training you use when you ask your dog to sit up and speak and then reward him with a snack.

MARGERY PACKLAM, *Wild Animals, Gentle Women*

4. A Balancing Act

Deep-sea divers are in balance between the internal pressure of their bodies and the external pressure of the sea. This state may fairly well be illustrated by comparison with that of a tire on a loaded truck. So long as the tire is inflated with sufficient air, it stays rounded and supports the load pressing down on it. If the tire "blows out," down comes the weight of the truck upon it and flattens it. In the same way, if the diver's suit by any chance loses its air pressure, down comes the weight of the sea, instantly crushing the diver as flat as any blown-out tire.

CAPTAIN EDWARD ELLSBERG, *The Bends* (ADAPTED)

5. Something Deeply Hidden

I experienced a wonder of nature as a child of four or five years, when my father showed me a compass. That this needle behaved in such a determined way did not at all fit into the nature of events. I can remember—or at least I believe I can remember—that this experience made a deep and lasting impression on me. Something deeply hidden had to be behind things. ALBERT EINSTEIN

WRITING ACTIVITY 12 *Choosing a Method of Development*

Write the method of development that would be most suitable for each of the following main ideas. Refer to the examples and the chart on pages 101–102.

1. There are about 250 different kinds of sharks in the world's oceans today.
2. To understand how astronomers measure the distance between stars, try this simple experiment.
3. My first day as a hospital volunteer taught me the value of teamwork.
4. The harpsichord and clavichord, although similar, produce sound in very different ways.
5. Advancements in the fields of transportation and communication have brought the far countries of the world closer together.
6. If you can picture the ripples around a pebble thrown into a pond, you can begin to understand how radio waves travel.
7. People are living longer now than ever before.
8. Imprinting is nature's way of assuring that young ducks and geese will be cared for.
9. There are many different types of computers.
10. The slash-and-burn process is one widely used method of clearing trees.

WRITING ACTIVITY 13 *Classifying Supporting Details*

Choose one of the following main ideas and brainstorm a list of details. Then decide on a method of development and make a chart similar to the one on page 102 to show the classification of your supporting details. You may wish to save these notes for a future composition.

1. I use several steps to prepare for a competitive event. *(For your answer choose an athletic or academic event or an event where you compete with a special talent.)*
2. Here are the directions for playing this game. *(Choose any game of skill.)*
3. I believe that there are several causes of pollution in my community.
4. Our community offers many different cultural events throughout the year.
5. This year's candidates certainly have their similarities and differences. *(Choose any two candidates.)*

WRITING ACTIVITY 14 *Writing on Your Own*

WRITING ABOUT THE THEME

Review the list of supporting details from Writing Activity 10 and the classifying examples on pages 101–102. Then choose a method of development for your paragraph and make a chart similar to the one on page 102 to classify your details. Save your work in your writing folder for later use.

Organizing Details in Logical Order

The final step in prewriting is to arrange your supporting details in a logical order. Well-organized details will help you write a clear explanation. Look for relationships among your supporting details and use one of the following methods of organization to arrange them.

Order of Importance, Interest, or Degree Arrange details in the order of least to most or most to least. Either way, the reader can take in ideas in a logical progression.

Developmental Order When your ideas are of equal importance, use *developmental order.* Arrange your supporting details in a logical order in which one idea grows out of another.

Chronological Order In *chronological order* arrange details in the order in which they occur over time. When chronological order is used to organize the steps in a process, or in a set of directions, it is sometimes called *sequential* order.

Spatial Order *Spatial order* places details in the order of *near to far, top to bottom, inside to outside, left to right,* and so on. Use this method to analyze what something is made of.

Writing Tip Choose the method of organization best suited to your supporting details.

WRITING ACTIVITY 15 *Identifying Methods of Organization*

Identify the method of organization in each paragraph as *order of importance, developmental order, chronological order,* or *spatial order.*

1. The Birth of a Car

The Packard was born around the turn of the century, brought into existence by one man's dissatisfaction with another automobile. In 1898, James Ward Packard, an engineer in Warren, Ohio, bought a brand-new Winton motorcar in nearby Cleveland. On the drive home, he had several breakdowns. When he complained to the manufacturer of the car, Alexander Winton, he got no results. In fact, Winton told Packard that if he didn't like the car, he should go out and build a better one himself. Packard accepted the challenge, and on November 6, 1899, the first Packard automobile rolled down the streets of Warren. It *was* a better product, and the newly formed company quickly established itself as a manufacturer of quality automobiles.

RICHARD L. KNUDSON, *Fabulous Cars of the 1920's and 1930's*

2. Four-Legged Remedies

Animals are helping people come out of their shells or recover from illnesses. Troubled young people who are given a pet to care for often develop a sense of responsibility. More important, people whose leg and back muscles have been seriously injured can get a therapeutic massage from riding a horse. Most important, people with heart disease or high blood pressure can actually lower their blood pressure by petting a dog. For these reasons pets are becoming just what the doctor ordered.

3. Defensive Architecture

The center of a medieval castle was the massive stone tower, which all the rest of the structures were designed to protect. Adjacent to the tower were lean-to sheds and surrounding these was a walled courtyard. Another courtyard, the outer bailey, surrounded the inner space. The outer bailey wall was built of stone and fortified with lookout towers. In addition to all these layers of protection, most castles also had a moat that encircled the outer wall. In an age when enemy attacks were commonplace, defense was the guiding principle in architecture.

4. The Mighty Queen

The queen is a key piece in a chess game. When it is on the board, it has great firepower because it can move in all directions to capture the opponent's pieces. Making the most of the queen's power also determines the way a player will move the other pieces. When both queens are out of play after having been captured or traded, the nature of the game changes. Without the queens, attacking and defending strategies must be tighter and more precise. The change is so drastic that this stage of the game has its own name: *endgame.*

WRITING ACTIVITY 16 *Arranging Details in Logical Order*

Arrange the details for each subject in *order of importance, developmental order, chronological order,* or *spatial order.* Write which you used.

1. Subject how the days of the week got their names

Details
- Friday—from Germanic god Freya
- Monday—moon's day
- Thursday—from Germanic god Thor
- Tuesday—from Germanic god Tiw
- Saturday—Saturn's day
- Wednesday—from Germanic god Woden
- Sunday—sun's day

Method of Development: Facts and examples

2. Subject negative effects of daylight saving time

Details
- people feel generally confused
- the number of automobile accidents increases
- people sometimes arrive late

Method of Development: Cause/effect

3. Subject parts of the brain stem

Details
- medulla oblongata—lowest part of the brain stem
- midbrain is the highest part of the brain stem
- medulla oblongata regulates heartbeat, breathing, and other reflexes
- pons is above the medulla oblongata
- midbrain is the center for hearing, seeing, and touching
- pons serves as a bridge between the lower and higher part of the brain stem

Method of Development: Analysis

4. Subject the first photograph

Details
- by 1780, scientists had discovered that chemically treated silver salts would retain an image made by light
- *camera obscura,* invented in 1500, projected an image onto a screen
- in 1826, Frenchman Joseph Niepce used chemically treated metal plates to take the very first photograph
- scientists needed to find a way to make permanent the image projected by *camera obscura*

Method of Development: Incident

WRITING ACTIVITY 17 *Writing on Your Own*

WRITING ABOUT THE THEME

Look over the supporting details you classified in Writing Activity 14. Then decide which logical order would best suit your details and arrange them accordingly. Save your work in your writing folder for later use.

WRITING ACTIVITY 18 *Evaluating Your Prewriting Work*

Before you write a draft and if your teacher permits, test your ideas by telling them to someone else. Form a small discussion group with other students. Take turns going around the group, telling your subject and your supporting details. As you talk through your prewriting work, comment on any parts that gave you difficulty. Ask for suggestions from others in the group about how they proceeded. Also ask them to tell you if your supporting details are sufficient and clear. If they are not, add or clarify them as needed.

Drafting

Writing Process

Once you have developed your subject, you are ready to write the first draft by transforming your notes into a topic sentence, supporting sentences, and a concluding sentence.

Drafting the Topic Sentence

A topic sentence can come anywhere in a paragraph, but drafting it before you draft your paragraph will help clarify your ideas. Follow the steps below to write your topic sentence.

Steps for Writing an Expository Topic Sentence

1. Look over your prewriting notes.
2. Express your main idea in one sentence.
3. Rewrite that sentence until it
   - tells the reader what you are going to explain.
   - controls, or binds together, all supporting details.

Suppose you had written the following prewriting notes.

SUBJECT the new high-speed train (MLV)

DETAILS
- engineers developed magnetic levitation vehicle (MLV)
- magnets on train motor and rail hold train four to six inches above single rail
- magnetic force also drives train forward
- may travel up to 300 miles per hour

You might start by writing a topic sentence like the following.

WEAK TOPIC SENTENCE The magnetic levitation vehicle can travel at up to 300 miles per hour.

This topic sentence, however, does not control all the supporting details; it focuses on only one aspect—speed. The following topic sentence is better because it also refers to the force that propels the train.

REVISED TOPIC SENTENCE A new type of train uses magnetic force to achieve high speeds.

WRITING ACTIVITY 19 *Revising Topic Sentences*

Revise each topic sentence until it accounts for all of the details.

1. Life in a big city offers many rewarding advantages.
- music, ballet, theater, art museums
- wide variety of other entertainments
- exposure to many different people and life-styles
- not much chance to experience natural beauty
- need for added security measures
- feeling of congestion

2. The eye is amazing.
- every person's eye has a unique pattern of blood vessels
- new machine has been invented to identify people by taking an eyeprint
- machine scans a person's eye and matches it with a previously recorded image stored in its memory
- forgery-proof method of identification

3. As amateurs, today's Olympic stars cannot be paid for their athletic performances.
- to earn money, some take jobs making commercials
- some receive gifts that do not affect their amateur status
- ancient Greeks also gave gifts to their Olympic winners
- prizes and gifts made athletes in ancient Greece wealthy

4. Two speakers are needed for stereo sound.
- in a stereo record, each groove is like two walls at right angles
- sound from one microphone is imprinted in one side of groove; sound from second microphone is imprinted on other side
- after recording, vinyl plastic is pressed between molds
- turntable stylus rides in groove, reproduces sounds on both sides of groove
- sends each side of sound independently through amplifier and two speakers

WRITING ACTIVITY 20 *Writing on Your Own*

WRITING ABOUT THE THEME

Review your prewriting notes from Writing Activity 17. Then follow the guidelines on page 110 to come up with a strong topic sentence. Continue revising until you feel the sentence ties together the details you intend to use in developing your paragraph. Save your work in your writing folder for later use.

Critical Thinking

Writing Is Thinking

Making Sound Generalizations

To write a topic sentence, you often use the thinking skill of **generalizing.** In other words you look at specific details, facts, and examples to form a general observation or principle. For example, after visiting several shopping malls at different times, you might form this generalization: *Most shopping malls are least crowded on Monday evenings.*

Not all generalizations are true. Suppose you know five people whose parents bought them cars for their sixteenth birthdays. To persuade your parents to buy you a car, you might pose this unsound generalization: *Parents of teenagers buy them cars when they turn sixteen!*

Making a chart like the one below can help you examine the soundness of your generalizations. Start by listing a preliminary generalization. Then list additional details based on research or experience and rewrite your generalization to reflect the new information. Limit your generalization by using words such as *some, many,* or *most.*

Revising a Generalization

Preliminary Generalization	All students who do not attend sports events lack school spirit.
Additional Research Details	Poll results: 10 students do not care to attend any school events but like the school; 15 students do not attend sports but belong to clubs; 10 students attend no school events and admit to no school spirit.
Qualifying Words *(some, many, most)*	some
Revised Generalization	Some students who do not attend sports events lack school spirit.

Thinking Practice Write a generalization using one of the following topics. Then use a chart like the one above to test and revise it.

1. how watching television can affect grades
2. why people show off at parties
3. how malicious rumors get started

Drafting the Body

If you planned your paragraph well, drafting the body should proceed smoothly. As you draft, you are simply changing your organized list of supporting details into sentences that clearly state your ideas. At this point you should not concern yourself about correctness in usage and mechanics since you will have opportunities for editing later. The following suggestions should also be helpful.

Tips for Drafting the Paragraph Body

1. Draft quickly, focusing on getting your ideas down on paper as clearly as possible.
2. Combine sentences that seem to go together. *(See pages 62–66)*
3. To keep your ideas developing logically, pause now and then to reread what you have just written.
4. Where necessary, add words and phrases to help one sentence lead smoothly into the next.

While drafting, try to develop the habit of showing the relationship among your ideas. You can use words and phrases called *transitions* to join sentences.

Writing Term A **transition** is a word or phrase that shows how ideas are related to one another.

The following chart shows some commonly used transitions that you can use to maintain the organization of your ideas.

Transitions for Four Types of Logical Order

IMPORTANCE	CHRONOLOGICAL	SPATIAL	DEVELOPMENT
even more	after	above	also
finally	as soon as	ahead	besides
first	first	behind	despite
more important	at last	below	for example
most important	second	higher	however
one reason	later	inside	therefore
to begin with	meanwhile	outside	while

WRITING ACTIVITY 21 *Writing on Your Own*

WRITING ABOUT THE THEME

Use the strategies on this page and your notes to draft the body of your expository paragraph. Include your topic sentence from Writing Activity 20 and remember to link sentences with transitions. Save your work in your writing folder for later use.

Drafting a Concluding Sentence

To complete your first draft, read over your topic sentence and paragraph body. Then think of a concluding sentence that will serve one or more of the following functions.

Functions of a Concluding Sentence

A concluding sentence

1. restates the main idea in fresh words.
2. summarizes the paragraph.
3. evaluates the supporting details.
4. adds an insight that emphasizes the main point.

Reread the first paragraph, "The Birth of a Car," in Writing Activity 15 on page 107. The concluding sentence restates the main idca in new words, but the writer might have written any of the following concluding sentences instead.

Student Model: *Alternate Concluding Sentences*

With one offhand comment, Alexander Winton had planted the seeds for a thriving competitor. [summarizes]

It would have been better for Winton if he had dealt more fairly with Packard's complaint. [evaluates details]

Many product improvements may result from a person's dissatisfaction with the old product. [adds an insight]

WRITING ACTIVITY 22 *Writing on Your Own*

WRITING ABOUT THE THEME

Write three possible concluding sentences for the expository paragraph you drafted in Writing Activity 21. Then read the draft aloud with each concluding sentence to choose the one that sounds the best. Save your work in your writing folder for later use.

Revising

Writing Process

As you revise your paragraph, look for wording that might confuse a reader or leave the reader in doubt as to your meaning.

Checking for Adequate Development

A common fault in expository writing is lack of adequate development. Readers of expository writing are looking for information and clear explanations, and you must meet their expectations by providing an ample number of specific details to support your ideas.

Writing Tip Achieve adequate development by adding any specific information that the reader will need to understand your subject.

In the first model below, not enough details are included.

Student Model: *Inadequately Developed Paragraph*

The Empire State Building in New York City is one of the most impressive buildings in the world. It once was the world's tallest building, and it still ranks as one of the tallest. Every year many people visit it. On a clear day, you can see far away. Besides its height the Empire State Building is impressive in other ways, for it has many windows and other things. People who are visiting New York City should be sure to see the Empire State Building.

Student Model: *Adequately Developed Paragraph*

The Empire State Building in New York City is one of the most impressive buildings in the world. Completed in 1931, it was the world's tallest building until 1972. At 1,250 feet it is now the third tallest building in the world. The two observation decks, which are on the 86th and 102nd stories, are visited by 1.5 million people every year. From the higher deck on a clear day, observers can see as far as 80 miles away. Besides its height, the Empire State Building is impressive in other ways. It has 6,500 windows, 7 miles of elevator shafts, and 60 miles of water pipes. People who are visiting New York City should be sure to see the Empire State Building.

WRITING ACTIVITY 23 *Revising*

The following paragraph lacks adequate development. Use your own knowledge or do some research to find specific supporting details that will strengthen the paragraph. Then revise the paragraph accordingly.

Memory Tricks

Memory tricks, called mnemonics, often succeed when unaided memory fails. For example, some people use a memory trick to remember the names of the Great Lakes. Others use a trick so they will remember the lines on a musical staff. Whenever you have to remember a series of items, make up a sentence with words that begin with the same letters as the items.

Checking for Unity

A paragraph that lacks *unity* can confuse readers. This problem occurs when one or more supporting sentences stray from the main point.

Writing Tip Achieve **unity** by making sure all the supporting sentences relate to the topic sentence.

The sentences that stray from the subject in the following paragraph are crossed out. Read the paragraph first with the crossed-out sentences. Then read it without them to see how the paragraph gains unity once the sentences that stray from the subject are eliminated.

Student Model: *Paragraph That Lacks Unity*

Predicting Earthquakes

Scientists face a difficult yet important task in trying to predict earthquakes. ~~Scientists are usually successful in the end, however.~~ Each year earthquakes take 10,000 to 15,000 lives and cause billions of dollars in damages. Many cities have been totally destroyed. In 1811 and 1812, a series of earthquakes in Missouri changed the course of the Mississippi River, shaking the earth enough to stop clocks in Boston. ~~Boston is also sometimes struck by tornadoes.~~ Recent efforts to predict earthquakes have met with only limited success. Chinese scientists predicted an earthquake in Haicheng in 1975, and Soviet scientists predicted an earthquake in 1978. To control destruction from earthquakes, scientists must find a way to predict them more consistently.

WRITING ACTIVITY 24 *Revising for Unity*

Decide which of the following paragraphs lacks unity, then revise it by writing it without the two sentences that stray from the subject.

1. Inventing Names

Many products are named after their inventors. The saxophone, for example, was named after Antoine Sax, a Belgian musical-instrument maker. The Geiger counter, used to detect radiation, was named for Hans Geiger, the German physicist who invented it. The macadam pavement that covers so many roadways is named for John McAdam, a British engineer. As long as these inventions are used, their creators' names will be remembered.

2. Pointed Toes

A fifteenth-century nobleman often tripped over his own feet. His shoes were long and pointed, and the toes extended as much as 24 inches beyond his feet. At the same time in history, noblemen's hats were also pointed. The points on the shoes became so inconvenient that they were sometimes attached with a decorative chain to the tops of the boots. Many of today's shoes have points, but they are not as long as those of the fifteenth century. After a law limited toe length, the style gradually died out and noblemen could again walk without tripping.

Checking for Coherence

Another confusing problem in a paragraph can be a lack of coherence. *Coherence* is the glue of the paragraph, the quality that makes each sentence seem connected to the one before and after it. Following are some tips for achieving coherence.

Tips for Achieving Coherence

1. Double-check your organization to make sure each detail fits logically into your method of organization.
2. Use transitional words and phrases. *(See page 113.)*
3. Every now and then repeat key words.
4. Use similar words or phrases in place of key words.
5. Use pronouns in place of key words.

In the following paragraph, the words and phrases that aid coherence are in bold type. The paragraph is in chronological order.

Student Model: *Transitions Aiding Coherence*

People are often slow to recognize good ideas. **For years** Tommy Rice, sportswriter for the *Brooklyn Eagle,* wrote about the need to have numbers on baseball players' shirts. **Without numbers** fans had a hard time identifying players. **Although** he wrote many columns, Rice always got the same reply from club owners—"Ridiculous!" Rice **finally** gave up. **In 1929,** the Yankees **suddenly** announced that they would assign their players numbers. Other teams **soon** followed. **Although** baseball managers were slow to see it, Tommy Rice's idea made good sense.

WRITING ACTIVITY 25 *Revising for Unity and Coherence*

After you read the following paragraph, answer the questions that follow. Then rewrite the paragraph according to your answers.

(1)Tsunamis, unlike all other sea waves, are created by a sudden and drastic change in the seafloor. (2)*Tsunami* is a Japanese word meaning "harbor wave." (3)In some cases tsunamis are created by an undersea landslide. (4)In other cases tsunamis occur as a result of an earthquake or a volcanic eruption. (5)The force of these earthquakes and volcanic eruptions disturbs and displaces the seafloor, sending gigantic tsunamis to far shores. (6)Tsunamis have occurred throughout history. (7)Understanding how tsunamis are formed has helped scientists develop a way to warn people living in the tsunamis' paths. (8)In May of 1983, 13 people on the coast of Honshu were killed by a tsunami. (9)Until better warnings are devised, the casualties from these tsunamis will continue to mount.

1. What two sentences in the paragraph stray from the main point?
2. What pronoun could replace the word *tsunamis* in sentence 4?
3. What one word could replace the words *earthquakes* and *volcanic eruptions* in sentence 5?
4. What term could replace the word *tsunamis* in sentence 5?
5. What transitional word is needed in sentence 8?
6. What words could replace the word *tsunamis* in sentence 9?

WRITING ACTIVITY 26 *Writing on Your Own*

WRITING ABOUT THE THEME

Look over the paragraph you finished in Writing Activity 22. Check it over carefully for adequate development, unity, and coherence. Revise as necessary to improve your draft and save your latest revision in your writing folder.

Using a Revision Checklist

Use the following checklist to guide you step-by-step through the process of revising your expository paragraphs.

Revision Checklist

CHECKING YOUR PARAGRAPH

1. Do you have a strong topic sentence? *(See pages 89–90.)*
2. Does your paragraph have adequate supporting sentences? *(See page 92.)*
3. Is your paragraph logically organized? *(See pages 106–107)*
4. Does your paragraph have unity? *(See page 116.)*
5. Does your paragraph have coherence? *(See pages 117–118.)*
6. Did you use transitions? *(See page 113.)*
7. Do you have a strong concluding sentence? *(See pages 93 and 114.)*

CHECKING YOUR SENTENCES

8. Do your sentences have variety? *(See pages 62–69)*
9. Did you combine related sentences? *(See pages 62–66.)*
10. Are your sentences concise? *(See pages 58–61.)*
11. Have you avoided faulty parallelism? *(See page 74.)*

CHECKING YOUR WORDS

12. Did you use specific words with appropriate connotations? *(See page 74.)*
13. Did you use figurative language where appropriate? *(See page 55.)*

WRITING ACTIVITY 27 *Writing on Your Own*

WRITING ABOUT THE THEME

Use the Revision Checklist above to make a thorough revision of the expository paragraph from Writing Activity 26. Save your paper in your writing folder for editing.

Integrating Language Skills

Editing and Publishing

Grammar in the Writing Process

> By the time he [Richard Rodgers] died, he was that rare man, someone who accomplished what he set out to do: "All I really want to do is to provide a hardworking man in the blouse business with a method of expressing himself. If he likes a tune, he can whistle it and it will make his life happier."

In this paragraph author Ellen Goodman uses three verb tenses, past, present, and future, so that readers will understand when different events occurred. The verbs that refer to Rodgers—such as *died* and *accomplished*—are in the past tense. They refer to events that occurred before the author wrote this piece. The quote by Rodgers, however, contains present tense verbs—such as *want* and *likes*—and one future tense verb, *will make*. Rodgers was talking about his present life and what he hoped for the future. You must use the correct verb tenses to avoid confusing readers about the order of events. *(For more information about tenses and practice in using them, see pages 672–673.)*

Shifts in Tense When you edit your writing, always look for shifts in tense. You could have started writing in the past tense, for example, and then shifted to the present tense. *(For more information about shifts in tense and for practice in correcting them, see pages 673–675.)*

SHIFT IN TENSE	When someone **praised** him, he **tells** of his love for music. [The writer shifts from past to present tense.]
CORRECT TENSES	When someone **praised** him, he always **told** of his love for music. [Both verbs are in the past.]

Principal Parts of Verbs The six tenses are formed from the principal parts of a verb. *(See pages 659–667.)* Most *regular verbs* form their past and past participle by adding *-ed* or *-d* to the present, while *irregular verbs* form their past and past participle in other ways. *(See pages 659–660.)* Following are examples of the principal parts of some irregular verbs. *(For lists of the principal parts of irregular verbs and for practice in using them, see pages 660–667.)*

Irregular Verbs			
PRESENT	**PRESENT PARTICIPLE**	**PAST**	**PAST PARTICIPLE**
put	putting	put	(have) put
lose	losing	lost	(have) lost
break	breaking	broke	(have) broken
see	seeing	saw	(have) seen
ring	ringing	rang	(have) rung
go	going	went	(have) gone

Active and Passive Voice Besides tense, some verbs have voice. *Active voice* indicates that the subject is performing the action. *Passive voice* indicates that the subject receives the action of the verb.

ACTIVE VOICE Richard Rodgers **wrote** that song.
PASSIVE VOICE The song **was written** by Richard Rodgers.

When you write, use the active voice whenever possible. Verbs in the active voice will make your writing forceful and your sentences concise. *(For more information about active and passive voice and for practice in changing the passive voice to the active voice, see pages 675–676.)*

Editing Checklist

1. Have you used correct tenses? *(See pages 672–673.)*
2. Are there any shifts in tense? *(See pages 673–675.)*
3. When forming tense, have you used the correct principal parts of verbs? *(See pages 659–667.)*
4. Have you used the active voice wherever possible? *(See pages 675–676.)*

WRITING ACTIVITY 28 *Writing on Your Own*

WRITING ABOUT THE THEME

Editing Using the above checklist, look at the verbs in your paragraph from Writing Activity 27. Review the Editing Checklist on page 35 and your Personalized Editing Checklist to find other errors. After reading for flow and clarity, make a final copy.

Publishing You may wish to consolidate all the paragraphs from the class and present a booklet to the music department in your school.

A Writer Writes

WRITING ABOUT THE THEME

An Expository Paragraph

PURPOSE: to use incidents and examples to support a general truth

AUDIENCE: your classmates and teacher

Prewriting The following three steps will help you prepare to write an expository paragraph that uses incidents and examples from your life to support this general statement.

> Try to play easy pieces well; it is better than to play difficult ones poorly. ROBERT SCHUMANN

Cellist Yo-Yo Ma

STEP 1: Answering Questions
In small cooperative learning groups, discuss the meaning of Robert Schumann's statement on the previous page by answering these questions.

1. Even though Schumann was advising young musicians when he made this statement, do you think it is *just* about music?
2. What general truth does this quotation seem to be implying?
3. To what other areas of life could this quotation apply?
4. What famous personalities or historical figures lived by this generalization?

STEP 2: Choosing and Limiting Your Subject
Using the answers to the questions above, write a summary of what you think the generalization means. Then, if necessary, limit your broad interpretation of the generalization so that your subject is appropriate for an expository paragraph.

STEP 3: Developing and Organizing Your Ideas
Using any of the brainstorming techniques, make a list of incidents or examples from your life that support the generalization. From that list choose those details that do the best job of illustrating and supporting the generalization. If necessary, classify your details. Finally, review pages 106–107 and think of the best way to organize your details clearly and effectively.

Drafting Write a first draft of your paragraph. Include the quotation very early in the paragraph and then use your supporting incidents and examples to develop your paragraph.

Revising As you read your first draft aloud, listen to it as if you had never heard it before. Is the broad meaning of the generalization clearly explained? Have you included enough examples and details to support the generalization, and are they arranged in a logical order? Make whatever changes are needed.

Editing and Publishing Using the Editing Checklists on pages 35 and 121 as guides, edit your paragraph. After you make a final copy, be prepared to read it aloud to classmates and to discuss various ideas that students developed in their paragraphs. Then, if your teacher permits, form small committees to brainstorm for ideas about the best way to collectively publish your paragraphs. *(For ideas about publishing your work, see page 40.)*

Independent Writing

Write an expository paragraph on one of the following subjects or on one of your own. Use the Checklist for Writing Expository Paragraphs on page 125 as a guide.

1. the layers of the earth
2. how to use a video camera
3. the differences between red giant and white dwarf stars
4. why certain cartoon characters became American institutions
5. how your hometown got its name
6. ways to overcome shyness
7. why the *Titanic* sank
8. Howard Hughes's *Spruce Goose*
9. how dress and grooming reveal personality
10. how ethnic cultures enrich American life

Creative Writing

The following poem, "Opposite," by Richard Wilbur is provocative. After reading it, write an "Opposite" of your own.

> The opposite of *standing still*
> Is *walking up or down a hill,*
> *Running backwards, creeping, crawling,*
> *Leaping off a cliff and falling,*
> *Turning somersaults in gravel,*
> Or any other mode of travel.

WRITING ABOUT THE THEME

Writing about Literature

Theme is the main idea in a piece of writing. You have responded to the theme of music in "The Sounds of Richard Rodgers." *Work* is another theme that could apply to this selection. Write a paragraph that explains the author's message about work.

Writing in Other Subject Areas

World History Write a paragraph explaining the ancient Egyptian attitude toward the pharaoh. To support your main idea, use specific information about Egyptian beliefs and practices.

Geometry Write a paragraph defining a parallelogram. Be sure to include an explanation of how a parallelogram differs from a rectangle and from a square.

Chapter

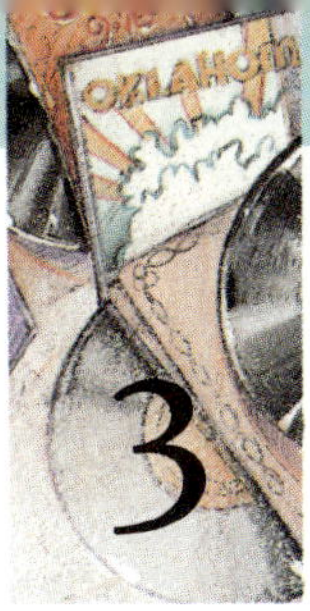

3 Checklist

Writing Expository Paragraphs

Prewriting

- ✔ Find ideas from your experiences or reading. *(See page 95.)*
- ✔ Choose and limit your subject. *(See pages 97–98.)*
- ✔ Determine your audience. *(See page 99.)*
- ✔ Develop a list of supporting details by reading and talking to knowledgeable people. *(See pages 99–100.)*
- ✔ Classify supporting details. *(See pages 101–102.)*
- ✔ Organize your details in a logical order. *(See pages 106–107.)*

Drafting

- ✔ Draft a topic sentence. *(See page 110.)*
- ✔ Change your organized list of details into sentences for the body of your paragraph. *(See page 113.)*
- ✔ Add a concluding sentence. *(See page 114.)*

Revising

- ✔ Using the Revision Checklist, check paragraph structure, adequate development, unity, coherence, transitions, sentences, and words. *(See pages 115–119.)*

Editing and Publishing

- ✔ Using the Editing Checklist, check your grammar, usage, spelling, and mechanics. *(See page 35.)*
- ✔ Prepare a neat final copy of your work and present it to an interested reader.

Chapter

4 Writing Other Kinds of Paragraphs

Part 1 Reading to Write

THEME: *Risk Takers*

"Would you rather be in an earthquake or work for a week digging mud out of a basement?" This question was just one of many that researchers at the University of Minnesota asked people in a poll designed to determine who were risk takers. What exactly is a *risk?* Ralph Keyes, the author of a book about risk takers, defines a risk as "something that causes fear and has the possibility of failure." However, this definition gets complicated because *fear* and *failure* do not mean the same to everyone. For example, swimming across the deep end of a pool is probably a greater risk to a beginning swimmer than parachuting out of a plane is to an experienced jumper. Only the risk taker can determine what is genuinely risky.

Nevertheless, that fear of failure, embarrassment, loss of money, injury, or even death keeps many people from taking risks. Most people seem content to sit back and enjoy taking risks by substituting video games, action-packed television shows, and sports programs for the real thing. There are a few people, however, like Beryl Markham, who take the genuine risk themselves. As you read about her and her adventure in the following selection from *West with the Night,* think about what personality traits you think risk takers must have.

Beryl Markham (1902–1986) was born in England and raised by her father, who took her to East Africa in 1906. In September 1936, she became the first person to fly solo westward across the Atlantic from England to America. This selection is from her account of that flight.

from

West with the Night

Beryl Markham

I have seldom dreamed a dream worth dreaming again, or at least none worth recording. Mine are not enigmatic dreams; they are peopled with characters who are plausible and who do plausible things, and I am the most plausible amongst them. All the characters in my dreams have quiet voices like the voice of the man who telephoned me at Elstree one morning in September of nineteen-thirty-six and told me that there was rain and strong head winds over the west of

England and over the Irish Sea, and that there were variable winds and clear skies in mid-Atlantic and fog off the coast of Newfoundland.[1]

"If you are still determined to fly the Atlantic this late in the year," the voice said, "the Air Ministry suggests that the weather it is able to forecast for tonight, and for tomorrow morning, will be about the best you can expect."

The voice had a few other things to say, but not many, and then it was gone, and I lay in bed half-suspecting that the telephone call and the man who made it were only parts of the mediocre dream I had been dreaming. I felt that if I closed my eyes the unreal quality of the message would be re-established, and that, when I opened them again, this would be another ordinary day with its usual beginning and its usual routine.

But of course I could not close my eyes, nor my mind, nor my memory. I could lie there for a few moments—remembering how it had begun, and telling myself, with senseless repetition, that by tomorrow morning I should either have flown the Atlantic to America—or I should not have flown it. In either case this was the day I would try.

So it didn't matter, I thought. It was silly to think about.

You can live a lifetime and, at the end of it, know more about other people than you know about yourself. You learn to watch other people, but you never watch yourself because you strive against loneliness. If you read a book, or shuffle a deck of cards, or care for a dog, you are avoiding yourself. The abhorrence of loneliness is as natural as wanting to live at all. If it were otherwise, men would never have bothered to make an alphabet, nor to have fashioned words out of what were only animal sounds, nor to have crossed continents—each man to see what the other looked like.

Being alone in an aeroplane for even so short a time as a night and a day, irrevocably alone, with nothing to observe but your instruments and your own hands in semi-darkness, nothing to contemplate but the size of your small courage, nothing to wonder about but the beliefs, the faces, and the hopes rooted in your mind—such an experience can be as startling as the first awareness of a stranger walking by your side at night. You are the stranger.

It is dark already and I am over the south of Ireland. There are the lights of Cork[2] and the lights are wet; they are drenched in Irish rain,

1. **Newfoundland:** An island in the Atlantic Ocean off the coast of Canada.
2. **Cork:** A seaport on the south coast of Ireland.

and I am above them and dry. I am above them and the plane roars in a sobbing world, but it imparts no sadness to me. I feel the security of solitude, the exhilaration of escape. So long as I can see the lights and imagine the people walking under them, I feel selfishly triumphant, as if I have eluded care and left even the small sorrow of rain in other hands.

It is a little over an hour now since I left Abingdon. England, Wales, and the Irish Sea are behind me like so much time used up. On a long flight distance and time are the same. But there had been a moment when Time stopped—and Distance too. It was the moment I lifted the blue-and-silver Gull from the aerodrome, the moment the photographers aimed their cameras, the moment I felt the craft refuse its burden and strain toward the earth in sullen rebellion, only to listen at last to the persuasion of stick and elevators, the dogmatic argument of blueprints that said she *had* to fly because the figures proved it.

So she had flown, and once airborne, once she had yielded to the sophistry of a draughtsman's board, she had said, "There: I have lifted the weight. Now, where are we bound?"—and the question had frightened me.

"We are bound for a place thirty-six hundred miles from here—two thousand miles of it unbroken ocean. Most of the way it will be night. We are flying west with the night."

So there behind me is Cork; and ahead of me is Berehaven Lighthouse. It is the last light, standing on the last land. I watch it, counting the frequency of its flashes—so many to the minute. Then I pass it and fly out to sea.

The fear is gone now—not overcome nor reasoned away. It is gone because something else has taken its place; the confidence and the trust, the inherent belief in the security of land underfoot—now this faith is transferred to my plane, because the land has vanished and there is no other tangible thing to fix faith upon. Flight is but momentary escape from the eternal custody of earth.

Rain continues to fall, and outside the cabin it is totally dark. My altimeter says that the Atlantic is two thousand feet below me, my Sperry Artificial Horizon says that I am flying level. I judge my drift at three degrees more than my weather chart suggests, and fly accordingly. I am flying blind.[3] A beam to follow would help. So would a radio—but then, so would clear weather. The voice of the man at the Air Ministry had not promised storm.

3. **flying blind:** Flying an airplane solely by the aid of instruments.

I feel the wind rising and the rain falls hard. The smell of petrol in the cabin is so strong and the roar of the plane so loud that my senses are almost deadened. Gradually it becomes unthinkable that existence was ever otherwise.

At ten o'clock P.M. I am flying along the Great Circle Course[4] for Harbour Grace, Newfoundland, into a forty-mile headwind at a speed of one hundred and thirty miles an hour. Because of the weather, I cannot be sure of how many more hours I have to fly, but I think it must be between sixteen and eighteen.

At ten-thirty I am still flying on the large cabin tank of petrol, hoping to use it up and put an end to the liquid swirl that has rocked the plane since my take-off. The tank has no gauge, but written on its side is the assurance: "This tank is good for four hours."

There is nothing ambiguous about such a guaranty. I believe it, but at twenty-five minutes to eleven, my motor coughs and dies, and the Gull is powerless above the sea.

I realize that the heavy drone of the plane has been, until this moment, complete and comforting silence. It is the actual silence following the last splutter of the engine that stuns me. I can't feel any fear; I can't feel anything. I can only observe with a kind of stupid disinterest that my hands are violently active and know that, while they move, I am being hypnotized by the needle of my altimeter.[5]

I suppose that the denial of natural impulse is what is meant by "keeping calm," but impulse has reason in it. If it is night and you are sitting in an aeroplane with a stalled motor, and there are two thousand feet between you and the sea, nothing can be more reasonable than the impulse to pull back your stick in the hope of adding to that two thousand, if only by a little. The thought, the knowledge, the law that tells you that your hope lies not in this, but in a contrary act—the act of directing your impotent craft toward the water—seems a terrifying abandonment, not only of reason, but of sanity. Your mind and your heart reject it. It is your hands—your stranger's hands—that follow with unfeeling precision the letter of the law.

I sit there and watch my hands push forward on the stick and feel the Gull respond and begin its dive to the sea. Of course it is a simple thing; surely the cabin tank has run dry too soon. I need only to turn another petcock . . .[6]

4. **Great Circle Course:** The shortest distance between any two points on the earth.
5. **altimeter** [al tim′ ə tər] *n:* An instrument for measuring altitude.
6. **petcock:** A small valve for letting out air, releasing compression, or draining.

But it is dark in the cabin. It is easy to see the luminous dial of the altimeter and to note that my height is now eleven hundred feet, but it is not easy to see a petcock that is somewhere near the floor of the plane. A hand gropes and reappears with an electric torch, and fingers, moving with agonizing composure, find the petcock and turn it; and I wait.

At three hundred feet the motor is still dead, and I am conscious that the needle of my altimeter seems to whirl like the spoke of a spindle winding up the remaining distance between the plane and the water. There is some lightning, but the quick flash only serves to emphasize the darkness. How high can waves reach—twenty feet, perhaps? Thirty?

It is impossible to avoid the thought that this is the end of my flight, but my reactions are not orthodox; the various incidents of my entire life do not run through my mind like a motion-picture film gone mad. I only feel that all this has happened before—and it has. It has all happened a hundred times in my mind, in my sleep, so that now I am not really caught in terror; I recognize a familiar scene, a familiar story with its climax dulled by too much telling.

I do not know how close to the waves I am when the motor explodes to life again. But the sound is almost meaningless. I see my hand easing back on the stick, and I feel the Gull climb up into the storm, and I see the altimeter whirl like a spindle again, paying out the distance between myself and the sea.

The storm is strong. It is comforting. It is like a friend shaking me and saying, "Wake up! You were only dreaming."

But soon I am thinking. By simple calculation I find that my motor had been silent for perhaps an instant more than thirty seconds.

I ought to thank God—and I do, though indirectly. I thank Geoffrey De Havilland who designed the indomitable Gipsy, and who, after all, must have been designed by God in the first place.

A lighted ship—the daybreak—some steep cliffs standing in the sea. The meaning of these will never change for pilots. If one day an ocean can be flown within an hour, if men can build a plane that so masters time, the sight of land will be no less welcome to the steersman of that fantastic craft. He will have cheated laws that the cunning of science has taught him how to cheat, and he will feel his guilt and be eager for the sanctuary of the soil.

I saw the ship and the daybreak, and then I saw the cliffs of Newfoundland wound in ribbons of fog. I felt the elation I had so long imagined, and I felt the happy guilt of having circumvented the stern authority of the weather and the sea. But mine was a minor triumph; my swift Gull was not so swift as to have escaped unnoticed. The night and the storm had caught her and we had flown blind for nineteen hours.

I was tired now, and cold. Ice began to film the glass of the cabin windows and the fog played a magician's game with the land. But the land was there. I could not see it, but I had seen it. I could not afford to believe that it was any land but the land I wanted. I could not afford to believe that my navigation was at fault, because there was no time for doubt.

South to Cape Race, west to Sydney on Cape Breton Island.[7] With my protractor, my map, and my compass, I set my new course, humming the ditty that Tom had taught me: "Variation West—magnetic best. Variation East—magnetic least." A silly rhyme, but it served to placate, for the moment, two warring poles—the magnetic and the true. I flew south and found the lighthouse of Cape Race protruding from the fog like a warning finger. I circled twice and went on over the Gulf of Saint Lawrence.

After a while there would be New Brunswick, and then Maine—and then New York. I could anticipate. I could almost say, "Well, if you stay awake, you'll find it's only a matter of time now"—but there was no question of staying awake. I was tired and I had not moved an inch since that uncertain moment at Abingdon when the Gull had elected to rise with her load and fly, but I could not have closed my eyes. I could sit there in the cabin, walled in glass and petrol tanks, and be grateful for the sun and the light, and the fact that I could see

7. **Sydney . . . Cape Breton Island:** Island off the coast of Nova Scotia in Canada.

the water under me. They were almost the last waves I had to pass. Four hundred miles of water, but then the land again—Cape Breton. I would stop at Sydney to refuel and go on. It was easy now. It would be like stopping at Kisumu[8] and going on.

Success breeds confidence. But who has a right to confidence except the Gods? I had a following wind, my last tank of petrol was more than three-quarters full, and the world was as bright to me as if it were a new world, never touched. If I had been wiser, I might have known that such moments are, like innocence, short-lived. My engine began to shudder before I saw the land. It died, it spluttered, it started again and limped along. It coughed and spat black exhaust toward the sea.

There are words for everything. There was a word for this—airlock,[9] I thought. This had to be an airlock because there was petrol enough. I thought I might clear it by turning on and turning off all the empty tanks, and so I did that. The handles of the petcocks were sharp little pins of metal, and when I had opened and closed them a dozen times, I saw that my hands were bleeding and that the blood was dropping on my maps and on my clothes, but the effort wasn't any good. I coasted along on a sick and halting engine. The oil pressure and the oil temperature gauges were normal, the magnetos working, and yet I lost altitude slowly while the realization of failure seeped into my heart. If I made the land, I should have been the first to fly the North Atlantic from England, but from my point of view, from a pilot's point of view, a forced landing was failure because New York was my goal. If only I could land and then take off, I would make it still . . . if only, if only . . .

The engine cuts again, and then catches, and each time it spurts to life I climb as high as I can get, and then it splutters and stops and I glide once more toward the water, to rise again and descend again, like a hunting sea bird.

I find the land. Visibility is perfect now and I see land forty or fifty miles ahead. If I am on my course, that will be Cape Breton. Minute after minute goes by. The minutes almost materialize; they pass before my eyes like links in a long slow-moving chain, and each time the engine cuts, I see a broken link in the chain and catch my breath until it passes.

The land is under me. I snatch my map and stare at it to confirm

8. **Kisumu:** A town in Kenya, East Africa.
9. **airlock:** A stoppage in the flow of liquid due to the presence of air.

my whereabouts. I am, even at my present crippled speed, only twelve minutes from Sydney Airport, where I can land for repairs and then go on.

The engine cuts once more and I begin to glide, but now I am not worried; she will start again, as she has done, and I will gain altitude and fly into Sydney.

But she doesn't start. This time she's dead as death; the Gull settles earthward and it isn't any earth I know. It is black earth stuck with boulders and I hang above it, on hope and on a motionless propeller. Only I cannot hang above it long. The earth hurries to meet me, I bank, turn, and side-slip to dodge the boulders, my wheels touch, and I feel them submerge. The nose of the plane is engulfed in mud, and I go forward striking my head on the glass of the cabin front, hearing it shatter, feeling blood pour over my face.

I stumble out of the plane and sink to my knees in muck and stand there foolishly staring, not at the lifeless land, but at my watch.

Twenty-one hours and twenty-five minutes.

Atlantic flight. Abingdon, England, to a nameless swamp—nonstop.

A Cape Breton islander found me—a fisherman trudging over the bog saw the Gull with her tail in the air and her nose buried, and then he saw me floundering in the embracing soil of his native land. I had been wandering for an hour and the black mud had got up to my waist and the blood from the cut in my head had met the mud halfway.

From a distance, the fisherman directed me with his arms and with shouts toward the firm places in the bog, and for another hour I walked on them and came toward him like a citizen of Hades blinded by the sun, but it wasn't the sun; I hadn't slept for forty hours.

He took me to his hut on the edge of the coast and I found that built upon the rocks there was a little cubicle that housed an ancient telephone—put there in case of shipwrecks.

I telephoned to Sydney Airport to say that I was safe and to prevent a needless search being made. On the following morning I did step out of a plane at Floyd Bennett Field[10] and there was a crowd of people still waiting there to greet me, but the plane I stepped from was not the Gull, and for days while I was in New York I kept thinking about that and wishing over and over again that it had been the Gull, until the wish lost its significance, and time moved on, overcoming many things it met on the way. ◆

10. **Floyd Bennett Field:** An airstrip in Brooklyn, New York.

Responding to the Theme

Risk Takers

Responding in Your Journal Life forces some risks on you. You naturally face more of these kinds of risks than older people because you have many new experiences: your first date, a first dance, or the first performance in a play. Firsts are risk-taking experiences.

In your journal this week, write about the many firsts you have already had in your life and the risks associated with them. Begin by brainstorming for a list of all of your first experiences. None of these firsts have to be great adventures. Rather, they probably will be simple experiences, such as the first time you were self-confident enough to express an unpopular opinion with your group of friends.

Today, in your journal, look over your list and write about your most recent first experience. Begin by relating the experience. Then explain how you felt during the experience and what you think, if anything, was gained from the experience. Follow that same procedure each day this week as you write about a different first.

Speaking and Listening Find information in either your history book or your literature book about another risk taker. Then, with your teacher's permission, meet in small discussion groups. After everyone in the group has discussed a risk taker, the group should discuss whether or not the risks were taken for a common good, for personal growth, or strictly for the personal glory of the risk taker.

Critical Thinking: Applying Beryl Markham faced and overcame severe odds during her risk-taking solo flight across the Atlantic Ocean. Write about an experience you have had when you took a risk that involved overcoming some odds. During your experience what traits do you think you shared with Beryl Markham?

Extending Your Vocabulary What are the meanings of the prefixes of the following words from *West with the Night?* How can you use the meaning of the prefixes to determine the meaning of the words? In your Learning Log, write a definition for each word. Then check the meaning of each in a dictionary.

irrevocably	contemplate	precision
protractor	indomitable	circumvent

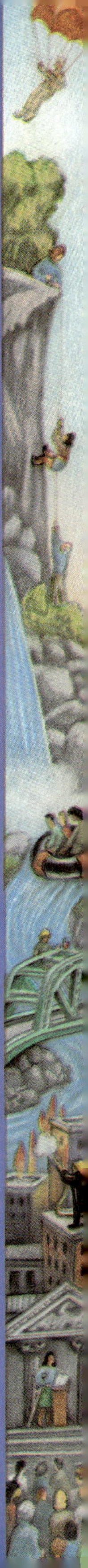

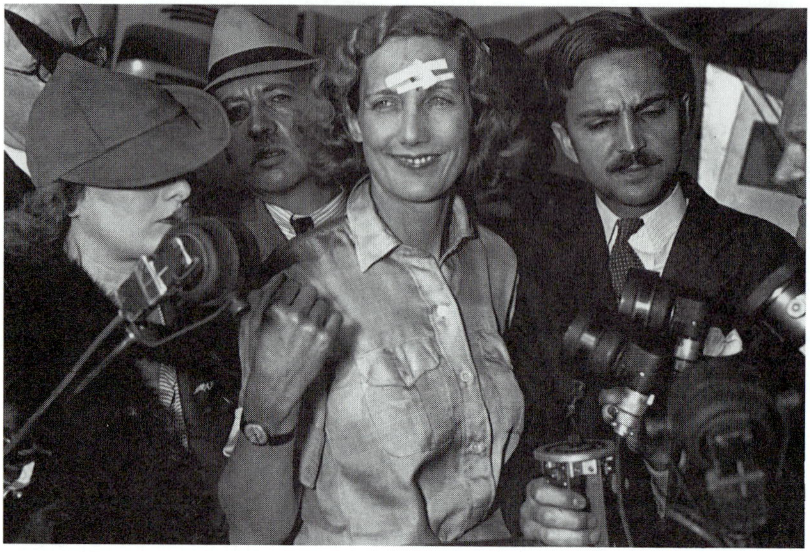

Beryl Markham

Part 2 *Writing*

Writing itself involves risks, but you can face them confidently if you follow certain steps. For example, before putting anything on paper, first consider your *audience* by asking, "Who are my readers? What do they find interesting? What do they need to know to understand my message?" Then determine your purpose by deciding which kind of writing best suits your goals. Many times, of course, you will have a combination of purposes. For example, you may wish to express strong feelings about an issue such as the destruction of the environment through human carelessness. You may decide that the best method of persuading the audience is to write a story with a setting in the wilderness. Then you may produce an eloquent description of a beautiful place and a strong narrative of the events leading to a crisis for the wilderness. In order to make such decisions, you would need to know how to compose various types of paragraphs.

In this chapter you will study the features of a narrative, a descriptive, and a persuasive paragraph. You will also learn specific skills for each type of paragraph. Once you have written various types of paragraphs, you too will be able to produce longer compositions that combine all types of writing.

Writing Narrative Paragraphs

Writing Process

If you want to tell about a series of events—in a letter, on a history test, or in a short story—you will be writing *narration*. You can learn the skills of narration and writing narrative paragraphs.

Writing Term A **narrative paragraph** tells a real or an imaginary story with a clear beginning, middle, and ending.

Each part of a narrative paragraph performs a specific function.

Structure of a Narrative Paragraph

1. The topic sentence captures the reader's attention and makes a general statement or sets the scene.
2. The supporting sentences tell the story event by event.
3. The concluding sentence shows the outcome, summarizes the story, or adds an insight.

Model: *Narrative Paragraph*

A Narrow Escape

TOPIC SENTENCE: MAKES A GENERAL STATEMENT

SUPPORTING SENTENCES: RELATE EVENTS ONE BY ONE

CONCLUDING SENTENCE: GIVES OUTCOME

We were young and sometimes we went beyond the limits of common sense. Once my comrade Philippe Tailliez was diving alone in December, with his dog Soika guarding his clothes. The water was 52 degrees Fahrenheit. Philippe was trying to spear some big sea bass but had to break off the chase when he could no longer stand the cold. He found himself several hundred yards from the deserted shore. The return swim was a harrowing, benumbed struggle. He dragged himself out on a rock and fainted. A bitter wind swept him. He had small chance of surviving such an exposure. The wolfhound, moved by an extraordinary instinct, covered him with its body and breathed hot air on his face. Tailliez awoke with near paralyzed hands and feet and stumbled to a shelter.

JACQUES COUSTEAU, "Menfish"

Italy, Francesco Clemente, 1983, Philadelphia Museum of Art
Hunt Manufacturing Co., Arts Collection Program

WRITING ACTIVITY 1 *Writing Topic Sentences*

Imagine how each event indicated below would take place. Then write a topic sentence for each one. Be sure that each sentence captures the reader's attention and makes a general statement or sets the scene.

1. struggling with your conscience
2. beginning a new friendship

3. meeting your favorite movie star
4. witnessing a street-corner drama
5. going to a concert (or sports event)

WRITING ACTIVITY 2 *Writing on Your Own*

WRITING ABOUT THE THEME

Reread the list of "first experiences" you wrote in your journal. *(See page 135.)* Choose one of them—the one you think you would like to develop into a narrative paragraph. Write freely about that experience on a separate sheet of paper. When you have finished, you may want to record how another person might remember that same experience. You might also express how your feelings are different today from what they were during the time of the experience. Then write a topic sentence for your narrative paragraph and save your work in your writing folder for Writing Activity 5.

Chronological Order and Transitions

A narrative paragraph tells about an event that occurs within a certain time. For this reason the most common organization for a narrative paragraph is *chronological order*. Words and phrases called *transitions* are used to show the relationship of events. The following chart lists transitions that are common in narrative writing.

Transitions for Chronological Order

after	meanwhile	during	last night
before	next	at last	on Monday
suddenly	then	at noon	the next day
just as	immediately	while	by evening

WRITING ACTIVITY 3 *Using Chronological Order*

Arrange the following events in chronological order. Then save your paper for Writing Activity 4.

- The passengers cheered when the engines started up again.
- The takeoff of Flight 81 from Los Angeles to Denver was normal.
- We flew into a thunderstorm above the Rocky Mountains.
- Passengers were relaxing and enjoying coffee and soft drinks after the captain turned off the seat belt sign.

- We heard a loud thump followed by a frightening silence.
- There was an even bigger cheer as the plane touched down safely.
- The pilots restarted the engines at 15,000 feet.
- The flight attendants said to prepare for an emergency landing.
- The plane began to descend without power at 20,000 feet.

WRITING ACTIVITY 4 *Using Transitions*

Write a narrative paragraph based on the events from Writing Activity 3. Use transitions to show how the events are related in time.

WRITING ACTIVITY 5 *Writing on Your Own*

WRITING ABOUT THE THEME

Review the freewriting you did in Writing Activity 2 about a first in your life. After you select details about the event to include in a narrative paragraph, list those details in chronological order. Save your work in your writing folder for Writing Activity 9.

Point of View

Every story has a *narrator,* the person whose voice is telling the story. If you tell a story about yourself and refer to yourself with first person pronouns—such as *I, we, us,* and *our*—you are using *first person* narration. If you use a narrator who does not participate in the events and refers to the characters with third person pronouns—such as *he, she,* and *they*—you are using *third person* narration. These different voices are called *point of view* because they indicate through whose eyes the story is being told.

FIRST PERSON **I** held **my** breath as the judge prepared to announce the winners. [narrator is participant]

THIRD PERSON **She** held **her** breath as the judge prepared to announce the winners. [narrator is observer]

Once you have chosen a point of view for a narrative, keep to it throughout the story.

Writing Tip: Use **first person point of view** if you are a character in the story. Use **third person point of view** if you are observing and reporting what happened to others.

WRITING ACTIVITY 6 *Identifying Points of View*

Write *first person* or *third person* to indicate the point of view of each of the following quotations.

1. Yes, he had practically saved my life. He had also practically lost it for me. JOHN KNOWLES, *A Separate Peace*
2. His lips curled in a smile and then opened with a short triumphant laugh. GEORGE ELIOT, *Middlemarch*
3. No scheme could have been more agreeable to Elizabeth, and her acceptance to the invitation was most ready and grateful.
JANE AUSTEN, *Pride and Prejudice*
4. The grocer opened later than usual this Saturday morning, but still it was early enough to make him one of the first walkers in the neighborhood. JAMES ALAN MCPHERSON, "A Loaf of Bread"
5. I think my honesty is the only sort in the world, and he thinks his is the only sort in the world as well.
ALAN SILLITOE, *The Loneliness of the Long-Distance Runner*

WRITING ACTIVITY 7 *Experimenting with Point of View*

The following paragraph is written in the third person. After you read it carefully, rewrite it in first person from the point of view of Angela.

Angela Gets a Computer

Angela had wanted a computer for a long time. One day she went into a computer store and found the computer of her dreams. Every day of the following week, she stopped in at the store to look at it and gently press its keys. Then she headed straight home to convince her parents that they should buy it for her. Her parents finally agreed, and they all went back to the store the following Saturday. The salesperson helped them pack it in its box, and off they drove with the computer jiggling around in the trunk. When they returned home, Angela and her father set up the machine and plugged it in. Immediately Angela inserted the training program and, following its directions, typed in her name. The computer kept calling her by name as she progressed step-by-step through the training program, with the words "Good job, Angela" appearing on the screen. Angela stayed up long past her usual bedtime that night, getting acquainted with her new friend.

WRITING ACTIVITY 8 *A Creative Point of View*

Rewrite the story about Angela from the point of view of the computer. Use first person to refer to the computer. Try to imagine what a computer might perceive if it could.

WRITING ACTIVITY 9 *Writing on Your Own*

WRITING ABOUT THE THEME

Choose the best point of view for the narrative paragraph you planned in Writing Activity 5 about a first in your life. Then draft your paragraph, using transitions where appropriate to make the chronological order of details clear. If time permits, revise and polish your paragraph, using The Process of Writing a Narrative Paragraph chart on page 143 for help. If not, place your paragraph in your writing folder so that you can revise and polish it later.

WRITING ACTIVITY 10 *Writing a First Person Narrative*

Prewriting Think of times when you tried something you did not think you would be able to do, such as skate boarding or using a telescope. Recall all the details about one event, including the outcome. Arrange your details in chronological order.

Drafting Use your notes to write a quick first draft of your story.

Revising If your teacher permits, exchange papers with a classmate. Offer helpful comments and suggestions about your partner's paragraph. Consider such features as word choice, sentence variety, interest level, and clarity of the details. Then use the chart on the next page and your partner's comments to improve your paragraph.

Editing and Publishing Use the chart on the next page to edit your work and correct any errors you may have made. Then share your finished work with the classmate who was your partner.

WRITING ACTIVITY 11 *Writing a Third Person Narrative*

Think of an incident from the life of a friend or relative that reveals an aspect of that person's character. For example, you might reveal a cousin's courage facing a serious illness. Write a narrative paragraph relating the incident. For help use the chart on the next page.

The Process of Writing a Narrative Paragraph

PREWRITING *(See pages 10–27.)*

1. Through brainstorming, clustering, freewriting, or any other technique, scan your memory for incidents that would make a good subject for a narrative paragraph.
2. Determine your audience by asking yourself questions about your readers' interests and level of knowledge.
3. Think back to the first incident that set the event in motion. Then list all the details about the event, including details of time and place.
4. Arrange your notes in chronological order and cross out any unnecessary details.

DRAFTING *(See pages 28–29.)*

5. Write a topic sentence that captures the reader's attention and that makes a general statement about the story or sets the scene.
6. Use your prewriting notes to write the supporting sentences, which tell the story event by event.
7. Add a concluding sentence that summarizes the story or makes a point about the meaning of the event.

REVISING *(See pages 30–34.)*

8. Does your paragraph have all the elements shown in the Structure of a Narrative Paragraph chart on page 137?
9. Should you delete anything to strengthen the unity? *(See page 116.)*
10. Should you add anything to strengthen the development?
11. Should you rearrange anything to strengthen the coherence? *(See pages 117–118.)*
12. Do your sentences have variety? *(See pages 62–69.)*
13. Did you avoid rambling sentences? *(See page 73.)*
14. Can you substitute any specific, vivid words for general ones? *(See page 53.)*

EDITING AND PUBLISHING *(See pages 35–40.)*

15. Check for errors in grammar and usage.
16. Check spelling, capitalization, and punctuation.
17. Did you indent correctly? Are your margins even?
18. Is your handwriting clear?
19. Present a neat final copy to a reader and check page 40 for other publishing ideas.

Writing Descriptive Paragraphs

Writing Process

If you want to help your reader picture a person, an object, or a place, you will be writing description. Good descriptive writing helps your reader see, hear, smell, taste, and feel all the details you are describing.

Writing Term A **descriptive paragraph** paints a vivid picture of a person, an object, or a scene by stimulating the reader's senses.

Like a narrative paragraph, a descriptive paragraph has three main parts. In a good descriptive paragraph, all these parts work together to create one main impression of the subject.

Structure of a Descriptive Paragraph

1. The **topic sentence** makes a general statement about the subject, often suggesting an overall impression.
2. The **supporting sentences** supply specific details that help readers use their five senses to bring the picture to life.
3. The **concluding sentence** summarizes the overall impression of the subject.

Student Model: *Descriptive Paragraph*

The Riverwalk

TOPIC SENTENCE

The Riverwalk in San Antonio, Texas, is a favorite noon-hour getaway for workers in nearby offices.

BODY OF SUPPORTING SENTENCES: PROVIDES SENSORY DETAILS

Below street level the green river winds leisurely between the promenades on either side, carrying occasional boatloads of sightseers in brightly colored gondolas. Lining the river are bakeries, art and handicraft stores, ice-cream stands, and restaurants, where lunchtime shoppers and idlers under the hot sun browse and sample the goods.

CONCLUDING SENTENCE

As the lazy hour draws to a close, the relaxed workers slowly climb the stone stairs to the busy streets of the city.

WRITING ACTIVITY 12 *Recognizing the Overall Impression*

Write *positive* or *negative* to indicate the type of overall impression suggested by each topic sentence.

1. Davis Street was like a well-tended garden in the middle of a war zone.
2. The house was a remarkable mixture of inspiration and boldness.
3. The team members dragged themselves off the field as if they wore iron shoes.
4. The vacant lot was a slap in the face of decency.
5. The kite festival turned the pale blue sky into a colorful, modern painting.

WRITING ACTIVITY 13 *Writing Topic Sentences*

Write a topic sentence for a descriptive paragraph about each of the following subjects. Make each topic sentence suggest the overall impression indicated in brackets.

1. a dog [positive]
2. a gymnasium [negative]
3. a parade [positive]
4. a subway station [negative]
5. a friend's face [positive]
6. an oil slick [negative]
7. walking [positive]
8. trash [negative]
9. books [positive]
10. dancing [positive]

WRITING ACTIVITY 14 *Writing on Your Own*

WRITING ABOUT THE THEME

Because first experiences involve risk, they usually are memorable. Can you remember, for example, where your first job interview took place? Was your interview in an office, in a store, or in a barn? Do you remember where you sat and what was on the wall behind the person interviewing you? Choose an indoor location where one of your most unforgettable first experiences occurred. Then close your eyes and picture that place in your mind. Once you see it clearly, jot down every detail you can remember. When you have finished, read over your notes and summarize the overall impression of that place. For example, was it gloomy or bright? Formal or friendly? Save your work in your writing folder for Writing Activity 18.

Specific Details and Sensory Words

Often the topic sentence of a descriptive paragraph indicates the overall impression you wish to create. The body of the paragraph then fleshes out that overall impression by providing specific details and sensory words—words that appeal to the reader's five senses. *(See pages 53 and 55.)* If you choose your details well, your paragraph will *show* the person, place, or thing being described—rather than merely telling about it.

Writing Tip Make descriptions show rather than tell by using **specific details** and **sensory words.**

The specific details and sensory words in the following paragraph are in heavy type.

Model: *Paragraph with Specific Details and Sensory Words*

He was a **stout tallish** young man. The **high color** of his **cheeks pushed** upwards even to his **forehead** where it **scattered** itself in a few **formless patches of pale red;** and on his **hairless face** there **scintillated restlessly** the **polished lenses** and the **bright gilt rims** of the **glasses** which **screened** his **delicate** and **restless** eyes. His **glossy black hair** was parted in the middle and brushed in a **long curve behind his ears** where it **curled slightly** beneath the **groove** left by his hat.

JAMES JOYCE, "The Dead"

WRITING ACTIVITY 15 *Recognizing Details and Sensory Words*

Write at least ten specific details or sensory words from the following paragraph.

Then in the evening he stood in the doorway of his house and looked across the land, his own land, lying loose and fresh from the winter's freezing, and ready for planting. It was full spring and in the shallow pool the frogs croaked drowsily. The bamboos at the corner of the house swayed slowly under a gentle night wind and through the twilight he could see dimly the fringe of trees at the border of the near field. They were peach trees, budded most delicately pink, and willow trees thrusting forth tender green leaves. Up from the quiescent, waiting land a faint mist rose, silver as moonlight, and clung about the tree trunks.

PEARL S. BUCK, *The Good Earth*

Figurative Language Sometimes the best way to help readers see a subject is to compare it to something else, using figurative language. The two most common figures of speech are the *simile* and the *metaphor.* Both invite the reader to see similarities between two things that are essentially unlike. The simile uses the comparing word *like* or *as.* The metaphor implies a comparison without using *like* or *as.*

SIMILE **Like illumined pearls** the lamps shone from the summits of their tall poles. JAMES JOYCE

METAPHOR The **soft rope** of her hair tossed from side to side. JAMES JOYCE

Some comparisons have been used so often that they have become worn-out. These trite expressions, called *clichés,* no longer call a vivid image to mind. Avoid such clichés as "they are like two peas in a pod" or "her eyes twinkled like stars." If you have heard a simile or metaphor many times before, do not use it. Search for fresh comparisons.

Writing Tip Make descriptions vivid by using **similes** and **metaphors.** Avoid using **clichés.**

WRITING ACTIVITY 16 *Using Figurative Language*

Write a sentence containing a fresh simile or metaphor to describe each subject.

EXAMPLE clouds before a storm

POSSIBLE ANSWER With full sails the clouds raced across the darkening sea of air.

1. the starry sky
2. a wild colt
3. autumn trees
4. a snowfall
5. a baby's smile
6. twilight in the city
7. an older man's face
8. a beautiful melody
9. an athlete's body
10. a friend's new car

Spatial Order and Transitions

A well-organized description usually leads the reader from point to point until the picture is complete. This method of organization is called *spatial order*.

Writing Term **Spatial order** arranges details according to their location.

In a descriptive paragraph, transitions show where each item fits into the larger picture. The following chart shows transitions used for each specific type of spatial order.

Transitions for Spatial Order

SPATIAL ORDER	TRANSITIONS
top to bottom (or the reverse)	higher, lower, above, below, at the base (top), in the middle, halfway
side to side	at the left (right), in the middle, next to, beside, at one end, at the other end
inside out (or the reverse)	within, in the center, on the outside, innermost, in the middle
near to far (or the reverse)	in front of, nearby, farther, beyond, across, to the north (etc.), in the distance

Many descriptive paragraphs use a special spatial order that is different from those shown in the chart. In this special type of order, writers describe details in the order in which they strike them rather than in a set pattern such as top to bottom. Transitions make this order clear.

WRITING ACTIVITY 17 *Recognizing Transitions*

Write all the transitional words and phrases in the paragraph on the next page. Then write *top to bottom* (or the reverse), *side to side, inside out* (or the reverse), or *special* to indicate the type of spatial order.

From my window here in Bellaggio, Italy, I have a view of the other side of the lake, which is as beautiful as a picture. A scarred and wrinkled precipice rises to a height of eighteen hundred feet. On a tiny bench halfway up its vast wall sits a little snowflake of a church, no bigger than a martin box apparently. Skirting the base of the cliff are a hundred orange groves and gardens, flecked with glimpses of the white dwellings that are buried in them. In front, three or four gondolas lie idle upon the water. In the burnished mirror of the lake, mountain, chapel, houses, groves, and boats are counterfeited so brightly and so clearly that one scarce knows where reality leaves off and the reflection begins!

MARK TWAIN, *The Innocents Abroad*

WRITING ACTIVITY 18 *Writing on Your Own*

WRITING ABOUT THE THEME

Review the notes you wrote in Writing Activity 14 about the location of one of your first experiences. Then arrange your descriptive details in a logical order, including only those that support the overall impression you wish to leave in the reader's mind. After you write a topic sentence that gives a general impression, draft your descriptive paragraph. When you have finished, revise your paragraph, using The Process of Writing a Descriptive Paragraph chart on page 153 for assistance. Save your work in your writing folder for Writing Activity 22.

WRITING ACTIVITY 19 *Describing a Person*

Write a detailed and well-organized description of someone who has played a special role in your life. For example, if you participate in sports, you might write about a coach. Use the chart on page 153 for help with prewriting, drafting, and revising. Save your work in your writing folder for Writing Activity 21.

WRITING ACTIVITY 20 *Describing Nature*

Prewriting Describe a scene in nature with a focal point, such as a mountain, a lake, a splendid garden, or a specific object. Search for details that make the focal point you chose unique. Then, after careful observation, form an overall impression of the focus. Through freewriting or clustering, develop a list of descriptive details and arrange them in spatial order.

Drafting Write a quick first draft of your paragraph. Give your readers the impression that they are by your side observing the focal point in your scene.

Revising Set your description aside for a day or two. Then pick it up, pretend that you are someone else, and read the paragraph. Close your eyes. Can you picture the focal point in the scene? What additional details would help you picture it better? How might the details be organized more effectively? Using your answers to these questions and the chart on page 153, revise your paragraph. Save your work in your writing folder for Writing Activity 21.

Language Integrating Skills

Grammar in the Writing Process

Editing and Publishing

Throughout the selection *West with the Night,* Beryl Markham described what she was seeing so vividly that you almost feel as if you are there beside her.

> It is dark already and I am over the south of Ireland. There are the lights of Cork and the lights are wet; they are drenched in Irish rain, and I am above them and dry. I am above them and the plane roars in a sobbing world . . .

The underlined words in the description above are *adjectives*—words that describe nouns and pronouns and add color and exactness.

In her description Markham used many adjectives. Adjectives like *dark* are regular adjectives. *Irish* is a proper adjective, and *sobbing* is a verb form called a *participle,* which is used as an adjective. *(For more about adjectives and participles, see pages 563–567 and 607.)*

Comparison of Adjectives When you compare two people or things, add *er* to most one-syllable adjectives and to some two-syllable adjectives. Add *more* to those two-syllable adjectives that sound awkward with *er* and to all adjectives with three or more syllables.

The *Gull* was **swifter** than other planes Markham had flown.
Markham experienced many risks in **earlier** trips.
She felt **more alone** on this flight than on others.
A blind flight was **more dangerous** at night than during the day.

When you compare three or more people or things, add *-est* to most one-syllable adjectives and to some two-syllable adjectives. Add *most* to two-syllable adjectives that sound awkward with *-est* and to all adjectives with three or more syllables. *(For more about comparison of adjectives and practice in writing them correctly, see pages 725–728.)*

Her plane was the **newest** model made available by an enthusiastic sponsor.
This was the **riskiest** flight she had ever made.
The *Gull* had the **most accurate** instruments for a small craft.

Capitalization of Proper Adjectives Like the proper nouns from which they are formed, proper adjectives begin with a capital letter. *(For other examples of proper adjectives and for practice in writing them correctly, see pages 563 and 756–757.)*

PROPER NOUNS	Ireland	Canada
PROPER ADJECTIVES	**Irish** rain	**Canadian** coast

Punctuation with Adjectives When a conjunction does not connect two adjectives before a noun, a comma is sometimes used. To decide if you should use a comma, read the sentence with *and* between the adjectives. If the sentence sounds natural, a comma is needed. *(For practice in writing adjectives correctly, see page 775.)*

COMMA NEEDED	I felt the strong, wet wind inside the cabin. [*Strong and wet* sounds natural.]
COMMA NOT NEEDED	I felt the strong October wind inside the cabin. [*Strong and October* does not sound natural.]

Editing Checklist

1. Have you used the correct form when writing the comparison of adjectives? *(See pages 725–728.)*
2. Are proper adjectives capitalized? *(See pages 756–757.)*
3. Have you correctly punctuated two adjectives before a noun? *(See page 775.)*

WRITING ACTIVITY 21 *Editing Descriptive Paragraphs*

Use the checklist above and the chart on the next page to edit your work for Writing Activities 19 and 20. Then make neat final copies.

WRITING ACTIVITY 22 *Writing on Your Own*

WRITING ABOUT THE THEME

Editing and Publishing Use the checklist above and the chart on the next page as guides to editing your paragraph from Writing Activity 18. After you make a neat final copy, go back to the setting or look at a photograph to see how accurate your description is. You might wish to make a drawing and submit it with your writing.

The Process of Writing a Descriptive Paragraph

PREWRITING *(See pages 10–27.)*

1. Through brainstorming, clustering, freewriting, or any other technique that works for you, scan your memory and experience for persons, scenes, or objects that lend themselves to vivid description.
2. Ask yourself whether your audience is likely to be familiar with the person, place, or thing you are going to describe.
3. Form an overall positive or negative impression of your subject. Then list all the specific details and sensory words you can use to show that overall impression.
4. Arrange your details in an appropriate form of spatial order and cross out any details that do not support your overall impression.

DRAFTING *(See pages 28–29.)*

5. Write a clear topic sentence that states an overall impression.
6. Use your prewriting notes to draft the supporting sentences, which reveal the details one by one.
7. Add a concluding sentence that summarizes your description.

REVISING *(See pages 30–34.)*

8. Does your paragraph have all the elements shown in the Structure of a Descriptive Paragraph chart on page 144?
9. Should you delete anything to strengthen unity? *(See page 116.)*
10. Should you add anything to strengthen the paragraph's development?
11. Should you rearrange anything to strengthen coherence? *(See pages 117–118.)*
12. Do your sentences have variety? *(See pages 62–69.)*
13. Did you avoid rambling sentences? *(See page 73.)*
14. Can you substitute any vivid words for general ones? *(See page 53.)*

EDITING AND PUBLISHING *(See pages 35–40.)*

15. Check for errors in grammar and usage.
16. Check spelling, capitalization, and punctuation.
17. Did you indent correctly? Are your margins even?
18. Is your handwriting clear?
19. Present a neat final copy to a reader and check page 40 for other publishing ideas.

Writing Persuasive Paragraphs

Writing Process

If your purpose is to express an opinion—whether in a letter to your mayor, in a newspaper editorial, or in a letter of complaint about a faulty product—you will be writing *persuasion*. Audience is an important consideration in persuasive writing since many of your readers may hold different views from yours.

Writing Term A **persuasive paragraph** asserts an opinion and uses facts, examples, and reasons to convince readers.

The following chart and model show how each element in a persuasive paragraph functions.

Structure of a Persuasive Paragraph

1. The **topic sentence** asserts an opinion.
2. The **supporting sentences** back up the opinion with facts, examples, reasons, and testimonies of experts.
3. The **concluding sentence** restates the opinion and often makes a final appeal to the reader.

Student Model: *Persuasive Paragraph*

Pennies from Heaven?

TOPIC SENTENCE: ASSERTS AN OPINION

SUPPORTING SENTENCES: BACK UP OPINIONS

The $12.5 million granted to NASA for the search for life in outer space is a waste of taxpayers' dollars. Since 1959, when the first organized search for extraterrestrial life began, not one single piece of evidence has been found that life exists anywhere but on Earth. Frank J. Tipler, a physicist at Tulane University, points out that if intelligent beings existed, they would already have contacted us. So convincing were these arguments that in 1978 Congress withdrew its support of the search for life in outer space. A movement led by Carl Sagan, however, gained wide popular support, based largely on the emotional appeal of finding life in outer space. As a result Congress restored millions of dollars that could have been better spent on much-needed social programs. While the expensive radio telescopes continue to detect nothing, people right here on Earth continue worrying about housing and medical care—problems the government should be solving.

CONCLUDING SENTENCE: MAKES A FINAL APPEAL

WRITING ACTIVITY 23 *Recognizing Opinions*

Some of the following topic sentences assert an opinion and are suitable for a persuasive paragraph. Others state a fact and are suitable for an expository paragraph. Identify each sentence by writing *P* for *persuasive* and *E* for *expository.*

1. The best way to protest against bad television programs is to boycott the products of the sponsors.
2. Advertising jingles sometimes become a deep-rooted part of a nation's popular culture.
3. Movie theaters should bring back ushers to keep the noise down during a movie.
4. A trained dog is a happy dog.
5. Some trees are actually giant weeds.
6. Carpooling helps conserve natural resources.
7. To encourage carpooling, toll roads should offer reduced rates to cars with two or more passengers.
8. Public buses should be equipped with automatic lifts for people in wheelchairs.
9. In recent years the nursing profession has attracted an increasing number of men.
10. Praise and rewards are effective ways to encourage good behavior.

WRITING ACTIVITY 24 *Writing on Your Own*

WRITING ABOUT THE THEME

The risks that you have been writing about in this chapter have all been healthy, positive risks. There is, however, another kind of risk. This kind of risk is foolhardy and dangerous, and it is based on a false belief that the risk taker is invincible. The best example of this kind of risk is driving while drunk. Brainstorm for a list of other examples of bad risks. Then save your work in your writing folder for use in Writing Activity 27.

Critical Thinking

Writing Is Thinking

Solving Problems

When writing persuasion, you often use the thinking skill of *solving problems* to examine issues. The solution then serves as the main idea of your persuasive writing. To solve problems, follow these steps.

1. State the problem.
2. Think of several possible solutions.
3. List the reasons for (*pros*) and reasons against (*cons*) each solution.
4. Decide on the best solution—the one with the most pros.

The following chart shows how these steps can be applied to a problem involving the search for life in outer space.

Solving a Problem

1. *State the problem.*
   How can money be found to search for life in outer space?
2. *List several possible solutions.*
   Solution 1: Raise taxes
   Solution 2: Find backers in private sector
3. *Evaluate solutions.*
   Solution 1: *Pro:* would raise money
   Con: unpopular with people and lawmakers
   Solution 2: *Pro 1:* would not be taxpayers' money
   Pro 2: corporations manage very large projects
   Con: would take time to raise money
4. *Make a decision:* Raise money through private sector

Use the decision as a basis for a topic sentence: *Raising money in the private sector is the best way to fund a search for life in outer space.*

Thinking Practice Make a similar chart to find a solution to one of the problems listed below or to one of your choice.

1. the amount of violence in movies
2. the wasteful consumption of oil to operate automobiles
3. the dangers of fad diets

The Tools of Persuasion

To establish your *credibility*, or believability, as a persuasive writer, use the following techniques for making an argument persuasive.

Tools of Persuasion

1. Use reasonable language rather than highly charged words.
2. If the opposition has a good point, admit it but then show why it failed to convince you.
3. Refer to experts who agree with your position.

WRITING ACTIVITY 25 *Analyzing a Paragraph*

Answer the questions that follow this draft of a persuasive paragraph.

> **(1)** The search for extraterrestrial life is well worth the $12.5 million the government has granted NASA for this purpose. **(2)** In the first place, if the giant radio telescopes did pick up a signal from an intelligent civilization, the practical benefits would be enormous. **(3)** In order to send the signals, such a civilization would have to be highly advanced. **(4)** Our own planet could benefit from the knowledge of how another advanced civilization manages its precious resources and avoids destroying itself. **(5)** Shortsighted and unimaginative opponents argue that the chances of finding intelligent life are very slim. **(6)** As physicists Philip Morrison and Giuseppi Cocconi point out, however, "If we never search, the chance of success is zero." **(7)** Furthermore, while it is true that life has not yet been found, the search for it has led to other discoveries, including the detection of pulsars in 1967. **(8)** The annual cost per taxpayer of this program is only a few pennies. **(9)** Whether or not life is found, the knowledge gained along the way makes this program a great bargain.

1. List all facts that support the writer's opinion.
2. Revise sentence 5 to eliminate the emotional language.
3. Write the sentence where the writer shows why an opposing point is not convincing.
4. How does the writer use information given by authorities?
5. Reread the paragraph on pages 154–155. Which side of the issue are you on? Explain your position in a paragraph.

Order of Importance and Transitions

Another important tool of persuasion is a logical organization. The most common way to organize supporting details in a persuasive paragraph is order of importance. For example, in both paragraphs about the value of the search for life in outer space, the details are arranged in the order of most to least important.

Writing Term **Order of importance** arranges supporting points in the order of least to most important or the reverse.

Writers use transitions to show the relative importance of ideas. That is, these transitions show the relationship among their supporting points. Some of the most common transitions used with order of importance are listed in the following chart.

Transitions for Order of Importance

also	moreover	for this reason
another	furthermore	more important
besides	in addition	most important
finally	similarly	in the first place
first	likewise	to begin with

When you wish to show that your opponents' arguments can be overcome, you must point out contrasting ideas. Doing so is called giving a *rebuttal.* The following transitions are useful for showing contrast.

Transitions Showing Contrast

but	however	nevertheless
yet	instead	in contrast
or, nor	still	on the other hand

EXAMPLE OF A REBUTTAL You say that compact cars are less than safe in collisions, **but** designers have already corrected many of these problems.

WRITING ACTIVITY 26 *Using Transitions*

In the following paragraph, the ideas are arranged in order of importance, but the transitions are missing. Using the charts on the previous page, add a transition for each blank. Write the transitions on a separate piece of paper. Use commas as needed. *(See page 784.)*

Relieving Congestion

As convenient as automobiles are, all privately owned automobiles should be banned from the downtown sections of congested cities such as New York and Chicago. _______ automobiles create air pollution, especially smog. Such conditions are dangerous for everyone, particularly children and the elderly. _______ banning automobiles would force people to use public transportation such as buses and trains. Such means of transportation create less pollution than cars do. _______ cities would be much less congested without automobiles. Police cars, fire trucks, and ambulances could all move more freely. People may claim that automobiles are more convenient than public transportation. _______ the inconvenience of a few people is a small price to pay for making cities cleaner, more livable places.

WRITING ACTIVITY 27 *Writing on Your Own*

WRITING ABOUT THE THEME

Review the list of bad risks you made in Writing Activity 24. Choose one example and through freewriting, explore facts, examples, and illustrations you could use to convince someone that such a risk was not only illogical but also extremely dangerous. You may even want to get some statistics from the library to add to your notes. Once you have developed a convincing argument for a persuasive paragraph, draft it, revise it, and edit it, using the Process of Writing a Persuasive Paragraph chart on page 161. Then share your paragraph with a friend who you think might actually take such a risk at some time. You and your classmates may also wish to arrange to present skits of your paragraphs to elementary classes.

WRITING ACTIVITY 28 *Writing an Editorial*

Prewriting Through freewriting explore opinions you have about different aspects of school, such as the effects of part-time jobs on grades. Choose one opinion you think worthy of developing into an editorial for the school newspaper. Brainstorm a list of supporting facts and examples you could use to make your point. Arrange your details in logical order.

Drafting Write a quick first draft of your editorial.

Revising If your teacher permits, exchange papers with a classmate. Offer one another suggestions for making your arguments more convincing. Using your partner's comments and the chart on the next page, revise your editorial.

Editing and Publishing Use the Process of Writing a Persuasive Paragraph chart on the next page to edit your work. Then make a neat final copy of your editorial and submit it to your school newspaper for possible publication.

WRITING ACTIVITY 29 *Writing a Product Review*

Think of a product you use regularly. Then write a review of it for a consumer magazine. Include an overall evaluation of the product as well as specific features of the product that determined your evaluation. Use the Process of Writing a Persuasive Paragraph chart on the next page for assistance.

The Process of Writing a Persuasive Paragraph

PREWRITING *(See pages 10–27.)*

1. Through brainstorming, clustering, freewriting, or any other strategy that works for you, explore opinions that you hold and challenge the assumptions underlying them.
2. Determine your audience by asking yourself questions about their attitudes, beliefs, and opinions.
3. Choose one opinion you feel strongly about. Then gather whatever information you need to persuade people that your opinion is worthwhile. Define the problem carefully, identify possible solutions, evaluate each solution, and finally choose the solution you think best. In the course of gathering your thoughts, also note opposing views and explain to yourself why you do not share them.
4. Arrange your ideas in a logical order.

DRAFTING *(See pages 28–29.)*

5. Write a topic sentence stating your opinion.
6. Use your prewriting notes to write the supporting sentences—providing facts, examples, and reasons to back up your claim.
7. Add a concluding sentence that makes a final appeal to readers.

REVISING *(See pages 30–34.)*

8. Does your paragraph have all the elements shown in the Structure of a Persuasive Paragraph chart on page 154?
9. Should you delete anything to strengthen unity? *(See page 116.)*
10. Should you add anything to strengthen development?
11. Should you rearrange anything to strengthen coherence? *(See pages 117–118.)*
12. Do your sentences have variety? *(See pages 62–69.)*
13. Did you avoid rambling sentences? *(See page 73.)*
14. Can you substitute any vivid words for general ones?

EDITING AND PUBLISHING *(See pages 35–40.)*

15. Check for errors in grammar and usage.
16. Check spelling, capitalization, and punctuation.
17. Did you indent correctly? Are your margins even?
18. Is your handwriting clear?
19. Present a neat final copy to a reader and check the chart on page 40 for other publishing ideas.

A Writer Writes

WRITING ABOUT THE THEME

Paragraphs for Different Purposes

Prewriting: Writing for Different Purposes Using different writing purposes, explore the subject of people who take risks—not for their own sake but to benefit others. This technique may help you to understand such risk takers more fully.

1. Writing a Narrative Paragraph

PURPOSE: to relate an experience of a modern-day risk taker—either someone you know or someone you have read or heard about—whose risk has affected others positively

AUDIENCE: general

Use The Process of Writing a Narrative Paragraph chart on page 143 to tell the story of a risk taker. Remember, the risk taker does not have to be a great scientist or artist. He or she could be a friend or neighbor whose risk benefited others, or it could be someone you have read or heard about who took a risk.

2. Writing a Descriptive Paragraph

PURPOSE: to describe a scene associated with the risk taker's experience

AUDIENCE: general

Use The Process of Writing a Descriptive Paragraph chart on page 153 to create a vivid scene in writing that describes a key aspect of the risk taker's experience. If necessary, do some research in the library for supporting details.

3. Writing a Persuasive Paragraph

PURPOSE: to assert and back up an opinion

AUDIENCE: general

Use The Process of Writing a Persuasive Paragraph chart on page 161 to develop a paragraph on a risk worth taking. Then persuade someone to take that risk.

Independent Writing

Write a paragraph on one of the following subjects or on one of your own.

Subjects for Narrative Paragraphs

1. the first time you cooked dinner
2. surprising yourself with success
3. an embarrassing moment
4. finding something valuable
5. helping someone in need

Subjects for Descriptive Paragraphs

1. an unusual birthday present
2. a Halloween costume
3. a remodeled car
4. your favorite record-album or compact-disk cover
5. an outdoor concert

Subjects for Persuasive Paragraphs

1. creating a drug-free society
2. improving the quality of television shows
3. saving wilderness lands from development
4. women playing on football teams
5. the need for privacy

Creative Writing

Use the picture on page 19 as a springboard for writing a story. In your story tell all the events that led up to the pictured happening and carry the story through to its outcome. Use first person or third person point of view.

WRITING ABOUT THE THEME

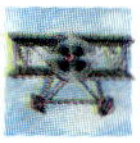

Writing about Literature

Mood is the atmosphere or feeling a work of literature creates for the reader. Write a paragraph that explains the mood that Beryl Markham creates when she describes flying alone in a plane at night in *West with the Night.* What words does she use to create that mood? How, do you think, does the mood she creates contribute to the suspense of her account?

Writing in Other Subject Areas

Geometry Write a persuasive paragraph arguing whether or not it is useful for a high school graduate to have studied geometry. Before you write, reflect on the process of proving a theorem. Make a list of the pros and cons of studying geometry to help you anticipate your opponents' views. Then write your paragraph.

World History Write a paragraph describing a historic monument you have seen, such as the Capitol building in Washington, D.C. Use vivid details that appeal to the senses to create an overall impression.

Chapter  4

Checklist

Writing Other Kinds of Paragraphs

Narrative Paragraphs

- ✔ Draft a topic sentence that captures the reader's attention and makes a general statement about the story or sets the scene. *(See page 137.)*
- ✔ Have the supporting sentences tell the story event by event. *(See page 137.)*
- ✔ Use a logical order, such as chronological order, with appropriate transitions. *(See page 139.)*
- ✔ Use a consistent point of view appropriate to the story. *(See page 140.)*
- ✔ Have the concluding sentence summarize the story or make a point about its meaning. *(See page 137.)*

Descriptive Paragraphs

- ✔ Draft a topic sentence that makes a general statement about your subject and suggests an overall impression. *(See page 144.)*
- ✔ Have the supporting sentences supply specific details that appeal to the five senses. *(See page 144.)*
- ✔ Use figurative language with striking comparisons. *(See page 147.)*
- ✔ Use a logical order, such as spatial order, with appropriate transitions. *(See page 148.)*
- ✔ Have the concluding sentence summarize the overall impression. *(See page 144.)*

Persuasive Paragraphs

- ✔ Draft a topic sentence that asserts an opinion. *(See page 154.)*
- ✔ Use the tools of persuasion. *(See page 157.)*
- ✔ Use a logical order, such as order of importance, with appropriate transitions. *(See page 158.)*
- ✔ Have the concluding sentence make a final appeal. *(See page 154.)*

Chapter 5

Writing Effective Essays

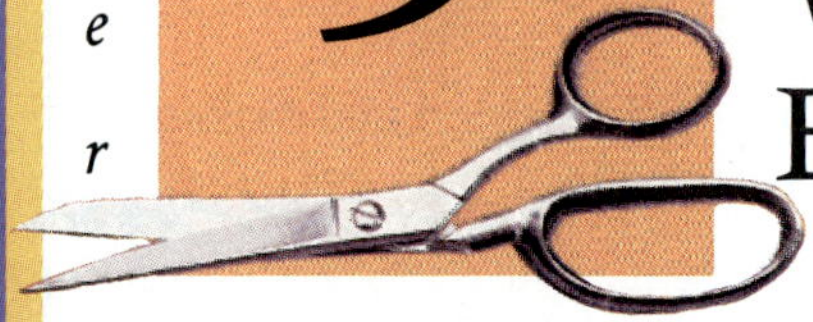

Part 1 *Reading to Write*

THEME: *Cultures*

Something inside you is affecting what you think, what you say, what you do, and even how you do what you do. This powerful force is called *culture*. While there is a long, complicated definition in the dictionary, the word *culture* basically means "the way of life of a specific group of people." In fact, you learn most aspects of culture from members of your family and the group of people that has most strongly influenced them. Consider the effects of culture—even on the basic need for food. Your particular culture determines what food you eat, how it is cooked, and in what manner you eat the food. In Western cultures, for instance, people eat with knives and forks; but in some Eastern cultures, people eat with chopsticks.

In the following selection from the book *Fifth Chinese Daughter*, the author relates how she and her family balanced two different cultures at the same time. As you read this selection, think about what makes up your culture. For instance, what traditions, beliefs, actions, and ideas have you learned from your family that set you apart from people of another culture?

Jade Snow Wong wrote a book about growing up in Chinatown in San Francisco during the 1930's—the years of the Great Depression. In the following excerpt she tells about the Oriental and Western influences she experienced.

from

Fifth Chinese Daughter

Jade Snow Wong

From infancy to my sixteenth year, I was reared according to nineteenth century ideals of Chinese womanhood. I was never left alone, though it was not unusual for me to feel lonely, while surrounded by a family of seven others, and often by ten (including bachelor cousins) at meals.

My father (who enjoyed our calling him Daddy in English) was the unquestioned head of our household. He was not talkative, being preoccupied with his business affairs and with reading constantly otherwise. My mother was mistress of domestic affairs. Seldom did these two converse before their children, but we knew them to be a united front, and suspected that privately she both informed and influenced him about each child.

In order to support the family in America, Daddy tried various occupations—candy making, the ministry to which he was later ordained—but finally settled on manufacturing men's and children's denim garments. He leased sewing equipment, installed machines in a basement where rent was cheapest, and there he and his family lived and worked. There was no thought that dim, airless quarters were terrible conditions for living and working, or that child labor was unhealthful. The only goal was for all in the family to work, to save, and to become educated. It was possible, so it would be done.

My father, a meticulous bookkeeper, used only an abacus, a brush, ink, and Chinese ledgers. Because of his newly learned ideals, he pioneered for the right of women to work. Concerned that they have economic independence, but not with the long hours of industrial home work, he went to shy housewives' apartments and taught them sewing.

My earliest memories of companionship with my father were as his passenger in his red wheelbarrow, sharing space with the piles of blue-jean materials he was delivering to a worker's home. He must have been forty. He was lean, tall, inevitably wearing blue overalls, rolled shirt sleeves, and high black kid shoes. In his pockets were numerous keys, tools, and pens. On such deliveries, I noticed that he always managed time to show a mother how to sew a difficult seam, or to help her repair a machine, or just to chat.

I observed from birth that living and working were inseparable. My mother was short, sturdy, young looking, and took pride in her appearance. She was at her machine the minute housework was done, and she was the hardest-working seamstress, seldom pausing, working after I went to bed. The hum of sewing machines continued day and night, seven days a week. She knew that to have more than the four necessities, she must work and save. We knew that to overcome poverty, there were only two methods: working and education.

Having provided the setup for family industry, my father turned his attention to our education. Ninety-five percent of the population in China had been illiterate. He knew that American public schools would take care of our English, but he had to be the watchdog to nurture our Chinese knowledge. Only the Cantonese tongue was ever spoken by him or my mother. When the two oldest girls arrived from China, the schools of Chinatown received only boys. My father tutored his daughters each morning before breakfast. In the midst of a foreign environment, he clung to a combination of the familiar old standards and what was permissible in the newly learned Christian ideals.

My eldest brother was born in America, the only boy for fourteen years, and after him three daughters—another older sister, myself, and my younger sister. Then my younger brother, Paul, was born. That older brother, Lincoln, was cherished in the best Chinese tradition. He had his own room; he kept a German shepherd as his pet; he was tutored by a Chinese scholar; he was sent to private school for American classes. As a male Wong, he would be responsible some day for the preservation of and pilgrimages to ancestral graves—his privileges were his birthright. We girls were content with the unusual opportunities of working and attending two schools.

For by the time I was six, times in Chinatown were changing. The Hip Wo Chinese Christian Academy (in the same building as the Methodist Mission) had been founded on a coeducational basis, with nominal tuition. Financial support came from three Protestant church boards: the Congregational, Presbyterian, and Methodist churches contributed equal shares. My father was on the Hip Wo School Board for many years. By day, I attended American public school near our home. From 5:00 P.M. to 8:00 P.M., on five weekdays and from 9:00 A.M. to 12 noon on Saturdays, I attended the Chinese school. Classes numbered twenty to thirty students, and were taught by educated Chinese from China. We studied poetry, calligraphy, philosophy, literature, history, correspondence, religion, all by exacting memorization. The Saturday morning chapel services carried out the purposes of the supporting churches.

Daddy emphasized memory development; he could still recite fluently many lengthy lessons of his youth. Every evening after both schools, I'd sit by my father, often as he worked at his sewing machine, sing-songing my lessons above its hum. Sometimes I would stop to hold a light for him as he threaded the difficult holes of a specialty machine, such as one for bias bindings. After my Chinese lessons passed his approval, I was allowed to attend to American homework. I was made to feel luckier than other Chinese girls who didn't study Chinese, and also luckier than Western girls without a dual heritage. . . . There was little time for play, and toys were unknown to me. In any spare time, I was supplied with embroidery and sewing for my mother. The Chinese New Year, which by the old lunar calendar would fall sometime in late January or early February of the Western Christian calendar, was the most special time of the year, for then the machines stopped for three days. Mother would clean our living quarters very thoroughly, decorate the sitting room with flowering branches and fresh oranges, and arrange candied fruits or salty melon seeds for callers. All of us would be dressed in bright new clothes, and relatives or close friends, who came to call, would give each of us a red paper packet containing a good luck coin—usually a quarter. I remember how my classmates would gleefully talk of *their* receipts. But my mother made us give our money to her, for she said that she needed it to reciprocate to others.

Yet there was little reason for unhappiness. I was never hungry. Though we had no milk, there was all the rice we wanted. We had hot and cold running water—a rarity in Chinatown—as well as our own bathtub. Our sheets were pieced from dishtowels, but we had sheets. I was never neglected, for my mother and father were always at home. During school vacation periods, I was taught to operate many types of machines—tacking (for pockets), overlocking (for the raw edges of seams), buttonhole, double seaming; and I learned all the stages in producing a pair of jeans to its final inspection, folding, and tying in bundles of a dozen pairs by size, ready for pickup. Denim jeans are heavy—my shoulders ached often. My father set up a modest nickel-and-dime piecework reward for me, which he recorded in my own notebook, and paid me regularly.

Only Daddy and Oldest Brother were allowed individual idiosyncrasies. Daughters were all expected to be of one standard. To allow each one of many daughters to be different would have posed enormous problems of cost, energy, and attention. No one was shown physical affection. Such familiarity would have weakened my parents and endangered the one-answer authoritative system. One standard from past to present, whether in China or in San Francisco, was simpler to enforce.

Thirty-five years later, I have four children, two sons and two daughters. In principle we remain true to my father's and mother's tradition, I believe. Our children respect my husband and me, but it is not a blind obedience enforced by punishment. It is a respect won from observing us and rounded by friendship. My parents never said "please" and "thank you" for any service or gift. In Chinese, both "please" and "thank you" can be literally translated as "I am not worthy" and naturally, no parent is going to say that about a service which should be their just due. Now I say "thank you," "please," and "sorry" to my children, in English, and I do not think it lessens my dignity. The ultimate praise I ever remember from my parents was a single word, "good." We do not abhor a show of affection. Each child looks forward to his goodnight kiss and tuck-in. Sometimes one or more of them will throw his arms around one of us and cry out, "I love you so."

Traditional Chinese parents pit their children against a standard of perfection without regard to personality, individual ambitions, tolerance for human error, or exposure to the changing social scene. It never occurred to that kind of parent to be friends with their children on common ground. Unlike our parents, we think we tolerate human error and human change. Our children are being encouraged to develop their individual abilities. They all draw and can use their hands in crafts, are all familiar with our office and love to experiment with the potter's wheel or enameling supplies at our studio. Sometimes I have been asked, "What would you like your children to be?" Let each choose his or her career. The education of our girls will be provided by us as well as that of our boys. ◆

Responding to the Theme

Cultures

Responding in Your Journal In the selection from *Fifth Chinese Daughter,* Jade Snow Wong told about several cultural influences in her early life. For example, she explained how her older brother had special privileges because he would some day be responsible for "the preservation of and pilgrimages to ancestral graves . . ." She wrote about the traditions of Chinese New Year and also explained why her parents never showed any affection.

Think about the cultural influences that have shaped your life. What aspects of your family life, for instance, are different from those of another culture? Some specifics you might think about are your family's attitudes and behavior in the areas of parental authority, interactions with relatives, dating, fashion, sports, money, education, dietary habits, and celebrations for special occasions, such as birthdays, holidays, and festivals. Begin by listing in your journal any specific details that you think are significant enough to write about. Then, each day this week in your journal, describe a different cultural aspect of your life and tell when you learned it, why you think it is important, and how it has influenced your life.

Speaking and Listening Research an interesting characteristic or habit of another culture. Condense your information into a two-to-three-minute report that you should be prepared to deliver, not read, to your classmates—as an informal speech or as a minireport in a small discussion group.

Critical Thinking: Interpreting In her autobiography Jade Snow Wong said that she was raised "according to the nineteenth century ideals of womanhood." Write a paragraph explaining some of the changes that Western culture brought to her adult life.

Extending Your Vocabulary Because one of the meanings of the prefix *-in* is "not," the definition of *informal* is "not formal," or "casual." After writing a definition for each of the following words—based on the meaning of the prefix—check each one in the dictionary. Then write a sentence using each word.

infancy independence inevitably inseparable

Mardi Gras Carnival, Binche, Belgium

Part 2 Writing

If you wanted to explain in writing what is unique about your cultural heritage or what you saw and did at a cultural festival in your town, you would need to write more than one paragraph. To include all your facts and details, you would need to write a longer composition called an *essay*.

Writing Term An **essay** is a composition that presents and develops one main idea in three or more paragraphs.

Essays can be written for a wide variety of purposes. You might describe the changes that have taken place in your neighborhood and express your feelings about those changes. You might analyze the motivation of a character in a short story or persuade your school to offer better lunches. You might explain how Alexander the Great conquered a vast part of Asia by the time he was thirty-two years old. Whatever the purpose and subject, it is your personal outlook that makes any essay you write interesting.

Exploring Essay Structure

Carefully constructed essays have three main parts: an introduction, a body, and a conclusion. These three parts of an essay parallel the three-part structure of a paragraph.

PARAGRAPH STRUCTURE	ESSAY STRUCTURE
topic sentence that expresses the main idea	introduction that states the main idea in a thesis statement
body of supporting sentences	body of supporting paragraphs
concluding sentence	conclusion

As you read the essay on cryptanalysis below and on the next page, notice how the three main parts and the thesis statement work together to present a unified subject.

Model: *Essay*

Cryptanalysis: Breaking Codes

INTRODUCTION

There are no easy ways to crack a code. In fact, no one has yet discovered a shortcut that will bypass the hard work. Breaking a code requires certain qualities on the part of the cryptanalyst.

THESIS STATEMENT

BODY

The first quality is the ability to study. Before anyone can hope to break a code, he or she must know how codes are put together. There may be a similarity between a system one has studied and the system one has to break. Therefore, the wider one's knowledge of various code systems, the more likely it is that one will begin to recognize messages at a first or second look.

The second quality required is patience. Consider the story of the patience of the Arab cryptanalyst who studied an intercepted message to

Rosetta stone

the Sultan of Morocco for 15 years before success was achieved! A particular code may reveal nothing, even after precious hours of searching for a clue. That's because good codes can be uncrackable. Short cryptograms with only a few letters or words often fall into this category. The only hope of breaking short coded messages sometimes is to know something about the sender and the intended recipient and to accumulate a collection of messages from the sender.

The third quality required by the cryptanalyst is a vivid imagination. When breaking codes, one has to be prepared for almost anything. A good imagination helps when the time has come to make wild or calculated guesses and when nothing but imagination can hope to get answers.

CONCLUSION

With all this, the cryptanalyst still needs luck. A little luck can bring answers that all the logical thinking in the world could never achieve.

JULIAN A. BIELEWICZ, *Secret Languages* (Adapted)

WRITING ACTIVITY 1 *Analyzing an Essay*

Use the essay "Cryptanalysis" on pages 173–174 to answer the following questions.

1. What is the main idea of the essay?
2. How do the paragraphs in the body support the main idea?
3. Summarize the conclusion.
4. How does the conclusion recall the introduction?

WRITING ACTIVITY 2 *Writing on Your Own*

WRITING ABOUT THE THEME

Refer to the journal activities on page 171 or brainstorm for unique aspects of your culture. Consider, for example, what things your culture values the most, what unique traditions you observe, and what foods, pastimes, or customs you regard as important or special. When you have a list of several possible subjects, explore each one through freewriting. Then save your work for later use.

The Introduction of an Essay

The introduction of an essay has five functions. You should keep these in mind as you plan your approach to your subject.

Functions of the Introduction

The introduction of an essay

1. introduces the subject.
2. captures the reader's attention and prepares the reader for what is to follow.
3. establishes the tone—the writer's attitude toward both the subject and the audience.
4. presents the main idea in a thesis statement.
5. states or implies the purpose for writing.

When beginning the introduction, you might use any one of a number of strategies to capture the reader's attention. For example, you could use a lively quotation, cite a little known statistic or fact, provide an anecdote, quote from a conversation you heard, or just relate an arresting bit of information.

Tone

In the introduction of an essay, writers often reveal the attitude they have taken toward their subject and audience. This attitude is called *tone.*

Writing Term **Tone** is the writer's attitude toward the subject and audience.

In setting the tone of an essay, consider your positive or negative feelings about your subject. For example, your tone may be serious or comical, admiring or critical, scary or reassuring, sympathetic or mocking, or joyful or sad. The tone of Jade Snow Wong's autobiographical essay is reflective, or thoughtful and serious. *(See pages 167–170.)* In contrast, the paragraph on the next page—which is taken from an essay—reveals an enthusiastic, admiring tone.

Model: *Paragraph with Admiring Tone*

Baseball is a truly American game . . . In its speed, skill, and brevity, it seems particularly adapted to our high nervous tension. It lasts about as long as a theater play and resembles that form of entertainment in more ways than one. The mystery of hero and villain is discovered in about two hours, sometimes at the rate of a thrill a minute. Frequently the unexpected happens. Victory suddenly emerges from the very core of defeat.

William Phelps
"The Great American Game"

The next paragraph, from an essay by Woody Allen, sets a humorous tone about a subject many people take seriously—the existence of UFO's.

Model: *Paragraph with Humorous Tone*

All UFO's may not prove to be of extraterrestrial origin. Experts do agree, however, that any glowing, cigar-shaped aircraft capable of rising straight up at 12,000 miles per second would require the kind of maintenance and spark plugs available only on Pluto. If these objects are indeed from another planet, then the civilization that designed them must be millions of years more advanced than our own. Either that, or they are very lucky. Professor Leon Speciman theorizes a civilization in outer space that is more advanced than ours by approximately 15 minutes. This, he feels, gives them a great advantage over us, since they needn't rush to appointments.

Woody Allen
"The UFO Menace" (Adapted)

WRITING ACTIVITY 3 *Identifying Tone*

Read each opening sentence for an essay about cars. Then write an adjective—such as *reflective, humorous,* or *enthusiastic*—to describe the tone of each one.

1. I regard driving a car as a responsibility, not a right.
2. My first car was a used-parts shop on wheels.
3. I was thrilled when I got my first car.
4. My new car was a symbol of my deep desire for freedom.
5. The scientific community would be stunned to see that my ancient car follows its own laws of motion.

WRITING ACTIVITY 4 *Writing on Your Own*

WRITING ABOUT THE THEME

Review the work you developed in Writing Activity 2. Choose one of your ideas about culture as a subject for an essay and, if necessary, limit the subject. (*See pages 15–16.*) Think about your writing purpose and your attitude toward your subject. Then decide on an appropriate tone and write a word or phrase describing that tone. Save your work in your writing folder for later use.

The Thesis Statement

Besides introducing the subject and setting the tone, the introduction also contains the *thesis statement.*

Writing Term The **thesis statement** states the main idea and makes the purpose of the essay clear.

Notice how each of the following thesis statements makes the main idea and purpose of an essay clear.

Model: *Thesis Statements*

The first time I drove a car I was a jumble of nerves and fear. [The purpose is to express a feeling about an experience.]

The Japanese Tea Ceremony reveals the beauty in everyday routine. [The purpose is to explain a factual subject.]

The roller rink comes to life on Saturday afternoon. [The purpose is to describe.]

A healthy society depends on a high degree of citizen participation in the government. [The purpose is to persuade.]

The thesis statement is the controlling idea of the essay. It should be broad enough to include the main points in the essay yet should be limited enough to allow you to cover your subject adequately in the number of paragraphs you plan to write. When you write your thesis statement, you might state an idea that is too vague or general for an essay. It will then be necessary to refine your thesis. Refining and revising your thesis statement guarantees that it will fit your subject perfectly.

The thesis statement usually creates the strongest impression when it is the first or last sentence of the introduction.

WRITING ACTIVITY 5 *Identifying Thesis Statements*

Write the thesis statement from each of the following introductory paragraphs. Then indicate the writer's purpose: *to explain a factual subject, to express a feeling about a personal experience, to describe,* or *to persuade.*

1.

San Juan, Puerto Rico, is really two cities in one. Old San Juan is rich in Spanish history. It has walled forts and stunning cathedrals dating back hundreds of years. The new city has skyscrapers, international banks and businesses, and the thrill of modern cities everywhere. For tourists as well as residents, the two-in-one city provides a seemingly endless variety of enjoyable activities.

2.

A single knoll rises out of the plain in Oklahoma, north and west of the Wichita Range. For my people, the Kiowas, it is an old landmark, and they gave it the name Rainy Mountain. I returned to Rainy Mountain in July. My grandmother had died in the spring, and I wanted to be at her grave. Although my grandmother lived out her long life in the shadow of Rainy Mountain, the immense landscape of the continental interior lay like memory in her blood. She could tell of the Crows, whom she had never seen, and of the Black Hills, where she had never been. I wanted to see in reality what she had seen more perfectly in the mind's eye, and traveled 1,500 miles to begin my pilgrimage.

N. SCOTT MOMADAY, *The Way to Rainy Mountain* (Adapted)

3.

It is hard to find a movie theater these days where a comedy is playing. In the days of the silent films, it was equally hard to find a theater which was not showing one. The laughs today are pitifully few, far between, shallow, quiet, and short. They almost never build, as they used to, into something combining the jabbering frequency of a machine gun with the delirious momentum of a roller coaster. Saddest of all, there are few comedians now below middle age, and there are none who seem to learn much from picture to picture, or to try anything new.

JAMES AGEE, "Comedy's Greatest Era"

4.

Millions of years before people walked the surface of the earth, moles were tunneling beneath it. Today, the meandering surface runways made by these animals in their constant search for food are a familiar sight to many Americans. Few people, however, have more than a vague understanding of the creatures that inhabit them. Of the many mole species living today, none is more bizarre than the semiaquatic, star-nosed mole.

TERRY L. YATES, "The Mole That Keeps Its Nose Clean"

WRITING ACTIVITY 6 *Writing a Thesis Statement*

For each of the following subjects and lists of details, write a thesis statement.

1. Subject energy consumption

Details
- Early people used fuel for light and heat.
- The use of fuel for mechanical power was a big change.
- The present rate of energy consumption is the greatest in all of history.
- The world's resources are depleting.
- People must change the way they use energy.

2. Subject transportation in America in the 1830's

Details
- People liked fast horses.
- Harnessed pairs of horses pulled wagons.
- Hackney coaches were available for hire.
- Omnibuses were used in cities.
- Horse-drawn stagecoaches carried nine passengers.
- Steamboats were popular for river travel.
- Railroads traveled at 14 to 16 miles per hour.

WRITING ACTIVITY 7 *Writing on Your Own*

WRITING ABOUT THE THEME

Based on your work in Writing Activities 2 and 4, write a working thesis statement about a unique aspect of your culture. Then build on that thesis statement by drafting two or three possible introductions for your essay. Place your thesis statement both at the beginning and at the end of your introduction to see which position is better. Also experiment with different ways of setting your tone and capturing the reader's attention. After you select your most effective introduction, save it in your writing folder for later use.

The Body of an Essay

After you have written the introduction, your next task is to develop your preliminary working thesis statement, idea by idea, in the body of your essay.

Supporting Paragraphs

The paragraphs that make up the body of an essay develop the main idea presented in the thesis statement. Although all the supporting paragraphs relate to the thesis, each one deals with one aspect of that thesis. Like any good paragraph, each has its own topic sentence and supporting sentences.

Writing Term The **supporting paragraphs** in the body of an essay develop the thesis statement.

Following is the introduction and body of an essay. Notice how each of the supporting paragraphs develops the thesis statement.

Student Model: *Introduction and Body of an Essay*

Why I Like Going to the Movies

INTRODUCTION

When the windchill factor is 62 degrees below zero and most people are keeping warm indoors, I am likely to be standing in a line to buy movie tickets, determined to see the latest release. On a warmer day, when the lines circle around the block, I will be waiting patiently, planning my purchases at the refreshment counter to help the time pass. To me going to the movies is worth any amount of hardship. The experience of seeing a movie satisfies me in a way few other experiences can match.

THESIS STATEMENT

BODY

TOPIC SENTENCE

Once I purchase a ticket, I feel a thrill of anticipation. In the darkened theater, leaning back and settling low into my seat, I am transported from the real world into another world. The sound wraps me in a shield that deflects the noises of the outside world. Eyes riveted to the screen, I float comfortably into a world of sheer imagination. For two hours I can escape the cares of life beyond the theater walls.

TOPIC SENTENCE During a good movie, the isolated feeling is so complete that I lose the sense of viewing the movie and begin to feel that I am actually in it. In one scene I am the romantic hero; in another, the tortured villain. I am all of the characters: comic and tragic, noble and selfish, aging and youthful. As I identify with the characters, my personality stretches and bends. I feel what they feel and experience what they experience.

Even a mediocre movie is worth the price of admission. The track and zoom of the camera, the light and darkness and colors, the settings and scenery and costumes—all these are enjoyable to see.

TOPIC SENTENCE Although the familiar sights of school, home, and neighborhood are pleasant to me, I hunger for new colors and images as well. Movies serve up a feast for my eyes and my mind.

The body of "Why I Like Going to the Movies" can be presented in a simple outline that shows how the main idea of each paragraph supports the thesis statement of the entire essay.

THESIS STATEMENT The experience of the movies satisfies me in a way few other experiences can match.

I. Transports me into another world
II. Allows me to identify with the major and minor characters
III. Offers a feast for my eyes and mind

WRITING ACTIVITY 8 *Analyzing Supporting Paragraphs*

Reread the thesis statement and the paragraphs that make up the body in Julian A. Bielewicz's essay "Cryptanalysis" on pages 173 and 174. After you see how each paragraph supports the thesis of the essay, develop an outline like the one above. In your outline use Roman numerals to show the main idea of each paragraph and how each supports the thesis statement.

WRITING ACTIVITY 9 *Developing Supporting Ideas*

Under each of the following thesis statements, write three ideas that could be developed into three supporting paragraphs for the body of an essay. Write them in the form of the preceding outline.

1. I have some advice for incoming ninth graders on the art of adjusting to high school.
2. Judging others by their appearance may lead to big mistakes.
3. Three of my favorite songs have different moods.
4. People need to learn early in life the importance of saying no.
5. Becoming an accomplished _____ takes special training. (Fill in the blank.)

WRITING ACTIVITY 10 *Writing on Your Own*

WRITING ABOUT THE THEME

Return to the freewriting about a unique aspect of your culture that you did in Writing Activity 2. After sorting through your ideas, select those details that support the thesis statement you wrote in Writing Activity 7. First group your details into meaningful categories, trying out several possible classifications to find the best one. *(See pages 101–102 and Writing Is Thinking on page 184.)* Then arrange your categories in an order that accurately reflects their importance. *(See pages 106–107.)* Make a simple outline of your ideas that you can use as a guide to writing the body of your essay. Save your outline in your writing folder for later use.

Critical Thinking

Writing Is Thinking

Classifying

Once you generate a list of details and ideas that support your thesis statement, your next step is to group, or *classify,* those ideas into meaningful categories that you can use to organize the body of your essay. When you classify, you group details and ideas together on the basis of shared features or characteristics. The following chart shows one way that details for an essay on your favorite recreational activities might be classified.

Classification Chart

Thesis: Although my favorite recreations are an odd assortment, together they give me year-round pleasure.

DETAILS	CLASSIFICATION
Rock climbing	I. Done by myself
Taping music	A. Kite making
Kite making	B. Collecting comic books
Bowling	C. Taping music
Watching videos	II. Done indoors with friends
Collecting comic books	A. Bowling
Playing soccer	B. Watching videos
	III. Done outdoors with friends
	A. Rock climbing
	B. Playing soccer

Thinking Practice Choose one of the following subjects or one of your own. Through freewriting, brainstorming, or clustering, list as many details as you can that relate to the subject. Then classify your list of details by making a chart like the one above.

1. preparations for a camping trip
2. the contents of your closet
3. the range of television programming available in your area
4. the ideal collection of records, tapes, or compact discs
5. part-time jobs available for teenagers in your community

Unity, Coherence, and Emphasis

An essay has *unity* when all the supporting paragraphs relate to the main idea in the thesis statement. As a result, in an essay with unity, readers are not distracted by sentences or paragraphs that seem to wander off the main point.

Essays should also have *coherence*—the quality that makes the ideas in the paragraphs flow logically and naturally from one to the next. When your essay has a coherent organization, readers can easily follow the sequence of your ideas.

You can create coherence in your essays by using transitional words and phrases to connect supporting paragraphs. *(For lists of transitions, see pages 139, 148, and 158.)* You can also achieve coherence by repeating key words or by using pronouns and synonyms to refer to key words. *(See pages 117–118.)*

Emphasis, another important quality of an essay, helps readers recognize your most important ideas. You can show your emphasis by writing more about one idea, by discussing it first, or by using transitional words and phrases to highlight it.

Writing Tip Check your essays for the qualities of **unity, coherence,** and **emphasis.**

Unity, coherence, and emphasis

Festival of La Tirana, Chile

Julian Bielewicz's essay "Cryptanalysis" on page 173 shows all three of these qualities. It has unity because all the supporting paragraphs describe what qualities a cryptanalyst needs to break a code. It has coherence because in each of the supporting paragraphs, the author uses introductory transitions such as *the first quality, the second quality,* and *the third quality* to make the organization clear. Finally, he reveals his emphasis by placing his most important idea in his first supporting paragraph.

WRITING ACTIVITY 11 *Analyzing Unity, Coherence, and Emphasis*

Reread the introduction and the body of the student model essay, "Why I Like Going to the Movies," on pages 181–182. Then write answers to each of the following questions.

1. What characteristic of the three supporting paragraphs gives this essay unity?
2. What transitional phrase in the second supporting paragraph links it to the first supporting paragraph?
3. What aspect of the experience of going to the movies is probably most important to this writer? How do you know this author's emphasis?
4. How do transitions from each paragraph to the next one give the essay coherence?
5. What three transitional phrases give coherence to the second paragraph of the body of the essay?

WRITING ACTIVITY 12 *Writing on Your Own*

WRITING ABOUT THE THEME

Return to the outline about a unique aspect of your culture, which you prepared in Writing Activity 10. Then, using the supporting details that support your thesis statement, draft the body of your essay. As you write, follow the organization you decided on for your supporting paragraphs. Be sure to use transitional words and phrases to connect your supporting paragraphs.

If your teacher permits, discuss your draft of the introduction and the body of your essay with a classmate. Sharing your writing with a partner will often give you some good ideas for improving your essay. After incorporating any improvements, save your work in your writing folder for later use.

The Conclusion of an Essay

No essay is complete without a conclusion that sums up the ideas in the body and reminds readers of the thesis statement. A good conclusion often ends with a clincher statement that rings in the reader's memory.

Writing Term The **conclusion** completes the essay and reinforces the thesis statement.

The following paragraph is the conclusion to "Why I Like Going to the Movies." *(See pages 181–182.)* It reinforces the thesis stated in the introduction, restates the ideas in the supporting paragraphs, and has an excellent clincher statement.

Student Model: *Conclusion of an Essay*

As I see more and more movies, I recognize the acting and filmmaking techniques that mark a great movie. Still, all my new critical skills are nothing compared to the fundamental pleasure I experience at the movies. Although the images disappear with the last click of the projector, they find a lasting home in me. As I leave the theater, I feel as if I have discovered a great treasure, or captained a starship, or danced to a driving rock beat. I like living in my everyday world, but movies give me exciting new worlds to enjoy.

CLINCHER STATEMENT

WRITING ACTIVITY 13 *Writing on Your Own*

WRITING ABOUT THE THEME

Add a strong conclusion to the body of your essay about a unique aspect of your culture that you drafted in Writing Activity 12. Then, when you have finished drafting, check your essay for the qualities of unity, coherence, and emphasis. If some of your paragraphs do not support your thesis statement, think of what you could delete or add to provide unity. If some paragraphs do not follow clearly from one to another, add transitional words or phrases that will make them coherent. If your readers could misunderstand what your most important idea is, think of a way to add emphasis. Revise your conclusion, if necessary, and save your work for later use.

Language Integrating Skills

Editing and Publishing

Grammar in the Writing Process

In the selection from *Fifth Chinese Daughter,* Jade Snow Wong explained that she needed to know two languages: Cantonese, the language of her ancestors, and English, the language of her new home. Learning a second language is never easy. You must not only study and learn the words of the new language, but you also must understand how those words work together to form sentences.

Sentence Fragments A *sentence fragment* is a group of words that does not work as a sentence. Instead of a complete sentence, you have only a fragment, or a part, of a sentence. In Chapter 1 on page 38, you reviewed sentence fragments that were missing either a subject or a verb. The most common type of sentence fragment, however, is a phrase that does not have either a subject or a verb.

SENTENCE FRAGMENTS In the dim, rented basement.
Riding in a wheelbarrow full of fabric.
To improve life as much as possible.

If you read your writing aloud as you edit, you will be able to detect most sentence fragments. Reading aloud is helpful because when you finish reading most sentence fragments, your voice is still up—expecting more information to follow. If you read the first example above, for instance, you end on a note of anticipation. You think you will find out what happened in the dim rented basement, but you never do. Therefore, to correct most fragments, add whatever information is missing—whatever information you anticipated would be there. *(For examples of different kinds of sentence fragments and practice in correcting them, see pages 647–651.)*

SENTENCES In the dim, rented basement, **you could hear the hum of sewing machines.**

Riding in a wheelbarrow full of fabric, **I spent some special moments with my father.**

To improve life as much as possible, **my mother became a hardworking seamstress.**

Run-on Sentences A run-on sentence is a mistake that happens when there are no words or punctuation to stop one sentence from running into another sentence. Therefore, to correct a run-on sentence, you have to separate the two sentences. You can do this (1) with a period and a capital letter or (2) with a comma and a conjunction.

RUN-ON SENTENCE — We learned English in the American schools my father taught us Cantonese at home.

CORRECTED SENTENCE — We learned English in the American schools**.** **M**y father taught us Cantonese at home.

CORRECTED SENTENCE — We learned English in the American schools**,** **but** my father taught us Cantonese at home.

Another way to correct a run-on sentence is to make one of the sentences into a subordinate clause.

RUN-ON SENTENCE — We learned English in the American schools my father taught us Cantonese at home.

CORRECTED SENTENCE — **Although we learned English in the American schools,** my father taught us Cantonese at home.

Using either a coordinating or a subordinating conjunction to correct a run-on sentence helps show the relationship between the two sentences. *(For other examples of run-on sentences and for practice in writing them correctly, see pages 651–654.)*

Editing Checklist

1. Are there any sentence fragments? *(See pages 647–650.)*
2. Are there any run-on sentences? *(See pages 651–653.)*

WRITING ACTIVITY 14 *Writing on Your Own*

WRITING ABOUT THE THEME

Editing Using the checklist above and the Editing Checklist on page 35, correct any mistakes in your essay. Then write a final copy.

Publishing With your teacher's help and permission, bind all of the essays in a handbook of cultures for everyone to read.

A Writer Writes

WRITING ABOUT THE THEME

An Essay about a Shared Experience

PURPOSE: to relate an incident involving you and someone from a culture different from your own

AUDIENCE: your classmates and teacher

Prewriting Brainstorm or talk to friends and family members to help you recall any experiences throughout your life that you have shared with someone whose cultural background was different from your own. As you remember various incidents, focus on any revelation, or new understanding, you may have gained as a result. (If you have never had such an experience, choose a different culture and imagine what the incident would be like.)

STEP 1: Through freewriting or brainstorming, recall details about your shared experiences. For instance, perhaps you tasted some new foods, heard a different kind of music, or observed a previously unknown custom or tradition. Then concentrate on one particularly meaningful incident that you could develop into an essay.

STEP 2: After writing a preliminary working thesis statement, list all the facts and details you can recall about your experience. If possible, gather additional information by reviewing the experience with someone who shared it with you. Then, after you group your details and ideas into meaningful categories, use a simple outline to arrange your categories into a logical order.

Drafting As you begin the first draft of your essay, write an introduction that will capture your readers' attention. Your introduction should also establish your tone and include a thesis statement that states your main idea and makes your purpose clear. Then, after you use your outline to write your supporting paragraphs, end with a strong conclusion.

Revising In addition to checking your draft for unity, coherence, and emphasis, use the Revision Checklist on page 31 to revise your writing further. Examine the vividness of your word choice and the variety of your sentence structure. Wherever necessary, add, substitute, delete, or rearrange to improve the clarity and forcefulness of your work.

Editing and Publishing Use the Editing Checklists on pages 35 and 189 as guides to editing your draft and make a neat final copy. With your teacher's permission, you may wish to plan and videotape a cultural festival where students dress in the native costume of their culture, play appropriate music, serve ethnic food, and share their papers. If this publishing idea is impossible,you may wish to consult the Ways to Publish Your Writing Chart on page 40 for publishing ideas.

Independent Writing

Write an essay based on one of the following thesis statements.

1. I thought learning to drive would be easy.
2. Efforts to save the planet are vitally important.
3. I had never thought of myself as being superstitious.

4. I will never forget my ____ birthday! (Fill in the blank.)
5. My pet ____ was one of the best friends I have ever had. (Fill in the blank.)
6. A successful war on drugs will help end violence in the streets.
7. Every student should become computer literate as early as possible.
8. Our community needs a corp of teenage volunteers for clean-up.
9. More low-income housing will help the homeless.
10. I wish courses like knitting, sewing, and cooking were required.

Creative Writing

Several years ago, in a book called *Cultural Literacy,* E. D. Hirsch listed 4,500 names, dates, and words and phrases that he believed were recognized by all educated people. Choose one of the following words, phrases, or sentences from his book and use it as the springboard for an idea that you can use to develop a short story.

abominable snowman	fair-weather friends	Live and learn.
brainwashing	gamma rays	nuclear energy
conformity	Ignorance is bliss.	Shangri-la
Dutch treat	insomnia	unicorn

Writing about Literature

An *autobiography* is a person's written account of his or her life. Write a paragraph that explains why you think the selection from *Fifth Chinese Daughter* leaves a more lasting impression because it is written as an autobiography rather than as a fictional story.

Writing in Other Subject Areas

Health Use the *Readers' Guide to Periodical Literature* to find articles about the field of sports medicine. Then write an essay about a current issue in that field that interests you. Use specific details and examples to explain why you think that issue is important.

World History Within a short period of time, traffic on the highways of some large cities will grind to a halt because of too many cars with a single passenger. This type of congested traffic is also the greatest cause of air pollution in those same cities. Write an essay that explains some alternatives in transportation that the next generation may have to take to resolve these problems.

Chapter 5 Checklist

Writing Effective Essays

Prewriting

- ✔ Find subjects by drawing on your personal experiences and insights and choose one to develop into an essay. *(See page 15.)*
- ✔ Limit your subject. Focus your ideas by asking yourself questions about your writing purpose, your audience, and the tone you have decided to use. *(See pages 15–16, 17, and 176–177.)*
- ✔ Brainstorm, freewrite, or cluster to develop supporting ideas.
- ✔ Sort through your ideas and classify them in meaningful groups. Organize your groups into a simple outline. *(See pages 101–102.)*

Drafting

- ✔ Write a working thesis statement that expresses your main idea and states or implies your writing purpose. *(See page 178.)*
- ✔ Write an introduction that catches the attention of your audience, establishes your tone, and includes your thesis statement. *(See pages 176–178.)*
- ✔ Write the supporting paragraphs of the body. *(See pages 181–182.)*
- ✔ Use transitional words and phrases to link your supporting paragraphs. *(See pages 185–186.)*
- ✔ Add a concluding paragraph with a clincher statement. *(See page 187.)*
- ✔ Add a title. *(See page 28.)*

Revising

- ✔ Revise your essay for structure, well-developed paragraphs, unity, coherence, emphasis, and varied, lively sentences and words. *(See pages 53–81, 173–182, and 185–186.)*

Editing and Publishing

- ✔ Check your grammar, spelling, mechanics, and standard manuscript form. Present your finished essay to a reader. *(See pages 35, 40, 189, 470–479.)*

Unit 2
Achieving the Writer's Purpose

Chapter 6

Writing Essays to Inform

Part 1 *Reading to Write*

THEME: *Progress*

You and your parents and grandparents have lived through an amazing time of change. When your grandparents were your age, for example, there were no computer games because no homes had computers. There were no push-button phones, no microwaves, and no home air conditioners. Many homes did not even have a television set, and the sets there were took several minutes to warm up before a picture appeared. You see, at that time there were no transistors. There also were no lasers. As a result people who had had surgery on eye cataracts had to convalesce by lying perfectly still for six weeks in a dark room. Now people with cataracts can walk into a hospital, have laser surgery, and be home several hours later. All of these kinds of changes can be classified under the heading "Progress."

When you hear the word *progress,* you normally think of a forward movement—life becoming better than it used to be. However, Isaac Asimov, the author of the next selection called "Dial versus Digital," thinks that sometimes progress may actually be one step forward and two steps backward. As you read his essay, think about progress. Everyone knows it has its positive side, but could it possibly have a negative side as well?

Dial versus Digital

Isaac Asimov

There seems no question but that the clock dial, which has existed in its present form since the seventeenth century and in earlier forms since ancient times, is on its way out. More and more common are the digital clocks that mark off the hours, minutes, and seconds in ever-changing numbers. This certainly appears to be an advance in technology. You will no longer have to interpret the meaning of "the big hand on the eleven and the little hand on the five." Your digital clock will tell you at once that it is 4:55. And yet there will be a loss in the conversion of dial to digital, and no one seems to be worrying about it.

When something turns, it can turn in just one of two ways, clockwise or counterclockwise, and we all know which is which. Clockwise is the normal turning direction of the hands of a clock and counterclockwise is the opposite of that. Since we all stare at clocks (dial clocks, that is), we have no trouble following directions or descriptions that include those words. But if dial clocks disappear, so will the meaning of those words for anyone who has never stared at anything but digitals. There are no *good* substitutes for clockwise and counterclockwise. The nearest you can come is by a consideration of your hands. If you clench your fists with your thumbs pointing at your chest and then look at your fingers, you will see that the fingers of your right hand curve counterclockwise from knuckles to tips while the fingers of your left hand curve clockwise. You could then talk about a "right-hand twist" and a "left-hand twist," but people don't stare at their hands the way they stare at a clock, and this will never be an adequate replacement.

Nor is this a minor matter. Astronomers define the north pole and south pole of any rotating body in such terms. If you are hovering above a pole of rotation and the body is rotating counterclockwise, it is the north pole; if the body is rotating clockwise, it is the south pole. Astronomers also speak of "direct motion" and "retrograde motion," by which they mean counterclockwise and clockwise, respectively.

Here is another example. Suppose you are looking through a microscope at some object on a slide or through a telescope at some view in the sky. In either case, you might wish to point out something to a colleague and ask him or her to look at it, too. "Notice that object at eleven o'clock," you might say—or five o'clock or two o'clock. Everyone knows exactly where two, five, or eleven—or any number from one to twelve—is located on the clock dial, and can immediately look exactly where he is told. (In combat, pilots may call attention to the approach of an enemy plane or the location of antiaircraft bursts or the target, for that matter, in the same way.)

Once the dial is gone, location by "o'clock" will also be gone, and we have nothing to take its place. Of course, you can use directions instead: "northeast," "southwest by south," and so on. However, you will have to know which direction is north to begin with. Or, if you are arbitrary and decide to let north be straight ahead or straight up, regardless of its real location, it still remains true that very few people are as familiar with a compass as with a clock face.

Here's still another thing. Children learn to count and once they learn the first few numbers, they quickly get the whole idea. You go

URSA M
BOOTES
Vega
MILKY

from 0 to 9, and 0 to 9, over and over again. You go from 0 to 9, then from 10 to 19, then from 20 to 29, and so on till you reach 90 to 99, and then you pass on to 100. It is a very systematic thing and once you learn it, you never forget it. Time is different! The early Sumerians[1] couldn't handle fractions very well, so they chose 60 as their base because it can be divided evenly in a number of ways. Ever since, we have continued to use the number 60 in certain applications, the chief one being the measurement of time. Thus, there are 60 minutes in an hour.

If you are using a dial, this doesn't matter. You simply note the position of the hands and they automatically become a measure of time: "half past five," "a quarter past three," "a quarter to ten," and so on. You see time as space and not as numbers. In a digital clock, however, time is measured *only* as numbers, so you go from 1:01 to 1:59 and then move directly to 2:00. It introduces an irregularity into the number system that is going to insert a stumbling block, and an unnecessary one, into education. Just think: 5.50 is halfway between 5 and 6 if we are measuring length or weight or money or anything but time. In time, 5:50 is nearly 6, and it is 5:30 that is halfway between 5 and 6.

What shall we do about all this? I can think of nothing. There is an odd conservatism among people that will make them fight to the death against making time decimal and having a hundred minutes to the hour. And even if we do convert to decimal time, what will we do about "clockwise," "counterclockwise," and locating things at "eleven o'clock"? It will be a pretty problem for our descendants. ◆

1. **Sumerians** [Sü'mer ē ənz] (2600–2400 B.C.): An ancient people from Babylon who are thought to have developed the cuneiform system of writing.

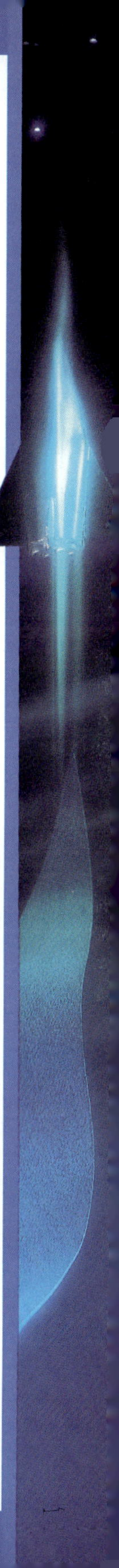

Responding to the Theme

Progress

Responding in Your Journal Progress in flight has been amazing. Consider these facts. Orville and Wilbur Wright arrived at Kitty Hawk in 1903, and just 66 years later the first Americans arrived on the moon! This week in your journal, write about the areas of progress that fascinate you the most—anything from progress in medicine to progress in the making of movies. Which ones have changed your life the most? Which ones have added to your enjoyment of life the most? Then, toward the end of the week, also consider very seriously the two-sided nature of progress. Will you and your future children have to pay a price for the progress made in the past few decades? For example, you may experience bad effects from air conditioners—which everyone enjoys on hot days—because they are one of the causes of the hole in the ozone layer.

Speaking and Listening To appreciate fully the benefits of progress, you really need to know how things were before the existence of all the modern conveniences that you take for granted today. The best way to see the differences between "way back then" and now is to record the oral history of someone who lived before computers and microwaves were invented. Find anyone fifty years old or older—preferably a relative—and take notes or use a tape recorder to take down an oral history of how his or her life used to be. Ask which of the modern conveniences available now has had the greatest impact on this person's life and why.

Critical Thinking: Classifying Brainstorm for a list of gadgets in your household that reflect the latest technology. Create appropriate categories, such as gadgets for communication, gadgets for the kitchen, and gadgets for the office into which you can group all the details. Then list each gadget under the proper category.

Extending Your Vocabulary In "Dial versus Digital" author Isaac Asimov writes about the meaning of *counterclockwise.* Add the prefix *counter,* which means "against," to the following words. Then use each new word in a sentence. Consult a dictionary if necessary.

point   sign   offer   intelligence

Part 2 Writing

If you are going to write an essay about the theme of progress, you will find that you have an almost limitless number of topics you could choose. You might explain, for example, how the police are able to use DNA testing to identify a criminal—based on a single strand of hair; or you might tell about the discoveries of *Pioneer 10*. Essays such as these and any others that present information or offer an explanation are called *expository essays.*

Writing Term An **expository essay** informs or explains.

In writing an essay for the purpose of explaining or informing, you will be able to use several types of writing that you have already learned about, including *narrative writing* and *descriptive writing.* *(See pages 137–150.)* In addition, you will be able to use *classification.* *(See pages 101–103.)* Finally, you may be able to use the skill of *evaluating.* *(See Writing Is Thinking on page 255.)*

Writing Process

Prewriting

Planning an expository essay is a very important step, which may also be an informative and enjoyable step. As you explore a subject, you undoubtedly will learn some new, fascinating facts and details. First, though, you have to choose a subject.

Discovering Subjects

The first step in discovering subjects for expository essays is to take an inventory of subjects you already know from your own experience and study. For example, in science class you may have learned enough about the hole in the ozone layer to write about its effects on the environment. If you are a musician, you may want to explain how your favorite instrument works. The following strategies may also serve as springboards for discovering subjects.

Strategies for Discovering Expository Subjects

1. Use the clustering technique, starting with the phrase *things I could explain*.
2. Freewrite to discover what is on your mind.
3. Use the method of inquiring to ask yourself questions about your interests and skills.
4. Review your journal—particularly your Learning Log—for subjects suitable for explaining or informing. *(See page 13.)*
5. Browse through the library and skim books, newspapers, or magazines for subjects that interest you.
6. Consider your favorite subjects in school and read your notes to find possible subjects.
7. View educational television programs—such as documentaries—for issues or events you would like to explore in writing.

WRITING ACTIVITY 1 *Writing on Your Own*

WRITING ABOUT THE THEME

Review your remarks in your journal about aspects of progress that interest you. Using the strategies above and the techniques of clustering and brainstorming, explore possible subject ideas for an expository essay about some aspect of progress.

Choosing and Limiting a Subject

After you think about possible subjects, the next step is to choose the one that interests you the most and limit it until it is manageable. To make your choice, use the following guidelines.

Guidelines for Choosing an Expository Subject

1. Choose a subject that you will enjoy writing about.
2. Choose a subject that will interest your readers.
3. Choose a subject that you know about or can readily find information about.
4. Choose a subject that you can develop in a short essay.
5. Choose a subject about which you have achieved some insight.

Limiting a Subject A broad subject is like a lump of clay that needs to be shaped before it takes on clearly defined features. To shape, or narrow, a subject for an expository essay so that it is manageable, answer the following questions.

Questions for Limiting a Subject

1. What about my subject do I want to explain?
2. What possible approaches can I choose to explain my subject?
3. What insight or understanding can I draw from my subject?

Suppose your broad subject is the Big Dipper. Using the Questions for Limiting a Subject above, you might limit your subject as follows.

> *What about my subject . . . ?* I want to explain the importance of the Big Dipper to travelers and stargazers.
>
> *What possible approaches . . . ?* I could tell how people viewed the Big Dipper in history or how people use it today, or I could compare it with other constellations.
>
> *What insight or understanding . . . ?* Constellations like the Big Dipper help people feel less overwhelmed by space.

The example on the following page shows how the broad subject has been limited to a more manageable one.

BROAD SUBJECT	the Big Dipper
LIMITED SUBJECT	the importance of the Big Dipper to travelers and stargazers

WRITING ACTIVITY 2 *Limiting a Subject*

For each of the following subjects, suggest possible answers to the three Questions for Limiting a Subject on page 204. Use the examples on the previous page as a guide. Then save your work in your writing folder for use in Writing Activity 6.

1. the exploration of space
2. fads
3. country and western music
4. recycling
5. the Bill of Rights
6. educational television
7. cost of health care
8. nutritional food
9. motorcycles
10. national parks

WRITING ACTIVITY 3 *Writing on Your Own*

WRITING ABOUT THE THEME

Using your notes from Writing Activity 1 or any fresh ideas, make a list of ten possible subjects for an expository essay about some aspect of progress. Put a check next to the subject that comes closest to following the Guidelines for Choosing an Expository Subject on the previous page. Then narrow the subject you chose by answering the Questions for Limiting a Subject on page 204. Save your work in your writing folder for later use.

The Armand Hammer Collection, Los Angeles, CA

Unfruitful Search for the Planet Leverrier,
Honoré Daumier

Determining Your Audience

Before going further, think about who will be reading your essay. Ask yourself the following questions about your readers.

- What do my readers already know about my subject? What questions might they ask about the subject?
- What are my readers' attitudes toward my subject? If their attitudes differ from mine, how can I address those differences?

For example, who will read your essay about the Big Dipper? Will your audience be a class of fifth graders at the elementary school or the members of an astronomy club that you belong to? If the fifth graders are your audience, you could assume that they do not know too much about the Big Dipper. Therefore, your explanations should be simple, basic, and straightforward. However, if your audience is made up of members of an astronomy club, you could assume that they already know quite a bit about the Big Dipper. Therefore, you would need to look for a new or different focus for your essay.

WRITING ACTIVITY 4 *Writing on Your Own*

WRITING ABOUT THE THEME

Write a brief paragraph in which you profile your audience. Determine as best you can your readers' knowledge, attitudes, and needs regarding the subject you chose in Writing Activity 3. Save your work for later use.

Gathering Information

Once you have a limited subject, you should gather information for an essay of three or more paragraphs. Using brainstorming, free-writing, charting, or clustering to explore your subject, collect as much information as possible. *(For more about gathering information, see pages 18–23.)* The following chart shows some of the most common types of supporting details used in expository essays. *(See pages 101–103 to see how these types of details can be used to develop exposition.)*

Types of Supporting Details

facts	incidents	analogies
examples	comparisons	causes and effects
reasons	contrasts	steps in a process

As you collect your information, jot down any details you think of or come upon—without concerning yourself about the order of your ideas. The following prewriting notes list facts and examples for an essay about the Big Dipper.

Student Model: *Gathering Information*

LIMITED SUBJECT: the importance of the Big Dipper to travelers and stargazers

- Stars pointing to the North Star and the last star on the handle are moving away from each other; the Big Dipper will lose its shape in 50,000 years.
- In ancient times shepherds along the Tigris and Euphrates rivers and Iroquois Indians along Lake Ontario saw the dipper as a bear.
- The seven stars in Ursa Major are seen as a dipper or a plough.
- Two stars opposite the handle at the front of the dipper point to the North Star.

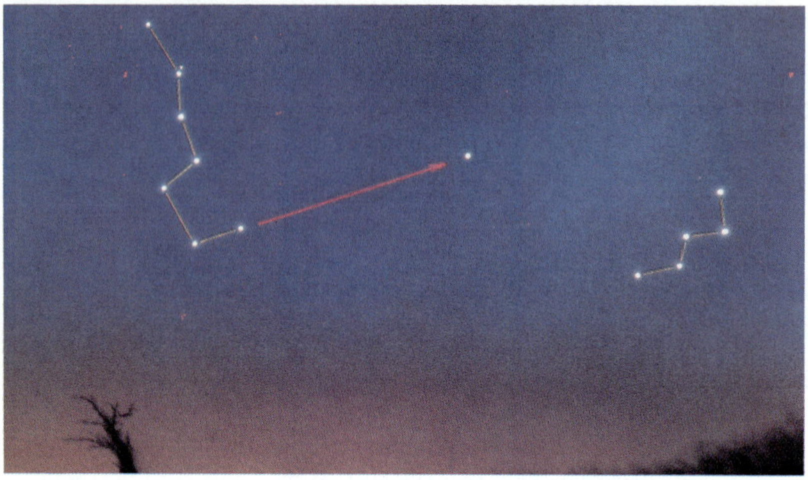

- The constellation helps stargazers get oriented in the night skies.
- The handle points to Arcturus—a bright star in the constellation Boötes.
- From Arcturus you can find the bright star Spica in the constellation Virgo.
- Virgo contains the double star (Mizar and Alcor), which ancient Arabs saw as a horse and rider and Indians saw as a squaw carrying a papoose.
- The stars at the top of the dipper, near the handle, point to Vega in the constellation Lyra (the harp).
- In the 1800's, slaves escaping from the South to the North were told to follow the drinking gourd.
- Navigators in northern seas use the dipper to find the North Star.
- The dipper is bright enough to be seen from cities, where lights brighten the sky too much to see many stars.
- Stars move at a rate of one million miles a day.
- On winter evenings the Big Dipper's handle points down but reverses its position on summer evenings.

WRITING ACTIVITY 5 *Writing on Your Own*

WRITING ABOUT THE THEME

Review your work from Writing Activity 3. Then use any of the prewriting techniques you have learned to gather information for your essay about progress. If you do not have all the information you think you need, use the library or other resources. Save all your information in your writing folder for later use.

Writing Is Thinking

Critical Thinking

Constructing Analogies

When you write an expository essay, you may need to explain something unfamiliar to your audience. In such a case, you may find it helpful to make a comparison, or an **analogy,** between an unfamiliar process or situation and facts or concepts more familiar to your reader. For example, suppose you want to explain the process of running for office. Suppose, too, that you have knowledge and skills as a runner in track and field events. You might focus on the similarities between the two situations and build an analogy between running in track and running for office. Keep in mind that an analogy is never exact. Running for office is not running in track, but the similarities are close enough to be helpful to your readers.

When you are comparing familiar and unfamiliar ideas, making a chart like the one below will help you think through the analogy.

Analogy Chart

Essay subject: running for office
Familiar situation: running in track

Runner's needs	Candidate's needs
1. proper training and equipment	1. background and job skills, a campaign staff, and funds
2. physical and mental stamina for the race	2. competitive spirit, stamina for campaigning
3. sense of timing and pacing in the race	3. well planned schedule of speeches and media events

Thinking Practice Select an essay subject from the left column below or choose one of your own. Then use the knowledge or skill from the right column or another familiar one to make an analogy chart that would help you explain the subject to your reader.

Essay Subjects	**Familiar Knowledge/Skills**
1. writing a poem	1. auto mechanics
2. building a friendship	2. cooking or baking

Developing a Working Thesis

As you gather information, you will begin to see connections between the facts and examples. At this point you should focus your thoughts more precisely by drafting a *working thesis*—a complete sentence that announces your subject and expresses a main idea. For example, notice that several facts on pages 207–208 indicate that the Big Dipper has been an important marker in the sky for a long time. With this idea in mind, you could write the following working thesis.

Student Model: *Developing a Working Thesis*

LIMITED SUBJECT	the importance of the Big Dipper to travelers and stargazers
WORKING THESIS	For centuries the Big Dipper has served as an important beacon to travelers and stargazers.

The working thesis will guide you in selecting information to use in your essay. That is, you would select from the list only those facts, examples, and incidents that explain the historical importance of the Big Dipper. If you decide later to include other information or refine your ideas, you will have to revise your working thesis. Formulating a working thesis now, however, helps you keep your purpose and ideas on track as you develop your essay.

Writing Term A **working thesis** is a preliminary thesis statement that is refined in the process of writing an essay.

WRITING ACTIVITY 6 *Developing a Working Thesis*

Review the work you did in Writing Activity 2 and write a possible working thesis for each item. If your teacher permits, compare your versions with those of your classmates.

WRITING ACTIVITY 7 *Writing on Your Own*

WRITING ABOUT THE THEME

Review the information you collected on your limited subject in Writing Activity 5. Then focus your thoughts more precisely by formulating a working thesis that is a complete statement expressing your main idea about your subject. Save your working thesis in your writing folder for later use.

Organizing Your Essay

Once you have gathered your information and have a working thesis statement, you will use the thinking skills of classifying and ordering to organize the information. *(See pages 101–103 and 184.)*

Grouping Supporting Details into Categories To group your list of supporting details into categories, ask yourself what one item has in common with another. The groupings that follow show three categories that can be made from the list of supporting details about the Big Dipper.

Student Model: *Classifying Details*

CATEGORY 1: People's interpretations of the star pattern in the Big Dipper

- Ancient shepherds along the Tigris and Euphrates rivers and Iroquois Indians along Lake Ontario saw the shape of a bear.
- When just the seven stars are included in the constellation, people see a dipper or a plough.
- Ancient Arabs saw a horse and rider in the double star (Mizar and Alcor), while Indians saw a squaw carrying a papoose.

CATEGORY 2: Use of the Big Dipper in locating the North Star

- Navigators in northern seas use the dipper to find the North Star.
- In the 1800's, slaves escaping from the South to the North were told to follow the drinking gourd in the sky.
- Two stars at the front of the dippei point to the North Star.

CATEGORY 3: Use of the Big Dipper in locating other stars

- It helps stargazers get oriented in the night sky.
- You can follow the handle to Arcturus, a bright star in the constellation Boötes.
- If you continue following the handle from Arcturus, you can find the bright star Spica in the constellation Virgo.
- The stars at the top of the dipper, closest to the handle, point to Vega in the constellation Lyra (the harp).

Some of the details from the original list were not placed in any category. Keep such leftover details because you might be able to use them in the introduction or conclusion of the essay.

WRITING ACTIVITY 8 *Creating Categories*

The following prewriting notes are on the subject of amusement parks and why people enjoy them. Create three categories into which you can group all the details. Then list the details under the proper category. Save your work in your writing folder for Writing Activity 10.

WORKING THESIS: People enjoy amusement parks for many reasons.

- Roller coaster gives a thrill without any real danger.
- Shooting gallery lets you practice your aim harmlessly.
- Special wide-screen films make you feel like you're actually riding in an airplane without ever leaving the ground.
- Monorail and Ferris wheel give you total view of park.
- Reenactments of train robberies and other scenes from the Old West provide entertainment.
- Tilt-a-whirl seems to defy gravity.
- Some games let you test your skill and strength.
- Singers and musicians perform in special areas.
- Games of chance with good prizes are challenging.
- Water rides are cooling because of the spray.

Arranging Categories in a Logical Order After establishing categories, the next step is to decide on the order in which to present them. The chart that follows lists five commonly used types of logical order.

Types of Logical Order	
CHRONOLOGICAL ORDER	Items are arranged according to when they happened in time.
SPATIAL ORDER	Items are arranged according to their location.
ORDER OF IMPORTANCE	Items are arranged in order of importance, interest, or degree.
DEVELOPMENTAL ORDER	Items of equal importance are arranged in an order made clear to the reader.
COMPARISON AND CONTRAST	Items are arranged according to similarities (comparisons) and differences (contrasts).

Organizing Comparison and Contrast A common type of expository essay is one of *comparison and contrast.* When you *compare,* you explain how two items are similar. For example, you might explain how an orange is like a grapefruit. When you *contrast,* on the other hand, you emphasize differences rather than similarities. For example, you might explain how an orange differs from a grapefruit. In an expository essay of comparison and contrast, you include *both* similarities and differences between two items.

If you have chosen to write an essay of comparison and contrast, you have two ways to organize your information. One way is to write about one subject first and then to write about the other subject. For example, if you were comparing outdoor camping (subject A) to vacationing in motels (subject B), you would first write all your information about subject A (camping) and then all your information about subject B (motel stays). For convenience this is called the *AABB pattern* of comparison and contrast.

You can use the *AABB* pattern in two ways. You can organize the pattern within one paragraph by discussing *A* in the first half of the paragraph and *B* in the second half. You can also use an alternative organization in two paragraphs by discussing *A* in one paragraph and *B* in the second paragraph. The following portion of an essay about vacation options shows the *AABB* pattern, which starts after the essay's introduction.

Student Model: *AABB Pattern of Organization*

Vacation Options

After World War II, dramatic new options for family vacations appeared on the American scene. Two of these options—**(A)**the family outdoor camping vacation and **(B)**the on-the-spot motel vacation—show the contrasting tastes of vacationers.

Suddenly, in the 1950's, shoppers began to see a variety of goods available for a new way to vacation—outdoor camping for the whole family. **(A)**The camping trailer and the motor home equipped with sleeping and cooking accommodations showed up in car dealers' lots and on the television screen. Hundreds of varieties of **(A)**camping gear—such as sleeping bags, cookers, tents, backpacks, and hiking boots—flooded the marketplace. People became aware of the **(A)**National Park Service and the development of private land into **(A)**camping facilities. American families were on the move out into the fresh air to enjoy the peace and pleasure of the country's wilderness, lakes, and seashores. "Let's go, America!" became the battle cry of **(A)**camping vacationers by the millions.

On the other hand, there loomed a whole population of **(B)**noncampers, who were allergic to campsites, to bugs, and perhaps to exertion. Their attention was soon captured by a new kind of vacation possibility. Road signs and neon lights and paper flyers in mailboxes announced the arrival of the **(B)**roadside motel. **(B)**Beautiful air-conditioned rooms with television and—wonder of wonders—a door leading directly to one's automobile beckoned the curious. Forget all that camping gear! **(B)**After a long drive, conveniences such as a swimming pool, a restaurant, a dance floor, miniature golf, and shuffleboard were within immediate reach. Moreover, these **(B)**complexes were available at all the pleasure spots of America! Such a splendid vacation option had never before existed.

The second way to organize comparison and contrast is called the *ABAB pattern.* In this pattern you discuss your two subjects together instead of separately. That is, first you compare *both A* and *B* in terms of one similarity or one difference. Then you compare both of them in terms of another similarity or difference. The following portion of the essay on vacation options switches to the *ABAB* pattern.

Student Model: *ABAB Pattern of Organization*

Even today families planning a trip often face the decision whether to go **(A)**camping or to stay in **(B)**motels along the way. Families would do well to weigh the advantages and disadvantages of each option by considering three major items. The first item, expense, is an important one, for **(A)**a camping vacation is much less expensive than **(B)**a vacation using motels. **(A)**Overnight camping accommodations will probably average a tenth of the expense of **(B)**motel accommodations. The second item is convenience. Although fortunate **(A)**campers may bathe in a quiet lake at sunset, many people prefer a hot shower in **(B)**a motel at the end of a long day of sightseeing. The third item to consider is accessibility to beautiful scenery. **(A)**Campers can pitch tents on wooded mountain slopes, near cool streams, in pine forests, or on the seashore. Most **(B)**motel sites are situated on crowded, noisy highways. After weighing the pros and cons, most families must make an intelligent compromise for a successful vacation for all.

WRITING ACTIVITY 9 *Comparison and Contrast*

Choose one of the following pairs of subjects and list three similarities and three differences. Then organize your information according to the *AABB* or the *ABAB* pattern.

1. tennis and badminton
2. two popular TV comedians
3. a halogen bulb and a conventional light bulb

Making an Outline

As a final step before writing a first draft, consider making an outline. An outline is a helpful plan for drafting the body of your essay. The form of an outline allows you to use a numbering and lettering system to show the order of your ideas. Each large category of information becomes the main topic of a supporting paragraph in the body of the essay and is assigned a Roman numeral. For example, the beginnings of an outline for an essay on the Big Dipper might look like this.

FIRST MAIN TOPIC	I. People's interpretations of star pattern in the Big Dipper
SECOND MAIN TOPIC	II. Use of Big Dipper to locate North Star
THIRD MAIN TOPIC	III. Use of Big Dipper to locate other stars

The supporting details for each category become the subtopics and supporting points of the outline. As you add subtopics and supporting points under each main topic, order them logically within each category of thought. *(See page 213 to review types of logical order.)* The following outline for the body of an essay on the Big Dipper shows logical developmental order.

Student Model: *Outline of the Body of an Essay*

MAIN TOPIC — I. People's interpretations of star pattern in Big Dipper
SUBTOPIC — A. Largest shape—Great Bear
SUPPORTING POINTS — 1. Shepherds in the Tigris-Euphrates area
2. Iroquois Indians near Lake Ontario

- I. People's interpretations of star pattern in Big Dipper
  - A. Largest shape—Great Bear
    1. Shepherds in the Tigris-Euphrates area
    2. Iroquois Indians near Lake Ontario
  - B. Seven stars only
    1. Dipper
    2. Plough
  - C. Double star within dipper
    1. Horse and rider to Arabs
    2. Squaw and papoose to Indians
- II. Use of Big Dipper in locating North Star
  - A. Pointers at front of dipper
  - B. Use by navigators
  - C. Use by land travelers—importance to slaves
- III. Use of Big Dipper in locating other stars
  - A. Arcturus
  - B. Spica
  - C. Vega

After finishing an outline, check its form. The following questions will help you see if you have consistency and balance in each part.

Checking an Outline

1. Did you use Roman numerals for main topics?
2. Did you use capital letters for subtopics?
3. Did you use Arabic numerals for supporting points?
4. If you included subtopics under topics, did you have at least two of them for each topic?
5. If you included supporting points under subtopics, did you have at least two of them for each subtopic?
6. Did you indent the outline as shown in the model?
7. Did you list your ideas in logical order?

WRITING ACTIVITY 10 *Outlining*

Write an outline using the categories about an amusement park that you created in Writing Activity 8. The outline should show three main topics, each with a Roman numeral and at least three subtopics.

WRITING ACTIVITY 11 *Writing on Your Own*

WRITING ABOUT THE THEME

Review all your prewriting work for your essay about progress from Writing Activity 7 and sort your supporting details into meaningful categories. Then arrange those categories in a logical order, using one of the types of order listed on page 213. Create an outline for the body of your essay, using the checklist above. Save your outline in your writing folder for later use.

WRITING ACTIVITY 12 *A Writer's Roundtable*

With your teacher's permission, participate in a writer's roundtable. This is a discussion group in which five or six students share their insights into their own writing processes. A writer's roundtable can help if you are having trouble with any part of your essay. For example, if you are unable to find good groupings for your supporting ideas, another student writer may have some useful ideas. A roundtable discussion will help you apply to your essay what you have learned from previous writing activities, as well as what you learn from other members of the group.

Drafting

Writing Process

When you draft, you convert the items in your outline into sentences and paragraphs. If you discover some new ideas you would like to include, keep your original purpose in mind so that any new ideas you add relate clearly to your main idea. When writing a first draft, focus on getting your ideas on paper without worrying about spelling and punctuation.

Drafting Your Thesis Statement

In drafting your thesis statement, you may have to refine your working thesis to take into account any new ideas you wish to include in your essay. Use the following guidelines to help you.

Guidelines for Drafting a Thesis Statement

1. Review your prewriting notes and your working thesis.
2. Revise your thesis until it covers all your supporting ideas.
3. Avoid such expressions as "In this paper I will . . . " or "This paper will be about . . . "

Review the information about the Big Dipper on pages 207 and 208 and the working thesis on page 210, which does not cover the various shapes people see in the Big Dipper's star pattern. If you want to include these details, you could expand the thesis statement as follows.

REFINED THESIS STATEMENT The stars in and near the Big Dipper are a distinguishing feature of the northern skies and a beacon for travelers and stargazers.

WRITING ACTIVITY 13 *Evaluating Thesis Statements*

Reread the prewriting notes for the essay on the Big Dipper on pages 207 and 208. Then, on a separate sheet of paper, explain why each of the following thesis statements is inadequate.

1. This essay will be about the Big Dipper.
2. The Big Dipper can be used to locate many stars.
3. People have seen many shapes in the stars near the Big Dipper.

Drafting the Introduction

In an expository essay, the introduction captures the reader's attention, sets the tone, and states the thesis. A direct and matter-of-fact tone is appropriate for an expository essay. The following suggestions will help you draft your introduction.

Ways to Begin an Essay

1. Give some background information or relate an incident that shows how you became interested in your subject.
2. Cite an example or incident that catches the reader's attention.
3. Give one or two of the original details that did not fit into your outline.
4. Always include your thesis statement, preferably as the last sentence of the introduction.

In the following introduction to the essay on the Big Dipper, the writer sets the tone, captures attention, and includes a slightly altered version of the thesis statement.

Student Model: *Essay Introduction*

INTRODUCTION

On a clear night in the country, the sky blazes with countless points of light. An earthbound observer like me feels small and lost until I find the Big Dipper, the familiar, easy-to-spot shape that was for most of us our first-known constellation. Even in a city sky illuminated by the bright lights below, the seven stars that form the Big Dipper are easy to see. Their pattern is a distinguishing mark of the northern skies and a centuries-old beacon for travelers and stargazers.

THESIS STATEMENT

WRITING ACTIVITY 14 *Writing on Your Own*

WRITING ABOUT THE THEME

Read over the working thesis and outline that you developed in Writing Activities 7 and 11 and revise the working thesis if needed. Then draft an introduction for your essay about progress, using one of the suggestions for beginning an essay and working in your thesis statement. Save your work for later use.

Drafting the Body

When you draft the body of your essay, follow the order of your outline and include all the points you have listed. Each main topic (Roman numeral) in your outline becomes one paragraph in the body of your essay. If covering all the points under a main topic makes an extremely long paragraph, use two or more paragraphs to cover the points. Be sure, however, that all paragraphs in the body relate to the thesis statement.

Guidelines for Adequately Developing an Essay

1. Include enough supporting points or ideas to fully explain your thesis statement.
2. Leave no question unanswered that readers might ask.
3. Include enough information to fully explain each topic and subtopic.
4. Use specific details and precise language to fully explain each piece of information.

As you draft your essay, move smoothly from sentence to sentence and paragraph to paragraph. Use the following strategies to connect your thoughts and to achieve coherence. *(See pages 117–118 for more information about coherence.)*

Strategies for Achieving Coherence

1. Use transitional words and phrases. *(See pages 113, 139, 148, and 158 for lists of transitions.)*
2. Repeat a key word from an earlier sentence.
3. Use synonyms for key words from an earlier sentence.
4. Repeat an idea from an earlier sentence, using new words.
5. Use a pronoun in place of a word used earlier.

Compare the outline on page 216 with the body of the essay on the Big Dipper, which follows. As you read, you will see how the words and phrases in heavy type make ideas flow smoothly. Notice how the repetition of key words—such as *shape, pattern, stars,* and *constellation*—is also used as a connecting device.

Student Model: *Essay Body*

FROM I IN OUTLINE

People have made different interpretations of **this pattern** of lights near the North Star. Many observers, including the ancient shepherds along the Tigris and Euphrates rivers and the Iroquois Indians near Lake Ontario, saw the seven stars as part of a larger **shape**, a great bear. In **this shape**, called Ursa Major, the handle of the dipper forms the tail of the bear. The **smaller** form made by the seven stars **alone** has been seen both as a dipper, or drinking gourd, and a plough. **Inside the dipper** is a double star, including the bright star Mizar and the tiny star Alcor. Ancient Arabs saw **this pair** as a horse and rider. Early American Indians saw **it** as a squaw with her papoose. **All** of the various interpretations, **from** the strong Great Bear **to** the nurturing squaw, are positive images.

FROM II IN OUTLINE

Aside from stirring people's imagination, the Big Dipper **also** serves as a practical guide for travelers. Navigators in northern waters have long used **it** to locate the North Star. The **stars** that form the front of the dipper point directly to the North Star. Travelers on land can **also** find north by tracing a line from the Dipper to the North Star. Historians note that slaves escaping from the South on the Underground Railroad were told to "follow the drinking gourd."

FROM III IN OUTLINE

The Big Dipper can **also** be used as a guidepost for finding **other stars** and **constellations.** If you trace a line extending from the handle of the dipper, you can easily find the bright star Arcturus in the constellation Boötes (the shepherd). Extend **that** line **even farther** in the **same** direction and you can see Spica, the bright star in the constellation Virgo (the maiden). The stars forming the top of the dipper nearest its handle point to the very bright star Vega in the **constellation** Lyra (the harp). A stargazer, **therefore,** can rely on the Big Dipper **throughout** the year for help in finding **other patterns** in the sky.

WRITING ACTIVITY 15 *Identifying Connecting Devices*

Number your paper 1 to 10. Then identify each numbered and underlined connecting device as a *repeated word,* an *earlier idea in new words,* a *pronoun,* or a *transitional word or phrase.*

The Flying Disk

While other sports have become commercialized, Frisbee has grown in popularity for the sake of pure sport. From (1) <u>its</u> earliest days to present-day tournaments, the sport of Frisbee has symbolized fun, individual skill, and the dream of flight.

The (2) <u>flying disk</u> is believed to have originated in the early 1900's, when students at Yale University treated themselves to the bakery goods of the Frisbee Pie Company. All over campus students tossed both pie tins and the lids of cookie tins. The thrower would always yell "Frisbee!" to alert the catcher that the (3) <u>metal disk</u> was on its way. The game was noncompetitive. It was played purely for (4) <u>fun</u>, which is still true of Frisbee.

(5) <u>In the 1940's</u>, designers came out with a much more flyable disk made of plastic. Continued improvements in design made the (6) <u>disk</u> a marvel of aeronautics. Throwers began developing intricate techniques to control the flight pattern of this amazing (7) <u>saucer</u>. (8) <u>Unlike requirements for athletes in</u>

other sports, the size and strength of the thrower are unimportant. A Frisbee is easy to throw, and its flight can be mastered through skill instead of muscle power.

(9) Perhaps the greatest appeal of Frisbee is its link with flight itself. Although the thrower is earthbound, the well-controlled Frisbee can soar and glide and sweep and arc with all the beauty of a bird. The power for its soaring is not a battery or an engine but a human hand. For many players the thrill of creating and controlling flight is the main pleasure of the game.

The fun and art of Frisbee helped to make it a respected sport. National tournaments offer Frisbee fans a chance to match their skills with those of others. People who have grown tired of other sports and are looking for both fun and a challenge should pick up a (10) flying disk and toss it around for a while. They may find, as so many others have, one of the most refreshing games in town.

WRITING ACTIVITY 16 *Writing on Your Own*

WRITING ABOUT THE THEME

Working from the outline you developed in Writing Activity 11, draft the body of your essay about progress. Make sure you write one paragraph for each main topic in your outline. As you write, refer to the Strategies for Achieving Coherence on page 220. Then save your work in your writing folder for later use.

Drafting the Conclusion

The conclusion to an expository essay should be strong and leave a final impression with your audience. Following is a list of ways to end an essay.

Ways to End an Essay

1. Summarize the body of the essay.
2. Restate the thesis statement in new words.
3. Draw a conclusion based on the body of the essay.
4. Add an insight about the thesis.
5. Refer to details from your prewriting notes not used in the body or introduction but which support your thesis.
6. Refer to ideas in the introduction to bring the essay full circle.
7. Write a memorable clincher statement.

In the following example, the basis for the conclusion of the essay on the Big Dipper was a detail that was not used anywhere else.

Student Model: *Essay Conclusion*

CONCLUSION

Although they appear stationary, the stars above are really speeding through space at the rate of one million miles a day. Five stars in the Big Dipper are moving in the same direction, so they will keep their positions relative to one another. Two of the stars, however—the star nearest the North Star and the last star in the handle—are speeding away from each other in opposite directions. Stargazers 50,000 years from now will no longer be able to see a dipper shape. No doubt they will find meaningful shapes in the new pattern of stars. They must find a new and equally important compass and guide at night as they try to understand the distant heavens and their own small place within them.

CLINCHER SENTENCE

The clincher sentence brings the essay full circle by referring to an idea in the introduction. It also fixes in the reader's mind the main idea that the Big Dipper is a familiar sight and practical guide.

Drafting a Title When you are satisfied with your conclusion, think of a title for your essay. Read over each paragraph, looking for words and phrases you could use as a title. A good title should make your readers curious enough to want to read your essay.

Student Model: *Creating a Title*

Clear Skies (boring)
Star Dust (??: doesn't really fit)
Clear Nights (not on the mark)
On a Clear Night (pretty good)
When You Can See Forever (I like it!)

WRITING ACTIVITY 17 *Writing a Conclusion*

Reread the essay on the Big Dipper, including the conclusion. *(See pages 221 and 224.)* Then write a different conclusion, using one of the other ways to end an essay listed on page 224.

WRITING ACTIVITY 18 *Thinking of Titles*

Make a list of five titles for the essay about the Big Dipper. Think of catchy titles that would make *you* want to read the essay.

WRITING ACTIVITY 19 *Writing on Your Own*

WRITING ABOUT THE THEME

Look over the first draft of your introduction and body for your essay about progress. Using the Ways to End an Essay chart on the previous page as a guide, draft a suitable conclusion and then read the entire essay aloud. More than likely you wrote your first draft quickly without too much concern for minor problems. Now keep your first draft at your side as you write a second draft of your essay. Line by line look for ways to expand, delete, rearrange, or substitute to improve the quality of your second draft. Take the time to think about the best possible ways to express your ideas. Now that your thoughts are securely on paper, you can concentrate on clarifying and refining them. If necessary, experiment with several different introductions and conclusions and then choose those that you think make the greatest impact. When you are satisfied that you have an acceptable second draft, think of a catchy title for your essay and write it at the top. Save your paper in your writing folder for revising at a later time.

Revising

Writing Process

Many writers put away their first or second draft for a few hours or overnight before they revise it. In this way they have a fresh outlook and can more easily see what needs to be improved. As you revise your essay, think of your readers and find ways to make your message as clear as possible.

Checking for Unity, Coherence, and Emphasis

If your essay has *unity*, your readers will not be distracted by paragraphs or sentences that stray from your main idea. If your essay has *coherence*, readers will take in your ideas in a logical order with smooth progressions. If your essay has *emphasis*, your readers will understand which points are the most important. The following questions will help you check your essay for unity, coherence, and emphasis.

Checking for Unity, Coherence, and Emphasis

CHECKING FOR UNITY

1. Does every idea and detail relate to the subject?
2. Does every paragraph in the essay support the thesis statement?
3. Does every sentence in each paragraph support its topic sentence?

CHECKING FOR COHERENCE

4. Did you write the paragraphs in the body of your essay in a logical order?
5. Did you use transitions between paragraphs?
6. Did you write the sentences within each of the paragraphs in a logical order?
7. Did you use transitions between the sentences within each paragraph?

CHECKING FOR EMPHASIS

8. Do your transitional words show the relative importance of your ideas?
9. Did you give an adequate amount of space to important and complex ideas?

Using a Revision Checklist

In addition to checking for unity, coherence, and emphasis, you should use a revision checklist to help you keep track of all the specific points you need to check in your essay. As you use the following checklist, read through your essay several times, focusing on different points each time.

Revision Checklist

CHECKING YOUR ESSAY

1. Do you have a strong introduction that sets the tone and captures attention?
2. Does the thesis statement express the main idea clearly?
3. Does your essay have unity, coherence, and emphasis?
4. Do you have a strong conclusion?
5. Did you add a title?

CHECKING YOUR PARAGRAPHS

6. Does each paragraph have a topic sentence?
7. Does every sentence in each paragraph support the topic sentence?
8. Is each paragraph unified and coherent?

CHECKING YOUR SENTENCES AND WORDS

9. Are your sentences varied? *(See pages 62–69.)*
10. Did you combine sentences that go together? *(See pages 62–66.)*
11. Are your sentences clear and concise? *(See page 58.)*
12. Have you avoided faulty sentences? *(See pages 70–74.)*
13. Did you use specific words with correct connotations? *(See pages 53–54.)*
14. Did you use figurative language? *(See page 55.)*

WRITING ACTIVITY 20 *Writing on Your Own*

WRITING ABOUT THE THEME

Carefully read over the second draft of your essay on some aspect of progress that you wrote in Writing Activity 19. Are you satisfied that your essay is the best it can be? Is your meaning as clear as it can be? Refer to the Revision Checklist several times to make a final revision. Save your paper for editing later.

Integrating Language Skills

Editing and Publishing

Grammar in the Writing Process

In "Dial versus Digital," Isaac Asimov points out the importance of the words *clockwise* and *counterclockwise* in making directions or descriptions clear. Writers and speakers often use other tools—such as the prepositional phrase and the appositive phrase—to make directions and descriptions clear.

Prepositional Phrases A *prepositional phrase* is a group of words that has no subject or verb and is used to modify, or describe, another word in the sentence. A prepositional phrase usually adds important information to the sentence. Just look at all the information that the six prepositional phrases in heavy type add to the following sentence. *(For information about kinds of prepositional phrases and practice in recognizing them, see pages 599–603. For the correct punctuation of prepositional phrases, see page 602.)*

> Suppose you are looking **through a microscope/at some object/on a slide/**or **through a telescope/at some view/in the sky.**

Appositive Phrases An *appositive phrase* is a group of words that identifies or explains a word in the sentence. Appositive phrases are often used in expository writing to define an unfamiliar term or to give identifying information about an unknown person. *(For more information about appositive phrases and practice in recognizing them, see pages 603–606.)*

> In his essay Asimov mentions the Sumerians**, an ancient people from Babylon.**
>
> Isaac Asimov**, the author of "Dial versus Digital,"** is worried about the disappearance of clocks with hands.

Punctuation of Appositive Phrases Most appositive phrases are punctuated like the two preceding examples. Notice that when the phrase comes in the middle of the sentence, a comma goes before and after the appositive phrase. *(For more information about the punctuation of appositive phrases and practice in writing them correctly, see page 605.)*

Combining Sentences with Phrases Once you understand prepositional phrases and appositive phrases, you can use them to combine two short sentences into one fluid, mature sentence. *(For other examples of sentences combined with phrases and practice in combining sentences, see pages 618–619.)*

TWO SENTENCES	The elimination of clocks with hands is a serious problem. It is a problem for our descendants.
COMBINED	The elimination of clocks with hands is a serious problem **for our descendants.**
TWO SENTENCES	Digital clocks will soon replace clocks with hands. Digital clocks are clocks with changing numbers.
COMBINED	Digital clocks, **clocks with changing numbers,** will soon replace clocks with hands.

Editing Checklist

1. Have prepositional phrases and appositive phrases been used to incorporate additional information into sentences? *(See pages 599–606.)*
2. Are all the phrases punctuated correctly? *(See pages 602–605.)*
3. Could phrases be used to combine any sentences? *(See pages 618–619.)*

WRITING ACTIVITY 21 *Writing on Your Own*

WRITING ABOUT THE THEME

Editing Read aloud your essay about progress from Writing Activity 20 and listen for any sentence fragments or run-on sentences. Then use the checklist above and the Editing Checklist on page 35 to help you find and correct any spelling, usage, or mechanics errors. Once you are pleased with your results, write a final copy.

Publishing If you recorded the oral history of someone you know for the Speaking and Listening activity on page 201, give that person your essay to read. If you did not take down anyone's oral history, give your paper to your grandparents or someone around their age. People who are fifty or older should enjoy reading your paper because they have seen many dramatic changes in their lifetime—changes that have taken place in the name of progress.

A Writer Writes

WRITING ABOUT THE THEME

An Expository Essay about Progress

PURPOSE to explain that progress sometimes has a negative side
AUDIENCE an adult

Carhenge, Nebraska (copy of Stonehenge, England)

Prewriting In your journal you wrote about the two-sided nature of progress. For example, nuclear energy does not pollute the air. That is progress over fossil fuels like coal and oil. However, now Americans must try to find a safe solution for the disposal of nuclear wastes. Look over your notes and brainstorm about each area of progress you had previously thought about. Consider if there was at least one step backward for each step forward.

Then choose one or several examples you would like to develop into supporting paragraphs in an essay about the two-sided nature of progress. Think about your purpose and audience and be sure to limit your subject so that it is manageable. If necessary, use the library to find additional, specific facts to use in your essay. After you develop a working thesis that states your main idea, group your details and arrange them in a logical order. Then write an outline from your notes that you can use as a guide to the drafting of your essay.

Drafting Using your outline, write a first draft of the introduction, body, and conclusion of your essay. Keep writing, never stopping to worry about any spelling or grammatical errors. Then, if time permits, experiment with different introductions and conclusions. Remember, you want to capture your reader's attention in the introduction. Also make sure that your thesis statement is clearly stated in your first paragraph.

Revising Use the Revision Checklist on page 227 to revise your essay. You may want to read your essay aloud, listening for the flow of your words.

Editing and Publishing The checklists on pages 35 and 229 should help you prepare an error-free essay. Once you have written a final copy of your essay, give it to your science teacher or some adult to read and then discuss that person's reactions to your ideas.

Independent Writing

Use the Checklist for Writing Essays to Inform on page 233 as a guide for writing an essay about one of the following subjects or one of your own choice.

1. how bricks are made
2. the Appalachian Mountain Trail
3. the origins of the Smithsonian Institution
4. a comparison of Aztec and Inca contributions to civilization
5. the future of NATO
6. artificial intelligence
7. causes and effects of the fall of the Berlin Wall
8. the fiords of Norway
9. how the United Nations is organized
10. how to use a video camera professionally

WRITING ABOUT THE THEME

Creative Writing

If you had told people 50 years ago that they would be able to fly across the Atlantic in three hours in a superfast airplane, they would have said that you were dreaming. Well, do some dreaming now! Brainstorm for one new invention that you would like to see developed in the next 50 to 100 years. Then write a short composition that describes that one small part of your vision of progress.

WRITING ABOUT THE THEME

Writing about Literature

Comparison/contrast is a device used in writing to show the similarities and differences between two things. Write a paragraph that explains how Isaac Asimov effectively uses this technique to emphasize his main idea in "Dial versus Digital."

Writing in Other Subject Areas

Geometry Write an essay explaining how astronomers use triangulation to determine the distances to heavenly bodies. After you carefully identify an audience for this assignment, decide how much technical explanation to include.

World History Write an essay explaining how the invention of the wheel brought about a turning point in world history. Be sure to arrange your ideas logically and use transitions to keep the reader on track.

Gary Larson, *The Far Side*,

Chapter 6 Checklist

Writing Essays to Inform

Prewriting

- ✔ Find subjects by drawing on your experiences and reading. *(See page 203.)*
- ✔ From a list of possible subjects, choose one to develop into an essay. *(See page 204.)*
- ✔ Limit your subject. Focus your ideas by asking yourself questions about your purpose, audience, and tone. *(See pages 204 and 206.)*
- ✔ Develop a list of supporting ideas. *(See pages 207–208.)*
- ✔ Develop a working thesis. *(See page 210.)*
- ✔ Organize your list of ideas into categories and an outline. *(See pages 211–217.)*

Drafting

- ✔ Refine your thesis statement. *(See page 218.)*
- ✔ Write an introduction that includes your thesis statement. *(See page 219.)*
- ✔ Use your outline to write the paragraphs of the body. *(See pages 220–221.)*
- ✔ Use connecting devices to link your thoughts. *(See page 220.)*
- ✔ Add a concluding paragraph. *(See page 224.)*
- ✔ Add a title. *(See page 225.)*

Revising

- ✔ Using the Revision Checklist, revise your essay for structure, well-developed paragraphs, unity, coherence, emphasis, and varied, lively sentences and words. *(See pages 226–227.)*

Editing and Publishing

- ✔ Using the Editing Checklist, check your grammar, spelling, mechanics, and manuscript form. *(See pages 35 and 40.)* Present your finished work to a reader.

C h a p t e r 7

Writing Essays to Persuade

Part 1 *Reading to Write*

THEME: *The Environment*

Imagine that you were taking an early morning hike through a beautiful forest filled with filtered sunlight and dewy green glow, the sounds of bird calls, the fresh smell of pine, and the sudden pleasures of wildflowers. Later during science class, however, your teacher explains how whole forests are dying as a result of acid rain. Imagine then an exciting trip to Los Angeles followed by a radio announcer's health warning as the result of a dark, hazy cloud of pollution hanging over the city. Imagine soaring over the planet Earth in a space capsule. Scientists, in the meantime, are discussing one of the disastrous results of PCB's in the atmosphere—the global warming that is taking place.

As these and other examples show, the environment is being threatened as it has never been before. Rachel Carson, the author of the following selection "The Obligation to Endure," believed that the future of life as you know it now is in jeopardy because the earth may be undergoing permanent damage from "universal contamination of the environment." The air, earth, rivers, and sea have been ruinously damaged by chemical poisons. As you read her essay, decide how you feel about what is happening to the environment and what—if anything—is your responsibility in this regard.

The Obligation to Endure

Rachel Carson

The history of life on earth has been a history of interaction between living things and their surroundings. To a large extent, the physical form and the habits of the earth's vegetation and its animal life have been molded by the environment. Considering the whole span of earthly time, the opposite effect, in which life actually modifies its surroundings, has been relatively slight. Only within the moment of time represented by the present century has one species—man—acquired significant power to alter the nature of his world.

During the past quarter century this power has not only increased to one of disturbing magnitude but it has changed in character. The most alarming of all man's assaults upon the environment is the contamination of air, earth, rivers, and sea with dangerous and even lethal materials. This pollution is for the most part irrecoverable; the chain of evil it initiates not only in the world that must support life but in living tissues is for the most part irreversible. In this now universal contamination of the environment, chemicals are the sinister and little-recognized partners of radiation in changing the very nature of the world—the very nature of its life. Strontium 90, released through nuclear explosions into the air, comes to earth in rain or drifts down as fallout, lodges in soil, enters into the grass or corn or wheat grown there, and in time takes up its abode in the bones of a human being, there to remain until his death. Similarly, chemicals sprayed on croplands or forests or gardens lie long in soil, entering into living organisms, passing from one to another in a chain of poisoning and death. Or they pass mysteriously by underground streams until they emerge and, through the alchemy of air and sunlight, combine into new forms that kill vegetation, sicken cattle, and work unknown harm on those who drink from once pure wells. As Albert Schweitzer[1] has said, "Man can hardly even recognize the devils of his own creation."

It took hundreds of millions of years to produce the life that now inhabits the earth—eons of time in which that developing and evolving and diversifying life reached a state of adjustment and balance with its surroundings. The environment, rigorously shaping and directing the life it supported, contained elements that were hostile as well as supporting. Certain rocks gave out dangerous radiation; even with the light of the sun, from which all life draws its energy, there were short-wave radiations with power to injure. Given time—time not in years but in millennia—life adjusts, and a balance has been reached. For time is the essential ingredient; but in the modern world there is no time.

The rapidity of change and the speed with which new situations are created follow the impetuous and heedless pace of man rather than the deliberate pace of nature. Radiation is no longer merely the background radiation of rocks, the bombardment of cosmic rays, the ultraviolet of the sun that have existed before there was any life on

1. **Albert Schweitzer** ['shuīt-sər] (1875–1965): French philosopher, physician, theologian, and music scholar who became a missionary physician in Africa and won the Nobel Prize in 1952.

earth; radiation is now the unnatural creation of man's tampering with the atom. The chemicals to which life is asked to make its adjustment are no longer merely the calcium and silica and copper and all the rest of the minerals washed out of the rocks and carried in rivers to the sea; they are the synthetic creations of man's inventive mind, brewed in his laboratories, and having no counterparts in nature.

To adjust to these chemicals would require time on the scale that is nature's; it would require not merely the years of a man's life but the life of generations. And even this, were it by some miracle possible, would be futile, for the new chemicals come from our laboratories in an endless stream; almost five hundred annually find their way into actual use in the United States alone. The figure is staggering and its implications are not easily grasped—500 new chemicals to which the bodies of men and animals are required somehow to adapt each year, chemicals totally outside the limits of biologic experience.

Among them are many that are used in man's war against nature. Since the mid-1940's over 200 basic chemicals have been created for use in killing insects, weeds, rodents, and other organisms described in the modern vernacular as "pests"; and they are sold under several thousand different brand names.

These sprays, dusts, and aerosols are now applied almost universally to farms, gardens, forests, and homes—nonselective chemicals that have the power to kill every insect, the "good" and the "bad," to still the song of birds and the leaping of fish in the streams, to coat the leaves with a deadly film, and to linger on in soil—all this though the intended target may be only a few weeds or insects. Can anyone believe it is possible to lay down such a barrage of poisons on the surface of the earth without making it unfit for all life? They should not be called "insecticides," but "biocides."

The whole process of spraying seems caught up in an endless spiral. Since DDT[2] was released for civilian use, a process of escalation has been going on in which ever more toxic materials must be found. This has happened because insects, in a triumphant vindication of Darwin's[3] principle of the survival of the fittest, have evolved super races immune to the particular insecticide used, hence a deadlier one has always to be developed—and then a deadlier one than that. It has happened also because, for reasons to be described later, destructive insects often

2. **DDT:** An insecticide that tends to accumulate in ecosystems, with toxic effect.
3. **Charles Darwin** (1809–1882): An English naturalist who developed the theory of evolution and published it in a book entitled *The Origin of the Species*.

undergo a "flareback," or resurgence, after spraying, in numbers greater than before. Thus the chemical war is never won, and all life is caught in its violent crossfire.

Along with the possibility of the extinction of mankind by nuclear war, the central problem of our age has therefore become the contamination of man's total environment with such substances of incredible potential for harm—substances that accumulate in the tissues of plants and animals and even penetrate the germ cells to shatter or alter the very material of heredity upon which the shape of the future depends.

It is not my contention that chemical insecticides must never be used. I do not contend that we have put poisonous and biologically potent chemicals indiscriminately into the hands of persons largely or wholly ignorant of their potentials for harm. We have subjected enormous numbers of people to contact with these poisons, without their consent and often without their knowledge. If the Bill of Rights contains no guarantee that a citizen shall be secure against lethal poisons distributed either by private individuals or by public officials, it is surely only because our forefathers, despite their considerable wisdom and foresight, could conceive of no such problem.

I contend, furthermore, that we have allowed these chemicals to be used with little or no advance investigation of their effect on soil, water, wildlife, and man himself. Future generations are unlikely to condone our lack of prudent concern for the integrity of the natural world that supports all life.

There is still very limited awareness of the nature of the threat. This is an era of specialists, each of whom sees his own problem and is unaware of or intolerant of the larger frame into which it fits. It is also an era dominated by industry, in which the right to make a dollar at whatever cost is seldom challenged. When the public protests, confronted with some obvious evidence of damaging results of pesticide applications, it is fed little tranquilizing pills of half truth. We urgently need an end to these false assurances, to the sugar coating of unpalatable facts. It is the public that is being asked to assume the risk that the insect controllers calculate. The public must decide whether it wishes to continue on the present road, and it can do so only when in full possession of the facts. In the words of Jean Rostand,[4] "the obligation to endure gives us the right to know." ◆

4. **Jean Rostand** (1868–1918): A French playwright who wrote *Cyrano de Bergerac* in 1897.

Responding to the Theme

The Environment

Responding in Your Journal The more you hear about the environment, the more you can become confused. What is the most important, life-threatening issue? Is it air pollution? Water pollution? Disposal of contaminated waste? The extinction of wildlife and natural resources like the rain forests? This week in your journal, write freely about all of these environmental issues and any others you can think of. Explore which ones have the greatest impact on your local area and which ones may cause the greatest global destruction. In addition, answer these questions in your journal. Can one person make a difference? Do you think that a single person—like you—can do anything to slow down the destructive process or to lessen the effects of damage that have already occurred? You may want to list any specific steps you can take right now to reduce the negative effects you observe in your immediate environment.

Speaking and Listening Look over the TV schedule this week to find a program about the environment on public television or on one of the other stations. As you watch at least one show, take notes. Then be prepared to share what you have learned with other members of your class. *(For information about taking notes, see pages 501–502.)*

Critical Thinking: Synthesizing As you hear about the different environmental issues, it is impossible not to form opinions about them. One vital thinking skill used in forming an opinion is the ability to *synthesize,* or summarize, available information—that is, to cover the main points clearly. After you review "The Obligation to Endure," write a brief paragraph that summarizes the author's opinions about pesticides.

Extending Your Vocabulary Some words convey an emotional meaning, or *connotation.* A word can have a positive or a negative connotation. For example, in the following sentence, Rachel Carson emphasized her argument by specifically choosing each of the underlined words. "The most alarming of all man's assaults upon the environment is the contamination of air, earth, rivers, and sea with dangerous and even lethal materials." Find at least ten words with similar emotionally charged connotations.

Part 2 Writing

What is the most life-threatening environmental issue today? People hold many different opinions about this issue. One of the best ways to express your position about an important issue is to write a persuasive essay. When you write essays for the purpose of persuading others to see your point of view, you will be able to use several types of writing including *narrative writing* and *descriptive writing*. *(See pages 137–150.)* You will also be able to use different methods of *classification* to organize the facts, reasons, and examples that support your opinions. *(See pages 101–103.)* Finally, you will find the skill of *evaluating* helpful in writing persuasively. *(See Writing Is Thinking on page 255.)*

Writing Term A **persuasive essay** states an opinion on a subject and uses facts, reasons, and examples to convince readers.

Persuasive Essay Structure

Like all essays, a persuasive essay has three main parts: an introduction, a body, and a conclusion. The chart below shows how each of these parts contributes to the essay.

The Structure of a Persuasive Essay

1. The **introduction** captures the audience's attention and presents the issue and expresses the writer's opinion in a thesis statement.
2. In an effective persuasive essay, the **body of supporting paragraphs** presents reasons, facts, examples, and expert opinions to support the writer's opinions.
3. The **conclusion** presents a summary or strong conclusive evidence—logically drawn from the arguments—that drives home the writer's opinion.

As you read the following persuasive essay, notice how each part carries out the purpose of persuading the reader.

Model: *Persuasive Essay*

Talking Chimps

INTRODUCTION: PROVIDES BACKGROUND INFORMATION ON THE ISSUE

In the past several decades, a number of chimps have been taught the gestures of American Sign Language (Ameslan). The results of these studies are hotly debated. A recent survey asked scientists to name the most significant discovery in recent years. Many replied that it was the failure of chimps to acquire language. About an equal number, however, believed the most significant discovery was the *success* of chimps in learning and using language. These opinions arise from differing definitions of language use. The first group of scientists see too much simple imitation or reward seeking in chimp language to call it true language learning. The success of chimps in mastering sign language, however, indicates that they have indeed learned a simple language.

THESIS STATEMENT

The chimpanzee Nim signs *eyes*.

FIRST BODY PARAGRAPH: USES FACTS, EXAMPLES, AND REASONS

To use language, it is first necessary to understand that a word—or a sign—is a symbol. It is a symbol of the thing it names, not the thing itself. Humans know, for example, that the word *cup* is a symbol for the thing they drink from. The five chimpanzees, Washoe, Moja, Pili, Tatu, and Dar, reared by Professors R. A. and B. T. Gardner at the University of Nevada acquired between 100 and 200 signs by age five. They were able to name things in pictures, showing another level of understanding. In addition to learning the names of things, such as *cat, hat,* and *tree,* they also learned the names of actions, such as *chase, hug,* and *tickle* and of qualities, such as *dirty* and *hot.*

SECOND BODY PARAGRAPH: ANSWERS OPPONENTS' OBJECTION

Critics of the early experiments argued that since chimps did not understand the concept of negating, they were not really using language. (Negating is adding a negative, such as *no* or *not,* to a thought, as in "I do *not* want a banana.") Sarah, a chimp trained at the University of California, Santa Barbara, showed an understanding not only of negating but also of compound and complex sentences. Sarah learned to compose and read sentences by placing metal symbols on a metallic board. She once asked herself, "What is an apple not?" and correctly—and creatively—replied, "Bread."

THIRD BODY PARAGRAPH: ANSWERS OPPONENTS' OBJECTION

Many critics also doubt the use of language by chimps on the grounds that the animals are cued by their trainers. Sarah's trainers decided to test the chimp's ability to use language without the help of cues. They sent an inexperienced person in to "converse" with Sarah—a person who did not know Sarah's language. That person was unable to cue Sarah to do something that she could then imitate. Sarah did not do as well as she usually did, probably because she was confused by the appearance of a new human partner. Still she scored high enough on her test to convince her trainers that she could use language without being cued.

CONCLUSION: DRIVES HOME THE MAIN POINT

Those who doubt that chimps have successfully learned a simple language place too much emphasis on comparing chimps to humans. Our language has developed over a long period of time, while chimps have only recently been exposed to language learning. Given their short exposure to language, chimps have demonstrated remarkable mastery. Any creature who can sign to himself, "Cry me; me cry" after his trainer has left him for the day surely can handle simple language.

WRITING ACTIVITY 1 *Analyzing a Persuasive Essay*

The essay on the following pages takes the opposite position on the question of a chimp's ability to use language from that presented in the model essay, "Talking Chimps," which you have just read. Read the next essay carefully and then write answers to the questions that follow it. The paragraphs are numbered for easy reference.

Monkey See, Monkey Do, Monkey Get

(l) The experiments in which chimps were taught the ingredients of language are fascinating and thought provoking. They do not, however, convince all experts that chimps have acquired a humanlike grasp of language. While the chimps have learned more than one hundred words, they do not use these words well enough to be called true language users.

(2) Dr. Herbert S. Terrace conducted an experiment for almost four years with a chimp named Nim. At first Nim's seeming success delighted him. Nim readily gestured many Ameslan signs. Then Dr. Terrace studied the videotapes of Nim and his trainers. He made several discoveries that led him to question Nim's use of language. One was that only 10 percent of Nim's utterances were uncued, whereas 40 percent were imitations of gestures the trainer had just used. Another discovery was that Nim, unlike human children, did not take turns in a conversation. He frequently interrupted his trainer to express his needs and desires. Dr. Terrance also discovered as he examined Nim's progress that the number of words in Nim's "sentences" did not increase with time. Children build increasingly longer sentences as they learn more words. Nim's sentences stayed at an average level of about 2.5 words per sentence.

(3) The combining of words into one utterance is often viewed as a real use of language. Many experts point to clever word combinations in chimps as signs of their mastery of language. Washoe, for example, gave a sign meaning "water bird" when she saw a swan for the first time in a pond. To the trainers this expression seemed like one word. Another explanation, however, is that Washoe was simply naming two things she saw, and the trainers, not Washoe, combined the two symbols into one.

(4) Finally many of the language experiments with chimps involve the use of rewards—a banana, a piece of chocolate, a tickle—for a correct answer. At the Yerkes Primate Center in Atlanta, Georgia, a chimp named Lana was taught a computer language called Yerkish. If she used the correct word order for requests, the machine would give her the item she requested. Sarah, a chimp at the University of California, was also rewarded with a treat if she "composed" a proper sentence on her magnetic board. The link between communication and reward is too strong in these cases to prove mastery over language. Until chimps

can convey information instead of seeking a reward, they cannot be said to be language users.

(5) Nonetheless, the chimp experiments revealed much to delight even those who doubt. The chimps' engaging personalities and intelligence suggest that future studies would be fruitful. For now, however, despite the dramatic use of individual signs, the evidence does not prove that chimps can truly use language.

1. What is the thesis statement?
2. Explain the controversy expressed in paragraph 1.
3. What three facts about the chimp named Nim are offered as support in paragraph 2?
4. What chimp in the first essay is a counter-example to Nim?
5. What example is used in paragraph 3 to support the point about word combinations?
6. Both essays report the use of tickling in the chimp experiments. In the first essay, what does the detail about tickling suggest? How is it used to make a different point in the second essay?
7. How many specific chimps are used as examples in the second essay?
8. How does paragraph 4 support the thesis?
9. What is the author of the second essay's conclusion?
10. Write a paragraph to express your view of this subject.

The chimpanzee Lana uses the computer board.

Facts and Opinions

Persuasive essays are primarily made up of two types of statements: facts and opinions. When you write a persuasive essay, you should be aware of the difference. *Facts* are statements that can be proved. *Opinions,* on the other hand, are beliefs or judgments that can be supported but not proved.

Writing Terms A **fact** is a statement that can be proved. An **opinion** is a belief or judgment that cannot be proved.

You can test whether a statement is factual in two ways. One way is to ask yourself whether you would be able to prove the statement through your own observation and experience.

FACT There are three chimpanzees at our local zoo. [You could go to the zoo and observe this.]

The second way is to ask yourself whether you could prove it by consulting accepted authorities.

FACT The chimpanzee is an anthropoid ape with a high degree of intelligence. [You cannot use your experience to test this statement, but you can verify it by consulting a recognized expert or by consulting an encyclopedia.]

Writing Tip Use your own experiences and observations as well as reliable authorities to verify facts.

Unlike facts, opinions cannot be proved. They are personal judgments, interpretations, preferences, and predictions that differ from person to person. Following are some examples.

War movies are **too violent.**
Mr. Ling is the **best** candidate for mayor.
I believe that nuclear energy plants are a **terrible** threat to the atmosphere.
Computer programming is the **most valuable** course at my school.

Sometimes you can recognize opinions in what you hear, read, and write by listening and watching for some of the following words that are often used in statements of opinion.

Opinion Words		
should	good, better, best	probably
ought	bad, worse, worst	might
can	beautiful	perhaps
may	terrible	maybe

In persuasive essays the soundest opinions are those that are supported by factual evidence, logical arguments, or both.

UNSUPPORTED OPINION Chimps can be taught to speak our language. [No supporting facts back up this statement.]

SUPPORTED OPINION Chimps are an endangered species. [African environmentalists support this statement.]

Writing Tip Support your opinions with convincing factual evidence.

WRITING ACTIVITY 2 *Identifying Facts and Opinions*

State whether each sentence below is a *fact* or an *opinion*. If you are in doubt about a statement, verify it by checking its validity in the library or with a reliable authority.

1. Recycling is not worth the expense.
2. The American Eagle is still an endangered species.
3. The United States expects major fuel shortages in the future.
4. Toxic wastes have often been disposed of in populated areas.
5. Cutting down forests diminishes the oxygen supply in the air.

WRITING ACTIVITY 3 Supporting Opinions

Write one fact that could be used to back up each of the following opinions. If necessary, use library resources to find supporting evidence.

EXAMPLE Teenagers benefit from employment.
POSSIBLE ANSWER Some jobs teach many useful skills.

1. Nutrition should be a required course in elementary school.
2. Using illegal drugs is self-destructive.
3. Many citizens are careless about energy consumption.

WRITING ACTIVITY 4 *Checking the Facts*

Think of one strong opinion you have about your city, town, school, or favorite pastime. List three facts you could use to back up your opinion. Check your supporting facts by asking the following two questions. Then rework any statements that cannot be verified.

- Can I verify each supporting fact?
- Can each fact be verified by my own experience or do I need to consult a reliable source?

Reasoning

When you write a persuasive essay, your ability to win over your reader usually depends on your reasoning skills. Facts and opinions cannot argue by themselves. Instead, you must create a logical argument by fitting the facts together so that they lead to a reasonable conclusion.

Generalizing When you state a rule or a principle based on fact and experience, you are *generalizing.* For example, suppose you have visited Washington, D.C., three times in July and August, and each time the weather was hot and muggy. From this experience you could generalize that Washington, D.C., is hot and muggy in the summer.

Generalizing is an important reasoning skill that will help you develop a strong thesis statement for your essay. However, you must use it carefully so that you do not overlook those important exceptions that will make a generalization false.

Hasty Generalizations When you reason, beware of the pitfall of *hasty generalizations*—broad generalizations based on insufficient evidence. Such hasty generalizations often lead to misleading or false conclusions. To avoid this fallacy, you must examine *enough* particular experiences to draw a sound conclusion.

HASTY GENERALIZATION	All professional athletes are healthy. [Has the writer examined enough athletes to conclude that they *all* are healthy?]
HASTY GENERALIZATION	Chlorine in swimming pools causes earaches. [Does *everyone* who swims in chlorinated pools have earaches?]

You can make the previous hasty generalizations more sound if you limit them to *some, many,* or *most* cases instead of *all* cases.

SOUND GENERALIZATION	**Most** professional athletes are healthy.
SOUND GENERALIZATION	**Some** people experience earaches from swimming in chlorinated pools.

You can avoid hasty generalizations if you follow these guidelines.

Avoiding Hasty Generalizations

1. Examine several facts or examples.
2. Be sure your examples represent the whole group.
3. If necessary, check reliable authorities to confirm your generalization.
4. Be able to explain any exceptions.
5. Avoid words like *all, complete, always, never,* and *none,* because they suggest that there are no exceptions.
6. Limit your generalization by using words like *some, many, most, probably, often,* and *sometimes.*

Writing Tip Avoid **hasty generalizations** by limiting generalizations to *some, many,* or *most* cases.

WRITING ACTIVITY 5 *Writing Sound Generalizations*

Choose one of the following hasty generalizations. Limit the statement to an opinion with which you agree.

1. Any rural area is less polluted than a city.
2. Chimps are more intelligent than any other animal.
3. Adults are responsible for more litter than teenagers.
4. Education is the only avenue to success.
5. Television shows are too violent.
6. Two boys from Webster High School crossed Mr. Kim's lawn and broke a shrub. Students from that school are destructive.
7. An Italian friend made this pizza. Italians are terrific cooks.
8. Lying in the sun causes skin cancer.
9. Boys are not interested in baby-sitting.
10. Politicians have the greatest impact on life in the United States.

Writing a Persuasive Essay

As you write a persuasive essay, keep in mind that your purpose is to influence the opinions and the behavior of your readers. In other words you want to persuade your readers to adopt your point of view and perhaps elect a course of action that you suggest. Your first step in accomplishing this purpose is to develop a logical and reasonable argument that supports your opinion.

Prewriting

Most of the success of a persuasive essay depends on careful planning during the prewriting stage. Choose a subject with care and take the time to prepare your argument thoroughly. The following strategies will help you plan a logical and convincing argument.

Choosing a Subject The subject you choose should be meaningful to you. The stronger your interest, the more convincing your persuasive essay will be. The subject you choose should also be controversial—one about which people tend to disagree. For instance, the treatment of the homeless in American society, the effectiveness of the President's war on drugs, teenagers' tastes in music, and the care of American seashores are all issues about which people hold opposing points of view. Brainstorm for a list of issues that you care about strongly—about which you can say, "I think," or "I believe." Next narrow your choices by using brainstorming, freewriting, or clustering on each of the issues under consideration. Then use the following guidelines to choose the best subject for your persuasive essay.

Guidelines for Choosing a Persuasive Essay Subject

1. Choose a subject about an issue that is important to you.
2. Choose a subject about an issue on which people hold very different opinions.
3. Choose a subject that you can support with examples, reasons, and facts from your own experience or from other reliable sources.
4. Choose a subject for which there is an audience whose beliefs or behavior you would like to influence.

Identifying Your Audience Sometimes when you write a persuasive essay, you may have to address an audience outside of the classroom. Learn as much as possible about that audience in advance in order to decide whether you can successfully persuade them or move them to action. Knowing your audience well also helps you choose the best material to support your argument. The following questions should help you zero in on your audience.

Questions for Analyzing an Audience

1. What does my audience already know about my subject?
2. What is my audience's point of view about my subject? Do they already agree or disagree with my position?
3. What are the chances of changing the opinions and behavior of my audience?
4. Are there any sensitive issues I should be aware of?

WRITING ACTIVITY 6 *Identifying Your Audience*

With your teacher's permission, form a small group and identify five possible audiences for each of the following persuasive essay subjects.

EXAMPLE establishing a large green space in town
ANSWER joggers, day-care helpers, landscape architects, senior citizens, gardeners

1. establishing a clean-up committee for riverbanks
2. establishing bird sanctuaries
3. establishing walking trails in conservation land

WRITING ACTIVITY 7 *Writing on Your Own*

WRITING ABOUT THE THEME

Review your journal notes and the facts and opinions listed in Writing Activity 2. Then brainstorm for any ideas you have about some pressing environmental concern or problem in your local area that will make a good subject for a persuasive essay. As you consider different subjects, list those that have two sides and will permit you to recommend some type of action or resolution to the problem. Use the guidelines on page 250 to make your final choice. Then place a star beside your choice and put your paper in your writing folder for later use.

Developing a Thesis Statement Once you have chosen a subject and identified your audience, you are ready to develop a thesis statement. This is a statement of the point of view you will argue for in your essay. Avoid a statement of fact or of personal preference, for these do not make suitable thesis statements for a persuasive essay. Look carefully at the opinion you have about your subject; it should be a supportable opinion and worth the consideration of others. Also avoid hasty generalizations by limiting your thesis statement. Keep in mind that often the thesis statement will take the form of a recommendation for action.

FACT	Throughout history, some companies have polluted water resources in the United States.
OPINION	I think my town should form a watchdog committee to protect the reservoir.
THESIS STATEMENT	Cleaning up the water resources will be a long, costly process that this town should start at once.

Use the following guidelines to develop your thesis statement.

Guidelines for Developing a Thesis Statement for a Persuasive Essay

1. Choose a debatable opinion—one that has two sides.
2. State the thesis simply and directly in one sentence.
3. Avoid hasty generalizations by limiting your statement.
4. Give a supportable opinion or a recommendation for action.
5. As you collect more information, continue to revise the thesis statement until it is clear-cut and defensible and covers all the evidence.

If your thesis does not meet all of these guidelines, you need to rethink your position or look for a more appropriate issue.

WRITING ACTIVITY 8 *Choosing a Suitable Thesis Statement*

Write whether each of the following statements would be suitable or unsuitable as a thesis statement for a persuasive essay. Use the guidelines above as you evaluate each statement.

1. It really makes me angry and discouraged to see so much trash on the city's streets.
2. The United Nations should provide funds for research in global-warming trends.
3. Our science club should volunteer to plant 1,000 tree saplings around the town dump.
4. Developing solar energy is a waste of time.
5. This nation's wilderness areas should be completely preserved even if it takes an act of Congress.

WRITING ACTIVITY 9 *Writing on Your Own*

WRITING ABOUT THE THEME

Return to the subject for a persuasive essay about the environment that you chose in Writing Activity 7. Identify your audience by using the Questions for Analyzing an Audience on page 251. Then use the guidelines above to write a clear thesis statement and save your work in your writing folder for later use.

Developing an Argument

After you have defined your position in a thesis statement, you are ready to develop the argument that will defend your thesis. You should first consider your audience. You will want to use evidence—the facts, examples, and expert opinions—that your audience will find convincing. Be sure to select factual evidence that supports your opinion (pro) and also evidence that refutes it (con) so that you can address opposing views in your essay. However, keep in mind that as you collect this evidence and your argument develops, you may have to revise your thesis statement. Once you have collected your evidence, use the following guidelines to help you develop your argument.

Guidelines for Developing an Argument

1. List pros and cons in separate columns in your prewriting notes. Be prepared to address the opposing views point by point.
2. Use facts and examples rather than more opinions to support your opinions.
3. If those with the opposing view have a good point, admit it. Then show why the point is not enough to sway your opinion. Such an admission is called *conceding a point,* and it will strengthen your believability.
4. Use polite and reasonable language rather than words that show bias or overcharged emotions.
5. Refer to well-respected experts and authorities who agree with your position.

Writing Is Thinking

Critical Thinking

Evaluating Evidence

In order to make an argument in a persuasive essay as convincing as possible, use evidence consisting of facts, examples, statistics, anecdotes, incidents, and opinions of qualified experts. Before you decide to include a piece of evidence, however, you should *evaluate,* or critically judge, it. To do so, use the following criteria to decide whether the piece of evidence will truly support your argument.

- Is this evidence clearly related to my thesis?
- Is this a fact or an expert opinion?
- Is my source reliable?
- Is my evidence up-to-date?
- Is the evidence unbiased and objective?
- Is this a fact my audience will readily grasp?

Suppose, for example, that you are arguing for longer public library hours. Here is how you could evaluate evidence on this issue.

Evidence	Evaluation
Students and workers need access to information.	Supports thesis—shows need for longer hours
Some taxpayers object to homeless people using libraries for sanctuaries.	Does not support thesis—evidence is not related to the thesis
Some librarians need longer hours to supplement earnings.	Does not support thesis—evidence is not related to the thesis

Thinking Practice Choose one of the arguable opinions below or one based on an issue that is important to you. Make a chart like the one above to evaluate the evidence for your position.

1. Skateboarding is not a public menace.
2. Safer working environments for teenagers are needed.
3. Biodegradables cost little more than other paperware.

WRITING ACTIVITY 10 *Listing Pros and Cons*

For each of the following thesis statements, list three facts, examples, incidents, reasons, or authoritative opinions that support the thesis (pros) and three that oppose it (cons). Save your work for Writing Activity 11.

1. Everyone should attend college for at least two years.
2. Retail stores should replace plastic shopping bags with paper bags.
3. The price of gasoline should be raised dramatically to force people to conserve energy.
4. Every tax-paying citizen should elect to have one dollar from tax returns contributed to environmental controls.
5. Homemade gifts are better than those bought in stores.

Organizing an Argument After gathering and evaluating the evidence for your argument, you should organize your material in a logical way. The most common order for persuasive essays is *order of importance*—beginning with the least important point and working up to the most important point at the end. With this emphasis your audience is likely to remember the last, most convincing point of your argument.

As you develop your argument, also remember to use transitional words and phrases to guide the reader from one point to the next. *(See pages 139, 148 and 158 for more information about transitions.)* The following transitions are especially strong when conceding a point or showing contrasting ideas.

Transitions for Persuasive Writing

although	instead	on the other hand
admittedly	nevertheless	still
however	nonetheless	while it is true that

WRITING ACTIVITY 11 *Organizing Persuasive Evidence*

Choose one of the thesis statements from Writing Activity 10 and decide which side of the issue you wish to support. Then follow the instructions below.

1. Revise the thesis statement, if necessary, to express your view. (If you agree with the thesis statement given in the exercise, you may use it.)
2. Review the supporting evidence you prepared in Writing Activity 10. Then list the three points that support your position in the order of least to most important. Leave two blank lines under each point.
3. Assign each of your three points a Roman numeral as in an outline.
4. Add at least two supporting points under each Roman numeral. Your outline should look like this.

I. (Least important point)
  A. (Supporting point)
  B. (Supporting point)
II. (More important point)
  A. (Supporting point)
  B. (Supporting point)
III. (Most important point)
  A. (Supporting point)
  B. (Supporting point)

WRITING ACTIVITY 12 *Writing on Your Own*

WRITING ABOUT THE THEME

Return to the thesis statement you wrote in Writing Activity 9. Using the guidelines on pages 254 and 255, gather and evaluate evidence to develop your argument about a pressing problem in the environment. Then organize your ideas into an outline like the one you completed in Writing Activity 11. Save your work in your writing folder for later use.

Drafting

As you write your first draft, remember that you will have an opportunity to review and revise it later. Use your outline and prewriting notes to express your ideas as quickly as possible and note any place where your information seems weak and where new facts may be required. If necessary, revise your working thesis to cover any new information you may use.

An effective way to capture your audience's attention is to begin with a startling fact or a probing question. You can give the reader a sense of how important the issue is by making sure that your thesis statement is a strong statement of your position. Experiment with emphasis, for example, by placing the thesis statement at the end of the introduction for the most dramatic effect.

As you draft the body of your essay, devote one paragraph to each main point in your outline. In addition to presenting your own supporting evidence, include the opposition's position where appropriate and show why this position has not changed yours. Remember to use transitional words to guide the reader through your argument. *(See page 257.)*

Finally, draft a conclusion that summarizes your position and restates your thesis. If you want to persuade the readers to take some action, make a recommendation. Then add a title that is lively and challenging.

Persuasive Language The strong, emotional words used in high-pressure advertising get attention; but if those words are offensive, they will never convince people to buy the product. Keep this in mind as you write your persuasive essay. If you use sincere, straightforward language, you will more likely convince your audience.

EMOTIONAL LANGUAGE	The oily lake is full of **dead** fish, and **dirty little kids dump junk** all over the beach.
FORCEFUL LANGUAGE	Once the lake was **blue** and **sparkling.** Now fish **die** in its oily waves, and **youngsters litter** the beach with **trash.**

WRITING ACTIVITY 13 *Writing on Your Own*

WRITING ABOUT THE THEME

Write a first draft of the persuasive essay about the environment that you planned in Writing Activity 12. Use sincere but reasonable language to present your argument. Save your work in your writing folder for later use.

Revising

One purpose for revising your persuasive essay is to make each point as clear and persuasive as possible. You will be most successful if you read your essay several times, each time addressing a different aspect of the writing. Does your introduction challenge your audience? Is your thesis statement a strong and clear statement of your position on the issue? Can your facts be strengthened by better examples? Are there any important points that you have overlooked? Have you conceded a point? In other words have you admitted that an opposing point has validity but is not strong enough to sway you? Are there words you might use that have more impact? Does your conclusion work? Once you have refined your language and strengthened your argument, read your essay again to check your logic and eliminate any of the following logical fallacies.

Eliminating Logical Fallacies A *fallacy* is an error in logic. You have already seen how to avoid hasty generalizations on page 249. Following are several other fallacies that can creep into your reasoning and weaken your argument.

Writing Tip Eliminate **logical fallacies** in your writing.

Attacking the Person instead of the Issue In Latin this fallacy is called *argumentum ad hominem* ("argument against the man"). Writers who fall into this trap criticize the character of their opponent instead of concentrating on the issue.

AD HOMINEM FALLACY	The clean-water study was doomed to failure because Mayor Reed is always out of town. [Unless the mayor is personally conducting the study, his absence had very little to do with its doom.]

It is just as illogical for a writer to use positive aspects of a person's personality as a basis of the argument.

AD HOMINEM FALLACY	The clean-water study should have been a great success because Mayor Reed is interested in everything—especially Little League. [In this case the mayor's interests had little to do with the study's success.]

WRITING ACTIVITY 14 *Recognizing an* Ad Hominem *Fallacy*

Identify which of the following sentences contain an *ad hominem* fallacy.

1. Tim Lee drives a big car, so he isn't concerned about energy conservation.
2. Because Ron is always tardy, he should not be given the Most Friendly Class Member award.
3. Anna White is a good choice for chairperson of the Halloween party committee.
4. The senator is so dignified that he should give a wonderful persuasive speech.
5. I don't see how Christopher's proposal for a class budget can work.

The Either-Or Fallacy Sometimes a writer of a persuasive essay assumes that there are only two sides to an argument. In fact, there may be many alternative opinions situated between the two extremes.

EITHER-OR FALLACY	Senator Wing must be willing to risk disastrous oil spills because she is against the use of atomic energy. [Senator Wing may actually support several other alternative sources of energy.]

WRITING ACTIVITY 15 *Avoiding the Either-Or Fallacy*

Write a sentence that offers a third alternative to the extreme opinions of each of the following either-or fallacies.

1. If you care about the environment, you will not own a car.
2. If we are to help farm animals, we must all become vegetarians.
3. Either we stop using oil, coal, and gas for fuel; or we will never breathe clean air again.

Confusing Chronology with Cause and Effect Writers fall into this trap when they assume that whatever happens after an event was caused by that event. In many cases the relationship between the two events is merely coincidental.

CAUSE-EFFECT FALLACY	Every time Chris and his family go on vacation it rains, so they must plan poorly. [Chris and his family are unlikely to plan for the rain. They may be victims of unlucky coincidence, or they may unknowingly vacation in the rainy season of particular areas.]

WRITING ACTIVITY 16 *Supplying Logical Causes*

In each of the following sets of circumstances, chronology is confused with cause and effect. Write a more likely cause of the second event in each case.

1. Every time I try to grow corn in our backyard, it fails. I must be doing something wrong.
2. Tom found a big black rock in his yard. Since it wasn't there yesterday, it must have been a meteorite.
3. Immediately after the new computers were installed, we had a big power failure. We must have bought the wrong computers for this building.
4. Our world history class had a discussion about the Berlin Wall yesterday. Tonight the news announced that German citizens were tearing down the wall. My teacher must have been alerted by someone in Germany.
5. Martin and Justin had an argument before school. That's why Martin fell off his bike on the way to school.

False Analogies An *analogy* is a comparison between two things that are alike in some important ways. A writer or speaker can use an analogy to communicate an unfamiliar idea by showing how it is very much like a more familiar one. You could, for example, explain the effect of acid rain to a small child by using the following analogy.

ANALOGY Acid rain hurts trees the way the salt on the road last winter hurt my bicycle. [The unfamiliar idea—*acid rain hurts trees*—is compared to the quite familiar idea—*salt on the road hurt my bicycle last winter.*]

A false analogy is an attempt to compare two things that are alike in some ways but too far apart in others to be logically compared.

FALSE ANALOGY Since this desert wilderness is just a great big sandbox, environmentalists should stop worrying about preserving it. [Both a desert and a sandbox contain sand, but a desert is a complex ecosystem that is home to many forms of life. A person's concept of a desert, based on one's knowledge of the contents of a sandbox, would have nothing to do with reality.]

FALSE ANALOGY Misty Hamlin owns a new skateboard. Why can't I have one too? [Misty Hamlin may have a different level of ability on a skateboard and may also have more money to buy a new one.]

WRITING ACTIVITY 17 *Finding the Flaws in False Analogies*

Write a sentence that explains the logical flaw in each of the following false analogies.

1. If a chimp can learn sign language, I should be able to teach my dog to do the same.
2. Long Beach High School has a water-skiing club. Why can't we have one?
3. Since driving a car is just like riding a bicycle, a driver's license should not be required.

Using a Revision Checklist Use the checklist on the following page to help you revise your persuasive essay.

Revision Checklist

CHECKING THE INTRODUCTION

1. Does the thesis statement present your opinion effectively?
2. Will your introduction convince the readers that your topic is important?
3. Is the language you use both persuasive and objective?

CHECKING THE BODY PARAGRAPHS

4. Does each paragraph have a topic sentence? *(See page 89.)*
5. Have you supported your main points with verified facts, examples, and authoritative opinions? *(See pages 246–247.)*
6. Have you developed your arguments well and organized them in the most appropriate way? *(See pages 254–257.)*
7. Have you dealt with opposing views effectively? *(See page 258.)*
8. Have you used sound reasoning and avoided logical fallacies? *(See pages 248–249 and 259–262.)*
9. Have you used transitions to help your reader follow your argument from point to point? *(See pages 256–257.)*

CHECKING YOUR CONCLUSION

10. Does your conclusion summarize your main points? *(See page 241.)*
11. Did you restate your thesis? *(See page 258.)*
12. Is your conclusion logically drawn from your arguments? *(See pages 248–249.)*

CHECKING YOUR WORDS AND SENTENCES

13. Are your sentences varied? *(See pages 67–69.)*
14. Have you avoided biased, emotionally charged words? *(See page 258.)*

WRITING ACTIVITY 18 *Writing on Your Own*

WRITING ABOUT THE THEME

Return to the persuasive essay about the environment that you drafted in Writing Activity 13 and correct any logical fallacies. Then, if your teacher permits it, exchange essays with a classmate and provide each other with suggested improvements. When your paper is returned, use your partner's comments and the above checklist to revise your essay. Save your work in your writing folder for editing later.

Integrating Language Skills

Editing and Publishing

Grammar in the Writing Process

In "The Obligation to Endure," Rachel Carson writes, "This is an era of specialists, each of whom sees his own problem and is unaware of or intolerant of the larger frame into which it fits." In a broad sense, this sentence can be applied to any usage or mechanical errors you make in your writing. One little problem here or one little problem there probably would not have any major effect on most of your readers. However, the sum of all of the errors could—without question—diminish the effect of your writing on your audience.

This textbook has a chapter called "A Writer's Glossary of Usage" that will help you find and correct many of these small, but significant, errors. You can use the glossary as a reference tool. Following are a few examples of the items you will find in the glossary. As you look at them, you will occasionally see the words *STANDARD* and *NONSTANDARD*. *Standard* is the form you should use when you write; *nonstandard* should be avoided in most writing. *(For more information about standard and nonstandard English, see pages 738–753.)*

advice, advise *Advice* is a noun that means "a recommendation." *Advise* is a verb that means "to recommend."

ADVICE In her essay Rachel Carson gives some good **advice.**
ADVISE She **advises** people to demand the truth about the chemicals that are applied to the environment.

amount, number *Amount* refers to a quantity. *Number* refers to things that can be counted.

AMOUNT Even a small **amount** of poison can contaminate the water supply for an entire area.
NUMBER Carson blames a **number** of hazardous chemicals for disastrous conditions in the environment.

bad, badly *Bad* is an adjective that often follows a linking verb. *Badly* is used as an adverb and often follows an action verb. In the first two examples, *feels* is used as a linking verb. *(For more information about adverbs and the comparison of adverbs, see pages 725–728.)*

NONSTANDARD Carson feels **badly** that Americans have been kept in the dark so long about pesticides.
STANDARD Carson feels **bad** that Americans have been kept in the dark so long about pesticides.
STANDARD According to Carson, we have treated the environment **badly.**

double negative Words such as *hardly, never, no, not,* and *nobody* are considered negatives. Do not use two negatives to express one negative meaning. *(See page 731 for a complete list of negative words.)*

NONSTANDARD We should**n't never** blindly accept all new chemicals as we have in the past.
STANDARD We should**n't** blindly accept all new chemicals as we have in the past.
STANDARD We should **never** blindly accept all new chemicals as we have in the past.

than, then *Than* is usually a conjunction and is used for comparisons. *Then* is an adverb that means "at that time" or "next."

THAN We have recycled our newspapers longer **than** they have.
THEN Call me and **then** we will visit the recycling plant.

(For other glossary entries and practice in writing all of the glossary items correctly, see pages 738–753.)

Editing Checklist

1. Is your essay written in standard English? *(See page 738.)*
2. Have you checked your writing with "A Writer's Glossary of Usage"? *(See pages 738–753.)*

WRITING ACTIVITY 19 *Writing on Your Own*

WRITING ABOUT THE THEME

Editing Use the Editing Checklist above and the Editing Checklist on page 35 to edit your persuasive essay about the environment. Then prepare a final draft in the correct manuscript form shown on page 41.

Publishing Attach a letter to your essay and send it into the editorial department of your local newspaper, requesting its publication.

A Writer Writes

WRITING ABOUT THE THEME

A Persuasive Essay

PURPOSE to persuade teenagers that one person can or cannot make a difference in the battle against environmental destruction

AUDIENCE anyone concerned about the environment

Prewriting What is the solution to the environmental crisis facing the United States today? Is the only solution massive doses of federal and local money poured into clean-up and prevention? Are there any other solutions or partial solutions now? Could you alone or with a few friends make a difference? Are there any things that you could

do in your local area to correct some damage that has already taken place, to stop some ongoing damage, or to prevent future damage from ever taking place? Are there enough facts, examples, and illustrations to convince others that the environment could at least be improved by the efforts of a few people here and a few there?

Before you take a stand on this issue, read some magazine and newspaper articles that describe what individuals and small groups have accomplished in their efforts to make the environment a better, cleaner place to live. Then form your opinion about whether or not a grass roots movement could have a positive effect on the environment and identify the audience you wish to persuade. At this point you should write a working thesis statement that makes clear the purpose of your essay and establishes your main idea.

Gather more information if necessary—listing both the pros and cons of your position. When you have enough information, if necessary, revise your thesis statement to cover all the facts. Then choose an organizing scheme and outline the body of your essay.

Drafting Write the first draft of your persuasive essay, beginning, perhaps, by capturing your readers' attention with a startling fact or illustration. Then, after you write a strong introduction around your thesis statement, follow your outline to develop the arguments that support your opinion in the body paragraphs. Your arguments may take the form of examples and illustrations of successful or unsuccessful efforts that individuals or small local groups have made locally or nationally. Remember to confront opposing arguments and show why your arguments are more reasonable. In your conclusion reaffirm your position and suggest any ways that convinced readers could take action.

Revising If time permits, set your essay aside for a day or so and then read it over carefully. Following the Revision Checklist on page 263, revise your essay to make it as persuasive as possible.

Editing and Publishing After you use the checklists on pages 35 and 265 to polish your essay, write a final draft and add a cover letter to it, explaining how and why you wrote the essay. Then send both to one of the following places: the mayor's office, the office of a local environmental group, or the office of one of your state representatives in Congress. You might also ask your local librarian to create space so you and your classmates can exhibit your essays.

Independent Writing

Choose one of the following subjects or one of your own and then follow the checklist on the next page as you write a persuasive essay.

1. Would longer school days improve education?
2. Should sports celebrities earn such colossal salaries?
3. Is lying to avoid hurting someone's feelings acceptable?
4. Should there be any type of censorship of TV?
5. Is a part-time job more important than higher grades?

WRITING ABOUT THE THEME

Creative Writing

Haiku is a form of poetry that was developed in Japan in the early 1900's. A haiku is usually written about a beautiful image of nature such as a flower or a cloud. You could make an impact today, however, by writing a haiku about an image of pollution. To write a haiku, include five syllables in the first line, seven syllables in the second line, and five syllables in the third line. After you read the following example, write a haiku of your own.

Acid rain falling
Gently over trees and lakes,
Killing everything.

WRITING ABOUT THE THEME

Writing about Literature

Tone reflects the author's attitude toward the subject. Tone can vary, for example, from the humor and irony of Bill Cosby in "No Problem, but It Needs a Solution" to the earnest alarm of Rachel Carson in "The Obligation to Endure." Write a paragraph explaining how Rachel Carson communicates this attitude toward pesticides.

Writing in Other Subject Areas

Science Many people see space exploration as vital to our future. Others feel that the huge amounts of time and money spent on space projects are wasteful. Write a persuasive essay in which you present arguments either for or against continuing the exploration of space.

World History Pretend you are chairperson of an international environmental council and write a persuasive essay on one of the most pressing problems you see awaiting the council's attention.

Chapter 7 Checklist

Writing Essays to Persuade

Prewriting

- ✔ Use brainstorming, freewriting, or clustering to identify issues about which you have strong opinions. *(See page 250.)*
- ✔ Choose one subject and identify the audience you want to persuade. Avoiding hasty generalizations, write a thesis statement that accurately presents your opinion. *(See pages 248–253.)*
- ✔ Brainstorm a list of supporting ideas.
- ✔ Evaluate your evidence. *(See page 255.)*
- ✔ Develop a defensible argument by considering pros and cons, by supporting the thesis with facts and examples, and by acknowledging any weak points in your opinion. *(See pages 254–255.)*
- ✔ Organize the details of your argument in an outline in order of importance. *(See pages 256–257.)*

Drafting

- ✔ If necessary refine the thesis statement and write an introduction that includes your thesis statement. *(See pages 252 and 258.)*
- ✔ Use your outline to write the body of your essay. *(See page 216.)*
- ✔ Use connecting devices to link your thoughts. *(See pages 256–257.)*
- ✔ Add a concluding paragraph and a title. *(See pages 224–225.)*

Revising

- ✔ Avoid highly charged, emotional language. *(See page 258.)*
- ✔ Revise your essay to eliminate logical fallacies: hasty generalizations, personal attacks, either-or fallacies, false analogies, or any confusion of chronology with cause and effect. *(See pages 248–262.)*
- ✔ Use the Revision Checklist. *(See page 263.)*

Editing and Publishing

- ✔ Use the Editing Checklist to check your grammar, usage, spelling, and mechanics. *(See page 35.)*
- ✔ Make a neat final copy of your essay in standard manuscript form and consult the Ways to Publish Your Writing chart for ideas about publishing. *(See pages 40 and 41.)*

Chapter 8 Writing Personal Essays

Part 1 Reading to Write

THEME: *Belongings*

What is your most prized belonging? Is it an object, such as a trophy or award that you won? Is it a group of things, such as a collection of cassette tapes? Perhaps the possession you value most is something that you wear, such as a special pair of sneakers or a piece of jewelry. Knowing what things you place great importance on is usually easy to determine, but understanding why you feel the way you do about an object or a piece of clothing may not be quite so obvious.

In the following selection, called "The Jacket," Gary Soto relates a time in his past when he felt that one possession—a jacket—was responsible for several years of unhappiness. The jacket was the wrong kind of jacket, for one thing. Because it was not smooth black leather with silver studs and belts all over it, he believed that girls did not like him, that teachers laughed at him, and that people—especially the people who mattered—did not want to be around him.

Is it possible that one piece of clothing could be the cause of so many feelings and reactions? As you read "The Jacket," think about your belongings—and what they mean to you. Is there one thing, such as a guitar, that helps you express your individuality or that brings back important memories? Such reflection's may help you understand better why a jacket was so important to Gary Soto.

The Jacket

Gary Soto

My clothes have failed me. I remember the green coat that I wore in fifth and sixth grades when you either danced like a champ or pressed yourself against a greasy wall, bitter as a penny toward the happy couples.

When I needed a new jacket and my mother asked what kind I wanted, I described something like bikers wear: black leather and silver studs with enough belts to hold down a small town. We were in the kitchen, steam on the windows from her cooking. She listened so long while stirring dinner that I thought she understood for sure the kind I wanted. The next day when I got home from school, I discovered draped on my bedpost a jacket the color of day-old guacamole.[1] I threw my books on the bed and approached the jacket slowly, as if it were a stranger whose hand I had to shake. I touched the vinyl sleeve, the collar, and peeked at the mustard-colored lining.

1. **guacamole** [gwäk ə' mo le]: Mashed avocados.

From the kitchen mother yelled that my jacket was in the closet. I closed the door to her voice and pulled at the rack of clothes in the closet, hoping the jacket on the bedpost wasn't for me but my mean brother. No luck. I gave up. From my bed, I stared at the jacket. I wanted to cry because it was so ugly and so big that I knew I'd have to wear it a long time. I was a small kid, thin as a young tree, and it would be years before I'd have a new one. I stared at the jacket, like an enemy, thinking bad things before I took off my old jacket whose sleeves climbed halfway to my elbow.

I put the big jacket on. I zipped it up and down several times, and rolled the cuffs up so they didn't cover my hands. I put my hands in the pockets and flapped the jacket like a bird's wings. I stood in front of the mirror, full face, then profile, and then looked over my shoulder as if someone had called me. I sat on the bed, stood against the bed, and combed my hair to see what I would look like doing something natural. I looked ugly. I threw it on my brother's bed and looked at it for a long time before I slipped it on and went out to the backyard, smiling a "thank you" to my mom as I passed her in the kitchen. With my hands in my pockets I kicked a ball against the fence, and then climbed it to sit looking into the alley. I hurled orange peels at the mouth of an open garbage can and when the peels were gone I watched the white puffs of my breath thin to nothing.

I jumped down, hands in my pockets, and in the backyard on my knees I teased my dog, Brownie, by swooping my arms while making bird calls. He jumped again and again, until a tooth sunk deep, ripping an L-shaped tear on my left sleeve. I pushed Brownie away to study the tear as I would a cut on my arm. There was no blood, only a few loose pieces of fuzz. Damn dog, I thought, and pushed him away hard when he tried to bite again. I got up from my knees and went to my bedroom to sit with my jacket on my lap, with the lights out.

That was the first afternoon with my new jacket. The next day I wore it to sixth grade and got a D on a math quiz. During the morning recess Frankie T., the playground terrorist, pushed me to the ground and told me to stay there until recess was over. My best friend, Steve Negrete, ate an apple while looking at me, and the girls turned away to whisper on the monkey bars. The teachers were no help: they looked my way and talked about how foolish I looked in my new jacket. I saw their heads bob with laughter, their hands half-covering their mouths.

Even though it was cold, I took off the jacket during lunch and played kickball in a thin shirt, my arms feeling like braille from goose

bumps. But when I returned to class I slipped the jacket on and shivered until I was warm. I sat on my hands, heating them up, while my teeth chattered like a cup of crooked dice. Finally warm, I slid out of the jacket but a few minutes later put it back on when the fire bell rang. We paraded out into the yard where we, the sixth graders, walked past all the other grades to stand against the back fence. Everybody saw me. Although they didn't say out loud, "Man, that's ugly," I heard the buzz-buzz of gossip and even laughter that I knew was meant for me.

And so I went, in my guacamole jacket. So embarrassed, so hurt, I couldn't even do my homework. I received Cs on quizzes, and forgot the state capitals and the rivers of South America, our friendly neighbor. Even the girls who had been friendly blew away like loose flowers to follow the boys in neat jackets.

I wore that thing for three years until the sleeves grew short and my forearms stuck out like the necks of turtles. All during that time no love came to me—no little dark girl in a Sunday dress she wore on Monday. At lunchtime I stayed with the ugly boys who leaned against the chainlink fence and looked around with propellers of grass spinning in our mouths. We saw girls walk by alone, saw couples, hand in hand, their heads like bookends pressing air together. We saw them and spun our propellers so fast our faces were blurs.

I blame that jacket for those bad years. It was a sad time for the heart. With a friend I spent my sixth-grade year in a tree in the alley waiting for something good to happen to me in that jacket, which had become the ugly brother who tagged along wherever I went. And it was about that time that I began to grow. My chest puffed up with muscle and, strangely, a few more ribs. Even my hands, those fleshy hammers, showed bravely through the cuffs, the fingers already hardening for the coming fights. But that L-shaped rip on the left sleeve got bigger; bits of stuffing coughed out from its wound after a hard day of play. I finally scotch-taped it closed, but in rain or cold weather the tape peeled off like a scab and more stuffing fell out until that sleeve shriveled into a palsied arm. That winter the elbows began to crack and whole chunks of green began to fall off. I showed the cracks to my mother, who always seemed to be at the stove with steamed-up glasses, and she said that there were children in Mexico who would love that jacket. I told her that this was America and yelled that Debbie, my sister, didn't have a jacket like mine. I ran outside, ready to cry, and climbed the tree by the alley to think bad thoughts and watch my breath puff white and disappear.

But whole pieces still casually flew off my jacket when I played hard, read quietly, or took vicious spelling tests at school. When it became so spotted that my brother began to call me "camouflage," I flung it over the fence into the alley. Later, however, I swiped the jacket off the ground and went inside to drape it across my lap and mope.

I was called to dinner: steam silvered my mother's glasses as she said grace; my brother and sister with their heads bowed made ugly faces at their glasses of powdered milk. I gagged too, but eagerly ate big rips of buttered tortilla that held scooped up beans. Finished, I went outside with my jacket across my arm. It was a cold sky. The faces of clouds were piled up, hurting. I climbed the fence, jumping down with a grunt. I started up the alley and soon slipped into my jacket, that green ugly brother who breathed over my shoulder that day and ever since. ◆

Responding to the Theme

Belongings

Responding in Your Journal In your journal this week, think and write about belongings. Begin today by listing those possessions that mean the most to you. Then analyze why they are important. Do your friends have similar ones? Are any of your possessions important to you because they are expressions of your individuality? Are any valuable because you associate them with important memories?

As the chapter progresses, also write in your journal about experiences that you associate with belongings. Has an article of clothing played a central role in an episode in your life, as it did for Gary Soto? When you were younger, did receiving a gift, such as a bicycle, lead to any experiences that stand out in your mind? Are there any experiences that involve fads or fashions—clothing or objects that are "in" for a short period of time?

Speaking and Listening Take a survey of your friends, neighbors, and family members. Ask at least 15 people what their most prized possession is. Then ask them to explain why that one possession means so much to them. When you are finished, categorize your answers. Then, if time permits, your teacher will have some students share their results with the rest of the class.

Critical Thinking: Imagining An important thinking skill is being able to imagine. What do you imagine happened to the narrator of "The Jacket" in the months following the end of this selection? Do you think he was able to overcome his unhappiness at having to wear the jacket? Write a sequel to the selection, continuing the narrative from the first person point of view.

Extending Your Vocabulary In "The Jacket" Gary Soto refers to two Mexican foods: *guacamole* and *tortillas*. Use a dictionary or an encyclopedia to find out what these foods are and then write an explanation of each one. In addition, read about these other foods from various cultures and write an explanation of what each one is.

crepes suzette (French)
cassava (Brazilian)
tamales (Mexican)
ziti (Italian)
sorghum (Chinese)

Coathangers, Sandy Skoglund

Part 2 Writing

In "The Jacket" Gary Soto has written about a personal experience in which a green jacket played a major role. This experience, of course, is only one of thousands of experiences he has had over the years that he could have written about in a type of composition called a personal essay.

Writing Term A **personal essay** expresses the writer's personal point of view on a subject drawn from the writer's own experience.

As the definition states, a personal essay can be about any personal experience. You could, for example, write about the first time you tried to ice-skate or a time you went to a Halloween party. Since a personal essay expresses your feelings and reflections about a subject, you should use the pronoun *I*. In addition, you should write in a natural, personal style and follow a less formal structure than in most of the other writing you do.

Prewriting

Writing Process

The starting point for thinking of a subject for a personal essay is your own experience, reflections, and observations. Writers have written essays about a tremendous variety of personal subjects—everything from taking driving lessons to expressing the importance of a friendship. In the following excerpt from a personal essay, the writer Annie Dillard wrote about a childhood experience that had personal significance for her.

Model: *Personal Essay*

When I was six or seven years old, growing up in Pittsburgh, I used to take a precious penny of my own and hide it for someone else to find. It was a curious compulsion; sadly, I've never been seized by it since. For some reason I always "hid" the penny along the same stretch of sidewalk up the street. I would cradle it at the roots of a sycamore, say, or in a hole left by a chipped-off piece of sidewalk. Then I would take a piece of chalk, and, starting at the other end of the block, draw huge arrows leading up to the penny from both directions. After I learned to write I labeled the arrows: SURPRISE AHEAD or MONEY THIS WAY. I was greatly excited, during all this arrow-drawing, at the thought of the first lucky passerby who would receive in this way, regardless of merit, a free gift from the universe. But I never lurked about. I would go straight home and not give the matter another thought, until, some months later, I would be gripped again by the impulse to hide another penny.

Annie Dillard
Pilgrim at Tinker Creek

Drawing on Personal Experience

To think of a subject for a personal essay, look through your journal entries and try clustering or freewriting to recall experiences, people, places, and objects that have personal significance for you. For instance, you might recall a coach or a teacher who has had a strong influence on you. You might visualize a special place that has always provided you pleasure. Even a simple object such as an old baseball mitt or a pair of dance shoes can be the starting point for a personal essay. The sources on the following page can all lead to appropriate subjects.

Sources of Subjects for Personal Essays

photograph albums	school newspapers
letters from friends	newspapers and magazines
family stories	souvenirs from vacations
friends' stories	school yearbooks
scrapbooks	items in your desk

WRITING ACTIVITY 1 *Writing on Your Own*

WRITING ABOUT THE THEME

Using your journal entries and the sources suggested in the box above, create a list of five possible subjects for a personal essay on the theme of belongings. On your list include both possessions that are important to you and experiences that you associate with possessions. Then, from your list, choose the one subject that appeals to you most. It should be one that you remember vividly and that is meaningful to you. Save your subject in your writing folder for later use.

Determining the Meaning of an Experience

While a personal essay may not have a thesis statement, it does communicate a main idea to the audience. This main idea usually grows out of the meaning that the experience had for you. For instance, suppose that you acted in a school play in your freshman year in high school and want to write about that experience. In the resulting personal essay, you could turn any of the following interpretations of that experience into the main idea of your essay.

- The experience helped you build self-confidence.
- The experience stimulated an interest in theater as a career.
- The experience introduced you to a group of talented people.

In the following excerpt, notice how Annie Dillard explains the meaning of her childhood experience of hiding pennies.

Model: *Excerpt from Personal Essay*

The world is fairly studded and strewn with pennies cast broadside from a generous hand. But—and this is the point—who gets excited by a mere penny? If you follow one arrow, if

> you crouch motionless on a bank to watch a tremendous ripple thrill on the water and are rewarded by the sight of a muskrat kit paddling from its den, will you count that sight a chip of copper only, and go on your rueful way? It is dire poverty indeed when a man is so malnourished and fatigued that he won't stop to pick up a penny. But if you cultivate a healthy poverty and simplicity, so that finding a penny will literally make your day, then, since the world is in fact planted in pennies, you have with your poverty bought a lifetime of days. It is that simple. What you see is what you get.
>
> ANNIE DILLARD
> *Pilgrim at Tinker Creek*

As Dillard makes clear, the experience taught her a lesson about the importance of noticing the small things in life, which the pennies symbolize. As a result, that lesson serves as the main idea of her personal essay.

WRITING ACTIVITY 2 *Writing on Your Own*

WRITING ABOUT THE THEME

Think about the possession or experience that you chose as your subject in Writing Activity 1. In a sentence or two, write what the experience or object means to you—what has made it important. *(See Writing Is Thinking on page 280.)* Save your work in your writing folder for later use.

Critical Thinking

Writing Is Thinking

Interpreting Experience

When you are in the middle of an experience, you are often too caught up in it to understand fully its impact on your life. Therefore, when planning a personal essay, you need to interpret an experience in order to decide what is important about it that makes it worth writing about. To help you, you might complete a checklist, like the one below, that helps you explore each aspect of the experience. You should modify the checklist to suit your own needs.

Checklist for Interpreting Experience

Experience: *when we moved to a new town between seventh and eighth grades.*

This experience is important to me now because it

____ helped me see something in a new way.
_✓_ changed the way I feel about myself.

I will always remember this experience because it

_✓_ strongly affected my attitudes.
____ had important consequences.

This experience is worth writing about because it

____ will be familiar to many readers.
_✓_ gave me an insight that may help other people.

Interpretation: *This experience helped me become more outgoing with people. I had to make an effort to make friends, and it worked!*

Thinking Practice Choose one of the following experiences or one of your own choice. Then interpret that experience by developing a checklist like the one above.

1. a humorous episode you had while on vacation
2. an experience that gave you an insight about a person
3. an incident that gave you an insight into your neighborhood

Determining Purpose and Audience

Once you have decided on the meaning of an experience, you need to think about the purpose and audience of your essay. Usually you will write a personal essay for the general purpose of entertaining your readers. However, you can combine this general purpose with specific purposes, which you achieve by including different kinds of paragraphs. For example, listed in the following box are possible specific purposes for an essay about being in the freshman class play.

Personal Essays

General Purpose: to express thoughts and feelings about being in the freshman class play

EXAMPLES OF SPECIFIC PURPOSES	KINDS OF PARAGRAPHS
• to explain the challenges of playing a particular role	expository
• to tell an anecdote about a humorous person in the cast	narrative
• to describe the director of the play	descriptive

Considering Your Audience When writing personal essays, you need to give special attention to making the subject as appealing and significant for your audience as it is for you. Suppose, for instance, that you are writing about white-water rafting on the Colorado River. Since most readers have not had this experience, you should describe the river and the process of rafting in sufficient detail so that your readers will be able to understand and visualize the experience.

WRITING ACTIVITY 3 *Determining Purpose and Audience*

Choose three of the following five subjects for personal essays and write an appropriate purpose and audience for each one.

1. helping a close friend achieve a goal
2. watching a younger brother or sister do well in a special activity
3. getting on a varsity team
4. moving to a new home
5. starting a new part-time job

WRITING ACTIVITY 4 *Writing on Your Own*

WRITING ABOUT THE THEME

Review the possible main idea on the theme of possessions that you explained in Writing Activity 2. Does that statement still accurately explain what the experience meant to you? If not, revise it. After you make notes on the purpose of your essay and your audience, put the notes in your writing folder for later use.

Developing and Selecting Details

An important part of developing a personal essay is using details that will flesh out your experience and give it life. Therefore, after deciding on your purpose and audience, you should think of and write down a list of details that make readers feel that they are at the scene of the experience with you. *(For strategies on recalling, see Writing Is Thinking on page 11.)* If you are writing about a person, think about how the person smiled or frowned, the look in his or her eyes, and so forth. If you are writing about a place, think of details about the smell in the air, the feel of the ground—all that you saw, heard, touched, tasted, and smelled.

After making a list of details, you should select those details you want to include when you draft your essay. Weed out details that, while interesting, are not relevant to the main idea of your essay. The following additional guidelines will help you select the most effective details.

Guidelines for Selecting Details

1. Choose details that are appropriate for your purpose and audience.
2. Use factual details to provide background information.
3. Use vivid descriptive and sensory details to bring your experience to life.

In the following excerpt from a personal essay, the writer E. B. White describes his return to a favorite childhood haunt—a camp at a lake in Maine. Notice how he has selected details that develop the main idea—that the week at the camp was memorable.

Model: *Sensory Details in a Personal Essay*

We had a good week at the camp. The bass were biting well and the sun shone endlessly, day after day. We would be tired at night and lie down in the accumulated heat of the little bedrooms after the long hot day and the breeze would stir almost imperceptibly outside and the smell of the swamp drift in through the rusty screens. E. B. WHITE, "Once More to the Lake"

Now look at how another writer, Eudora Welty, introduces her long selection "Listening" with details that you can almost hear. The details develop the main idea, which is that listening was important in her family when she was young.

Model: *Auditory Details in a Personal Essay*

When I was young enough to still spend a long time buttoning my shoes in the morning, I'd listen toward the hall: Daddy upstairs was shaving in the bathroom and Mother downstairs was frying the bacon. They would begin whistling back and forth to each other up and down the stairwell. My father would whistle his phrase, my mother would try to whistle, then hum hers back. It was their duet. EUDORA WELTY

One Writer's Beginnings

WRITING ACTIVITY 5 *Finding Examples of Details*

Review "The Jacket" by Gary Soto on pages 271–274. Find details in that essay that the author uses to give life to the experience he wrote about. Then on your paper, write at least ten details under the title "Examples of Specific Details."

WRITING ACTIVITY 6 *Writing on Your Own*

WRITING ABOUT THE THEME

List details that you want to include in your personal essay on the theme of possessions. Pay particular attention to details that will assist the reader to understand and visualize the experience. To develop your list of details, use clustering, freewriting, brainstorming, or other techniques you learned about in Chapter 1, "The Writing Process." Keep your list of details in your writing folder.

Organizing Your Essay

The overall organization of your personal essay will probably be developmental order. That is, ideas will be arranged in a progression so that one idea grows out of the previous idea and leads to the next idea. However, within this overall pattern of organization, you will usually use individual paragraphs that are narrative, descriptive, or expository. Within each paragraph, you should use an appropriate method of organizing your details, as the following chart shows. *(For more information about types of order, see pages 139, 148, and 158.)*

Types of Order

TYPE OF PARAGRAPH	KIND OF DETAILS	TYPE OF ORDER
narrative	events in a story, narrated from beginning to end	chronological order
descriptive	details to help readers visualize from top to bottom, right to left, or vice versa	spatial order
expository	background details and details explaining the meaning of an experience	order of importance

WRITING ACTIVITY 7 *Writing on Your Own*

WRITING ABOUT THE THEME

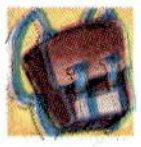

Select and organize the details that you listed in Writing Activity 6 for your personal essay about possessions. After you use the Guidelines for Selecting Details on page 282 to choose your details, arrange them into groups for specific paragraphs and order them, using the above Types of Order chart to assist you. In ordering details, you may find it helpful to write organized notes consisting of phrases or sentences. Save your organized notes in your writing folder for later use.

Drafting

Writing Process

Even though a personal essay is less formal in structure than other types of essays, it should still have all the parts of any good piece of writing: an interesting introduction, an effective body, and a memorable conclusion.

Drafting the Introduction

You should introduce your personal essay in a way that convinces your readers that this experience, person, place, or thing had a strong impact on you. To achieve this goal, your introduction should not only tell readers what your essay is about; it should also give them a clue as to how you feel about your subject. Consequently, your introduction should set the tone of your essay.

Tone in Personal Essays The *tone* of an essay expresses the writer's attitude toward the subject. To choose an appropriate tone for your essay, think about the effect that you want the essay to have on your readers. Do you want them to laugh with you, cry with you, or share the pleasure of a special time or place? Notice how the writer of the following three paragraphs has used three different tones—humorous, angry, and reflective—to deal with the same subject.

Student Model: *Humorous Tone*

Who knew what lurked in those pale waters? All around me happy snorkelers surfaced, crowing with glee about the rainbow of fish that had nibbled at their fingertips. I looked at my own fingers with a sense of doom, absolutely certain that a razor-toothed barracuda was preparing to greet me when *I* went below. Grimly I locked my bloodless lips over the mouthpiece, ducked my head, breathed in water, and came up choking. *Why* in the world was I doing this?

Student Model: *Angry Tone*

It was a raw, windy day, and I was furious. I hate swimming! Since I'm too skinny to look good in a bathing suit, I never go to the beach if I can help it. Here I was, though, all signed up for a free lesson in snorkeling—a sport I'd never wanted to try. Ow! Was that a sea urchin I stepped on?

Beach Umbrella, 1971, acrylic on canvas, 48" × 35 1/4" © David Hockney

Student Model: *Reflective Tone*

This little bay is my favorite spot in the world. When I go out very early in the morning before the crowds, it is like paradise. I never grow tired of the magic in that clear and silent world as I swim and am surrounded by bright blue and yellow fish. In their world I cannot help feeling at peace.

WRITING ACTIVITY 8 *Analyzing for Tone*

Look once again at "The Jacket" by Gary Soto. What do you think is the author's tone? In other words, what attitude does he have about the events he describes? Is he happy? Nostalgic? Sad? Bitter? Write a paragraph in which you explain what you think the tone is. Be sure to support your opinion by including examples—including specific quotations—from the selection.

WRITING ACTIVITY 9 *Writing on Your Own*

WRITING ABOUT THE THEME

Draft three possible introductions to the essay that you have been planning on the theme of belongings. Select a different tone for each introduction and use that tone consistently. Save your work in your writing folder.

Drafting the Body

Once you have introduced the subject and set a tone appropriate for your purpose, you are ready to draft the body of your essay. As you write, make your interpretation of the experience clear and use sensory details to add richness, interest, and individuality to your writing. The following guidelines will also help you draft the body of your personal essay.

Guidelines for Drafting the Body

1. Make sure that each supporting paragraph has a topic sentence that supports the main idea.
2. Follow a logical order of ideas and details.
3. Use transitions between sentences and paragraphs to give your essay coherence.
4. If you discover new ideas and details as you write, go back and make changes in those sections of the essay that are affected by the new insights or details.

In a personal essay, you may use different types of writing, such as narration, description, or exposition, to accomplish your purpose. *(See pages 82–125 for expository writing, pages 137–143 for narrative writing, and pages 144–153 for descriptive writing.)* For instance, in "The Jacket" Gary Soto uses description and narration to express his feelings about the jacket. Early in the essay, he uses description to imply his initial feelings about it.

Model: *Description in a Personal Essay*

The next day when I got home from school, I discovered draped on my bedpost a jacket the color of day-old guacamole. I threw my books on the bed and approached the jacket slowly, as if it were a stranger whose hand I had to shake. I touched the vinyl sleeve, the collar, and peeked at the mustard-colored lining.

A few paragraphs later Soto uses narration to tell what he did when he was alone with the jacket.

Model: *Narration in a Personal Essay*

I put the big jacket on. I zipped it up and down several times, and rolled the cuffs up so they didn't cover my hands. I put my hands in the pockets and flapped the jacket like a bird's wings. I stood in front of the mirror, full face, then profile, and then looked over my shoulder as if someone had called me. I sat on the bed, stood against the bed, and combed my hair to see what I would look like doing something natural. I looked ugly.

GARY SOTO, "The Jacket"

WRITING ACTIVITY 10 *Writing on Your Own*

WRITING ABOUT THE THEME

Select one of the three introductions that you wrote in Writing Activity 9. Draft the body of your personal essay on the theme of possessions, continuing in the same tone that you established in your introduction. Be sure to use the details that you collected in Writing Activity 6. In the course of drafting, stop occasionally and read over what you have written to see whether you are using a consistent tone in your writing.

Drafting the Conclusion

The conclusion of a personal essay should give readers a sense of completion and a lasting impression of the personal experience or insight that you have written about. Following are several appropriate ways to end a personal essay.

Ways to End a Personal Essay

1. Summarize the body or restate the main idea in new words.
2. Add an insight that shows a new or deeper understanding of the experience.
3. Add a striking new detail or memorable image.
4. Refer to ideas in the introduction to bring your essay full circle.
5. Appeal to the reader's emotions.

The following paragraph concludes a student essay that was introduced in the last model paragraph on page 286. The essay was given the title "Early Morning Magic." This conclusion both summarizes the experience and restates the main idea.

Student Model: *Conclusion*

After an early morning swim like this, I come out of the water and spread out on the sand to dry off. The sound of the waves soothes me, and I continue to picture the fish I have seen and the reef that I have explored. Days and even weeks later, I'm able to reflect back on that time and feel a moment of peace in the middle of a hectic day.

WRITING ACTIVITY 11 *Writing on Your Own*

WRITING ABOUT THE THEME

Reread the introduction and body of your essay on the theme of possessions, which you drafted in Writing Activities 9 and 10. Decide what kind of conclusion would be most appropriate. Is there an additional insight or perception that would make an effective conclusion? Should you summarize the experience you have shared? After you draft at least two possible conclusions for your personal essay, choose the one that seems to work better. Then, if time allows, set aside your completed draft for a day or two.

Revising

Writing Process

At this point you have turned the raw materials of your personal perceptions and reflections into a rough draft. Your draft is far from a polished piece of writing, though. As Donald M. Murray, a well-known teacher of writing, wrote, "When a draft is completed, the real job of writing can begin." In a personal essay, this job involves the important task of adding details for adequate development.

Revising for Adequate Development

An effective personal essay should touch the reader in some way. For instance, if you have narrated a personal experience, your narrative should make the reader feel the way you did during that experience and see and touch everything as you did. To evaluate whether you have achieved this effect, check your essay for vivid and interesting details. The following strategies will help you think of additional details as you revise your personal essay.

Strategies for Revising for Adequate Development	
EVENTS	Close your eyes and slowly visualize the experience that you are writing about. Write down the details as you "see" them in your mind's eye.
PEOPLE	Visualize each person that you are writing about. Start by visualizing the head and face of each person and slowly move down to the feet. Write down details as you "see" them.
PLACES	Visualize the place you are describing. Start at the left side of the setting and visualize slowly to the right. Then visualize the place from top to bottom or vice versa.
FEELINGS	Imagine yourself once again undergoing the experience that you are writing about. This time focus on your feelings, thoughts, and impressions as you move through the experience.

WRITING ACTIVITY 12 *Revising for Adequate Development*

Read the following paragraph from a personal essay. What questions does the writer leave unanswered? What details are missing that would help a reader truly understand the experience? After considering these questions, revise the paragraph.

> As I walked home from school yesterday, I decided this had been one of the worst days of my life. Not one thing had gone right. I looked at the book in my hand. I didn't understand the homework assignment, so tomorrow was going to be bad too. Just then it started to rain, and that made me feel worse.

Using a Revision Checklist

After you have revised for adequate development, check the style of your personal essay. Specifically, supply any needed transitions to help your writing flow more smoothly. The following checklist will help you identify a few other problems.

Revision Checklist

1. Does your introduction capture the reader's interest? If not, what might make a better beginning?
2. Have you held the reader's interest to the end? If not, how can you add to the interest level of your essay?
3. Does your feeling about your subject come through? If not, how can you make the point more clearly?
4. Does your ending give the reader a sense of completion? If not, how might you make it more effective?
5. Write a title for your personal essay.

WRITING ACTIVITY 13 *Writing on Your Own*

WRITING ABOUT THE THEME

Return to the personal essay on the theme of belongings that you finished drafting in Writing Activity 11. Revise it, using the Revision Checklist above as a guide. Pay attention to whether you have provided enough details and kept the tone consistent.

Language Integrating Skills

Editing and Publishing

Grammar in the Writing Process

In "The Jacket" Gary Soto wrote, "I stared at the jacket, like an enemy, thinking bad things . . ." The words *thinking bad things* make the sentence dramatic because they emphasize what the writer's feelings were. Notice how much less dramatic the sentence would be without that group of words.

I thought bad things about the jacket.

The words *thinking bad things* form a phrase. Like all phrases it has no subject or verb. However, this is a special kind of phrase called a *verbal phrase.* A *verbal,* which is a verb form that is used as an adjective or a noun, is often combined with modifiers or complements to form a verbal phrase. Writers use verbal phrases frequently to create lively and dramatic sentences, as Gary Soto did in the example above. By using verbal phrases to combine sentences, you can also vary your sentences and eliminate a choppy writing style.

Participial Phrases One kind of verbal phrase is a participial phrase. A *participle* is a verb form used as an adjective to describe nouns or pronouns. *Present participles* end in *-ing,* and *past participles* end in *-ed, -n, -t,* or *-en.* A *participial phrase,* therefore, is a participle plus its modifiers and complements. In the following examples, the participial phrases not only add liveliness to each sentence, but they also supply important additional information. *(For other examples of participial phrases and practice in using them correctly, see pages 608–609.)*

PARTICIPIAL PHRASES **Smiling a "thank you" to my mother,** I went outside.

I saw their hands **covering their mouths** and their heads **bobbing with laughter.**

Punctuation with Participial Phrases When a participial phrase comes at the beginning of the sentence, as in the first example above, place a comma after it. In addition, set off a nonessential participial phrase from the rest of the sentence with commas. A participial phrase is *nonessential* when you can remove it from the sentence without changing the meaning of the sentence. *(For more information about punctuating nonessential phrases and practice in writing them correctly, see pages 609 and 786–790.)*

NONESSENTIAL PHRASE The ugly boys**, leaning against the fence,** watched the couples walk by. [The participial phrase, *leaning against the fence,* is nonessential because it can be removed without changing the meaning of the sentence.]

Combining Sentences by Using Participial Phrases You can use participial phrases to combine sentences, thus eliminating wordiness from your writing. *(For other examples of sentences combined with phrases and practice in combining sentences, see pages 62–63 and 618–619.)*

TWO SENTENCES I spent my sixth-grade year in a tree. I was waiting for something good to happen.

COMBINED I spent my sixth-grade year in a tree **waiting for something good to happen.**

Editing Checklist

1. Have participial phrases been used to add liveliness to sentences and to incorporate additional information? *(See pages 69 and 608.)*
2. Are all participial phrases punctuated correctly? *(See pages 609 and 786.)*
3. Could participial phrases be used to combine any sentences? *(See pages 62 and 618.)*

WRITING ACTIVITY 14 *Writing on Your Own*

WRITING ABOUT THE THEME

Editing If you have the opportunity, read aloud your essay about a possession, which you revised in Writing Activity 13. As you read, listen for the smooth flow of your words. Then edit your essay by using the checklist above and the one on page 35.

Publishing After you have written a neat final copy, give your essay to your teacher, who may choose several to be read aloud in class.

A Writer Writes

WRITING ABOUT THE THEME

A Personal Experience Essay

PURPOSE: to express your thoughts and feelings about a personal experience

AUDIENCE: your classmates and teacher

Prewriting In "The Jacket" Gary Soto wanted a black leather jacket, the kind that many of the other boys were wearing. Without that kind of a jacket, he did not feel confident or attractive. In school, students often place a great importance on looking alike and wearing the same things. Think about an experience you have had during your

school years in which a fad or a fashion played a part. Perhaps you wore a type of clothing in order to follow a fad. On the other hand, there may have been a time when you resisted a fad because you wanted to express your independence. As you explore ideas by reading over your journal, brainstorming, and freewriting, think about how each experience was meaningful to you. What did you learn about yourself or learn about others as a result of each experience?

After you have a list of several possible subjects, choose the best, most meaningful experience. Then brainstorm, freewrite, or cluster to gather all of the details that you will need to include in a retelling of your experience.

Drafting Write a first draft of your personal essay, including an introduction that states or implies your main idea, a body of supporting paragraphs, and a conclusion.

Revising Have you left out any details that will make your essay clearer? Have you stated or implied a main idea about your experience? Will the reader's interest be maintained throughout the essay? Have you developed the essay with adequate details regarding the events, people, places, and things that are included in your essay? Finally, is the tone of the essay consistent from beginning to end? Make revisions and add transitions that will make your essay flow more smoothly.

Editing and Publishing Use the checklists on page 35 and page 293 to edit your essay. Copy your corrected essay neatly onto a spirit duplicating master or reproduce it in some other way so that all your classmates can read a copy. You may wish to include a photograph collage for added interest.

Independent Writing

Write a personal essay about one of the following subjects or one of your own choice. As you plan and write your essay, follow the Checklist for Writing Personal Essays on page 297.

1. a job-related experience
2. the first time you went to a particular place
3. a school-related experience
4. an experience on an athletic team
5. an encounter with an animal
6. an experience with a new friend

7. an unusual accomplishment
8. an encounter with nature
9. an experience with solitude
10. an experience with music

Creative Writing

The more you are familiar with the people, places, and events about which you are writing, the more believable your writing will be. As a result, writers often base their fictional characters on people they know and include experiences they personally have had. Write a short fictional story, limited to two characters involved in one incident or experience. Base the characters on real people you know—or combined parts of real people—to develop your characters. Then create a story line based on an experience you have had. *(For help in developing a short story, see pages 380–419.)* When you have finished, your teacher will include your story in a class anthology of short stories.

WRITING ABOUT THE THEME

Writing about Literature

A *symbol* is a person, place, thing, or action that represents an idea, value, condition, belief, or attitude. For example, a rainbow often symbolizes hope for the future. What do you think the jacket symbolizes in "The Jacket"? Explain your answer in a paragraph, referring to specific passages in the selection that will support your opinion.

Writing in Other Subject Areas

History Choose a time in history that interests you and pretend that you are living in that time. Think of the kinds of personal experiences you might have lived through and choose one experience as the subject of a personal essay. Be sure to make the main idea about the experience clear to readers.

Natural Science Even if you live in the middle of a city, there are important parts of the natural world in your environment. Write a personal essay in which you describe in detail a phenomenon of nature that you see around you—a bird, an insect, a storm, or a plant. Do a little research on your subject to add facts to your observations. Consider what special meaning this natural phenomenon has for you and make that meaning the point of your essay.

Chapter

Checklist

Writing Personal Essays

Prewriting

- ✔ Sift through your memories for experiences, reflections, and observations about which you would like to express your thoughts and feelings. *(See pages 277–278.)*
- ✔ Decide on the meaning that a particular subject has for you. *(See pages 278–280.)*
- ✔ Determine your purpose and audience. *(See pages 16 and 281.)*
- ✔ Choose the most suitable means of developing your subject: narration, description, exposition, or perhaps a combination of all three. *(See page 284.)*
- ✔ List the details that will best develop your main idea and share the meaning of the experience. *(See pages 282–283.)*

Drafting

- ✔ Introduce your subject in a way that catches the reader's interest and sets the tone of the essay. *(See pages 285–286.)*
- ✔ Build the body of your essay from the details you have chosen so that you make the point you wish to share. *(See page 287.)*
- ✔ Add a conclusion that leaves your reader with the idea or feeling that you wish to convey. *(See page 289.)*

Revising

- ✔ Revise your essay for adequate development. *(See page 290.)*
- ✔ Revise your essay for unity, coherence, emphasis, and transitions that make your writing flow smoothly. *(See pages 116–118.)*
- ✔ Choose a title that is true to the tone of your essay. *(See page 225.)*

Editing and Publishing

- ✔ Use the Editing Checklist to polish your grammar, spelling, and mechanics. *(See pages 35 and 293.)*
- ✔ Refer to Ways to Publish Your Writing for ideas on how to present your personal essay. *(See page 40.)*

Chapter

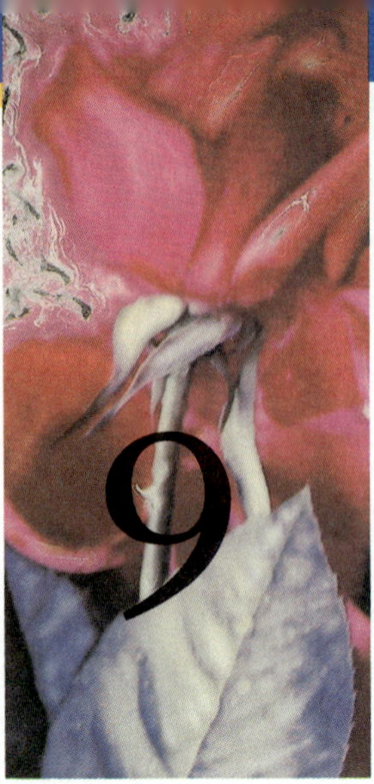

9 Writing Essays about Literature

Part 1 Reading to Write

THEME: *Courage*

History books are filled with stories of bravery—bold deeds in the face of urgent, ominous danger. Recorded in the histories of humankind are tales of extraordinary heroes, such as daring explorers on the icy sea, prisoners under extreme hardship, and pioneers in a harsh and violent wilderness.

In everyday life, bold deeds are rarely required. Yet day by day, you perform smaller acts of courage: admitting you were wrong no matter what the consequences, for example, or overcoming the grief of a deep disappointment. Quiet, courageous acts like these have also been recorded through the centuries. They fill the pages of literature—novels, plays, stories, and poems. Reading in literature about the quiet struggles of the human heart can help you grow in courage.

Reading literature can also help you grow as a writer. Samuel Johnson wrote: "The greatest part of a writer's time is spent in reading, in order to write; a [writer] will turn over half a library to make one book." As a reader you sit side by side with the writers you read and gain appreciation of how they solve their writing problems. As you read and study the following poems, imagine you are sitting elbow to elbow with each poet as she tries to express in poetry her insights into courage.

Courage

Anne Sexton

It is in the small things we see it.
The child's first step,
as awesome as an earthquake.
The first time you rode a bike,
wallowing up the sidewalk.
The first spanking when your heart
went on a journey all alone.
When they called you crybaby
or poor or fatty or crazy
and made you into an alien,
you drank their acid
and concealed it.

Later,
if you faced the death of bombs and bullets
you did not do it with a banner,
you did it with only a hat to
cover your heart.
You did not fondle the weakness inside you
though it was there.
Your courage was a small coal
that you kept swallowing.
If your buddy saved you
and died himself in so doing,
then his courage was not courage,
it was love; love as simple as shaving soap.

Later,
if you have endured a great despair,
then you did it alone,
getting a transfusion from the fire,
picking the scabs off your heart,
then wringing it out like a sock.

Next, my kinsman, you powdered your sorrow,
you gave it a back rub
and then you covered it with a blanket
and after it had slept a while
it woke to the wings of the roses
and was transformed.

Later,
when you face old age and its natural conclusion
your courage will still be shown in the little ways,
each spring will be a sword you'll sharpen,
those you love will live in a fever of love,
and you'll bargain with the calendar
and at the last moment
when death opens the back door
you'll put on your carpet slippers
and stride out.

The Courage That My Mother Had

Edna St. Vincent Millay

The courage that my mother had
Went with her, and is with her still:
Rock from New England quarried;
Now granite in a granite hill.

The golden brooch my mother wore
She left behind for me to wear;
I have no thing I treasure more:
Yet, it is something I could spare.

Oh, if instead she'd left to me
The thing she took into the grave!—
That courage like a rock, which she
has no more need of, and I have.

Responding to the Theme

Courage

Responding in Your Journal No doubt you have heard people say, "I got my blue eyes from my mother and my red hair from my father." You can usually trace physical features back to their source in your family. From where, though, do you get the inner qualities like courage that make you who you are? Anne Sexton provides some answers in her poem. Today, in your journal, explore the "history" of courage as she presented it and summarize the growth of courage experienced at each stage of life. On following days also write about the personal history of your courage. For example, when in your childhood did your courage first show itself "in the small things"?

Edna St. Vincent Millay, in contrast to Anne Sexton, seems to tell where courage does not come from. She suggests that courage—unlike blue eyes, red hair, or a golden brooch—may not be passed on to offspring. Do you agree? Explore in your journal what inner qualities you are likely to inherit from your family—and how they are passed on.

Finally, take some time to record in your journal any words, phrases, or images from the two poems that startled you or moved you in unexpected ways. Try to explain—as if you were a coauthor of the poems—why those startling elements were included.

Speaking and Listening Have you ever seen a very bad actor trying to read Shakespeare? Chances are that actor would present the lines in a sing-song, meaningless patter. "The Courage That My Mother Had" has a very regular rhythm. Practice reading this poem aloud and avoid a monotonous sing-song of uninteresting "da-dum's." Focus on the meaning of the words, and let them—and the emotions they convey—sing out more clearly than the patterned rhythm.

Critical Thinking: Applying In her poem "Courage," the poet Anne Sexton says that it "is in the small things" that we see courage. Think of someone in your immediate or extended family who has exhibited courage and give examples of that person's admirable behavior.

Extending Your Vocabulary Trace the etymology, or history, of the word *courage*. Then read today's newspaper and find five news reports of people's courageous behavior. List ten words or phrases used by the journalists to describe courage.

Edna St. Vincent Millay

Gwendolyn Brooks

Robert Frost

Anne Sexton

Part 2 Writing

In some ways each act of writing is a small act of courage. Every time you write, every time you commit your thoughts to paper, you open yourself to questions, disagreements, and even criticism from your readers. The writer Samuel Butler went as far as to compare readers to judges and juries: "Books should be tried by a judge and jury as though they were crimes." Submitting your writing to the judgment of readers requires courage. Each time you do so, however, your confidence as a writer grows.

When you go a step further and write about what you have read, you enter even more fully into the writer's world. When writing about a poem, for example, you discover and explore the poem's meaning for you. At the same time, however, you "stand in the shoes" of the poet. As you try to explain how the poem communicates, you reconstruct the poet's choices and begin to understand—sometimes only dimly—how the poem came to be.

Writing about literature, then, can deepen your understanding of a work. Before you analyze and evaluate that work, however, you should understand how its genre fits into the general body of literature.

Literature can be divided into three major divisions, or genres: *poetry, prose,* and *drama;* and each of these major genres can be subdivided into smaller genres. For instance, prose can be divided into *fiction* (short stories and novels) and *nonfiction* (biographies, autobiographies, essays, and reports). Poetry and drama each have several smaller genres as well.

In school you have many opportunities to analyze and evaluate some of these different genres. This process will not be new to you. In fact, it is not much different from the effort you make to understand and appreciate two very different friends or family members. This chapter will show you how to explore in writing your personal responses to a work of literature and to combine that personal response statement with your knowledge of literary elements. The result, or finished product, will be a critical essay that shares your evaluation and understanding of a literary work.

Writing Term A **critical essay** presents an interpretation of a work of literature and supports that interpretation with appropriate details and quotations.

The structure of a critical essay is similar to that of other kinds of essays.

Structure of an Essay about Literature

TITLE	The title identifies which aspect of the work the writer will focus on.
INTRODUCTION	The introduction names the author and the work and contains a thesis statement expressing an interpretation of some aspect of the work.
BODY	The body supports the thesis statement with details and direct quotations from the work. In some instances the body also contains some quotations from other respected sources, such as literary critics, biographers, or the author's personal comments and letters.
CONCLUSION	The conclusion summarizes, clarifies, or adds an insight to the thesis statement.

Prewriting

Writing Process

Reading literature is a creative process in which you, the reader, interact with a literary work. Therefore, before you can write formally about a work, you need to experience this creative process by responding openly to what you read. Furthermore, it is important to understand that your response comes from several sources.

Sources of a Reader's Response to Literature

1. individual characteristics, such as age, sex, and personality
2. cultural or ethnic origins, attitudes, and customs
3. personal opinions, beliefs, and values
4. life's experiences and general knowledge
5. knowledge of literature and literary genres
6. knowledge of the historical and social climate in which an author has written a work
7. reading and language skills

All of these sources contribute to your ability to *identify* with the characters and understand the theme, setting, and message of a piece of literature. Who you are, what you know, what you believe, and

where, when, and how you live all help you to understand the content of the story, novel, play, or poem you are reading. The more you identify, the better your enjoyment of the literary work.

Responding from Personal Experience

A writer once commented, "You will not find poetry anywhere unless you bring some of it with you." To understand the meaning of this statement, think back to poems you have read that have had a lasting impact on you. Chances are that each of those poems calls to mind something—an experience, wish, dream, mood, hope—of personal importance to you. Your willingness to let yourself go and personally respond to a poem is the way you can "bring poetry with you." The poet contributes the words and structure of the poem; you and your memories contribute to what the poem's special meaning and its structure will convey to you.

A similar interaction occurs with any literary work you are reading: a story, play, or novel—as well as a poem. Your ability to identify with characters, to let the work serve as a mirror to your own world, makes you an integral part of each literary work you read. As a result your reactions to literature may not always be positive; sometimes a work will irritate, disturb, or even bore you. A negative response, however, is just as important as a positive one, and it also deserves to be explored.

Strategies for a Personal Response to Literature All of the following techniques will help you respond and will help you make sense out of those responses to literature.

Personal Response Strategies

1. In your journal freewrite answers to the following questions:
   a. When you approached this reading, did you have any expectations of the text? In other words, did you expect to be bored? To experience pleasure? To be stimulated? To have difficulty? Were your expectations met? How? Were you surprised? If so, explain why.
   b. Where in the poem, story, novel, or play do you see yourself? In other words, with what character or characters do you most closely identify? Why? Do your feelings about the character or characters stay the same? Do they change? If so, when and why do they change?
   c. What characters remind you of other people you know? In what ways are they like those real people? In what ways are they different? How has your experience with those real people influenced your reactions to the characters in the work?
   d. If you were a character in the work, would you have behaved any differently? Why or why not? What actions or behaviors puzzle you?
   e. What experiences from your own life come to mind as you read this work? How are they similar to the events portrayed? How are they different? What feelings do you associate with the experiences? Are those feelings in any way represented in the work?
   f. What moved you in the work? How and why did it move you?
2. Write a personal response statement explaining what the work means to you.
3. In small discussion groups, if possible, share your personal response statement and your various reactions to the questions in item 1 above. Listen carefully to the reactions of your classmates and, if appropriate, contrast them with your own. Be open to changing your responses if you find other points of view convincing. Afterward, write freely about whether your ideas changed and why.

The model on page 309 shows how a typical student, who read the following two poems, used the Personal Response Strategies to write a personal response statement about the works.

Model: *Poems Selected for a Personal Response Statement*

The Explorer

Somehow to find a still spot in the noise
Was the frayed inner want, the winding, the frayed
  hope
Whose tatters he kept hunting through the din.
A satin peace somewhere.
A room of wily hush somewhere within.

So tipping down the scrambled halls he set
Vague hands on throbbing knobs. There were
  behind
Only spiraling, high human voices,
The scream of nervous affairs,
Wee griefs,
Grand griefs. And choices.
He feared most of all the choices, that cried to be
  taken.

There were no bourns.
There were no quiet rooms.

GWENDOLYN BROOKS

The Subway, George Tooker, 1950 Egg tempera on composition board, 18" x 36" (45.7 cm x 91.4 cm). Coll. of Whitney Museum of American Art. Juliana Force Purchase 50.23

The Road Not Taken

Two roads diverged in a yellow wood,
And sorry I could not travel both
And be one traveler, long I stood
And looked down one as far as I could
To where it bent in the undergrowth;

Then took the other, as just as fair,
And having perhaps the better claim,
Because it was grassy and wanted wear;
Though as for that, the passing there
Had worn them really about the same,

And both that morning equally lay
In leaves no step had trodden black.
Oh, I kept the first for another day!
Yet knowing how way leads on to way,
I doubted if I should ever come back.

I shall be telling this with a sigh
Somewhere ages and ages hence;
Two roads diverged in a wood, and I—
I took the one less traveled by.
And that has made all the difference.

ROBERT FROST

The Puddle, M. C. Escher

Student Model: *Personal Response Statement*

I had just read Gwendolyn Brook's poem "The Explorer" twice and felt really depressed and anxious. The poem makes life sound so scary and grim. After a while I read Robert Frost's "The Road Not Taken" and must admit I felt calmer, yet a bit let down. That poem makes life sound ho-hum and very business-like without any enthusiasm or fun. The traveler speaks as though all you have to do is "case" things and then make up your mind. Everything will work out. Then I decided to read both poems aloud. After that I had a few different feelings and thoughts.

I can't say I strongly prefer the Frost poem; it's just that I like its message better. The view of life and choice seems more helpful to anyone who's wondering what life's all about or needs direction.

Both poems talk about choices. As a sophomore in high school, I have a lot of choices I have to make soon. I must decide what college to go to--if I do go--and what to study. If I don't go to college, I have to decide what else to do with my life. Besides worrying about these practical matters, I guess I'm in the process of deciding just who I am. My choice of friends and my choice of clothes and pastimes tell who I am. I guess everything we do one way or another is a choice, which is a little scary to think of. However, I don't feel as fearful about the choices as the explorer does in the first poem. Still, I wish I knew as much about choice as the traveler in the Frost poem does. That person already knows the consequences of choice and isn't afraid to grab the one "less traveled by." This poem means more to me because I realize, too, that the choices I make now will have a lasting effect on my life. As I read it, I kept saying to myself, "Yeah, that's how it is!"

WRITING ACTIVITY ◆ 1 ◆ *Responding from Personal Experience*

Reread your work from Responding in Your Journal on page 301. Then complete the following activity in your journal and save it.

1. Read "Courage," by Anne Sexton, on pages 299–300. Then write freely about the poem, addressing the following questions.
   a. Did you like the poem? Why or why not?
   b. What in your own life comes to mind when you read this poem?

2. Write a personal response statement explaining what "Courage" means to you.

3. Read the poem "The Courage That My Mother Had," by Edna St. Vincent Millay, on page 300. Then write freely about the poem, addressing the following questions.
   a. Did you like the poem? Why or why not?
   b. Can you identify with the character in the poem? If so, how?
   c. Does the poem bring any personal experiences to mind? If so, what are they and how do you feel about them?

4. Write a personal response statement explaining what "The Courage That My Mother Had" means to you.

Responding from Literary Knowledge

Each story, poem, and novel that you have read has probably taught you something about literary traditions and literary elements—the parts and characteristics of a literary work. For example, when you were just a child and were read your first fairy tale, you probably were nervous about how it would come out in the end. Because you had never heard a fairy tale before, you had no way of knowing that the good characters in fairy tales always "live happily ever after." The more fairy tales you heard or read, the more you learned about that literary tradition, and the more you came to expect happy endings!

The same process has taken place over the years as you have read other types of literature, including poems, novels, and plays. You have learned more about what you can expect in the various genres of literature and how literary elements work.

The chart on the next page shows the main elements of fiction, poetry, and drama. The elements listed under drama show only the features that differ from those of other kinds of fiction.

Elements of Literature

FICTION

PLOT—events that lead up to a *climax*, or high point, and either resolve a central struggle called the *conflict* or explain the outcome
SETTING—when and where the story takes place
MOOD—prevalent feeling or atmosphere in the work
CHARACTERS—people in the story whose thoughts and actions advance the story
DIALOGUE—conversations among characters that reveal personalities, actions, and motivations
TONE—the writer's attitude toward his or her characters
POINT OF VIEW—the "voice" telling the story—*first person (I)* or *third person (he* or *she)*
THEME—the main idea or message of the story

POETRY

PERSONA—the person whose "voice" is saying the poem
METER—the pattern of stressed and unstressed syllables in each line of the poem
RHYME SCHEME—the pattern of rhymed sounds in the poem or at the ends of lines
SOUND DEVICES—ways to use sounds to create certain effects and images, such as *alliteration* and *onomatopoeia*
FIGURES OF SPEECH—imaginative language, such as *similes* and *metaphors (See page 55.)*
IMAGERY—the descriptive or figurative language that creates word pictures, or images, for the reader
THEME—the underlying meaning of the poem

DRAMA

SETTING—time of action, lighting, costumes, and stage sets described by the stage directions
CHARACTERS—the people of the action played by a cast of actors and actresses whose appearances are described by the stage directions
PLOT—the story of the play—which is divided into acts and scenes and developed only through the characters' action and dialogue
THEME—the meaning of a play revealed only through the characters' words and actions

How Literary Elements Contribute to Meaning The elements of each genre of literature contribute to the meaning of a work. In poetry, for example, a poet may use figurative language, sound devices, meter, and sometimes rhyme. On the other hand, a poet may use *free verse*—which has no regular meter or rhyme—to reveal his or her message to readers. One strategy you can use to find meaning in a work of literature, therefore, is to analyze how the author has used such elements in the creation of the work. The following charts list questions you can ask yourself as you explore the meaning of a short story, a novel, a poem, and a play.

Questions for Finding Meaning in Fiction

PLOT

1. How does each event in the plot affect the characters?
2. What do details in the plot reveal about the central conflict?
3. What do the climax and the ending reveal about the theme?

SETTING

4. How does the setting contribute to the tone or mood of the story? How do details of the setting help define the characters?
5. Which details of the setting are most important in the development of the plot?

CHARACTERS

6. How do the characters respond to their setting?
7. How does each character contribute to the development of the plot? Who or what does each character represent? How do the details of characterization reveal personalities?
8. What does the dialogue reveal about the characters' personalities and motivations? How does the point of view of the story affect the characterization?

THEME

9. What passages and details in the story best express the main theme? Are there other recurring ideas that contribute to the meaning?
10. How effectively does the author communicate the theme through the development of setting, characters, and plot? How does this theme have meaning for me? What else have I read that has the same or a similar theme?

Questions for Finding Meaning in a Poem

1. Who is the poet's persona? How does the persona relate to the subject, mood, and theme of the poem?
2. How does the meter affect the rhythm of the poem? How does that rhythm express the mood?
3. How does the rhyme scheme, if any, affect the expression of thoughts and feelings?
4. What sounds do alliteration and onomatopoeia create? What images do those sound devices suggest?
5. What images do figures of speech create? What feelings do those images suggest?
6. How does the shape of the poem relate to the subject, mood, or theme?
7. What feeling, theme, or message does the poem express?
8. What meaning does the poem have for me?

L.A. County Museum of Art, *Photo-Transformation*, 11/1/73, Lucas Samaras
United States, b. Greece 1936–. Ralph M. Parsons Fund

Questions for Finding Meaning in a Play

1. What details of setting and character do the stage directions emphasize? How do those details contribute to the meaning?
2. What are the key relationships among the characters? How do those relationships reveal the central conflict? What changes in the relationships help resolve the conflict?
3. How does the dialogue alone advance the plot? What developments in the plot occur with each change of act and scene?
4. What is the subject and theme of the play? What meaning does the play have for me?

WRITING ACTIVITY 2 *Responding from Literary Knowledge*

Reread "Courage" and "The Courage That My Mother Had" on pages 299–300. Then complete these activities in your journal.

1. Who is the persona in "Courage"? To whom is he or she talking? What can you infer about the kind of life the persona has led?
2. What figures of speech does the poet use in "Courage"? What do they add to the poem?
3. What effect does the repeated line "Later" have on the feeling and meaning of the poem?
4. What, do you think, is being said about life in this poem? In other words, what is the theme of the poem?
5. Who is the persona in "The Courage That My Mother Had"? How is this persona like or unlike the persona in "Courage"?
6. Identify the rhyme scheme of "The Courage That My Mother Had" by noting the final sound in each line. How does the rhyme scheme affect the feeling of the poem?
7. Around what metaphor is "The Courage That My Mother Had" built? Do you feel it is a convincing metaphor? Why or why not?
8. What is the theme of "The Courage That My Mother Had"? How is it like or unlike the theme of "Courage"?

Evaluating a Work of Literature Analyzing the elements in literature helps you make judgments about the work. However, your personal judgment and the judgment of others may not agree. Following are some of the criteria by which great literature is judged.

Some Characteristics of Great Literature

1. Explores great themes in human nature and the human experience that many people can identify with—such as growing up, family life, love, the courageous individual's struggle against oppression, and war.
2. Expresses universal meanings—such as truth or hope—that people from many different backgrounds and cultures can appreciate.
3. Conveys a timeless message that remains true for many generations of readers.
4. Creates vivid impressions of characters and settings that many generations of readers can treasure.

The literary work you are reading may or may not meet the criteria for great literature, but you can still apply other standards of evaluation. When you are making judgments about a work, ask yourself the following questions.

Questions for Evaluating Literature

1. How original and inventive is the work?
2. How effectively does the writing achieve the purpose?
3. How vividly and believably are the characters, settings, dialogue, actions, and feelings portrayed? In fiction and drama, how well structured is the plot? Does it have a satisfying resolution of the central conflict?
4. How strongly did I react to the work? Did I identify with a character, situation, or feeling? Did the work stir my memories and emotions?
5. Does the message of the work have meaning for me? Will I remember anything about it a year from now?

WRITING ACTIVITY 3 *Evaluating Literature*

In your journal write an evaluation of the poems "Courage" and "The Courage That My Mother Had" by applying the above criteria for great literature and by answering the previous Questions for Evaluating Literature.

Choosing a Subject

The prewriting work you have completed so far has helped you explore your responses—both personal and literary—to the work or works you are reading. You can now use these responses to help you focus on a subject for your critical essay.

Although your teacher may assign you a subject, most often he or she will expect you to think of your own. The following questions will help you think of subjects that are personally important to you and appropriate for a critical essay.

Questions for Choosing a Subject

1. What parts of the work puzzle me? What would I like to understand better?
2. What parts of the work move me especially? Why do they have that effect on me?
3. What images or details made a strong impression on me? What do they contribute to the overall work?
4. With which character do I identify and why?
5. What message does the work convey to me? What new insight or understanding have I gained from this work?
6. How do the characters in the work differ? What motivates each one?
7. Are there elements of humor in the work that I can relate to? What are they?
8. What other works am I reading (or have I read) that are similar to this work? What elements of these works might I compare in some meaningful way? *(See page 311.)*

For subjects you might like to develop further, search through all the responses to literature that you have recorded thus far in your journal and that you might have saved in your writing folder from previous chapters. See if any ideas come up repeatedly. If they do, these ideas undoubtedly intrigue you in some way. Developing a critical essay around such intriguing ideas would probably be a very satisfying writing challenge.

Before you choose a subject for a critical essay, be sure to consider your audience. In this chapter you usually will be writing for your teacher and classmates. Therefore, you can assume that your audience is familiar with the literature you are analyzing.

Writing Is Thinking

Critical Thinking

Synthesizing

When choosing a subject for your critical essay on literature, remember that while your subject should reflect your personal response to the literary work, it cannot ignore the literary elements in the work. By using a critical thinking process called *synthesizing,* which means "combining or bringing together," you can include both responses in your subject.

Suppose you have decided to write about the two poems, "The Explorer" and "The Road Not Taken," on pages 307 and 308. Make a chart like the one below to track your personal responses to both poems. Then look for a focus. In the chart below, the idea of *choices* clearly intrigues the reader.

Now you must *synthesize* your personal responses with a literary element. You may decide on the element of *theme,* since the theme of both poems deals with choices. Then take brief notes on the right side of the chart about the theme of each poem.

Personal Response	Literary Element
Choices are so important in life. Can be scary. Career? Friends? My future life? I'm not as afraid as the explorer. I'm more like the person in "Road." I know that my choices, like college, could lead to lots of other choices. Some I might regret later.	*Theme of "Explorer":* Life is a journey with choices that bring conflict, depriving us of peace and quiet. *Theme of "Road":* We stumble upon choices, try to see consequences, but can see only so far. We must make the choice, or never know how it might have been.

SYNTHESIS: The subject is the theme of choice in two modern poems.

Thinking Practice In your journal make a chart like the one above to combine your personal responses with the literary elements of the poems "Courage" and "The Courage That My Mother Had."

WRITING ACTIVITY 4 *Choosing Subjects*

Review the Elements of Poetry on page 311. Then, for each of the following literary elements, think of a possible subject for a critical essay on "The Explorer," "The Road Not Taken," or both poems.

EXAMPLE persona

POSSIBLE ANSWER how the character in "The Explorer" differs from the persona in "The Road Not Taken"

1. figures of speech
2. rhyme and meter
3. theme
4. imagery

WRITING ACTIVITY 5 *Writing on Your Own*

WRITING ABOUT THE THEME

For your critical essay, you will be writing a comparison/contrast on "Courage"and "The Courage That My Mother Had." It is up to you, however, to find the focus for this comparison/contrast. For example, you may choose to compare and contrast an element of both poems—such as the persona of each poem, the treatment of theme, or the use of figurative language. Review your personal and literary responses to the poems that you recorded in your journal and synthesize your responses to identify which element of the two poems interests you the most. Then write your subject on a piece of paper and save it in your writing folder for later use.

Limiting a Subject

Before you have thought of a subject for your critical essay, you may sometimes feel as if you have nothing at all to say about a work of literature. Once you have focused on a subject, however, ideas often begin to flood your mind. To be sure your main idea does not drown in the flood, take the time to limit your subject appropriately.

One good way to limit your subject is to try to express it in a phrase instead of a single word. To develop a single-word subject into a phrase-length subject, ask yourself, "What do I plan to say about my subject?" When you can express the answer to that question in a phrase, you probably have a suitably limited subject.

If you were writing about "The Explorer" and "The Road Not Taken," you might go through the following thought process.

TOO GENERAL	theme
ASK YOURSELF	What do I plan to say about the theme?
POSSIBLE ANSWER	In both poems the theme has to do with choice, but the poems seem to have a different attitude toward choice.
SUITABLY LIMITED	the differing attitudes toward choice in the two poems

WRITING ACTIVITY 6 *Limiting Subjects for a Critical Essay*

Each of the following subjects is too unfocused for a brief critical essay comparing and contrasting "The Explorer" and "The Road Not Taken." Write a suitably limited subject for each one.

EXAMPLE	choice
POSSIBLE ANSWER	differing attitudes toward choice

1. regret
2. fear
3. peacefulness versus chaos
4. hope
5. views of life

WRITING ACTIVITY 7 *Writing on Your Own*

WRITING ABOUT THE THEME

Review the subject you chose for your critical essay in Writing Activity 5. Ask yourself, "What do I want to say about my subject?" until you have a clearly focused phrase. Then save your limited subject in your writing folder for later use.

Developing Your Thesis

Every good critical essay has a thesis at its core. This thesis, or proposition, is the main point the writer is making about some part of a literary work. Since interpretations of literary works do differ from one reader to another, your task in a critical essay is to convince your audience that your thesis is valid and that your interpretation makes good sense based on the evidence you have found in the work to support that thesis. The foundation of a critical essay is, therefore, a soundly reasoned thesis.

As you have been limiting your subject, you have also been slowly homing in on your thesis. In fact, your limited subject is just a step away from your thesis statement. To develop your limited subject into a clear thesis statement, you simply have to express your main idea in a complete sentence, instead of in a phrase.

In the following example about "The Explorer" and "The Road Not Taken," the thesis statement makes a definite proposition that was only hinted at in the limited subject.

FOCUSED, LIMITED SUBJECT	the differing attitudes toward choice in the two poems
THESIS STATEMENT, OR PROPOSITION	"The Explorer" presents a fearful attitude toward choice, while "The Road Not Taken" presents a calmer, more resigned attitude toward choice.

To convert your limited subject into a clear thesis statement, you can repeat the technique of asking yourself, "What *exactly* do I want to say about my subject?" The thesis statement at this stage should be precise enough to guide you through the rest of your planning. However, you should regard it as a working thesis statement only. As a result, you can change or adjust it as you continue to develop your essay.

WRITING ACTIVITY 8 *Writing on Your Own*

WRITING ABOUT THE THEME

Review your focused, limited subject from Writing Activity 7. If you are satisfied that your limited subject homes in on your thesis, you are ready to proceed. To develop your working thesis statement, cast your limited subject in the form of a complete sentence and write it on your paper. Keep in mind that you can change or adjust it as needed. Then save your work in your writing folder.

Gathering Evidence

What happens when you read a poem or some other work of literature? If you are like most readers, you probably pay little conscious attention to such elements as character, theme, imagery, style, or form. Instead, you probably lose yourself in the work and let it speak to you on an emotional level.

Nonetheless, even though you may not be aware of it, the only way a work can succeed in moving you is through the details it uses. These details form an overall impression, touching off memories and surges of emotion. This overall impression helps you formulate your ideas about a literary work and express them in a thesis statement.

Once you have a clear thesis statement, however, you can go back over the work and take a closer, more conscious look at what exactly in the poem or story created the overall impression. Ask yourself, "Why did the work make me feel this way?" and then review the work to find the quotations and details to back up what you want to say about your feelings and reactions. For example, the student who wrote the personal response on page 309 to "The Explorer" and "The Road Not Taken" decided to write about the different attitudes toward choice in the two poems and looked for all the references to choice in each work. The student also looked for ways in which the other elements of the poems reinforce the attitudes toward choice. Below is a summary of the basic steps to follow when you are gathering evidence for a critical essay on a literary work.

Gathering Supporting Details for a Critical Essay

1. As you scan the work, look for quotations and other details that support your interpretation.
2. Write each detail on a note card or piece of paper. If it is a quotation, indicate who said it and write the page number on which it appears. If it is a quotation from a poem, write the number of the line from which it comes.
3. Tell how a particular detail supports your interpretation.
4. Use a separate card or piece of paper for each detail.

The model cards on the following pages show how one writer gathered evidence to support the thesis that "The Explorer" and "The Road Not Taken" express sharply contrasting views toward choice.

Student Model: *Notes for "The Road Not Taken"*

Text Portion

Two roads diverged in a yellow wood,
And sorry I could not travel both
And be one traveler, long I stood
And looked down one as far as I could
To where it bent in the undergrowth;

Note Cards

1. Seems to welcome choices only wishes he could take both roads and still "be one traveler." "Looks down road, thinks through consequences of choices.

Then took the other, as just as fair,
And having perhaps the better claim,
Because it was grassy and wanted wear;
Though as for that, the passing there
Had worn them really about the same,

2. 2nd stanza confusing. Says one road is "just as fair" but then they're "really about the same." Suggests how hard choice is.

And both that morning equally lay
In leaves no step had trodden black.
Oh, I kept the first for another day!
Yet knowing how way leads on to way,

3. Sigh "Oh" in line 13 is important — suggests traveler feels regret at not traveling both roads. Lines 14-15 accept that "way leads on to way."

I doubted if I should ever come back.
I shall be telling this with a sigh
Somewhere ages and ages hence;
Two roads diverged in a woods, and I—
I took the one less traveled by.
And that has made all the difference.

4. Last stanza mentions sigh. Dash at end of line 18 suggests another sigh — more regret. Yet he expects to tell his story someday.

Student Model: *Notes for "The Explorer"*

Text Portion

Somehow to fill a still spot in the noise

Was the frayed inner want, the winding, the frayed hope
Whose tatters he kept hunting through the din.
A satin peace somewhere.
A room of wily hush somewhere within.

So tipping down the scrambled halls he set
Vague hands on throbbing knobs.
There were behind
Only spiraling, high human voices,
The scream of nervous affairs,
Wee griefs,
Grand griefs. And choices.

He feared most of all the choices, that cried to be taken.

There were no bourns.
There were no quiet rooms.

Note Cards

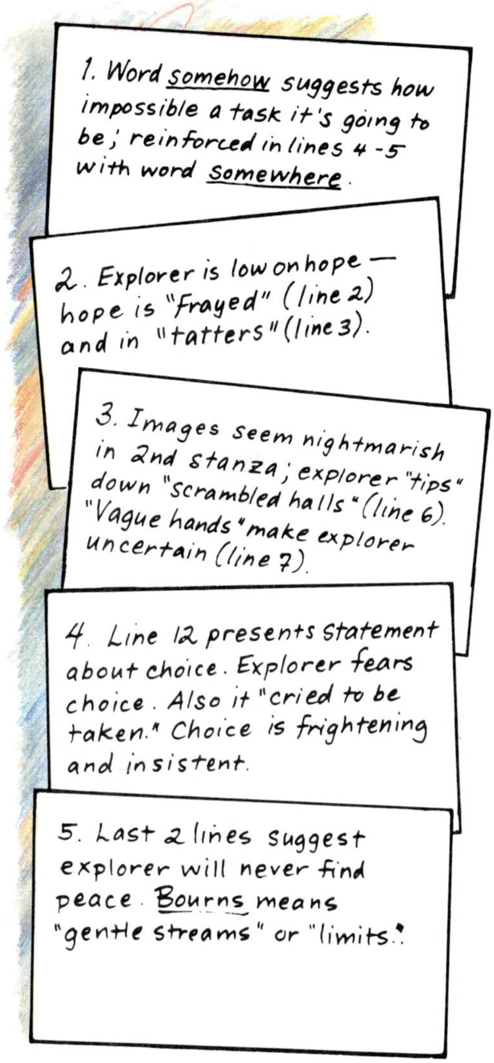

WRITING ACTIVITY 9 *Writing on Your Own*

WRITING ABOUT THE THEME

Gather evidence to support your thesis by skimming the poems "Courage" and "The Courage That My Mother Had." On separate paper or note cards, jot down each supporting detail you find and write a brief note explaining the significance of that detail. Save your work in your writing folder for later use.

Organizing Supporting Details

When gathering your evidence, you probably will jot down supporting details in the order in which they appeared in the literary work. In most cases you may wish to keep your evidence in that order when writing your paper. For example, when writing about a single poem, you may wish to present your evidence line by line. If you are showing how a character changed over time, following the chronology of the story would be the best way to show the changes.

On the other hand, if you give reasons why a character behaves in a certain way, using cause and effect or order of importance would be a more effective way to organize your details. With some other subjects you might have to use comparison and contrast—one of the best ways to support an interpretation of two works. In all cases you need to reorder your supporting details so that they are arranged in the most effective way possible to support your thesis.

Comparison and Contrast A common type of critical essay is one that discusses the similarities and differences between two works of literature. In this type of essay, comparison and contrast is the most appropriate way to organize your supporting evidence. *(See pages 213–215 for more information about organizing an essay of comparison and contrast.)*

You can organize details in a comparison and contrast essay in two different ways. To understand how these methods work, assume that you are comparing and contrasting "The Explorer" and "The Road Not Taken." The first pattern of organization is called *AABB.* In this pattern you would make all your points about "The Explorer" (poem *A*). Then you would make all your points about "The Road Not Taken" (poem *B*). As you discuss the second work, you would explain how it is similar to and different from the first work. Such an approach is called "whole by whole" because you examine the whole of one work before moving on to the other work.

Another way to organize comparison and contrast is called *ABAB,* or "point by point." In this pattern, you make one point about both literary works. This point could be either a similarity or a difference. For instance, you might discuss how the tone of "The Explorer" (poem *A*) is similar to or different from that of "The Road Not Taken" (poem *B*). Then you move on to make another point about the two poems. You might compare and contrast the imagery in the two poems, for example.

Outlining Once you organize your details, write an outline to guide you as you draft. The outline below shows the plan one writer used for a critical essay about "The Explorer" and "The Road Not Taken."

Model: *Outline for a Critical Essay (AABB Pattern)*

Introduction: includes thesis statement as well as points of similarity and difference between two poems

Body

I. "The Explorer" shows hopeless feelings about choice.
   - A. line 1: *somehow* = impossible task
   - B. lines 2–3: "frayed inner want" and "frayed hope in tatters" = hopelessness
   - C. line 5: *somewhere* = impossible place

II. "The Explorer" shows fearfulness about choice.
   - A. lines 6–7: "scrambled halls" and "vague hands on throbbing knobs" = desperation
   - B. line 12: "choices . . . cried to be taken" = fear

III. "The Road Not Taken" shows acceptance of difficulties of choice.
   - A. line 2–3: "travel both and be one traveler" = wants both choices
   - B. line 4: "looked down as far as I could" = thinks about choices

IV. "The Road Not Taken" shows awareness of choice and need for action.
   - A. line 6: "as just as fair" = options are very similar
   - B. line 8: "it was grassy and wanted wear" = second choice is less traveled

V. "The Road Not Taken" shows acceptance of all the consequences of choice.
   - A. line 14: "how way leads on to way, I doubted if I should ever come back"
   - B. line 16: "telling this with a sigh" = regret and resignation

Conclusion: ties both poems together, emphasizing differences in their attitude toward choice

WRITING ACTIVITY 10 *Writing on Your Own*

WRITING ABOUT THE THEME

Review your work from Writing Activity 9. After deciding on an *AABB* or an *ABAB* order for your supporting details, create an outline showing a plan for your critical essay. Save your work.

Writing Process

Drafting

Your outline will prove to be a valuable guide as you draft your critical essay. The following suggestions may also help.

Guidelines for Drafting a Critical Essay

1. Use present tense verbs throughout your essay.
2. In the introduction be sure to identify the author and the title of the work you are discussing.
3. Include your thesis statement somewhere in the introduction. Refine it as needed and work it in as smoothly as possible.
4. In the body of your essay, include your clearly organized supporting details, using transitions to show how one detail relates to another. Throughout your essay use direct quotes from the work if they strengthen the points you are trying to make. (Always enclose direct quotes in quotation marks.)
5. In the conclusion draw together the details you have included to reinforce the main idea of your essay. Then add a title that suggests the focus of your essay.

Writing Direct Quotations The best supporting evidence for a critical essay about literature comes from the work itself. You should plan to have your essay full of references to the literature, with plenty of quotations. To give strong support to your thesis statement, however, be sure your quotations make a strong point rather than just fill space.

Since quotations are so important in an essay analyzing literature, learn to punctuate them correctly. The examples below show how quotations in different positions in a sentence are punctuated. Notice that quotations in the middle of a sentence, for example, are not usually capitalized.

BEGINS SENTENCE	"Two roads diverged in a yellow wood," observes the persona in Robert Frost's poem.
INTERRUPTS SENTENCE	Since one road in the Frost poem is "just as fair" and worn "really about the same," the persona suggests that the options for choice are not that different.

If you need to show that words have been left out of a quotation, use an *ellipsis*—a series of three dots—for the missing words. *(For more information about punctuating quotations, see pages 796–804.)*

ELLIPSES "Oh . . . I doubted if I should ever come back."

If the quotation is two lines or longer, set it off by itself without quotation marks. Indent it and leave space above and below.

EXAMPLE The persona in "The Road Not Taken" shows resignation and perhaps regret in the final stanza.

> I shall be telling this with a sigh
> Somewhere ages and ages hence;
> Two roads diverged in a wood, and I—
> I took the one less traveled by,
> And that has made all the difference.

The model critical essay on the following pages, which has already been revised and edited, will give you an idea of how to create a convincing presentation of your interpretation. Notice that this essay of comparison and contrast uses the *AABB* pattern of organization.

Student Model: *A Critical Essay*

Choice in "The Explorer" and "The Road Not Taken"

INTRODUCTION: PRESENTS POINTS OF SIMILARITIES BETWEEN BOTH POEMS

"The Explorer," by Gwendolyn Brooks, and "The Road Not Taken," by Robert Frost are both poems that express the confusion people often face when confronted with choice. Both poems focus on a person traveling through life. One is searching for peace and quiet, and the other for all the richness that life can offer. Both poems also suggest that what the travelers seek can never be found. Despite these similarities the two poems are starkly different in their attitude toward choice. "The Explorer" represents a fearful, desperate attitude, while "The Road Not Taken" presents a calmer, more resigned attitude toward choice and its consequences.

THESIS STATEMENT

MAIN TOPIC I FROM OUTLINE: (POEM *A*)

From the very first word in "The Explorer," the reader senses that hopelessness and fear lie ahead. The word *somehow* suggests a virtually impossible task, just as *somewhere*, repeated in lines 4 and 5, suggests an impossible place. The explorer's hope for a quiet spot amid the noise and chaos of life is far from strong. In fact, it has worn so thin that it is "frayed" and in "tatters."

MAIN TOPIC II FROM OUTLINE: (POEM *A*)

The desperation increases in the second stanza of the poem. In lines 6 and 7, for example, the explorer unsteadily tips down "scrambled halls" as if in a nightmare of tilted, frightening reality. His "vague hands" make him seem almost random in his efforts to find his way through the chaos. At each turn he finds only more of the same: "high human voices, wee griefs, grand griefs, and choices." In line 12 the poem makes its strongest, clearest point about choice; the explorer fears the choices. The choices do not beckon temptingly; instead, they "cried to be taken." To the explorer any choice would be painful, since it would lead again only to grief, "wee or grand." No matter how hard he searches or what choices he makes, the explorer will not find his peace. This fact is clearly stated in the final lines of the poem.

MAIN TOPIC III FROM OUTLINE: (POEM *B*)

In sharp contrast to "The Explorer," Robert Frost's famous poem presents a calm, accepting attitude toward the choices life offers. The persona in "The Road Not Taken" does not fear each choice before him; instead, he wishes he could take both roads and still "be one traveler." He thinks long and hard about which road to take, trying to follow each as far as his eye will take him. He acts like many people who, before they act, think through all the consequences of a choice they have to make.

MAIN TOPIC IV FROM OUTLINE: (POEM *B*)

The second and third stanzas raise a question familiar to anyone who has ever faced a choice. How different, really, are the options? The poem never clearly resolves this question. First the traveler says the second road is "just as fair." Then he suggests in lines 7–8 that the second road is less traveled; "it was grassy and wanted wear." Just as quickly he turns around and admits in lines 9–11 that the two roads are "really about the same" and "both that morning equally lay." The traveler's inability to tell for sure how different the roads are reinforces the theme of the poem. Unless one actually makes a choice and follows it through, one can never know for sure how the choice would have come out.

MAIN TOPIC V FROM OUTLINE: (POEM *B*)

As stanza three continues, the traveler makes his choice but also recognizes that he will probably never come back to try the other road. He knows—and seems to accept—"how way leads on to way." Frost's language and style suggest regret but resignation. The sigh "Oh" at the beginning of line 13 is the first of several to come. Indeed, the word *sigh* appears in the first line of stanza four, and the dash at the end of line 18 signals another sigh. All the sighs add up to a sense of resigned regret.

CONCLUSION: TIES BOTH POEMS TOGETHER AND CONTRASTS THE TRAVELERS' ATTITUDES TOWARD CHOICE

How different, though, is the traveler's sigh in "The Road Not Taken" from the explorer's fear and misery in the poem by Gwendolyn Brooks. In "The Road Not Taken," the persona realizes that little by little through the choices he makes, he gradually limits his options and defines his life in narrower terms. Although he accepts this inevitability, he regrets that he cannot follow several different choices at once. The traveler in "The Road Not Taken" is left at least with the mixed pleasure and regret of telling his tale "ages and ages hence." The explorer, in contrast, is left with nothing—neither "bourns" nor "quiet rooms," where a weary wanderer could tell his tale.

WRITING ACTIVITY 11 *Writing on Your Own*

WRITING ABOUT THE THEME

Using the guidelines on page 326 and your work from Writing Activity 10, write a first draft of your critical essay on "Courage" and "The Courage That My Mother Had." To keep your ideas on track, stop occasionally and read over what you have written. Save your draft in your writing folder for later use.

Writing Process

Revising

When you are reasonably satisfied with your first draft, you may want to share your essay with a peer reader to find out whether or not your points are clearly expressed. Then, using your partner's comments and the following checklist, you can revise your work.

Revision Checklist

CHECKING YOUR ESSAY

1. Does you have a strong introduction that identifies the author and work you will discuss? *(See page 303.)*
2. Does your introduction contain a clearly worded thesis statement? *(See page 303.)*
3. Does the body of your essay provide ample details from the work to support your thesis well? *(See pages 320–323.)*
4. Did you use quotes from the work to strengthen your points? *(See page 303.)*
5. Does your conclusion summarize the details in the body of your essay and reinforce your thesis statement? *(See page 303.)*
6. Does your whole essay have unity and coherence? *(See pages 185–186.)*
7. Did you add a title showing the focus of your essay?

CHECKING YOUR PARAGRAPHS

8. Does each paragraph have a topic sentence? *(See page 89.)*
9. Is each paragraph unified and coherent? *(See pages 116–118.)*

CHECKING YOUR SENTENCES AND WORDS

10. Are your sentences varied and concise? *(See pages 58–69.)*
11. Did you use lively, specific words? *(See pages 53–54.)*

WRITING ACTIVITY 12 *Writing on Your Own*

WRITING ABOUT THE THEME

If your teacher permits, exchange your critical essay with a partner. Comment on the strengths and weaknesses of your partner's paper. Then keep your partner's comments in mind as you use the Revision Checklist above to improve your draft. Save your work for later use.

Integrating Language Skills

Editing and Publishing

Grammar in the Writing Process

In the poem "Courage," Anne Sexton writes that if sorrow is powdered, given a back rub, and has had time to sleep, it will wake up to the wings of the roses and be transformed. Like sorrow your writing can be "transformed," or changed, once you know and understand clauses. An *independent clause* can stand alone as a sentence, but a *subordinate clause* cannot stand alone as a sentence. It must be attached to an independent clause. In addition to adding information to sentences, subordinate clauses also can transform your writing if you use them to combine short choppy sentences into smooth-flowing, mature sentences.

Adverb Clauses An *adverb clause* is a subordinate clause used as an adverb to describe mainly a verb. Adverb clauses add information to sentences by answering questions such as *Where? When? How?* and *Why?* An adverb clause at the beginning of a sentence also provides sentence variety.

The following examples are about "The Pedestrian," the story on pages 339–344 about which you will soon write a critical essay. *(For more examples of adverb clauses and for practice in using them correctly, see pages 627–629.)*

WHY? **If he wore hard heels,** the dogs would bark.

WHEN? He paused but went on **when nothing happened.**

Adjective Clauses An *adjective clause* is a subordinate clause that is used as an adjective to describe a noun or a pronoun. Adjective clauses add information to sentences by answering questions such as *Which one? What kind?* and *How many?* *(For more examples of adjective clauses and for practice in using them correctly, see pages 630–633.)*

WHICH ONE? Along the street they passed one house **that was brightly lit.**

WHAT KIND? He peered into the back seat, **which was a little black cell with bars.**

Punctuation with Clauses Place a comma after an introductory adverb clause—like the first example on the previous page. Also use commas to set off a nonessential adjective clause from the rest of the sentence. A *nonessential adjective clause* could be removed from the sentence without changing its meaning. *(For more information about punctuating nonessential adjective clauses, see pages 633 and 786–790.)*

NONESSENTIAL CLAUSE The cloverleaf, **where two main highways crossed the town,** stood silent. [The nonessential clause could be removed: *The cloverleaf stood silent.*]

Combining Sentences with Clauses Once you understand clauses and how they work in a sentence, you can use them to improve your writing style. When revising or editing, you can show the relationship between two short sentences by combining them into one sentence. *(For other examples of sentences combined with clauses and practice in combining sentences, see pages 64–68 and 640–641.)*

TWO SENTENCES He passed the car. He looked inside.
COMBINED **As he passed the car,** he looked inside.
TWO SENTENCES The cell smelled of antiseptic. It was hard.
COMBINED The cell, **which smelled of antiseptic,** was hard.

Editing Checklist

1. Have subordinate clauses been used to incorporate additional information and add sentence variety? *(See pages 627–633.)*
2. Are all clauses punctuated correctly? *(See pages 779 and 786.)*
3. Could subordinate clauses be used to combine any sentences? *(See pages 66 and 640–641.)*

WRITING ACTIVITY 13 *Writing on Your Own*

WRITING ABOUT THE THEME **Editing** Use the checklist above and the Editing Checklist on page 35 to edit your critical essay. Pay special attention to the punctuation of quotations.

Publishing Enter your essay in a literary contest. Write to the National Council of Teachers of English, 1111 Kenyon Road, Urbana, IL 61801, for information.

A Writer Writes

WRITING ABOUT THE THEME

A Critical Essay

PURPOSE: to explain your understanding of "The Pedestrian," by Ray Bradbury

AUDIENCE: your teacher and classmates

Prewriting In your reading about all the stages of history, you will find accounts of many courageous men and women. Will the future produce courageous people like the past did? In the story "The Pedestrian," you will travel into the future—into the year 2053 to be exact—and meet just one man with some old-fashioned courage.

After you read "The Pedestrian" on pages 339–344, record your personal reactions to it in your journal—as well as your reaction to author Ray Bradbury's treatment of courage. Use the elements of fiction in the chart on page 311 as the basis for exploring your literary responses. Consider, for example, discussing setting, character, or theme. Then, after synthesizing your personal and literary responses, choose a subject and narrow it, if necessary. After writing your thesis statement, gather evidence to support it. *(See Gathering Supporting Details for a Critical Essay on page 321.)* After you arrange your facts into a logical order, prepare a simple outline.

Drafting Using your outline as a guide, draft your critical essay. As you write, you also may find it helpful to refer to the Checklist for Writing Essays about Literature on page 337.

Revising: Peer Conferencing With your teacher's permission, exchange papers with a partner and share one another's responses to the story, commenting on both the strengths and weaknesses of your partner's paper. Pay special attention to how effectively the supporting details strengthen the ideas in the thesis statement. After your discussion make any changes to your essay that you think are appropriate. Then, when you are finished, use your partner's comments and the Revision Checklist on page 331 to revise your essay.

Editing and Publishing Use the checklists on pages 35 and 333 as a guide to editing your critical essay. Also make sure that you have consistently used the present tense throughout your essay and check for the correct punctuation of quotations. When you are pleased with your essay, write a neat final copy. Then give your essay to an interested reader who is familiar with the selection.

Independent Writing

Write a critical essay on the poem on the next page, "The Coach of Life" by Alexander Pushkin, one of Russia's greatest poets. After you read it, write down your personal and literary responses. For example, why, do you think, did Pushkin use a coach to symbolize life? Then follow the Checklist for Writing Essays about Literature on page 337.

The Coach of Life

Though often somewhat heavy-freighted,
The coach rolls at an easy pace;
And Time, the coachman, grizzly-pated,
But smart, alert—is in his place.

We board it lightly in the morning
And on our way at once proceed.
Repose and slothful comfort scorning,
We shout: "Hey, there! Get on! Full speed!"

Noon finds us done with reckless daring,
And shaken up. Now care's the rule.
Down hills, through gulleys roughly faring,
We sulk, and cry: "Hey, easy fool!"

The coach rolls on, no pitfalls dodging.
At dusk, to pains more wonted grown,
We drowse, while to the night's dark lodging
Old coachman Time drives on, drives on.

ALEXANDER PUSHKIN

Creative Writing

Write a two- or three-stanza poem about courage that follows the rhyme scheme of *abab*, like the poem above. You may, for example, want to write about a courageous act that you personally know about or have read about.

Writing about Literature

Free verse is poetry that has no rhyme scheme, meter, stanza form, or line length. The language in free verse, however, is usually more rhythmic than ordinary language. Reread aloud "Courage," by Anne Sexton, on page 299, a poem written in free verse. Then rewrite in free verse "The Courage That My Mother Had," by Edna St. Vincent Millay, on page 300.

Writing in Another Subject Area

World History Choose a novel or short story about a period and place you have studied, such as Charles Dickens's novel *A Tale of Two Cities* about the French Revolution. Write a critical essay analyzing the work as a mirror of the people, time, and place it is about.

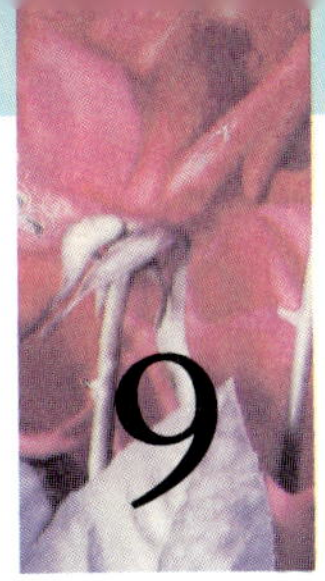

Chapter 9 Checklist

Writing Essays about Literature

Prewriting

- ✓ Read the work carefully and respond to it from both your personal experience and your literary knowledge. *(See pages 304–315.)*
- ✓ By synthesizing your personal and literary responses, choose and limit a subject for your essay. *(See pages 316–319.)*
- ✓ Shape your limited subject into a working thesis statement that will guide you as you write. *(See page 320.)*
- ✓ Skim the work again, looking for details from it that will support your thesis statement. On a note card or separate paper, jot down each detail with a page reference after it. If you are writing about poetry, cite the number of the line of the poem. *(See pages 321–323.)*
- ✓ Organize your supporting details into an informal outline. *(See pages 324–325.)*

Drafting

- ✓ Use the guidelines on page 326 to help you draft your critical essay.

Revising

- ✓ Use the Revision Checklist to help you make a thorough revision of your essay. *(See page 331.)*

Editing and Publishing

- ✓ Use the Editing Checklist to check your grammar, spelling, usage, and mechanics. *(See page 35.)*
- ✓ Pay special attention to the punctuation of direct quotations. *(See pages 326–327.)*
- ✓ Prepare a neat final copy of your work and present it to an interested reader in an appropriate way. *(See pages 40–41.)*

Chapter 10 Writing Research Papers

Part 1 Reading to Write

THEME: *Freedom*

It is a fact of life that you tend to forget about or at best take for granted a privilege you have had all the time, particularly if you have not had to earn it. Unfortunately, because you live in the United States, you may tend to take your freedom for granted. It is quite possible that you do not even know how much freedom you actually have. Can you, for example, tell what ten freedoms citizens are guaranteed by the Bill of Rights? In fact, can you even define *freedom*?

The *American Heritage Dictionary* says freedom is "the condition of being free of restraints." It is "liberty of a person from slavery, oppression, or incarceration" and "immunity from the arbitrary exercise of authority." It is also "the capacity to exercise choice" and the "ease and facility of movement."

In the following story, "The Pedestrian," there is no "ease and facility of movement." In fact, taking a simple walk outside at night is forbidden. This story, by science-fiction writer Ray Bradbury, takes place in the United States in the year 2053 A.D. At that time people no longer take their freedom for granted—because there no longer is any freedom. Could this actually happen here in the land of the free? Answer that question as you read the story.

The Pedestrian

Ray Bradbury

To enter out into that silence that was the city at eight o'clock of a misty evening in November, to put your feet upon that buckling concrete walk, to step over grassy seams and make your way, hands in pockets, through the silences, that was what Mr. Leonard Mead most dearly loved to do. He would stand upon the corner of an intersection and peer down long moonlit avenues of sidewalk in four directions, deciding which way to go, but it really made no difference; he was alone in this world of 2053 A.D., or as good as alone, and with a final decision made, a path selected, he would stride off, sending patterns of frosty air before him like the smoke of a cigar.

Sometimes he would walk for hours and miles and return only at midnight to his house. And on his way he would see the cottages and homes with their dark windows, and it was not unequal to walking through a graveyard where only the faintest glimmers of firefly light appeared in flickers behind the windows. Sudden gray phantoms seemed

to manifest upon inner room walls where a curtain was still undrawn against the night, or there were whisperings and murmurs where a window in a tomblike building was still open.

Mr. Leonard Mead would pause, cock his head, listen, look, and march on, his feet making no noise on the lumpy walk. For long ago he had wisely changed to sneakers when strolling at night, because the dogs in intermittent squads would parallel his journey with barkings if he wore hard heels, and lights might click on and faces appear and an entire street be startled by the passing of a lone figure, himself, in the early November evening.

On this particular evening he began his journey in a westerly direction, toward the hidden sea. There was a good crystal frost in the air; it cut the nose and made the lungs blaze like a Christmas tree inside; you could feel the cold light going on and off, all the branches filled with invisible snow. He listened to the faint push of his soft shoes through autumn leaves with satisfaction and whistled a cold, quiet whistle between his teeth, occasionally picking up a leaf as he passed, examining its skeletal pattern in the infrequent lamplights as he went on, smelling its rusty smell.

"Hello, in there," he whispered to every house on every side as he moved. "What's up tonight on Channel 4, Channel 7, Channel 9?

Where are the cowboys rushing, and do I see the United States Calvary over the next hill to the rescue?"

The street was silent and long and empty, with only his shadow moving like the shadow of a hawk in mid-country. If he closed his eyes and stood very still, frozen, he could imagine himself upon the center of a plain, a wintry, windless Arizona desert with no house in a thousand miles, and only dry riverbeds, the streets, for company.

"What is it now?" he asked the houses, noticing his wristwatch. "Eight-thirty P.M.? Time for a dozen assorted murders? A quiz? A revue? A comedian falling off the stage?"

Was that a murmur of laughter from within a moon-white house? He hesitated, but went on when nothing more happened. He stumbled over a particularly uneven section of sidewalk. The cement was vanishing under flowers and grass. In ten years of walking by night or day, for thousands of miles, he had never met another person walking, not one in all that time.

He came to a cloverleaf intersection, which stood silent where two main highways crossed the town. During the day it was a thunderous surge of cars, the gas stations open, a great insect rustling, and a ceaseless jockeying for position as the scarab beetles, a faint incense puttering from their exhausts, skimmed homeward to the far directions. But now these highways, too, were like streams in a dry season, all stone and bed and moon radiance.

He turned back on a side street, circling around toward his home. He was within a block of his destination when the lone car turned a corner quite suddenly and flashed a fierce white cone of light upon him. He stood entranced, not unlike a night moth, stunned by the illumination, and then drawn toward it.

A metallic voice called to him:

"Stand still. Stay where your are! Don't move!"

He halted.

"Put up your hands!"

"But—" he said.

"Your hands up! Or we'll shoot!"

The police, of course, but what a rare, incredible thing; in a city of three million, there was only one police car left, wasn't that correct? Ever since a year ago, 2052, the election year, the force had been cut down from three cars to one. Crime was ebbing; there was no need now for the police, save for this one lone car wandering and wandering the empty streets.

"Your name?" said the police car in a metallic whisper. He couldn't see the men in it for the bright light in his eyes.

"Leonard Mead," he said

"Speak up!"

"Leonard Mead!"

"Business or profession?"

"I guess you'd call me a writer."

"No profession," said the police car, as if talking to itself. The light held him fixed, like a museum specimen, needle thrust through chest.

"You might say that," said Mr. Mead. He hadn't written in years. Magazines and books didn't sell any more. Everything went on in the tomblike houses at night now, he thought, continuing his fancy. The tombs, ill-lit by television light, where the people sat like the dead, the gray or multicolored lights touching their faces, but never really touching them.

"No profession," said the phonograph voice, hissing. "What are you doing out?"

"Walking," said Leonard Mead.

"Walking!"

"Just walking," he said simply, but his face felt cold.

"Walking, just walking, walking?"

"Yes, sir."

"Walking where? For what?"

"Walking for air. Walking to *see*."

"Your address!"

"Eleven South Saint James Street."

"And there is air *in* your house, you have an *air conditioner,* Mr. Mead?"

"Yes."

"And you have a viewing screen in your house to see with?"

"No."

"No?" There was a crackling quiet that in itself was an accusation.

"Are you married, Mr. Mead?"

"No."

"Not married," said the police voice behind the fiery beam. The moon was high and clear among the stars and the houses were gray and silent."

"Nobody wanted me," said Leonard Mead with a smile.

"Don't speak unless you're spoken to!"

Leonard Mead waited in the cold night.

"Just *walking,* Mr. Mead?"

"Yes."

"But you haven't explained for what purpose."

"I explained; for air, and to see, and just to walk."

"Have you done this often?"

"Every night for years."

The police car sat in the center of the street with its radio throat faintly humming.

"Well, Mr. Mead," it said.

"Is that all?" he asked politely.

"Yes," said the voice. "Here." There was a sigh, a pop. The back door of the police car sprang wide. "Get in."

"Wait a minute, I haven't done anything!"

"Get in."

"I protest!"

"Mr. Mead."

He walked like a man suddenly drunk. As he passed the front window of the car he looked in. As he had expected, there was no one in the front seat, no one in the car at all.

"Get in."

He put his hand to the door and peered into the back seat, which was a little cell, a little black jail with bars. It smelled of riveted steel. It smelled of harsh antiseptic; it smelled too clean and hard and metallic. There was nothing soft there.

"Now, if you had a wife to give you an alibi," said the iron voice. "But—"

"Where are you taking me?"

The car hesitated, or rather, gave a faint whirring click, as if information, somewhere, was dropping card by punch-slotted card under electric eyes. "To the Psychiatric Center for Research on Regressive Tendencies."

He got in. The door shut with a soft thud. The police car rolled through the night avenues, flashing its dim lights ahead.

They passed one house on one street a moment later, one house in an entire city of houses that were dark, but this one particular house had all of its electric lights brightly lit, every window a loud yellow illumination, square and warm in the cool darkness.

"That's *my* house," said Leonard Mead.

No one answered him.

The car moved down the empty riverbed streets and off away, leaving the empty streets with the empty sidewalks and no sound and no motion all the rest of the chill November night. ◆

Responding to the Theme

Freedom

Responding in Your Journal What were your reactions to "The Pedestrian?" Were you stimulated? Curious? Outraged? Scared? Why? Do you think Americans could ever lose all of the freedoms they enjoy at this time? Today in your journal, freewrite your thoughts and feelings about this and any other ideas and concerns you have about freedom. Then later in the week, look up the Bill of Rights in a book in the library and write about any discoveries you make. For example, did you learn anything new about your basic human rights? Which rights had you forgotten? Do you think you forgot them because they are not so important? You also may want to think about some of the people who participated in the writing of the Constitution and the Bill of Rights. For instance, why do you think they had the vision to create a government and a society so dedicated to the human rights spelled out in both of those documents?

Speaking and Listening With your teacher's permission, meet in small discussion groups and share your ideas about the following question: *What do you think it would take to make citizens more appreciative—and even more conscious—of their rights and freedoms under the Constitution of the United States?* At the end of the discussion, one person from each group should share with the rest of the class the results of his or her group's discussion. Be sure to observe courtesy and respect for members of the group as you speak and listen during the discussion.

Critical Thinking: Extending Write a paragraph in which you predict what will happen when Leonard Mead of "The Pedestrian" arrives at the Psychiatric Center for Research on Regressive Tendencies.

Extending Your Vocabulary Ray Bradbury uses several words with negative connotations to establish the setting of "The Pedestrian." Use some of these words from the selection to write a setting for a short story of your own. Save your work in your writing folder for a possible short story later.

phantoms	dead	tomblike
whisperings	murmurs	cell
graveyard	skeletal	bars
jail	metallic	antiseptic

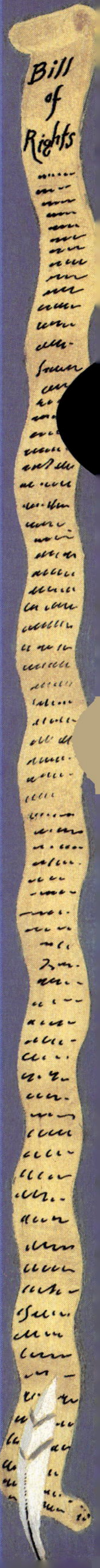

Part 2 Writing

In "The Pedestrian" author Ray Bradbury pictures a future without any available writing. Instead of being free to read the ideas and opinions of different writers, people watched only "viewing screens" controlled by the government.

Today you not only have the right to read what you want, but also the right to write whatever you want. In an essay, for example, you draw on your own experiences and knowledge to express personal opinions and ideas. On the other hand, when you write a *research paper,* or report, you can freely read and draw on the knowledge and experience of others to create a more factual piece of writing.

Writing Term A **research paper** is a composition based on research drawn from books, periodicals, and interviews with experts.

In school you will be writing research papers on many different subjects. Since the main purpose of reports is to inform, you will use the skills of expository writing to write them. You will also use your library skills as you hunt for information for your research papers. *(See Chapter 16 to review the use of the library and its resources.)*

Writing Process

Prewriting

Since you will be collecting information from a number of different sources, keep your notes organized from the beginning. Use a folder with pockets, and also index cards, paper clips, and rubber bands.

Discovering Subjects

Browsing through the library stacks, skimming through magazines, and taking ideas from television shows are all good ways to think of subjects for a report. You can also, of course, refer to the Learning Log in your journal for ideas. *(See page 13.)* If these strategies do not produce a subject, freewrite or brainstorm to complete the following statement: *I've always wondered why . . .* The best reports usually grow out of the writer's genuine desire to learn more about a subject.

WRITING ACTIVITY 1 *Writing on Your Own*

WRITING ABOUT THE THEME

To think of possible subjects for a research paper on the subject of freedom, look over what you have recently written about freedom in your journal and apply the strategies above. For example, you may want to skim a magazine article from July 1976, the bicentennial of the Declaration of Independence, or look for articles about the breaking down of the Berlin Wall in December 1989. You also may want to browse through the history section of the library or read what an encyclopedia says about *freedom.* When you have a list of five to ten possible subjects, put them in your writing folder for future use.

Choosing and Limiting a Subject

When you have five to ten possible subjects, choose one that you think best suits your purpose and audience. The following guidelines will help.

Guidelines for Choosing a Subject

1. Choose a subject you would like to know more about.
2. Consider your audience by choosing a subject your readers would like to know more about.
3. Consider your purpose by choosing a limited subject that can be covered thoroughly in a short research paper.
4. Choose a subject on which there is sufficient information in the school or local library.

Limiting a Subject The next step is to limit your subject by finding a clear, specific focus with which to approach the subject. One good way to find a focus is to create a cluster. *(See page 22.)* In the following cluster, the general subject is about families, and each offshoot from the center is a more limited version of that subject.

Model: *Limiting a Subject by Clustering*

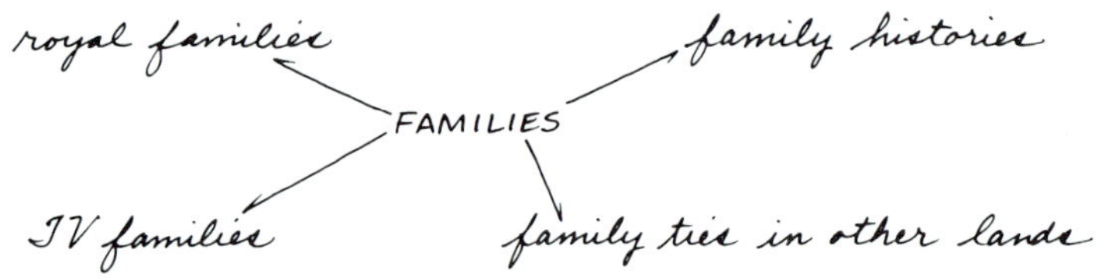

To limit the subject even further, you can create another cluster, using one of the offshoots in the middle.

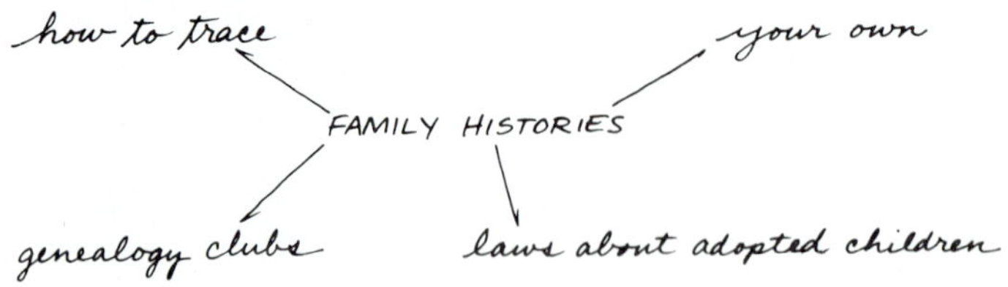

Any one of the offshoots in the second cluster is a suitably limited subject for a research paper. Each has a specific enough focus to provide the writer an angle on the subject.

WRITING ACTIVITY 2 *Evaluating Subjects*

Decide which of the following subjects are suitable for a short research paper and which are too broad. Indicate your answer by writing *suitable* or *too broad.*

1. the Industrial Revolution
2. how computers are used in cockpits
3. how Oscar-winning movies are chosen
4. outer space
5. the impact of major television networks on presidential campaigns
6. ecology
7. how the Trans-Alaska Pipeline affected animal life in the area
8. the record industry
9. how Olympic athletes are chosen to represent the United States
10. bowling

WRITING ACTIVITY 3 *Limiting a Subject*

After you choose one of the offshoots in the following cluster, create a second cluster with at least four new offshoots. Each offshoot should be a suitably limited subject for a research paper.

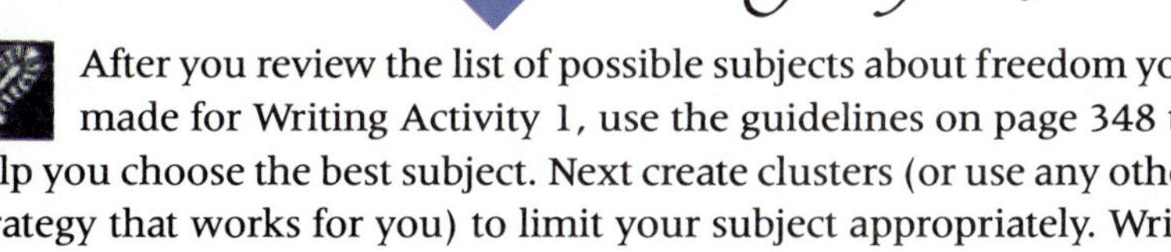

WRITING ACTIVITY 4 *Writing on Your Own*

WRITING ABOUT THE THEME

After you review the list of possible subjects about freedom you made for Writing Activity 1, use the guidelines on page 348 to help you choose the best subject. Next create clusters (or use any other strategy that works for you) to limit your subject appropriately. Write the limited subject you choose for your research paper at the top of your worksheet and then save your paper in your writing folder for future use.

Gathering Information

Once you have limited your subject, the next step is to jot down a few questions that you want your research to answer. These questions will serve as a guide for gathering information and, therefore, eliminate the possibility of wasting time. As you develop these questions, keep the purpose of your report and a profile of your audience clearly in mind so that the direction of your research is appropriate and on the mark. On the subject of family histories, for example, the preresearch questions that the writer could consider might be as follows.

Model: *Preresearch Questions*

- What basics does a novice family researcher need to know to start tracing his or her ancestry?
- What kinds of documents are needed in the search for family roots?
- Which libraries around the country have special aids for family researchers?
- What problems might an inexperienced family researcher encounter?
- Who are some experts in family history I might be able to interview?

With your preresearch questions clearly in mind, you can begin to find the information you need by using the following steps.

Steps for Gathering Information

1. Use a general reference work such as an encyclopedia to gain an overview of your subject. *(See pages 486–489.)*
2. Use the subject cards in the library to find books on your subject. *(See pages 483–485.)*
3. Consult the *Readers' Guide to Periodical Literature* to find magazine articles on your subject. *(See pages 487–488.)*
4. Make a list of all sources available on your subject. Include the author, title, copyright year, publisher and location, and call number for each source.
5. Assign each source on your list a number that will easily identify it when you take notes.

WRITING ACTIVITY 5 *Gathering Information*

Use the library to list five sources for each of the following subjects. If possible, include at least one magazine article for each subject. Remember to record all the information listed in step 4 in the Steps for Gathering Information.

1. solar energy
2. new uses for the home computer
3. gorillas as an endangered species
4. earthquakes along the San Andreas fault
5. the most recent World Series

WRITING ACTIVITY 6 *Writing on Your Own*

WRITING ABOUT THE THEME

Use the library to find at least eight sources for the subject about freedom you are researching. If possible, at least two of the sources should be magazine articles. After you follow all the Steps for Gathering Information listed on page 350, save your work in your writing folder for later use.

Taking Notes and Summarizing

Before you take any notes from your library sources, review your preresearch questions. Then, by referring to the index or by skimming, see if your source contains the information you need. Next, record the source number in the upper right-hand corner of each note card. As you begin to take notes, keep the following goals in mind.

Writing Tip The **goals of note-taking** are to summarize the main points in your own words and to record quotations that you might use in your research paper.

Notice how the following information about tracing a family tree is summarized on a note card.

> "Genealogy, like charity, begins at home," says Dr. Kenn Stryker-Rodda of the New York Genealogical and Biological Society in New York City. "Begin by digging into the memories of all your living relatives and by checking family records—letters in an old trunk in the attic, for instance, or entries in a family Bible—for records of births, marriages, and deaths. This information will be the skeleton of your family tree."

Model: *Note Card with Summary*

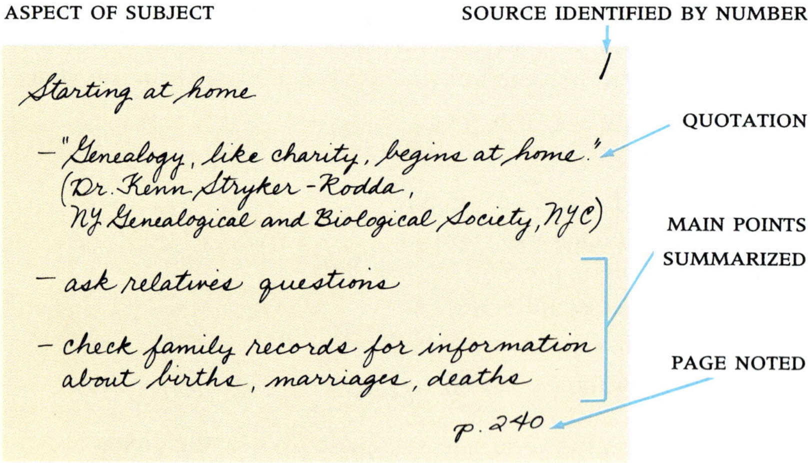

Clip together with a paper clip all the note cards from one source and keep them in your folder. Make sure, however, that the source is identified on each card. Later you will re-sort your note cards.

Writing Is Thinking

Critical Thinking

Summarizing

When you research a report, you should not copy word for word everything that you read about your topic. Instead summarize the key ideas and details from your sources onto your note cards. *Summarizing* means identifying the main idea of a passage and restating it accurately, concisely, and in your own words. When you summarize, you use several important thinking processes. First, you *translate,* or make sense of, what you have read. Then, you *analyze,* or identify, the parts of the passage and *evaluate,* or decide, which points are the most important to your report. Finally, in your own words, you *synthesize,* or put back together, these important points in a concise summary—often no longer than a phrase or a sentence.

If you look back at the sample note card on the previous page, you will see a clear, simple summary of a paragraph. After reading the paragraph, the writer decided that there were two main points about how to proceed in making a family tree. One is to ask relatives questions, and the other is to check family records. The writer then concisely reworded the main points—leaving out the other details, such as the letters in an attic trunk and the family Bible.

Thinking Practice Write a one-sentence summary of the following paragraph. First read the paragraph to make sure you understand it. Then, when you decide which are the most important points, include those points in your sentence. Omit all the unnecessary details.

> Though most people would name the wood or the fruit of a tree as its most useful part, a surprising number of trees are valued chiefly for their bark. The bark of the cork oak, for example, found chiefly in Portugal, provides the world with cork. Every eight years the cork is stripped away from the tree. Another tree, the cinnamon tree, which grows in Sri Lanka and India, has bark that curls as it dries. The curled bark becomes cinnamon sticks and can be ground for use as a spice. The aroma and flavor of cinnamon are savored around the world. In addition, a tree, the *cinchona,* is related to the poplar tree and has bark that contains the chemical quinine. This chemical protects the tree from pests and is used in the treatment of malaria.

WRITING ACTIVITY 7 *Taking Notes and Summarizing*

The following article is from page 123 of the February 1985 issue of *Word Power* magazine. Take notes on the article for a report called "Esperanto: The Universal Language." *(Assume the source has been assigned the number "2" for identification.)* On your note card, identify the aspect of the subject being discussed. Then summarize the main points in your own words and record any good quotations. Use the note card on page 352 as a model.

A Language of Hope

Bialystok is a city that has been part of several countries, held at first by one and then by another warring nation. When Ludwig Zamenhof (1859–1917) was growing up there, it was in Poland, although the Russians occupied the area. Throughout Zamenhof's upbringing, people of different backgrounds—Russians, Poles, and Germans—were in political and social conflict all around him. He believed strongly that their language differences were causing a division among them.

One reason for his belief was the rising tide of nationalism in world affairs. Nationalism is the belief that the good of one's country surpasses all other values, including peaceful coexistence with neighbors. Nationalism stresses the ties that bind a nation's people together: native music, literature, folk traditions, and—most importantly—language. Zamenhof believed that if language differences were done away with, humanity instead of nationality would become the tie that binds.

Under the pen name Doktoro Esperanto, Zamenhof published a book outlining an international language he had carefully worked out. The name he chose for himself means "one who hopes." The language itself is known by that name. For the thousands who have learned Zamenhof's language, it still speaks of hope for a peaceful future.

WRITING ACTIVITY 8 *Writing on Your Own*

WRITING ABOUT THE THEME

Follow the procedures described in Writing Activity 7 for taking notes from the sources that you found in Writing Activity 6 for your report about freedom. Save your note cards in your writing folder for future use.

Developing a Working Thesis

Your limited subject is probably already fairly well fixed to permit you to begin your research, but focusing your thoughts even further will save you time and effort as you organize your research. The best way to focus your thoughts at this stage is to develop a *working thesis* that expresses the main ideas your research revealed. A working thesis is a tentative proposition; you can revise it as needed if you discover more information that you wish to include in your research paper.

To develop your working thesis, think carefully about what you know about your subject. For example, after gathering information about tracing family histories, the writer of that research paper learned that there are some basic sources and documents each genealogist should consult and also discovered that there are a number of common mistakes beginners make. Consequently, she developed a working thesis statement that accounts for this information.

Student Model: *Developing a Working Thesis Statement*

LIMITED SUBJECT — how to trace a family history

WORKING THESIS STATEMENT — The best way to study one's family history is to know the sources of genealogy and to avoid some common mistakes.

WRITING ACTIVITY 9 *Writing on Your Own*

WRITING ABOUT THE THEME

Formulate a working thesis from the limited subject about freedom that you selected in Writing Activity 4. Summarize the main points of the information you have gathered and express your thesis in the form of a complete sentence. Save your work in your writing folder.

Outlining

After you have answered all of the preresearch guide questions on page 350 and written a working thesis statement, you can begin to organize your notes and plan the structure of your research paper. Then you can use your notes to develop an outline.

Organizing Your Notes The first step in organizing your notes is to group your note cards into categories. Notice how the following categories for the subject of family histories come from the preresearch questions on page 350.

CATEGORY 1	general information: popularity of genealogy, events that madc gcnealogy popular
CATEGORY 2	kinds of public documents needed
CATEGORY 3	famous library collections of genealogies
CATEGORY 4	problems to avoid from the start
CATEGORY 5	the family itself as a starting point

After grouping your note cards into three or more main categories of information, clip together the cards in each category and bind each set with a rubber band. Cards that do not fit into any of your categories should be clipped separately. You may be able to use some of those notes in the introduction or conclusion of your report.

WRITING ACTIVITY 10 *Creating Categories*

Write three main categories into which the following tips for staying healthy can be grouped. Then write each item under the appropriate category. Save your work for Writing Activity 11.

Tips for Staying Healthy

1. Eat fresh fruits and vegetables.
2. Exercise to strengthen the heart and lungs.
3. Avoid foods high in fat content.
4. Follow a regular sleeping schedule.
5. Exercise for 20 minutes, 3 times a week.
6. Avoid foods high in sugar (empty calories).
7. Clear your mind before sleeping.
8. Stretch muscles before and after exercise to avoid injury.
9. Get plenty of sleep to maintain your resistance to germs.
10. Mix foods from the four basic food groups.

The Bicycle Race, Lyonel Feininger, National Gallery of Art, Washington, D.C.

Structuring Your Outline The categories you created when organizing your notes will be the basis for your outline. You can begin structuring your outline by deciding which type of logical order suits your subject: *chronological order, spatial order, order of importance,* or *developmental order.* *(See pages 106–107.)* Then, after you assign each category a Roman numeral, arrange the categories according to the type of order you have chosen.

Following is the beginning of an outline for a research paper about family history. As you will see, the main categories are arranged in developmental order. *(See page 106.)*

Student Model: *Categories in Developmental Order*

I. Collecting family data
II. Using library collections
III. Using public documents
IV. Avoiding common mistakes

The next step is to go back over your notes and add subtopics (capital letters) and supporting points (Arabic numerals) to fill out the outline. Following is the resulting outline for a research paper about how to trace a family history.

Student Model: *Outline*

MAIN TOPIC / SUBTOPIC / SUPPORTING POINTS

- **I.** Collecting family data
  - **A.** Asking the right questions
    - **1.** Basic facts
    - **2.** Family stories
  - **B.** Interpreting family photographs
- **II.** Using library collections
  - **A.** Library of the Church of Jesus Christ of Latter-Day Saints
    - **1.** Size
    - **2.** Scope of information available
  - **B.** Other good libraries
    - **1.** Newberry Library, Chicago
    - **2.** Fort Wayne Public Library, Indiana
    - **3.** Free Library of Philadelphia
    - **4.** New Orleans Public Library
- **III.** Using public documents
  - **A.** Types of documents
    - **1.** Local records
    - **2.** Federal records
  - **B.** How to request information
- **IV.** Avoiding common mistakes
  - **A.** Lack of organization
  - **B.** Lack of focus
  - **C.** Lack of critical approach to documents

WRITING ACTIVITY 11 *Outlining*

Write a simple outline, using the categories you wrote in Writing Activity 10 on page 356 on the subject about staying healthy. You should have three main topics (Roman numerals), with at least three subtopics (capital letters) under each one. Remember that each entry in the outline should be a phrase rather than a sentence.

WRITING ACTIVITY 12 *Writing on Your Own*

WRITING ABOUT THE THEME

Look back over all your research notes. After you organize your note cards into categories, select a logical order that suits your subject and use those categories to write an outline for the body of your report about some aspect of freedom. Then save your outline in your writing folder to use as a guide when drafting.

Drafting

Writing Process

A well-written report, like any good piece of writing, has a lively and engaging style. *(See pages 48–81.)* As you draft your report from your notes and outline, also strive for sentence variety, precise words, and fresh comparisons to make your report more interesting.

Writing a Thesis Statement

Now that you have an outline with clear categories of information, check your working thesis once again to make sure it is broad enough to cover the categories in your outline but also accurately expresses the main idea of the report. The following guidelines will help you refine your working thesis into an appropriate thesis statement.

Guidelines for Refining a Thesis Statement

1. A thesis statement should make the main point of your research paper clear to a reader.
2. A thesis statement should cover all the main topics listed in your outline.
3. A thesis statement should fit smoothly into the introduction of your research paper.

The writer of the report about studying family history wanted to make the additional point that the inexperienced person studying family history is a "budding genealogist." She also wished to use smoother wording than she had used in her working thesis. The model below shows how she accomplished these goals.

Model: *Refining a Working Thesis*

WORKING THESIS	The best way to study one's family history is to know the sources of genealogy and to avoid some common mistakes.
THESIS STATEMENT	Before becoming a family detective, a budding genealogist should become familiar with the basic sources of genealogy and the common mistakes beginners make.

Henry Art Gallery, U. of Washington, gift of the artist

The Builders No. 1, Jacob Armstead Lawrence, 1970

WRITING ACTIVITY 13 *Refining Thesis Statements*

Rewrite each of the following thesis statements so that it covers all the main topics listed in the outline accompanying it.

1. The construction of a building begins with the substructure, or foundation.

I. Substructure—construction below ground
II. Superstructure—construction above ground

2. The sun may be the main source of energy in the future.

I. Fossil fuels
II. Solar energy
III. Nuclear energy

3. Watching a solar eclipse can be very hazardous unless it is done in the proper way.

I. Dangers
II. Proper way to watch
III. Watching a lunar eclipse

4. Jazz trumpeter Miles Davis now plays music that blends the jazz and rock styles.

I. Early years—bebop style
II. Middle years—cool style
III. Recent years—jazz/rock style

5. The trumpet and bugle are very similar instruments.
   I. Tubing
   II. How sound is produced
   III. Differences

Structuring the Research Paper

The following chart will help you structure your research paper as you write your first draft. Notice that a research paper contains special features.

The Structure of a Research Paper

PARTS	**PURPOSE**
TITLE	• suggests the subject of the research paper
INTRODUCTION	• captures attention • provides background information • contains the thesis statement
BODY	• supports the thesis statement with information drawn from research • contains well-developed paragraphs
CONCLUSION	• brings the research paper to a close by restating the thesis or by referring to earlier ideas with fresh emphasis
SPECIAL FEATURES	
CITATIONS	• give credit to other authors for ideas
WORKS CITED	• lists sources used in preparing the research paper • appears at the end of the research paper on a separate page

The following model report was written from the outline on page 358. Although it is more polished than your first draft will be, it shows you how each part in the report contributes to the whole. Notice that whenever words or ideas are borrowed, a citation in parentheses refers the reader to the proper source on the works cited page.

Student Model: *Research Paper*

TITLE

Climbing a Family Tree

INTRODUCTION:
BACKGROUND INFORMATION

Since the United States celebrated its 200th birthday in 1976, the study of family history, called *genealogy*, has gained many devoted followers. According to John H. Tennent of the National Genealogical Society in Washington, D.C., "tracing your ancestry is like eating peanuts--once you get started, it's hard to stop" ("Trace Your Family Tree" 240).

THESIS STATEMENT

Before becoming a family detective, become familiar with the basic sources of genealogy and the traps that could leave you dangling from a branch in someone else's tree.

MAIN TOPIC I FROM OUTLINE

The first basic source of information for your family tree is your family. Useful questions to ask family members include these: "Who were my ancestors? Where and when were they born? Where and when did they die? What was their relationship to one another?" (Lichtman 18). The Smithsonian Institution in Washington, D.C., also recommends a good question for family reunions: "Are there any stories about how a great fortune was lost or almost, but not quite, made? Do you believe them?" (Shenker 27). Family photographs are another excellent source. To learn as much as you can, ask yourself, "What conclusions about the past can explain why the picture looks the way it does?" (Lichtman 111). Tracing a family history, of course, is more than filling in a chart. You must learn as much as you can about how life really was for people in the past.

MAIN TOPIC II FROM OUTLINE

After you have explored family sources, consult the genealogical library of the Church of Jesus Christ of Latter-Day Saints in Salt Lake City, Utah. This collection is considered the greatest in the world. It has the equivalent of "more than 1.5 billion book pages" on over a million rolls of microfilm (Westin 60). If you cannot go to Salt Lake City, you can use one of the more than 200 branch libraries around the country. The library of Latter-Day Saints is open to all people and includes records on more than 60 million people from 126 different countries (Westin 60). Other libraries with excellent family-history collections are the Newberry Library in Chicago, the Fort Wayne (Indiana) Public Library, the Free Library of Philadelphia, and the New Orleans Public Library (Westin 71-77).

MAIN TOPIC III FROM OUTLINE

If these family records do not include your ancestors, you should search through local and federal records to track down your forebears. Vital records include birth, marriage, and death certificates. Other useful records are wills, church records, census reports, military records, ships' passenger lists, and immigration files. Your local library will have the addresses of public offices you can write to for information. "In writing for records," Gilbert [illegible] Doane and James B. Bell suggest, "you should always offer to pay any fee that the clerk may charge. It is also a good policy to enclose a stamped, self-addressed envelope for a reply" (Doane and Bell 82). If you state your questions clearly, you will be more likely to receive the information you need to add a missing piece to the family puzzle (Heimberg 23).

MAIN TOPIC IV FROM OUTLINE

To beginning family detectives, the great number and variety of sources can seem overwhelming. David Thackery, Librarian of Local and Family History at the Newberry Library, points out three common mistakes that people often make. The first is "not having a good system of organizing" research. With so many sources, keeping well-organized and accurate notes is critical to putting the pieces together later. The second problem is "a lack of focus." It is best not to attempt everything at once. Thackery suggests that researchers should "focus on one particular branch for a month or two" before moving on to the next. The third problem is "the lack of a critical approach" to the documents. Many documents have errors, omissions, or exaggerations. A careful researcher will learn to question the accuracy of every source until it can be verified by another (Thackery, telephone interview).

CONCLUSION

Despite the pitfalls, Thackery is enthusiastic about family research. In his mid-teens he began to trace his roots. He has found all of his great-great-great-grandparents on his father's side and 12 of his great-great-great-great-great-grandparents on his mother's side, as far back as the early 1700's. "We're all part of hundreds of families," says Thackery, and tracing one's roots is a "means of self-discovery." With the help of family memories, library collections, and the expert guidance of librarians, anyone with the patience and motivation can discover the pleasures of climbing the family tree.

RESTATEMENT OF THESIS

Works Cited

Doane, Gilbert H., and James B. Bell. Searching for Your Ancestors. Minneapolis: U of Minnesota P, 1980.

Heimberg, Marilyn Markham. Discover Your Roots. San Diego: Communication Creativity, 1977.

Lichtman, Allan J. Your Family History. New York: Vintage Books, 1978.

Shenker, Israel. "Smithsonian Urges Public to Dig at the Family Tree." New York Times 17 June 1976, sec. 1: 27.

Thackery, David. Telephone interview. 23 Nov. 1983.

"Trace Your Family Tree." Good Housekeeping Oct. 1976: 240.

Westin, Jeane Eddy. Finding Your Roots. Los Angeles: J.P. Tarcher, Inc., 1977.

Notice that only sources consulted and actually cited in the report can be included on the works cited page. *(See page 370.)*

WRITING ACTIVITY 14 *Writing on Your Own*

WRITING ABOUT THE THEME

Based on your outline from Writing Activity 12, write a first draft of your report about some aspect of freedom. After you polish your thesis statement according to the guidelines on page 359, draft the introduction to your report. (Notice how the thesis statement about tracing family history was polished to fit in smoothly with the rest of the introduction.) Then follow your outline to draft the body of your report. For this first draft, do not worry about using the correct form for your citations. Every time you include a direct quote or a specific piece of information you wish to credit to a source, identify in parentheses the source and page number fully enough so that you know which source you mean. Later you will go back over these citations and place them in proper form. At that time you can also put together your works cited page. When you have finished, save your draft in your writing folder for later use.

Using and Citing Sources

The model report on pages 362–365 shows the different kinds of borrowings that need to be credited to the original authors. Failure to give proper credit for direct quotations and borrowed facts and statistics is called *plagiarism,* a serious and unlawful offense. In some cases you may want to *paraphrase* an author's idea, or rewrite an author's idea in your own words. Even if you paraphrase, however, you must credit the author for the idea.

Using Sources When you borrow material from sources, work it smoothly into your research paper. The following suggestions will help you improve the flow of your research paper.

Quoting and Paraphrasing Information

1. Use a quotation to finish a sentence you have started.
   EXAMPLE Tracing your family history is a "means of self-discovery."
2. Quote a whole sentence.
   EXAMPLE "We're all part of hundreds of families," says Thackery.
3. Quote just a few words.
   EXAMPLE Many researchers lack a "critical approach" to their sources.
4. Paraphrase information from a source.
   EXAMPLE According to Thackery all of us are part of many families.

WRITING ACTIVITY 15 *Using Sources*

Read the following excerpt about the geyser Old Faithful. Then use it as a source to complete the assignment that follows it.

Old Faithful

Every day of the year, at intervals that average a little over an hour, a plume of steam and boiling water bursts out of the ground. For two to five minutes, it thrusts straight upward, a total of 8,000 gallons forming a tower 180 feet high. Then it subsides, waiting for pressure to rebuild and a fresh crowd of tourists to gather. It has recurred without fail for the more than 110 recorded years and, geologists say, for thousands of years before that.

Although it is a metaphor for punctuality and power, Old Faithful is neither the most regular nor the most spectacular of the geysers in Yellowstone National Park. Steamboat Geyser, the most powerful in the world, can explode to a height of 300 feet. Some small geysers—squirting only a foot or two in the air—erupt every minute or so, like clockwork; Old Faithful's rest periods vary from three minutes to two hours.

1. Write a sentence that ends with a quotation.
2. Write three sentences about geysers of different sizes. One of the sentences should be a direct quotation.
3. Write a sentence about Steamboat Geyser that quotes just a few words from the source.
4. Write a sentence paraphrasing part of the passage.

Citing Sources Notes that tell the original source of words or ideas you have used in your report are called *citations.* Although several formats for citing sources are available, this textbook uses the guidelines established by the Modern Language Association (MLA) for *parenthetical citations*—the preferred way to give credit to your sources. Parenthetical citations identify the source briefly *in parentheses* immediately after the borrowed material. *Footnotes* are another type of citation. Instead of identifying sources *within* the report in parentheses, footnotes use a number next to the borrowed material that refers to a source listed at the bottom, or foot, of the page. A similar type of citation is the *endnote*. Instead of identifying sources at the foot of the page, endnotes come at the end of the report, after the conclusion but beforc the works cited page.

Writing Tip Cite the sources of information you include in your research paper by using parenthetical citations, footnotes, or endnotes.

Your teacher will tell you which type of citation to use in your research papers.

Parenthetical Citations When you use parenthetical citations, you give readers only enough information to identify the source of the borrowed material. Readers then refer to your works cited page for complete information on each source. The following examples show the correct form for using parenthetical citations.

BOOKS BY ONE AUTHOR	Give author's last name and page number(s): (Lichtman 18).
BOOKS WITH MORE THAN ONE AUTHOR	Give both authors' names and page number(s): (Doane and Bell 82).
ARTICLE WITH AUTHOR NAMED	Give author's last name and page number(s): (Shenker 27–30).
ARTICLE WITH AUTHOR UNNAMED	Give a shortened form of the title of the article (unless title is short to begin with) and page number(s): ("Trace Your Family Tree" 240).
ARTICLE FROM GENERAL REFERENCE WORK/AUTHOR UNNAMED	Give title (or shortened form of title); no page number(s) needed if article is single page or from an encyclopedia arranged alphabetically: ("Genealogy").

A parenthetical citation placed at the end of a sentence goes after a closing quotation mark and before the period. Titles of works should be enclosed in quotation marks within the parentheses. *(See the model research paper for examples.)*

Footnotes and Endnotes If your teacher tells you to use footnotes or endnotes, you need to follow a different form for citing sources. With either footnotes or endnotes, place a small number, called a *superscript*, halfway above the line and immediately after the borrowed material.

EXAMPLE The collection in Salt Lake City has the equivalent of "more than 1.5 billion book pages"[1] on over a million rolls of microfilm.

The number refers readers to the proper footnote or endnote. The following examples show the correct form for footnotes and endnotes.

Model: *Correct Form for Footnotes and Endnotes*

REFERENCE WORKS	[1] Joseph Charles Wolf, "Genealogy," <u>World Book Encyclopedia</u>, 1983 ed.
BOOKS WITH SINGLE AUTHOR	[2] Marilyn Markham Heimberg, <u>Discover Your Roots</u> (San Diego: Communication Creativity, 1977) 23.
BOOKS WITH MORE THAN ONE AUTHOR	[3] Gilbert H. Doane and James B. Bell, <u>Searching for Your Ancestors</u> (Minneapolis: U of Minnesota P, 1980) 82.
MAGAZINE ARTICLES	[4] "Trace Your Family Tree," <u>Good Housekeeping</u> Oct. 1976:240. [Note: If the author is given, list the first name first.]
NEWSPAPER ARTICLES	[5] Israel Shenker, "Smithsonian Urges Public to Dig at the Family Tree," <u>New York Times</u> 17 June 1976, sec. 1:27.
INTERVIEWS	[6]David Thackery, telephone interview, Newberry Library, 23 Nov. 1983.

For repeated references to a work already cited, you can use a shortened form of footnote.

REPEATED REFERENCES [1] Heimberg 69.
[2] Doane and Bell 36.

Preparing a Works Cited Page Sources cited in the research paper must also be listed on a separate works cited page at the end of the paper. The author's last name comes first and the indentation and punctuation are different. In a works cited page, the entries are listed in alphabetical order by the author's last name. If no author is given for a work, the entry is alphabetized by the title.

Model: *Form for the Works Cited Page*

BOOKS WITH MORE THAN ONE AUTHOR	Doane, Gilbert H., and James B. Bell. Searching for Your Ancestors. Minneapolis: U of Minnesota P, 1980.
BOOKS WITH SINGLE AUTHOR	Heimberg, Marilyn Markham. Discover Your Roots. San Diego: Communication Creativity, 1977.
	Lichtman, Allan J. Your Family History. New York: Vintage Books, 1978.
NEWSPAPER ARTICLES	Shenker, Israel. "Smithsonian Urges Public to Dig at the Family Tree." New York Times 17 June 1976, sec. 1: 27–30.
INTERVIEWS	Thackery, David. Telephone interview. 23 Nov. 1983.
MAGAZINE ARTICLES	"Trace Your Family Tree." Good Housekeeping Oct. 1976: 240.
BOOKS WITH SINGLE AUTHOR	Westin, Jeane Eddy. Finding Your Roots. Los Angeles: J.P. Tarcher, Inc., 1977.
REFERENCE WORKS	Wolf, Joseph Charles. "Genealogy." World Book Encyclopedia. 1983 ed.

Your teacher may require a works consulted page—often called a *bibliography*—on which you include all works you consulted but did not necessarily cite in the actual report. A works consulted list, or bibliography, uses the same form as the works cited list.

WRITING ACTIVITY 16 *Preparing a Works Cited Page*

The following sources were used for a report on sharks. Using the model on the previous page, write a works cited page that includes all the sources.

1. Jacques Y. Cousteau, The Shark: Splendid Savage of the Sea (Garden City: Doubleday, 1970).
2. "Sharks Slay Half of Those Attacked," New York Times, 10 Aug. 1975, sec. 1, page 42.
3. Paul Budker, The Life of Sharks (New York: Columbia University Press, 1971).
4. "A Bum Rap for Sharks," Changing Times, Jan. 1982, page 6.
5. Sharon Begley, "Giving Sharks a Good Name," Newsweek, 2 Aug. 1982, pages 64–65.

WRITING ACTIVITY 17 *Using Parenthetical Citations*

Write a parenthetical citation for each of the following references to the works cited page developed in Writing Activity 16.

EXAMPLE A description by Jacques Cousteau
ANSWER (Cousteau 72)

1. An example of a shark attack from the New York Times article
2. A little-known fact about sharks from the article in Newsweek
3. A choice quote from the article in Changing Times
4. Information from The Life of Sharks

WRITING ACTIVITY 18 *Writing on Your Own*

WRITING ABOUT THE THEME

Review what you have learned about using and citing sources correctly. Then read over the first draft of your research paper about some aspect of freedom. Apply any tips for using sources that you think would improve the flow of your report and your use of borrowed material. Next correct the form of your parenthetical citations and prepare your works cited page. If you have a source that does not fit one of the categories described on pages 368 or 369, find information on how to cite it correctly by referring to the *MLA Handbook for Writers of Research Papers*, third edition, by Joseph Gibaldi and Walter S. Achtert. Save your work in your writing folder for later use.

Writing Process

Revising

A report writer's desk is usually messy with piles of books in one corner, note cards fanned out in another, and maybe an outline taped to the wall. When you are researching and drafting your report, you are busy keeping together all your sources of information and writing guides. In an effort to pull together the bits and pieces of your research into a first draft, you may not have composed the smoothest flowing piece of writing you can produce. Revising is the stage during which you should clear your desk and read over your report with a fresh eye and a keen sense of concentration. Your first concern is whether your research paper has effectively satisfied its purpose. Does the report *inform* the audience as fully and accurately as possible?

Checking for Adequate Development One especially important feature to look for in your draft is adequate development. A good research paper will have ample supporting material, enough so the thesis is well documented. If certain sections seem thin and weak, you may have to return to the library and do additional research to bolster these sagging parts of your report.

Checking for Accuracy Another important feature of a factual research paper is accuracy. Whenever you borrow material from another source, you need to take special care that you are accurately representing the views of the author of that source. Be careful that in your zeal to support your thesis, you have not quoted an authority out of context or failed to include some important information that would cast your thesis in doubt.

WRITING ACTIVITY 19 *Writing on Your Own*

WRITING ABOUT THE THEME

If your teacher permits, share your first draft with a peer. Ask him or her to tell you where your report may need supporting material. If necessary, complete any needed research and add those portions to your report. Then take a careful, objective look at the sources you quoted. Have you quoted the material exactly? Furthermore, have you been accurate in representing the information you obtained while researching? If not, provide the citations that may be missing. Save your revised draft in your writing folder for later use.

Using a Revision Checklist The following checklist will help you spot places in your report that need improvement. The first section of the checklist will help you polish the most important aspect of your report, its content. The second section will help you refine each paragraph within your report to make it as sharp and concise as it can be. The final section will help you weave into your writing the words and sentence rhythms that are sure to hold your reader's attention.

Revision Checklist

CHECKING YOUR RESEARCH PAPER

1. Does your introduction contain a thesis statement that makes the main point of your research paper clear? *(See page 359.)*
2. Does the body of your research paper support the thesis statement? *(See page 361.)*
3. Does your research paper have unity? *(See page 226.)*
4. Does your research paper have coherence? *(See page 226.)*
5. Is your emphasis clear? *(See page 226.)*
6. Does your conclusion add a strong ending? *(See page 224.)*
7. Does your research paper have parenthetical citations and a list of sources on a works cited page? *(See pages 366–370.)*
8. Does your research paper have a title that suggests the subject of the report?

CHECKING YOUR PARAGRAPHS

9. Does each sentence have a topic sentence? *(See pages 89–90.)*
10. Is each paragraph unified and coherent? *(See pages 116–118.)*
11. Did you use transitions so that one paragraph leads smoothly into the next? *(See page 113.)*

CHECKING YOUR SENTENCE AND WORDS

12. Are your sentences varied? *(See pages 62–69.)*
13. Are your sentences concise? *(See page 58.)*
14. Did you avoid faulty sentences? *(See pages 70–74.)*
15. Did you use specific words? *(See pages 53–54.)*

WRITING ACTIVITY 20 *Writing on Your Own*

WRITING ABOUT THE THEME

Using the Revision Checklist above, revise the first draft of your report about some aspect of freedom. Then save your paper in your writing folder for editing later.

Language Integrating Skills

Editing and Publishing

Grammar in the Writing Process

When Ray Bradbury, the author of "The Pedestrian," was twelve, he received a toy typewriter. Eight years later he published his first story, and since then he has written over 1,000 other stories. He has a large audience because he writes stimulating science-fiction stories in a clear, engaging style. Part of the effectiveness of his style—and the style of any good writer—is the variety of sentence structure he includes in his writing. Just as eating the same dinner—night after night—would be dull and boring, so would be writing that contained only the same sentence structure—sentence after sentence.

Kinds of Sentence Structure Sentences are classified according to the number and kind of clauses within each of them. The four basic kinds of sentences are simple, compound, complex, and compound-complex. A *simple sentence* consists of one independent clause. A *compound sentence* consists of two or more independent clauses. A *complex sentence* consists of one independent clause and one or more subordinate clauses, and a *compound-complex sentence* consists of two or more independent clauses and one or more subordinate clauses.

When you revise, always include a variety of different sentence structures so that your writing will flow at a lively, interesting pace. *(For practice in classifying sentences, see pages 638–639.)*

SIMPLE SENTENCE	He felt alone in this world of 2053 A.D.
COMPOUND SENTENCE	He would stride off, and patterns of frosty air rose like the smoke of a cigar.
COMPLEX SENTENCE	On this evening he went in a westerly direction, which took him toward the sea.
COMPOUND-COMPLEX SENTENCE	The street was silent and long and empty, and he made no noise as he moved along.

Punctuation with Compound Sentences Join the two independent clauses in a compound sentence with a comma and a conjunction or with a semicolon. *(For other examples and for practice in writing compound sentences correctly, see pages 777–778.)*

COMMA AND CONJUNCTION In ten years he had walked thousands of miles, **but** he had never met another person.

SEMICOLON He stumbled over an uneven section of the sidewalk**;** the cement was vanishing under the grass.

(For information about punctuating complex sentences and for practice in writing them correctly, see pages 786–790.)

Capitalization and Punctuation of Titles When you write a research paper, apply the following rules to the titles you include in your citations and in your list of works cited. *(For more information about titles, see pages 764 and 795–797.)*

1. **Capitalize** the first word, the last word, and all important words in the titles of books, newspapers, magazines, stories, poems, movies, plays, and other works of art.
2. **Underline** the titles of long written or musical works that are published as a single unit—such as books, newspapers, magazines, full-length plays, and long poems.
3. **Use quotation marks** to enclose the titles of chapters, articles, stories, one-act plays, short poems, and songs.

TITLES Besides short stories like "The Pedestrian," Ray Bradbury has written novels, such as The Martian Chronicles.

Editing Checklist

1. Have different sentence structures been included to create variety? *(See pages 62–69 and 638–639.)*
2. Are all the sentences punctuated correctly? *(See pages 771–772.)*
3. Are all titles written correctly? *(See pages 764, 795–797.)*

WRITING ACTIVITY 21 *Writing on Your Own*

WRITING ABOUT THE THEME

Editing After you edit your research paper, using the checklists above and on page 35, write a neat final copy.

Publishing To protect your report, bind it in plastic or cardboard covers or place it in a folder where the pages will be protected. Then share your research paper with someone interested in the subject. You have worked hard; be proud of sharing what you have written.

A Writer Writes

WRITING ABOUT THE THEME

A Research Paper

PURPOSE to inform or explain
AUDIENCE a teacher and a state senator

Statue of Liberty Crying, Cosimo

Prewriting Because the theme of freedom is so broad, there are literally dozens of subjects you could write about. For this report consider those many heroes and heroines who, throughout history, have had a lasting impact on personal freedom. Write a report about one of the following such people—or choose one of your own.

1. Susan B. Anthony
2. Rosa Parks
3. Winston Churchill
4. Anne Frank
5. Thomas Jefferson
6. Martin Luther King, Jr.
7. Abraham Lincoln
8. General Douglas MacArthur
9. Nelson Mandela
10. Harriet Tubman

When you have decided on your subject, limit it so that it is manageable and gather information on note cards from as many different sources as possible, such as reference books, biographies, magazines, newspapers, and even interviews. After you develop a working thesis, organize your notes into categories. Then decide on a logical order for your information and create an outline.

Drafting Once you refine your thesis, if that is necessary, write an introduction, body, and conclusion. Cite sources wherever necessary to give proper credit to any borrowed ideas or information. When you have completed your draft, add a title and write the works cited page.

Revising Once you have checked for adequate development and accuracy, use the Revision Checklist on page 373 as your guide to revising your research paper.

Editing and Publishing After you have used the Editing Checklists on pages 35 and 375 to polish your final draft, write or type two final copies, bind them if you wish, and share one copy with your teacher. Find the name and address of one of your state senators and send the second copy to him or her.

Independent Writing

Write a report on one of the following subjects or one of your own. Use the Checklist for Writing Research Papers on page 379 for help.

1. comedy stars of silent movies
2. the public duties of Britain's royal family
3. current theories about the meaning of dreams
4. the voyages of Thor Heyerdahl
5. space stations
6. the American Indians known as the Mound Builders
7. Henri Matisse's cutout compositions
8. the Beatles
9. Steven Spielberg
10. Robert A. Moog and the invention of the synthesizer
11. the mystery of Stonehenge
12. Attila the Hun
13. the influence of Frank Lloyd Wright
14. the Appalachian Mountain Trail
15. the Gothic Cathedral

Creative Writing

No one knows what will happen tomorrow. This unpredictability about the future is exactly what makes thinking about it so interesting. How is your view of the future, for example, different from Ray Bradbury's view in "The Pedestrian"? In your future world, will everyone be living on Earth, or will some be living in colonies on other planets, in huge spacecrafts, or in cities under the sea? What futuristic machinery will people need in order to exist? Create a cluster for your ideas and then write freely about all your imaginings about the future. Once your world of the future is clear in your mind, write the setting for a short story. Save your notes and setting in your writing folder to develop a short story at a later time.

Writing about Literature

A *narrator* is the person from whose point of view a story is told. A narrator may be a character in a story or an *omniscient narrator*—the external observer of the characters and the action, such as the narrator of "The Pedestrian." Write a paragraph that explains why you think this story would have or would not have been more interesting if the narrator had been Leonard Mead.

Writing in Another Subject Area

World History Write a report on child labor conditions in England during the Industrial Revolution. Include vivid, descriptive language in your report so that readers have an accurate picture.

C h a p t e r 10

Checklist

Writing Research Papers

Prewriting

- ✔ Use a variety of strategies to discover ideas to write about that require research. *(See page 347.)*
- ✔ Make a list of possible subjects and choose one to report on. Then limit your subject. *(See pages 348–349.)*
- ✔ Gather information on note cards from reference books and other books, magazines, and newspapers. *(See pages 350–353.)*
- ✔ Develop a working thesis. *(See page 355.)*
- ✔ Organize your notes into categories, decide on a logical order for your information, and create an outline for your research paper. *(See pages 356–358.)*

Drafting

- ✔ If necessary, refine your working thesis. Then write an introduction that includes your thesis statement, body, and conclusion. *(See pages 359–365.)*
- ✔ Avoid plagiarism by using and citing sources carefully. *(See page 366.)*
- ✔ Prepare parenthetical citations and a works cited page. *(See pages 368–370.)*
- ✔ Add a title.

Revising

- ✔ Check your research paper for adequate development and accuracy. *(See page 372.)*
- ✔ Using the Revision Checklist, check your research paper for structure, well-developed paragraphs, unity, coherence, emphasis, and varied and lively sentences and words. *(See page 373.)*

Editing and Publishing

- ✔ Using the Editing Checklist, check your grammar, spelling, mechanics, manuscript form, and citation and works cited form. *(See pages 35, 41, and 375.)*
- ✔ Share your finished work with an interested reader. *(See page 40.)*

Chapter 11

Creative Writing

Part 1 *Reading to Write*

THEME: *The Unexpected*

Going to an amusement park is great fun because it is full of unexpected occurrences. When you go into the house of horrors, for example, you never know what will jump out at you or what image will flash in front of you to make you scream with surprise. Even the unexpected images of you in distorted mirrors that make you look tall and thin or short and fat surprise you.

Life with its unexpected twists and turns could be compared to these amusement park experiences. For example, think about the many times that an unexpected person or event has changed your life just as the distorted mirrors in a house of horrors change your physical appearance. Also think about how writers of science fiction and mysteries use unexpected events to capture and hold your interest.

The story you are about to read—called "Ghost Town," by Jack Schaefer—is neither science fiction nor a mystery. It is not even about ghosts. However, the ghost town does not turn out to be what you expect it to be, and the story does not end the way you expect it to end. As you read this story, think about how things in your life have not always turned out the way you expected them to.

From

Ghost Town

Jack Schaefer

I owned a whole town once—what was left of it anyway—a ghost town. It was one of the mining camps back in the hills that must have been quite a place when the gold rush was on. Then the diggings there petered out and people began moving on.

This old town of mine was up a narrow gulch that wasn't good for a thing once the gold was gone. It was only about a half mile from a modern main highway, though, and the old dirt road leading to it was still passable. I drove in there one day and was poking around when another car loaded with tourists pulled up, and people piled out and were oh-ing and ah-ing as if they were seeing something wonderful. That's when I had my idea.

It took time, but I ran that town down on the tax books and found out all about it. When I offered to buy it, the county officials thought I was crazy and jumped to make a deal. They hadn't expected ever to get another nickel out of the place. I paid $800 and I owned a town.

I cleaned out the old buildings enough so you could walk around inside them. I painted names on them telling what they had been. I plastered signs along the highway for maybe five miles in each direction and a big one where the dirt road turned off. I roofed over one room of the old jail for my own quarters. I charged fifty cents a head for a look-see through the old place—and I was in business.

Sometimes I'd have four or five cars at a time parked by the entrance and a dozen or more people listening to my talk. I'd check the license plates and temper the talk accordingly. If they were from the home state or one nearby, I'd go easy on the fancy trimmings. Those people might know too much real history. If they were from far states, though, I'd let loose and make it strong. I'd tell about fights in the saloons—shootings and knifings and big brawls with bottles flying. What if all of it happened only in my head? There wasn't anything anyone could do to me so long as I made up the names too. The town belonged to me.

It was a good business—for three years. Then it collapsed the way the old town itself did way back then. The state started straightening the highway and knocked off the loop that came near my ghost town. My business started skidding. I tried to unload it on the historical society, and they just laughed at me.

I was stuck with that town. The summer season started, and I was lucky to average a single car a day. I was figuring I'd have to swallow the loss and move on when late one afternoon this pink-cheeked young fellow came along. He was pink-cheeked like a boy with maybe a little fuzz on his chin that hadn't begun to be whiskers yet. I was so lonesome for customers, or just anyone to talk to, that I stuck close and kept words bouncing back and forth with him. He looked so young and innocent, I figured he was a college kid seeing some of the country on vacation time. But no. He said he'd had all the college he could absorb. He was a mining engineer by profession, but there wasn't much professing to be done in that field about then, so he was knocking around looking over the old camps. Maybe he'd write a book on it sometime.

"Mighty interesting town you have here," he said. "Those buildings. Brick. Don't see much brick in the old camps. They haul them in here?"

"Why no," I said. "They had a kiln right here—you can see where it was behind the blacksmith shop. They dug the clay out of the bank over there." Right away this young fellow had to see that too.

"Mighty interesting business you're in," he said.

"Playing nursemaid to an old town like this and having people pay to look it over. Must be kind of a nice life." That's when I had another idea.

I took that pink-cheeked young fellow into my jail-room and persuaded him to stay for supper. I began coughing at strategic intervals during the meal. I told him my health was bad and the climate bothered me; otherwise I wouldn't even be thinking of maybe leaving such a nice life in such an interesting business. I played it clever with indirect questions and got out of him the fact that he had a bit of cash to invest. Then I really went to work on him.

"Stay here tonight," I said, "and stick around tomorrow. You'll see what a good business this really is." He said he would, and I worked on him some more. After a while I asked him to keep an eye on the place while I drove over to the county seat to tend to a few things.

I tended to the things all right but not at the county seat. I burned up the roads getting to various men I knew around about. "There's ten dollars in it for you," I said, "if you'll take the time tomorrow to put the missus and anyone else handy in the car and drive over to the old town and make like a tourist gawking around some."

Come morning everything clicked just right. My young visitor just watched what was going on and spent some time poking around in what was left of the kiln. About the middle of the afternoon, when the last of the cars had left, I figured it was time to hook him.

"Not bad," I said. "Eleven cars and forty-one people. Twenty dollars and a fifty-cent piece left over. Good enough for a week day, but you should see the weekends. Saturdays double it. And Sundays! Why Sundays triple it."

It was just a matter of price after that, and on price I always was a tough one. I'd pushed him up to a thousand bucks. He looked so young and innocent tagging after me into the notary's office that I was almost ashamed of myself.

It wasn't a week later I saw this baby-faced sucker I thought I'd trimmed coming toward me along a street. I ducked quick into a bar. He followed me in and cornered me.

"How's business?" I said, hoping to get any unpleasantness over with fast.

"Business?" he said. "Now that's mighty interesting. Do you really think you fooled me with those fake tourists?" He grinned—the same innocent grin he had the first time I saw him. "Let me buy you a drink. No hard feelings. Your so-called business didn't interest me at all. It was the buildings. I've got a crew tearing them down now."

"Tearing them down?" I said.

"Certainly," he said. "Those bricks. That clay was the best pocket of pay dirt in the whole gulch—only those old miners didn't know it. There was gold dust in that clay and it's right there in the bricks. I'm having them crushed and washing the gold out. There's close to a hundred tons of those bricks, and they're panning about eight hundred dollar to the ton." ◆

Responding to the Theme

The Unexpected

Responding in Your Journal Were you surprised at the ending to "Ghost Town"? Why, do you think, do people like to be surprised by unexpected events and endings in stories? This week, in your journal, write answers to these questions as well as observations about different aspects of the unexpected. Begin today, for example, by jotting down the most unexpected things that have happened throughout your life. For example, have you ever unexpectedly won a contest or an award? Have you ever found something? Have you ever struggled with a serious loss? During the rest of the week, write about unexpected incidents in the lives of others—real people you know or even characters in the science fiction or mysteries you have read. For instance, have you ever known someone who suddenly inherited a large sum of money? Also jot down the details about unexpected occurrences in nature, such as a tornado that demolishes one home but does not touch another right next door.

Speaking and Listening Rewrite the first part of "Ghost Town" as a dialogue between the storyteller and a friend of his. Then, with your teacher's permission, meet in a small group and assign the parts of the storyteller, his friend, and the young man who bought the town. Any other lines should be assigned to a narrator. Finally, have all parts read aloud clearly and with expression.

Critical Thinking: Comparing and Contrasting Write an essay in which you compare and contrast the two men in "Ghost Town." *(For information about writing such essays, see pages 324–325.)*

Extending Your Vocabulary As part of his narrative technique, Jack Schaefer has his narrator use many idiomatic and slang expressions. Find each of the following expressions in the story and decide its meaning, based on its context in the story. Then rewrite each expression with a word or words in standard English. *(For information about standard and nonstandard English, see pages 738–753.)*

temper the talk	stick around
playing nursemaid	cornered me
burned up the roads	let loose
everything clicked just right	poking around

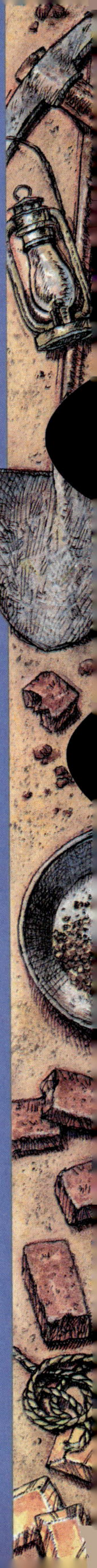

Beancils, Bruno Photography

Part 2 Writing

Most of the writing that you do throughout your life will have a very practical purpose: to explain or pass along information. From time to time, however, you may want to kick off your shoes, lean back, and let your imagination loose. You may want to create imaginary people who accomplish amazing feats in uncharted places. Your purpose for writing such imaginary stories, poems, or plays will be simply to create a work and to entertain your reader.

Coming up with ideas for successful fiction is not always easy. Sitting and waiting for inspiration may work occasionally, but you cannot count on it. Instead, as Jack London once said, "You have to go after it [inspiration] with a club." This chapter will supply you with the "club" you need to explore your imagination and shape your ideas into a short story.

Writing Term A **short story** is a well-developed fictional account of characters resolving a conflict or problem.

The Elements of a Short Story

A short story has three major sections: a beginning, a middle, and an end. The beginning identifies the person telling the story, describes the place and time when the story takes place, and gradually introduces the major and minor characters. In addition the writer creates a problem or obstacle that the main character must overcome. The middle of the story relates a chain of events that result as the characters try to resolve the problem. The ending of the story usually explains how everything turns out. *(For more information about how the elements of a short story contribute to its meaning, see pages 311–312.)*

The Plot and the Central Conflict

The *plot* of a short story is like a play-by-play account of a sporting event. It tells who does what as the story unfolds. It also tells how the characters behave in the face of a *conflict*—the struggle or major problem—around which the story is built. In a sporting event, the conflict is between two opponents; and it usually boils down to the simple question of who will win. In a short story, the conflict is rarely so simple. It usually grows between the main character and some other force in the story, such as another character or a natural force, like a storm or a drought. On the other hand, the conflict could center around a force within the main character—such as a driving, unmet desire or a bitter struggle with his or her conscience. This central conflict drives the plot, from which all the action and dialogue of the story flow. The plot, therefore, usually begins with an event that triggers the conflict.

Once the central conflict is revealed, the plot moves briskly on to the greatest part of the conflict—the *climax*. Finally the plot settles or resolves the conflict or presents another outcome if the conflict remains unresolved.

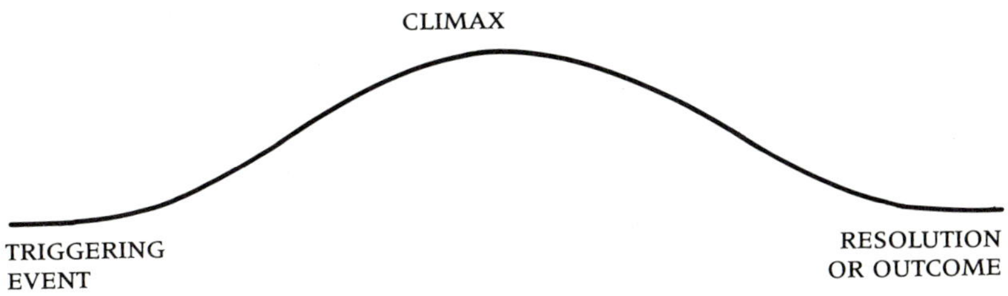

The Characters

Believable characters struggling through the twists and turns of a plot are the hallmarks of an effective short story. In most stories the spotlight is on one main character who is trying to resolve the conflict, or problem. Other characters either help or hinder the main character. Well-written short stories present lifelike characters behaving in believable ways so that readers can identify with them and become involved in the story.

To create lifelike, memorable characters, base your characters on yourself or people you know but give each one a separate, unique identity. Short-story writer Shirley Jackson cautions, ". . . I want to emphasize that people in stories are called characters because that is what they are. They are not real people." The challenge for you is to make the characters as believable as possible. You must create lifelike, unique qualities for the characters through narration, description, and dialogue.

The Setting

The setting of a story is the environment in which the action takes place but it is more than a simple location. It includes the time and the historical or cultural context in which the story occurs. The setting also establishes a mood or atmosphere that reflects the events of the story. *Mood* is the overall feeling that the story conveys.

Writers rely on vivid sensory details to establish their setting and often to reflect the characters' thoughts and feelings. For example, a brooding, angry character may spend a lot of time sitting in a dark room listening to the wailing winds and thunder of a violent storm and contemplating an unpleasant encounter with an enemy. As the story progresses, some elements of the setting may change to match the changes in action and in the characters' feelings. A frightening story, for example, may begin at the stroke of midnight on a rainy night. By the end of the story—if it has a happy ending—dawn might be breaking on a clear new day.

The Narrator

The narrator is the storyteller—the "voice" that tells what happens. The reader follows the events of the story through the eyes or *point of view* of that narrator. The following chart represents the different points of view a narrator may assume to tell a story.

Point of View	Narrator's Role in a Story
FIRST PERSON	Observes or participates in the story's action; uses *I, we,* and other first person pronouns.
EXAMPLE	Before breaking the wishbone, **I** phrased **my** wish carefully in **my** mind, for never before had a wish been so important to **me.**
THIRD PERSON OBJECTIVE	Observes but does not participate in the story's action; relates the words and actions of the characters but not their thoughts and feelings; uses *he, she, him, her, his, hers, they, them, their,* and *theirs.*
EXAMPLE	Before breaking the wishbone, **the contenders** were silent for a moment, **their** brows knit.
THIRD PERSON OMNISCIENT ("ALL-KNOWING")	Observes but does not participate in the story's action; relates the words and actions as well as the thoughts and feelings of all the characters.
EXAMPLE	Before breaking the wishbone, **Alexis** repeated **her** wish silently to **herself,** while **her** sister **Connie, with equal fervor, hoped** that **her sister's** wish would come true.

Each point of view has certain advantages. The first person narrator not only narrates as a participant in the story but also responds to the other characters. With a first person narrator, the reader experiences all of the story through that narrator's observations, thoughts, and feelings. The third person objective narrator can relate two events happening simultaneously in two different places. This technique permits the reader to see the connections between those events. The third person omniscient narrator can relate not only simultaneous events but also all the characters' inner thoughts and outer actions at the same time. This technique gives the reader a broader opportunity to identify with all the characters and see the connections between the events of the story.

The Theme

Most stories have a *theme,* or main idea, of some kind. For instance, a story may be about hope or despair, love or hate, courage or fear, peace or war, life or death. Its outcome may also imply some lesson or moral or make some meaningful observation or conclusion about life. Still other stories present a twist or surprise that is a lesson or moral in itself. In "Ghost Town," for instance, the author does not say anything about the consequences of the narrator's manipulation of people. Schaefer simply lets the events suggest their own story. The reader is then left to reflect on the moral that may lie behind the unpleasant surprise that hits the wily narrator.

WRITING ACTIVITY 1 *Understanding Elements of a Short Story*

Write answers to the following questions about the story "Ghost Town" on pages 381–384.

1. What event triggers the action of the story?
2. What is the central conflict and what event brings about that conflict?
3. At what point does the story reach its climax?
4. How does the owner of the ghost town resolve his problem?
5. What is the outcome of the story? Does the outcome suggest a theme, or message, about life? If so, what is it?
6. Who are the characters in the story?
7. Who is the main character?
8. What is the setting of the story? Describe it in a few sentences.
9. How do you think the setting contributes to the overall effect of the story?
10. What point of view does the writer use?

Prewriting

Writing Process

Writers approach the task of beginning a short story in different ways. For many the process begins with an urge to write. William Faulkner followed a different process. "With me, a story usually begins with a single idea or memory or mental picture. The writing of the story is simply a matter of working up to that moment, to explain why it happened or what caused it to follow." The following prewriting strategies will no doubt help you discover the best approach for getting your story started.

Developing Story Ideas

"What will my story be about?" Many people waste too much time worrying about subjects for their stories. Famous writer of short stories Shirley Jackson offers the following explanation.

> People are always asking me—and every other writer I know—where story ideas come from. Where *do* you get your ideas, they ask; how do you ever manage to think them up? It's certainly the hardest question in the world to answer, since stories originate in everyday happenings and emotions, and any writer who tried to answer such a question would find himself telling over, in some detail, the story of his life. Fiction uses so many small items, so many little gestures and remembered incidents and unforgettable faces, that trying to isolate any one inspiration is incredibly difficult, but basically, of course, the genesis of any fictional work has to be human experience . . . A bald description of an incident is hardly fiction, but the same incident, carefully taken apart, examined as to emotional and balanced structure, and then as carefully reassembled in the most effective form, slanted and polished and weighed, may very well be a short story. SHIRLEY JACKSON, *Experience and Fiction*

Short stories, then, may be based on real-life happenings or forged in a writer's imagination. Whatever the source, a good story will hold a reader in suspense until the problem or conflict that the characters face is finally resolved. The strategies on the following page provide possible sources for story ideas and may even directly stimulate a few ideas.

Strategies for Developing Story Ideas

1. Review your journal writings for conflicts or turning points in your life that may be worth developing into a story.
2. Whenever you think of a story idea, write it in your journal.
3. If possible, form a small discussion group to generate story ideas.
4. Scan newspaper headlines and news items for an event you could build into a fictional story. Some pieces of information, for example, might suggest a mystery, a romance, an adventure, or a comic tale.
5. Observe people in your daily life. Sometimes even small events or snatches of conversation, such as an incident that you noticed in a shopping mall or a conversation you overheard in a pizza parlor, for example, will suggest a conflict around which you can build a plot.

Whatever approach you take, concentrate on finding an event that triggers a conflict for you or for someone else. Do not discard events that seem ordinary or humdrum. Well told, stories about the simple pains or pleasures of daily life can be effective and moving.

WRITING ACTIVITY 2 *Writing on Your Own*

WRITING ABOUT THE THEME

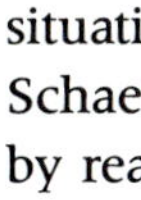

Reread the above Strategies for Developing Story Ideas and adapt them to the theme of the unexpected. Start by reading over all the ideas about the unexpected that you have written in your journal. If possible, share your ideas about the unexpected with others and brainstorm together for more ideas. Also scan newspapers for stories with unexpected endings or twists and turns and use ordinary situations as the basis for imagining unexpected happenings. Jack Schaefer, for example, could have gotten his idea for "Ghost Town" by reading a newspaper article about gold's having been discovered in the bricks of an old ghost town. From there he would have developed his idea for a short story, with its unexpected developments.

Once you have used the strategies above to generate several ideas, think about each one to see if any can trigger a conflict. After you evaluate each idea and its potential, select the one you like best—the one you think you can use to create the most imaginative story. Then save your work in your writing folder for later use.

Developing a Plot

After you have settled on an event related to a conflict, you can begin building the plot. Because a plot usually unfolds from the event that triggers the conflict to the event that resolves that conflict, you need to arrange the details of your plot so that they unfold *naturally* as your tale progresses. The following chart shows several strategies for developing the events of a plot—along with a few examples.

Strategies for Unfolding a Plot

1. Introduce the event or circumstance that triggers the action.

FROM WITHIN A CHARACTER	• a decision to try something new • an uncomfortable or painful feeling
FROM THE OUTSIDE WORLD	• an accident • a meeting with a stranger

2. Develop details that describe the nature of the conflict.

CONFLICT WITH SELF	• a struggle with conscience or desires • a struggle against old ways
CONFLICT WITH OTHERS	• friends, family members • authority figures, enemies, strangers
CONFLICT WITH NATURE	• storms and floods • fire, pollution, or famine

3. Develop details about the obstacles the characters will struggle against or overcome to resolve the conflict.

WITHIN A CHARACTER	• fears or habits of the past • illness
IN THE OUTSIDE WORLD	• misfortunes • challenges from nature

4. Develop details concerned with how the main character will overcome obstacles.

BY THE CHARACTER	• strength of character or growth • perseverence and new skills
THROUGH OUTSIDE EVENTS	• luck or change of circumstances • others' decisions

5. Develop details concerned with the resolution, or solution to the problem, and the outcome.

OVERCOMING OBSTACLES	• new wisdom • success, feeling at peace
FAILING TO OVERCOME	• acceptance of shortcomings • decision to try again

WRITING ACTIVITY 3 *Developing Plots*

Each of the following sentences can serve as an event that triggers the action of a story. After the appropriate number, briefly describe a possible plot for each triggering event. Use the chart on page 394.

1. Amy is stranded on her way home from school when a winter storm closes all roads and knocks out power lines.
2. A teenager walking the dog hears a human voice coming from it.
3. Both Mike and his best friend Mario want the lead in the play.
4. Sarah and Ramona vow that nothing will ever come between them, and then Jason moves to town.
5. Dennis discovers Alicia won the scholarship he hoped was his.

WRITING ACTIVITY 4 *Writing on Your Own*

WRITING ABOUT THE THEME

Review your prewriting work from Writing Activity 2 on a story idea related to the theme of the unexpected. Refer to Strategies for Unfolding a Plot on page 394 and then sketch out the steps in the development of your plot by completing the following chart. Let your imagination reign and freely create possibilities. When you are satisfied that you have some good ideas for your plot, save your notes in your writing folder for later use.

CENTRAL CONFLICT: ______________________

EVENT TRIGGERING ACTION: ______________________

HOW CHARACTER FACES CONFLICT: ______________________

STRUGGLE TO RESOLVE CONFLICT: ______________________

OUTCOME: ______________________

Sketching Characters

In her autobiography famous mystery writer Agatha Christie explained that she often used real people she saw on the bus as the basis for many of her characters. She knew that to be believable, characters in a story must ring true to a reader. In other words they must look and walk and talk like real people.

To create such imaginary "real" people you should always visualize your characters in your mind—or on paper—until you have added enough details to turn the characters into flesh and blood. For example, you would want to consider such aspects as a character's name, age, physical appearance, voice, mannerisms, background, and personality traits and eccentricities. The following description shows how the specific details of physical features contribute to a characterization.

Model: *Characterization*

> Elisa Allen, working in her flower garden, looked down across the yard . . . She was thirty-five. Her face was lean and strong and her eyes were as clear as water. Her figure looked blocked and heavy in her gardening costume, a man's black hat pulled down over her eyes, clod-hopper shoes, a figured print dress almost completely covered by a big corduroy apron with four big pockets and the knife she worked with. She wore heavy leather gloves to protect her hands while she worked.
>
> JOHN STEINBECK, "The Chrysanthemums"

The following chart will help you create a preliminary sketch of your characters so that they will be realistic and believable to your reader.

Character Sketch

Name: ______________________
Age: ______________________
Role in story: ______________________
Physical appearance: ______________________
Most important personality traits: ______________________
Mannerisms: ______________________
Background information: ______________________
Strengths: ______________________
Weaknesses: ______________________

Writing Is Thinking

Critical Thinking

Elaborating

One way to reveal character is through precise description. To help your readers see characters exactly as you see them, you may need to call on the skill of *elaborating.* When you elaborate on a character, you work out the details suggested by the general idea you already have of that character.

To assist in the elaborating of your characters, construct a chart like the one below. Visualize an aspect of the character for each heading on the chart. Then list as many details as you can to reveal your character's age, coloring, facial expressions, voice, style of talking, style of walking, clothing, habits, even smells. When you write your story, you can select those details from the chart that contribute to the impression you want to create for your character.

Character Elaboration Chart

CHARACTER	teenager Mark Stevens
APPEARANCE (age, eyes, hair, face, physical build)	sixteen, lean but muscular, strong features, brilliant blue eyes, gleaming white teeth, long blond curly hair, unusually long arms with huge hands
CLOTHING	baseball cap, basketball shoes, cutoff jeans, baggy T-shirt with neon colors, black sunglasses
MANNERISMS, ACTIONS (ways of walking, talking, voice)	chews gum, squints and looks at training track; shoulders hunched, hands jammed in pockets; speaks in rapid half-sentences with low voice
POSSESSIONS	camera around neck

Thinking Practice Select a character from your journal or originate a new one and then elaborate about him or her with as many details as possible. Construct a chart like the one above to help you visualize the character more completely.

Witness, Joyce Treiman, 1988, Collection ARA Services, Inc.

WRITING ACTIVITY 5 *Sketching Characters*

Complete the Character Sketch chart on page 396 for each of the following imaginary characters. Save your work for possible stories.

1. a practical joker
2. a banker who always behaves very properly
3. an attractive but self-centered teenage girl or boy

WRITING ACTIVITY 6 *Writing on Your Own*

WRITING ABOUT THE THEME

Review your prewriting notes from Writing Activity 4 for your short story about the unexpected. Using the chart on page 396, create a preliminary character sketch for each of the characters that will appear in your story. Then, referring to the Character Elaboration chart on the previous page, elaborate on each of your main characters. Save your sketches to use when drafting your story.

Creating a Setting

When planning the setting of your story, remember that the most effective settings are those that establish a mood that mirrors the characters' feelings and the action.

Writing Tip Match the **setting** of your story to the characters' feelings and the action.

Notice the mood of fear that the author develops in his story about the taboos and beliefs of people in a primitive hunting society.

Model: *Details of Mood in a Setting*

> My father is a priest; I am the son of a priest. I have been in the Dead Places near us, with my father—at first, I was afraid. When my father went into the house to search for the metal, I stood by the door and my heart felt small and weak. It was a dead man's house; a spirit house. It did not have the smell of man, though there were old bones in a corner. But it is not fitting that a priest's son should show fear. I looked at the bones in the shadow and kept my voice still.
>
> STEPHEN VINCENT BENÉT, "By the Waters of Babylon."

Also strive for as much realistic detail in your setting as possible to help the action unfold believably. As English writer Ford Maddox Ford said, "Unless I know what sort of doorknob his fingers closed on, how shall I—satisfactorily to myself—get my character out-of-doors?"

Model: *Realistic Details in a Setting*

> It was a narrow, little shop, not very well lit, and the doorbell pinged again with a plaintive note as we closed it behind us. For a moment or so we were alone and could glance about us. There was a tiger in *papier-maché* on the glass case that covered the low counter—a grave, kind-eyed tiger that waggled his head in a methodical manner. There were several crystal spheres, a china hand holding magic cards, a stock of magic fishbowls in various sizes, and an immodest magic bat that shamelessly displayed its springs. On the floor were magic mirrors; one to draw you out long and thin, one to swell your head and vanish your legs, and one to make you short and fat like a draught; and while we were laughing at these the shopman, as I suppose, came in.
>
> H. G. WELLS, "The Magic Shop"

WRITING ACTIVITY 7 *Choosing Settings*

Number your paper 1 to 5. Then write the letter of the setting that is best suited to each character and explain your choice.

Characters

1. a shy boy who is afraid to come out of his shell
2. a girl who tests her strength against nature
3. a boy who does not feel a sense of belonging in his family
4. a girl who dreams of going places and making it big in show business
5. a miser who values riches above friendship

Settings

a. a room added onto the main house
b. a room with closed windows and doors
c. a small town on a river near a bridge leading to the big city
d. a room decorated in black and gold
e. the mountains of Montana

WRITING ACTIVITY 8 *Sketching Settings*

Visualize interesting and appropriate settings for three of the following imaginary situations. Then write a brief sketch of each setting that reflects the situation or relates to the character's mood.

1. While waiting for the coach to call her into the game, Lottie felt panic rising in her throat.
2. Rob's wondering eyes saw the great expanse of ocean and horizon ahead.
3. Pushing her pen tensely against the examination paper, Marge struggled to concentrate.
4. Jeff, his heart pounding, approached Katie for a dance.
5. Mrs. Gagen frowned as she entered the subway station.

WRITING ACTIVITY 9 *Writing on Your Own*

WRITING ABOUT THE THEME

Review your prewriting work on your short story about the unexpected and create an appropriate setting for your characters and the events you have developed for your plot. Remember to establish a mood. Freewrite, brainstorm, or cluster to include as many details as possible. Then save your notes in your writing folder to refer to later when you draft your story.

Choosing a Point of View

The power you have as a writer is both fun and challenging. You can make anything happen that you want, such as changing the characters, the mood, and the setting. You also have complete control over the point of view you choose for your story. As you learned on page 390, you can choose one of three points of view when telling your stories: first person, third person objective, or third person omniscient. Even if the story is about an experience you have had, for example, you could tell it from the third person objective or omniscient point of view, referring to yourself as *he* or *she.* In a similar way, if your story is actually about your best friend, you could tell it in the first person, referring to the main character as *I.* Choose whatever point of view is most suitable for your story, but be sure to use it consistently throughout the story, without switching back and forth.

If you choose a point of view that does not allow you to enter the minds of all your characters, remember that a character's actions and dialogue can reveal what he or she is feeling.

Model: *Third Person Objective Narrator*

ACTION Anna gripped the wood armrests tightly as she awaited the news. [Anna's actions show that she feels nervous.]

DIALOGUE "I won!" Loren shouted triumphantly as he approached his mother in the kitchen. [The dialogue shows that Loren feels proud and happy.]

WRITING ACTIVITY 10 *Revealing Feeling through Actions*

Imagine that you have just come upon a friend of yours sitting under a tree. Write five sentences that describe the person's actions. Choose actions that reveal the following feelings.

EXAMPLE surprise

POSSIBLE ANSWER My friend's huge eyes became still larger when he noticed me.

1. surprise
2. discouragement
3. fear
4. excitement
5. anger

WRITING ACTIVITY 11 *Choosing Point of View*

While riding her new bicycle, Rhoda collides with Mrs. Schneider who is carrying a large bag of groceries. Choose two of the following points of view to relate the incident, writing a paragraph for each.

1. first person as Rhoda
2. first person as Mrs. Schneider
3. third person objective as a witness

WRITING ACTIVITY 12 *Writing on Your Own*

WRITING ABOUT THE THEME

Review all your prewriting notes for the story about the unexpected that you have been developing. Imagine how your story would read if it was told from the point of view of your main character, or from the third person objective or omniscient point of view. Review the chart on page 390 and then choose the most appropriate point of view for your story. Make a note of your choice and save it.

Listing Events in Order

When you sketched out the events in the unfolding of your plot, you probably placed them in chronological order, the order in which they happen. If you plan to tell your story in chronological order, look over your list of events to make sure each happening progresses logically from the one before it. Also consider all the events you wish to include in your story and add any new event to your list, in proper sequence. Your final list might look like the one below.

Model: *Events in Chronological Order*

- At the breakfast table, Anthony's father teases him about the Band-Aid on his face and says he's too young to shave.
- Anthony leaves the table and slams the door on his way out.
- Hurrying angrily to school, Anthony crosses the street without noticing an approaching car.
- The car slams on its brakes but knocks Anthony down.
- Police come and take Anthony to the hospital, where his broken arm is put in a cast.
- Police call Anthony's father at work and report the accident.
- Anthony's father heads straight for the hospital with a gift.
- Anthony's father gives him the gift: an electric razor.

Gregory Walking, Venice, California, Feb. 1983
photographic collage, 12" x 23" © David Hockney

Understanding Flashback Sometimes when drafting your story, you may want a variation from chronological order. You may, for example, begin at the end of the story and use flashbacks to show the events leading up to your ending. A *flashback* is a memory sequence that interrupts the chronological order of events for the purpose of telling what happened at some time in the past. You could also begin your story at the moment of highest tension, use flashbacks to tell what came before that moment, and then continue in chronological order—on through the resolution and outcome.

WRITING ACTIVITY 13 *Using Flashbacks*

The details for the story about Anthony on page 402 are arranged in chronological order. Reorder the events of the story by beginning with either the final detail or a detail that shows the moment of highest tension. Then tell the rest of the story with flashbacks or a combination of flashbacks and chronological order.

WRITING ACTIVITY 14 *Writing on Your Own*

WRITING ABOUT THE THEME

Make a complete list of all the events you want to include in your story about the unexpected. If you decide to present your story in strict chronological order, be sure your details are arranged accordingly. If you decide to use flashbacks, make a list showing where you will start in the story and in what order you will present the other events from the past. Save your work in your writing folder.

Drafting

Writing Process

Most writers have their own special strategy and style of drafting. Some, for example, use their prewriting work rigorously, referring often to their list of organized details as a guide. Others find that they have a clear enough idea of their story to sit down and write it from start to finish without once looking back at their notes. Experiment until you find a drafting style that is effective for you.

Drafting the Beginning

As you draft your story, keep your audience and purpose in mind. While your basic writing purpose is to create and be inventive, you may have another more specific goal. For example, you may want to have your audience strongly identify with a particular character that you have created. On the other hand, your goal may be to influence your reader by providing an insight about life. To reach your audience successfully, use the following strategies to begin your story.

Strategies for Beginning a Story

1. Be inventive and capture the reader's attention by using sensory details to describe the setting and to create a mood.
2. Establish the narrator's point of view and use it consistently.
3. Use vivid language and interesting details to introduce the characters and the central conflict.
4. Provide any background information about the time and place of the story that the reader may need.
5. If you are using strict chronological order, include the triggering event that starts the story in motion. If you are using flashbacks, however, begin with an incident in the story that reflects the central conflict.

WRITING ACTIVITY 15 *Writing on Your Own*

WRITING ABOUT THE THEME

Look over all your prewriting work from earlier writing activities. Use that work as you see fit to help you draft the beginning of your story, referring to the strategies above to make sure your beginning captures the reader's attention and interest. Save your work.

Drafting the Middle

A good beginning will help you write the middle of your story as well. Once the plot is set in motion in well-written stories, the events seem to unfold somewhat naturally. As you draft the middle of your story, present those events as smoothly as possible and make your characters live and breathe. The following strategies will help you draft the middle of your story.

Strategies for Drafting the Middle

1. Include only those events that have a direct bearing on the plot and the central conflict.
2. Tell the events in a logical, dramatic order (either strict chronological order or a variation using flashbacks) and use transitions to connect the events smoothly and show the passage of time.
3. Build on the conflict until the action reaches a climax.
4. Use narration, description, dialogue, and action to show—not just tell—what the characters are thinking and to advance the plot.
5. Maintain a clear and consistent point of view.

Connecting the Events in the Story When you draft the middle of your story, you simply pick up where you left off and show how each event follows from the triggering event at the beginning of your story. Keep in mind that the story's events should not just follow each other but should build on each other, with each event adding to the tension until the plot reaches its climax. Use transitions to show the passage of time between events as well as the buildup of tension as your story approaches its climax. The transitions will also keep your story flowing smoothly from one event to another. *(See page 113 for a list of common transitions used in chronological order.)*

Using Flashbacks If you are using flashbacks, how do you accomplish the same smooth-flowing results? In movies or on television, directors sometimes indicate that a flashback is about to start by playing dreamlike music and making the screen look dim, fuzzy, and wavy. When you write, you have several options. You can simply skip a line or use a row of stars or asterisks to indicate a break in the chronology.

Model: *Showing Flashback with Spacing*

Anthony was still thinking about his father's teasing as he charged across the street. He didn't even see the car at first—he just heard a heart-stopping screech of brakes. Without thinking he was in the middle of the street himself, feeling the crunch of the car's fender.

* * * * * * * * * * * * * *

Anthony had come down for breakfast—feeling good and ready and eager for the day ahead, which he knew included a chance to sit next to Julie at lunch . . .

With an appropriate point of view, you can make the connections even smoother by using narration to introduce the flashback so that the events will be smoothly connected.

Model: *Showing Flashback with Narration*

Anthony was still thinking about his father's teasing as he charged across the street. He didn't even see the car at first—he just heard a heart-stopping screech of brakes. Without thinking he was in the middle of the street himself, feeling the crunch of the car's fender. For a while all was a blur of pain. Little by little Anthony began to remember how the day had begun.

He had come down for breakfast—feeling good and ready and eager for the day ahead, which he knew included a chance to sit next to Julie at lunch . . .

Notice that in both cases the verb tense changes from simple past to past perfect when the flashback begins. This change in tense indicates to the reader that the events in the flashback have occurred earlier.

Using Dialogue Besides using narration to tell your story, you can also use dialogue to show how the plot unfolds. For instance, Jack Schaefer used dialogue for the first time in "Ghost Town," to show the heightening of the conflict as the ghost-town owner tries to interest the "pink-cheeked young fellow" in buying his town. *(See page 382.)* Using natural-sounding dialogue as Schaefer does is also one of the best ways to bring your characters to life and to let your reader "hear" as well as visualize the people in your story. As you read the following two versions of an event, notice how much livelier the one with the dialogue is.

NARRATIVE	He shyly handed her a tiny white package tied with a narrow gold ribbon, explaining that he was sorry he had missed her birthday and hoped she liked it. She beamed with pleasure.
DIALOGUE	"Here," he said shyly as he thrust the slim white package at her. "I'm real sorry I didn't come around last night for your birthday but I had to work." "Oh Josh," she breathed. "What's this?" "Not much, actually," he gulped. "Hope you like it." "Cool, it's just the charm I wanted! How could you have known?"

The Artist and His Mother, Arshile Gorky, c. 1926–36. Oil on canvas, 60" x 50" (152.4 cm x 127 cm). Coll. of Whitney Museum of American Art. Gift of Julien Levy for Maro and Natasha Gorky in memory of their father. 50.17

WRITING ACTIVITY 16 *Writing Dialogue*

After imagining each of the following situations, select one and write a dialogue of about 15 lines between the characters. To review the punctuation and the correct form for writing dialogue, refer to page 805.

1. a confrontation between a sales clerk and a dissatisfied customer
2. an offer to assist a young child across a busy intersection
3. a discussion of a major news story
4. a dinner-table discussion about curfews
5. an argument about a play on the sports field

WRITING ACTIVITY 17 *Writing on Your Own*

WRITING ABOUT THE THEME

After you review the beginning of your short story about the unexpected that you drafted in Writing Activity 15, use the strategies on page 405 to draft the middle of your story. As you write, let your imagination flow freely and add fresh details and new ideas that you think are appropriate. If you get stuck in one part, continue on to another incident in the plot where you are more confident. In other words, writing the middle of the story is a flexible process; you can return to the difficult part later. If your teacher permits, use peer conferencing to test your ideas or to get help with any trouble spots. When you are satisfied with your draft to this point, save it in your writing folder for future use.

Drafting the Ending

The mystery writer Mickey Spillane wrote, "I write the ending first. Nobody reads a book to get to the middle." The ending of a story is, after all, the payoff. Especially in a mystery story, it is where the conflicts are resolved and everything is explained. Keep in mind, though, that the ending of a short story does not have to be upbeat, with all the characters living happily ever after. In any kind of story, however, the ending must bring the events to a fitting close. To write an effective ending to your short story, you may want to use the following strategies.

Strategies for Ending a Story

1. Resolve the conflict and complete the action of the story.
2. If the conflict is not to be resolved, present an outcome that is logical and believable.
3. Continue to use dialogue, action, or description to show, not just tell, what happens.
4. Match the mood of the story.
5. Leave the reader feeling satisfied.

Writing Tip End your short story by showing how the conflict is resolved and by telling the final outcome of events. Remember to leave a strong emotional impression on your readers.

Drafting a Title Once you are satisfied with your story, read it aloud and think of a title that will enliven your story and capture your reader's attention. A successful title will simultaneously invite and challenge the reader to give up some time to spend reading your story.

WRITING ACTIVITY 18 *Writing on Your Own*

WRITING ABOUT THE THEME

Add a strong ending to your short story, using the strategies above to guide you. Then think of a title that will enliven your story and capture the reader's attention. You may wish to test several possible titles with members of your family to see which is the strongest. Save your work in your writing folder for revising and editing later.

Revising

Writing Process

When you revise a short story, spend some of your time checking for believability. Are your characters walking, talking people that your reader can identify with? Does your setting seem real? Even extremely imaginative settings like another planet should have a ring of authenticity to them. As you revise, look for any missing details needed to make your story ring true to your reader.

Sharpening Characterizations

When revising, take a good hard look at each and every one of your characters. Does each convey a distinct, memorable personality? Have you fallen into the trap of presenting a "type" instead of a real person (a kindly grandmother, for example, rather than a living, breathing elderly person with unique characteristics)? Focus on sharpening your characterizations to make your story more memorable and believable. The following strategies will help you create lifelike characters.

Strategies for Revealing Character

1. Avoid stereotypes.
2. Use dialogue with natural-sounding speech that reflects the personality of your characters.
3. Use descriptions rich in sensory details to help readers see your characters.
4. Use narration to record significant actions—such as little gestures, particular turns of speech, and automatic reactions of surprise, fear, or anger.
5. With a third person omniscient narrator, use narration to record thoughts and feelings.

WRITING ACTIVITY 19 *Matching Dialogue to Character*

The statements on the following page all express the same general meaning. Each one, however, creates a different image and would therefore be suitable to reveal a different kind of character. Choose one statement. Then, avoiding stereotypes, write a one-paragraph description of the character that the statement leads you to visualize. Save your work for Writing Activity 21.

1. "Yup," I says again, "that was one fine meal you rustled up."
2. "Wow! That was like really dee-lish!"
3. "That was a wonderful dinner indeed."
4. "I am beholden to you for a fine meal."
5. "Please! I'd love the recipes. What a meal!"

WRITING ACTIVITY 20 *Revealing Character*

Write one paragraph telling what goes on in Brenda's mind when she learns her family must move out of state by the end of the month. Use a third person omniscient narrator. The first sentence is provided for you.

> Brenda grew steadily more angry at being wrenched from her friends, her new job, and—worst of all—her lifelong confidant, cousin Burt.

Tightening the Descriptions

When some people are learning how to write fiction, they tend to overwrite, or to use *purple prose.* In other words they use too many unnecessary or redundant words to describe a character or a setting. One function of revising, therefore, is to look for any purple prose and reduce it to clear, uncluttered description. Following is an example of how purple prose can call such attention to itself that it distracts the reader from becoming involved with the character. Reread John Steinbeck's description of his character Elisa Allen on page 396. Contrast that effective description with the purple prose below and then consider the effects of the purple prose if it had appeared in Steinbeck's story.

> Elisa Allen worked in her flower garden. And what a garden it was! Fragrant roses blushed hot pink in the glimmering sunshine and sent their roots ever deeper and deeper into the fertile, life-giving mud beneath the surface. Lambent lilies arched their slender backs and reached toward the sunshine, drawn as if to a gigantic burning magnet in the cloudless, endless, brilliant blue sky . . .

As you can see, purple-prose Elisa becomes lost as the focus in this rambling, self-conscious description. Although elaborating is useful to paint sharp, accurate pictures of your characters, limitless descriptive details that serve no purpose will only cloud the picture. Tighten your descriptions so that you say as much as possible in a few, well-chosen words.

> In her flower garden, Elisa Allen poked the fertile soil around the hot-pink roses, yanked the weeds, and then stood, staring at the tall, brilliant lilies.

WRITING ACTIVITY 21 *Tightening Descriptions*

Write a two-paragraph passage of purple prose about the character you described in Writing Activity 19. Have fun. Try to make your description as overdone and rambling as possible. Then trim it back to an effective three- or four-sentence description. With your teacher's permission, select a partner and exchange papers. Revise your partner's description so that the writing is even tighter and discuss your changes.

Using a Revision Checklist

After sharpening your characterizations and tightening your descriptions, you are ready to check over your whole story and look for ways to make it even better. The following checklist will help you revise your short stories.

Revision Checklist

1. Does the beginning of your story give the setting, capture attention, introduce the characters, and include the triggering event? *(See page 404.)*
2. Does the middle present events directly related to the central conflict? Are the events arranged in strict chronological order, or a variation with flashbacks? Are they connected by smooth transitions? *(See page 405.)*
3. Does your story build on the conflict until the action reaches a climax? *(See page 387.)*
4. Did you use dialogue and description to bring your characters to life? *(See pages 388 and 406–407.)*
5. Does the ending of your story show how the conflict was resolved or present an outcome and bring the story to a close? *(See page 409.)*
6. Is the narrator's point of view consistent throughout the story? *(See page 404.)*

WRITING ACTIVITY 22 *Writing on Your Own*

WRITING ABOUT THE THEME

If your teacher permits, break up into small discussion groups and take turns reading aloud your stories about the unexpected. Comment on what is especially strong about them and what could be improved, paying special attention to sharp characterizations and tight descriptions. Then return to your seat and use your listeners' comments and the Revision Checklist above to make a complete and thorough revision of your short story.

If time permits, repeat the process of meeting in small groups or share your story with new test readers, including friends or family members. Different audiences can sometimes have different responses to your work that will help you approach your revisions with new insights. Then save your work in your writing folder for editing and publishing.

Language Integrating Skills

Editing and Publishing

Grammar in the Writing Process

"Mighty interesting town you have here," he said. "Those buildings. Brick. Don't see much brick in the old camps. They haul them in here?"

"Why no," I said. "They had a kiln right here—you can see where it was behind the blacksmith shop. They dug the clay out of the bank over there."

When you write fiction, an extremely useful tool is dialogue. You can use it to move the plot along, which is what the above dialogue from "Ghost Town" does. You can also use dialogue to reveal character traits and to add realism to a story. However, you will need to know which pronouns to use and how to punctuate your dialogue correctly.

Cases of Pronouns A *pronoun* is a word that takes the place of a noun. *Nominative case* pronouns, used as subjects and predicate nominatives, are *I, you, he, she, it, we,* and *they. Objective case* pronouns used as objects are *me, you, him, her, it, us,* and *them. Possessive case* pronouns, used to show ownership or possession, are *my, mine, your, yours, his, her, hers, its, our, ours, their,* and *theirs.* *(For more information about pronouns and practice in using them correctly, see pages 681–690.)*

NOMINATIVE CASE	If **they** knew too much history, **I**'d go easy on the fancy trimmings.
OBJECTIVE CASE	Some of the customers would ask **me** to tell **them** about the big brawls.
POSSESSIVE CASE	People stopped spending **their** money in **my** town when the highway was built.

Quotation Marks with Dialogue When you are writing dialogue, enclose a person's exact words—and nothing else—inside quotation marks. Put the opening quotation marks before the first word a person says and put the closing quotation marks after the last word a person says—even if the person says several sentences.

"Mighty interesting business you're in. Playing nursemaid to an old town like this. Must be kind of nice.**"**

Capital Letters with Dialogue Begin each sentence of a direct quotation with a capital letter.

> **"H**ow's business?" I said.
> He said, **"Y**ou didn't fool me with those fake tourists."

Commas and End Marks with Dialogue Use a comma to separate a direct quotation from a speaker tag, such as *he said.* Place the comma *inside* the closing quotation marks. Also an end mark usually should be placed inside the closing quotation marks when the end of the quotation comes at the end of the sentence. *(For more information about punctuating dialogue and for practice in writing direct quotations correctly, see pages 798–807.)*

> He said, **"**Your so-called business didn't interest me at all. It was the buildings. I've got a crew tearing them down now**."**
> "Tearing them down**?"** I said.
> "Certainly**,"** he said.

Indentation with Dialogue Begin a new paragraph each time the speaker changes so that the reader will know who is speaking. For an example, look at the previous lines of dialogue.

Editing Checklist

1. Has the correct case of each pronoun been used? *(See pages 681–689.)*
2. Has all dialogue been punctuated, capitalized, and indented correctly? *(See page 805.)*

WRITING ACTIVITY 23 *Writing on Your Own*

WRITING ABOUT THE THEME

Editing Use the checklist above and the one on page 35 to edit your story. When you are pleased with it, make a final copy.

Publishing Before submitting your story to your teacher, make an audiotape of it—if possible. You may wish to assume the different voices of your characters yourself. On the other hand, you could invite others to take on roles and give a dramatic reading. Then give your tape to the school library.

A Writer Writes

WRITING
BOUT THE
THEME

A Short Story

PURPOSE: To create and to entertain with a science-fiction or mystery story

AUDIENCE: lovers of suspense

Prewriting Most everyone loves to read mysteries and science-fiction stories because they usually surprise and baffle readers with unexpected happenings and events. In fact, an entire science-fiction story may revolve around an unexpected creature or character. On the other hand, some of the best mysteries are based on ordinary people who are unexpectedly caught up in a less than ordinary situation and one that often is frightening.

To find a subject for a mystery or science-fiction story, read over your journal entries about the unexpected and review the Strategies for Developing Story Ideas on page 393. You also could make a cluster with the word *unexpected* in the center of a page and see what additional possibilities you discover. Then choose one and decide whether it would work better in a science-fiction story or a mystery.

After you have established the theme and a point of view for your story, sketch the setting and characters, keeping the number of the latter as few as possible. Decide on what conflict your characters will face and outline the steps of the plot: the triggering event, the buildup of tension to the climax, the resolution, and the outcome. In the case of a mystery, also be sure that before you begin to write your first draft, you carefully plan several clues to include in your story. Then decide whether you will tell the story in strict chronological order or use a flashback and list the events accordingly.

Drafting Use your prewriting work to draft an effective beginning, middle, and end to your story. At all times make your characters behave in ways that match the personalities you established for them. Also remember to use dialogue, description, and narration to bring your characters and action to life.

Revising Use the checklists on pages 31 and 413 and the following questions as guides to your revision. Is the sequence of events clear? If you are writing a mystery, have you given enough clues so that your reader can figure it out? Do all the events lead to the climax of the mystery? Where can you add figurative language and sensory words to help you tell the story? Where can you add sound devices to heighten the effect of a suspenseful moment? Now read your dialogue aloud. Does it sound like an everyday conversation between real people?

Editing and Publishing Using the checklists on pages 35 and 415, edit your story. Then copy it neatly and be prepared to read it to your classmates. If time permits, your teacher may hold a writing contest, in which everyone in your class votes on the best story.

Independent Writing

Write a short story about one of the subjects on the following page or on a subject of your own choice. Use the Checklist for Creative Writing on page 419 as a guide.

1. a neighborhood incident
2. moving to a new town
3. colonizing a new planet
4. a time machine
5. the Bermuda Triangle
6. a computer with feelings
7. a voice from the past
8. finding a secret passageway
9. an unexpected meeting
10. one footprint in the sand

WRITING ABOUT THE THEME

Creative Writing

The unexpected form in a poem is almost sure to catch a reader's attention. After you think about the following poem, create a crossword poem of your own.

```
D
U
S     D
T H O U G H T S
Y     S
      T H I N G S
      Y       E
              T
              T
            R I D
              N
              G O I N G
                      O
                      I
                      N
                      G O N E
```

Writing about Literature

A *protagonist,* the main character in a literary work, is always involved in the major conflict of a short story. The protagonist is also the character with whom most readers sympathize. In a paragraph state who the protagonist of "Ghost Town" is and explain how this character is the driving force in the story.

Writing in Another Subject Area

World History Write a dramatic story about the trial and death of Socrates. Refer to your history textbook and a library for information you will need to present all the relevant details in the story.

Chapter

11 Checklist

Creative Writing

Prewriting

- ✔ Drawing on your own experiences or imagination, think of a conflict worthy of developing in a short story. *(See pages 392–394.)*
- ✔ Write a brief character sketch for each person in your story and create a setting appropriate to the mood you have chosen. *(See pages 388–389 and 396–399.)*
- ✔ Choose an appropriate point of view from which to tell your story. *(See page 390.)*
- ✔ List all the events in the plot of your story in strict chronological order or a variation using flashbacks. *(See pages 402–403.)*

Drafting

- ✔ Write the beginning of your story. Be sure to capture attention, introduce characters, give the setting, and include the triggering event. Strive to be inventive and keep your purpose and audience in mind. *(See page 404.)*
- ✔ Write the middle of your story. Tell the events in chronological order, with appropriate transitions to connect the story events smoothly. If you use flashbacks, adjust your chronology appropriately. Build on the conflict and bring the action to a climax, using dialogue and description. *(See pages 405–407.)*
- ✔ Write the ending. Tell how the conflict is resolved or, if not, present another outcome and bring the story to a close. *(See page 409.)*
- ✔ Write a catchy title. *(See page 409.)*

Revising

- ✔ Look for ways to sharpen your characterizations. *(See page 410.)*
- ✔ Tighten your descriptions by omitting purple prose. *(See page 412.)*
- ✔ Use the Revision Checklist on page 413.

Editing and Publishing

- ✔ Use the Editing Checklists on pages 35 and 415 to polish your final draft and if possible make an audiotape of your story.

...the author set the stage
Traveling along
risk takes here,
of speech
refuse its burden
momentary
denial of natural

Unit 3
Applying Communication and Study Skills

Chapter

12 Letters and Applications

Perhaps some time in the future, people in business will communicate exclusively through a worldwide network of home and office computers. Until that time, however, the business letter will remain an effective way to communicate. For the price of stationery and a stamp, you can request information, order merchandise, register a complaint, apply for a job, or apply to college.

Writing letters for these and other purposes will become increasingly important to you as you move closer to graduation from high school and make plans for the future. If you plan to continue your education, you will use letters to obtain college applications, seek information about courses, and explain your qualifications to potential schools. When you seek employment after graduation, you will write letters to show your qualifications to best advantage to potential employers.

This chapter will help you by showing you how to write business letters that follow the correct form and are clear, to the point, and convincing. In the chapter you will also see how to compose effective résumés and fill out application forms.

Writing Business Letters

Most of the business letters you write will call for some action on the part of the receiver. To make sure the busy people you write to understand your purpose or request, make your letters neat and easy to read.

A few simple guidelines will help your letter be as neat as possible in appearance. First, use white paper, preferably 8-½ by 11 inches in size. On your paper leave margins that are at least one inch wide. Whenever possible, you should type your letter, and if you do so, you should also type the envelope. Finally, fold your letter neatly to fit into the envelope.

Correct Form for Business Letters

HEADING

2220 Peachtree Drive
Atlanta, GA 30314
December 12, 1992

INSIDE ADDRESS

Customer Service
J & H Videos, Inc.
113 Clayton Street
Mount Aetna, PA 19544

SALUTATION

Dear Sir or Madam:

BODY

CLOSING

Yours truly,

SIGNATURE

Leroy Washington

Leroy Washington

The parts of a business letter are the heading, inside address, salutation, body, closing, and signature. The following guidelines will help you with each part.

Parts of a Business Letter	
HEADING	Write your full address, including your ZIP Code. Write out the name of your state in full or use the two-letter postal abbreviation.
INSIDE ADDRESS	Write the receiver's address two to four lines below the heading. Include the name of the person if you know it, using *Mr.*, *Ms.*, *Mrs.*, *Dr.*, or some other appropriate title. If the person has a business title, such as *Manager*, write it on the next line. Use the same way of identifying the state that you used in the heading.
SALUTATION	Start the salutation two lines below the inside address. Use *Sir* or *Madam* if you do not know the person's name. Otherwise use the person's last name preceded by *Mr.*, *Ms.*, *Mrs.*, or other title. Use a colon after the salutation.
BODY	Start two lines below the salutation. Double-space and indent a single paragraph. For longer letters, single-space each paragraph, skipping a line between paragraphs and indenting each new one.
CLOSING	Start two or three lines below the body. Line up the closing with the left-hand edge of the heading. Use a formal closing, such as *Sincerely, Sincerely yours,* or *Yours truly.* The closing is followed by a comma.
SIGNATURE	Type (or print, if your letter is handwritten) your name four or five lines below the closing. Then sign your name in the space between the closing and your typed name.

Keep a record of each business letter you write. You can make a copy with carbon paper or use a copying machine.

Use the form shown below for your envelope.

Correct Form for a Business Envelope

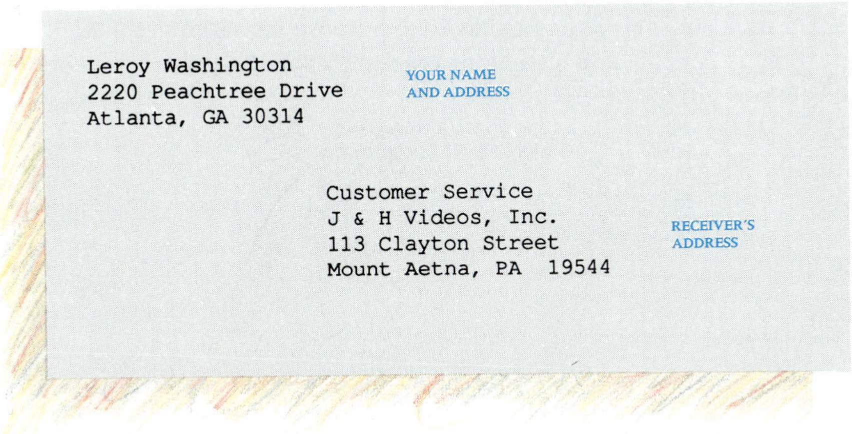

Language *Integrating* Skills

Capitalizing Proper Nouns and Proper Adjectives

Follow these rules for capitalizing words in the different parts of your letter. As you write the business letters in this chapter, proofread each one for correct capital letters.

1. In the **heading** and **inside address,** capitalize all names of people, companies, streets, cities, states, and months. Also capitalize titles such as *Mr.* and *Mrs.*

   2119 **S**pring **S**treet
   Skokie, **IL** 60025
   October 24, 1992

   Mr. **N**eil **S**aperstein
   Movie **M**emories, **I**nc.
   521 **M**aple **G**rove **R**oad
   Lawrence, **KS** 66044

2. In the **salutation** capitalize the first word, titles, and names.

   Dear **M**r. **S**aperstein:

3. In the **closing** capitalize the first word, and in the **signature,** capitalize your name.

   Sincerely yours,
   Sandra **G**raber

Letters of Request

A common type of business letter is the *request letter,* in which you ask for information or for an item such as a pamphlet, brochure, or application. In such letters make your purpose for writing apparent as soon as possible and state your request clearly. Be sure to include all six parts of the business letter.

Letter of Request

2719 Lincoln Avenue
Chicago, IL 60657
May 11, 1992

Director
Tourist Information
State of Wisconsin
Box 7921
Madison, WI 53707

Dear Sir or Madam:

Our club, the Chicago Backpackers, is planning a hiking trip for the first week in July. We are interested in the Tuscobia Trail and would like to have more information about it. Would you please send me a pamphlet describing the trail and the stopping points along the way?

I would also be interested in learning the rules and regulations about backpacking in Wisconsin state lands. Please send this information so we can plan accordingly.

Thank you for your assistance.

Sincerely yours,

Salvatore Cabasino

Salvatore Cabasino

Order Letters

When ordering merchandise from a catalog or an advertisement, be sure to include the order number, price, quantity, and size for each item. If you are enclosing a check or money order, identify that enclosure in your letter. Remember to add any shipping and handling charges to the total cost of the merchandise.

Order Letter

1015 Brookside
San Anselmo, CA 94960
January 7, 1992

Pacific Publishing Company
Box 9998
Centralia, WA 98531

Dear Sir or Madam:

Please send me the following books from your 1992 winter catalog:

1	Programming in BASIC, #77-B	$9.95
1	Guide to Computer Games, #78-C	$6.95
	Shipping and handling	$3.00
		$19.90

A check for $19.90 is enclosed.

Sincerely,

Maureen O'Connor

Maureen O'Connor

Letters of Complaint

Reputable companies stand behind their merchandise and services and are prepared to make amends if a mistake has been made. Express yourself courteously if you are registering a complaint and recommend a reasonable solution. Notice how clearly the following letter describes the problem.

Letter of Complaint

603 Pine Hill Road
Sleepy Eye, MN 56085
February 11, 1992

Customer Service
Northern Electronics
3278 Elson Avenue
St. Paul, MN 55109

Dear Sir or Madam:

On January 5 of this year, I ordered a set of Walkie-Talkies from your catalog (#AA-573). A check for $22.75 to cover $20.00 for the merchandise and $2.75 for the shipping charges was enclosed with the order. I received the Walkie-Talkies on January 19, but a bill was enclosed in the package.

As you can see from the enclosed photocopy of my canceled check, I have paid in full for the merchandise I ordered. Please adjust your records to show my payment and request the billing department to remove my name from the billing list.

Thank you for your cooperation.

Sincerely,

Edward Swanson

Edward Swanson

EXERCISE 1 *Writing a Letter of Request*

Write a letter to the Baseball Hall of Fame. Request information on the founding of the Hall of Fame and the people who have been recognized there. Then prepare a sample envelope.

ADDRESS Baseball Hall of Fame
Main Street
Cooperstown, NY 13326

EXERCISE 2 *Writing a Letter of Request*

Think of an interest of yours about which you would like to find more information. For example, you may be interested in a career and would like to find out more about it. By using the library, determine what organization would best provide you with information. Then write a letter requesting information from that organization and, with your teacher's permission, mail the letter.

EXERCISE 3 *Writing an Order Letter*

Use the following information to order merchandise from a catalog. Unscramble the information for the inside address and write it in the proper order. Use your own name and address and today's date for the heading. Add $3.00 for shipping and handling.

INSIDE ADDRESS Order Department, Medina, Olympic Sporting Goods, 44256, Ohio, 3237 Arlington Avenue

MERCHANDISE 1 sweat shirt, #45589, blue, size small, $10.50; 1 sweat pants, #45590, blue, size medium, $8.00; 3 pairs tube socks, #5667, $1.25 each

EXERCISE 4 *Revising a Letter of Complaint*

Rewrite the following letter of complaint, revising the tone so that it is polite but firm.

Don't the people in your order department know how to read? I ordered a telephoto lens to use on my Sharpshooter A-220 camera, and your store sent me a wide-angle lens instead. So much for having fun with my new lens over the school holidays! I demand that you ship me either the correct lens or my money back within one week.

Application Letters

Often a business letter is the first contact you have with someone when you apply for a job or for admission to a school. Try to make as good an impression as possible by being neat, correct, and specific about your qualifications. Use the following letter as a guide when you are writing to apply for a job.

Letter of Application for Employment

145 Cannon Drive
Concord, MA 01742
May 15, 1992

Ms. Helen Carter
Patriot Pharmacy
2112 Greenway
Concord, MA 01742

Dear Ms. Carter:

I am writing to apply for the full-time summer position advertised in the Boston Globe. The enclosed résumé will give you an overview of my background and previous experience. Since my goals include studying to become a pharmacist, I am very interested in finding a job at a drugstore.

I will be available to start work on June 7, when school will be out for the summer. Until then, I will be available for an interview after four o'clock on weekdays and any time on Saturday. I look forward to hearing from you.

Sincerely,

Michael Robinson

Michael Robinson

If you are applying for admission to a college, a university, or a special program, your application letter should resemble a letter of request. Be specific about the information you request. For instance, you may want to request a list of courses and information about financial aid. Since schools require you to fill out applications, be sure to request an application form in your letter.

Letter of Application to a School

312 Lake Avenue
Lake Forest, IL 60045
May 15, 1992

Director
Cherub Program
Drama Department
Northwestern University
Evanston, IL 60201

Dear Sir or Madam:

I am interested in applying for admission to your summer program for high school students. I have acted in two drama productions at Lake Forest High School and intend to major in theater in college.

Please send me information about the program, including schedules, available classes, costs, and financial aid. I would also like an application form.

Thank you very much.

Sincerely,

Janet Chen

Janet Chen

EXERCISE 5 *Correcting an Application Letter*

In the following letter, each line preceded by a number contains an error. Rewrite the letter, correcting each mistake.

1 Deborah Schuster
2 463 Elm street
Richmond VA 23240
3 August 19th, 1992

4 Mr. Alan Bishop,
The Charts Record Store
5 1396 Fairfax Avinue
Richmond, VA 23217

6 Dear Mr. Bishop,

I am writing to apply for the part-time
7 cashier's position advertized in the Richmond Times.
The enclosed résumé will inform you of my educational
background and previous experience. Since my goal is
8 to pursue a career in retailing. I am especially
interested in working in a store. I am good with
numbers and throughout high school have received a
B-plus average in my math courses.

I can come to your store for an interview after
3:30 during the week and at any time on Saturdays. In
9 addition, I am available to start workeing at any
time. I will look forward to hearing from you.

10 Yours truly

Deborah Schuster

Deborah Schuster

EXERCISE 6 *Writing an Application Letter*

Write a letter to the Undergraduate Admissions department of a college. Request a catalog and an application form.

Writing a Résumé

A résumé is a summary of your work experience, education, and interests. The purpose of a résumé is to give a potential employer a brief but positive overview of your qualifications for a job. The following guidelines and model will help you write your own résumé. You should update your résumé on a regular basis to include information about recent educational or work experiences.

How to Write a Résumé

FORM

1. Use one sheet of white 8½- by 11-inch paper.
2. Use even margins and leave space between sections.

WORK EXPERIENCE

1. List your most recent job first.
2. Include part-time, summer, and volunteer jobs.
3. For each job list the dates you worked, your employer's name, your title, and your primary responsibilities.

EDUCATION

1. List the name and address of each school and the years you attended.
2. List any special courses you have taken that would help make you a valuable employee.

SKILLS, ACTIVITIES, AWARDS, INTERESTS

1. List skills, such as typing, computer programming, or fluency in a foreign language, that relate to the position.
2. List school or community activities in which you have participated, such as music lessons or volunteer work.
3. List awards or certificates of merit you have earned.
4. Include your hobbies and special interests.

REFERENCES

1. Give the names and addresses of people who have agreed to give you a recommendation, or state that references are available upon request.
2. As references list one previous employer, one teacher or school administrator, and one family friend.

Model of a Résumé

Jennifer Conn
314 South Madison Avenue
Cyrius, Maine 04735
Telephone: (207) 357-8642

WORK EXPERIENCE	
1991 - present	Craftmasters, 240 Moore Road, Cyrius, Maine 04735 Position: Free-lance carver of miniature wooden animals Responsibilities: Supplied store with carvings on commission
1988 - 1991	Aroostook Forum, 3 Main Street, Wiggins, Maine 04730 Position: Delivery person Responsibilities: Delivered daily newspapers to 35 homes
EDUCATION	
1991 - present	Hamlin High School, 170 High Street, Cyrius, Maine 04735 Special courses: graphic design, advanced photography
1989 - 1991	Blaine Middle School, Shays Lane, Cyrius, Maine 04735
SPECIAL SKILLS	Speak French, operate word-processing equipment, type 45 words per minute
ACTIVITIES	Tenth-grade class secretary, Math Club
AWARDS	Various photography prizes
SPECIAL INTERESTS	Art, photography
REFERENCES	Available on request

Completing a Job Application

When you apply for a job, you may be asked to fill out an application form. Application forms vary, but most of them ask for similar kinds of information. You may wish to prepare your information ahead of time so that you will be ready to complete the form when you apply for a job. The following is a list of items you will most likely need to know to complete a job application.

- The current date
- Your complete name, address, and telephone number
- Your date and place of birth
- Your Social Security number
- Names and addresses of schools you have attended, dates you attended them, and your year of graduation
- Any special courses or advanced degrees
- Names and addresses of employers for whom you have worked and the dates you were employed
- Any part-time, summer, and volunteer jobs
- Names and addresses of references (Obtain permission beforehand from each person you intend to list as a reference.)

When you are filling out a job application, use the following general guidelines.

Completing a Job Application

1. Print all information neatly and accurately.
2. Be sure your answers are accurate and complete.
3. Do not leave blanks. If a section does not apply to you, write *N/A* ("not applicable").
4. List schools attended and work experience in order, giving the most recent first.
5. If you mail the application form, include a brief cover letter stating the job you are applying for.

The sample on the next page shows a completed job application. Note that the applicant did not leave any blank spaces and supplied all the information required. Also notice that the applicant wrote neatly and legibly.

Sample of a Completed Job Application

LAKESIDE COMPUTER CENTER
EMPLOYMENT APPLICATION

Date *November 7, 1992*

Name *Paul* (FIRST) *Evan* (MIDDLE) *Kolba* (LAST)

Address *39 Park Street* (STREET), *Rutledge*, (CITY) *South Carolina* (STATE) *29503* (ZIP CODE)

Phone *(803) 720-1132* Social Security Number *178-35-2180*

Have you ever been employed here before? ___ Yes *✓* No If so, when? *N/A*

Date of Birth *June* (MONTH) *30*, (DAY) *1978* (YEAR) Place of Birth *Ames*, (CITY) *Iowa* (STATE)

Work Permit Number (if under 18) *7632*

Married? ___ Yes *✓* No Number of Children *N/A*

EDUCATION

College or University	*N/A*	From *N/A*	to *N/A*
Vocational Training	*N/A*	From *N/A*	to *N/A*
Senior High School	*Gervais High School*	From *1992*	to *present*
Junior High School	*Haven Junior High*	From *1990*	to *1992*
Elementary School	*Edisto School*	From *1983*	to *1990*

PREVIOUS WORK EXPERIENCE

Year	Employer	Address	Postion
1991–present	*Gemini Video, Inc.,*	*Rte. 43, Rutledge,*	*Window washer*
1989	*Allen Rescue Squad*	*22 Broadway, Rutledge,*	*Fund raiser*
1988–1989	*Rutledge News*	*7 Pine Road, Rutledge,*	*Messenger*

REFERENCES

1. *Jay O'Neil Gevais High School, 6 Glen Rodd, Rutledge, Principal*
2. *Gale Reafern Gemini Video, Inc., Rte. 43, Rutledge, Plant Manager*
3. *Phyllis Acardi 13 Gray Street, Rutledge, Registered Nurse*

Applicant's Signature *Paul Evan Kolba*

Chapter 12 Review

A Letters to a Department Store Use the following address to write four letters to a department store, as described below. Then prepare one sample envelope.

Goodman's Department Store
333 Hazelcrest Drive
Centerbrook, CO 06409

1. Write a letter to the mail-order department, requesting the store's latest catalog.
2. Write a letter to the mail-order department, ordering the following merchandise from the catalog. Include $1.50 for shipping and handling charges.

   Merchandise: 1 record shelf, #45578, $15.98;
   2 sets of bookends, #35567, $3.75 per set

3. Write a letter to the mail-order department to complain when only one set of bookends arrives with your order.
4. Write a letter to the director of personnel to apply for a summer job as a sales clerk in the sports department. Be sure to include a résumé with your letter of application. Refer to the model on page 434 to help you write a résumé of your work experiences and educational qualifications.

B Completing a Job Application Write a letter requesting a job-application form from a place of employment that you think would be interesting to work for. For example, if you like sports, a sporting-goods store might be interesting. When you receive the job-application form, fill it out, following the guidelines on page 435. Ask your teacher to look at your completed application for neatness, thoroughness, and correctness. Then, if appropriate, send your completed application to the place of employment.

C Writing an Order Letter Imagine you live in twelfth-century Venice. Write an order letter to a local merchant requesting goods from Asia. Use the library or your world history textbook to include accurate details about the merchandise and shipping time.

Chapter

13 Speaking and Listening

During his Inaugural Address in 1961, President John F. Kennedy spoke the famous words, ". . . ask not what your country can do for you—ask what you can do for your country." These words, communicated to the entire nation, inspired people to work for social causes, and they set a patriotic tone for Kennedy's presidency. Through effective communication—a process in which speakers speak clearly and forcefully and listeners hear and understand what is being said—words can make people laugh, cry, become angry, or take action. This chapter explains how you can become a more effective speaker and a better listener.

Preparing a Speech

In school as well as in your future career, you may often find yourself in a situation where you must give a formal speech. In school you may make a speech to a group of students, parents, or teachers. In your career you may make a formal presentation to a group of coworkers at a small meeting or a large convention.

Preparing and delivering speeches for a variety of purposes is similar to preparing and writing a report, a persuasive essay, or a short story. To prepare a speech, therefore, you follow the prewriting steps in the writing process. In both speaking and writing, you choose and limit a subject, gather information, and organize your ideas into an outline. Instead of editing and publishing an essay, however, you will practice and deliver a speech to an audience for oral presentation.

Knowing Your Audience and Purpose

Your audience may be a small group of friends or a large assembly of parents or voters. They may already know something about your subject or have particular views on it. It is important, therefore, to consider your listeners as you define your purpose and limit the subject of your speech. The following strategies will help you.

Strategies for Considering Audience and Purpose

1. Find out the interests of your audience. Decide how you can limit your subject to match their interests.
2. Try to determine what your audience already knows about your subject. Consider what your audience may expect to hear.
3. Decide whether your purpose is to inform, to persuade, or to entertain by expressing your thoughts or by telling a story. *(See Chapter 6, pages 196–233; Chapter 7, pages 234–269; and Chapters 8 and 11, pages 270–297 and pages 380–419 for more information about these specific purposes for written and oral compositions.)*

The following examples illustrate three ways to limit the subject of cooking according to the purpose of your speech.

Purposes of Speeches

PURPOSE	EXAMPLES
to inform	explaining the benefits of cooking with a wok
to persuade	persuading school administrators to offer cooking classes in school
to entertain	telling about the first time you prepared dinner for your family

EXERCISE 1 *Determining Purpose*

Write an example of a subject for a speech you might give for each of the three purposes—to inform, to persuade, and to entertain.

Choosing and Limiting a Subject

After choosing an interesting subject, you should limit the subject. Limiting the subject enables you to present it fully for a given audience within a limited period of time. As a rule of thumb, it takes about as long to deliver a ten-minute speech as it does to read aloud slowly four pages of a typed, double-spaced, written composition. The strategies for choosing and limiting a subject for a speech are the same as the strategies you would use to choose and limit a subject for an essay. *(See pages 15 to 16.)*

Strategies for Choosing and Limiting a Subject

1. Choose a subject that interests you and is likely to interest your audience.
2. Choose a subject that you know well or can research thoroughly.
3. Limit the subject by choosing one aspect of it. For example, for a ten-minute speech on endangered species, you could limit the subject to the American bald eagle.

EXERCISE 2 *Finding a Subject*

For each of the following items, write a subject for a speech.

1. personal experiences
2. experiences of others
3. current events or issues
4. past events or people
5. how to do something
6. how to make something
7. jobs or professions
8. school-related subjects
9. ideas for inventions
10. ideas about the future

EXERCISE 3 *Limiting a Subject*

Limit each subject so that it would be suitable for a ten-minute speech.

1. earthquakes
2. zoos
3. education
4. astronomy
5. bears
6. postage stamps
7. space travel
8. weather
9. good health
10. football

Gathering and Organizing Information

After you have chosen and limited your subject, begin to gather information. Begin by brainstorming everything you already know about the subject. Then consult other useful sources of information including encyclopedias, books, and periodicals in the library. You might also consider interviewing people who are knowledgeable about your subject.

Taking Notes Take notes on note cards throughout your research. Note cards are best for recording ideas because the information can be easily organized later as you prepare to make an outline of your speech. Use a separate card to summarize each important idea and include facts and examples to support the idea. Record accurately any quotations you plan to use. If you conduct an interview, take notes or use a tape recorder and then transfer the information to note cards.

Collecting Audiovisual Materials While gathering information, collect or create visual materials such as pictures, maps, charts, slides, or props. These will help you make your points and also capture the interest of your audience.

Strategies for Organizing a Speech

1. Arrange your note cards by topics and subtopics. Then use the cards to make a detailed outline of your speech and draft an introduction and a conclusion. *(See pages 356–358.)*
2. To make your introduction interesting, begin with an anecdote, an unusual fact, a question, or an interesting quotation. As part of your introduction, include a thesis statement that makes clear the main idea and the purpose of your speech. *(See page 178.)*
3. The body of your speech should include several ideas with facts and examples to support each one. Arrange the ideas in a logical order and think of the transitions you will use to connect your ideas. *(See pages 113, 139, 148, and 158.)*
4. Write a conclusion for your speech that summarizes your important ideas and signals to the audience that you have finished. Try to conclude your speech with a memorable sentence or phrase. *(See page 187.)*

EXERCISE 4 *Gathering and Organizing Information*

Choose and limit a subject for a ten-minute speech in which the purpose is to inform. Write what you know about the subject on note cards. Next, go to the library and find additional information for ten more note cards. Then organize your cards, outline your speech, and use your outline to draft an introduction and a conclusion. Save your work for Exercise 5.

Practicing Your Speech

Although rehearsing your speech is important, in most cases you should not attempt to write it out or to memorize it. Instead, use your outline or convert your outline and note cards into cue cards. Cue cards include your main points along with key words, phrases, and quotations listed in the order you want to follow in your speech. While you are delivering your speech, your cue cards will help you to remember your important points and supporting details. Following are some strategies for practicing your speech.

Strategies for Practicing a Speech

1. Practice in front of a long mirror so that you will be aware of your gestures, facial expressions, and posture.
2. As you practice, look around the room as if you were looking at your audience.
3. Time your speech. If it is too long, cut some information. If it is too short, find additional information and add it to your speech.
4. Practice using your cue cards and any visual aids or props that are part of your speech.
5. Practice over a period of several days. Your confidence will grow each time you practice, and your nervousness will decrease as your confidence increases.

Revise your speech as you practice by experimenting with choosing the right words and adding or deleting information to make your main points clearer. You may find it helpful to practice your speech with a friend. This listener's comments may help you revise and improve your speech.

EXERCISE 5 *Practicing and Revising Your Speech*

Prepare cue cards for the speech you started preparing in Exercise 4. Then, using the Strategies for Practicing a Speech, practice your speech before a relative, friend, or classmate. Use your listener's comments to make improvements and then practice your revised speech in preparation for Exercise 6.

Delivering Your Speech

If you have researched your subject well, planned the content carefully, and rehearsed sufficiently, you will deliver your speech with confidence. When the time comes to give your speech, recall the following Strategies for Delivering a Speech.

Strategies for Delivering a Speech

1. Have ready all the materials you need, such as your outline or cue cards and audiovisual materials or props.
2. Wait until your audience is quiet and settled.
3. Relax and breathe deeply before you begin your introduction.
4. Stand with your weight evenly divided between both feet. Avoid swaying back and forth.
5. Look directly at the people in your audience, not over their heads. Try to make eye contact.
6. Speak slowly, clearly, and loudly enough to be heard.
7. Be aware of using correct grammar and well-formed sentences.
8. Use appropriate gestures and facial expressions to emphasize your main points.
9. Remember to use your audiovisual aids, making sure everyone in your audience can see them.
10. After finishing your conclusion, take your seat without making comments to people in the audience.

Evaluating an Oral Presentation After you have finished delivering your speech, evaluate it yourself while your listeners evaluate it. Through self-evaluation and the sharing of others' evaluations, you can improve your speaking skills and help your classmates to improve theirs. You may wish to use the Oral Presentation Evaluation Form on page 444.

Oral Presentation Evaluation Form

SUBJECT: ______________________________

SPEAKER: ______________________ **DATE:** __________

CONTENT

Is the subject appropriate for the audience?
Is the main point clear?
Are there enough details and examples?
Do all the ideas clearly relate to the subject?
Is the length appropriate (not too long or too short)?

ORGANIZATION

Does it begin with a clear and interesting introduction?
Do the ideas in the body follow a logical order?
Are transitions used between ideas?
Does the conclusion summarize the main points?

PRESENTATION

Does the speaker use good word choice?
Does he/she speak loudly and clearly enough?
Is the rate appropriate (not too fast or too slow)?
Does the speaker make eye contact with the audience?
Does he/she use gestures and pauses effectively?
Are audiovisual aids or other props used effectively?
Are cue cards or an outline used effectively?

COMMENTS: ______________________________

____

____

____

____

EXERCISE 6 *Delivering and Evaluating Your Speech*

Using the Strategies for Delivering a Speech, and with your teacher's permission, give the speech you prepared and practiced in Exercise 5. Then listen to the speeches of your classmates as well. After each speech, including your own, complete an Oral Presentation Evaluation Form. Each speaker should then collect and read the listeners' evaluations of his or her speech. After reading the assessments, identify speaking skills and techniques that you would like to improve in future oral presentations.

Listening

Skillful listening requires that you pay close attention to what you hear. In addition, when listening for information or ideas, you must be able to evaluate what the speaker says and record the information in an organized way so that you will be able to remember and use the information later.

Listening to Directions

Every day in school and elsewhere, you are given directions to follow. When listening to directions, always listen carefully from beginning to end, without assuming that you already know what to do. Then practice the following listening strategies.

Strategies for Listening to Directions

1. Write down the directions while the speaker is presenting them.
2. After listening to the directions, ask specific questions to help clarify the directions.
3. When you finish an assignment, review the directions once more to make sure you have followed them correctly.

EXERCISE 7 *Following Directions*

Have paper and pencil ready. As your teacher reads you a set of directions, follow them carefully.

Listening for Information

Much of your time as a student is spent listening, but you should not take this important skill for granted. Listening for the purpose of learning includes more than merely hearing words. You must be able to understand what you hear so that you can evaluate and apply the information. When listening to learn, you may find the following strategies helpful.

Listening Strategies

1. Sit comfortably but stay alert. Try to focus on what the speaker is saying without being distracted by people and noises.

2. Determine whether the speaker's purpose is to inform, to persuade, or to entertain by expressing thoughts and feelings.

3. Listen for verbal clues to identify the speaker's main ideas. Often, for example, a speaker emphasizes important points by using such phrases as *first . . . , finally . . . , also consider . . . , most importantly . . . , remember that . . . ,* or *in conclusion . . .*

4. Watch for nonverbal clues such as gestures, pauses, or changes in the speaking pace. Such clues often signal important points.

5. Determine the speaker's point of view about the subject. For example, is the speaker expressing positive or negative attitudes or arguing for or against an issue?

6. Take notes to organize your thoughts and to help you remember details. Your notes provide a basis for further discussion. You may also want to use your notes to outline your speech or write a summary of it. If the speech is a course lecture, notes will help you study for a test on the subject. (*See pages 352 and 501–502.*)

EXERCISE 8 *Listening and Taking Notes*

As your teacher delivers a prepared lecture, listen carefully and take notes. After the lecture form a small group with other students and compare notes. Try to explain why group members all recorded certain points and why in other cases everyone wrote different information. Then combine your notes to write a complete outline of the lecture. Compare your outline with the outlines other groups wrote.

Recognizing Propaganda

People who listen carefully and critically learn that the words they hear can sometimes be misleading. This happens when speakers use propaganda techniques instead of facts and examples as they try to get you to accept their point of view. A speaker may use propaganda to distort or misrepresent information or disguise opinions as facts. Propaganda can also be used to appeal to listeners' emotions by using strongly emotional language, stereotypes, and exaggerations. To evaluate the content or message of a speech and make judgments about what you hear, you must be able to recognize various kinds of propaganda devices.

Confusing Fact and Opinion A *fact* is a statement that can be proved to be true or accurate, while an *opinion* is a personal feeling or judgment about something. When opinions are stated as facts, misunderstanding or confusion often results for the listener. You can avoid confusion by listening critically to distinguish between facts and opinions.

FACT My sister is on the soccer team.
OPINION Soccer players are the most talented athletes.

EXERCISE 9 *Distinguishing between Facts and Opinions*

Label each of the following statements *F* for *fact* or *O* for *opinion*.

1. Harrisburg is the capital of Pennsylvania.
2. Animals in shelters should not be put to sleep, even if homes cannot be found for them.
3. My sister Shari made straight *A*'s in math throughout high school and college.
4. The longest day of the year occurs in June.
5. Harrisburg is the best place to live in Pennsylvania.
6. Watching television is a waste of time.
7. Animal shelters have caring employees.
8. Men make better scientists than women.
9. My brother watches about two hours of television a day, usually after dinner.
10. Summer is the most carefree time of the year.

Bandwagon Appeals The *bandwagon appeal* tries to get people to do or think the same thing as everyone else. Bandwagon appeals in advertising often try to make consumers feel inferior if they do not conform. Political parties and candidates use bandwagon appeals to win votes. Common slogans associated with this type of propaganda include *Get on board! Join the crowd! Everyone loves . . .* and *Don't be left out!*

> Everyone who's in the know wears Toe-Stomp'n Sneakers. Don't be an outsider; get your Toe-Stomp'ns today!

Testimonials A famous person's endorsement, or support, of a product, candidate, or policy is called a *testimonial.* A testimonial can be misleading because it suggests that a famous person's opinions must be right or that a product must be good if a celebrity recommends it.

> Hi! I'm Tiffany, star of the recent blockbuster film, *Fire in the Desert*. You probably wonder how I can keep my hair so shiny while working under such harsh conditions. Well, it's easy with Shampoo Shazam. It works wonders on my hair, and it can do the same for your hair.

Unproved Generalizations A *generalization* is a conclusion based on many facts and examples. However, generalizations based on only one or two facts or examples are unproved, or unsound. Unproved generalizations can mislead you by suggesting that they are based on facts and examples that apply to all cases. Unproved generalizations usually contain words such as *always, never, all,* or *none.*

UNPROVED GENERALIZATION	**All** the buys in this store are better than you can find in any other store.
ACCURATE GENERALIZATION	**Many** of the buys in this store are better than you can find in any other store.

EXERCISE 10 *Using Propaganda Techniques*

Choose one of the three propaganda techniques described on this page and use it in a written advertisement for a real or an imaginary product. With your teacher's permission, ask a classmate to read your advertisement and identify the propaganda technique used.

EXERCISE 11 *Recognizing Propaganda Techniques*

Label each statement *B* for *bandwagon, T* for *testimonial,* or *U* for *unproved generalization.*

1. Glow Bright never lets you down! In one simple step you can wash, wax, and polish your kitchen floor. Glow Bright always leaves your kitchen floor as bright as the sun.

2. As host of *Wheels of Wealth,* I need fresh breath when I talk to the contestants. That's why I use Mighty Mints, the mouth freshener I can depend on. If I can depend on Mighty Mints, you can too.

3. Join the crowd for Joe Barnes and vote for a winner. The polls predict Barnes will win, so don't waste your vote by casting your ballot for the losing candidate. Get on the winning side.

4. For a short trip across town or a long trip across the world, contact A-One-A Travel Service. We have the best service, the lowest prices, and the nicest travel agents in town.

5. You trusted me when I hosted the Olympic Games for your favorite television network, so trust me now when I say that for a long life you need a lifetime membership in the Lifelong Health Club.

6. In today's world opportunities for education and advancement are shrinking fast. But now there's hope. At little cost to you, the Banker's Bank will finance your child's future.

7. As a three-time winner at Kentucky Downs, I know a good race when I see one. This election looks like a close one to me, but I'm behind the best candidate, Francis Dickson. As jockey of the year, believe me when I say that I can spot a winner.

Integrating Language Skills

Recognizing Misleading Information Read magazines and newspapers to find examples of the use of propaganda in advertising and in editorials. Identify hidden messages through the use of opinions as facts, unproved generalizations, bandwagon appeals, and testimonials. Then select an example of propaganda and write an essay describing the propaganda and its impact. With your teacher's permission, share and discuss your work with other students and jointly publish your essays.

Group Discussion

Group discussion is a means of communicating ideas, exchanging opinions, solving problems, and reaching conclusions. Group discussions may be informal or formal. In informal discussions you freely express your views and share your experiences. In formal discussions, on the other hand, you may present information you researched or use evidence to argue an issue.

You use the same group discussion skills in many learning contexts as well. When you are using the writing process, group brainstorming may help you during the prewriting stage; and peer conferencing is an effective technique to help you revise your work. You may also use discussion and communication skills in preparing a speech or an oral report or in working with other students to prepare for a test. Learning group discussion skills will help you to present your ideas effectively and to listen thoughtfully to others' ideas. *(See pages 21, 33, and 446.)*

Strategies for Participating in Group Discussions

1. Listen carefully and respond respectfully to others' views.
2. Ask questions to make sure you understand others' views or information.
3. State or express your own ideas clearly. Present examples or evidence to support your ideas.
4. Keep in mind that everyone in the group should have an equal opportunity and equal time to speak.
5. Make sure your contributions to the discussion are constructive and relevant to the subject.
6. Try to help your group to draw a conclusion or to reach a consensus.

Duties of Discussion Leaders

A discussion leader—also called a moderator or a chairperson—is chosen to guide and direct a group discussion. This role requires additional responsibilities as described in the list of Strategies for Discussion Leaders on page 451.

Strategies for Discussion Leaders

1. Introduce the topic, question, or problem.
2. With the group's help, state the purpose or goal of the discussion.
3. Keep the discussion on track to help the group reach agreement and accomplish its goals.
4. Encourage everyone to participate.
5. Make sure that everyone has an equal opportunity and equal time to speak.
6. Keep a record of the group's main points and decisions, or assign this task to a group member.
7. At the end of the discussion, summarize the main points and restate any conclusions the group reached.

EXERCISE 12 *Conducting a Group Discussion*

With your teacher's permission, form small groups and have a group discussion. Begin by choosing a current subject or issue concerning your school, such as study hall policies, dress codes, student privileges, extracurricular activities, or school improvement. Then choose a discussion leader and establish a goal. During the discussion take turns practicing the responsibilities of a discussion leader. At the end of the discussion, review the main points and summarize your conclusions.

Cooperative Learning

In a *cooperative learning* group, members work together to achieve a goal. A subject is divided into manageable tasks and then the tasks are assigned to individuals in the group. For this reason cooperative learning groups are sometimes called task groups. After the tasks are accomplished, members put together and organize the results of their individual efforts. For example, members of a task group in a biology class may cooperate to prepare an oral presentation on organisms that cause diseases. One member of the group may research viruses, another member may find information on bacteria, a third member may investigate fungi, and a fourth member may research parasites. As another option, the group may choose to share the work by assigning different types of diseases to be researched by individual members.

In addition to performing tasks, members of cooperative learning groups may have special roles, such as acting as the group discussion leader. The leader of a cooperative learning group helps coordinate the group's efforts. After performing their tasks, group members meet with the leader, share their information, discuss their plans, and reach decisions about their presentation.

Strategies for Cooperative Learning

1. Observe the Strategies for Participating in Group Discussions. *(See page 450.)*
2. Participate in planning the project and in assigning roles.
3. If you have been assigned a task, do not let your group down by coming to meetings unprepared.
4. Cooperate with others in the group to resolve conflicts, solve problems, reach conclusions, and make decisions.
5. Help your group achieve its goals by taking your fair share of responsibility for the group's success.

EXERCISE 13 *Organizing a Cooperative Learning Group*

With your teacher's permission, form cooperative learning groups of five to seven members and plan a presentation on one of the following subjects or on one of your own. Begin by deciding your purpose and establishing a goal. Then choose a leader and divide the work into manageable tasks. After assigning tasks, gather and share information, meeting several times to coordinate your efforts. Finally, make your presentation to the class. Follow the steps in preparing and delivering an oral presentation. *(See pages 438–444.)*

1. careers in science
2. endangered species
3. the Seven Wonders of the World
4. the signers of the Constitution
5. ways to become physically fit
6. rock musicians of the 1960's
7. the Arctic
8. women in government

Chapter 13

Review

A Giving a Speech Prepare a ten-minute speech about one of the following subjects or one of your own choosing. Decide whether your purpose will be to inform, to persuade, or to entertain. Your teacher may ask you to deliver your speech to the class.

1. the value of a part-time job
2. recycling efforts in your community
3. traveling in a foreign country
4. fast-food restaurants

B Listening for Information Practice your listening skills by tuning in to an educational or documentary television program and taking notes. Make an outline from your notes and share or discuss your results with other students who chose the same program.

C Listening for Directions Practice your skills in giving and receiving complex directions. Begin by writing a set of directions involving many steps or landmarks, such as how to get from the school to your home. Then, working with a partner, take turns giving and listening to the directions. See if the listener can repeat the directions accurately.

D Recognizing Propaganda As you listen to the radio or watch television this week, listen for propaganda techniques that are used to convince you to buy or use certain products, to make certain decisions, or to take certain actions. Keep notes on your observations and discuss them with other members of your class.

E Conducting a Group Discussion With your teacher's permission, form small groups and discuss the advantages and disadvantages of nuclear power plants. Each group should select a leader who will direct the discussion and summarize its results.

F Cooperative Learning Form a cooperative learning group to develop a presentation on the subject of television advertising. Decide what your main point will be and plan how you will make that point. Then assign tasks and choose a leader to help coordinate the group's work. With your teacher's permission, give your presentation.

Chapter

14 Vocabulary

Words are tools for expressing your thoughts and feelings precisely, vividly, and effectively. The more words you know, therefore, the better equipped you are to enjoy reading and conversation and to write compositions.

Language Integrating Skills

Recording Unfamiliar Words for Writing In your writer's notebook, write any unfamiliar words in the following list and include a brief dictionary definition. Continue to add to this list with unfamiliar words you find in your reading. By looking at the words often, you will eventually make them a part of your everyday vocabulary. Then, as your vocabulary increases, you will have more words to choose from when you write.

Vocabulary List

abnormality	devalue	idiosyncrasy	readjust
alliteration	diminish	inconsistent	reconsider
antiseptic	equestrian	lustrous	stipend
auxiliary	extinct	meditate	surmise
boisterous	fable	misinterpret	tantalize
clamorous	fortuitous	paradox	untenable
colossal	galvanize	populous	validate
deodorize	hilarity	pseudonym	visualize

The History of English

The Celts, who arrived in England sometime before the beginning of the Christian era, brought with them the first Indo-European language to be spoken in that country. (Today, all the major languages of Europe—except for Finnish, Hungarian, and Basque—are of Indo-European origin.) In spite of this strong early influence and the fact that the Celts occupied England for hundreds of years, relatively few Celtic words are in the English language today. Among the few remaining place names are *Avon* and *Dover*.

The Celts were eventually driven out around 55 B.C. by Julius Caesar and his Roman armies. The Romans established a stable Roman society, which lasted for several hundred years. In 410 A.D., however, trouble at home caused the Roman legions to withdraw.

Because they were no longer under the protection of the Romans, the people of England asked some Germanic tribes across the English Channel to help them fight off an invasion of Picts and Scots from Scotland. Three tribes—the Angles, the Saxons, and the Jutes—responded. After driving out the invading troops, these tribes decided to stay in England.

Anglo-Saxon, the language they brought with them, is the foundation of modern English. Many frequently used words, such as *home, friend,* and *brother,* come from this parent language. Almost all the pronouns, prepositions, conjunctions, articles, and auxiliary verbs are also carryovers from the Anglo-Saxon language. Old English is the name most scholars call this period of the English language, from 410 to 1066 A.D.

Middle English

Middle English began around 1066 A.D. as a result of the Battle of Hastings. At that time, William the Conqueror, who came from northwestern France, won a decisive victory over the Anglo-Saxons. Within a few years of the battle, he became the ruler of all of England. His Norman lords and followers, who became the ruling class, spoke only French in government and in the courts. Nevertheless, throughout the next three centuries, the conquered English people and their language survived. Eventually French and English began to merge, and a richer, more expressive language was the result.

Finally, in 1362, English—with its many French words—became the official language of the courts and shortly afterward the official language of the schools. To cement the permanence of English, Geoffrey Chaucer, the greatest poet in England at the time, began to write in English. Another factor in the establishment of English was the introduction of William Caxton's printing machine in 1476. As a result of his invention, the rules for grammar and the spelling of words in English became standardized.

Modern English

The period from around 1500 to the present is often called Modern English. During this time English grammar has not changed much, but there have been great changes in pronunciation. During the English Renaissance, the number of English words also grew rapidly. Many Greek and even more Latin words were added to the English language at that time.

Today the English language is still changing and growing. Words are added, words become obsolete, and through use, words change in form and meaning. Knowing how a word was adopted into English and what its original meaning was can often help you understand its current meaning. The *etymology* of a word is the history of that word from its earliest recorded use. Dictionary entries often contain very brief etymologies. *(See page 495.)* The following is an example of a dictionary etymology.

counsel [Middle English *conseil,* from Old French *conseil,* from Latin *consilium, consulere:* to consult]

The most recent form of the word appears first—in this case the Middle English form. Next come the earlier forms of the word and finally the original meaning.

Some words have interesting histories. The word *chauvinism,* for example, comes from the name of a patriotic character in a nineteenth-century French play. The following entry explains the history of the word.

chauvinism [French, *chauvinisme,* from Nicolas *Chauvin,* patriotic French soldier extremely devoted to Napoleon]

Knowing the origin of this word may help you to remember its current meaning: blind patriotism or attachment to a group or place to which one belongs or has belonged. One of the words that follows was derived from the name of a real person, and one comes from a fictional character.

Words with Unusual Origins

WORD	MEANING	ETYMOLOGY
boycott	refuse to deal with, as a form of protest	[After Charles C. Boycott, a land agent in Ireland ostracized by tenants for refusing to lower rents]
gargantuan	of tremendous size or volume	[After Gargantua, a giant king in French literature who had a huge appetite]

EXERCISE 1 *Recognizing Word Origins*

Number your paper 1 to 10. Write the letter of the phrase you think explains the origin of each numbered word. Then check your answers in the dictionary.

1. colossal	**a.** outline drawing, named for a French politician
2. galvanize	**b.** long footrace, named after a city in Greece
3. limerick	**c.** enormous, as was the statue in ancient Rhodes
4. marathon	**d.** destruction, named after the tribe that sacked Rome
5. mentor	**e.** of great power or size, from a family in Greek mythology
6. paisley	**f.** shock with electric current or coat with zinc, from an Italian scientist's name
7. quixotic	**g.** fabric with swirled designs, named after a city in Scotland
8. silhouette	**h.** tutor, named after a character in Greek mythology
9. titanic	**i.** short verse, named after a county in Ireland
10. vandalism	**j.** rashly idealistic, like the legendary hero Don Quixote

Colloquialisms, Idioms, Slang, and Jargon

Words and phrases also come into the English language in another way—through everyday conversation and usage. Such expressions include colloquialisms, slang, idioms, and jargon. All three types of informal language are usually not appropriate for formal written English. *(See pages 738–753 about levels of usage.)*

Colloquialisms *Colloquialisms* are expressions that are used in conversation but usually not in writing because they are too informal. In writing dialogue in short stories or in plays, however, you may use colloquialisms.

Without her calculator she was **in a bind.** [had a problem]

I **don't get** [don't understand] why we can't use the gym now.

Idioms An *idiom* is a phrase or expression that has a meaning different from what the words suggest in their usual meaning. Idioms often do not make sense when taken literally, yet they are still meaningful to most people who speak a particular language.

Everyone **made the bus** [got to the bus] on time.

Bao refused to **give in** [submit] to threats.

Slang *Slang* consists of colorful or exaggerated expressions and phrases—usually in nonstandard English—that are used by particular groups, such as teenagers. Although slang constantly changes and quickly goes out of fashion, some slang expressions, like the following ones, have become widely known.

That movie was a real **tearjerker** [sad, intended to make viewers cry].

The **guy** [man] playing accordion was a real **cornball** [sentimentalist].

Jargon *Jargon* is the specialized vocabulary used in a technical, scientific, or professional field. Computer jargon, for example, includes *glitches, menus, input,* and *computer virus.* Jargon allows scientists and other professionals to share information with one another precisely and concisely. However, when jargon is used for a general audience, it often obscures meaning. A jargon-filled sentence like the following one is needlessly difficult to understand.

The vehicle was rendered inoperative by a discharged battery mechanism.

This sentence can easily be revised so that its meaning is clear to the general reader.

The car would not start because of a dead battery.

EXERCISE 2 *Using Appropriate English*

Substitute words or phrases in standard English for the underlined colloquialisms, idioms, and slang expressions in the following sentences.

1. Will you please hit the light on your way out?
2. I'm really burned up at Victor for keeping me waiting so long.
3. The All-Pro running back decided to hang up his cleats after his best season.
4. Pauline and Marcia did not hit it off at first, but now they are close friends.
5. The final football game was a real squeaker, but our team won, 14–13.
6. The director asked the cast not to goof off during rehearsals.
7. Maria burned the midnight oil to finish her science project in time for the beginning of the science fair on Friday.
8. Peter's nose is out of joint because he didn't receive an invitation to the party.
9. Moving pianos is back-breaking work!
10. During the figure-skating finals, Laura took a spill.

Determining Word Meanings

Even if you have an excellent vocabulary, you know only a small percentage of the 600,000 words in an unabridged dictionary. Once you have learned a new word, however, it is yours for life. Aside from looking up words in a dictionary, you have other ways of finding out the meaning of an unfamiliar word. The remainder of this chapter shows you several ways to discover and remember word meanings. These methods will all add to the storehouse of ideas upon which you can draw when you write or speak.

Using Context Clues

Context clues can help you learn the meaning of a word. The *context* of a word is the sentence, the surrounding words, or the situation in which the word appears. Context clues can also improve your vocabulary. Notice how the following kinds of context clues can help you understand or discover the meanings of unfamiliar words.

Kinds of Context Clues	
DEFINITION OR RESTATEMENT	We read a collection of *fables*, **short tales that teach a lesson.** [The word *fable* is defined in the sentence as a short tale that teaches a lesson.]
EXAMPLE	Bombay is a *populous* city; **one way the Indian government has tried to ease the overcrowding there is to build a second Bombay.** [The meaning of *populous* is made clear by the example of a way India has dealt with the overcrowding in Bombay.]
COMPARISON	Joseph Briggs has always been *amiable*—**almost as friendly as his older brother Stephen.** [*As* introduces a comparison between Joseph's disposition and that of his older brother Stephen.]
CONTRAST	Mayor Luzinski's popularity **soared to its highest point, but** the city council's **dropped** to its *nadir*. [A contrast is drawn between the highest point of Mayor Luzinski's popularity and the lowest point, the *nadir*, of the city council's.]

EXERCISE 3 *Using Context Clues*

Write the letter of the word that is closest in meaning to the underlined word. Then identify the type of context clue you used.

1. Using flattery, she tried to <u>cajole</u> him into singing "The Yellow Rose of Texas."
(A) discourage (B) persuade (C) annoy (D) command
(E) mistreat

2. The leading actor's <u>vapid</u> performance sharply contrasted with the supporting actor's lively one.
(A) fast (B) sparkling (C) ridiculous (D) dull (E) vivid

3. Joan has won many awards for her <u>aquatic</u> ability, especially her diving and freestyle swimming.
(A) hidden (B) wasted (C) water-related (D) flight-related
(E) average

4. A <u>schism</u>, a separation caused by differences of opinion, split the group into two opposing factions.
(A) division (B) crystal (C) treaty (D) scheme
(E) nightmare

5. Her gray hair was <u>lustrous</u>, like the glow of pewter.
(A) false (B) important (C) gleaming (D) foggy
(E) unattractive

6. The brothers were opposites; one was <u>wily</u>, while the other was honest and open in his dealings with others.
(A) brilliant (B) crafty (C) innocent (D) funny
(E) stubborn

7. The day's <u>equestrian</u> event featured yearling colts and fillies.
(A) gymnastic (B) clown-related (C) soothing (D) amateur
(E) horse-related

8. They <u>gibed</u> him over his new haircut, mildly making fun of him in a joking way.
(A) amused (B) disliked (C) entertained (D) teased
(E) protected

9. Her <u>hilarity</u> matched the laughter and good cheer of the other people at the party.
(A) merriment (B) ambition (C) outspokenness (D) gloom
(E) honesty

10. Two <u>auxiliary</u> law enforcement officers were hired temporarily to help out whenever an emergency arose.
(A) full-time (B) city (C) assistant (D) untrained
(E) unqualified

Prefixes, Roots, and Suffixes

If you know words and parts of words borrowed from Latin and Greek, you will understand the meanings of many English words. The three word parts that offer clues to word meanings are the root, the prefix, and the suffix. A *root* is the part of a word that carries the basic meaning. A *prefix* is one or more syllables placed in front of the root to modify the meaning of the root or to form a new word. A *suffix* is one or more syllables placed after the root to help shape its meaning and often to determine its part of speech. The following examples illustrate how the meaning of each word part contributes to the meaning of a word as a whole.

Word	**Prefix**	**Root**	**Suffix**
abnormality	ab- (away from)	-normal- (typical)	-ity (state of)
deodorize	de- (remove from)	-odor- (smell)	-ize (cause to be)
disagreement	dis- (not)	-agree- (get along together)	-ment (act or fact of doing)
nonfictional	non- (not)	-fiction- (invented story)	-al (characterized by)
postoperative	post- (later than)	-operate- (perform surgery)	-ive (that tends toward action)

As the examples above show, word parts usually provide only clues, not exact meanings. Following are dictionary definitions of these words.

abnormality:	state of not being typical
deodorize:	eliminate a smell
disagreement:	the act of failing to agree
nonfictional:	factual, realistic
postoperative:	following a surgical operation

Knowing the meanings of prefixes, roots, and suffixes can help you figure out the definitions of numerous words.

Common Prefixes and Suffixes

PREFIX	MEANING	EXAMPLE
anti-	against, opposing	anti + freeze: protection against icing
de-	do opposite of, reduce, remove	de + vitalize: deprive of vigor or effectiveness
ex-	out of, outside	ex + clude: shut out
extra-	beyond, outside	extra + ordinary: going beyond what is usual
in-	not	in + tolerable: not bearable
mis-	badly, wrongly	mis + inform: give wrong or untrue information
pre-	before	pre + historic: occurring before written history
re-	again, back	re + enter: go in again

SUFFIX	MEANING	EXAMPLE
-able, -ible	capable of	break + able: capable of being broken
-ate	cause to become	valid + ate: cause to become legal or official
-en	cause to be or to have	sharp + en: cause to be more pointed
-ion	act or process	construct + ion: act or process of building
-ist	one who does something	harp + ist: one who plays the harp
-ity	quality, state	equal + ity: state of being equal
-ize	cause to be formed into, conform to	visual + ize: form a mental image of
-ness	state, condition	neat + ness: state of being neat and orderly
-ous	full of	clamor + ous: full of noise

EXERCISE 4 *Combining Prefixes and Roots*

Write the prefix that has the same meaning as the underlined word. Then write the complete word defined after the equal sign.

EXAMPLE badly + pronounce = say incorrectly
ANSWER mis—mispronounce

1. beyond + terrestrial = outside the earth's atmosphere
2. again + adjust = arrange or put in order again
3. before + determine = decide ahead of time
4. against + septic = preventing the growth of germs
5. remove + hydrate = take water away from
6. out of + cavate = hollow out
7. not + compatible = not capable of existing in harmony
8. again + enact = repeat the actions of an event or incident
9. badly + interpret = understand or explain wrongly
10. not + variable = not changing or not capable of change

EXERCISE 5 *Using Prefixes, Roots, and Suffixes*

Number your paper 1 to 10. Then write the letter of the phrase that is closest in meaning to the word in capital letters.

1. HAUGHTINESS: (A) state of being proud and scornful (B) one who is arrogant (C) result of vanity
2. ACCESSIBLE: (A) cause to be reached (B) action of gaining entry (C) capable of being approached
3. RECONSIDER: (A) state of thinking (B) think carefully about again (C) deny responsibility
4. ANTAGONIST: (A) one who opposes another (B) state of competition (C) quality of dislike
5. UNTENABLE: (A) favoring defense (B) capable of defending (C) not able to be defended
6. SYSTEMIZE: (A) one who studies a plan (B) conform to a definite plan (C) capable of a plan
7. BOISTEROUS: (A) crafty (B) full of noise (C) immature
8. DEVALUE: (A) reduce the worth of (B) be opposed to wealth (C) fill with something again
9. INCONSISTENT: (A) capable of regulating (B) state of being without (C) not regular or steady
10. DIFFERENTIATION: (A) act of finding differences (B) make similar (C) be capable of being unlike

Synonyms and Antonyms

A *synonym* is a word that has the same or nearly the same meaning as another word. An *antonym* is a word that has the opposite or nearly the opposite meaning of another word.

SYNONYMS	verbose: wordy	diminish: lessen
ANTONYMS	verbose: concise	diminish: increase

To find synonyms, use a book of synonyms or a specialized dictionary called a *thesaurus*. Both resources list words and their synonyms. The words in a book of synonyms usually appear in alphabetical order, as in a dictionary. A thesaurus, which is not alphabetical, provides a thorough index to make words easy to find. A thesaurus also may give antonyms. One advantage of consulting a thesaurus is that you become aware of the many shades of meaning a word may have and, therefore, of the complexity of the English language.

EXERCISE 6 *Recognizing Synonyms*

Write the letter of the word or words closest in meaning to the word in capital letters. Then check your answers in the dictionary.

1. EXTINCT: (A) brief (B) clear (C) inactive (D) imperfect (E) poor

2. THWART: (A) love (B) frustrate (C) defend (D) grow (E) advance

3. STIPEND: (A) plant (B) financier (C) fluid (D) bank (E) payment

4. PRECLUDE: (A) prevent (B) avoid (C) promise (D) listen (E) imagine

5. FOIBLE: (A) story (B) flaw (C) strength (D) tradition (E) good-bye

6. MEDITATE: (A) compromise (B) reject (C) agree (D) ponder (E) repair

7. PARADOX: (A) occurrence (B) heaven (C) approval (D) contradiction (E) example

8. SURMISE: (A) guess (B) daybreak (C) provide (D) shock (E) govern

9. PSEUDONYM: (A) falsehood (B) forgery (C) elephant (D) pen name (E) writer

10. ECCENTRIC: (A) trustworthy (B) truthful (C) prompt (D) earnest (E) unusual

EXERCISE 7 Recognizing Antonyms

Number your paper 1 to 10. Write the letter of the word that is most nearly opposite in meaning to the word in capital letters. Then check your answers in the dictionary.

1. OPAQUE: (A) heavy (B) decorative (C) transparent (D) empty (E) sensible
2. PLIABLE: (A) rigid (B) honest (C) flexible (D) loose (E) mysterious
3. AMBIGUOUS: (A) friendly (B) generous (C) clear (D) lazy (E) clever
4. DEJECTED: (A) joyous (B) released (C) downcast (D) satisfied (E) reckless
5. BENEVOLENT: (A) determined (B) unkind (C) foolish (D) worthy (E) informal
6. RECEDE: (A) advance (B) retreat (C) proclaim (D) unite (E) offer
7. FASTIDIOUS: (A) sloppy (B) precise (C) small (D) cautious (E) restful
8. SURLY: (A) uncertain (B) amiable (C) doubting (D) rude (E) helpful
9. FRUGAL: (A) magnificent (B) friendly (C) wasteful (D) doubtful (E) trivial
10. DEPLETE: (A) begin (B) succeed (C) fold (D) demonstrate (E) fill

Analogies

Your ability to recognize synonyms and antonyms of words is sometimes tested in analogies on standardized tests. *Analogies* ask you to identify relationships between pairs of words. The following example shows the standard format for an analogy test item.

ARTIFICIAL:FAKE : : (A) enormous:minute
(B) isolate:group (C) drowsy:sleepy

Your first step in answering an analogy item is to identify the relationship between the first two words. In the example above, the words *artificial* and *fake* are synonyms, because they have similar meanings. The next step is to find the pair of words among the choices that have the same relationship. The first pair of words, *enormous* and *minute,* are antonyms because they have opposite meanings. The next pair of words, *isolate* and *group*, are also antonyms. The final pair, *drowsy* and *sleepy*, is the correct answer. *Drowsy* and *sleepy* are synonyms. *(See pages 506–507 for more information about analogies.)*

EXERCISE 8 *Recognizing Analogies*

Number your paper 1 to 15. Write the letter of the word pair that has the same relationship as the word pair in capital letters. Then identify the type of relationship by writing *synonym* or *antonym*.

1. ACCESSIBLE:REACHABLE : : (A) exotic:common (B) expand:amplify (C) lazy:industrious
2. DEPLETE:REPLENISH : : (A) foremost:primary (B) affluent:wealthy (C) optimist:pessimist
3. VERBOSE:WORDY : : (A) invisible:concealed (B) fortunate:unlucky (C) found:lost
4. PREDETERMINE:UNPLANNED : : (A) defect:imperfection (B) fallacy:truthfulness (C) congestion:overcrowding
5. OPAQUE:TRANSPARENT : : (A) chamber:room (B) dissent:agreement (C) disrespectful:rude
6. DIMINISH:ENLARGE : : (A) musical:melodic (B) stipulate:specify (C) mute:noisy
7. FRUGAL:THRIFTY : : (A) stratum:layer (B) quarrelsome:harmonious (C) beginning:outcome
8. EXCAVATE:DIG OUT : : (A) lucrative:unprofitable (B) fleeting:permanent (C) improvise:ad-lib
9. GARGANTUAN:TINY : : (A) thoroughly:completely (B) equip:furnish (C) ruthless:merciful
10. RECEDE:EXTEND : : (A) intriguing:interesting (B) intricate:simple (C) dwindle:fade
11. FORTUITOUS:UNEXPECTED : : (A) lateness:tardiness (B) mirth:sadness (C) persist:discontinue
12. EXTRAORDINARY:NORMAL : : (A) quench:satisfy (B) magnify:decrease (C) faint:swoon
13. VALIDATE:DISAPPROVE : : (A) exhibit:display (B) fleeting:passing (C) perishable:indestructible
14. LUSTROUS:SHINY : : (A) protest:agree (B) haggle:bargain (C) modern:ancient
15. CAJOLE:COAX : : (A) reside:dwell (B) dynamic:inactive (C) increase:dwindle

Chapter 14 Review

A **Synonyms** Number your paper 1 to 10. Then write the letter of the word that is closest in meaning to the word in capital letters.

1. ECCENTRIC: (A) peculiar (B) conceited (C) clever (D) lost (E) large
2. THWART: (A) inquire (B) encourage (C) frustrate (D) smash (E) insist
3. MENTOR: (A) genius (B) artist (C) tutor (D) soldier (E) politician
4. SURMISE: (A) shock (B) guess (C) forget (D) sweep (E) return
5. GIBE: (A) jeer (B) agree (C) disbelieve (D) glitter (E) answer
6. ANTAGONIST: (A) medicine (B) opponent (C) boxer (D) hero (E) deserter
7. MEDITATE: (A) interfere (B) argue (C) compromise (D) think (E) join
8. CAJOLE: (A) joke (B) trust (C) defeat (D) coax (E) promise
9. HILARITY: (A) fear (B) freedom (C) glee (D) luck (E) power
10. DIMINISH: (A) argue (B) threaten (C) lessen (D) demand (E) grow

B **Antonyms** Write the letter of the word that is opposite in meaning to the word in capital letters.

1. BOISTEROUS: (A) calm (B) unusual (C) mournful (D) specific (E) forceful
2. AMBIGUOUS: (A) eager (B) vague (C) playful (D) specific (E) false
3. PRECLUDE: (A) divide (B) listen (C) decide (D) prevent (E) permit

4. WILY: (A) honest (B) shrewd (C) foolish (D) insane (E) tragic

5. LUSTROUS: (A) vigorous (B) beautiful (C) dull (D) magical (E) shining

6. DEPLETE: (A) lessen (B) wrinkle (C) postpone (D) fill (E) deceive

7. AMIABLE: (A) sorrowful (B) sickly (C) successful (D) unfriendly (E) incorrect

8. GARGANTUAN: (A) grotesque (B) gigantic (C) snakelike (D) tiny (E) distorted

9. INVARIABLE: (A) tired (B) agreeable (C) changing (D) lively (E) nervous

10. BENEVOLENT: (A) charitable (B) unkind (C) accidental (D) unprofitable (E) boastful

C **Analogies** Write the letter of the word pair that has the same relationship as the word pair in capital letters.

1. CONCEAL:UNCOVER : : (A) misplace:lose (B) miserly:stingy (C) retrievable:unrecoverable

2. UNDERSTAND:COMPREHEND : : (A) imperil:endanger (B) impede:assist (C) fabulous:ordinary

3. LEGAL:ILLEGITIMATE : : (A) exultation:triumph (B) discrepancy:equality (C) disappear:vanish

4. RELIABLE:UNDEPENDABLE : : (A) promote:encourage (B) hoax:trick (C) morose:jovial

5. REVOKE:ANNUL : : (A) flatter:compliment (B) entire:partial (C) decease:continue

6. SMUG:CONCEITED : : (A) disheveled:dismantle (B) contentment:satisfaction (C) build:dismantle

7. HOODLUM:THUG : : (A) aroma:odor (B) private:public (C) makeshift:permanent

8. RESILIENT:INFLEXIBLE : : (A) prologue:introduction (B) meddle:interfere (C) peeved:pleased

9. PROWESS:COWARDLINESS : : (A) lethal:deadly (B) macabre:hideous (C) prosecute:pardon

10. PLUNGE:IMMERSE : : (A) pursue:retreat (B) scarcity:lack (C) serene:troubled

Chapter

15 Spelling

Good spelling helps you to communicate effectively in writing. Your readers can understand your message more easily when your writing is not filled with misspellings. This chapter will help you communicate clearly by improving your spelling.

Language Integrating Skills

Recognizing Commonly Misspelled Words *Spelling demons* are words that are frequently used but are commonly misspelled. Go over the following list of demons and, in your journal, write any words you find hard to spell.

Spelling Demons

accommodate	counterfeit	naturally	rehearse
accumulate	definitely	noticeable	repetition
adequate	dissatisfied	nuclear	ridiculous
ascend	excitable	nuisance	schedule
athletics	humorous	opinion	separate
awkward	hygiene	original	strategy
boulevard	incidentally	pamphlet	subtle
bulletin	indispensable	paralyze	temperature
category	jealousy	preferable	tomorrow
colonel	leisure	pursue	tragedy
conscience	lieutenant	questionnaire	unanimous
criticism	likelihood	recognize	vacuum

Spelling Improvement

If you apply the following strategies, you can improve your spelling.

Strategies for Improving Your Spelling

1. In your journal list the words you find difficult to spell. By reviewing that list often, you will master the words.
2. When writing, use the dictionary to check words you are unsure how to spell. Guessing is unreliable.
3. Carefully proofread your work.
4. Sound out each syllable to avoid dropping any letters.
   ath let ics   sep a rate   main te nance
5. Use memory tricks to master some difficult words.

Following are some examples.

bicycle: Do not bi**cy**cle when it is **icy**.
volunteer: Will **you** (*u*) volunteer?

EXERCISE 1 *Recognizing Misspelled Words*

Write the letter of each misspelled word. Then write the word correctly.

1.	(A) leather	(B) Wensday	(C) surgeon
2.	(A) changable	(B) schedule	(C) practical
3.	(A) awkward	(B) postpone	(C) develope
4.	(A) transferred	(B) category	(C) obsticle
5.	(A) labratory	(B) accommodate	(C) jealous
6.	(A) maneuver	(B) marriage	(C) basicly
7.	(A) preferred	(B) movement	(C) disatisfied
8.	(A) fiery	(B) twelth	(C) equipment
9.	(A) naturally	(B) martyr	(C) dominent
10.	(A) fulfill	(B) heroic	(C) advertisment

Spelling Rules

Some spelling rules are based on spelling patterns, such as the choice between *ie* and *ei*. Other rules are concerned with forming plurals and adding prefixes and suffixes.

Spelling Patterns

The following spelling patterns are useful to know because they apply to many words.

Words with *ie* and *ei* A simple rule will help you spell words with the *ie* or *ei* pattern.

Put *i* before *e*:	achieve	chief	hygiene
Except after *c*:	ceiling	conceivable	deceit
	perceive	receipt	conceited
Or when sounded like *a*:	feign	neighbor	reindeer
	sleigh	weight	vein

Although this rule applies to most words, there are exceptions.

ancient	either	leisure	sovereign
conscience	foreign	neither	sufficient
counterfeit	forfeit	protein	their
efficient	height	seizure	weird

Notice that the rule for spelling the *ie/ei* pattern applies only when these letters appear in the same syllable. The rule does not apply when the *i* and the *e* appear in separate syllables.

de ify	juici er	re inforce	soci ety

Words with *-sede, -ceed,* and *-cede* The following information will help you eliminate any confusion you may have about words that end in the "seed" sound.

1. Only one word—*supersede*—has the ending *-sede.*
2. Three words—*exceed, proceed,* and *succeed*—have the ending *-ceed.*
3. All other words that end in this sound have the ending *-cede,* including *accede, concede,* and *precede.*

EXERCISE 2 *Using Spelling Patterns*

Write each word, adding either *ie* or *ei.*

1. hyg__ne	**6.** conc__t	**11.** f__gn	**16.** l__utenant
2. dec__t	**7.** bel__ve	**12.** ch__f	**17.** conc__vable
3. sl__gh	**8.** th__r	**13.** p__rce	**18.** s__zure
4. for__gn	**9.** med__val	**14.** n__ghbor	**19.** counterf__t
5. s__ge	**10.** perc__ve	**15.** w__ght	**20.** rec__pt

EXERCISE 3 *Using Spelling Patterns*

Number your paper 1 to 10. Write each word, adding *-sede, -ceed,* or *-cede.*

1. pro__	**3.** con__	**5.** se__	**7.** pre__	**9.** suc__
2. re__	**4.** super__	**6.** ac__	**8.** ex__	**10.** inter__

Plurals

There are several spelling rules that can help you form the plural of most nouns.

Regular Nouns Add *s* to form the plural of most nouns. If a noun ends in *s, ch, sh, x,* or *z,* add *es* to form the plural.

SINGULAR	dentist	character	column	niece
PLURAL	dentist**s**	character**s**	column**s**	niece**s**
SINGULAR	genius	clutch	sash	waltz
PLURAL	genius**es**	clutch**es**	sash**es**	waltz**es**

Nouns Ending in *y* Add *s* to form the plural of a noun ending in a vowel and *y.*

SINGULAR	tray	holiday	attorney	decoy
PLURAL	tray**s**	holiday**s**	attorney**s**	decoy**s**

For a noun ending in a consonant and *y*, change the *y* to *i* and add *es.*

SINGULAR	tendency	family	accessory	delivery
PLURAL	tenden**cies**	famil**ies**	accessor**ies**	deliver**ies**

EXERCISE 4 Forming Plurals

Write the plural of each noun.

1. salary	**6.** society	**11.** glass	**16.** juror
2. turkey	**7.** constable	**12.** ranch	**17.** alloy
3. computer	**8.** waltz	**13.** dash	**18.** blue jay
4. college	**9.** army	**14.** delay	**19.** lunch
5. fox	**10.** fossil	**15.** speech	**20.** jockey

Nouns Ending in *o* Add *s* to form the plural of a noun ending in a vowel and *o*.

SINGULAR	radio	ratio	rodeo	portfolio
PLURAL	radio**s**	ratio**s**	rodeo**s**	portfolio**s**

The plural of a noun ending in a consonant and *o* may end in either *s* or *es*. There is no regular pattern.

SINGULAR	ditto	silo	photo	hero	potato
PLURAL	ditto**s**	silo**s**	photo**s**	hero**es**	potato**es**

Add only *s* to form the plural of a musical term ending in *o*.

SINGULAR	piano	solo	soprano	trio	piccolo
PLURAL	piano**s**	solo**s**	soprano**s**	trio**s**	piccolo**s**

When you are in doubt about a plural, consult the dictionary. If the dictionary does not give a plural form, the plural of that word usually ends in *s*.

Nouns Ending in *f* or *fe* Add *s* to form the plural of some nouns ending in *f* or *fe*.

SINGULAR	chief	roof	waif	clef	belief
PLURAL	chief**s**	roof**s**	waif**s**	clef**s**	belief**s**

For other nouns ending in *f* or *fe*, change the *f* to *v* and add *es*.

SINGULAR	calf	self	thief	wife	life
PLURAL	cal**ves**	sel**ves**	thie**ves**	wi**ves**	li**ves**

Because there is no sure way to tell which method you should use, check the dictionary for the plural form of words ending in *f* or *fe*.

EXERCISE 5 *Forming Plurals*

Write the plural of each noun. Check your answers in the dictionary.

1. cello	**11.** belief
2. ego	**12.** shelf
3. ratio	**13.** loaf
4. tomato	**14.** gulf
5. alto	**15.** knife
6. igloo	**16.** half
7. cameo	**17.** sheaf
8. duo	**18.** chef
9. studio	**19.** elf
10. echo	**20.** fife

Other Plural Forms Following are some examples of nouns that form their plurals in irregular ways.

Irregular Plurals

child, children	louse, lice	man, men
woman, women	mouse, mice	ox, oxen
tooth, teeth	foot, feet	goose, geese

Same Form for Singular and Plural

Chinese	salmon	trousers	series
Japanese	deer	scissors	politics
Sioux	sheep	headquarters	species
Danish	moose	surf	shad

Compound Nouns The plurals of most compound nouns are formed in the same way as other noun plurals.

SINGULAR	baby-sitter	go-between	chairwoman	rooftop
PLURAL	baby-sitter**s**	go-between**s**	chairwom**e**n	rooftop**s**

In some compound nouns, however, the main part of the word appears first. This main word is the part of the compound that becomes plural.

SINGULAR	son-in-law	bill of sale	runner-up	passerby
PLURAL	son**s**-in-law	bill**s** of sale	runner**s**-up	passer**s**by

EXERCISE 6 *Forming Plurals*

Write the plural of each noun.

1. pliers	**6.** co-star	**11.** Swiss	**16.** seat belt
2. drive-in	**7.** passerby	**12.** series	**17.** windshield
3. louse	**8.** Japanese	**13.** child	**18.** teaspoonful
4. corps	**9.** snowman	**14.** goose	**19.** son-in-law
5. squash	**10.** hot rod	**15.** byline	**20.** looker-on

Prefixes and Suffixes

A *prefix* is one or more syllables placed in front of a root to form a new word. When you add a prefix to a root, do not change the spelling of the root.

dis + array = disarray	trans + oceanic = transoceanic
re + type = retype	dis + similar = dissimilar
over + rule = overrule	il + literate = illiterate
re + enact = reenact	pre + eminent = preeminent

A *suffix* is one or more syllables placed after a root to help shape its meaning or to determine its part of speech. The spelling of the root does not change when the suffixes *-ness* and *-ly* are added.

thin + ness = thinness	love + ly = lovely
same + ness = sameness	natural + ly = naturally

When you add suffixes other than *-ness* or *-ly*, you sometimes change the spelling of the root. The following rules explain how.

Words Ending in *e* Drop the final *e* of a root before a suffix that begins with a vowel.

recite + ing = reciting	fame + ous = famous
excite + able = excitable	liberate + ion = liberation

When adding a suffix to a word that ends in *e*, keep the final *e* if the suffix begins with a consonant.

fate + ful = fateful	name + less = nameless
home + like = homelike	move + ment = movement

Also, keep the final *e* in a word that ends in *ce* or *ge* if the suffix begins with *a* or *o*. Notice in the following words how the *e* keeps the sound of the *c* or *g* soft.

manage, manageable	trace, traceable
notice, noticeable	courage, courageous

You will find some exceptions to the spelling rules for adding suffixes to words ending in *e*, including the following.

dye, dyeing	awe, awful	argue, argument
die, dying	true, truly	judge, judgment

EXERCISE 7 *Adding Prefixes and Suffixes*

Write each word, adding the prefix or the suffix shown. Remember to make any necessary spelling changes.

1. dis + appear
2. lean + ness
3. hike + ing
4. sane + ity
5. under + rate
6. special + ly
7. re + examine
8. tribe + al
9. state + hood
10. ripe + est
11. care + ful
12. strive + ing
13. quote + able
14. same + ness
15. rare + ity
16. de + emphasize
17. outrage + ous
18. co + operate
19. bride + al
20. guide + ance

Words Ending in *y* For most words ending in a vowel and *y*, keep the *y* when adding a suffix.

buy + er = buyer	obey + ing = obeying
joy + ous = joyous	play + ful = playful

For most words ending in a consonant and *y*, change the *y* to *i* before adding a suffix.

hazy + ness = haziness	steady + ly = steadily
friendly + er = friendlier	twenty + eth = twentieth

Following are some exceptions to the spelling rules for adding suffixes to words ending in *y*.

SUFFIX BEGINNING WITH *i*	carrying	babyish	denying
SOME ONE-SYLLABLE WORDS	daily	paid	dryness

EXERCISE 8 *Adding Suffixes*

Write each word, adding the suffix shown. Remember to make any necessary spelling changes.

1. worry + er
2. tray + ful
3. dizzy + ly
4. gray + est
5. study + ing
6. rely + able
7. toy + like
8. funny + ness
9. thirty + eth
10. pay + er
11. shy + ness
12. sunny + er
13. deny + al
14. ally + ance
15. dairy + ing
16. supply + ed
17. lazy + ly
18. prey + ing
19. early + ness
20. scary + est

Doubling the Final Consonant Double the final consonant before a suffix beginning with a vowel if the word satisfies both of the following conditions.

- The word has only one syllable or is stressed on the final syllable.
- The word ends in one consonant preceded by one vowel.

ONE-SYLLABLE WORD	let + ing le**tt**ing	dim + ed di**mm**ed	big + est bi**gg**est
FINAL SYLLABLE STRESSED	occur + ing occu**rr**ing	regret + able regre**tt**able	defer + al defe**rr**al

EXERCISE 9 *Adding Suffixes*

Write each word, adding the suffix shown. Remember to make any necessary spelling changes.

1. sit + ing
2. prefer + ed
3. fast + est
4. glad + en
5. transfer + ing
6. affirm + ative
7. can + ed
8. stop + able
9. leap + ing
10. slip + age
11. build + er
12. red + ish
13. begin + er
14. perfect + ion
15. infer + ed
16. sad + est
17. ton + age
18. hot + est
19. roof + ing
20. offer + ed

Chapter 15 Review

Recognizing Misspelled Words Write the letter of the misspelled word in each group. Then write the word, spelling it correctly.

1. (A) cemetery (B) brilliant (C) foreign
(D) arguement (E) obstacle

2. (A) disarray (B) perceive (C) dissimilar
(D) exceed (E) seperate

3. (A) excitable (B) potatoes (C) temperture
(D) siege (E) attorneys

4. (A) seizure (B) families (C) occuring
(D) bicycle (E) courageous

5. (A) conscience (B) vinegar (C) tommorrow
(D) weird (E) foxes

6. (A) friendlier (B) illiterate (C) athletics
(D) subtle (E) maintainance

7. (A) baby-sitter (B) Wednesday (C) concede
(D) pianoes (E) awkward

8. (A) achieve (B) noticable (C) nuisance
(D) thieves (E) bookkeeper

9. (A) tradgedy (B) sophomore (C) reenact
(D) fulfill (E) sleigh

10. (A) transmittal (B) either (C) neighbor
(D) twelfth (E) passerbys

11. (A) original (B) volunteer (C) permanent
(D) suceed (E) radios

12. (A) armies (B) overrule (C) dairying
(D) celloes (E) precede

13. (A) syllabel (B) ceiling (C) dissatisfied
(D) elves (E) solos

14. (A) writing (B) runners-up (C) traceable
(D) foggyness (E) irresistible

15. (A) preempt (B) ancient (C) medieval
(D) misstate (E) lovly

Chapter

16 Reference Skills

The library is a storehouse of information that you can use to your advantage if you know how. This chapter shows you how to tap the library's many resources and how to find information in various types of reference books, in a dictionary, or in a magazine.

Language Integrating Skills

An Information File for Writing To get ideas for writing topics, you really do not have to do much more than wander through a library, look at book covers, flip through newspapers or magazines, or observe the people in the library. These simple tasks, however, may not always be convenient. That is why you should develop your own personal information file as a part of your journal.

In this file you should write or include anything and everything that catches your interest or piques your curiosity. You might include a newspaper article about an old-time football great, a funny poem, or a magazine article about the diminishing wolf population in the United States. If you make sure that you include the source of each item you put into your information file, then you will be able to find the original source again easily. Then refer to your file when you need a convenient source of information for writing topics.

The Library

When people think about libraries, they mostly think of books, but in addition to books, most libraries have magazines, newspapers, pamphlets, and other printed materials. Today many libraries also have nonprint materials—such as records, tape recordings and videotapes, slides and filmstrips, and computer software. All of these sources of information are arranged so that people can find them easily.

Library Arrangement

Most libraries have separate sections for fiction, nonfiction, magazines and newspapers, and reference works. In each section the materials are organized either alphabetically or numerically. Browse through your library to learn where each section is located.

Fiction and Nonfiction In many libraries, works of fiction, such as short stories and novels, are marked with the symbol *F* or *FIC.* Books in the fiction section are arranged alphabetically by the authors' last names. In special cases the following rules apply.

Guide for Finding Fiction

- Two-part names are alphabetized by the first part of the name. (**Mac**Donald, **O'**Malley, **Van** Dyke)
- Names beginning with *Mc* and *St.* are alphabetized as if they began with *Mac* and *Saint.*
- Books by authors with the same last name are alphabetized by the authors' first names.
- Books by the same author are alphabetized by title, skipping *a, an,* and *the.*
- Numbers in titles are alphabetized as if they were written out. (*50–Fifty*)

Nonfiction books are usually arranged according to the *Dewey decimal classification system,* developed by American librarian Melvin Dewey in the 1870's. In this system each book is assigned a number according to its subject.

Main Subject Areas in Dewey Decimal System	
000–099	General Works (reference books)
100–199	Philosophy
200–299	Religion
300–399	Social Science (law, education, economics)
400–499	Language
500–599	Science (mathematics, biology, chemistry)
600–699	Technology (medicine, inventions)
700–799	Fine Arts (painting, music, theater)
800–899	Literature
900–999	History (biography, geography, travel)

Each main subject area has ten subdivisions. The subdivisions for science follow, as an example.

500–599 Science			
500–509	Pure sciences	550–559	Earth sciences
510–519	Mathematics	560–569	Paleontology
520–529	Astronomy	570–579	Anthropology
530–539	Physics	580–589	Botany
540–549	Chemistry	590–599	Zoology

The subdivisions of a main subject are further subdivided through the use of decimal numbers and other symbols. Together these numbers and letters form a book's call number, which is displayed on the book's spine.

In addition to the call number, some works carry a special label to show the section of the library in which they are shelved. Biographies and autobiographies may be identified by *B* or *92* (short for *920* in the Dewey decimal system). These books are arranged in alphabetical order by the name of the subject, rather than by the name of the author. The following chart lists other works that are often given special labels.

CATEGORIES	SPECIAL LABELS
Juvenile Books	J or X
Reference Works	R or REF
Records	REC
Filmstrips	FS

EXERCISE 1 ***Understanding the Dewey Decimal System***

Using the list of classifications on page 482, write the subject numbers for each book. If the title is marked with an asterisk (*), also write the science subdivision.

EXAMPLE *Chemistry Made Easy**
ANSWER *500–599, 540–549*

1. *What to Listen For in Music*
2. *The Story of Speech and Language*
3. *Thinking Machines*
4. *Astronomy: The Cosmic Journey**
5. *Black Images in American Literature*
6. *Earth's Valuable Minerals**
7. *A Guide to Solo Travel*
8. *Technology and the Future*
9. *Introduction to Geometry**
10. *Asimov on Physics**

The Card Catalog

The card catalog is a cabinet of small file drawers that contain cards for every book in the library. Each book usually has an *author card*, a *title card*, and a *subject card*, and all of these cards are arranged alphabetically.

Author Cards When you want to find books by a particular author, look under the author's last name in the card catalog.

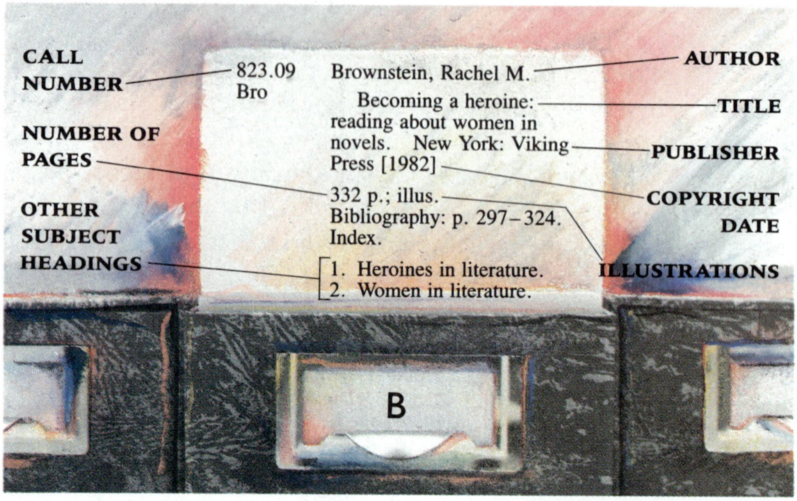

Title Cards When you know the title of a book but not the author, you can find the book by looking up the title card. Title cards are alphabetized by the first word in the title except for *a, an,* and *the.*

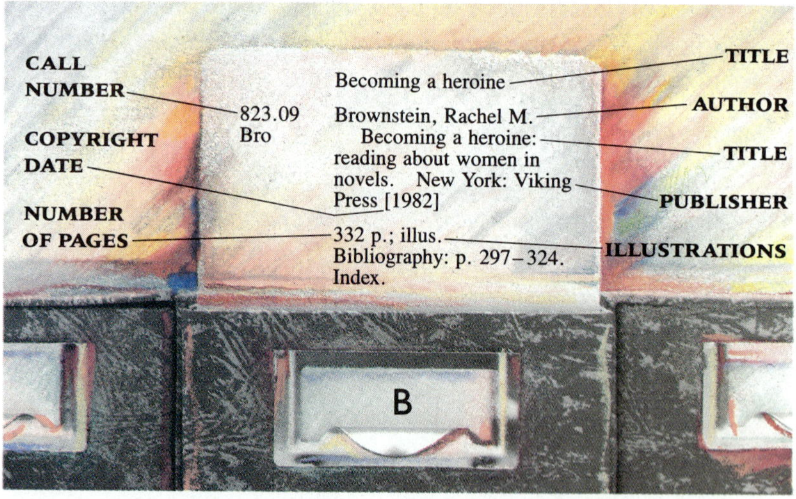

Subject Cards If you do not know the author of a book or its title, subject cards are particularly helpful. The subject is printed at the top of each card in capital letters. Subject cards are arranged alphabetically according to the first main word in the subject heading.

Cross-Reference Cards In addition to three cards for each book, the catalog contains *See* and *See also* cards—also called *cross-reference cards*. A *See* card tells you that the subject you have looked up is under another heading. A *See also* card lists other subjects you could look up for additional titles.

EXERCISE 2 *Understanding Catalog Cards*

Using the catalog card below, write the answers to the questions on the next page.

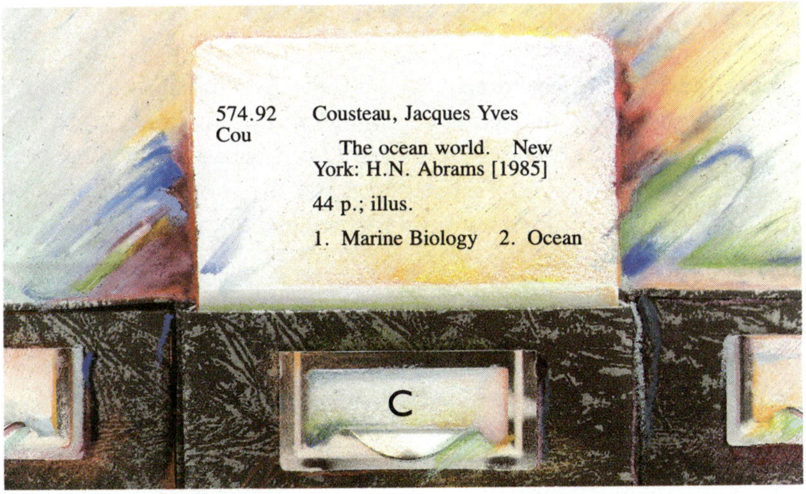

1. Is the catalog card on the previous page an author card, a subject card, or a title card?
2. Who is the author of this book?
3. What is the call number for this book?
4. Who is the publisher?
5. What is the copyright date?
6. How many pages does this book have?
7. Does the book contain illustrations?
8. Under what letter would you look to find the title card?
9. Would the title card *Dolphins: Playful Mammals of the Sea* be filed before or after the title card for this book?
10. Under what two subject headings is this book filed?

Reference Materials

Most libraries keep current reference materials in a separate section because these materials cannot be taken out of the library. Following is a review of the kinds of reference materials you may find most helpful.

General Encyclopedias Encyclopedias provide basic information on a wide variety of subjects. These subjects are arranged alphabetically in a number of volumes. An encyclopedia is a good reference to start with when you begin to collect information for a report. Two examples of general encyclopedias are *Collier's Encyclopedia* and *Encyclopaedia Britannica*.

Specialized Encyclopedias Specialized encyclopedias are available on almost every subject. For example, most libraries contain the *Encyclopedia of Mythology* and *The Baseball Encyclopedia*. Because a specialized encyclopedia concentrates on a specific subject area, it provides more detailed information on that subject than you will find in a general encyclopedia.

Biographical References Information about famous people of the past and of the present may be found in biographical reference books. Some biographical references contain only a paragraph of facts about each person, while others, such as *Current Biography*, contain long articles. The following excerpt about the American writer Maya Angelou is from *Who's Who in America 1986–1987*.

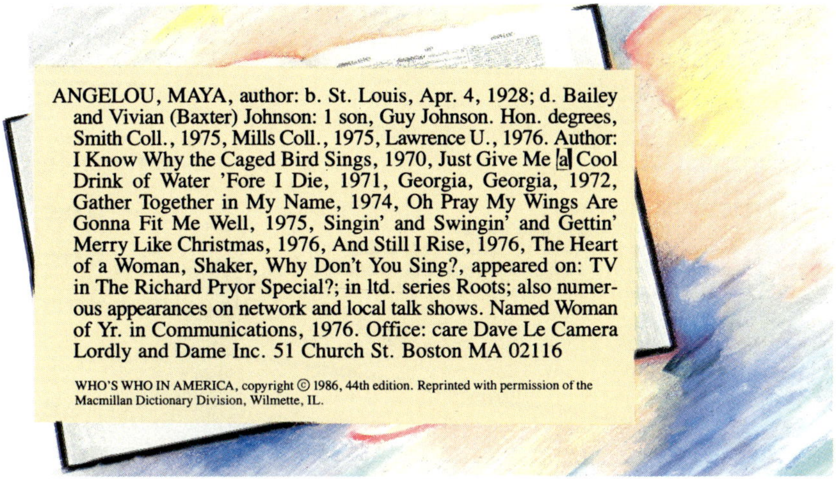

ANGELOU, MAYA, author: b. St. Louis, Apr. 4, 1928; d. Bailey and Vivian (Baxter) Johnson: 1 son, Guy Johnson. Hon. degrees, Smith Coll., 1975, Mills Coll., 1975, Lawrence U., 1976. Author: I Know Why the Caged Bird Sings, 1970, Just Give Me a Cool Drink of Water 'Fore I Die, 1971, Georgia, Georgia, 1972, Gather Together in My Name, 1974, Oh Pray My Wings Are Gonna Fit Me Well, 1975, Singin' and Swingin' and Gettin' Merry Like Christmas, 1976, And Still I Rise, 1976, The Heart of a Woman, Shaker, Why Don't You Sing?, appeared on: TV in The Richard Pryor Special?; in ltd. series Roots; also numerous appearances on network and local talk shows. Named Woman of Yr. in Communications, 1976. Office: care Dave Le Camera Lordly and Dame Inc. 51 Church St. Boston MA 02116

Atlases These books of maps present information about the regions of the world. Special-purpose maps and tables may show a region's physical geography, cities, population, climate, industries, natural resources, and systems of transportation. Historical atlases show maps of the world during different periods of history. In addition, some specialized atlases focus on the geography and history of a specific country or state. *Goode's World Atlas* and *The Times Atlas of the World* are found in most libraries.

Almanacs and Yearbooks Because almanacs and yearbooks are published once a year, they are reliable sources for up-to-date information on a wide range of subjects, as well as for information about famous people, unusual achievements, and sports. The *Information Please Almanac* and the *Guinness Book of World Records* are two widely used and read almanacs.

Specialized Dictionaries A dictionary of synonyms, or a thesaurus, such as *Roget's Thesaurus in Dictionary Form,* will help you make exact word choices. Another type of specialized dictionary contains words about a particular subject. An example of this kind of specialized dictionary is the *Harvard Dictionary of Music.*

Readers' Guide to Periodical Literature The *Readers' Guide to Periodical Literature* indexes articles, short stories, and poems published in more than 175 magazines and journals. Articles are listed in alphabetical order by subject and author. On the next page is an example of an entry from the *Readers' Guide.*

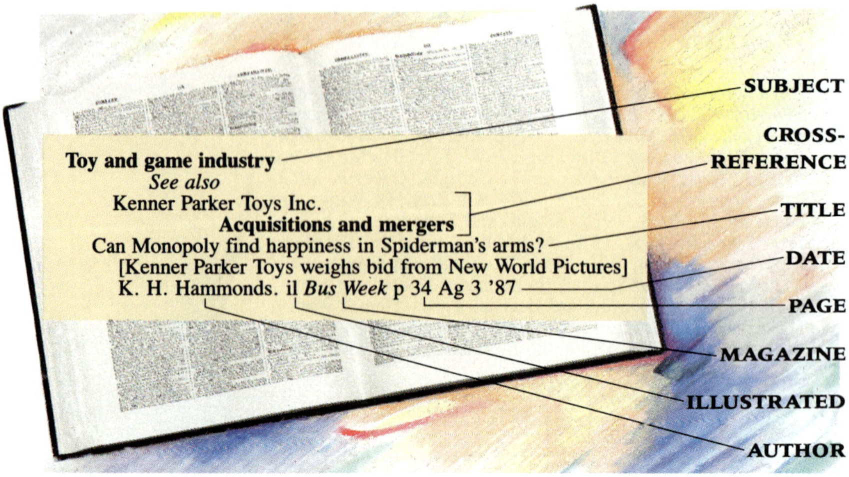

Note: *Readers' Guide* entries use many abbreviations, which are all listed at the front of each volume. For example, *Ag* stands for *August*.

Vertical File Libraries often store pamphlets, catalogs, and newspaper clippings alphabetically in a filing cabinet called the vertical file.

EXERCISE 3 *Using Reference Materials*

Write one kind of reference work—other than a general encyclopedia—that would contain information about each subject.

1. magazine articles about the 1988 presidential election
2. famous young Americans
3. Olympic records in alpine skiing events
4. location of active volcanoes in North America
5. college catalogs
6. the meaning of the term *allegro* in music
7. the name and location of the capital of Hawaii
8. pamphlets on eating disorders
9. information about a scientific discovery this year
10. information about Supreme Court Justice Sandra Day O'Connor

Reference Materials about Language and Literature For your English class, you may need to consult reference books specifically on the subjects of language and literature. Following are examples.

SPECIALIZED DICTIONARIES	*Webster's New Dictionary of Synonyms; Dictionary of Literary Terms*

SPECIALIZED ENCYCLOPEDIAS	*Cassell's Encyclopedia of World Literature; Reader's Encyclopedia of American Literature*
BIOGRAPHICAL REFERENCES	*Contemporary Authors* *American Authors 1600–1900* *Contemporary Poets of the English Language* *Black American Writers Past & Present*

Handbooks, or companions, are another kind of literary reference. Some handbooks give plot summaries or describe characters. Others explain literary terms or give information about authors. For example, most libraries carry *The Oxford Companion to American Literature* and *The Oxford Companion to English Literature.*

Books of quotations, such as *Bartlett's Familiar Quotations,* tell you the source of a particular quotation. These books also list complete quotations as well as other quotations on the same subject.

Indexes are useful for finding a particular poem, short story, or play. An index such as *Granger's Index to Poetry* lists the books that contain the particular selection you are looking for.

EXERCISE 4 *Understanding Literary Reference Works*

Write one kind of reference work about language and literature that you could use to find the answer to each question.

EXAMPLE What collections of poetry contain Robert Frost's "The Road Not Taken"?

POSSIBLE ANSWER index to poetry

1. What does the term *unreliable narrator* mean?
2. Who defined a coward as "one who in a perilous emergency thinks with his legs"?
3. What was the real name of George Eliot, a British novelist?
4. Where could you find the short story "A Bottle of Milk for Mother" by Nelson Algren?
5. What is a synonym for *determine?*
6. Which play contains the line "Parting is such sweet sorrow"?
7. How many books did the American author Ralph Ellison write?
8. In what collections is the play *Pygmalion* published?
9. J. D. Salinger is a twentieth-century American author. What do the initials *J. D.* stand for?
10. What is the meaning of the term *denouement?*

The Dictionary

Most libraries have a large, *unabridged* dictionary that sits on a stand in the reference section. Unabridged, or unshortened, dictionaries usually contain more than half a million words and have long, complete definitions. Smaller dictionaries are *abridged* (shortened), *college*, or *school dictionaries*. Whatever its size, a dictionary is one of your most valuable resource tools.

Information in an Entry

You will probably use a dictionary most often to check the spelling, pronunciation, or meaning of a word. However, dictionaries contain much additional information. Through the use of symbols and abbreviations, dictionaries also tell the history of a word, its division into syllables, its part or parts of speech, its usage in idioms, and its synonyms and antonyms.

The word itself is called an *entry word.* All the information about each word entry is called a *main entry.* The following list shows the different kinds of entry words and how they would be listed in alphabetical order in the dictionary.

HYPHENATED WORD	ill-humored	PREFIX	ir-
COMPOUND WORD	ion exchange	SINGLE WORD	iris
SUFFIX	-ious	PROPER NOUN	Iron Age
ABBREVIATION	IQ		

Preferred and Variant Spellings The entry word, printed in heavy type at the beginning of each main entry, shows the correct spelling of a word. When words can be spelled in more than one way, the most commonly used spelling, called the *preferred spelling,* is listed first. Less common spellings, called *variants,* follow. In some cases a variant spelling may be listed as a separate entry but does not include a full definition. For the complete information, the entry refers you to the preferred spelling of the word. Always use the preferred spelling of words in your writing.

PREFERRED SPELLING ⟶ ⟵ VARIANT SPELLING

cal·o·rie, *also* **calory**

EXERCISE 5 *Finding Preferred Spellings*

Find the variant spelling of each word in a dictionary. Then write the preferred spelling.

1. theatre **2.** judgement **3.** moveable **4.** practise **5.** chaperone

Syllable Division of Words The entry words in a dictionary show how to break words into syllables.

phe•nom•e•non grad•u•ate dy•nam•ic

Pronunciation Following the entry word is the phonetic spelling of that word, which shows you how to pronounce the word.

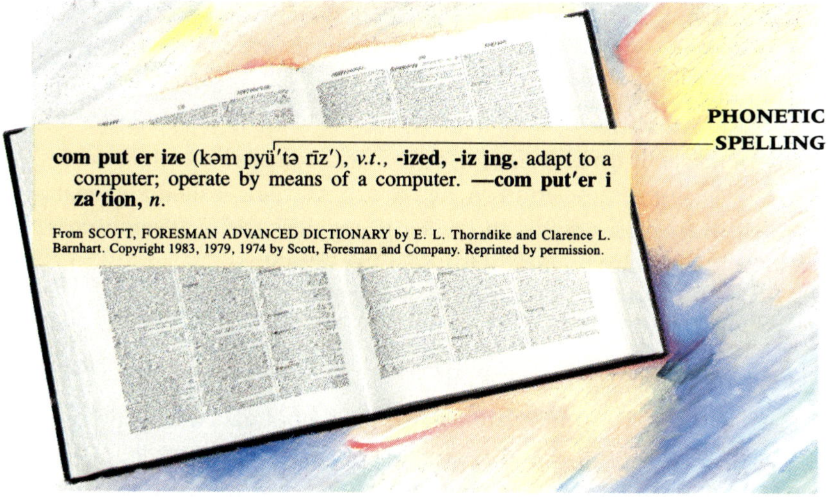

com put er ize (kəm pyü′tə rīz′), *v.t.*, **-ized, -iz ing.** adapt to a computer; operate by means of a computer. **—com put′er i za′tion,** *n.*

A listing of phonetic symbols is at the beginning of a dictionary. Most dictionaries also provide a partial pronunciation key on each page.

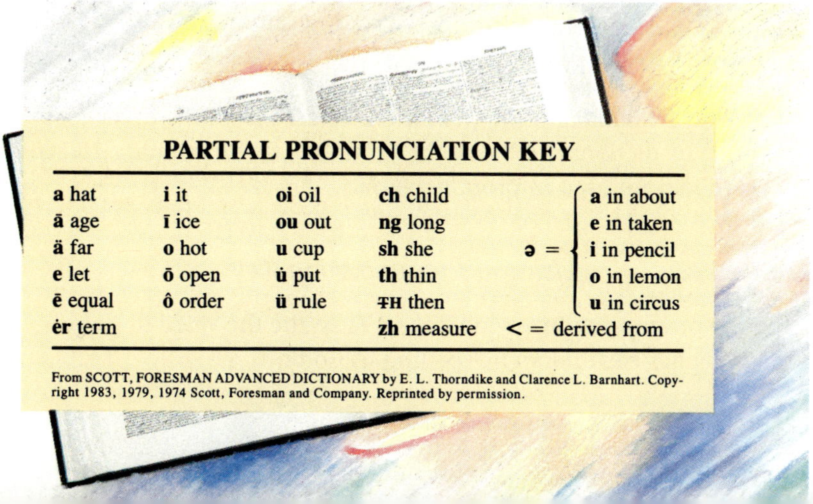

PARTIAL PRONUNCIATION KEY

a hat	**i** it	**oi** oil	**ch** child	**ə** =	**a** in about
ā age	**ī** ice	**ou** out	**ng** long		**e** in taken
ä far	**o** hot	**u** cup	**sh** she		**i** in pencil
e let	**ō** open	**ů** put	**th** thin		**o** in lemon
ē equal	**ô** order	**ü** rule	**ŦH** then		**u** in circus
ėr term			**zh** measure	< = derived from	

To find out how to pronounce the vowel in the second syllable of the word *computerize*, for example, look for the symbol *u* in the pronunciation key. You can see that it is pronounced like the *u* in *rule*.

To distinguish one vowel sound from another, phonetic spellings include diacritical marks above the vowels. The letter *u*, for instance, can be pronounced three different ways.

DIACRITICAL MARKS

u as in *cup* **u** as in *pu̇t* **u** as in *rüle*

The letter *u* and other vowels are sometimes pronounced *uh*. This sound is represented by a symbol (ə), called the *schwa*. In the word *computerize*, both the *o* and the first *e* are pronounced *uh*. A schwa is used in the phonetic spelling to represent this sound.

SCHWA

kəm pyü'tə rīz'

Phonetic spellings also have accent marks to show which syllables are stressed in pronunciation. A heavy accent mark, called a *primary stress*, shows which syllable in the word receives the most emphasis. *Secondary stresses* are marked with a lighter accent.

PRIMARY STRESS SECONDARY STRESS

kəm pyü'tə rīz'

If a word can be pronounced more than one way, the dictionary will show both pronunciations. The first one shown, however, is preferred. In some dictionaries only the parts of a word that differ in an alternate pronunciation are given.

ALTERNATE PRONUNCIATIONS

da · ta (dā' tə, dat' ə, dä' tə)
pro · gram (prō' gram, -grəm)

Phonetic symbols and the placement of accent marks differ from dictionary to dictionary. Check the front of your dictionary to see what symbols are used in pronunciation.

EXERCISE 6 *Using a Pronunciation Key*

Using the pronunciation key on page 491, write the word in Column B that matches each phonetic spelling in Column A.

COLUMN A	COLUMN B
1. ə māz′	subside
2. är′ ju əs	caucus
3. ô dā′ shəs	quadrant
4. kô′ kəs	writhe
5. ek′ sə kyüt	amaze
6. eg zil′ ə rāt′	arduous
7. in ô′ gyə rāt′	execute
8. kwod′ rənt	inaugurate
9. səb sīd′	audacious
10. rīᴛʜ	exhilarate

Part-of-Speech Labels Each word entry in a dictionary also contains an abbreviation that indicates what part of speech the word can be used as. Because some words can function as more than one part of speech, some entries will contain several part-of-speech labels.

PART-OF-SPEECH LABELS		
	n. = noun	*v.* = verb
	pron. = pronoun	*prep.* = preposition
	adj. = adjective	*conj.* = conjunction
	adv. = adverb	*interj.* = interjection

Multiple Meanings Many words have more than one meaning. Most dictionaries list the most common meaning first, although some list the meanings in historical order, showing the oldest meaning first.

Dictionaries use *restrictive labels* to help explain differences in meaning. These labels restrict a given definition to a particular subject area, dialect, or usage—such as *informal* or *slang*. The last part of an entry is often a list of synonyms—with an explanation of their different shades of meaning.

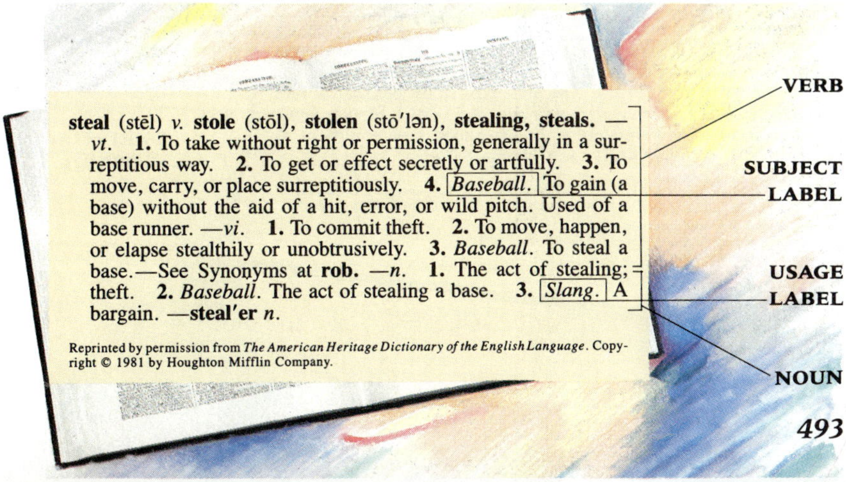
steal (stēl) *v.* **stole** (stōl), **stolen** (stō′lən), **stealing, steals.** —*vt.* **1.** To take without right or permission, generally in a surreptitious way. **2.** To get or effect secretly or artfully. **3.** To move, carry, or place surreptitiously. **4.** *Baseball.* To gain (a base) without the aid of a hit, error, or wild pitch. Used of a base runner. —*vi.* **1.** To commit theft. **2.** To move, happen, or elapse stealthily or unobtrusively. **3.** *Baseball.* To steal a base.—See Synonyms at **rob.** —*n.* **1.** The act of stealing; theft. **2.** *Baseball.* The act of stealing a base. **3.** *Slang.* A bargain. —**steal′er** *n.*

EXERCISE 7 *Recognizing Multiple Meanings*

Use the entry on the previous page to write the part of speech of the word *steal* as it is used in each sentence. Then write the number of the definition that matches that use of the word.

EXAMPLE Who stole the last piece of pie?
ANSWER transitive verb, 2

1. Do you think the runner on first will try to steal second base?
2. You bought that dress for 20 dollars? It was a steal!
3. The rock star, hoping that no one would recognize him, stole out of the store through a side exit.
4. Debbie claimed that Jimmy stole her pen while she wasn't looking.
5. All the reviewers agreed that the new actress stole the show from her more experienced colleagues.

Inflected Forms and Derived Words The dictionary shows endings, or *inflections*, that change the form of the word but not its part of speech. Verbs, for example, can be inflected with *-ed* or *-ing* to change the principal part of the verb. Adjectives can be inflected with *-er* or *-est* to show the comparative and superlative degrees. Nouns have plural forms, but most dictionaries show only those plural forms that are formed irregularly.

Derived words are made by adding endings that change the part of speech of a word. For example, by adding the suffix *-ment* to the verb *resent*, the noun *resentment* is formed. Most dictionaries list derived words at the end of a main entry.

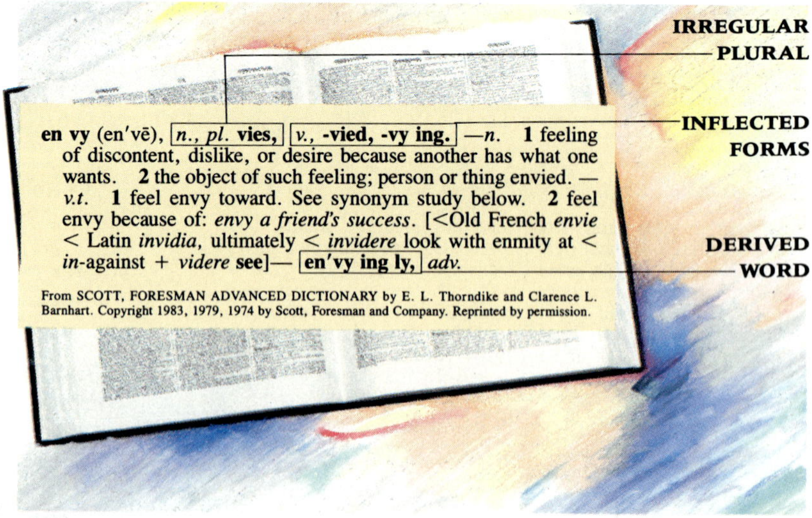

en vy (en′vē), *n., pl.* **vies,** *v.,* **-vied, -vy ing.** —*n.* **1** feeling of discontent, dislike, or desire because another has what one wants. **2** the object of such feeling; person or thing envied. —*v.t.* **1** feel envy toward. See synonym study below. **2** feel envy because of: *envy a friend's success.* [<Old French *envie* < Latin *invidia,* ultimately < *invidere* look with enmity at < *in-*against + *videre* see]— **en′vy ing ly,** *adv.*

Etymologies A dictionary gives the *etymology,* or history, of a word. The etymology is usually explained in an entry through the use of abbreviations and symbols. The abbreviations stand for languages from which the word developed. The symbols stand for such phrases as *derived from* (<) and *equivalent to* (=). A chart at the beginning of the dictionary lists all the abbreviations and symbols used in showing the etymology of a word. In an etymology the most recent source of the word is listed first. *(See also pages 455–457 for more information about the histories of words.)*

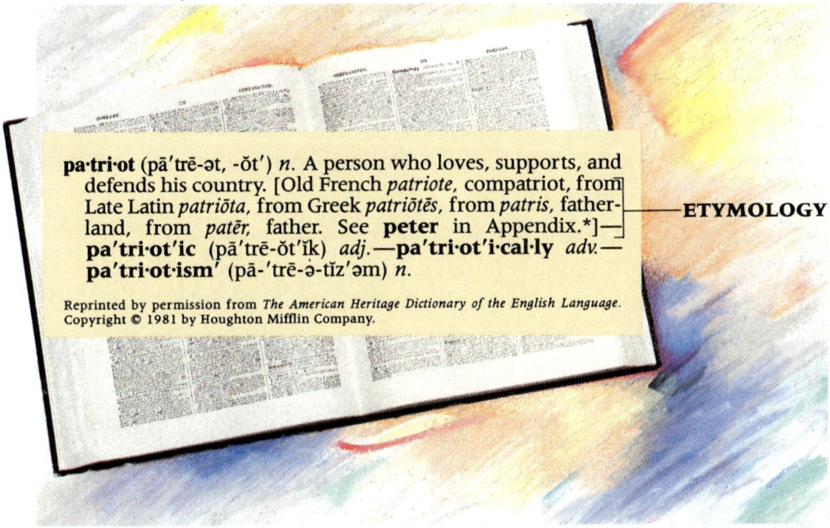

pa·tri·ot (pā'trē-ət, -ŏt') *n.* A person who loves, supports, and defends his country. [Old French *patriote,* compatriot, from Late Latin *patriōta,* from Greek *patriōtēs,* from *patris,* fatherland, from *patēr,* father. See **peter** in Appendix.*] —**pa'tri·ot'ic** (pā'trē-ŏt'ĭk) *adj.* —**pa'tri·ot'i·cal·ly** *adv.* —**pa'tri·ot·ism'** (pā-'trē-ə-tĭz'əm) *n.*

The etymology of *patriot* can be translated as follows: The modern word *patriot* comes from the Old French *patriote,* which meant *compatriot.* The Old French word was derived from the Late Latin *patriōta,* which came from the Greek *patriōtēs.* The Greek word *patriōtēs* was derived from *patris,* meaning *fatherland,* which in turn came from *pāter,* meaning *father.*

EXERCISE 8 *Tracing Word Origins*

Number your paper 1 to 10. Then use the dictionary to trace the etymology of each word. Write the etymology on your paper.

1. brave
2. chariot
3. infant
4. comet
5. eccentric
6. comedy
7. mob
8. rebel
9. calisthenics
10. shambles

Chapter 16

Review

A **Choosing Reference Material** Number your paper 1 to 15. Then, using the following list of library resources, write the best resource for finding the answer to each question.

card catalog	book of quotations
general encyclopedia	index to poetry
specialized encyclopedia	atlas
biographical reference	almanac
specialized dictionary	*Readers' Guide*

1. How did Mark Twain (Samuel Clemens) learn about steamboating on the Mississippi?
2. Who wrote the poem that begins, "Hold fast to dreams"?
3. What mountain range separates Europe and Asia?
4. To whom did Beethoven originally dedicate his third symphony?
5. Who was the youngest major-league baseball player of all time, and how old was he when he started?
6. What are three synonyms for the word *income?*
7. What are two call numbers for books by Carl Sagan?
8. What three rivers meet at Pittsburgh, Pennsylvania?
9. For what is Louis Sullivan famous?
10. Where is the natural home of the duckbill platypus?
11. Who wrote, "The education of a man is never completed until he dies"?
12. What magazine articles were written about cable TV in the last six months?
13. What do physicists mean by a *subatomic particle?*
14. How many light-years away is the nearest star?
15. Who won the Grammy award for male pop vocalist in 1990?

B **Finding Information** Use the resources in your library to find the answers to the first ten questions of Part A above.

C **Using the Dictionary** Number your paper 1 to 15. Then, using the entries on page 497, write the answer to each question.

1. What is the preferred spelling for *pixie?*
2. What is the plural of *pizzicato?*

pit ter-pat ter (pit'ər pat'ər), *n.* a rapid succession of light beats or taps: *the pitter-patter of rain.* —*adv.* with a rapid succession of beats or taps. —*v.i.* go pitter-patter. Also, **pitapat.**

Pitts burgh (pits'bėrg'), *n.* city in SW Pennsylvania, a center of the iron and steel industry. 424,000.

pit y (pit'ē), *n., pl.* **pit ies,** *v.,* **pit ied, pit y ing.** —*n.* **1** sorrow for another's suffering or distress; feeling for the sorrows of others; compassion: sympathy. See synonym study below. **2** cause for pity or regret; thing to be sorry for: *It is a pity to be kept in the house in good weather.* **3 have pity on** or **take pity on, show pity for.** —*v.t.* feel pity for. —*v.i.* feel pity. [<Old French *pite* < Latin *pietatem.* Doublet of PIETY.] —**pit'y ing ly,** *adv.*
Syn. *n.* **1 Pity, compassion, sympathy** mean a feeling for the sorrows or suffering of others. Pity means a feeling of sorrow for someone who is suffering or in distress, and often felt to be weak or unfortunate: *The beggar's hungry look and ragged appearance aroused the stranger's pity.* **Compassion** adds the idea of tenderness and a strong desire to help or protect: *She felt compassion for the sobbing child.* **Sympathy** means a feeling with another in sorrow and sharing and understanding it: *His friends expressed great sympathy for him when his mother died.*

piv ot (piv'ət), *n.* **1** shaft, pin, or point on which something turns. **2** a turn on or as if on a pivot. **3** that on which something turns, hinges, or depends; central point. —*v.t.* mount on, attach by, or provide with a pivot. —*v.i.* turn on or as if on a pivot. [<French]

pix y or **pix ie** (pik'sē), *n., pl.* **pix ies.** fairy or elf. [origin uncertain]

Pi zar ro (pi zär'ō), *n.* **Francisco,** 1471?-1541, Spanish explorer, who conquered Peru.

piz zazz (pə zaz'), *n.* SLANG. pizazz.

piz ze ri a (pēt'sə rē'ə), *n.* restaurant or bakery where pizzas are baked and sold. [<Italian]

piz zi ca to (pit'sə kä'tō), *adj., n., pl.* **-ti** (-tē). in music: —*adj.* played by plucking the strings of a musical instrument with the finger instead of using the bow. —*n.* note or passage so played. [<Italian, picked, pinched]

pl., 1 place. **2** plate. **3** plural.

pla cate (plā'kāt, plak'āt), *v.t.,* **-cat ed, -cat ing.** soothe or satisfy the anger of; make peaceful; appease: *placate a person one has offended.* [<Latin *placatum* soothed] —**pla'cat er,** *n.* —**pla'cat ing ly,** *adv.* —**pla ca'tion,** *n.*

3. Which two syllables are accented in the pronunciation of *pizzeria?*
4. When did Francisco Pizarro die?
5. What is the population of Pittsburgh?
6. What are the two synonyms for the word *pity?*
7. What are the inflected forms of the verb *pity?*
8. As what three parts of speech can the word *pitter-patter* be used?
9. From what language is *pivot* derived?
10. What are the three meanings of the abbreviation *pl.?*
11. What is the usage label for *pizazz?*
12. How many schwas are in the phonetic spelling of *pizzeria*?
13. What three derived words are listed in the entry for *placate?*
14. Write an explanation of the etymology of *placate.*
15. What is the variant spelling for *pitter-patter?*

Chapter

17 Study and Test-Taking Skills

During the next few years, you will take many tests—in high school subjects, for college entrance, and for job applications. Successful test taking requires more than knowing the material to be tested. It also requires mastering various test-taking strategies. In this chapter you will practice effective study and test-taking strategies to help improve your chances for success on important tests.

Learning Study Skills

Applying good study habits helps you in taking tests as well as in completing daily classroom assignments. Begin to improve your study habits by using the following strategies.

Strategies for Effective Studying

1. Choose an area that is well lighted and quiet.
2. Equip your study area with everything you need for reading and writing, including a dictionary and a thesaurus.
3. Keep an assignment book for recording assignments and due dates.
4. Allow plenty of time for studying. Begin your reading and writing assignments early.
5. Adjust your reading rate to suit your purpose.

Adjusting Reading Rate to Purpose

Your reading rate is the speed with which you read. Depending on your purpose for reading, you may appropriately choose to read certain materials quickly or slowly, using the techniques of *scanning, skimming,* or *close reading*.

For example, if your purpose is to get a quick impression of the contents of a newspaper, you should scan the headlines. If you want to learn the main ideas of a certain article, you should skim it. On the other hand, if your purpose is to learn new facts or understand the details, then you may choose to read the article closely.

Whether you are reading a newspaper, an article in a periodical, or a textbook, you can read with greater effectiveness and efficiency if you adjust your reading rate to suit your purpose for reading the material.

Suggestions for Adjusting Your Reading Rate

SCANNING	*Scanning* is reading to get a general impression and to prepare for learning about a subject. To scan, you should read the title, headings, subheadings, picture captions, words and phrases in boldface or italics, and any focus questions. Using this method, you can quickly determine what the reading is about and what questions to keep in mind. Scanning is also a way to familiarize yourself with everything a book has to offer. Scan the table of contents, appendix, glossary, and index of a book before reading.
SKIMMING	After scanning a chapter, section, or article, you should quickly read, or skim, the introduction, the topic sentence of each paragraph, and the conclusion. Skimming is reading to identify quickly the purpose, thesis, main ideas, and supporting ideas of a selection.
CLOSE READING	Close reading is for locating specific information, following the logic of an argument, or comprehending the meaning or significance of information. After scanning the selection or chapter, read it more slowly, word for word.

Reading a Textbook

In studying a textbook, the techniques of scanning, skimming, and close reading are combined in the "SQ3R" study strategy. This method helps you to understand and remember what you read. *S* in *SQ3R* stands for *Survey*, *Q* for *Question*, and *3R* for *Read, Recite,* and *Review.*

The SQ3R Study Strategy

SURVEY	First get a general idea of what the selection is about by scanning titles, subtitles, and words that are set off in a different type or color. Also look at maps, tables, charts, and other illustrations. Then read the introduction and conclusion or summary.
QUESTION	Decide what questions you should be able to answer after reading the selection. You can do this by turning the headings and subheadings into questions or by looking at any study questions in the book.
READ	Now read the selection. As you read, try to answer your questions. In addition, find the main idea in each section and look for important information that is not included in your questions. After reading, review the important points in the selection and take notes. *(See pages 501–502.)*
RECITE	Answer each question in your own words by reciting or writing the answers.
REVIEW	Answer the questions again without looking at your notes or at the selection. Continue reviewing until you answer each question correctly.

Taking Notes

Taking notes when reading a textbook or listening to a lecture will help you identify and remember important points. Two methods of taking notes are the modified outline and the summary. In a *modified outline*, you use words and phrases to record main ideas and important details. Notes in this form are helpful in studying for an objective test because they emphasize specific facts.

In a *summary* you use sentences to express important ideas in your own words. A summary should not simply restate the ideas presented in the textbook or lecture. Instead, a good summary should express relationships between ideas and draw conclusions. For this reason summaries are useful in preparing for an essay test.

In the following passage from a history textbook, the essential information for understanding the Great Compromise is underlined. Following the passage are examples of notes in both modified outline and summary form.

Model: *Recognizing Important Information*

The Great Compromise, proposed by Roger Sherman of Connecticut at the Constitutional Convention of 1787, offered a way to ensure fair representation for all the states. The compromise provided that Congress have two houses, as the Virginia Plan had proposed. Voters in each state would choose representatives for two-year terms. The number of representatives from a state would be based on population, a provision that satisfied the larger states. Each state would also have two senators, regardless of the state's population. Like the New Jersey Plan, this provision gave all states an equal voice, at least in one branch of Congress. The provision satisfied the smaller states. Legislators in each state would choose senators for six-year terms.

The Great Compromise

MODIFIED OUTLINE

1. Satisfied large and small states by guaranteeing fair representation
2. Provided for two houses of Congress
3. Number of representatives in Congress based on state's population
4. Two senators in Congress regardless of state's population

SUMMARY

The Great Compromise

The Great Compromise satisfied both the large and the small states by guaranteeing fair representation. The compromise provided for two houses of Congress. The number of representatives in Congress from each state would vary according to each state's population, but the number of senators from each state would be the same regardless of population.

Whichever note-taking method you use, the following strategies will help you make those notes clear and well-organized.

Strategies for Taking Notes

1. Label your notes with the title and page numbers of the chapter or the topic and date of the lecture.
2. Record only the main ideas and important details.
3. Use the titles, subtitles, and words in special type to help you select the most important information.
4. Use your own words; do not copy word for word.
5. Use as few words as possible.

MODIFIED OUTLINE

- Use words and phrases.
- Use main ideas for headings.
- List any supporting details under each heading.

SUMMARY

- Write complete sentences, using your own words.
- Show the relationship between ideas, being careful to use only the facts stated in the textbook or lecture.
- Include only essential information.
- Organize ideas logically.

EXERCISE 1 *Taking Notes*

Read the selection "Dial versus Digital," by Isaac Asimov, on page 197. Then take notes on this selection, using either modified-outline or summary form. If time permits, form small groups and compare your results.

Preparing Subject-Area Assignments

The strategies you have learned in this chapter for reading textbooks and taking notes can be applied to assignments in any subject area. In addition, you will find that each subject area has specialized learning aids.

Mathematics, geometry, algebra, and science textbooks, for example, often list rules, formulas, equations, or models. In these subjects, therefore, focus on applying the rules or models to solve a problem or to show the truth of a scientific principle.

Social studies courses, on the other hand, emphasize reading and interpreting maps, charts, graphs, time lines, documents, and statistical data. In preparing for social studies assignments or tests, pay attention to information provided in those formats.

Strategies for Preparing Subject-Area Assignments

1. Carefully read and follow directions. *(See page 445.)*
2. Adjust your reading rate to suit your purpose.
3. In reading your textbook, use the SQ3R method. *(See page 500.)*
4. Take notes from readings and lectures. Organize your notebook by keeping reading notes and lecture notes on the same topic together in your notebook.
5. For review keep a separate list of vocabulary, key terms and concepts, or rules and equations.
6. Keep a list of questions you think of as you read, listen, or review. Seek answers promptly.
7. Participate in study groups, following the principles of cooperative learning. *(See pages 451–452.)*
8. Leave ample time to study for tests. Anticipate and answer the questions you think will be asked.

EXERCISE 2 *Preparing for a Subject-Area Test*

Select any subject area other than English. Prepare for the next quiz or test in that subject by applying the Tips for Preparing Subject Area Assignments. After the test explain in your journal how these tips did or did not help you to improve your grade.

Taking Standardized Tests

A standardized test measures your academic progress, skills, and achievement in such a way that results can be compared with those of other students who have taken the same test. Standardized tests that assess your ability to use language—or verbal—skills, include vocabulary tests, analogy tests, sentence-completion tests, and tests of standard written English.

The best way to do well on standardized tests is to work consistently on your school subjects throughout the year, to read as much as possible from a variety of sources, and to learn the strategies of test taking. In addition, when you take standardized tests, apply the following strategies.

Strategies for Taking Standardized Tests

1. Read the test directions carefully, always taking time to answer the sample questions to be sure you understand what the test requires.
2. Relax. Although you can expect to be a little nervous, concentrate on doing the best you can.
3. Preview the whole test quickly by skimming. This procedure will give you an overview of the kinds of questions on the test.
4. Plan your time carefully, allotting a certain amount of time to each part of the test.
5. Answer first the questions you find easiest. Skip questions you find too hard, coming back to them later if you have time.
6. Read and reread all choices before you choose an answer. If you are not sure of the answer, try to eliminate choices that are obviously wrong. Making an educated guess is usually a good idea in cases where you have narrowed the choices to two or three possible answers.
7. If you have time, check your answers. Watch out for omissions and careless errors. Be sure you have not made a mistake in marking your answer sheet.

Vocabulary Tests

One kind of vocabulary test asks you to find antonyms—words most nearly opposite in meaning. For instance, in the following test item, you must find the antonym for *temporary* among the five choices.

> TEMPORARY: (A) portable (B) permanent (C) reliable (D) patriotic (E) momentary

The answer is *B* because *permanent* is an antonym for *temporary*. The other choices are wrong for various reasons. The word *momentary* is a synonym for *temporary*, not an antonym. None of the other three word choices means the opposite of *temporary*.

Always consider carefully every choice. You can often figure out the meaning of a word by using a prefix, a root, or a suffix as a clue.

EXERCISE 3 *Recognizing Antonyms*

Write the letter of the word that is most nearly opposite in meaning to the word in capital letters.

EXAMPLE MASSIVE: (A) major (B) common (C) bulky (D) false (E) slight

ANSWER E

1. TRANQUIL: (A) old-fashioned (B) troubled (C) pleasant (D) steady (E) famous

2. DEVIOUS: (A) tricky (B) reckless (C) handsome (D) straightforward (E) skillful

3. ORNATE: (A) plain (B) amusing (C) fancy (D) strong (E) variable

4. RELINQUISH: (A) upset (B) surrender (C) disagree (D) keep (E) praise

5. NOVICE: (A) beginner (B) coward (C) veteran (D) bravery (E) praise

6. AGILE: (A) free (B) inactive (C) speedy (D) fearful (E) dishonest

7. HUMANE: (A) unwilling (B) moody (C) absurd (D) caring (E) unsympathetic

8. OVERT: (A) strong (B) brave (C) innocent (D) terrible (E) hidden

9. CONVENE: (A) dismiss (B) oppose (C) assemble (D) refuse (E) select

10. PRECARIOUS: (A) brilliant (B) postponed (C) safe (D) foreseen (E) dangerous

11. LUCID: (A) polite (B) vague (C) simple (D) clear (E) strange

12. URBANE: (A) rude (B) quick (C) stylish (D) polite (E) invisible

13. REBUKE: (A) hire (B) convince (C) join (D) praise (E) repay

14. VERBOSE: (A) outstanding (B) bitter (C) wordy (D) brief (E) calm

15. SERENE: (A) unlikely (B) excited (C) humble (D) clever (E) courageous

Analogies

Analogy questions test your skill at figuring out relationships between words. Your first step on an analogy question is to decide how the given words—the first, capitalized pair of words—are related to each other. The next step is to read several other pairs of words and decide which pair has the same kind of relationship as the given pair.

The single colon in an analogy question stands for the words *is to*, and the double colon stands for the word *as*.

FURNACE:FIRE :: reservoir:water

The above example reads, "A furnace *is to* fire *as* a reservoir *is to* water." That is, a furnace has the same relationship to fire as a reservoir has to water. A furnace and a reservoir are both containers for natural elements—fire and water. Explaining an analogy to yourself in one sentence can help you to figure out the answer. In the following item, for example, you might say to yourself, "One kind of flower is a tulip."

FLOWER:TULIP :: (A) deer:buffalo (B) fever:virus
(C) automobile:station wagon (D) plumber:wrench
(E) oak:tree

The answer, *(C) automobile:station wagon*, expresses the same relationship: One kind of car is a station wagon. The given word pair expresses a category-to-item relationship. That is, *flower* is a category in which *tulip* is an item or example. The word pair *automobile:station wagon* is the answer because it is the only choice that expresses the same category-to-item relationship.

The other choices are incorrect for a variety of reasons. *Deer:buffalo* expresses an item-to-item relationship—two examples of kinds of animals. *Fever:virus* shows an effect-to-cause relationship rather than category-to-item. *Plumber:wrench* refers to the relationship of a worker to a tool. In the pair *oak:tree*, the order of the relationship is item-to-category rather than category-to-item.

Keep in mind that the word order in an analogy is very important. If the given pair of words in the analogy expresses a part-to-whole order, for example, the words in the correct answer should also be in the order of part to whole.

Common Types of Analogies

ANALOGY	EXAMPLE
word:synonym	slim:slender
word:antonym	exciting:dull
part:whole	wing:airplane
cause:effect	drought:famine
worker:tool	carpenter:hammer
worker:product	baker:bread
item:purpose	ruler:measure
item:category	robin:bird

EXERCISE 4 *Recognizing Analogies*

Write the letter of the word pair that has the same relationship as the word pair in capital letters.

1. TARNISH:SILVER :: (A) tape:music (B) ending:story (C) salesperson:bonus (D) decay:organism (E) peace:treaty

2. PUBLISHER:NEWSPAPER :: (A) ink:paper (B) book:writer (C) farmer:crops (D) hockey:puck (E) needle:thread

3. CRIME:PUNISHMENT :: (A) chinchilla:fur (B) rat:rodent (C) client:attorney (D) game:tennis (E) tornado:destruction

4. COBRA:SNAKE :: (A) tree:leaves (B) run:baseball (C) collie:dog (D) water:dissolve (E) greasy:oily

5. JUBILANT:MOROSE :: (A) car:tire (B) passive:active (C) pencil:lead (D) meddle:interfere (E) pilot:plane

6. TAXI:TRANSPORT :: (A) president:democracy (B) scene:play (C) fence:enclose (D) evade:avoid (E) architecture:profession

7. ENGINE:AUTOMOBILE :: (A) teacher:student (B) dog:cat (C) sail:boat (D) lamp:light (E) telephone:message

8. OUTDATED:STAGECOACH :: (A) portion:segment (B) popular:uncoventional (C) picture:frame (D) computer:printer (E) extinct:dinosaur

9. LEASH:DOG :: (A) rein:horse (B) bicycle:tire (C) gold:money (D) key:chain (E) hand:finger

10. MODERATE:REASONABLE :: (A) jeweler:gem (B) flag:nation (C) conquer:vanquish (D) spoon:chef (E) silver:ore

"We're gettin' old, Jake."

EXERCISE 5 *Recognizing Analogies*

Write the letter of the word pair that has the same relationship as the word pair in capital letters.

1. BANDAGE:PROTECT :: (A) paint:paintbrush (B) knife:cut (C) page:read (D) breathe:gill (E) magazine:sell

2. CONDEMN:APPROVE :: (A) rain:flood (B) accuse:blame (C) amuse:applaud (D) pity:sympathize (E) accept:reject

3. FLOUR:BREAD :: (A) debt:payment (B) shoe:sole (C) cloth:flag (D) farmer:land (E) bank:money

4. ELECTRICIAN:PLIERS :: (A) surgeon:scalpel (B) nurse:patient (C) mayor:election (D) friend:enemy (E) ink:printer

5. FAN:BREEZE :: (A) star:galaxy (B) moon:satellite (C) clover:leaf (D) radio:sound (E) warmth:fire

6. BEETLE:INSECT :: (A) butterfly:moth (B) rodent:squirrel (C) snow:precipitation (D) fish:fowl (E) cup:saucer

7. RESULT:OUTCOME :: (A) chess:strategy (B) real:genuine (C) sword:shield (D) team:victory (E) wood:desk

8. TREE:PINE :: (A) clothes:trousers (B) river:sea (C) finger:hand (D) condor:bird (E) brick:stone

9. METAL:COPPER :: (A) zinc:tin (B) court:lawyer (C) luck:chance (D) shellfish:oyster (E) king:queen

10. HORSE:EQUINE :: (A) cloud:cumulus (B) marine:fish (C) cow:bovine (D) ship:submarine (E) soil:erosion

Sentence-Completion Tests

Sentence-completion tests measure your ability to comprehend what you read and to use context correctly. Each item consists of a sentence with one or more words missing. First read the entire sentence. Then read the answer choices and select the one that completes the sentence in a way that makes sense. For example, in the following item, read the sentence and then find the word that most appropriately completes the sentence.

> Our tour of the 200-foot Pyramid of the Sun in Mexico, which included climbing and ___ the steep stairs, took more than an hour.
>
> (A) completing (B) scaling (C) descending
> (D) constructing (E) ascending

The answer is *(C) descending,* the opposite of *climbing.* Because the sentence refers to *climbing* steep stairs, a choice of either *scaling* or *ascending* to complete the sentence is repetitive. *Scaling* and *ascending* both mean the same as *climbing.* A choice of either *completing* or *constructing* is incorrect because neither word makes sense in the context of the sentence.

EXERCISE 6 *Sentence-Completion Tests*

Write the letter of the word that best completes each of the following sentences.

1. Grackles are blackbirds with plumage so glossy it ___.
(A) glides (B) sheds (C) disappears (D) shimmers
(E) wrinkles

2. While to an observer the pitch of a train whistle seems to change as the train passes, to a passenger on the train the pitch remains ___.
(A) louder (B) constant (C) harsh (D) variable (E) faint

3. With the development of the tiny silicon chip, the ___ of electronic equipment proceeded rapidly.
(A) disappearance (B) banning (C) destruction
(D) shelving (E) miniaturization

4. James Thurber's humorous writings are among the most ___ and popular literary works of this century.
(A) awkward (B) delightful (C) incomprehensible
(D) serious (E) threatening

5. Far north of Fairbanks, Alaska, on the icy shores of the Arctic Ocean, lies the ___ village of Prudhoe Bay.
(A) barren (B) tropical (C) inland (D) popular (E) foreign

6. To picture the ___ size of the sequoia tree, consider that a single branch can be longer than the tallest American elm.
(A) unknown (B) immense (C) imagined (D) historical (E) limited

7. In the early 1900's, a Texas League baseball player set a ___ record; he hit eight home runs in eight times at bat.
(A) remarkable (B) humdrum (C) daily (D) broken (E) common

8. Ida Tarbell led the muckraking movement, which attacked dishonesty and other ___ in business and politics.
(A) debt (B) corruption (C) freedom (D) fairness (E) progress

9. The invention of barbed wire, a ___ in the history of the American West, transformed the cattle industry, ending the era of the open range and bringing about great change.
(A) plan (B) surprise (C) mistake (D) landmark (E) misfortune

10. Today the ___ city of Williamsburg, Virginia, looks much as it did in the eighteenth century.
(A) active (B) local (C) restored (D) major (E) crowded

Tests of Standard Written English

A test of standard written English is a standardized test that measures writing ability. Your task is to decide if any one of the underlined parts in a sentence includes an error in punctuation, capitalization, grammar, usage, or word choice. For example, identify the error in the following sentence.

The <u>bay</u> (A) of Fundy, between Nova Scotia and New Brunswick<u>,</u> (B) <u>has</u> (C) the highest tides in the <u>world</u> (D). <u>No error</u> (E)

The answer is *A*. The word *bay* should be capitalized because it is part of the name of a specific body of water, the Bay of Fundy. The following list identifies some of the errors you should look for on a test of standard written English.

- lack of agreement between subject and verb
- lack of agreement between pronoun and antecedent
- incorrect spelling or use of a word
- missing, misplaced, or unnecessary punctuation
- missing or unnecessary capitalization
- misused or misplaced italics or quotation marks

Some sentences contain no errors. Before you choose answer *E (No error)*, however, be sure that you carefully examine every part of the sentence. Sentence errors are easy to overlook. As you search for answers, keep in mind that the parts of the sentence that are not underlined are correct.

EXERCISE 7 *Recognizing Errors in Writing*

Number your paper 1 to 10. Write the letter of the underlined word or punctuation mark that is incorrect. If the sentence contains no error, write *E*.

1. A large amount (A) of modern transportation routes follow (B) old Indian (C) trails. (D) No error (E)
2. The New York State (A) Thruway, (B) for example, (C) parrallels (D) the path once used by the Iroquois. No error (E)
3. Like the Iroquois who (A) preceded (B) them, early explorers traveling west (C) often made a journey by canoe up the Mohawk river (D). No error (E)
4. When the river became (A) unnavigable, (B) these (C) explorers decided that the Indian foot trails were preferrable (D). No error (E)
5. The Erie Canal (A) opened in 1825; (B) following the route that the Iroquois had (C) been using for centuries (D). No error (E)
6. Eventually (A) railroads were built close (B) to the canal, (C) and began to (D) take business away from it. No error (E)

7. Roads for horses, wagons, (A) and stagecoaches followed this route (B); (C) one road became route (D) 5. No error (E)

8. Those who (A) planned the state thruway found that their (B) was no better path than (C) the old familiar (D) one. No error (E)

9. Parallel waterways, (A) roads, and railroad tracks now follows (B) the original (C) Iroquois route. (D) No error (E)

10. Only the airways, heedless of the lay of the land, have (A) broke (B) the pattern set (C) so long ago. (D) No error (E)

EXERCISE 8 *Recognizing Errors in Writing*

Write the letter of the underlined word or punctuation mark that is incorrect. If the sentence contains no error, write *E.*

1. The task of exploring the depths (A) of the Ocean (B) has (C) seen great (D) advances over the past 50 years. No error (E)

2. The first bathysphere, (A) built in 1934, (B) carried two (C) men more than (D) half a mile under the sea. No error (E)

3. This (A) two-ton (B) steel ball was attached to a heavy cable and then was lowered (C) in (D) the ocean. No error (E)

4. Next came (A) the bathyscaphe, (B) a research vessel that (C) had a cabin on it's (D) underside. No error (E)

5. On January 23, 1960, [A] two [B] researchers take [C] the bathyscaphe *Trieste* down 35,800 feet [D]. No error [E]

6. The craft descended [A] further [B] than [C] any other craft ever had, to the deepest place in the Pacific Ocean [D]. No error [E]

7. When the bathyscaphe touched bottom seven miles beneath the surface, [A] the researchers saw [B] a fish swimming [C] passed [D] them. No error [E]

8. While 200,000 tons [A] of water pressed on the cabin, [B] the researchers observed marine [C] life. [D] No error [E]

9. Modern "submarines," the newer [A] of the three types of undersea research vessels, are [B] more maneuverable [C] than [D] bathyspheres or bathyscaphes. No error [E]

10. These [A] latest ships for deep-sea exploration occasionally [B] doubles [C] as [D] submarine rescue vehicles. No error [E]

Taking Essay Tests

Another type of test that measures writing ability is the essay test. The questions on an essay test are designed to assess your understanding of important ideas and your ability to see connections, or relationships, between those ideas. To do well, you must be able to organize your thoughts quickly and to express them logically and clearly in writing.

Understanding Essay Questions

In taking an essay test, begin by carefully reading all the instructions, or directions. This important first step enables you to plan your time and to determine precisely what each question asks of you. In planning the amount of time you will need to spend on each question, allot more time to the questions that are worth the most points. In interpreting each question, look for key direction words, which tell you exactly what kind of answer you are expected to write.

Key Direction Words in Essay Questions	
Analyze	Separate into parts and examine each part.
Compare	Point out similarities.
Contrast	Point out differences.
Define	Clarify meaning.
Discuss	Examine in detail.
Evaluate	Give your opinion.
Explain	Tell how, what, or why.
Illustrate	Give examples.
Summarize	Briefly review main points.
Trace	Show development or progress.

Sometimes you may find it helpful to make notes on the kind of answer that a question requires or to underline key direction words in the instructions. In the following example, instructions are circled and key requirements for the answer are underlined.

Model: *Interpreting an Essay Question*

(Explain) the theory of geographic determinism, the process by which the climate and the geography of the earth determines the distribution of the world's population centers. (Write three paragraphs,) giving specific (examples) or illustrations.

EXERCISE 9 *Interpreting Essay Test Items*

Write the key direction word in each item. Then write one sentence explaining what the question asks you to do.

EXAMPLE Trace the life cycle of a frog.

POSSIBLE ANSWER Trace—Show the development, in order, of the stages in the life of a frog.

1. In your own words, define *plate tectonics*.
2. How does the appearance of a timber rattlesnake compare with that of a diamondback rattlesnake?

3. Briefly summarize one of the acts in Shakespeare's play *Julius Caesar*.
4. Trace the history of the United States flag.
5. James Thurber wrote, "Humor is emotional chaos remembered in tranquility." Discuss his meaning.
6. Explain how a tornado forms and moves.
7. Briefly analyze the scientific contributions of Marie Curie.
8. Evaluate one of Edgar Allan Poe's short stories.
9. Briefly contrast a desert and a tundra.
10. From your study of literature, explain and illustrate either the simile, the metaphor, or personification.

Writing an Effective Essay Answer

The steps in writing a well-constructed essay are the same for an essay test as they are for a written assignment. The only difference is that in a test situation you have a strict time limit for writing. As a result you need to plan how much time you will spend writing each answer and how much time you will devote to each step in the writing process. As a rule of thumb, for every five minutes of writing, allow two minutes for planning and organizing and one minute for revising and editing.

Prewriting Begin planning your answer by brainstorming for main ideas and supporting details. Then organize your main ideas into a simple modified outline. Your outline will help you to present your ideas in a logical order, to cover all your main points, and to avoid omitting important details.

Shoe by Jeff MacNelly. Reprinted by permission. Tribune Media Services, © 1990.

Model: *Modified Outline of an Essay Test Answer*

Geographic Determinism

1. explanation of theory
2. climate as a determining factor
3. geography as a determining factor

Your next step is to write a thesis statement that states your main idea and covers all of your supporting ideas. *(See page 178.)* Often you can write a suitable thesis statement by rewording the test question. For example, to write a thesis statement for an essay explaining the theory of geographic determinism, you might rephrase the question in the following way.

Model: *Rewording an Essay Test Item*

ESSAY QUESTION	Explain the theory of geographic determinism, the process by which climate and the geography of the earth determined the distribution of the world's population centers.
THESIS STATEMENT	The theory of geographic determinism states that population distribution was determined by climate and by geography.

Drafting As you write your essay answer, keep the following strategies in mind.

Strategies for Writing an Essay Answer

1. Write an introduction that includes the thesis statement. *(See pages 178 and 219.)*
2. Follow the order of your outline. Write one paragraph for each main point, beginning with a topic sentence.
3. Be specific. Support each main idea by using supporting details such as facts and examples. *(See pages 181–182.)*
4. Use transitions to connect your ideas and examples. *(See page 113.)*
5. End with a strong concluding statement that summarizes your thesis. *(See page 187.)*
6. Write clearly and legibly because you will not have time to copy your work.

Model: *Essay Test Answer*

The theory of geographic determinism states that population distribution was determined by climate and by geography. One proof of this theory is the fact that the world's present population centers are not evenly distributed. Almost half of the world's populations live on less than 10 percent of the total land area. The two main causes of high population density in some areas and low population density in others are climate and geography.

Climate affects where people live. For example, few people live in far northern North America, because it is cold there for several months of the year. As a result, the growing season is too short to supply adequate food for a large population. Similarly, in parts of the Middle East and northern Africa, the climate is too hot and dry to produce enough food to feed large populations.

Geography also has a significant effect on where people live. For example, mountainous areas in North and South America have sparse populations. Because most farming is difficult in mountainous terrain, people who live in such areas support themselves mainly by animal husbandry. In contrast, broad, fertile river valleys and less mountainous land with abundant natural resources have always attracted large populations. Europe, for example, with its water supply, rich soil, and mineral wealth, is one of the most densely populated areas of the world. In conclusion, evidence shows that climate and geography have affected the distribution of the world's population centers. This evidence supports the theory of geographic determinism.

Revising Leave time to revise and edit your essay answer. To keep your paper as neat as possible, use proofreading symbols to mark any corrections or revisions. As you revise, think of the following questions.

- Did you follow the instructions completely?
- Did you interpret the question accurately?
- Did you begin with a thesis statement?
- Did you include facts, examples, or other supporting details?
- Did you sequence your ideas and examples logically in paragraphs according to your modified outline?
- Did you use transitions to connect ideas and examples?
- Did you end with a strong concluding statement that summarizes your thesis?

Editing After you have made any necessary revisions, quickly read your essay to check for mistakes in spelling, usage, or punctuation. As you edit, check your work for accuracy in the following areas:

- agreement between subjects and verbs *(See pages 704–723.)*
- forms of adjectives and adverbs when using comparative and superlative *(See pages 725–728.)*
- capitalization of proper nouns and proper adjectives *(See pages 756–757.)*
- use of commas *(See pages 774–787.)*
- use of apostrophes *(See pages 809–814.)*
- division of words at the end of a line *(See pages 822–823.)*

EXERCISE 10 *Answering an Essay Test Question*

Select any subject area such as English, science, or social studies. With your teacher's permission, form a small group with other students who are interested in the same subject. Brainstorm together a list of essay test questions related to a topic you are currently studying in the course. Then on your own, choose one of the questions and write an answer for it. Begin by brainstorming and then write a modified outline and a thesis statement. As you draft your essay, follow the Strategies for Writing an Essay Answer on page 516. Be sure to revise and edit your essay answer.

Midway through the exam, Allen pulls out a bigger brain.

Timed Writing

Throughout your school years, you will be tested on your ability to organize your thoughts quickly and to express them in a limited time. Your teacher may ask you to write a 20-minute, 200-word essay that will then be judged on how thoroughly you covered the topic and organized your essay. The more you practice writing under time constraints, the better you will be able to apply these effective writing strategies during timed tests.

Strategies for Timed Tests

1. Listen carefully to instructions. Find out if you may write notes or an outline on your paper or in the examination book.
2. Find out if you should erase mistakes or cross them out by neatly drawing a line through them.
3. Plan your time, keeping in mind your time limit.

Integrating Language Skills

Practicing a Timed Writing Test When you take a timed writing test, you will find that following the steps in the writing process is the best way to complete the assignment thoroughly and in an organized way. For example, suppose you were given 20 minutes to write on the following topic:

Discuss the character of one person, living or dead, whom you especially admire. Include specific facts and examples.

To complete this assignment, organize your time in the following way.

6 minutes: Brainstorm for ideas.
2 minutes: Arrange ideas in a logical order.
12 minutes: Write a draft.
5 minutes: Revise your work and edit it for any mistakes.

Using the topic given above or another topic your class chooses, follow these guidelines as you practice taking a timed writing test. Your teacher will tell you when to begin.

Chapter 17

Review

A **Antonyms** Write the letter of the word that is most nearly opposite in meaning to the word in capital letters.

1. MISER: (A) student (B) lawyer (C) spendthrift (D) clown (E) pauper
2. ZEALOUS: (A) unenthusiastic (B) envious (C) unhappy (D) good (E) radiant
3. FRAGILE: (A) original (B) delicate (C) illegal (D) frantic (E) sturdy
4. MONOTONY: (A) roughness (B) stability (C) variety (D) unity (E) motion
5. TRIUMPH: (A) victory (B) obedience (C) impurity (D) distrust (E) failure

B **Analogies** Write the letter of the word pair that has the same relationship as the word pair in capital letters.

1. JANUARY:MONTH : : (A) sheep:lamb (B) tree:leaf (C) tire:automobile (D) Tuesday:day (E) victory:defeat
2. NEWSPAPER:PRINTER : : (A) photographer:negative (B) drama:audience (C) sunset:evening (D) cup:saucer (E) shoes:cobbler
3. SPICE:SEASONING : : (A) snow:avalanche (B) bee:hive (C) flour:grain (D) margarine:butter (E) omelette:egg
4. HOSTILE:FRIENDLY : : (A) intentional:accidental (B) lost:discouraged (C) original:fresh (D) worried:uneasy (E) cool:chilly
5. COMPUTER:ELECTRONICS : : (A) yarn:wool (B) game:toy (C) telescope:optics (D) scientist:microscope (E) robot:invention
6. STADIUM:GAME : : (A) checkers:checkerboard (B) croquet:wicket (C) racetrack:jockey (D) theater:play (E) picture:frame

7. IMAGINARY:UNICORN : : (A) experiment:scientific
(B) rainbow:colorful (C) extinct:dinosaur (D) owl:wise
(E) comedian:funny

8. STAR:GALAXY : : (A) dictionary:encyclopedia
(B) bicycle:motorcycle (C) beach:pebble (D) ant:colony
(E) fire:heat

9. TALKATIVE:GARRULOUS : : (A) athletic:competitive
(B) sensible:foolish (C) sly:courageous (D) often:seldom
(E) miserable:unhappy

10. MACHINIST:LATHE : : (A) weaver:loom (B) mason:brick
(C) photographer:picture (D) farmer:crops (E) pilot:runway

C Tests of Standard Written English

Write the letter that is below the underlined word, phrase, or punctuation mark that is incorrect. If the sentence contains no error, write E.

1. On January 24, 1848, a workmen at Sutter's Mill in California
A B C
discovered gold. No error
D E

2. Within months the news had spread everywheres, and a stampede
A B C
began. No error
D E

3. San Francisco, a tiny village, quickly developed into a sizable city,
A B C
where eggs suddenly cost as much as ten dollars a dozen.
D
No error
E

4. Over the course of the next few years, probably more fortunes
A
were made in farming and business than was made in mining.
B C D
No error
E

5. The gold rush was certainly responsible for hastening California's
A B
admission to the Union, which occured in the year 1850. No error
C D E

Unit 4
Language Skills Resource

Grammar

Usage

Mechanics

Chapter

18 The Sentence

Diagnostic Test

Number your paper 1 to 10. Then write the subjects and the verbs in the following sentences.

EXAMPLE Mia and Peter have finished their term papers.
ANSWER Mia, Peter—have finished.

1. You should treat mild burns with ice water.
2. A red light on the rocket's control panel was blinking rapidly.
3. In the ninth inning, the hitter smashed the ball over the wall and scored a home run.
4. Why didn't you go to the awards ceremony?
5. At 5:00 A.M. Mark and I headed for the trout stream.
6. There are 30 students in my homeroom.
7. The diamond appeared real to me.
8. On the surface of the pool floated a big red ball.
9. Until last night I had never driven Gram's new car.
10. Mel and his brother operate a tackle shop and rent boats during the summer.

Recognizing Sentences

Recognizing complete thoughts as sentences is the first step in communicating your ideas clearly.

Rule 18a **A sentence is a group of words that expresses a complete thought.**

The groups of words below do not express complete thoughts. They are called *sentence fragments*.

The horse in the barn. Typing my term paper.
Cooked dinner last night. After the game was over.

Fragments become sentences when each idea is expressed completely.

The horse in the barn **belongs to Jeff.**
Jamie cooked dinner last night.
Typing my term paper **took two hours.**
After the game was over, **everyone came to my house.**

Note: For more information about sentence fragments, see pages 647–650.

EXERCISE 1 *Recognizing Sentences*

Number your paper 1 to 10. Write *S* if a group of words is a sentence or *F* if it is a fragment.

1. Slamming the ball with all her strength. F
2. Since school has begun. F
3. The radio blared. S
4. Mr. Henry, my geometry teacher. F
5. The phone just rang. S
6. After a night without sleep. F
7. A balanced diet is important. S
8. Just as the train thundered by. F
9. The lightning during the storm. F
10. After we ate dinner. F

EXERCISE 2 *Completing Sentences*

Add the information needed to make each fragment in Exercise 1 a sentence. Include capital letters and correct punctuation.

Subjects and Predicates

To express a complete thought, a sentence must have a subject and a predicate.

Rule 18b A sentence has two main parts: a **subject** and a **predicate.** A subject names the person, place, thing, or idea the sentence is about. A predicate tells something about the subject.

	SUBJECT	PREDICATE
PERSON	My sister Roberta	works at Kenny's Market.
PLACE	The downtown bank	will be open on Saturdays.
THING	The blue notebook	belongs to Carlos.
IDEA	His attitude	was positive.

Complete and Simple Subjects

Every sentence has a subject. The *complete subject* is the group of words that names the person, place, thing, or idea the sentence is about. To find a subject, ask yourself *Whom?* or *What?* the sentence is about.

Many forest animals have sharp eyesight. [*Many forest animals* tell what this sentence is about.]

Mrs. Mason of the history department has become the new principal. [*Mrs. Mason of the history department* tells whom this sentence is about.]

In both of the preceding examples, one word—more than the others—answers the question *Whom?* or *What?* This main word in the complete subject is called the *simple subject.* When finding a simple subject, keep in mind that a subject is never part of a prepositional phrase. *(See pages 599–602 for more information about prepositional phrases.)*

Rule 18c A **simple subject** is the main word in the complete subject.

In the following examples, the simple subjects are in heavy type.

complete subject: Many forest animals

Many forest **animals** have sharp eyesight. [*Animals* is the main word that tells what the sentence is about.]

complete subject
Mrs. Mason of the history department has become the new principal. [*Mrs. Mason* tells whom the sentence is talking about.]

Even though *Mrs. Mason* is two words, it is considered the simple subject because it is the name of one person.

Sometimes the complete subject and the simple subject are the same.

She answered the math question correctly.
Brad Willis went sailing yesterday.

Note: Throughout the rest of this book, the simple subject will be called the *subject.*

EXERCISE 3 *Finding Complete and Simple Subjects*

Number your paper 1 to 15. Write the complete subject in each sentence. Then underline each simple subject.

Creatures' Features

1. A grown circus lion consumes about 30 pounds of horse meat each day.
2. A male kangaroo is called a boomer.
3. Four hours are needed to boil most ostrich eggs.
4. The skin of the hippopotamus is about two inches thick.
5. The age of a mountain sheep is shown by the number of rings on its horns.
6. Salmon swim downstream tailfirst.
7. A long-distance race between a camel and a horse would be won by the camel.
8. A large female cod can lay more than nine million eggs in a lifetime.
9. Hogs eat all kinds of snakes.
10. Each quill of a porcupine has about 1,000 tiny, sharp barbs.
11. A dog's normal temperature runs between 101 and 102 degrees.
12. The fastest fish is a swordfish, swimming at about 68 miles per hour.
13. A whale's heart beats only nine times per minute.
14. A milk cow in good health will give nearly 6,000 quarts of milk every year.
15. Male moose have antlers 7 feet across, often weighing up to 60 pounds.

Complete and Simple Predicates

In addition to a subject, every sentence needs a predicate. The *complete predicate* is a group of words that tells something about the subject. To find a predicate, first find the subject. Then ask, *What is the subject doing?* or *What is being said about the subject?*

Donna **drove to Houston last week.** [The subject is *Donna. Drove to Houston last week* tells what Donna did.]

The pears on the tree **are nearly ripe.** [The subject is *pears. Are nearly ripe* tells something about the pears.]

Complete predicates usually have one main word or phrase that tells what the subject is doing or that tells something about the subject. This main word or phrase is called the *simple predicate* or *verb.*

Rule 18d A **simple predicate,** or **verb,** is the main word or phrase in the complete predicate.

In the following examples, the verbs are in heavy type.

complete predicate
Donna **drove** to Houston last week.

complete predicate
The pears on the tree **are** nearly ripe.

Verbs that tell what a subject is doing are usually easy to find because they show action. Verbs that tell something about the subject are harder to find. Following is a list of common verb forms that are used to make statements about subjects.

Verbs That Make Statements							
am	is	are	was	were	be	being	been

EXERCISE 4 *Finding Complete Predicates and Verbs*

Number your paper 1 to 15. Write the complete predicate in each sentence. Then underline each verb.

1. Linda wrote the editorial in the school newspaper.
2. The report of the tornado blared from the radio.

3. Glaciers occupy about 10 percent of the world's land surface.
4. A nova is a suddenly brilliant star.
5. The Andean capital city of Ecuador sits almost directly on top of the equator.
6. The textile mill near the river employs many residents from our town.
7. Bryan earned the best score on the biology test.
8. The lead in last year's school play was my sister.
9. Twenty bales of hay dotted an open field near a farm.
10. Mavis was once the president of our class.
11. Most varieties of spiders have eight eyes.
12. Two out of three members of the softball team play football in the fall.
13. High humidity on a warm day causes great discomfort to many people.
14. The average adult American's vocabulary contains close to 10,000 words.
15. A car operates at maximum economy at speeds between 25 and 35 miles per hour.

Verb Phrases

More often than not the main verb of a sentence is composed of more than one word. Auxiliary verbs, or *helping verbs,* are added to the main verb to form a *verb phrase.* In the following examples, the helping verbs are in heavy type.

verb phrase

We **will be** spending next summer in Alaska.

verb phrase

The winners' names **must have been** announced already.

Following is a list of common helping verbs.

Common Helping Verbs	
be	am, is, are, was, were, be, being, been
have	has, have, had
do	do, does, did
others	may, might, must, can, could, shall, should, will, would

Sometimes a verb phrase is interrupted by other words. *Not* and its contraction, *n't,* often come between the parts of a verb phrase.

Sheila **has** never **entered** a contest in her life.
Will Tom **meet** us at the rink?
I **did**n't **need** a new pair of gloves.

Note: Throughout the rest of this book, the term *verb* will refer to the whole verb phrase.

EXERCISE 5 *Finding Verb Phrases*

Number your paper 1 to 10. Then write the verb in each sentence. Remember that other words may interrupt a verb phrase.

1. We have played shuffleboard every night this week.
2. Can you do ten knee bends?
3. Kenneth should never have joined the club.
4. Someone must have taken your notebook by mistake.
5. Haven't you ever eaten Mexican food?
6. Fish can be caught in underground streams in the Sahara.
7. No train has ever run on the tracks of the Hampden Railroad near Belchertown, Massachusetts.
8. Where did you put the ketchup?
9. The first radio station with a regular schedule did not appear until 1920.
10. The trunk of an elephant can hold six quarts of water.

EXERCISE 6 *Cumulative Review*

Number your paper 1 to 15. Then write the subject and the verb in each sentence.

Sequoya

1. Sequoya was a Cherokee Indian.
2. He was born in the late eighteenth century in Tennessee.
3. His family was admired for its knowledge of Indian customs.
4. As a young man, Sequoya was a hunter and a fur trader.
5. Eventually a leg injury kept him from his jobs.
6. This man then studied the Cherokee language.
7. At the time the Cherokee language was only spoken.
8. It could not be written without an alphabet.

9. By 1809, Sequoya was working on an alphabet for his language.
10. At the beginning he drew simple pictures.
11. After years of work, this Indian scholar developed an alphabet similar to the English alphabet.
12. His alphabet consisted of 85 characters.
13. The characters were adapted from English, Greek, and Hebrew symbols.
14. In later life Sequoya taught his alphabet in the schools of Oklahoma.
15. Other tribes have since adopted his alphabet.

Compound Subjects and Verbs

A sentence may have more than one subject, called a *compound subject.*

Rule 18e **A compound subject is two or more subjects in one sentence that have the same verb and are joined by a conjunction.**

In the following examples, each subject is underlined once, and each verb is underlined twice.

Fran or Meg will plant the seeds today.
Many rivers, lakes, and streams are filled with pollutants.

A sentence may also have more than one verb, called a *compound verb.*

Rule 18f **A compound verb is two or more verbs in one sentence that have the same subject and are joined by a conjunction.**

Henry has washed the car but will wax it tomorrow.
The bird paused on the branch, looked around, and then flew away.

A sentence may include both a compound subject and a compound verb.

My brother and I stacked the old magazines and placed them in boxes for storage.

Note: *And* and *or* can connect compound subjects. *And, or,* and *but* can connect compound verbs. *Either/or, neither/nor, not only/but also, both/and,* and *whether/or* may also be used with either compound subjects or compound verbs.

EXERCISE 7 *Finding Compound Subjects and Verbs*

Number your paper 1 to 15. Then write the subjects and the verbs in the following sentences.

EXAMPLE Dave and Meg sang a duet during the concert.
ANSWER Dave, Meg—sang

1. Both Amy and Chris have visited England.
2. Among my friends only Jennifer and Catherine can drive.
3. Either Tracy or Kevin will launder the sheets and fold them.
4. Good citizens study candidates and vote wisely in elections.
5. Both Missouri and Tennessee touch eight other states.
6. Water is leaking through the ceiling and will damage the new carpet.
7. Ducks and geese can fly at a speed of 70 miles per hour.
8. In the United States not only nickel and copper but also tin, zinc, and steel have been used in coins.
9. Terry and Marvin will take a trip to Vermont.
10. Your tests will be graded tonight and will be returned.
11. Kim exercises and jogs twice a day.
12. Bats and turtles sleep through the long winter months.
13. The squirrel and the chinchilla are both rodents.
14. Haven't you fed or walked the dog?
15. The starfish preys upon oysters and forces their shells open by means of suction cups.

Application to Writing

In sequence clearly explain the steps in making something you like to eat. At least one sentence in your explanation should have a compound subject, and one other sentence should have a compound verb. Be prepared to identify both sets of subjects and verbs.

Position of Subjects

Normally the subject comes before the verb in a sentence. To create sentence variety, you can sometimes change the subject-verb order. When this change occurs, the sentence is said to be in *inverted order.* In inverted sentences the subject is harder to find or may even seem to be missing.

To find a subject in an inverted sentence, first find the verb. Then ask, *Who or what is doing the action?* or *About whom or what is a statement being made?*

> Down the field raced the quarterback. [*Raced* is the verb. Who raced? *Quarterback* is the subject—even though it follows the verb.]

Finding the subject and the verb in an inverted sentence is easy if you turn the sentence around to its natural order. Each subject is underlined once and each verb is underlined twice in the following examples.

INVERTED ORDER	At the back of this book is an appendix.
NATURAL ORDER	An appendix is at the back of this book.

Questions Inverted order usually appears in questions. The subject often comes between parts of a verb phrase. To find the subject in a question, turn the question around so that it makes a statement.

QUESTION	Has Lani auditioned for the play?
STATEMENT	Lani has auditioned for the play.

Sentences Beginning with *There* or *Here* When a sentence begins with *there* or *here,* the subject will come after the verb. To find the subject, drop the word *there* or *here*. Then put the rest of the words in the sentence in natural order.

INVERTED ORDER	There are two apples in the refrigerator.
NATURAL ORDER	Two apples are in the refrigerator.

Understood Subjects Most often the subject *you* is not stated in a command or a request. It is, however, understood to be there.

> Lend me your bicycle. [If you ask who should lend, the answer is an understood *you*—the person requested or commanded to do something.]

Notice that *you* is the understood subject of each of the following sentences.

> **(you)** Answer the phone.
> **(you)** Clear the table after dinner.
> Dana, **(you)** please return my books to the library.

Note: Although the person receiving the request in the last example is called directly by name, *you* is still the understood subject.

EXERCISE 8 *Finding Subjects in Inverted Order*

Number your paper 1 to 15. Then write the subject and the verbs in the following sentences. If the subject is an understood *you,* write it in parentheses.

1. Find your seats quickly.
2. In 1816, there was frost or snow in the northeastern United States during every month of the year.
3. Have you heard the weather forecast for tomorrow?
4. Down the empty school corridor ran the tardy student.
5. Here come Paula and her younger sister.
6. Why didn't you or Walter sign the petition?
7. Rick, please bring in the groceries from the car.
8. There are 350 calories in a piece of apple pie.
9. Where did you find your sneakers?
10. Along the coast of Maine are found many beautiful rocky coves.
11. There are ten trillion living cells in the human body.
12. Answer the doorbell!
13. Will you work on your history project tonight?
14. Here is the most recent *Newsweek.*
15. Into the lake splashed the hot, tired hikers.

EXERCISE 9 *Cumulative Review*

Number your paper 1 to 10. Then write the subjects and the verbs in the following sentences. If the subject is an understood *you,* write it in parentheses.

Saving a Life

1. You and a friend are dining in a restaurant.
2. A man at the next table chokes on a piece of food.
3. Without help that person could die in four minutes.
4. What should you do?
5. Get behind the man and place your arms around him above his waist.
6. The man's head and torso will automatically lean forward.
7. Tightly grasp your own wrist and press your fist into his abdomen forcefully.
8. You shouldn't worry about damage to his ribs.
9. These actions should be repeated several times and should finally force the piece of food out.
10. This maneuver was successfully developed by Dr. H. J. Heimlich.

Integrating Language Skills

USING YOUR TEXT

Expository Paragraphs (82–125)

Grammar: Combining Sentences

Many sentences that contain different subjects but have the same verb are repetitive and dull to read. The same is true of sentences containing different verbs but the same subject. Combining sentences by using compound subjects or compound verbs can help you avoid unnecessary repetition in your writing.

TWO SENTENCES	Stairs cause accidents in the home. Doors also cause accidents.
COMPOUND SUBJECT	Stairs and doors cause accidents in the home.
TWO SENTENCES	Television provides entertainment. It also supplies up-to-the-minute news.
COMPOUND VERB	Television provides entertainment and also supplies up-to-the-minute news.

Checking Your Understanding Combine each pair of sentences into one sentence with a compound subject or a compound verb. Use *and* or *but* to connect the compound parts.

1. Police officers answered the call. Fire fighters also answered the call.
2. The car's engine sputtered. Then it died.
3. Fresh vegetables are good for you. Lean meats are also good for you.
4. The dish fell to the floor. It broke into a dozen pieces.
5. I looked for Mark in the library. I couldn't find him.

Writing an Explanation The moral, or lesson, of one of Aesop's fables is "It is possible to have too much of a good thing." What does this mean to you? Write freely for several minutes, jotting down all of your ideas. Next write the first draft of a paragraph explaining what you think Aesop's moral means. ***Application:*** As you revise, combine sentences by creating a compound subject or verb whenever possible. Then edit the paragraph for any errors and write a final copy.

Diagraming Subjects and Verbs

A *sentence diagram* may be used to show at a glance how a sentence is put together. Diagrams show the relationships among all the parts of a sentence.

Subjects and Verbs The subject and the verb are placed on a straight baseline and are separated by a short vertical line. Notice in the following diagrams that the capital letter is included, but not the punctuation. Notice also that the whole verb phrase is written on the baseline.

Traffic had stopped.

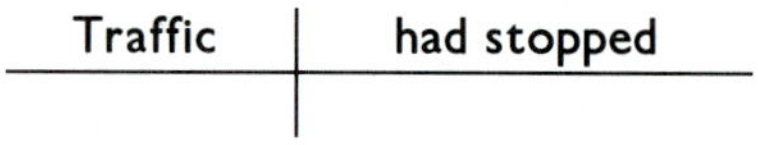

Inverted Order A sentence in inverted order is diagramed as if it were in natural order.

Did you sing?

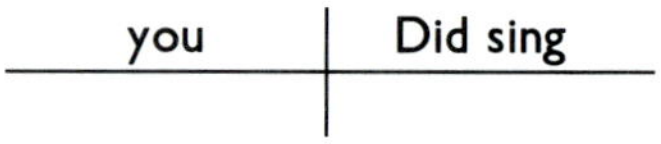

Understood Subjects An understood *you* as a subject is diagramed in the subject position—in parentheses.

Listen!

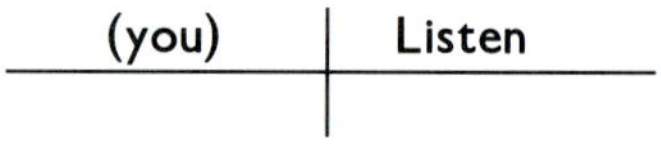

Compound Subjects and Verbs Compound subjects and verbs are placed on parallel lines. The conjunction or conjunctions connecting them are placed on a broken line between them.

Both hamburgers and ribs were sizzling.

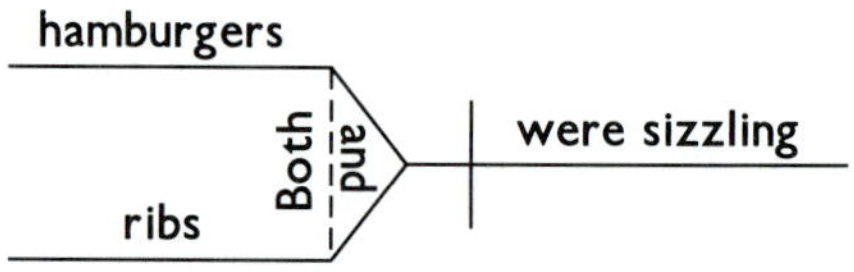

Joyce smiled and bowed.

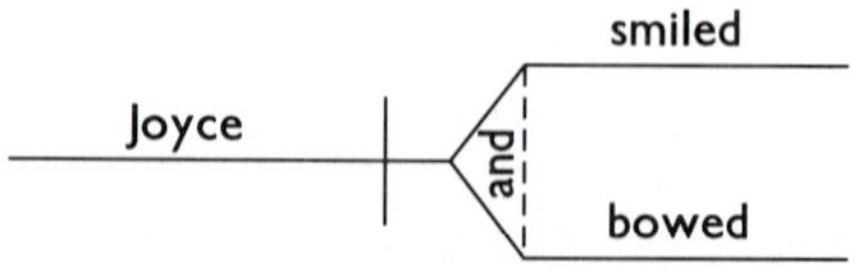

Turtles, parakeets, and rabbits are being sold.

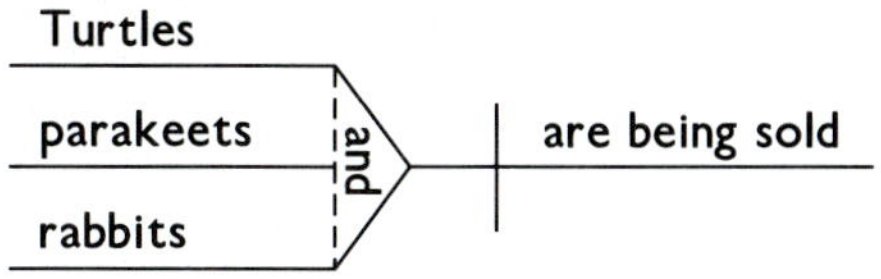

When different helping verbs are used in a compound verb, the helping verbs are placed on the parallel lines. When the same helping verb is used, it is placed on the baseline.

The radio and television are broken but will be fixed.

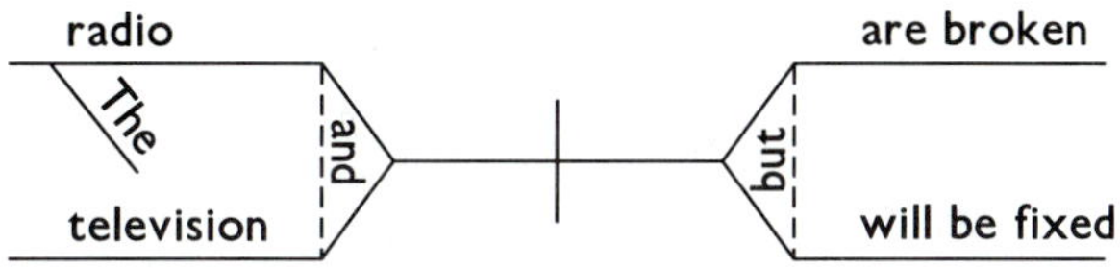

Hannah was sneezing and wheezing.

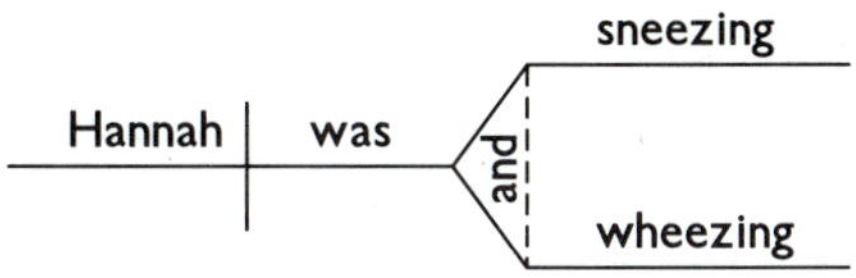

EXERCISE 10 *Diagraming Subjects and Verbs*

Diagram the following sentences or copy them. If you copy them, draw one line under each subject and two lines under each verb. If the subject is an understood *you,* write it in parentheses.

1. Pigeons were cooing.
2. Did you reply?
3. Hyenas were screaming and howling.
4. Wait!
5. Both dancers and singers should be rehearsing.
6. Rachel, Emma, and Eileen were talking.
7. Will you sing?
8. Roger and Tony dived and swam.
9. Can you stay?
10. Both meat and potatoes have been prepared.

Chapter 18

Review

A **Finding Subjects and Verbs** Number your paper 1 to 25. Then write the subjects and the verbs in the following sentences. If the subject is an understood *you,* write it in parentheses.

1. Around the sunken ship swam the divers.
2. There are 336 dimples on a golf ball.
3. Boxes and crates were filled with clothes and given to the shelter for the homeless.
4. Experienced electricians and carpenters are working in the new bank building.
5. Don't eat anything before dinner.
6. Isn't this scarf the color of your coat?
7. Amish men shave until their marriage and then grow a beard.
8. You must have heard the entire interview.
9. Why aren't you going to the dance on Saturday?
10. The queen in a beehive may live five years.
11. Navy cruisers are always named after cities.
12. The first seedless oranges in the United States came from Brazil and were then planted in California.
13. There are approximately 100 million dogs and cats in the United States.
14. Does the greyhound have better eyesight than any other breed of dog?
15. From the top of the hill, we could see the house.
16. Here are the tapes on sale.
17. All the planets in our solar system would fit inside the planet Jupiter.
18. Please make us a fruit salad for lunch.
19. For 186 days a year, the sun is not seen at the North Pole.
20. Until the time of the Caesars, all Romans were vegetarians.
21. Across the canyon galloped the wild horses.
22. Susan, don't step on the wet floor!
23. We should never have taken the shortcut!
24. All pencils and pens are on sale at the stationery store.
25. Spots on the sun appear and disappear in mysterious 22-year cycles.

B Finding Subjects and Verbs Number your paper 1 to 10. Then write the subjects and the verbs in the following sentences. If the subject is an understood *you,* write it in parentheses.

1. Turn the TV on to Channel 6.
2. Some people can sit in a chair and just push a button.
3. Children or adults can easily use a remote control.
4. Do you have a remote control for the TV or VCR in your home?
5. There are three different types of remote controls.
6. In the most popular type, commands are always relayed by invisible flashes of light.
7. Each command or button on the control box has a different number of flashes.
8. A computer inside the TV interprets the flashes and makes the necessary changes on the TV.
9. This type is called an infrared remote control.
10. Can you imagine other uses for a remote control?

Mastery Test

Number your paper 1 to 10. Then write the subjects and the verbs in the following sentences.

1. Kathleen has always answered my letters promptly.
2. Jean has been hired as a part-time secretary.
3. Today Patty bought her mother's birthday present and wrapped it.
4. Under the bed scurried the tiny kitten.
5. There are 206 bones in the human body.
6. Is the final episode of *Masterpiece Theatre* repeated tonight?
7. I didn't know the answer to the last question on the test.
8. London and Paris are two popular tourist attractions.
9. Why hasn't the rabbit been fed yet?
10. The actors and actresses learned their lines and rehearsed their scenes together.

Chapter

19 Nouns and Pronouns

Diagnostic Test

Number your paper 1 to 10. Make two columns on your paper. Label the first column *nouns* and the second column *pronouns*. Then, in the proper column, write each noun and pronoun.

EXAMPLE Will you go to the game with me after school?

ANSWER <u>nouns</u> <u>pronouns</u>

game, school you, me

1. A man in Scotland once walked 1,000 miles in 1,000 hours.
2. After you take Tippy for a walk, give her a bath.
3. I have great respect for him as a coach.
4. Mrs. Brown is a biology professor at the University of Virginia.
5. These are excellent directions you gave me to Hayes Park.
6. Everyone in the group should meet at City Hall.
7. Who put the groceries on the floor?
8. Someone left the door open, and Muffin sneaked out.
9. What should we do before the election?
10. If Larry and Peter don't get their reports in on Friday, they have only themselves to blame.

Nouns

There are eight parts of speech: *noun, pronoun, verb, adjective, adverb, preposition, conjunction,* and *interjection.* These parts of speech are the basic tools of grammar. To determine what part of speech a word is, you need to figure out what job the word does in a sentence. The job of a noun, for example, is to name a person, place, thing, or idea.

Rule 19a A **noun** is the name of a person, place, thing, or idea.

PEOPLE	man, singers, Senator James, astronaut, team
PLACES	park, Georgia, study hall, kitchen, kennel
THINGS	computers, saxophone, snow, trees, trophy, lamb
IDEAS	friendship, freedom, hope, goodness, loyalty

Some nouns, such as *study hall,* include more than one word. They are called *compound nouns.* Compound nouns can take three different forms. To know which form a particular compound noun takes, you should always check a dictionary.

SEPARATE WORDS	first aid, coffee maker, sleeping bag
HYPHENATED WORDS	ambassador-at-large, baby-sitter
SINGLE WORDS	turtleneck, officeholder, onlooker

Other nouns, such as *team* and *orchestra,* name groups of people or things. These nouns are called *collective nouns.*

EXERCISE 1 *Finding Nouns*

Number your paper 1 to 10. Then write the nouns in each sentence. There are 40 nouns.

1. Cinnamon comes from the bark of a laurel tree.
2. The gorilla was almost unknown to science less than 150 years ago.
3. When Cecilia was on vacation last summer, she rode a double-decker for the first time.
4. Diamonds are the hardest gems in the world.
5. According to a law, buried treasure belongs to the person who finds it, not to the owner of the land.
6. A wedding ring is a traditional symbol of love.

7. Cows throughout the world supply over 200 billion quarts of milk each year.
8. On warm days bees will fan the air with their wings to cool their hives.
9. To my surprise my little brother has no fear of bees.
10. More than 90,000 vehicles travel some 30 million miles each week to deliver daily newspapers.

Common and Proper Nouns

All nouns name people, places, things, or ideas. A *common noun* names any person, place, or thing; but a *proper noun* names a particular person, place, or thing. All proper nouns begin with a capital letter.

COMMON NOUNS	friend, city, spacecraft, holiday
PROPER NOUNS	Anne, Houston, *Voyager 2,* Presidents' Day

Some proper nouns, such as *Voyager 2* and *Presidents' Day,* include more than one word. They are still considered one noun. *Voyager 2* is the name of *one* spacecraft, and Presidents' Day is the name of *one* holiday.

EXERCISE 2 *Finding Common and Proper Nouns*

Number your paper 1 to 10. Write the nouns in each sentence. Then label each one *C* for common noun or *P* for proper noun.

Facts and Figures

1. The largest carousel in the world, ten stories high, can be found in Santa Clara, California.
2. From Earth the sun appears 400,000 times brighter than the full moon.
3. Americans eat about 18 million hot dogs a year.
4. Tornadoes are quite rare west of the Rocky Mountains.
5. "Dixie," a song associated with the South, was written by Daniel Emmett, a native of Ohio.
6. Edgar Allan Poe went to West Point.
7. Midway Island is so named because it is the body of land nearest to the geographical center of the Pacific Ocean.
8. The first movie of *Frankenstein* was produced by Thomas Edison.
9. Even during the Middle Ages, people served lemon with fish.
10. Bacteria left on the moon by *Surveyor III* were still alive three years later.

EXERCISE 3 *Cumulative Review*

Number your paper 1 to 15. Then write the nouns in each sentence. There are 60 nouns.

A True Story

1. Huge snowdrifts had prevented Jim Maxwell from arriving promptly at the auction on a cold day in December.
2. He arrived as a group of horses were being loaded onto a truck—headed for a slaughterhouse.
3. As Jim watched, he noticed Cassidy, a horse that had worked nine years on a farm.
4. The horse was in bad shape; his ribs stuck out, and mud covered his coat.
5. Jim paid the dealer a few dollars and returned to his family.
6. Because the children showed Cassidy so much affection, he soon fattened up and looked like a new animal.
7. With great sadness Jim had to sell him ten months later to a neighbor, Dr. Mason Adams.
8. Cassidy, however, didn't like that idea at all.
9. That night he jumped a fence, ran across a field, wandered through gardens and yards, and returned to Jim.
10. After higher fences still didn't stop Cassidy, Jim bought him back.
11. Impressed by his jumps, Jim started to train him.
12. By the following spring, Cassidy was ready.
13. After defeating thoroughbreds at exhibitions in nearby areas, Cassidy was entered in a national competition.
14. He became the winner, the best jumper in the United States.
15. Jim accepted the trophy before a crowd of cheering fans in Madison Square Garden.

Application to Writing

When you follow the same route every day, all too often you fail to notice much about it. For example, list all the things you usually see on your way to school. Tomorrow check your list. Add to it all the things you had never noticed before. Then write a paragraph that describes all those things that you used to pass, day after day, without really seeing them. Be prepared to identify each noun in the paragraph.

Integrating Language Skills

USING YOUR TEXT

Figurative Language (147)
Descriptive Paragraphs (144–153)

Grammar: Using Specific Nouns

Specific nouns create clear images in the reader's mind. Other nouns are so vague that they create only fuzzy images—at best. When you write, use specific nouns.

VAGUE NOUNS	SPECIFIC NOUNS
bird	wren
fruit	mangoes
book	*White Fang*
flower	lily

Checking Your Understanding Write at least one specific noun for each of the following vague nouns. Then write sentences using five of the specific nouns.

1. cat
2. car
3. school
4. insect
5. tool
6. food
7. river
8. grain
9. author
10. animal
11. building
12. planet
13. spice
14. country
15. fruit

Writing a Description Write freely about your last visit to a state fair or county fair, a theme park or amusement park, or a shopping mall. Recall not only what you saw but also whatever impressions you received through your other senses: what you ate, smelled, and touched while you were there. When you have finished, put your notes in a logical order. *(See pages 24–27, 106–107, 139, 148, and 158 for different ways to organize a paragraph.)*

Write a paragraph that describes your visit. Use colorful words and figures of speech so that the word pictures you create will be crystal-clear in your readers' minds. ***Application:*** As you revise your description, replace any vague, general nouns with specific ones. (A thesaurus can be a big help in finding specific nouns.) Then edit your paragraph and prepare a final copy. With your teacher's permission, read your description to a classmate.

Pronouns

Pronouns make it possible to eliminate awkward repetition in your writing. The second sentence in the following examples flows more smoothly and is easier to understand because pronouns were used.

Paul told Mary that Paul received an *A* on Paul's math test.
Paul told Mary that **he** received an *A* on **his** math test.

Rule 19b **A pronoun is a word that takes the place of one or more nouns.**

The noun that the pronoun replaces or refers to is called its *antecedent.* In the following examples, an arrow has been drawn from each pronoun to its antecedent.

The **report** is written, but **it** still must be typed.

Andrea and **Lynn** said **they** enjoyed the fair.

Personal Pronouns

Personal pronouns are the most common kind of pronoun. They are divided into the following three groups.

Personal Pronouns

FIRST PERSON	(The person speaking)
SINGULAR	I, me, my, mine
PLURAL	we, us, our, ours
SECOND PERSON	(The person spoken to)
SINGULAR	you, your, yours
PLURAL	you, your, yours
THIRD PERSON	(The person or thing spoken about)
SINGULAR	he, him, his, she, her, hers, it, its
PLURAL	they, them, their, theirs

You can meet **them** at **my** house.
We should take **your** tent with **us.**

EXERCISE 4 *Finding Personal Pronouns*

Number your paper 1 to 10. Write the personal pronouns in each of the following sentences. Then, beside each pronoun, write its antecedent.

EXAMPLE A bird is building its nest in the garage.
ANSWER its—bird

1. Stacy unexpectedly found her pink and white sweater at Marcy's house. Stacy - her
2. "I wish you could go with me," Gwen said to Kara.
3. Armon gave his speech after Karen gave hers.
4. The twins wrote poems and showed them to their parents.
5. Janice told Bonnie, "We should have brought our raincoats with us."
6. "Did Ari say that he would try out for the team?" Rob asked.
7. "Your report is fine, but I think it should be retyped," Mrs. Johnson told Leon.
8. The Hansons said that they are moving to South Carolina.
9. "Lani said she couldn't meet us," Lilly told Paula.
10. Did Kent take his parents out on their anniversary?

Other Kinds of Pronouns

In addition to personal pronouns, there are other kinds. This section will discuss *reflexive, indefinite, demonstrative,* and *interrogative pronouns. Relative pronouns* will be discussed in Chapter 25.

Reflexive Pronouns Reflexive pronouns are formed by adding *-self* or *-selves* to certain personal pronouns.

Jason makes **himself** breakfast every morning.

The guests could see **themselves** on the television screen.

We found **ourselves** with nothing to do.

Reflexive Pronouns	
SINGULAR	myself, yourself, himself, herself, itself
PLURAL	ourselves, yourselves, themselves

Indefinite Pronouns Indefinite pronouns quite often refer to unnamed people or things. Therefore, they usually do not have definite antecedents as personal pronouns do.

Everyone applauded after Grant's speech.
At the meeting **nothing** important happened.
After dinner **none** of the turkey was left.

Common Indefinite Pronouns

all	both	few	no one
another	each	many	nothing
any	either	most	others
anybody	everybody	neither	several
anyone	everyone	nobody	some
anything	everything	none	someone

Demonstrative Pronouns Demonstrative pronouns are used to point out specific people, places, or things.

This is my favorite pair of sneakers.
Can you also carry **these?**
We bought **those** at the discount store.

Demonstrative Pronouns

this	that	these	those

Interrogative Pronouns Interrogative pronouns are used to ask questions.

What did you find out about the accident?
Who is taking you to school today?
Whose are these?

Interrogative Pronouns

what	which	who	whom	whose

EXERCISE 5 Finding Pronouns

Number your paper 1 to 10. Then write the pronouns in each sentence.

1. Aren't these the ones you wanted?
2. Others may seem nicer than Willis, but no one could be.
3. Someone told me to give this to you.
4. What did you say to him?
5. Most of the books I need are not in the library.
6. These are difficult problems for me to solve.
7. They congratulated themselves on their victory.
8. Several of my friends stayed and helped me clean up.
9. Did you make that by yourself?
10. Which is the best car for my needs?

EXERCISE 6 Cumulative Review

Number your paper 1 to 15. Make two columns on your paper. Label the first column *nouns* and the second column *pronouns*. Then, in the proper column, write each noun and pronoun.

Pass Go. Collect $200.

1. During the Great Depression, Charles Darrow lost his job.
2. With time on his hands, he began to invent things like puzzles.
3. One day he got an idea for a game about Atlantic City, the place where he and his wife had spent their vacations.
4. First he drew the outline of the board on the tablecloth.
5. Then he built little houses and hotels from scraps of wood.
6. Colored buttons became tokens, and pieces of cardboard became deeds to the properties.
7. Next Charles bought play money and a pair of dice and named his game Monopoly.
8. Everyone loved the game and wanted one.
9. When he couldn't keep up with the orders, Darrow tried to sell his game to the people at Parker Brothers.
10. What do you think happened?
11. They came up with 52 reasons why no one would play it.
12. Darrow then arranged for a printer to make 5,000 copies of the game.
13. The success of Monopoly soon changed the minds of all at Parker Brothers.
14. This is now the most popular game in the world.
15. The rules are printed in 18 different languages.

Integrating Language Skills

USING YOUR TEXT

Persuasive Essays (234–269)

Grammar: Substituting Pronouns for Nouns

When you use pronouns to avoid repetition, you create a smoother flow in your writing. Using pronouns also makes your writing more coherent.

Checking Your Understanding The following paragraph repeats some nouns too often. Rewrite the paragraph by replacing nouns with pronouns where they are needed. Then underline the changes you have made.

> At 118 pounds Abbye Stockton looked petite and frail next to Abbye's 185-pound husband Les. That's what made Abbye and Les's act so amazing. In 1940, Abbye and Les toured the country, performing at athletic events. As Abbye stood upright, Les would stand on Abbye's shoulders. Les would then flip into a handstand, using Abbye's palms for a base. Abbye would hold Les up—with one hand—for as long as 30 seconds. Although this act had been done before, the act had never been done by a woman who weighed 67 pounds less than the person the woman was holding!

Expressing Your Opinion In a recent poll, parents stated what they thought their children worried about most. The answers most frequently given were (1) pollution, (2) crime, and (3) poverty. Brainstorm about whether you agree or disagree with these responses. As you brainstorm, think of reasons and evidence that supports your reasons. Your supporting material can be from personal observation and from research.

Write an essay in which you agree or disagree with the results of the poll. Be sure to draft a thesis statement for your introduction. Give reasons, facts, incidents, and examples to support your position. ***Application:*** As you edit your essay, make sure you have substituted pronouns for nouns, where appropriate, to avoid repetition. When you have finished, write a final copy. Exchange your composition with one other student in the class to see what viewpoint that student adopted.

Chapter 19

Review

A **Finding Nouns and Pronouns** Number your paper 1 to 20. Make two columns on your paper. Label the first column *nouns* and the second column *pronouns*. Then, in the proper column, write each noun and pronoun.

1. What did you tell everyone about the dude ranch?
2. During its incredible journey, the spacecraft will travel over a billion miles.
3. He prides himself in his ability to use the computer.
4. There are more people for the trip up the mountain than there are seats on the bus.
5. Who made the salad with blueberries and peaches in it?
6. Although the fabric feels soft enough to be called silk, it is actually rayon.
7. They helped themselves to the free brochures on the counter.
8. People had their first taste of tea with ice at a world's fair in St. Louis, Missouri.
9. "I prefer these to those," Dawn said, pointing to the bunch of tulips.
10. You share your birthday with about nine million others.
11. What does everybody want for dessert on Thanksgiving Day?
12. A tortoise would take about 4 years 6 months 18 days to crawl from New York City to Los Angeles.
13. Most of us have already seen the movie at Cinema Plaza.
14. I kept telling myself to keep my mouth shut!
15. A mountain on Mars is much taller than Mount Everest, the tallest mountain on Earth.
16. We must meet someone at the airport in Detroit.
17. No one has eaten any of that.
18. In the United States, more women than men are millionaires.
19. Whom did she choose to be her vice president of the Student Council?
20. A bee must make about 4,200 trips to a flower to produce a single tablespoon of honey.

B Finding Pronouns and Antecedents Number your paper 1 to 10. Write the personal pronouns in each sentence. Then, beside each one, write its antecedent.

1. Jim thought he should talk with his father first.
2. When Mr. Wong noticed that he had left his briefcase at home, he went back to get it.
3. Betty told Melissa, "You go now, and I will come later."
4. The Keiths will take their dog with them to Denver.
5. As Nina watched the parade, she saw Juan in it.
6. Carlos asked Bob, "Will you help me repair my car?"
7. Jody asked Mike if he would try out for the play with her.
8. Frank told Margie, "Chad can ride with you and me."
9. Mary said to Lisa, "I think the book is yours."
10. The Lees borrowed the rake, but they will return it soon.

Mastery Test

Number your paper 1 to 10. Make two columns on your paper. Label the first column *nouns* and the second column *pronouns*. Then, in the proper column, write each noun and pronoun.

1. Maine is the largest state in New England.
2. We spent three weeks of our vacation in California.
3. Lisa is the best skater at the rink.
4. When you finish with the dictionary, may I have it?
5. Who did you say is running for president of the Drama Club?
6. We went down the trails into the Grand Canyon on burros.
7. Those are the arrowheads we found in my backyard.
8. What would you like me to bring to the picnic on Saturday?
9. Nobody but Jake could fix the old lawnmower.
10. Use the rollers to paint the walls and the brushes to paint the trim.

C h a p t e r

20 Verbs

Diagnostic Test

Number your paper 1 to 10. Write the verb or the verb phrase in each sentence. Then label each one *action* or *linking*.

EXAMPLE Did the soup taste salty to you?
ANSWER did taste—linking

1. The moon moves about two inches away from the earth each year.
2. Did he show slow-motion pictures of the divers?
3. The person in the clown costume was Anne.
4. Melanie is an aggressive soccer player.
5. Most people have never seen the inside of a control tower.
6. The loud sirens sounded closer and closer.
7. A sprinter on our track team had run the 500-yard dash in record time.
8. The hamburgers and the shish kebab on the grill smelled delicious.
9. Do you feel tired?
10. The prizes at the fair were radios and TV's.

Action Verbs

In Chapter 18 you learned that the verb is one of the two main parts of a sentence. No sentence can be written without a verb. This chapter will explain the different kinds of verbs and show you how to use them effectively in your writing. Most of the verbs that you use when you speak or write are *action verbs*.

Rule 20a An **action verb** tells what action a subject is performing.

The action verbs in the following two sentences show physical action.

Martha **marched** down Main Street with the band.
Charlie **mailed** the package yesterday.

Action verbs can also show mental action or ownership.

I **thought** of his name the next day.
Jerry **has** the combination to the lock.

Action verbs can be used with helping verbs. *(See pages 529–530.)* The verb and any helping verbs form a *verb phrase*.

Rule 20b A **verb phrase** is a main verb plus one or more helping verbs.

Following is a list of common helping verbs.

Common Helping Verbs

be	am, is, are, was, were, be, being, been
have	has, have, had
do	do, does, did
others	may, might, must, can, could, shall, should, will, would

Notice in the following examples that a verb phrase may be interrupted by other words. *(See pages 529–530.)*

Kate **should** never **have taken** that job.
Terry **had** not **seen** the notice.
Haven't you **bought** your supplies?

EXERCISE 1 *Finding Action Verbs*

Number your paper 1 to 10. Write the verb or the verb phrase in each sentence. Include any helping verbs.

Airy Facts

1. In the United States, President George Washington wrote the first "airmail" letter.
2. Someone transported the letter by balloon from Pennsylvania to New Jersey.
3. During the Civil War, a citizen took the first aerial photograph from a balloon.
4. During the first space walk, an astronaut dropped a camera.
5. The camera will now orbit the earth indefinitely.
6. After the first moonwalk, Pan American Airlines accepted reservations for commercial flights to the moon.
7. More than 80,000 requests immediately poured in.
8. While in orbit, astronauts may see 16 sunrises and 16 sunsets each "day."
9. Hot-aır balloons are having a commercial comeback.
10. They are lifting huge loads of timber in the mountains of the Pacific Northwest.

Application to Writing

Write a paragraph that explains the possible problems of giving a dog or a cat a bath. Be prepared to identify each action verb.

Transitive and Intransitive Verbs

All action verbs fall within two general classes. They are either transitive or intransitive. An action verb that has an object is *transitive*. To find an object, say the subject and the verb and then ask the question *What?* or *Whom?* A word that answers either question is called an *object*. An action verb that does not have an object is *intransitive*.

TRANSITIVE **Have** you **seen** Ann? [You have seen what or whom? *Ann* is the object; therefore, *have seen* is a transitive verb.]

INTRANSITIVE The sun **sank** behind the mountains. [The sun sank what or whom? Since there is no object, *sank* is an intransitive verb.]

Some verbs may be transitive in one sentence and intransitive in another sentence.

TRANSITIVE Melinda **sang** a solo. [*Solo* is the object.]
INTRANSITIVE Melinda **sang** softly. [There is no object.]

EXERCISE 2 *Finding Transitive and Intransitive Verbs*

Number your paper 1 to 10. Write the verb or verb phrase. Then label each verb *transitive* or *intransitive.*

City Animals

1. Coyotes have howled along with the music at outdoor concerts in Los Angeles.
2. Beavers have built dams in the Potomac near Washington, D.C.
3. For a while a fox was living in New York's Yankee Stadium.
4. Most raccoons can tip garbage cans over.
5. The cans' contents provide food for the raccoons.
6. Falcons have lived on the tops of skyscrapers in big cities.
7. Many animals make their homes on center strips of highways.
8. In some cities police on horses patrol streets.
9. Don't forget the pigeons.
10. They have existed everywhere for centuries.

Linking Verbs

A verb that links or joins the subject with another word in the sentence is called a *linking verb.*

Rule 20c **A linking verb links the subject with another word in the sentence. The other word either renames or describes the subject.**

Chico **was** the winner of the race. [*Was* links *winner* and the subject *Chico*. *Winner* renames the subject.]

You **will be** happy with the results. [*Will be* links *happy* with the subject *you*. *Happy* describes the subject.]

Forms of the verb *be* are the most common linking verbs. *(See the list on the following page.)* In fact, any verb phrase ending in *be* or *been* can be a linking verb.

Common Forms of *Be*		
be	will be	has been
being	can be	had been
is	could be	could have been
am	should be	should have been
are	would be	would have been
was	may be	may have been
were	might be	might have been
been	must be	must have been
shall be	have been	

Mr. Hedren **could be** next year's tennis coach. [*Coach* renames the subject, *Mr. Hedren*.]

The weather **has been** damp and gloomy. [*Damp* and *gloomy* describe the subject, *weather*.]

The forms of the verb *be* are not always linking verbs. To be a linking verb, a verb must link the subject with another word that renames or describes the subject. In the following examples, the verbs simply make statements.

She **was** there. Her dress **is** on the ironing board.

EXERCISE 3 *Finding Linking Verbs*

Number your paper 1 to 10. Write the verb or the verb phrase in each sentence. Then write the two words that the verb links.

EXAMPLE The prize will be a new camera.
ANSWER will be prize—camera

1. Some dinosaurs were rather gentle creatures.
2. Robin has been the class secretary for two years.
3. The steak might be very tough.
4. The eyes of a horse are unusually large.
5. William could be a professional singer.
6. Jesse Owens was the hero of the 1936 Olympics.
7. The dishes in the sink are dirty.
8. The job may be very monotonous.
9. Queen Anne's lace is a wild carrot.
10. The story must have been true.

Additional Linking Verbs

The verbs in the following list may also be used as linking verbs. All these verbs can be used with helping verbs as well.

Additional Linking Verbs					
appear	feel	look	seem	sound	taste
become	grow	remain	smell	stay	turn

Carmen **will become** my sister-in-law. [*Sister-in-law* renames the subject, *Carmen*.]

The speaker on the stage **appeared** nervous. [*Nervous* describes the subject, *speaker*.]

EXERCISE 4 *Finding Linking Verbs*

Number your paper 1 to 10. Write the verb or the verb phrase in each sentence. Then write the two words that the verb links.

1. Your bicycle certainly looks sleek.
2. Raisins have become my favorite snack.
3. The surgery appeared quite successful.
4. The horse was feeling very frisky on the cool autumn day.
5. This locket will remain a reminder of our friendship.
6. Was Theodore Roosevelt president for eight years?
7. Jennifer turned pale during her ride on the roller coaster.
8. Peter seemed uneasy during tryouts.
9. Is everyone ready now?
10. His words sounded most unsympathetic.

Linking Verb or Action Verb? Most of the additional linking verbs can also be action verbs if they show action. They are linking verbs if they link the subject with another word that renames or describes the subject.

LINKING Mom **looked** beautiful in her evening gown.
ACTION Mom **looked** all over the house for her missing ring.

LINKING Steve **grew** quiet in the afternoon.
ACTION Steve **grew** tomatoes in the backyard last year.

EXERCISE 5 *Distinguishing between Linking Verbs and Action Verbs*

Number your paper 1 to 10. Write the verb or the verb phrase in each sentence. Then label each one *linking* or *action*.

1. The bell in the church steeple sounded mournful.
2. Have you ever tasted venison?
3. The air felt unusually raw and cold for this time of year.
4. Jackie could smell smoke from the building next door.
5. Did you feel the rabbit's soft fur?
6. A baked potato with sour cream always tastes delicious.
7. To everyone's surprise Jonathan appeared at the party.
8. The books in the basement will probably smell musty.
9. After a month the onions still appeared fresh.
10. The fire fighter urgently sounded the alarm.

EXERCISE 6 *Writing Sentences*

Write two sentences for each of the following verbs. First use the verb as a linking verb. Then use it as an action verb. Label each verb *linking* or *action*.

1. appear **2.** feel **3.** grow **4.** look **5.** sound

EXERCISE 7 *Cumulative Review*

Number your paper 1 to 10. Write the verb or the verb phrase in each sentence. Then label each one *linking* or *action*.

Facing the Ferocious

1. For many people Clyde Beatty has remained the greatest animal trainer of all times.
2. Without protection he would enter a cage with 12 to 24 animals.
3. His only weapon was a pistol with blanks in it.
4. During his long career, Beatty faced thousands of lions and tigers.
5. Once in a while, some of these animals would become uncontrollable.
6. Several times the 500-pound beasts clawed him.
7. In one act he handled 40 big cats at once.
8. This feat was unusually dangerous.
9. Beatty could not keep all the animals in his range of vision.
10. He performed this act only one time.

USING YOUR TEXT

Personal Essays *(270–297)*
Specific Words *(53–54)*

Grammar: Using Vivid Verbs

The verb is the most powerful word in a sentence. Carefully chosen verbs can make a sentence come alive. Notice the difference in the following sentences.

OVERUSED VERB	The young boy **came** into the room.
COLORFUL VERB	The young boy **bolted** *(darted, charged, shot)* into the room.

A dictionary and a thesaurus are good sources of colorful verbs. For example, under the verb *say,* you might find *utter, state, assert, declare,* and *disclose.*

Checking Your Understanding Number your paper 1 to 5. Then write two vivid verbs that complete each sentence. You may find it helpful to use a thesaurus.

1. The train ________ into the station.
2. The football team ________ onto the field.
3. The clouds ________ across the prairie.
4. The sudden noise ________ Emily.
5. The dog ________ against its leash.

Writing a Personal Essay Recall a time when you had to make a difficult decision. For example, did a family member need your help at home when you were about to go out with friends? Brainstorm about such an occasion, jotting down as many specific facts and details as you can remember.

After you arrange your notes in chronological order—the order in which things happened—write the first draft of an essay. Explain the steps you went through in making your decision. Be clear about your reasons for making it and tell the result. For example, did it turn out to be the right one? ***Application:*** As you revise your essay, use a dictionary or a thesaurus to find vivid verbs that express your ideas convincingly. Then edit your essay and make a final copy of your work.

Chapter 20

Review

A Finding Action Verbs and Linking Verbs

A **Finding Action Verbs and Linking Verbs** Number your paper 1 to 25. Write the verb or the verb phrase in each sentence. Then label each one *action* or *linking.*

1. One jelly bean has seven calories.
2. Fingernails grow faster than toenails.
3. Collies have always been my favorite breed of dog.
4. My parents named me after my grandmother.
5. My older sister and I have grown very close over the past several years.
6. He should not have taken the advanced math course during his sophomore year.
7. In 1874, Philadelphia became the first city in the United States with a zoo.
8. Have you been waiting very long for the bus?
9. The most popular street name in the United States is *Park.*
10. *Washington, Maple, Oak,* and *Lincoln* follow *Park.*
11. Did you join the marching band this year?
12. Have you looked for your baseball mitt in the basement and in the garage?
13. Patty stayed confident in spite of her disappointments.
14. Don't turn the page before the buzzer.
15. A snake's skin does not feel slimy.
16. I might never have noticed the new street sign.
17. Some deer in the Florida Keys are the size of a big dog.
18. Bart looked strange without his old baseball cap.
19. That after-shave lotion smells fresh and clean.
20. This year many students have elected industrial arts.
21. Jeffrey turned red with embarrassment.
22. At the petting zoo, the young children felt the soft fur of the rabbits.
23. I should never have eaten such a late snack.

24. On our trip across the country, we stayed in many motels along our route.

25. In an average lifetime, a person could probably read 14,000 newspapers, 6,000 magazines, and 1,000 books.

B **Transitive and Intransitive Verbs** Number your paper 1 to 10. Write the verb or the verb phrase in each sentence. Then label each one *transitive* or *intransitive*.

1. The kite soared upward as well as downward.
2. Tree swallows once raised a family on a ferryboat.
3. Tiger was waiting for us at the door.
4. Cats can get head colds—just like humans.
5. A number of books on space exploration have recently appeared in bookstores.
6. Concetta works at the car wash on Saturdays.
7. Medieval monks did invent the waterwheel.
8. Did you tear the recipe for barbecued pork out of the newspaper?
9. How can you determine the age of a giant redwood tree?
10. The young bride walked slowly down the aisle.

Mastery Test

Number your paper 1 to 10. Write the verb or the verb phrase in each sentence. Then label each one *action* or *linking*.

1. That man looks strangely familiar to me.
2. We should have measured those hailstones.
3. The black-eyed Susan is a common North American wildflower.
4. We didn't have electricity for three hours last night.
5. Did you leave a package on the back seat of the van?
6. They have always grown wheat on their farm.
7. You should be proud of your achievements.
8. Everyone looked happy after the ceremony.
9. A beaver can hold its breath for 15 minutes.
10. The Ribbon in California is the highest waterfall in North America.

C h a p t e r

21 Adjectives and Adverbs

Diagnostic Test

Number your paper 1 to 10. Make two columns on your paper. Label the first column *adjectives* and the second column *adverbs*. Then, in the proper column, write each adjective and adverb. Do not include articles.

EXAMPLE Laws protect many rare animals now.

ANSWER <u>adjectives</u> <u>adverbs</u>
many, rare now

1. I just bought some cotton T-shirts.
2. The moon could hardly be seen through the dark clouds.
3. The gold and purple sunset was quite spectacular.
4. The actress, tired but happy, bowed graciously.
5. The old phonograph works surprisingly well.
6. Everyone thoroughly enjoyed the first-class service in the hotel.
7. Swiss watches are known for extraordinarily fine workmanship.
8. These new street signs are too small.
9. Dale has already taken the history exam.
10. The enthusiastic audience cheered the two Spanish dancers.

Adjectives

Your best friend calls you on the phone and tells you that he or she now has a car. You probably would respond with a series of questions. *How old is it? What color is it? When did you get it? When can I have a ride in it?* The words used to answer these questions would all be *modifiers*. Modifiers make the meaning of other parts of speech more precise. Two kinds of modifiers, *adjectives* and *adverbs*, will be discussed in this chapter.

In the following example, the words in heavy type are adjectives. They all describe a car.

I just bought a **six-year-old blue Ford** sedan.

Rule 21a An **adjective** is a word that modifies a noun or a pronoun.

To find an adjective, first find each noun and pronoun in a sentence. Then ask yourself, *What kind? Which one(s)? How many?* or *How much?* about each one. The answers to these questions will be adjectives.

WHAT KIND?	**fresh** vegetables	**loud** noise
WHICH ONE(S)?	**these** windows	**red** ones
HOW MANY?	**ten** seats	**one** banana
HOW MUCH?	**great** relief	**much** help

There are two special kinds of adjectives that also answer these same questions. They are proper adjectives and compound adjectives. A *proper adjective* is formed from a proper noun and begins with a capital letter. A *compound adjective,* like a compound noun, can take different forms. The words in a compound adjective may be combined into one word, or they may be joined by a hyphen.

PROPER ADJECTIVES	**Swiss** watches	**Mexican** hat
COMPOUND ADJECTIVES	**cordless** beater	**third-class** mail

As you can see, most adjectives come in front of the nouns or the pronouns they modify. A few adjectives come after the nouns or the pronouns they modify, and some adjectives follow linking verbs. *(See pages 556 and 557 for lists of linking verbs.)* Notice in the examples on the following page that more than one adjective can modify the same noun or pronoun.

BEFORE A NOUN The **frisky, playful** kitten woke us.

AFTER A NOUN The kitten, **frisky** and **playful,** woke us.

AFTER A LINKING VERB The kitten is **frisky** and **playful.**

Note: The words *a, an,* and *the* form a special group of adjectives called *articles.* You will not be asked to list articles as adjectives in the exercises in this book.

EXERCISE 1 *Finding Adjectives*

Number your paper 1 to 15. Write the adjectives in each sentence. Then, beside each one, write the word it modifies. There are 33 adjectives.

EXAMPLE Common things often have unusual beginnings.
ANSWER common—things, unusual—beginnings

A Delicious Accident

1. The doughnut has been called a delicious accident.
2. Doughnuts were probably first made in a French hamlet in 1917 during World War I.
3. Nearly 1,000 American soldiers were stationed in a tiny out-of-the-way village.
4. Rain, cold and heavy, had fallen for many days.
5. The morale of the men was low.
6. Two top-notch representatives of the Salvation Army looked for a quick remedy.
7. According to the story, they mixed a pot of dough and rolled the lumpy mixture with a large bottle.
8. Then they cut round pieces of dough with a can.
9. The small pieces of dough were then fried on a crude, homemade stove.
10. The unusual results, warm and tasty, did the trick.
11. Temporarily the men didn't feel homesick.
12. Further experiments with the pastry resulted in the small center holes.
13. Creating holes was the easiest way to eliminate the soggy middles.
14. The name for the new pastry probably came from the nickname for the lonely soldiers—doughboys.
15. The tasty discovery eventually made an Atlantic crossing, and the modern doughnut was born.

Other Parts of Speech Used as Adjectives

The same word may be used as an adjective in one sentence and a noun in another sentence.

ADJECTIVE **Porch** furniture is on sale now. [*Porch* tells what kind of furniture.]

NOUN We built a **porch** on our house. [*Porch* is the name of a thing.]

ADJECTIVE **Name** tags were given to the people at the convention.

NOUN I can't think of a good **name** for the kitten.

Note: *Name* can also be used as a verb.

He will **name** the winner tomorrow.

Some words can also be used as pronouns or adjectives. The following words are adjectives when they come in front of a noun and modify a noun. They are pronouns when they stand alone.

Words Used as Pronouns or Adjectives

DEMONSTRATIVE	INTERROGATIVE	INDEFINITE	
that	what	all	many
these	which	another	more
this		any	most
those		both	neither
		each	other
		either	several
		few	some

ADJECTIVE **These** boots are too large for me.
PRONOUN **These** are too large for me.

ADJECTIVE **What** answer did he give you?
PRONOUN **What** did he give you?

Note: The possessive pronouns *my, your, his, her, its, our,* and *their* are sometimes called *pronominal adjectives* because they answer the adjective question *Which one(s)?* Throughout this book, however, these words will be considered pronouns.

EXERCISE 2 Determining How a Word Is Used in a Sentence

Number your paper 1 to 15. Write the underlined word in each sentence. Then label each word *adjective, noun,* or *pronoun.*

1. Allen found an unusual rock in his backyard.
2. Which pair of boots do you want?
3. Megan's Bay is full of plant life.
4. Some cross hairs in optical instruments are made of spider silk.
5. I sent all of the postcards from San Francisco.
6. Did you paint these pictures yourself?
7. Is your suit 100 percent wool?
8. I don't care for either.
9. All reports are due on Friday.
10. Fine wool fiber will stretch one third its original length.
11. I would like to have a plant like that.
12. That spider had to be three inches long!
13. Which is the one we should take?
14. Do you really have a rock collection?
15. Either plan will work.

EXERCISE 3 Cumulative Review

Number your paper 1 to 20. Write the adjectives in the following paragraph. Then beside each adjective, write the word it modifies.

The World's Icebox

The lowest temperature ever recorded was 90 degrees below zero. It was in a northern Siberian city. At this temperature someone outside for five minutes without proper clothing would become a stonelike statue. Few would choose this icy city for a winter vacation. However, this climate, icy and frigid, has certain advantages. No one can catch a cold in this germ-free environment. The air is too cold for germs to live. Also, food can be stored at a low temperature for many years without spoiling.

Application to Writing

Imagine that you are going to write a one-act TV mystery play. Write a paragraph that describes the setting for your drama. Be prepared to identify each adjective.

USING YOUR TEXT

Figurative Language (55 and 147)
Descriptive Paragraphs (144–153)

Grammar: Using Colorful Adjectives

Adjectives should make nouns more specific. Some adjectives, however, are used so often that they no longer can accomplish this purpose. When you write, use a dictionary or a thesaurus to find fresh, effective adjectives. They add life to your words.

OVERUSED ADJECTIVE	Her dorm room was **big.**
FRESH ADJECTIVES	Her dorm room was **enormous** *(vast, spacious, immense).*

Checking Your Understanding Write fresh, colorful adjectives that appropriately complete the following sentences.

1. The ______ animals darted for their homes after the ______ bolt of lightning.
2. The ______ oak near the porch shades our house from the ______ heat.
3. ______ footsteps could be heard from the hallway in the ______ house.
4. The ______ desk stood in a ______ corner of the ______ shed.
5. The ______ drizzle depressed the ______ hikers as they tramped through the ______ mud.

Writing a Description Imagine that you have just been invited to a New Year's Eve costume party at the governor's mansion. The theme is "Famous Movie Monsters." Brainstorm for ideas for a costume you could wear to the party. Then choose one idea and make a drawing of that costume—or list as many details about it as possible.

Write a paragraph in which you describe your famous movie monster costume and explain why you chose it. ***Application:*** As you revise your paragraph, ask yourself if readers will be able to picture your costume clearly in their minds. To add to the clarity of your description, replace any overused adjectives. Use fresh, specific ones that help describe details. Also, wherever appropriate, add interesting figures of speech to enliven your writing even more.

Adverbs

Just as an adjective adds more information to a noun or a pronoun, an adverb adds preciseness to a verb, an adjective, or another adverb.

Rule 21b An **adverb** is a word that modifies a verb, an adjective, or another adverb.

To find an adverb, ask yourself, *Where? When? How?* or *To what extent?* Words answering these questions will be adverbs. Another way to find adverbs is to look for words ending in *-ly*. Some adverbs, however, do not end in *-ly*.

Common Adverbs

again	ever	often	then
almost	here	perhaps	there
alone	just	quite	today
already	later	rather	too
also	never	seldom	very
always	not (n't)	so	yet
away	now	somewhat	
even	nowhere	soon	

Most adverbs modify verbs. An adverb that modifies a verb modifies the whole verb phrase.

WHERE?	looked **everywhere**	was found **here**
WHEN?	is **always** singing	has **never** arrived
HOW?	was **carefully** wrapping	is standing **quietly**

A few adverbs modify adjectives or other adverbs. The adverbs in the following examples answer the question *To what extent?*

MODIFYING AN ADJECTIVE The weather this winter has been **extremely** cold.

MODIFYING AN ADVERB My grandparents visit **quite often.**

EXERCISE 4 Finding Adverbs

Number your paper 1 to 15. Write the adverb or adverbs in each sentence. Then beside each one, write the word or words it modifies.

EXAMPLE Janice has never sung better.
ANSWER never—has sung, better—has sung

1. The candidate unexpectedly won by a very narrow margin.
2. Walk slowly and carefully over the ice on the sidewalk.
3. The coach has strongly disagreed with the referee.
4. Don't speak too rapidly during your speech.
5. The turtle's head moved in and out.
6. Later the hikers were wearily pitching camp.
7. The chipmunk scurried very quickly through the garden.
8. Sometimes our dog will bark angrily at the plumber.
9. The ex-mayor had not conceded graciously.
10. I think Bonita plays the piano extremely well.
11. Desserts are often too rich for me.
12. His arrival with the very colorful balloons was perfectly timed.
13. Sam was in an exceptionally good mood at the party.
14. I have always put the keys there.
15. Ellie drove too fast down the busy street.

EXERCISE 5 Cumulative Review

Make two columns on your paper. Label the first column *adjectives* and the second column *adverbs*. Then, under the proper column, write each adjective and adverb in the following paragraph. There is a total of 20.

A Tangled Tackle

Rice University and Alabama were extremely well matched in the Cotton Bowl in 1954. In the fourth quarter, Dicky Moegle was clear. With great speed he raced for a 95-yard touchdown. As Moegle passed the Alabama bench, Tommy Lewis suddenly jumped up. The fullback, anxious and eager, flung himself forcefully at Moegle. Moegle crashed to the ground. Lewis instantly realized what he had done. His face turned very red with embarrassment. Timidly he crawled back to the bench. The 75,000 fans in the bleachers were silent with disbelief. The referee declared a touchdown for Rice. Rice later won 28-6.

Language Integrating Skills

USING YOUR TEXT

Expository Paragraphs (82–125)
Order of Importance (113 and 158)

Grammar: Creating Sentence Variety

You can create variety in your writing by occasionally beginning a sentence with an adverb.

REGULAR ORDER The sun **quickly** dried the tents.
VARIETY **Quickly** the sun dried the tents.

Checking Your Understanding Choose ten of the following words and use each of them as an adverb in a sentence. Then change five of the sentences so that they begin with the adverb.

1. immediately
2. cleverly
3. suddenly
4. hastily
5. slowly
6. loudly
7. always
8. never
9. soon
10. now
11. silently
12. quickly
13. away
14. closer
15. timidly
16. easily
17. boldly

Writing a Newspaper Article Newspapers are often criticized for featuring so much bad news. Brainstorm for a recent event you have heard about that was good news. Decide on one that you think should have appeared in your local paper. After choosing the event you will report on, jot down facts about it by writing answers to the five *W*'s and *H*: *Who? What? When? Where? Why?* and *How?* Arrange the information in order of importance. Then write the first draft of a newspaper article about the event. Make your first sentence catch your readers' interest. Then add a headline that will make people want to read the article.

As you revise your article, make sure you have included enough facts and details to make it interesting. ***Application:*** Check the beginnings of your sentences. If most start with the subject, create variety by beginning a few with an adverb. Then edit your article carefully. Write a final copy and consider submitting it to the local or school paper.

Diagraming Adjectives and Adverbs

In a sentence diagram, adjectives and adverbs are connected to the words they modify by a slanted line. Two adjectives or adverbs are connected by a conjunction on a broken line.

The boisterous audience cheered wildly and happily.

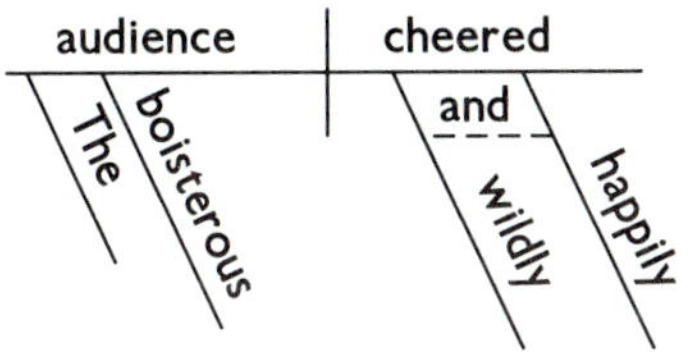

An adverb that modifies an adjective or another adverb is placed on a line parallel to the word it modifies.

The extremely hard worker was promoted.

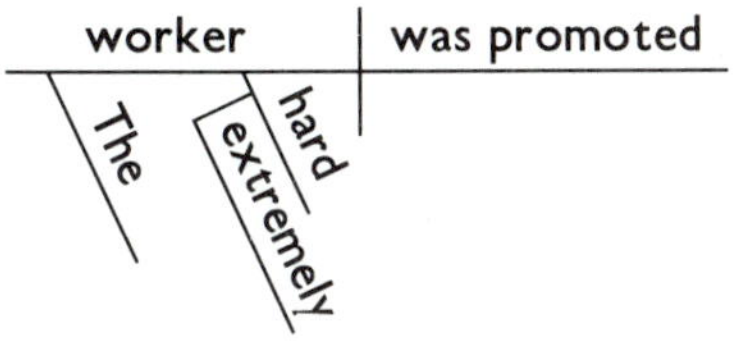

My sister writes quite often.

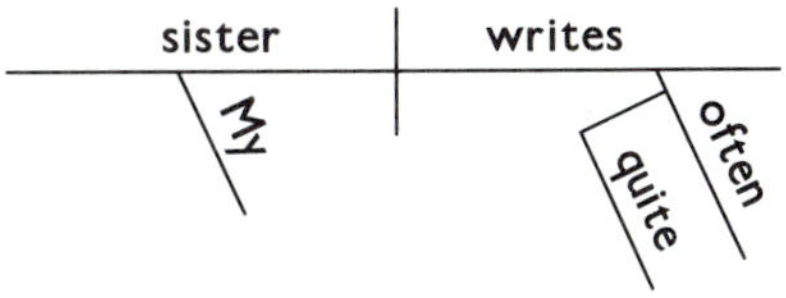

EXERCISE 6 *Diagraming Adjectives and Adverbs*

Diagram the following sentences or copy them. If you copy them, draw one line under each subject and two lines under each verb. Then label each modifier *adjective* or *adverb*.

1. The huge plane roared overhead.
2. The older but faster runner easily won.
3. The violets have bloomed unusually early.
4. Her very expensive dress was ruined.
5. The new secretary typed quickly and efficiently.
6. The enthusiastic fans waited eagerly.
7. The shy deer swiftly bounded away.
8. My energetic cousin jogs effortlessly.
9. The two lively gymnasts leaped nimbly.
10. The lovely dancers twirled extremely gracefully.

Chapter 21 Review

A Identifying Adjectives and Adverbs

Number your paper 1 to 20. Make two columns on your paper. Label the first column *adjectives* and the second column *adverbs*. Then, in the proper column, write each adjective and adverb.

1. The fresh paint has now dried completely.
2. That is an extremely smart outfit.
3. The vegetables from the Ortiz farm are fresher than those at the local store.
4. Don't come too early to the surprise party.
5. The shortest time the race has ever been run is approximately three hours.
6. Recently I took a two-day tour of the English countryside.
7. The price of the average American car doubled during a ten-year period (1968–1978).
8. The big black snake slithered slowly along the ground.
9. First-class seats on airplanes are very expensive.
10. My research paper is somewhat short.
11. Two states, Maine and Vermont, are the primary focus of the New England foliage tour.
12. The large white gulls flew noisily overhead and turned seaward.
13. Some whales often travel 4,000 miles in a single year.
14. The most northern point in the United States is Point Barrow, Alaska.
15. No Pilgrims were on the *Mayflower* on its return to England.
16. Margaret runs faster, farther, and more often than Chris.
17. My work is accomplished more easily in the early part of the day than in the late afternoon.
18. Tigers, ancestors of present-day Asian mammals, once roamed the American plains.
19. Did the hungry explorers actually eat octopus meat?
20. A completely blind chameleon will still assume the colors of the things around it.

B Determining a Word's Part of Speech Number your paper 1 to 10. Write the underlined words in each sentence. Then label each one *adjective, noun,* or *pronoun.*

1. Give <u>those</u> horses an <u>apple</u>.
2. <u>What</u> do you want for your <u>birthday</u>?
3. <u>That</u> is rather expensive <u>lawn</u> furniture.
4. <u>Neither</u> of the <u>turkey</u> legs was eaten.
5. <u>What</u> spices did you add to the <u>pie</u> filling?
6. <u>Several</u> of the <u>birthday</u> candles wouldn't light.
7. <u>Neither</u> man could catch the <u>turkey</u>.
8. I made <u>that</u> <u>pie</u> all by myself.
9. <u>Several</u> friends took care of our <u>lawn</u> while we were away on vacation.
10. <u>Those</u> were the best <u>apple</u> dumplings I have ever eaten.

Mastery Test

Number your paper 1 to 10. Make two columns on your paper. Label the first column *adjectives* and the second column *adverbs*. Then in the proper column, write each adjective and adverb.

1. Old family pictures have always hung here.
2. Several heads of state met secretly in a European city.
3. The three sophomore runners performed very well.
4. This black wool coat is too large for me.
5. The fast-food restaurant is known for crispy chicken.
6. What issue of the sports magazine do you have?
7. The downstream current, rapid and rough, could easily overturn a small boat.
8. The midwestern part of the country was severely hit by tornadoes.
9. The new mayor will speak soon.
10. Credit for the win goes entirely to Roger.

Chapter

22 Other Parts of Speech

Diagnostic Test

Number your paper 1 to 10. Write each underlined word. Then, beside each word, write its part of speech: *noun, pronoun, verb, adjective, adverb, preposition, conjunction,* or *interjection*.

EXAMPLE That smell reminds me of ozone.
ANSWER *smell* = noun *of* = preposition

1. Those are the candles from my birthday cake.
2. Which dog jumped over the fence?
3. That plant flowers in the spring.
4. We put the geranium outside.
5. The spring dance for sophomores will be held during school hours.
6. For her birthday Karen gave Betsy a shell necklace from Florida.
7. Which are the geranium seeds?
8. Did you grow those beautiful flowers?
9. That unusual shell is not found outside the Gulf of Mexico area.
10. Don't come over after school today, because I'm sick.

Other Parts of Speech

This chapter will cover three parts of speech: prepositions, conjunctions, and interjections. *Prepositions* show relationships between words, *conjunctions* connect words, and *interjections* show strong feeling. In addition, the chapter will review all eight parts of speech.

Prepositions

If your brother asked you to get a book for him from the living room, you would save time if he told you whether he wanted the book on the couch or the one beside the couch. *On* and *beside* are *prepositions.* They each show a different relationship between the book and the couch.

Rule 22a A **preposition** is a word that shows the relationship between a noun or a pronoun and another word in the sentence.

Following are lists of common prepositions.

Prepositions

aboard	before	down	off	till
about	behind	during	on	to
above	below	except	onto	toward
across	beneath	for	opposite	under
after	beside	from	out	underneath
against	besides	in	outside	until
along	between	inside	over	up
among	beyond	into	past	upon
around	but ("except")	like	since	with
as	by	near	through	within
at	concerning	of	throughout	without

Compound Prepositions

according to	by means of	instead of
ahead of	in addition to	in view of
apart from	in back of	next to
aside from	in front of	on account of
as of	in place of	out of
because of	in spite of	prior to

Prepositional Phrases A preposition is always part of a group of words called a *prepositional phrase.* A prepositional phrase begins with a preposition. It ends with a noun or a pronoun called the *object of the preposition.* A prepositional phrase may also contain modifiers.

> **In the early evening,** we rode **to the lake.**
>
> He wouldn't go **near the barn or the stable.** [The words *barn* and *stable* form a compound object of a preposition.]

Preposition or Adverb? Some prepositions can also be adverbs. They are prepositions when they are part of a prepositional phrase. They are adverbs when they stand alone.

PREPOSITION Put the card ***inside* the box.**

ADVERB Put the card **inside.**

EXERCISE 1 *Finding Prepositional Phrases*

Write each prepositional phrase in the following paragraph.

Climbing down Mountains

The greatest mountain range, called the Dolphin Rise, lies under the sea! It extends from the Arctic to the Antarctic. At certain points the tops of the mountains rise out of the water. Some of these points are the Azores and the Canary Islands. In some places the deepest valleys between these mountains descend five miles below the surface of the ocean. Mount McKinley is the highest mountain in North America. If it were dropped into such a spot, it would be completely covered with water on account of the great depth.

EXERCISE 2 *Writing Sentences*

Write two sentences for each of the following words. In the first sentence, use the word as a preposition. In the second, use the word as an adverb. Label the use of each one.

1. by **2.** inside **3.** below **4.** around **5.** near

Application to Writing

Write an expository paragraph. Tell why you do or do not watch sports on TV. Be prepared to identify each prepositional phrase.

Integrating Language Skills

USING YOUR TEXT

Creative Writing (380–419)

Grammar: Creating Sentence Variety

The usual way to begin a sentence is with the subject. However, your writing will seem monotonous if every sentence has the same kind of beginning. Make your writing interesting by occasionally starting or ending a sentence with a prepositional phrase.

Checking Your Understanding Number your paper 1 to 10. Write a prepositional phrase that completes each of the following sentences. Then rewrite each sentence, placing the prepositional phrase first.

1. I bought some roses ________.
2. An old automobile had been left ________.
3. The faithful dog stayed ________.
4. We officially became members ________.
5. We were very tired ________.
6. You will find a computer software store ________.
7. Gloria found the books she wanted ________.
8. The miniature glider flew ________.
9. The exhausted tennis player sat ________.
10. The missing homework assignment was ________.

Writing a Tall Tale Think of any tall tales you know, such as stories about Paul Bunyan. A tall tale is usually about a person who is in some way bigger than life—a hero with remarkable powers. The tale is told tongue in cheek, as a humorous form of entertainment.

Create a tall-tale character. Brainstorm for several minutes about possible traits, or abilities, for him or her. Choose one trait from your ideas and write a cluster around it, suggesting possibilities for using that trait.

Now put your character into a modern setting and write the first draft of your original tall tale. Have the hero reveal his or her powers in some surprising and amusing ways. ***Application:*** As you revise your tall tale, create sentence variety by beginning a few sentences with a prepositional phrase. Then edit your story and write a final draft. With your teacher's permission, read your tall tale to the class.

Conjunctions

You have already worked with conjunctions throughout the previous chapters of this book. Each time you studied a compound subject or a compound verb, you saw a conjunction.

Rule 22b **A conjunction connects words or groups of words.**

In English there are three kinds of conjunctions. *Coordinating conjunctions* are single connecting words. *Correlative conjunctions* are pairs of connecting words. *Subordinating conjunctions* are covered in Chapter 25.

Conjunctions

COORDINATING			CORRELATIVE	
and	nor	yet	both/and	not only/but also
but	or		either/or	whether/or
for	so		neither/nor	

A pen **or** pencil will do. [connects nouns]

Let's sit **and** rest for a short while. [connects verbs]

That road is **not only** dusty **but also** bumpy. [connects adjectives]

I remembered the date, **but** I forgot the time. [connects sentences]

Note: Notice that a comma comes before a conjunction connecting two sentences.

EXERCISE 3 *Finding Conjunctions*

Write the coordinating or correlative conjunction in each sentence.

1. Snakes have neither ears nor vocal cords.
2. I wanted to go to the game, yet I knew I should study.
3. Bats are not blind, but their vision is extremely poor.
4. Please drive me either to the bus stop or to the mall.
5. Each day I jog two miles or do exercises.
6. The Australian walking fish occasionally leaves the water and climbs a tree for a snack of insects.

7. The lecture was not only informative but also interesting.
8. I'm not going with you, for I saw that movie yesterday.
9. Both Chicago and New York City rank among the 20 most populated cities in the world.
10. I don't like sweets, nor do I like fatty foods.

Interjections

Surprise, disbelief, joy, disappointment—these and other emotions or feelings are often expressed by *interjections.*

Rule 22c **An interjection is a word that expresses strong feeling or emotion.**

An interjection is separated from the rest of the sentence by an exclamation point or a comma.

Ouch! That stove is hot.
Oh, I can't believe it!
Well! That's finally over.
Great! I like that idea.

EXERCISE 4 *Writing Sentences*

Number your paper 1 to 5. Then write a sentence using each interjection.

1. Oops! **2.** Wow! **3.** Yikes! **4.** Aha! **5.** Ugh!

EXERCISE 5 *Cumulative Review*

Make three columns on your paper. Label the first column *prepositional phrases*, the second column *conjunctions*, and the third column *interjections*. Then, in the proper column, write each one.

Before His Time

Quick! Make a choice. Which would you prefer to be: a painter, sculptor, musician, poet, or philosopher? Leonardo da Vinci was not only all of these but also an inventor, a biologist, an astronomer, a geologist, and a mathematician. Da Vinci was born near Florence, Italy, in 1492. In his early thirties, he painted *The Last Supper.* Within a short period of time, he also painted the *Mona Lisa*, the most famous painting in the world. During his lifetime he was a recognized artist, yet his notebooks also contain sketches of fantastic inventions. There are drawings of an airplane, a helicopter, and a submarine. Yes! Leonardo da Vinci was centuries ahead of his time.

Parts of Speech Review

You know that a word can be used as more than one part of speech. The way a word is used in a sentence determines its part of speech. For example, the word *well* can be used as five different parts of speech.

NOUN	There's a **well** in my uncle's backyard.
VERB	Tears sometimes **well** up in his eyes when he talks about his dog's accident.
ADJECTIVE	Don't you feel **well** today?
ADVERB	Stir the pudding **well,** or it will scorch.
INTERJECTION	**Well!** You should have told me that before.

Before deciding which part of speech a particular word is, ask yourself, *What is this word doing in the sentence?* The following summary with questions should help you.

NOUN Is the word naming a person, a place, a thing, or an idea?

The **roses** were a **symbol** of his **love.**

PRONOUN Is the word taking the place of a noun?

They presented the trophies to **her** and **me.**

VERB Is the word showing action?

Timothy **is planting** some tomatoes.

Does the word link the subject with another word in the sentence?

In many areas today, cars **are** a necessity.

ADJECTIVE Is the word modifying a noun or a pronoun? Does it answer the question *What kind? Which one(s)? How many?* or *How much?*

The **two American** flags were **brand-new.**

These few were donated.

ADVERB Is the word modifying a verb, an adjective, or another adverb? Does it answer the question *How? When? Where?* or *To what extent?*

The **somewhat** awkward child
dances **quite well.**

PREPOSITION Is the word showing a relationship between a noun or a pronoun and another word in the sentence? Is it part of a phrase?

According to the report, everyone **in** our area is free **of** danger.

CONJUNCTION Is the word connecting words or groups of words?

Take **either** the bus **or** the train, **for** you have plenty of time.

INTERJECTION Is the word expressing strong feeling?

Oh! I forgot my homework.

Whew! We worked on the scenery for the play until midnight.

EXERCISE 6 *Determining Parts of Speech*

Number your paper 1 to 25. Write the underlined word in each sentence. Then, beside each word, write its part of speech: *noun, pronoun, verb, adjective, adverb, preposition, conjunction,* or *interjection.*

1. The stop sign was missing.
2. This milk is sour.
3. Most are torn.
4. Why did you stop?
5. How large is your stamp collection?
6. Who spilled the ink?
7. Stamp the price on the boxes.
8. No! Don't move.
9. Ink the stamp pad.
10. Empty the trash, for it is spilling over.
11. What is that?
12. I bought several.
13. Give her the reward.
14. It is on the top shelf.
15. Is that a French stamp?
16. Most cats have short hair.
17. Please sing for us.
18. Waves tossed the small sailboat about.
19. This is for you.
20. He will top that score.
21. They walked about the new mall.
22. Turn left.
23. Stop and talk.
24. He looked carefully at himself.
25. Oh! I'm late again.

Chapter 22

Review

A Identifying Prepositions, Conjunctions, and Interjections Number your paper 1 to 10. Make three columns on your paper. Label the first column *prepositions*, the second *conjunctions*, and the third *interjections*. Then in the proper column, write these parts of speech.

1. In an emergency, dial the number on the front of the telephone book.
2. The sailor taught me the difference between a square knot and a granny knot.
3. Yum! Both dinner and dessert were delicious.
4. In spite of my protests, we went to the movie anyway.
5. The fire not only warmed us but also dried our wet clothes.
6. By the end of the day, Kathy didn't feel well.
7. Never! I won't go to another horror movie with you.
8. Apart from the huge crowds, I enjoyed the concert at the Civic Center very much.
9. Neither Melvin nor Roger could stop the noise inside the computer.
10. I like hamburgers with ketchup but no mustard.

B Finding Prepositional Phrases Number your paper 1 to 10. Then write the prepositional phrases in each sentence.

1. Without its trunk, an elephant could not manage very well on its own.
2. A trunk is an extremely useful appendage for an elephant.
3. Because of its 40,000 muscles, a trunk is very flexible.
4. An elephant can wrap its trunk around a bunch of leaves and stuff them into its mouth.
5. On the other hand, the trunk can carefully pick a single piece of fruit from a tree.
6. In addition to these actions, an elephant protects itself against enemies with its trunk.
7. With one swing an elephant's trunk can eliminate a tiger.
8. The trunk also serves as a faucet or shower.
9. An elephant can even use its trunk like a snorkel in deep water.
10. It can swim under the water for hours by means of this natural snorkel.

C Determining Parts of Speech Number your paper 1 to 25. Write each underlined word. Then, beside each word, write its part of speech: *noun, pronoun, verb, adjective, adverb, preposition,* or *conjunction.*

(1)In 1823, Captain John Cleves Symmes appeared(2)before (3)Congress. He wanted money for a ship and a few (4)extremely brave scientists to make a trip to the North Pole. (5)You see, Symmes (6)believed that the earth was (7)hollow. There's more. Not only (8)his research but also his documents seemed to prove that the (9)earth was open at the poles. (10)He was convinced that the (11)inside of the earth (12)was "a warm, (13)rich land, stocked (14)generously with (15)thrifty vegetables and animals—if not men." Symmes's proposal was defeated on the (16)House floor. Years (17)later, however, he (18)won the support of President John Quincy Adams. (19)Unfortunately, before Captain Symmes could set sail, Andrew Jackson came (20)into office. He (21)immediately quashed Captain Symmes's plan. People continued to believe Symmes's (22)ideas until Robert Peary (23)reached the North Pole in 1909 (24)and found (25)no hole!

Mastery Test

Number your paper 1 to 10. Write each underlined word. Then, beside each word, write its part of speech: *noun, pronoun, verb, adjective, adverb, preposition, conjunction,* or *interjection.*

1. The bucket is in the well.
2. These are your tickets to the first performance of the play at the civic center.
3. We looked at each of the jackets in that catalog.
4. Which is the right answer?
5. That works well, even though it is old.
6. Great! I've wanted these sneakers for a long time.
7. The top line on the answer sheet is for your name.
8. Which gift should we open first?
9. Without any hesitation the great athlete dived in.
10. Each top in that store was quite expensive, so we went somewhere else.

Chapter

23 Complements

Diagnostic Test

Number your paper 1 to 10. Write each complement. Then label each one *direct object, indirect object, predicate nominative,* or *predicate adjective*.

EXAMPLE Show me your new watch.
ANSWER me—indirect object watch—direct object

1. A pair of houseflies can produce 6.5 billion descendants in one year.
2. The books in the basement smelled damp and musty.
3. The Flying Falcons became famous acrobats.
4. Will you lend me a dollar?
5. Sue will bring the pickles and the relish to the picnic on Saturday afternoon.
6. Stack the dishes in the sink.
7. The lemonade was too sour for me.
8. Dan has carved some realistic-looking birds and ducks for the arts and crafts show.
9. Leonard will be the leader of our group.
10. Mr. Wong gave Steve a recipe for egg rolls.

Complements

Subjects and verbs often need another word to complete the meaning of a sentence. This word is called a completer, or *complement.*

Ira lifts **weights.**
The dinner rolls were **warm.**

There are four major kinds of complements. *Direct objects* and *indirect objects* follow action verbs. *Predicate nominatives* and *predicate adjectives* follow linking verbs. Together, a subject, a verb, and a complement are called the *sentence base.*

Direct Objects

Direct objects complete the meaning of action verbs.

Rule 23a A **direct object** is a noun or a pronoun that receives the action of the verb.

To find a direct object, first find the subject and the action verb. Then ask the question *What?* or *Whom?* The answer to either of these questions will be a direct object.

d.o.
I will take **Tammy** to school today. [I will take whom? *Tammy* is the direct object.]

d.o. d.o.
I ordered a **book** but received a **calendar** instead. [I ordered what? *Book* is the direct object of *ordered.* I received what? *Calendar* is the direct object of *received.*]

d.o. d.o.
Dan painted the **table** and **chairs**. [Dan painted what? *Table* and *chairs* are both direct objects.]

Note: Two or more direct objects following the same verb are called a *compound direct object.*

A complement is never part of a prepositional phrase.

d.o.
Do you want **any** of these old hats? [You do want what? *Any* is the direct object. *Hats* cannot be the direct object, since it is part of the prepositional phrase *of these old hats.*]

EXERCISE 1 *Finding Direct Objects*

Number your paper 1 to 10. Then write each direct object.

Clever Creatures

1. Sea otters love all kinds of shellfish.
2. Lying on their backs, they hold the unopened shells on their chests and smash them with a rock.
3. Termites do not like the sun.
4. They often make paper umbrellas and shade their heads outside of the mound.
5. Chimpanzees chew the ends of sticks and make brushes.
6. With the brushes they dig termites and other insects out of the ground.
7. An elephant holds a stick in its trunk and scratches its back.
8. The Egyptian vulture takes a rock in its beak and opens an ostrich egg with it.
9. Bowerbirds often build fancy nests for themselves.
10. They will use shells, leaves, and even clothespins.

EXERCISE 2 *Writing Sentences*

Number your paper 1 to 5. Write a sentence that answers each of the following questions. Then underline each direct object.

1. What do you see to your right?
2. Whom did you recently visit?
3. What did you eat for breakfast this morning?
4. What courses are you taking this year?
5. What are you holding in your hand right now?

Indirect Objects

An indirect object can be included in a sentence that already contains a direct object.

Rule 23b An **indirect object** answers the questions *To or for whom?* or *To or for what?* after an action verb.

To find an indirect object, first find the direct object. Then ask, *To or for whom?* or *To or for what?* about each direct object. The answer to either of these questions will be an indirect object. Notice in the following examples that an indirect object comes before a direct object.

i.o. d.o.
Jennifer built **Mom** a **birdhouse**. [*Birdhouse* is the direct object. Jennifer built a birdhouse for whom? *Mom* is the indirect object.]

i.o. d.o.
Jerry gave his **car** a **name.** [*Name* is the direct object. Jerry gave a name to what? *Car* is the indirect object.]

i.o. i.o. d.o.
Mrs. Reynolds assigned **Jeff** and **me** a special **project.** [*Project* is the direct object. Mrs. Reynolds assigned a project to whom? *Jeff* and *me* are the *compound indirect object.*]

An indirect object cannot be part of a prepositional phrase.

i.o.
Read **Dad** the ad in the newspaper. [*Dad* is an indirect object. It comes before the direct object *ad* and is not part of a prepositional phrase.]

Read the ad in the newspaper to Dad. [*Dad* is *not* the indirect object because it follows the direct object and is part of the prepositional phrase *to Dad.*]

EXERCISE 3 *Finding Indirect Objects and Direct Objects*

Number your paper 1 to 15. Write each indirect object and each direct object. Then label each one *indirect object* or *direct object.*

1. Mr. Leary assigned Mary a report on the effects of smoking.
2. Mother promised us chicken for dinner.
3. Joseph sold four quarts of paint to Mr. Baum.
4. Don't give Muffin or Tiger a snack now.
5. The faculty awarded a special prize to Carmella.
6. Make me an offer for my old bicycle.
7. My cousins loaned Patty and me their tennis rackets.
8. Draw the directions for me on this paper.
9. Did Ben give you his club dues?
10. Mr. Norris sold Elizabeth and Tad his slide projector.
11. Some people have an extra rib.
12. The Harrisons bought Barbara a sterling silver bracelet.
13. Tell Bart and him the joke about the elephants.
14. City Bank gives free investment advice to all its customers.
15. The Manx cat has no external tail.

Predicate Nominatives

The types of complements that follow linking verbs are called *subject complements*. One of these subject complements is the predicate nominative.

Rule 23c **A predicate nominative is a noun or a pronoun that follows a linking verb and identifies, renames, or explains the subject.**

To find a predicate nominative, first find the subject and the linking verb. *(See pages 556 and 557 for lists of linking verbs.)* Then find the noun or the pronoun that follows the verb and identifies, renames, or explains the subject. This word will be a predicate nominative.

p.n.

Hannah will be our new **treasurer.** [treasurer = Hannah]

p.n. p.n.

The nominees for class president were **Burt** and **she**. [Burt and she = nominees. *Burt* and *she* are the *compound predicate nominative.*]

A predicate nominative, like other complements, cannot be part of a prepositional phrase.

p.n.

Yvonne is **one** of my best friends. [One = Yvonne. *Friends* is part of the prepositional phrase *of my best friends.*]

EXERCISE 4 *Finding Predicate Nominatives*

Number your paper 1 to 10. Then write the predicate nominatives in the following sentences.

1. The solution to the problem remains a mystery to me.
2. Andrew Johnson became president after Lincoln.
3. The sun is one of the smallest stars in our galaxy.
4. The speakers will be Dr. Thomas and Ms. Hensen.
5. Letters were their only means of communication.
6. Surprisingly, elephants are excellent swimmers.
7. Allen Konigsberg is the real name of Woody Allen.
8. Lady Jane Grey was queen of England for only nine days.
9. With luck the winners of the debate will be Hank and I.
10. The earth's crust is a layer of rock about 40 miles thick.

Predicate Adjectives

A predicate adjective is also a subject complement.

Rule 23d A **predicate adjective** is an adjective that follows a linking verb and modifies the subject.

To find a predicate adjective, first find the subject and the linking verb. Then find the adjective that follows the verb and describes the subject. This word will be a predicate adjective.

p.a.
The highway was very **icy.** [*Icy* describes the highway—*the icy highway.*]

p.a. p.a.
The peaches were **soft** and **fuzzy.** [*Soft* and *fuzzy* describe the peaches—*the soft, fuzzy peaches. Soft* and *fuzzy* are the two parts of a *compound predicate adjective.*]

Do not confuse a regular adjective with a predicate adjective. A predicate adjective follows the linking verb and describes the subject.

REGULAR ADJECTIVE	Lee is such a **cheerful** person.
PREDICATE ADJECTIVE	Lee is always **cheerful**.

EXERCISE 5 *Finding Predicate Adjectives*

Number your paper 1 to 10. Then write the predicate adjectives in the following sentences. If a sentence does not have a predicate adjective, write *none* after the number.

1. Most domestic cats' eyes are green.
2. Limes should be tart and tangy.
3. The fresh vegetables on the glass tray were a delicious appetizer.
4. Dame Margot Fonteyn became famous in ballet.
5. The steak was unusually tough and tasteless.
6. No two fingerprints are exactly alike.
7. Jupiter looked brilliant last night.
8. The hyena is a cowardly but efficient scavenger.
9. For some people a bee sting can be fatal.
10. Are cactus blossoms delicate and colorful?

EXERCISE 6 *Finding Subject Complements*

Number your paper 1 to 20. Write each subject complement. Then label it *predicate nominative* or *predicate adjective.*

1. A pirouette is a rapid turn on the toe or ball of the foot.
2. The Hawaiian pineapple was first a native of South America.
3. The South Pole is colder than the North Pole.
4. After hanging outside, these sheets smell fresh and clean.
5. e.e. cummings's poetry is unconventional.
6. The rainiest spot on Earth is Mount Waialeale in Hawaii.
7. Those with the best chance of winning are he and Eva.
8. Nails were extremely scarce in Colonial days.
9. A major in engineering remains a good choice for students.
10. From the plane the cars and trucks looked tiny.
11. Bud and Kevin have been good friends since third grade.
12. The life expectancy of a dollar bill is approximately 18 months.
13. After a winter in the mountains, the trapper looked pale and haggard.
14. Swans are exceptionally fast fliers and swimmers.
15. Whales are huge, powerful, and warm-blooded.
16. The "horns" of a rhinoceros are really hard projections of closely impacted hair.
17. Mary is president of the class and captain of the swim team.
18. Tahiti is fragrant with tropical flowers.
19. Texas was once an independent republic.
20. That old canoe doesn't look seaworthy.

EXERCISE 7 *Writing Sentences*

Number your paper 1 to 10. Complete each of the following groups of words by adding a subject complement. Then underline each complement and label it *predicate nominative* or *predicate adjective.*

EXAMPLE Albert Einstein was
POSSIBLE ANSWER Albert Einstein was <u>one</u> of the world's greatest scientists. predicate nominative

1. The old piano sounds
2. John F. Kennedy was
3. That automobile looks
4. Tammy's dog is
5. John Lennon was
6. Our country is
7. Margo seems
8. Life today is
9. The milk became
10. Football is

Application to Writing

Write a paragraph that describes what you see from a window in your home. Keep glancing out the window as you write. Include in your paragraph the things that are always there—such as a tree or house. Also include the particular people and things that happen to be there while you are writing. Be prepared to identify all the complements in your paragraph.

EXERCISE 8 Cumulative Review

Number your paper 1 to 20. Write each complement. Then label each one *direct object, indirect object, predicate nominative,* or *predicate adjective.*

Thomas Alva Edison

1. Thomas Edison was not popular at his school in Port Huron, Michigan, in 1854.
2. He was sick much of the time.
3. Sometimes his fellow students called names at him.
4. After a time his mother ended his formal education.
5. From then on she taught him lessons at home.
6. At age ten Tom read a science book completely.
7. Immediately afterward he built himself a chemical laboratory in the basement of his home.
8. At twelve Edison started his own business.
9. On a train that ran between Port Huron and Detroit, he sold passengers newspapers.
10. The work was hard and tiring.
11. Surprisingly, Tom still found time for other ventures.
12. He published his own one-page newspaper and sold it for three cents a copy.
13. He learned Morse code and took a job in a telegraph office.
14. The pay was twenty-five dollars a month.
15. Often he was idle and bored at work.
16. At these times he did chemical experiments.
17. One day an experiment exploded and destroyed the office.
18. Tom became an inventor at the age of sixteen.
19. His best-known inventions are the electric light and the phonograph.
20. Later in life Thomas Edison became a millionaire.

Language Integrating Skills

USING YOUR TEXT

Personal Essays (270–297)
Punctuation with Dialogue (805)

Grammar: Using Sentence Patterns

Surprisingly, all written sentences follow a few basic sentence patterns. Sentences can vary greatly because each element in a given pattern can be expanded differently. Following are the most common sentence patterns. Knowing them will help you plan your writing effectively.

PATTERN 1: S-V *(subject-verb)*

S V
Icebergs drifted.

S V
The large icebergs with their towering crags drifted into the shipping lanes.

PATTERN 2: S-V-O *(subject-verb-object)*

S V O
Grubs destroy grass.

S V O
Fat grubs often destroy the grass in our lawn.

PATTERN 3: S-V-I-O *(subject-verb-indirect object-direct object)*

S V I O
Grandmother sent me jewelry.

S V I O
My grandmother in Colorado recently sent me silver jewelry with turquoise stones.

PATTERN 4: S-V-N *(subject-verb-predicate nominative)*

S V N
Porpoises are performers.

S V N
The friendly porpoises in Marineland are popular performers.

PATTERN 5: S-V-A ***(subject-verb-predicate adjective)***

S V A
Dragonflies are harmless.

S V A
The fierce-looking dragonflies are actually harmless to people.

Checking Your Understanding Write the sentence pattern that each sentence follows.

1. The quarterback's abilities were obvious to everyone.
2. The animal with the longest life span is the giant tortoise.
3. Roger Tory Peterson wrote many books about nature.
4. The baseball team practices daily in the early afternoon.
5. The teacher promised Jerry some extra help after school.
6. Mr. Murphy assigned us a new chapter in our history books.
7. The capital of Puerto Rico is San Juan.
8. Mauna Loa in Hawaii is the world's most active volcano.
9. Mary L. Petermann is an outstanding American scientist.
10. A griffin resembles a cross between an eagle and a lion.
11. Dolphins are really whales.
12. The guests wished the couple a long and prosperous life.
13. Southern Colonial homes are famous for their stately columns.
14. Jim gladly accepted the prize of one hundred dollars.
15. The Adams family of Massachusetts gave their country two United States presidents.
16. Australia is the home of many unusual creatures.
17. You can have the last slice of the roast.
18. The brain is the most complex group of cells on Earth.
19. David loaned his brother his new catcher's mitt.
20. The ears of the African elephant are the largest in the world.

Writing a Personal Essay Suppose you awoke one morning speaking a language that no one around you understood. Write a short narrative relating one incident that might occur. Use your imagination—as well as brainstorming and clustering techniques—to include specific details of your experience. ***Application:*** As you revise your paragraph, make sure you have included different kinds of sentence patterns. Then edit your work, looking for misspelled words and incorrect punctuation before you write a final copy.

Diagraming Complements

All complements except the indirect object are diagramed on the baseline—along with the subject and the verb—because they are part of the sentence base.

Direct Objects A direct object is separated from the verb by a short vertical line. Notice in the second example that the conjunction connecting the parts of the compound direct object is placed on a broken line between them.

Our car gets good mileage.

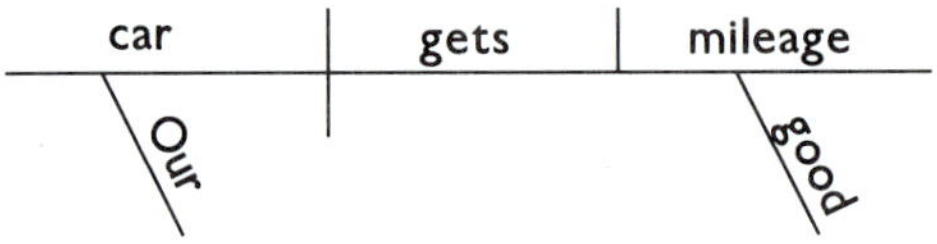

Tony served milk and sandwiches.

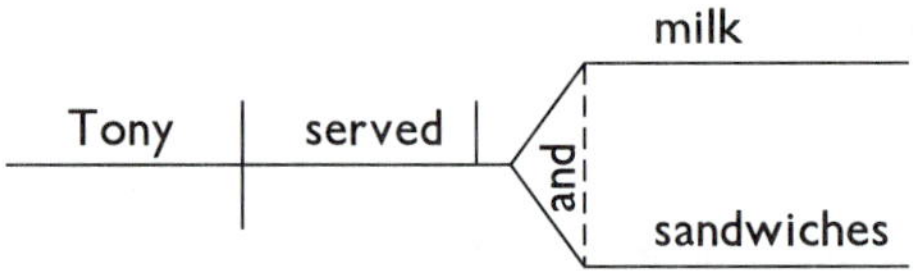

Indirect Objects An indirect object is diagramed on a horizontal line that is connected to the verb. In the second example, the conjunction connecting the parts of the compound indirect object is placed on a broken line between them.

Dad cooked me a hamburger.

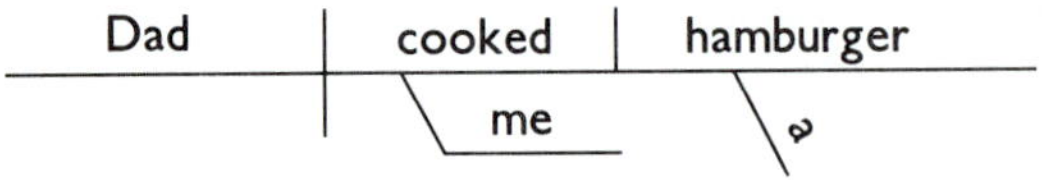

Teach Rob and me a few basic rules.

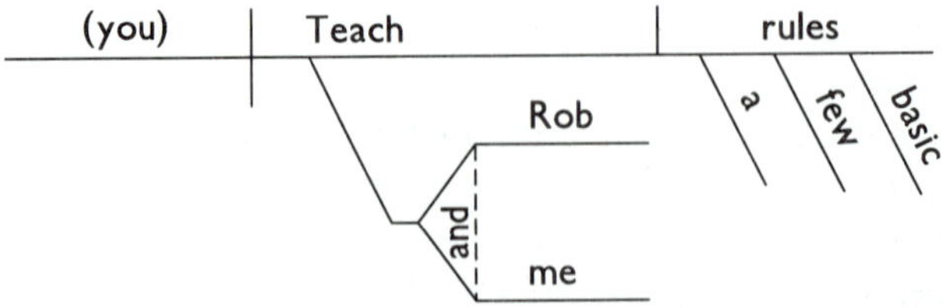

Subject Complements A predicate nominative and a predicate adjective are both diagramed on the baseline after the verb. They are separated from the verb by a slanted line that points back to the subject. The conjunction that joins a compound subject complement is placed on a broken line between the compound parts.

The first speaker was she.

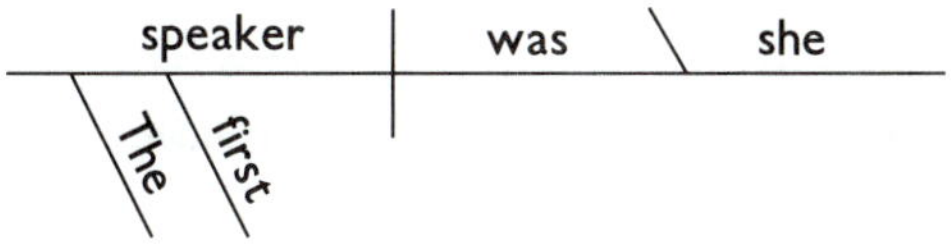

Her speech was very long.

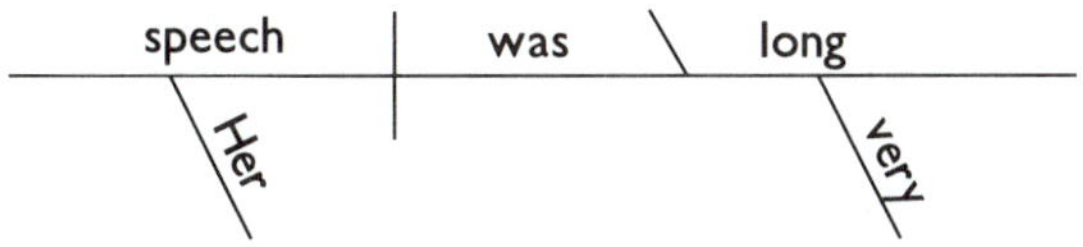

Our representatives will be Esther and Robert.

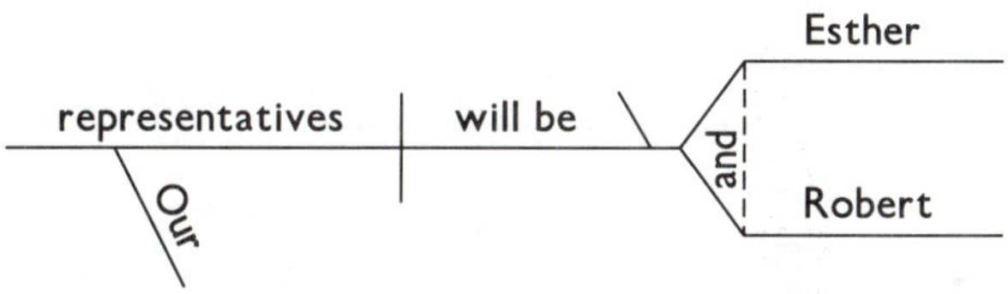

EXERCISE 9 *Diagraming Complements*

Diagram the following sentences or copy them. If you copy them, draw one line under each subject and two lines under each verb. Then label each complement *d.o.*, *i.o.*, *p.n.*, or *p.a.*

1. Shellfish are not fish.
2. Empty the trash.
3. Dad bought me a small computer.
4. The stallion was very high-strung.
5. Show Mike and him your new watch.
6. Opals are extremely beautiful but quite soft.
7. The coach gave the athletes new uniforms and sneakers.
8. Answer the letter soon.
9. Those birds are chickadees and sparrows.
10. The Australian outback is an extremely dry area.

Chapter 23

Review

A Identifying Complements

Number your paper 1 to 25. Write each complement. Then label each one *direct object, indirect object, predicate nominative,* or *predicate adjective.*

1. The birthstone for November is the topaz.
2. Forest fires destroy millions of acres of woodland every single year.
3. Stone walls and fences are favorite spots for poison ivy.
4. The penguins in the pool at the aquarium were comical but stately.
5. Jed showed my mother a picture of his new setter.
6. Tarantulas are dangerous to banana workers.
7. The mosquito is the carrier of many serious diseases.
8. In the legends about King Arthur and his court, knights gave their swords names.
9. Strawberries contain large amounts of vitamin C.
10. Four thousand years ago queens wore false beards as a sign of royalty.
11. Blood has many vitamins and minerals in it.
12. Rubber is one of the ingredients in bubble gum.
13. That centerpiece is colorful and attractive.
14. A woodpecker can pound its head against wood at the rate of 20 times a second.
15. Lettuce is the world's most popular green vegetable.
16. Dr. Staniford gave Les a prescription for his cough and fever.
17. This spinach seems unusually fresh and crisp.
18. An American typewriter has 43 keys and 84 symbols.
19. Tomás made Sally and me our favorite dinner.
20. Benjamin Franklin was the first head of the United States postal system.
21. A camel in Arabia once grew four humps.
22. Read the class your story about the latest space probe.
23. The stars were bright in the dark sky.
24. Before his term as president, Abraham Lincoln was a corporate lawyer.
25. In 1969, Neil Armstrong became the first person to walk on the moon.

B **Identifying Complements** Number your paper 1 to 10. Write each complement. Then label each one *direct object, indirect object, predicate nominative,* or *predicate adjective.*

1. In 1975, Margaret Thatcher became the leader of the British Conservative Party.
2. The Library of Congress celebrated its 175th birthday during that year.
3. The Steelers defeated the Vikings in the Super Bowl.
4. The New York Drama Critics gave the production *A Chorus Line* a prestigious award.
5. It was the best musical of 1975.
6. Andrei Sakharov was the winner of the Nobel Peace Prize.
7. Steven Spielberg gave the public a few scares with a new film, *Jaws.*
8. At 9.2 percent, the national unemployment rate was extremely high.
9. The postage for a first-class letter mailed in the United States became more expensive—25¢.
10. The United States began its bicentennial celebration with ceremonies at the Old North Church in Boston.

Mastery Test

Number your paper 1 to 10. Write each complement. Then label each one *direct object, indirect object, predicate nominative,* or *predicate adjective.*

1. The local newspaper will award a prize for the best editorial written in the past year.
2. Mrs. Maxwell showed us pictures of her vacation.
3. A cure for the common cold is still one of medicine's challenges.
4. The otters felt lively and frisky in the cool weather.
5. Have you ever thrown a boomerang?
6. The Indian costumes for the school pageant looked authentic.
7. The Grand Canyon is the largest gorge in the world.
8. The gym teacher assigned us 20 push-ups and 6 laps in the pool.
9. A cornered gorilla will give any opponent a hard fight.
10. We found shells along the beach.

Chapter 24

Phrases

Diagnostic Test

Number your paper 1 to 10. Write the phrase in each sentence. Then label each phrase *prepositional, appositive, participial, gerund,* or *infinitive.*

EXAMPLE I like walking in the rain.
ANSWER walking in the rain—gerund

1. Deserts cover nearly one third of our planet's land.
2. A beautiful silver cup engraved with the winner's name will be the prize.
3. Losing the first three games discouraged the team.
4. Mr. Murphy, an old friend, recently visited us.
5. I hope to visit Santa Fe this spring.
6. Those flowers, the colorful zinnias, will make a nice centerpiece.
7. Circling the dog, the fox maintained a safe distance.
8. We will use Japanese lanterns to light the patio.
9. Maria mentioned your being elected club secretary.
10. During the first inning, the pitcher had some trouble.

Prepositional Phrases

There are several kinds of phrases. In addition to *prepositional phrases* and *appositive phrases,* there is a group of phrases called *verbal phrases.* They include *participial phrases, gerund phrases,* and *infinitive phrases.* Although all phrases have unique characteristics, they do share some things in common.

Rule 24a **A phrase is a group of related words that function as a single part of speech. A phrase does not have a subject and a verb.**

All phrases have three things in common. First, all the words in a phrase work together as a single part of speech. Second, a phrase does not have a subject and a verb. Finally, all phrases can add variety and conciseness to your writing.

Prepositional phrases, which you learned about in Chapter 22, begin with a preposition. *(See page 575 for a list of common prepositions.)* A prepositional phrase ends with a noun or a pronoun called the *object of the preposition.* The prepositional phrases in the following examples are in heavy type.

The Babe Ruth Award **from the athletic club** will be presented **to Richard and Thomas.**

According to the announcement, lunch periods will be extended **by ten minutes.**

Look **for the cat** either **in the back of the sofa** or **underneath the bed.**

EXERCISE 1 *Finding Prepositional Phrases*

Number your paper 1 to 10. Then write the prepositional phrases in the following paragraph.

A New Sport

The only major sport with a totally American origin is basketball. It was invented in December 1891 by James Naismith. He was an instructor at the YMCA Training School in Springfield, Massachusetts. Because his students had continually complained about boring gym classes, he created a game with peach baskets and a soccer ball. In a few years, basketball was being played throughout the country. After World War I, it became a major international sport.

Adjective Phrases

Like a single adjective, a prepositional phrase can modify a noun or a pronoun. When it does, the phrase is called an *adjective phrase.*

SINGLE ADJECTIVES	**school** dance	**40-foot** depth
ADJECTIVE PHRASES	dance **at school**	depth **of 40 feet**

Rule 24b An **adjective phrase** is a prepositional phrase that is used to modify a noun or a pronoun.

A single adjective and an adjective phrase answer the same questions: *Which one(s)?* and *What kind?*

WHICH ONE(S)? Did you read the article **about our school?**

WHAT KIND? It was one chance **in a million.**

An adjective phrase usually modifies the noun or the pronoun directly in front of it. Occasionally that word will be the object of the preposition of a different phrase.

The house **across the street** has been painted a strange shade **of green.**

Some ***of* the tickets *to* the game** have been lost.

Two adjective phrases can modify the same noun or pronoun.

The loaf ***of* bread *on* the counter** should be used first.

EXERCISE 2 *Finding Adjective Phrases*

Number your paper 1 to 10. Write each adjective phrase. Then, beside each phrase, write the word it modifies.

1. That article about the Olympics was interesting.
2. The players on the tennis team have new uniforms.
3. Every puppy in the pet store has had its shot for distemper.
4. An elephant eats a quarter of a ton of food each day.
5. A single flash of lightning can carry a charge of 100 million volts.
6. The box underneath my bed contains winter clothes.

7. The string of pearls around her neck was a gift.
8. Mexican Hat is the name of a town in Utah.
9. The man opposite you is a teacher from our school.
10. The bowling record for the most strikes in a row is 29.

Adverb Phrases

A prepositional phrase can modify a verb, an adjective, or an adverb. When it does, it is an *adverb phrase*.

SINGLE ADVERBS	soared **upward**	looked **in**
ADVERB PHRASES	soared **into the sky**	looked **in the closet**

Rule 24c **An adverb phrase is a prepositional phrase that is used to modify a verb, an adjective, or an adverb.**

A single adverb and an adverb phrase answer the same questions: *Where? When? How? To what extent?* and *To what degree?* Adverb phrases also answer *Why?*

WHERE? Please drive me **to school.**

WHEN? **During dinner** the phone rang six times.

HOW? I drank the hot chocolate **with great pleasure.**

WHY? **Because of the heat,** we bought a fan.

Notice in the preceding examples that an adverb phrase does not always come next to the word it modifies.

When an adverb phrase modifies a verb, it modifies the whole verb phrase. Notice in the next example that more than one adverb phrase can modify the same verb.

At one o'clock the turkey should be placed **in the oven.**

Although most adverb phrases modify verbs, some modify adjectives and adverbs.

MODIFYING AN ADJECTIVE Susan was happy **with her grades.**

MODIFYING AN ADVERB His plane arrives late **in the evening.**

Punctuation with Adverb Phrases

If a short adverb phrase comes at the beginning of a sentence, usually no comma is needed. You should, however, place a comma after an adverb phrase of four or more words or after several introductory phrases.

NO COMMA **With their help** we finished early.
COMMA **According to the latest news release,** school will be closed tomorrow.

EXERCISE 3 *Finding Adverb Phrases*

Number your paper 1 to 10. Write each adverb phrase. Then, beside each phrase, write the word or words that the adverb phrase modifies.

1. The pony express existed for only 18 months.
2. Spaghetti was invented by the Chinese.
3. At any given moment, 2,000 thunderstorms may be brewing in the earth's atmosphere.
4. Throughout the evening the candidates presented their platforms to the audience.
5. Within the week your next book report must be given to Mr. Johnson.
6. During our history class, Anthony appeared nervous as the debate monitor.
7. In spite of the weather predictions, we will be driving to the lake.
8. After English class we put our books away and went to the cafeteria.
9. You should feed the cat late in the evening and refill its water bowl.
10. Before 1929, United States paper money was one third larger in size.

Application to Writing

Write a paragraph that gives directions from your home to another place in your city or town. The place should be one that you especially like. Be as specific as possible in your directions, mentioning landmarks where appropriate. Then be prepared to identify each adjective phrase and each adverb phrase.

EXERCISE 4 *Cumulative Review*

Number your paper 1 to 20. Write each prepositional phrase in the following paragraphs. Then label each one *adjective* or *adverb*.

Early Bikeways

A bicycle-riding craze hit the United States during the 1890's. On account of the enormous interest in bicycles, cities created miles of bikeways. In those days a bikeway was a narrow elevated road; it was similar to a boardwalk. Many of the routes wound their way through fields and between houses. Lamps were even installed for night riding.

One of the oldest bikeways in the nation stretched from Pasadena to Los Angeles. Riders could stop at bicycle rental and repair shops at each end of a bikeway. Stops were mandatory, however, at tollbooths along the routes. Many people think these bikeways were forerunners of the modern highway.

Appositives and Appositive Phrases

An *appositive* identifies or explains a noun or pronoun.

Rule 24d An **appositive** is a noun or pronoun that identifies or explains another noun or pronoun in the sentence.

An appositive usually follows the word it identifies or explains.

Raymond wrote his report on the Greek hero **Hercules.**

He mentioned his home state, **Nevada.**

An appositive usually includes modifiers. When it does, it is called an appositive phrase.

Rule 24e An **appositive phrase** is a group of words that contains an appositive and its modifiers.

Notice in the second example that an appositive phrase can include a prepositional phrase.

Her ring contained an emerald, **a sparkling green gem.**

The movie, **a thriller with special effects,** was exciting.

EXERCISE 5 Finding Appositives and Appositive Phrases

Number your paper 1 to 25. Write the appositive or the appositive phrase in each sentence. Then, beside each, write the word or words it identifies or explains.

1. People with arthritis often move to Arizona, a very dry state.
2. The Hoang typewriter, a device for typing Chinese, has 5,700 keys.
3. Beth was in the Shakespearean play *Romeo and Juliet.*
4. My sister Sharla is a professor at Memphis State.
5. Black Labradors, excellent retrievers, have webbed feet.
6. Everyone in the tenth grade must read the book *The Pearl.*
7. The capybara, the largest rodent in the world, weighs up to 160 pounds.
8. That is my favorite tree, a horse chestnut.
9. My birthday, March 26, falls on a Tuesday this year.
10. Salt, the most popular seasoning, has been used as money.
11. The wings of the ostrich, the largest living bird, are not equipped for flight.
12. Mercury, a silvery-white metal, is also called quicksilver.
13. I wrote a report about Robert Louis Stevenson, the author of *Treasure Island.*
14. For many years the largest city in the world was London, the capital of England.
15. Divers have raised the sunken submarine *Squalus.*
16. Grace Roberts, a Texan by birth, still speaks with an accent.
17. Soccer, the original version of football, was played in England as far back as A.D. 1100.
18. Have you met my neighbor Gretchen Mallory?
19. The oarfish, a long Australian fish, resembles the legendary sea serpent.
20. Hockey, by far the most popular team sport on ice, was enjoyed in some form as long ago as 1670.
21. Pumas, members of the cat family, jump as high as 23 feet.
22. Get permission from Coach Matthews, the baseball coach.
23. Millard Fillmore, the 13th president, belonged to the Whig Party.
24. We subscribe to the *Bee,* a newspaper in Fresno, California.
25. The Mile High Stadium, home of the Denver Broncos, seats over 75,000 fans.

Punctuation with Appositives and Appositive Phrases

If an appositive contains information essential to the meaning of a sentence, no punctuation is needed. Information is considered essential if it identifies a person, place, or thing. If an appositive or an appositive phrase contains nonessential information, a comma or commas should be used to separate it from the rest of the sentence. Information is nonessential if it can be removed without changing the basic meaning of the sentence.

ESSENTIAL The great stage actress **Sarah Bernhardt** had a wooden leg. [No commas are used because *Sarah Bernhardt* is needed to identify the actress.]

NONESSENTIAL Sarah Bernhardt, **the great stage actress,** had a wooden leg. [Commas are used because the appositive phrase could be removed without changing the meaning of the sentence.]

EXERCISE 6 *Writing Sentences*

Match a noun with an appropriate appositive phrase. Then write a sentence that includes both. Use commas where needed.

	NOUNS	APPOSITIVE PHRASE
1.	Alaska	a very popular name
2.	William	the largest state in the United States
3.	baseball	the brightest planet in the solar system
4.	Venus	the smallest continent in the world
5.	Australia	a national pastime in the United States

Application to Writing

Think of interesting people whom you have read about in history books. Decide which one you wish you had met and spoken with. Write a paragraph explaining who the person is—or was—and why you have chosen him or her. Include at least one appositive phrase. First, however, you may want to review some history or do some library research. Be prepared to identify any appositive phrases.

EXERCISE 7 Cumulative Review

Number your paper 1 to 20. Write the prepositional phrases and the appositive phrases in the following sentences. Then label how each one is used—*adjective, adverb,* or *appositive.*

Auto Info

1. The French Panhard, one of the first practical gasoline-powered cars, was designed in 1894.
2. In 1898, the total number of existing automobiles was only 50.
3. A Ford Model T sold for $295 in 1923.
4. In the 1970's, the most popular make of American car was the Chevrolet.
5. The total number of auto registrations in the United States is nearly 110 million.
6. Benz and Daimler, two German engineers, built the first gas-driven car in the 1800's.
7. Le Mans, a city in France, is known for its automobile races.
8. Formal regulation of motor-vehicle traffic was first instituted in New York City in 1903.
9. The tachometer, an instrument in some cars, shows the number of wheel revolutions per minute.
10. The exhaust from a motor vehicle consists mainly of carbon monoxide.
11. Because of the slow speed of the first automobiles, manufacturers saw no reason for a windshield.
12. Approximately one person in every 14,500 now owns a car in China.
13. The Duryea brothers, builders of the first American gasoline-powered car, had perfected their machine by 1895.
14. The B. F. Goodrich Company provided the first road signs for motorists.
15. For almost a century, the Rolls-Royce has been considered a symbol of luxury and wealth.
16. The average American car consumes 563 gallons of gasoline in a single year.
17. By the early 1900's, over 100 automobiles were reportedly on Massachusetts roads.
18. Before Henry Ford's assembly line, all cars were made by hand.
19. The Buick, the first General Motors car, was actually built by David Buick, a plumber.
20. Within twenty years, many people may own solar-powered cars.

Verbals and Verbal Phrases

A *verbal* is a unique word because it is a verb form that is used as some other part of speech. A verbal can be used alone, or it can be combined with modifiers or complements to form a *verbal phrase*. Verbals are part of your daily conversation. They add interest to your writing also. The three kinds of verbals are *participles, gerunds,* and *infinitives*.

Participles

When weather forecasters talk about *rising* tides or *howling* winds, they are using participles, one kind of verbal.

Rule 24f A **participle** is a verb form that is used as an adjective.

Used like an adjective, a participle modifies a noun or a pronoun. To find a participle, simply ask the adjective-questions *Which one(s)?* and *What kind?* A verb form that answers one of these questions and describes a noun or a pronoun will be a participle. The participles in the following examples are in heavy type. An arrow points to the word each participle modifies.

The **winning** team shook hands with the **defeated** team.

The **blazing** sun melted the **frozen** pond.

There are two kinds of participles. *Present participles* end in *-ing*. *Past participles* often end in *-ed,* but they can also have irregular endings such as *-n, -t,* or *-en*.

PRESENT PARTICIPLES	clinging, running, sinking, winding
PAST PARTICIPLES	reserved, buried, worn, bent, broken

Since a participle is a verb form, it is sometimes mistaken for the main verb of a sentence. There will always be a helping verb with the participle if it is used as the main verb.

PARTICIPLE	Tim carefully repaired his **torn** jacket.
VERB	He **had torn** his jacket in several places.

EXERCISE 8 *Finding Participles*

Write each participle. Then write the word it modifies.

1. Dark clouds warned of an approaching storm.
2. The number on the winning ticket is 652.
3. No one could find the hidden passageway.
4. The bent bicycle wheel could not be repaired.
5. Bette Davis used to be called a living legend.
6. Handle that cracked vase with care.
7. The decorated room was a lovely setting for the party.
8. The frozen dinner was still cold in the middle.
9. On the other end of the wire was a taped message.
10. Karen has a very worried expression on her face.

Participial Phrases

As a verb form, a participle can have modifiers and complements. Together these words form a participial phrase.

Rule 24g **A participial phrase is a participle with its modifiers and complements—all working together as an adjective.**

The following examples show variations of the participial phrase.

PARTICIPLE WITH AN ADVERB	**Purring softly,** the cat seemed content.
PARTICIPLE WITH A PREPOSITIONAL PHRASE	The instructions, **written in French,** were impossible for me to read.
PARTICIPLE WITH A COMPLEMENT	Every runner **winning a race** will receive a medal.

The participles *being* and *having* may be followed by a past participle.

Having read the story before, I just skimmed it.

EXERCISE 9 *Finding Participial Phrases*

Write each participial phrase. Then write the word it modifies.

1. The heaviest dog was a Saint Bernard weighing 295 pounds.

2. The country of Tonga issued a stamp shaped like a banana.
3. Insulin used for treatment of diabetes is taken from pigs and cows.
4. Introduced in 1938, nylon was used only for stockings.
5. Having trimmed the hedge, I began to mow the lawn.
6. That fabric, woven by my aunt, will be used for a coat.
7. In the first King Kong movie, made in 1933, the monster was really a model 18 inches high.
8. The letter used most in the English language is *e*.
9. Having packed our suitcases, we were ready to go.
10. An adult sitting in a relaxed position inhales about one pint of air with every breath.
11. Dates grown in the oases of the Sahara Desert are among the best.
12. Requiring heavy rainfall, tea does not grow very well in dry regions.
13. Paper money is a Chinese invention dating from the seventeenth century.
14. He found the articles packed with information.
15. The oldest tennis court, built in 1496, can be found in Paris.
16. Scampering off the field, the puppy escaped with the ball.
17. Clam chowder was invented by a group of hungry sailors shipwrecked off the coast of Maine.
18. That jacket, given to me last winter, still fits.
19. Having read the sports section, I headed for school.
20. Compact disks, totaling $2.4 million in sales in 1984, reached $33.4 million just four years later.

Punctuation with Participial Phrases

Always place a comma after an introductory participial phrase. If the information in an internal phrase is essential, no commas are needed. Information is essential if it identifies a person, place, or thing. If the information in an internal phrase is nonessential, commas are used to separate it from the rest of the sentence. A nonessential phrase contains information that could be removed without changing the basic meaning of the sentence.

ESSENTIAL — The person **talking to the coach** is my dad. [No commas are used because the phrase is needed to identify the person.]

NONESSENTIAL — Pete Jons, **talking to the coach,** is my friend. [Commas are needed because the phrase could be removed from the sentence.]

EXERCISE 10 *Writing Sentences*

Write two sentences for each word. The first should use the word as a verb. The second should use the same word as a participle in a participial phrase. Use punctuation correctly where needed.

EXAMPLE frozen

POSSIBLE ANSWER These beans were frozen last summer.
These beans, frozen last summer, will add extra fiber to the stew.

1. folding
2. buzzing
3. found
4. connecting
5. cracked
6. hidden
7. paid
8. glancing
9. sinking
10. painted

Gerunds

A gerund is another kind of verbal. Like a present participle, a gerund ends in *-ing*. Unlike a participle, however, a gerund is used as a noun, not as an adjective.

GERUND **Talking** is not allowed in study hall. [*Talking* is used as a noun—the subject of the sentence.]

PARTICIPLE The **talking** parrot amused everyone. [*Talking* is used as an adjective to describe *parrot*.]

Rule 24h A **gerund** is a verb form that is used as a noun.

A gerund can be used in all the ways in which a noun can be used.

SUBJECT **Pointing** is impolite.

DIRECT OBJECT Pamela likes **skating.**

INDIRECT OBJECT She gives her **running** one hour each day.

OBJECT OF A PREPOSITION My friend went a whole day without **speaking.**

PREDICATE NOMINATIVE This year my favorite winter sport was **skiing** at Loon Mountain.

APPOSITIVE Tim has a new major, **engineering.**

EXERCISE 11 *Finding Gerunds*

Number your paper 1 to 10. Write the gerund in each sentence. Then use one of the following abbreviations to label how each one is used.

subject = *subj.*	object of a preposition = *o.p.*
direct object = *d.o.*	predicate nominative = *p.n.*
indirect object = *i.o.*	appositive = *appos.*

1. Do you enjoy traveling?
2. Dancing was the highlight of the evening.
3. Lessons in weaving will be given on Tuesdays.
4. His favorite pastime is fishing.
5. Sarah signed up for swimming.
6. Practicing is very important to a successful team.
7. They gave rehearsing all of their free time.
8. Wipe your feet before entering.
9. She has a great talent, acting.
10. Sailing is my favorite sport.

Gerund Phrases

Gerunds, like participles, can be combined with modifiers and complements. Together the words form a gerund phrase.

Rule 24i A **gerund phrase** is a gerund with its modifiers and complements—all working together as a noun.

The following examples show some variations of the gerund phrase.

GERUND WITH AN ADVERB	**Traveling inexpensively** is a necessity for them.
GERUND WITH A PREPOSITIONAL PHRASE	Brian surprised us by **visiting for a week.**
GERUND WITH A COMPLEMENT	**Painting landscapes** is Rebecca's specialty.

Note: The possessive form of a noun or a pronoun is used before a gerund and is considered part of the phrase.

***Paul's* winning the tennis tournament** was a surprise.
They encouraged ***his* studying chemistry.**

EXERCISE 12 *Finding Gerund Phrases*

Number your paper 1 to 10. Write the gerund phrase in each sentence. Then underline each gerund.

1. Filling out a job application takes a long time.
2. Credit for introducing tennis to the United States is usually given to Mary Ewing Outerbridge.
3. Goldrenrod has been falsely accused of causing hay fever.
4. We appreciated Mr. Morrison's judging the art contest.
5. Until 1912, women were barred from participating in Olympic events.
6. Keith has a new goal, writing programs for his computer.
7. Landing a jet plane on the deck of an aircraft carrier is one of the most difficult maneuvers in aviation.
8. My weekend job is parking cars at a restaurant.
9. After Thanksgiving I like eating leftover turkey.
10. A grasshopper is capable of jumping a distance of two feet.

EXERCISE 13 *Determining the Use of Gerund Phrases*

Number your paper 1 to 15. Write the gerund phrase in each sentence. Then use the following abbreviations to label how each one is used.

subject = *subj.*
direct object = *d.o.*
object of a preposition = *o.p.*
predicate nominative = *p.n.*
appositive = *appos.*

1. A flea is capable of jumping 13 inches in a single leap.
2. I enjoy collecting old coins.
3. Using solar energy is one answer to fuel conservation.
4. Your next chore is taking out the trash.
5. Most snakes can go a year without eating anything.
6. Flying in a helicopter is very noisy.
7. I don't like going to the movies by myself.
8. The highlight of the party was watching the magician.
9. My uncle enjoys a different sport, hunting animals with a camera.
10. Dad was surprised at my entering the poetry contest.
11. For winning the contest, you get a free trip to Paris.
12. Your assignment is hanging posters in the mall.
13. The United States began using standard time in 1883.
14. We accomplished our goal, enlisting 100 parents as volunteers.
15. Painting the White House takes over 750 gallons of paint.

EXERCISE 14 *Writing Sentences*

Write two sentences for each of the following words. The first sentence should use the word as a gerund. The second sentence should use the same word as a participle. Use punctuation correctly where needed.

EXAMPLE broiling
POSSIBLE ANSWER Broiling meat is better than frying meat.
The meat broiling in the oven will be ready soon.

1. skiing
2. looking
3. wrestling
4. losing
5. debating
6. reading

Infinitives

The infinitive is the third kind of verbal. It is different in form from the other verbals because it usually begins with the word *to*. Unlike other verbals, though, it is used as more than one part of speech.

Rule 24j An **infinitive** is a verb form that usually begins with *to*. It is used as a noun, an adjective, or an adverb.

The following sentences show some of the ways in which an infinitive can be used.

NOUN **To err** is human. [subject]
Everyone should learn **to cook**. [direct object]

ADJECTIVE This year Danvers is the team **to beat.** [*To beat* modifies the noun *team*.]

ADVERB Chimpanzees are quick **to learn.** [*To learn* modifies the adjective *quick*.]

Because an infinitive begins with the word *to*, it is sometimes confused with a prepositional phrase. An infinitive ends with a verb form, but a prepositional phrase ends with a noun or a pronoun.

INFINITIVE This will be expensive **to repair.** [ends with a verb form]

PREPOSITIONAL PHRASE You should take this **to a repair shop.** [ends with a noun or pronoun]

EXERCISE 15 *Finding Infinitives*

Number your paper 1 to 10. Write the infinitive in each sentence. Then label how each one is used—*noun, adjective,* or *adverb.*

1. Those big, red, juicy strawberries are the ones to freeze for the winter.
2. The purpose of the story about Smokey the Bear was to instruct.
3. This weekend Kari plans to study.
4. Carnegie Hall, which is located in New York City, has a reputation to maintain.
5. That game is hard to play.
6. At our stable, the best horse to ride is Nice Boy because he is gentle and calm.
7. Pilar's desire to travel is strong.
8. Do you have to leave?
9. Human hair is almost impossible to destroy.
10. At an early age, children can learn to swim.

Infinitive Phrases

Like other verbals infinitives can be combined with modifiers and complements to form an infinitive phrase.

Rule 24k An **infinitive phrase** is an infinitive with its modifiers and complements—all working together as a noun, an adjective, or an adverb.

The following sentences show some of the variations of the infinitive phrase.

INFINITIVE WITH AN ADVERB	Everyone on the committee promises **to work hard.**
INFINITIVE WITH A PREPOSITIONAL PHRASE	**To win at chess** requires concentration and patience.
INFINITIVE WITH A COMPLEMENT	It's fun **to try different foods** in new restaurants.

Note: *To* is sometimes omitted when an infinitive follows such verbs as *dare, feel, hear, help, let, make, need, see,* or *watch.*

Will you help **collect** old newspapers? [to collect]

EXERCISE 16 *Finding Infinitive Phrases*

Write the infinitive phrase in each sentence. Then underline each infinitive. Remember that *to* is sometimes omitted.

1. As a reporter she had to verify his story.
2. It took da Vinci about five years to complete the *Mona Lisa*.
3. Snakes do not seem to care for one another's company.
4. Did you feel the room vibrate slightly?
5. Volcanic ash has been known to remain hot for nearly 100 years.
6. From the balcony we were unable to hear the actors.
7. To escape its enemies, the flying fish leaps out of the water.
8. A baseball can be made to curve six and a half inches from its original course.
9. It was very thoughtful of you to send me those flowers.
10. A snake is unable to close its eyes.

EXERCISE 17 *Determining the Use of Infinitive Phrases*

Number your paper 1 to 10. Write the infinitive phrase in each sentence. Then label how it is used—*noun, adjective,* or *adverb.*

1. We had two hours to finish the test.
2. I decided to serve tacos for dinner.
3. We plan to ride down the rapids of the Colorado River.
4. No one would dare begin without him.
5. To save time, we took the subway from the stadium.
6. To repair watches takes patience and skill.
7. Which is the best computer to buy for a teenager?
8. The lens of the eye continues to grow throughout a person's life.
9. His secret ambition was to climb Mount Everest.
10. He studied to become a surgical nurse.

Application to Writing

Write a short essay that explains why you would or would not like to be a comedian. What would be the advantages or the disadvantages? Include as many specific examples as possible. Also incorporate at least one participial phrase, one gerund phrase, and one infinitive phrase and be prepared to identify each one.

EXERCISE 18 *Cumulative Review*

Number your paper 1 to 15. Write each verbal phrase in the following paragraphs. Then label each one *participial, gerund,* or *infinitive.*

Why the Wall?

The Great Wall of China, twisting and turning for over 2,500 miles, is the only structure seen from the moon. Covering more than one twentieth of the earth's circumference, the Great Wall stretches over mountains, deserts, and plains. In the third century B.C., the first emperor of China began to build the Wall. However, the rulers during the Ming Dynasty (1368–1644) are responsible for constructing the major portion of the Wall. Built over a period of 1,700 years, the Great Wall is unquestionably an incredible feat. For example, the stone in the Wall is enough to construct an eight-foot wall encircling the globe at the equator.

Determining why the Great Wall was built is not easy. To defend China against hostile tribes to the north is one theory. This, however, may not have been the reason for creating the Wall. Many times armies were successful in breaching the Wall. To defend the limits of Chinese authority is a second theory. The Wall, in fact, did serve as a boundary between the Orient and the rest of the world for hundreds of years. To provide employment is still another theory. Of course, the real reason will probably never be known. Nevertheless, the Great Wall stands as one of the greatest—and certainly the largest—feats accomplished by humans.

Misplaced and Dangling Modifiers

A phrase that is used as a modifier should be placed as close as possible to the word it modifies. When a phrase is placed far away from the word it modifies, it often becomes a *misplaced modifier.*

MISPLACED Rick saw two owls camping on Mount Greylock.

CORRECTED **Camping on Mount Greylock,** Rick saw two owls.

Another problem arises when a phrase that is being used as a modifier lacks a word to modify. This kind of phrase is called a *dangling modifier.*

DANGLING	To build a good doghouse, plans are helpful.
CORRECTED	**To build a good doghouse,** you will need plans.

EXERCISE 19 *Correcting Misplaced and Dangling Modifiers*

Number your paper 1 to 20. Write the following sentences, correcting the error in each one. To do this, follow one of these methods: (1) Place a phrase closer to the word it modifies or (2) add words and change the sentence around so that the phrase has a noun or a pronoun to modify. Use punctuation correctly where needed.

1. We saw a large, graceful willow tree strolling around the lake.
2. We had our first glimpse of the Statue of Liberty sailing into New York Harbor.
3. Hanging on the wall, we saw a huge cartoonlike drawing of a cat.
4. That's my mother's van parked in the driveway with the red upholstery.
5. Clipping the hedge, a baby sparrow fell from the tree.
6. Flying at the end of a heavy cord, we saw a box kite.
7. Todd kept his eye on the big bass drum playing the bugle in the parade.
8. Mr. Como told his wife that he had had a good flight from a telephone booth.
9. To remove the wasps' nest from the attic, extreme care must be taken.
10. We saw a flock of geese riding along the turnpike.
11. Hearing the harsh command to halt, the soldier's legs were frozen in his tracks.
12. We could see Mount Rainier landing at the Seattle airport.
13. When playing chess, concentration is very important.
14. I could see lightning flashing from my room on the top floor.
15. Crying with pain, several splinters were removed from his hand.
16. We saw John hit a long home run from the bleachers.
17. Having been planted in poor soil, we moved the rosebushes nearer the fence.
18. While tuning up his car, my brother's fan belt seemed warm.
19. I saw a pheasant riding my ten-speed bicycle through the park.
20. After installing a skylight, the room looked not only brighter but also larger.

Integrating Language Skills

USING YOUR TEXT

Clustering (22)
Expository Essays (196–233)

Grammar: Combining Sentences

You can often achieve variety and conciseness in your writing by using phrases to combine two sentences.

TWO SENTENCES	We visited San Francisco. We stayed there for two weeks.
ONE SENTENCE	We visited San Francisco **for two weeks.** [prepositional phrase]
TWO SENTENCES	The column was written by Ellen Goodman. She is a syndicated columnist.
ONE SENTENCE	The column was written by Ellen Goodman, **a syndicated columnist.** [appositive phrase]
TWO SENTENCES	The old sea captain was seated in his boat. He was weaving a fishnet.
ONE SENTENCE	The old sea captain, **weaving a fishnet,** was seated in his boat. [participial phrase]
TWO SENTENCES	David earns money on weekends. He mows his neighbors' lawns.
ONE SENTENCE	David earns money on weekends by **mowing his neighbors' lawns.** [gerund phrase]
TWO SENTENCES	We need Willard's help. He could fix the computer.
ONE SENTENCE	We need Willard's help **to fix the computer.** [infinitive phrase]

Checking Your Understanding Combine each pair of sentences by expressing the information in one of the sentences in a phrase. Remember to use commas where needed.

1. Buzzard hawks are large birds. They have long, broad wings.
2. Epcot Center was built near Walt Disney World. It is a wonderful place to visit.
3. Meg started the campfire. She rubbed two stones together.

4. Tallahassee is the capital of Florida. It is located in the northern part of the state.
5. In ancient times black pepper was a luxury. It was valued greatly for its medicinal qualities.
6. We should get the score of last night's game. Ask Kevin.
7. We went for a swim. We went to Brockton Beach.
8. Five counties in Texas are larger than Rhode Island. Rhode Island is the smallest state.
9. We sat on the shore of the inlet. We watched the sailboats.
10. I prepared for the final exam. I studied my unit tests.
11. The Battle of Saratoga saved the American Revolution. It was fought in 1777.
12. Polar bears have very thick fur coats. They never get cold in the most frigid waters.
13. We lost the first three games of the season. Then we routed Springfield 42 to 6.
14. We made the shack weatherproof. We stuffed the cracks with old newspapers.
15. The Eiffel Tower was built in 1889. It is 984 feet high.
16. Dad shoveled snow for four hours. He decided to buy a snow-blower as soon as he could.
17. Scrappy wagged his tail eagerly. He watched Donna open the box of dog biscuits.
18. Frank Parsons works at the hardware store on weekends. This earns him money for college.
19. Route 1 is a picturesque but busy highway. It runs from Maine all the way to Florida.
20. The child ran into the house. The child was frightened by the sudden appearance of a dog.

Writing an Expository Essay A local radio station is holding an essay contest. The prize is a family trip to Orlando, Florida, home of many family attractions. Contest entries must be essays, three or more paragraphs long, explaining what the typical teenager is like today.

Gather ideas by making a cluster around the word *teenager.* Record likes and dislikes, such as clothes, entertainment, and "in" expressions. As you write your first draft, include details and examples to support what you say. ***Application:*** Revise the essay, using phrases to begin or combine some sentences. As you edit, check for correct punctuation; then proofread the essay before writing the final draft.

Diagraming Phrases

How a phrase is used in a sentence will determine how and where it is diagramed.

Prepositional Phrases An adjective phrase or an adverb phrase is always connected to the word it modifies. The preposition is placed on a connecting slanted line. The object of a preposition is placed on a horizontal line that is attached to the slanted line.

A loud round of applause came from the stands on the left.

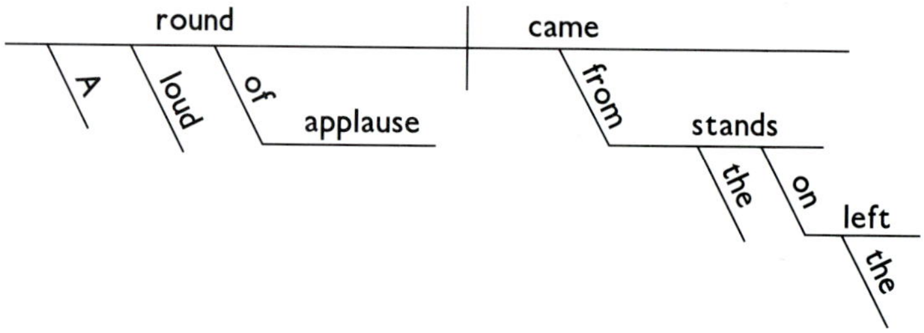

Appositive Phrases An appositive is diagramed in parentheses next to the word it identifies or explains.

I spoke with Mr. Monroe, the director of personnel.

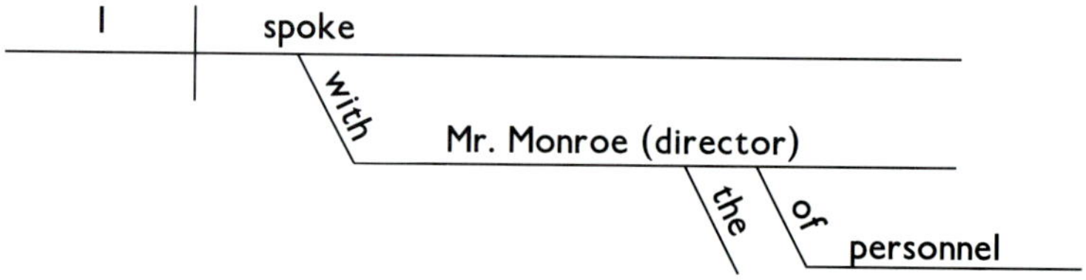

Participial Phrases A participial phrase is diagramed under the word it modifies. Participles are written in a curve.

Hiding in a bush, the rabbit was silent.

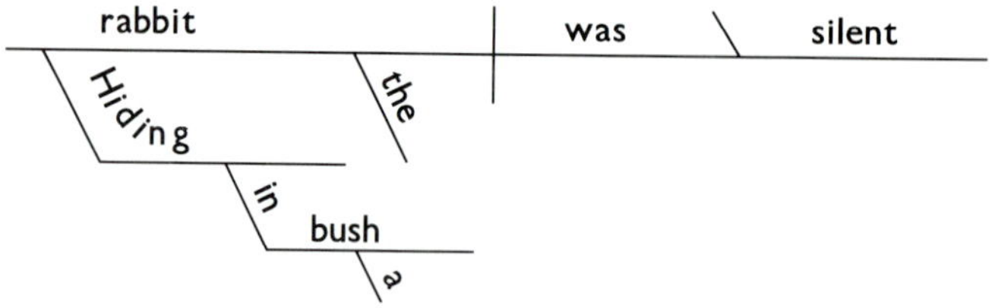

Gerund Phrases As a noun a gerund phrase can be diagramed in many places. In the diagram the gerund phrase is used as a direct object and diagramed on a pedestal. Notice that a complement is part of the gerund phrase.

Talbot enjoys discussing politics with everyone.

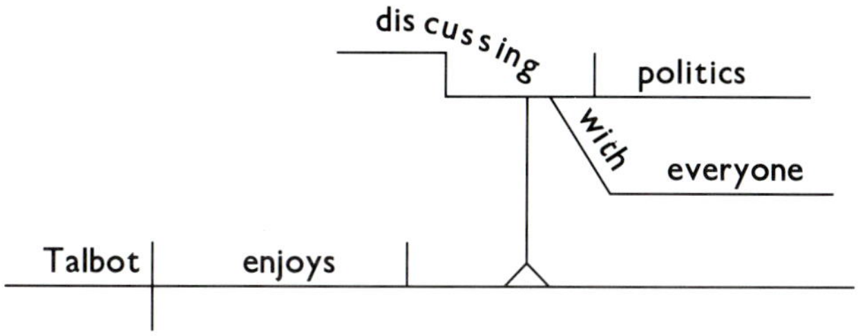

Infinitive Phrases An infinitive phrase that is used as an adjective or an adverb is diagramed like a prepositional phrase.

A foreign language can be hard to learn.

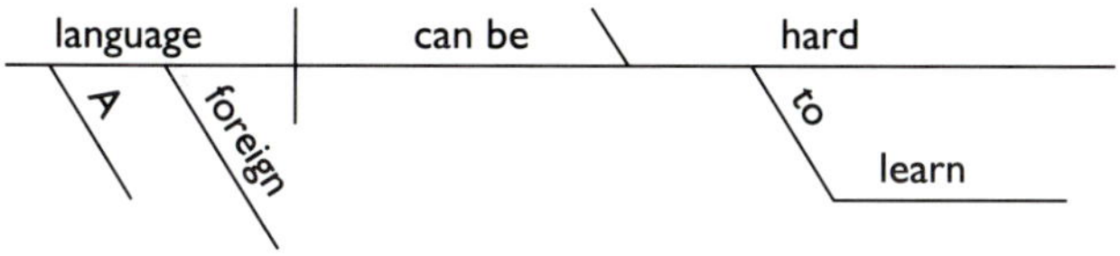

EXERCISE 20 *Diagraming Phrases*

Diagram the following sentences or copy them. If you copy them, draw one line under each subject and two lines under each verb. Put parentheses around each phrase. Then label each phrase *prepositional, appositive, participial, gerund,* or *infinitive.*

1. We enjoy swimming in the lake.
2. I will call you at six o'clock.
3. Daryl hopes to become the manager of the store.
4. I gave Lily a book about Broadway plays.
5. The huge pyramids built by the Aztecs are incredible monuments.
6. I wrote to Barbara, my oldest sister.
7. Do you dare dive from the high board?
8. The spot on his jacket can be removed without damage.
9. Nutritionists recommend eating a variety of foods.
10. The elm tree growing in our yard was planted by my grandfather.

Chapter 24

Review

A Identifying Phrases

A **Identifying Phrases** Number your paper 1 to 20. Write the phrases in the following sentences. Then label each one *prepositional, appositive, participial, gerund,* or *infinitive*.

1. Porpoises have been trained to play basketball.
2. I will be going to the library soon.
3. Built of mud, the oldest house in the United States stands in New Mexico.
4. Saccharin, one type of artificial sweetener, is a coal-tar product.
5. The Caseys told us about their moving to Indiana.
6. Camping in the mountains is my idea of a really great vacation.
7. Twenty-four percent of California is desert.
8. Tigers, the ancestors of present-day Asian mammals, once roamed the North American plains.
9. No one over six feet can qualify to become an astronaut.
10. Having read the chapter, Bernie answered the questions at the end.
11. I just heard about your winning a free, week-long trip to Washington, D.C.!
12. The fruit with the greatest number of calories is the delicious, rich avocado.
13. Almost everyone I know likes getting out of school early.
14. Are you going to refinish the surface of that old table?
15. Jupiter, the largest planet in the solar system, has the shortest day of all the planets.
16. According to the Nielsen ratings, the average American spends 49 hours a week in front of the TV set.
17. Arriving before anyone else, Yvette set up the projector in the auditorium.
18. Being elected to the National Baseball Hall of Fame establishes a player as a baseball immortal.
19. The koala, a marsupial of Australia, eats only eucalyptus leaves.
20. Moving cautiously under heavy packs, the mules slowly picked their way up the rocky mountain path.

B **Identifying Phrases** Number your paper 1 to 25. Write the phrases in the following paragraphs. Then label each one *prepositional, appositive, participial, gerund,* or *infinitive.*

Dinosaurs have not been seen for approximately 65 million years. To understand the animals' disappearance, scientists have turned to geology, the study of rocks. Credit for offering one interesting theory goes to Luis and Walter Alvarez, a father-and-son team. Digging down to a rock layer with dinosaur fossils in it, the Alvarezes discovered a thin layer of clay containing iridium. Iridium, a chemical rare on Earth, is common in outer space.

Making a connection between iridium and the extinction of the dinosaurs was the hard part of their job. Eventually the Alvarezes decided to try an educated guess. They proposed that a meteorite, a huge rock from outer space, landed on Earth and created tons of dust. Spreading around the planet, the thick dust eventually blocked the sunlight from reaching it. Earth fell into darkness, and temperatures dropped severely. As a result, the plant life on the planet died. Without any plants to eat for food, the dinosaurs died too.

Mastery Test

Number your paper 1 to 10. Write the phrase in each sentence. Then label each phrase *prepositional, appositive, participial, gerund,* or *infinitive.*

1. Diving from the boat, Melanie swam ashore.
2. Scientists study animals to learn more about humans.
3. Please drive me to Ellen's birthday party.
4. The cake baked by my sister won the first prize.
5. Computer programming, my favorite course, is fun and extremely interesting.
6. The coat with the fur collar needs new buttons.
7. Do you like cooking chicken on a grill?
8. It is very nice to see them so happy together.
9. Will you eat the leftovers, the potato and meat loaf?
10. Making her own wedding cake was an ambitious undertaking.

Chapter 25

Clauses

Diagnostic Test

Number your paper 1 to 10. Then label each sentence *simple, compound, complex,* or *compound-complex.*

EXAMPLE As I came closer, the colt ran away.
ANSWER complex

1. Your body contains about ten gallons of water.
2. My younger sister has blond hair, but my older sister is a brunette.
3. A rattlesnake gives a warning before it strikes.
4. We found a nice spot in the park and stayed well into the afternoon.
5. What started out as a snow flurry turned into a raging storm.
6. A shrub that is common in Florida is the hibiscus.
7. This sounds like a tall tale, but it's true.
8. When we finally reached the beach, I set up the umbrella, and Leroy inflated the raft.
9. I always wonder how ducks find their way north in the spring.
10. For two weeks searchers looked all over the state for the missing plane.

Independent and Subordinate Clauses

A phrase, as you learned in the last chapter, can be used as a noun, an adjective, or an adverb. Another group of words, called a *clause,* can also be used as these parts of speech. A clause, however, has a subject and a verb; a phrase does not.

Rule 25a A **clause** is a group of words that has a subject and a verb.

In the following examples, both the phrase and the clause are used as an adverb to modify *feed.*

PHRASE Feed the dog **before dinner.**

CLAUSE Feed the dog **before you eat dinner.** [*You* is the subject of the clause; *eat* is the verb.]

Understanding clauses and being able to include them in your writing is valuable because clauses show important relationships between ideas. Clauses also combine ideas and in that way create clearer sentences.

There are two kinds of clauses: the *independent clause* and the *subordinate clause.*

Rule 25b An **independent (or main) clause** can stand alone as a sentence because it expresses a complete thought.

When an independent clause stands by itself, it is called a *sentence.* When it appears in a sentence with another clause, it is called a *clause.* In the following examples, each subject is underlined once, and each verb is underlined twice. Notice that each of the independent clauses could stand alone as a separate sentence.

[independent clause] [independent clause]
Lynn trimmed the hedges, and Brian mowed the lawn.

[sentence] [sentence]
Lynn trimmed the hedges. Brian mowed the lawn.

The second kind of clause is the subordinate clause.

Rule 25c A **subordinate (or dependent) clause** cannot stand alone as a sentence, because it does not express a complete thought.

Notice in the examples that the subordinate clauses do not express complete thoughts—even though they have a subject and a verb.

subordinate clause | independent clause
After the horses had eaten, Nathan gave them water.

independent clause | subordinate clause
Are you going to watch the special that is on TV tonight?

EXERCISE 1 *Identifying Subordinate Clauses*

Number your paper 1 to 10. Then write the subordinate clause in each sentence.

1. Because we were late, we missed the first touchdown.
2. Take the umbrella that is hanging in the hall closet.
3. Did you know that the dance is Friday evening?
4. You should talk to the drama teacher, who is holding rehearsals in the auditorium.
5. We go to the beach whenever we get the chance.
6. While you were out, this package arrived for you.
7. I promised that she could sit with us.
8. Timmy wants a pet whom he can play with.
9. You will like what we bought for them.
10. We should take our lunch because we may not get home until late this afternoon.

EXERCISE 2 *Distinguishing between Independent and Subordinate Clauses*

Number your paper 1 to 10. Write each underlined clause in the following paragraph. Then label each one *independent* or *subordinate.*

Clean as Clean Can Be

The raccoon is not a very particular animal when it comes to food. This black-masked creature can make a meal of almost anything as long as the food is clean. Before it will eat anything, the raccoon first washes its food. A raccoon would go hungry before it would eat anything that had not first been washed. However, a raccoon will sometimes go through the motions of washing if no water is available. Because a raccoon's desire for cleanliness is so strong, it will often scrub pebbles until they shine. Then it will neatly stack the pebbles so they can dry in the sun. This is an unusual form of behavior that no other animal shares.

Uses of Subordinate Clauses

In a sentence a subordinate clause can be used as an adverb, an adjective, or a noun.

Adverb Clauses

Like a phrase, a subordinate clause can be used like a single adverb. The single adverb, the adverb phrase, and the adverb clause in the following examples all modify the verb *had worked.*

SINGLE ADVERB	He had worked **continuously.**
ADVERB PHRASE	He had worked **without a rest.**
ADVERB CLAUSE	He had worked **even though he was tired.**

Rule 25d **An adverb clause is a subordinate clause that is used like an adverb to modify a verb, an adjective, or an adverb.**

An adverb clause answers the same questions a single adverb answers: *How? When? Where? How much?* and *To what extent?* An adverb clause also answers the questions *Under what condition?* and *Why?* Notice that in the first two examples, the adverb clauses modify the whole verb phrase.

WHEN?	We will go **whenever you're ready.**
UNDER WHAT CONDITION?	We will attend the concert **if we can get tickets.**
WHY?	We left early **so that we wouldn't be late.**

Although most adverb clauses modify verbs, some modify adjectives or adverbs.

MODIFYING AN ADJECTIVE	Mike is taller **than I am.**
MODIFYING AN ADVERB	Jan arrived sooner **than I did.**

Subordinating Conjunctions A word called a *subordinating conjunction* begins an adverb clause. On the following page is a list of common subordinating conjunctions. Remember that words such as *after, before,* and *until* can also be used as prepositions.

Common Subordinating Conjunctions			
after	as soon as	in order that	until
although	as though	since	when
as	because	so that	whenever
as far as	before	than	where
as if	even though	though	wherever
as long as	if	unless	while

If you like jazz, you will enjoy my new album.

We arrived **after the movie started.**

She was speaking **as if she had laryngitis.**

EXERCISE 3 *Recognizing Subordinating Conjunctions*

Number your paper 1 to 20. Write each adverb clause. Then underline each subordinating conjunction.

1. The horned toad will lie quietly as long as its chin is being tickled.
2. While you empty the trash cans, I'll dust the furniture.
3. If the coils of a French horn were straightened out, the instrument would be 22 feet long.
4. That test was harder than the one we took last week.
5. A person cannot taste food unless it is mixed with saliva.
6. Twins are quite rare because only one in every 90 births results in twins.
7. Although the giraffe's neck is about seven feet long, it contains the same number of vertebrae as a mouse's.
8. They acted as though nothing had happened.
9. Joan of Arc was only seventeen when she led the French army to victory against the English at Orléans.
10. Some cicadas live underground all their lives and emerge for only a few weeks of sunshine before they die.
11. As far as I can see, we can begin whenever you're ready.
12. Call me as soon as they arrive.
13. I feel so much better since I have been exercising every morning.
14. As people age, their ability to taste sweet foods decreases.
15. In March the team practices more than it does in May.

16. If a car is moving at 55 miles per hour, it will travel 56 feet before the driver can shift his or her foot to the brake.
17. Speak more slowly so that I can understand you.
18. After we eat, let's study in the library.
19. Act as if you were enjoying yourself.
20. Your blood is blue until it encounters oxygen from outside.

EXERCISE 4 *Finding Adverb Clauses*

Number your paper 1 to 10. Write each adverb clause. Then beside each one, write the word or words it modifies.

1. After the horses had eaten, Lisa gave them some water.
2. Many fruits are shipped before they are ripe.
3. Quentin finished his report sooner than I did.
4. Fish can get seasick if they are kept aboard a ship.
5. As long as I have known him, Jeff has exercised daily.
6. Bea cannot paint the den until the walls are sanded.
7. Unless my plans change, I will wait for you at the gym.
8. I feel safe when the dog is in the house with me.
9. As soon as the election returns were in, we celebrated.
10. Although a dragonfly has six legs, it cannot walk.

Punctuation with Adverb Clauses

Place a comma after an introductory adverb clause.

If you win, what will you do with the prize money?

If an adverb clause interrupts an independent clause, place a comma before and after it.

The Senate**, after the President vetoed the bill,** overrode the veto.

EXERCISE 5 *Writing Sentences*

Using the following subordinating conjunctions, write five sentences that include adverb clauses. The first three sentences should begin with the adverb clause. Then underline each adverb clause. Use commas where needed.

1. since **2.** until **3.** while **4.** unless **5.** because

Adjective Clauses

When a subordinate clause is used like a single adjective, it is called an *adjective clause*. In the following examples, the single adjective, the adjective phrase, and the adjective clause all modify *business*.

SINGLE ADJECTIVE	Farming is a **risky** business.
ADJECTIVE PHRASE	Farming is a business **with many risks.**
ADJECTIVE CLAUSE	Farming is a business **that has many risks.**

Rule 25e An **adjective clause** is a subordinate clause that is used like an adjective to modify a noun or a pronoun.

An adjective clause answers the same questions a single adjective answers: *Which one(s)?* and *What kind?*

WHICH ONE(S)?	The person **who just rang the bell** left a package.
WHAT KIND?	Have you seen the new computer **that composes music?**

Relative Pronouns An adjective clause usually begins with a *relative pronoun.* A relative pronoun relates an adjective clause to its antecedent—the noun or pronoun the clause modifies.

Relative Pronouns				
who	whom	whose	which	that

Note: *Where* and *when* sometimes introduce an adjective clause.

The wallet **that you found** belongs to me.

Three o'clock is the time **when we'll leave.**

Occasionally the relative pronoun *that* is omitted from an adjective clause, but it is always understood to be there.

I have an assignment **I must do tonight.** [The entire adjective clause is *(that) I must do tonight.*]

EXERCISE 6 *Recognizing Relative Pronouns*

Number your paper 1 to 10. Write each adjective clause. Then underline the relative pronoun or the word introducing the adjective clause.

1. The fastest land animal in the world is the cheetah, which has been clocked at 72 miles per hour.
2. I haven't seen a jacket that I've liked.
3. This form must be signed by Mr. Alfonzo, whose room is at the end of this corridor.
4. Autumn is the time when we like to go camping.
5. Is this the person whom you saw in the store before the accident?
6. A tornado that hit St. Louis in 1927 caused $26 million worth of damage in five minutes.
7. In 1776, a man who made four thousand dollars a year was called wealthy.
8. The tarpon fish has scales that are almost four inches wide.
9. Ms. Henderson, whom I know from Seattle, will be the guest speaker at the convention.
10. The state where the average income is greatest is Alaska.

EXERCISE 7 *Finding Adjective Clauses*

Number your paper 1 to 10. Write each adjective clause. Then beside each one, write the word it modifies.

From Tents to Jeans

1. An item of clothing that is popular among people of all ages is the blue jean.
2. The first jeans, which were made in 1850, cost $13.50 a dozen!
3. They were made by a German immigrant whose name was Levi Strauss.
4. Strauss, who had a dream of success, went to San Francisco during the gold rush.
5. He took with him several bales of cloth, which he planned to use to make tents.
6. By the time he arrived, other people were already making tents.
7. San Francisco was still a place where ingenuity paid off.
8. He got an idea from a miner who complained of his trousers' wearing out too fast.
9. The heavy-duty material, which Strauss had intended for tents, soon became jeans.
10. The jeans that Strauss made are still copied today.

Function of a Relative Pronoun Besides introducing an adjective clause, a relative pronoun has another function. Within the adjective clause, it can serve as a subject, a direct object, or an object of a preposition. A relative pronoun can also show possession.

SUBJECT	Mrs. Brown, **who drove us to school today,** is my next-door neighbor. [*Who* is the subject of *drove.*]
DIRECT OBJECT	The school **she attends** is in Portland, Maine. [The understood *that* is the direct object of *she attends.*]
OBJECT OF A PREPOSITION	The book **from which I got most of my information** is in the library. [*Which* is the object of the preposition *from.* Notice that *from* is part of the clause.]
POSSESSION	My father is the person **whose opinions I respect and follow most.** [*Whose* shows possession of *opinion.*]

EXERCISE 8 *Finding Adjective Clauses*

Number your paper 1 to 15. Write each adjective clause. Then beside each one, write the word it modifies.

1. The third-place athlete in an Olympic event receives a medal that is made of bronze.

2. Jean Henri Dunant, who founded the Red Cross, was one of the first recipients of the Nobel Prize.

3. *South Pacific* is the only musical in which my sister sang a solo before a large audience.

4. We thanked Mr. Sanchez, whose ladder we borrowed.

5. Water eventually dissolves almost everything with which it comes in contact.

6. Give your receipts to the treasurer, whom you just met.

7. The female giraffe gives birth to a single calf, which is about six feet tall at birth.

8. The computer he owns has eight-inch disk drives.

9. Grover Cleveland was the only president who was married in the White House.

10. The city with the most snow in New York State is Buffalo, whose annual snowfall comes to more than 88 inches.

11. A pangram is a sentence that uses all the letters in the alphabet.
12. Alaska is the only state in which houseflies cannot survive.
13. You should speak to Catherine, whom the principal just hired.
14. Thomas Edison, whose inventions changed the world, patented 1,093 different ones during his lifetime.
15. Thomas Jefferson, who was our third president, was also an inventor of such things as a revolving chair and a plow.

EXERCISE 9 *Determining the Function of a Relative Pronoun*

Number your paper 1 to 15. Then use the following abbreviations to label the use of each relative pronoun in Exercise 8. If an adjective clause begins with an understood *that,* write *understood* after the number and then write how *that* is used.

subject = *subj.*	object of a preposition = *o.p.*
direct object = *d.o.*	possession = *poss.*

Punctuation with Adjective Clauses

No punctuation is used with an adjective clause that contains information that is essential to identify a person, place, or thing in a sentence. A comma or commas, however, should set off an adjective clause that is nonessential. A clause is nonessential if it can be removed from the sentence without changing the basic meaning.

ESSENTIAL The person **who invented the phonograph** was Thomas Edison. [No commas are used because the clause is needed to identify which person.]

NONESSENTIAL Thomas Edison**, who invented the phonograph,** was deaf. [Commas are used because the clause can be removed from the sentence.]

The relative pronoun *that* is usually used in an essential clause.

EXERCISE 10 *Writing Sentences*

Write a sentence for each of the relative pronouns in Exercise 8. Then underline each adjective clause. Use commas where needed.

Misplaced Modifiers

An adjective clause should be placed as near as possible to the word it modifies. A clause placed too far away from the word it modifies is called a *misplaced modifier.*

MISPLACED The huge maple tree fell against the house, which had been uprooted during the storm.

CORRECT The huge maple tree, **which had been uprooted during the storm,** fell against the house.

EXERCISE 11 *Correcting Misplaced Modifiers*

Write the following sentences, correcting each misplaced modifier. Use commas where needed.

1. We saw a reconstructed dinosaur at the museum which existed millions of years ago.
2. I spent Monday fixing a car which was windy and cool.
3. Mr. Hale donated his Stanley Steamer to a museum in New York which his father purchased in 1912.
4. We visited Sturbridge on Saturday morning where Colonial occupations are still practiced.
5. Today the coffee tree is grown in Asia and South America which originated in Africa.
6. The wild cherry tree provides a beautifully finished wood which grows throughout most of the East.
7. Una took her ten-speed bicycle on a trip to Canada which is ideal for long rides.
8. A hailstorm may strike unexpectedly in summer which often destroys crops.
9. The Jeffersons' dog turned over our trash can which is usually tied up.
10. We wrapped the fish in newspaper that we had caught.
11. I used the computer in the English room that sits on the small desk.
12. I got a book from the library that was written by Charles Dickens.
13. Find the melon in the refrigerator that is for dessert.
14. They got a dog from the humane society that was only six weeks old.
15. I rode the horse at the stable that has the long blond mane and tail.

Noun Clauses

A subordinate clause that is used like a single noun is called a *noun clause.* Both the single noun *news* and the noun clause in the following examples are used as objects of a preposition.

SINGLE NOUN	Bridget was elated by the **news.**
NOUN CLAUSE	Bridget was elated by **what she had heard.**

Rule 25f A **noun clause** is a subordinate clause that is used like a noun.

Within a sentence a noun clause can be used in the same ways in which a single noun can be used.

SUBJECT	**Whatever you choose** is fine with me.
DIRECT OBJECT	Did you know **that Lamar won?**
INDIRECT OBJECT	Give **whoever comes to the door** the samples.
OBJECT OF A PREPOSITION	Award the prize to **whoever sells the most tickets.**
PREDICATE NOMINATIVE	Helen's reason for visiting Seattle was **that she hadn't seen her sister for a year.**

Words in the following list often introduce a noun clause. *Who, whom, whose, which,* and *that* also introduce adjective clauses. For this reason, do not rely on an introductory word alone to identify a clause. Instead, determine how a clause is used in a sentence.

Common Introductory Words for Noun Clauses

how	whatever	which	whomever
if	when	who	whose
that	where	whoever	why
what	whether	whom	

EXERCISE 12 *Finding Noun Clauses*

Number your paper 1 to 10. Then write each noun clause.

1. Most people don't know that the yellow-footed armadillo can outrun a person.
2. Give whoever is in the office my excuse for being late.

3. I read that the oceans contain ten million tons of gold.
4. United States national parks are a fine example of how a country can preserve its resources.
5. We learned that the sweaters were handmade in Norway.
6. A prize will be given to whoever raises the most money.
7. My wish for you on your birthday is that you live a long life.
8. That Central High won the basketball tournament surprised most of the spectators.
9. Do you know who won a Pulitzer Prize recently?
10. What he told me this morning must be kept a secret.

EXERCISE 13 *Finding Noun Clauses*

Number your paper 1 to 20. Then write each noun clause.

1. Many people once thought that horseradish would cure baldness.
2. What we anticipate seldom occurs. DISRAELI
3. Keith will make dinner for whoever arrives.
4. The only trouble with that idea is that it won't work.
5. Give whoever calls the message.
6. Most of what we call classical music was written during a period of 47 years from 1781 to 1828.
7. The potter described how he shapes and molds the clay.
8. Tell me where you want the picture hung.
9. Some people once believed that a vein ran from the third finger of the left hand to the heart.
10. This is why the wedding ring is worn on that finger.
11. Farmers realize that the least frost will destroy their buckwheat crops.
12. The clerk gave samples to whoever would watch the demonstration.
13. How sound is stored on disks was explained in science class today.
14. Their opinion was that the fire had started in the basement.
15. Most psychologists believe that people's personalities cannot be revealed by their handwriting.
16. Did you know that all bananas are picked green?
17. What I do depends upon your plans.
18. The Franklin Scholarship will go to whoever has the highest academic record in the senior class.
19. In 1875, the director of the United States Patent Office resigned and asked that his department be closed.
20. He believed that there was nothing left to invent.

EXERCISE 14 *Labeling Noun Clauses*

Use these abbreviations to label each noun clause in Exercise 13.

subject = *subj.*
direct object = *d.o.*
indirect object = *i.o.*
object of a preposition = *o.p.*
predicate nominative = *p.n.*

EXERCISE 15 *Writing Sentences*

Complete the following sentences by adding noun clauses.

1. Mr. McPherson hoped ______.
2. The award for the most valuable player will go to ______.
3. Anne asked ______.
4. ______ was no surprise.
5. Has anyone told you ______?
6. The difficulty was ______.
7. Did you know ______?
8. I wonder ______.
9. Send ______ to the office.
10. His reason for leaving early was ______.

EXERCISE 16 *Cumulative Review*

Number your paper 1 to 10. Write the subordinate clauses. Then label the use of each one—*adverb, adjective,* or *noun.*

Killer Bees

Brazilian scientists knew that killer bees were fierce. They also knew that killer bees made more honey than European bees did. It seemed worth the chance to fly in some killer bees from Africa. If they could be crossed with European bees, the results might be gentle bees that would make a great deal of honey. Special hives from which the larger queen bees and drones could not escape were constructed. As long as the queen bees were locked up in the hives, the workers would come home to them.

Accidents, however, do happen. A beekeeper who didn't know about the killer bees removed the grids from the hives. Twenty-six queen bees escaped—along with all of their workers and drones. The killer bees, which have been traveling north at about 200 miles a year, should begin to reach the United States during the 1990's. Most experts say that people shouldn't worry. Killer bees can't live through cold winters.

Kinds of Sentence Structure

Sentences are classified according to the number and kind of clauses within them. The four basic kinds of sentences are *simple, compound, complex,* and *compound-complex.*

Rule 25g A **simple sentence** consists of one independent clause.

This letter just arrived for you.

A simple sentence can have a compound subject, a compound verb, or both.

Jason and **Luis finished** their work and **have gone** home.

Rule 25h A **compound sentence** consists of two or more independent clauses.

independent clause — independent clause
Penguins cannot fly, but they can dive into the ocean.

independent clause — independent clause
Football is an autumn sport; baseball is a spring sport.

Independent clauses should not be combined to make a compound sentence unless they are closely related.

Note: For the punctuation of a compound sentence, see pages 777 and 816.

Rule 25i A **complex sentence** consists of one independent clause and one or more subordinate clauses.

independent clause — subordinate clause
I enjoy a comedy more than I enjoy a heavy drama.

subordinate clause — independent clause — subordinate clause
Although I have tried many times, ice hockey is one sport that I cannot master.

Note: For the punctuation of a complex sentence, see page 786.

Rule 25j A **compound-complex sentence** consists of two or more independent clauses and one or more subordinate clauses.

subordinate clause

If a color-blind woman marries a man with normal vision, all

independent clause — independent clause

the daughters will have normal vision, but all the sons will be color-blind.

Note: To punctuate compound-complex sentences, follow the rules for both compound and complex sentences.

EXERCISE 17 *Classifying Sentences*

Number your paper 1 to 10. Then label each of the following sentences *simple, compound, complex,* or *compound-complex.*

An Unusual Animal

1. When you wash the dishes with a natural sponge, you are actually using the skeleton of an ocean animal.
2. The sponge is not a plant; it is an animal that is covered with flesh.
3. The skeleton is gradually formed as hard materials become imbedded in the body.
4. The sponge is alive, yet it has no legs or fins.
5. As a result it attaches itself to some firm object.
6. Nature's plan for the sponge was ingenious, for tiny holes exist in the sponge.
7. As water flows into these holes, food and oxygen are carried in.
8. Through the same holes, waste materials are carried out.
9. Some sponges can regenerate themselves; they can grow whole new sponges from small fragments.
10. People plant sponge fragments, and they are harvested two or three years later when they have grown large.

Application to Writing

Write a short persuasive essay that names your favorite musical group and explains why you like it so much. What type of music and showmanship does it offer an audience? Are teenagers eager to meet the performers? How do these musicians respond to their fans? In your essay, use at least one simple sentence, one compound sentence, and one complex sentence. Make sure you punctuate your sentences correctly and be prepared to identify an example of each kind of sentence.

Integrating Language Skills

USING YOUR TEXT
Brainstorming (20–21)
Persuasive Essays (234–269)

Grammar: Combining Sentences

Part of a mature writing style includes the use of all kinds of sentences. You can sometimes achieve variety by combining simple sentences into a compound or a complex sentence.

TWO SIMPLE SENTENCES	The warning lights flashed. The gates lowered into position.
A COMPOUND SENTENCE	The warning lights flashed, **and** the gates lowered into position.
TWO SIMPLE SENTENCES	My brother became a shell collector. Now our house looks like a beach.
A COMPLEX SENTENCE	**Since my brother has become a shell collector,** our house looks like a beach. [adverb clause]
TWO SIMPLE SENTENCES	The best perfumes contain large portions of animal oils. These perfumes are made mostly in France.
A COMPLEX SENTENCE	The best perfumes, **which are made mostly in France,** contain large portions of animal oils. [adjective clause]
TWO SIMPLE SENTENCES	Everyone had passed the math exam. Mr. Cohen made this announcement.
A COMPLEX SENTENCE	Mr. Cohen announced **that everyone had passed the math exam.** [noun clause]

Checking Your Understanding Combine the first five pairs of sentences into compound sentences. Then combine the last ten pairs into complex sentences. Use punctuation where needed.

1. A male walrus may weigh 3,000 pounds. A female rarely exceeds 2,000 pounds.
2. Homing pigeons have an incredible sense of direction. They have found their way home from 1,500 miles away.
3. Otters are awkward on land. In water they are graceful and speedy.
4. In the Southern Hemisphere, a cyclone moves clockwise. In the Northern Hemisphere, it travels counterclockwise.

5. A rabbit runs from danger. A hare leaps away.
6. Porpoises and whales are fishlike in appearance. They are really warm-blooded mammals.
7. Venus often rises in the morning before the sun. Amateur astronomers know this.
8. An Indian birch-bark canoe could easily be carried by one person. The canoe could still transport an entire family and its dogs and equipment.
9. Southern California has a very warm climate. The houses there are often built without furnaces.
10. Many people in early times wrote in hieroglyphics. These hieroglyphics were the origin of all alphabets.
11. Mother likes big dogs. We bought a collie.
12. A cow usually eats seven times as much as a sheep. This surprised me.
13. Many of the pioneers were rough individuals. They hated crowded cities and the restrictions of civilization.
14. In northern Scandinavia the sun doesn't set for nearly three months. Did you know that?
15. Retrievers are intelligent and fearless. They can be trained as excellent hunting dogs.

Writing a Persuasive Essay Since the nuclear accidents in the United States and the Soviet Union, some people have become wary of using nuclear energy. Safe disposal of nuclear wastes is a problem yet to be solved. However, scientists warn that the burning of fossil fuels, such as coal and oil, harms the earth's atmosphere. They warn that Earth's protective ozone layer could be permanently damaged.

Which course of action would you advise your country to follow, more use of nuclear energy or less? Brainstorm for any ideas you have already formed about nuclear energy. You may also want to read current information in magazines or newspapers. You may find it helpful to talk with others and get their opinions as well. Next write the first draft of an essay stating your position on using nuclear energy. In the essay encourage others to adopt your view. ***Application:*** As you revise your essay, strengthen some of your arguments by beginning them with an adverb clause. Also check to see if you can combine any simple sentences into compound or complex sentences. Then edit your essay and write the final copy.

Diagraming Sentences

A simple sentence is diagramed on a single baseline. In compound, complex, and compound-complex sentences, however, each clause is diagramed on a separate baseline.

Compound Sentences Each independent clause in a compound sentence is diagramed like a simple sentence. The clauses are joined with a broken line that connects the verbs. The conjunction is then placed on the broken line.

You make the salad, and I will make the dessert.

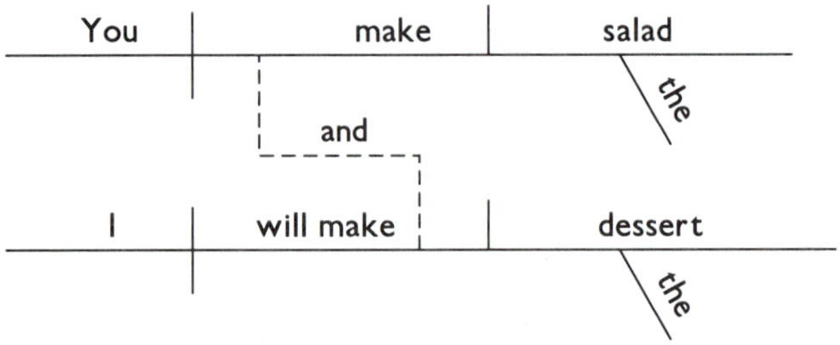

Complex Sentences In a complex sentence, an adverb clause is diagramed beneath the independent clause it modifies. The subordinating conjunction goes on a broken line that connects the verb in the adverb clause to the verb, the adjective, or the adverb that the clause modifies. In the following diagram, the adverb clause modifies the verb in the independent clause.

Take the dog out before you go to bed.

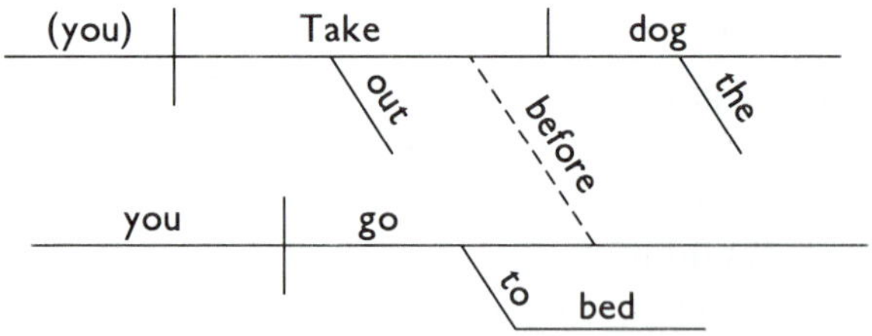

In a complex sentence, an adjective clause is also diagramed beneath the independent clause it modifies. The relative pronoun in the clause is connected by a broken line to the noun or the pronoun the clause modifies. In the following diagram, the adjective clause modifies the noun *book* in the independent clause.

This is the book that you should read.

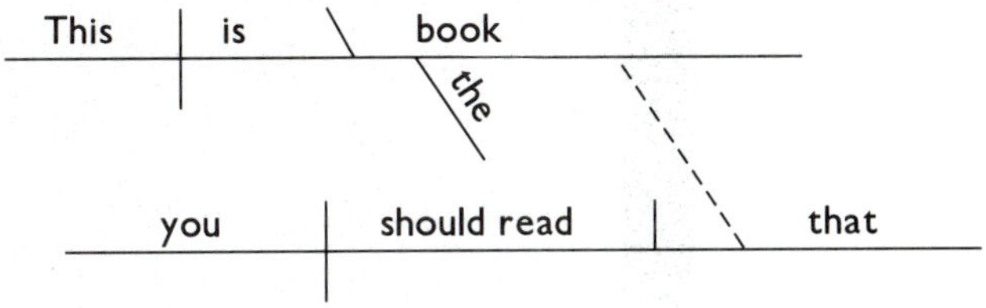

A noun clause is diagramed on a pedestal in the same place that a single noun would be if it had the same function. In the following diagram, the noun clause is used as the subject.

Whatever will be will be.

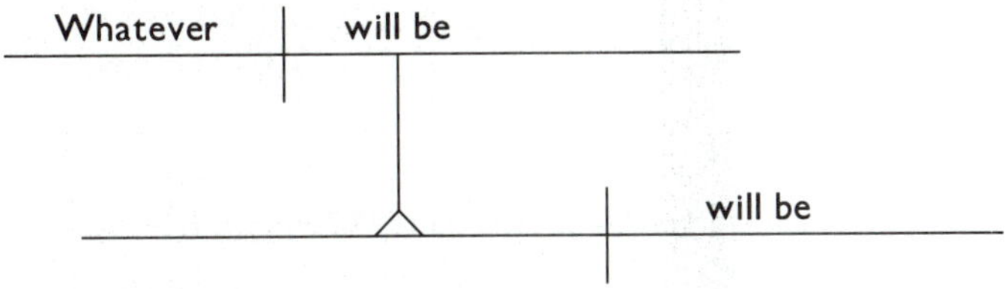

Compound-Complex Sentences To diagram these sentences, apply what you just learned about diagraming compound and complex sentences.

EXERCISE 18 *Diagraming Sentences*

Diagram the following sentences or copy them. If you copy them, draw one line under each subject and two lines under each verb. Then put parentheses around each subordinate clause and label each one *adverb, adjective,* or *noun.*

1. Tony is at the library, and Sally went to a meeting.
2. We will respond when we know all the facts.
3. Rows of houses now occupy land that was once a forest.
4. Whatever you donate will help.
5. Cut the grass before the rain starts.
6. The road is narrow, but it is the most direct route.
7. Can you replace the window that was broken?
8. The fire fighters battled the huge blaze, but the strong winds worked against them.
9. Tell me what you like about New York City.
10. The movie was long, but I liked it very much.

Chapter 25 Review

A **Identifying Subordinate Clauses** Number your paper 1 to 20. Write the subordinate clause in each sentence. Then label the use of each one—*adverb, adjective,* or *noun.*

1. A little-known invention by Thomas Edison was a doll that talked.
2. Although people eat the harmless eggplant, its vines are poisonous.
3. It is estimated that Niagara Falls will disappear into Lake Erie in about 23,000 years.
4. If diamonds are heated sufficiently, they will burn.
5. Venus, which is the third brightest object in the sky, can sometimes be seen clearly at noon.
6. Sailing is what I like best.
7. They agreed on a place where they would meet.
8. Whoever just called didn't leave a message.
9. When it is provoked, a rhinoceros can charge at a speed of 30 miles per hour.
10. Of the 60 million buffalo that once roamed North America, only about 5,000 now exist.
11. I don't know where I put my sunglasses.
12. A French astronomer found helium on the sun before anyone found it on the earth.
13. Napoleon had conquered Italy by the time he was twenty-six years old.
14. Stanley Lopez, whom you have not met, will be the new soccer captain.
15. Sir Arthur Conan Doyle, who created Sherlock Holmes, was a doctor.
16. Do you remember when the temperature stayed below zero for 33 straight days?
17. That we should meet like this after so many years have gone by is truly amazing!
18. The best apples are those that ripen on the tree.
19. I never saw an ocean until I was thirteen years old.
20. You shouldn't eat wild mushrooms because poisonous and non-poisonous species often look alike.

B **Identifying Kinds of Sentence Structure** Number your paper 1 to 10. Then label each of the following sentences *simple, compound, complex,* or *compound-complex.*

1. Records and tapes are out, and compact disks are in.
2. Compact disks are often called CD's.
3. Although a CD may look like a little record, it doesn't work like one.
4. Records have a thin groove, and different sounds are recorded as bumps and dents in the groove's sides and floor.
5. The sound is produced when a needle moves up and down and from side to side along the groove.
6. A CD, however, is covered with microscopic pits that make up a digital code.
7. When you play a CD, a laser bounces off the CD and reads the little pits; and the code is translated into sound.
8. In spite of the cost of CD's, they have many advantages.
9. They produce extraordinary sound; and since a needle never touches them, they last and last.
10. Some music lovers would rather not listen to anything but CD's.

Mastery Test

Number your paper 1 to 10. Then label each sentence *simple, compound, complex,* or *compound-complex.*

1. All the mountain climbers were extremely exhausted.
2. Juan dived from the board and arched gracefully toward the pool.
3. Most birds are asleep by dark, but the screech owl hunts all night.
4. Jane, whose brother you just met, lives next door.
5. I enjoyed what we had for dinner at your house.
6. The silkworm is not a worm; it's a caterpillar.
7. Last week Bart came home on leave, but I didn't see him because I was working as a camp counselor.
8. When the cat's away, the mice will play.
9. Does Marsha know that I need a ride?
10. Over the door of the inn hung a golden lion.

Chapter

26 Sound Sentences

Diagnostic Test

Number your paper 1 to 10. Then label each group of words *sentence*, *fragment*, or *run-on*.

EXAMPLE Spending the evening with friends.
ANSWER fragment

1. After leaving the air-conditioned department store.
2. On a branch of the apple tree near the house at the end of the block.
3. The day started out rainy, by noon the sun came out.
4. I haven't finished the Sunday crossword puzzle yet.
5. Winter is my favorite season, I like skiing and skating.
6. Yvette plays the violin in the community orchestra.
7. Since the fair starts at nine o'clock.
8. Colorful balloons, red and white streamers, and a huge welcoming sign.
9. Leave my lunch on the kitchen table.
10. On Saturday night my friends came over, we watched a movie on television.

Sentence Errors

Any written work that is filled with sentence errors can result in confusion and misunderstanding. The two most common types of sentences errors are sentence fragments and run-on sentences. A *sentence fragment* is not a sentence at all; it is an incomplete thought masquerading as a sentence. A *run-on sentence* is two or more sentences written as one sentence.

This chapter will cover these two common writing errors and will show you specific ways to avoid them. One of the best ways to eliminate these errors, however, is to read your written work aloud. The rhythm of your voice will often reveal any sentence errors.

Sentence Fragments

Sentence fragments are often the result of writing too fast. In a fragment only part of a sentence is actually written. Because a fragment does not contain all the needed information, a reader can easily become confused.

Rule 26a **A sentence fragment is a group of words that does not express a complete thought.**

Phrase Fragments Because a phrase does not have a subject and a verb, it can never stand alone as a sentence. Following are examples of different kinds of phrase fragments.

PREPOSITIONAL PHRASE

I have a meeting with Mr. Hayes. **During my study period on Thursday afternoon.**

After the game against Kenmore High. Everyone went to a celebration dance.

PARTICIPIAL PHRASE

The picnic will be held at Grange Park. **Located off Route 24 in Brighton.**

Washing cars on weekends. The club members raised money for Children's Hospital.

INFINITIVE PHRASE

I am going to Otis's house. **To study for the semester exam in history.**

To find the answer to the question. Gregory looked in five reference books.

APPOSITIVE PHRASE — Maria got a job at the First Century Bank. **The largest bank in town.**

Did you see the TV special report? **The one about Soviet-American relations.**

EXERCISE 1 *Finding Phrase Fragments*

Number your paper 1 to 10. Then label each group of words *sentence* or *fragment*. If a group of words is a fragment, add the words necessary to make it a sentence. Add capital letters and punctuation where needed.

EXAMPLE Laughing loudly in the backyard.
ANSWER fragment—The children, laughing loudly in the backyard, could be heard down the block.

1. As a result of a survey of the sophomores at Jefferson High School.
2. My appointment with the editor of the *Daily News* is today.
3. The newly elected mayor of Springfield.
4. To finish my work faster.
5. Throughout the entire television program about the Civil War.
6. Answer the telephone.
7. Diving into the pool from the high board.
8. That was my choice.
9. Delivered to the door of their apartment house on Main Street and Second Avenue.
10. The one assigned to us in history.

Clause Fragments All clauses have a subject and a verb, but only an independent clause can stand alone as a sentence. Because subordinate clauses do not express a complete thought, they are fragments when they stand alone.

ADVERB CLAUSE — The class trip was canceled. **Since not enough people signed up.**

Before you decide. Think carefully.

ADJECTIVE CLAUSE — Here is the notice. **That you wanted me to copy for you.**

Jennifer ordered stuffed filet of sole. **Which she never gets at home.**

EXERCISE 2 *Finding Clause Fragments*

Number your paper 1 to 10. Then label each group of words *sentence* or *fragment*. If a group of words is a fragment, add the words necessary to make it a sentence. Add capital letters and punctuation where needed.

1. While you were at the store.
2. Who is never on time.
3. Now is the time to decide.
4. Because the auditorium is so large.
5. Which was impossible to read.
6. Which one do you want?
7. After dinner and dessert, she will open all of her birthday presents.
8. Since daylight saving time starts tonight.
9. Who is making the decorations for the dance?
10. If the weather forecaster at noon on Channel 6 was correct.

Other Kinds of Fragments Other groups of words can also be mistakenly considered a sentence.

PARTS OF A COMPOUND VERB	Have you looked in your locker? **And checked in the lost-and-found?**
ITEMS IN A SERIES	We have everything we need. **Sleeping bag, tent, and warm clothing.**

EXERCISE 3 *Finding Sentence Fragments*

Number your paper 1 to 10. Then label each group of words *sentence* or *fragment*. If a group of words is a fragment, add the words necessary to make it a sentence. Add capital letters and punctuation where needed.

1. But left before the final touchdown.
2. Whenever I wash the car.
3. I will be finished in half an hour.
4. A jar of peanut butter, a loaf of bread, and a box of oat-bran cereal.
5. Driving much too slowly in the fast lane of the Pennsylvania Turnpike.
6. And smashed the ball over the ball park fence.
7. Tuesday afternoon, Wednesday morning, or Friday after school.

8. Which hasn't needed any repairs for a whole year.
9. As soon as I know the time of the meeting.
10. Turn the calendar page to the next month.

Ways to Correct Sentence Fragments

A fragment can be corrected in either of two ways. Words can be added to make the fragment a separate sentence, as you have done in the previous exercises. A fragment can also be attached to the sentence next to it.

SENTENCE AND FRAGMENT	We were startled by the cat's eyes. **Shining in the dark.**
SEPARATE SENTENCES	We were startled by the cat's eyes. **They were shining in the dark.**
ATTACHED	We were startled by the cat's eyes **shining in the dark.**
SENTENCE AND FRAGMENT	Have you met Lionel? **George's cousin from Los Angeles.**
SEPARATE SENTENCES	Have you met Lionel? **He is George's cousin from Los Angeles.**
ATTACHED	Have you met Lionel, **George's cousin from Los Angeles?**

EXERCISE 4 *Correcting Sentence Fragments*

Number your paper 1 to 20. Write the following sentences, correcting each sentence fragment. Add capital letters and punctuation where needed.

1. One of the rarest birds in the United States is the California condor. With a wingspread of at least nine feet.
2. The Mississippi River overflowed its banks. And ruined thousands of acres of farmland.
3. Cave dwellers tamed the horse and the ox. To draw heavy sleds for them.
4. Swimming is an excellent sport. Because it exercises muscles usually inactive in ordinary life.
5. For nearly an hour, we watched the gulls. Soaring above the dock.

6. A minority of drivers have a majority of accidents. According to a recent report by an insurance company.
7. You can't visit Yellowstone National Park in the winter. Because it is buried under ten feet of snow.
8. We had just stopped playing baseball. When lightning struck a nearby tree.
9. Last night I went to the meeting at school. To learn about the new sports program.
10. Many English words are derived from Indian languages. *Pecan, chipmunk, igloo, moose,* and *raccoon.*
11. The planet Mercury is smaller than Ganymede. One of Jupiter's moons.
12. We recently visited Martha's Vineyard. An island off the coast of Cape Cod.
13. I learned many interesting things about snakes. In the last issue of *Nature Magazine.*
14. Mom found some tiny mint leaves. Growing beside the house.
15. I picked two ripe tomatoes from the garden. And cut them up in a salad for dinner.
16. Have you ever written a palindrome? A sentence or group of sentences that reads the same backward and forward.
17. We took a shortcut on a dirt road. To get to the railroad station on time.
18. Stars in the sky have individual personalities. That are revealed in various ways.
19. Coca-Cola was originally sold as a medicine. For use against headaches.
20. According to scientists, gold exists on distant planets. Mars, Mercury, and Venus.

Run-on Sentences

Run-on sentences are often caused by writing too fast. One sentence flows into another. Someone can become confused by reading several pieces of information that are neither separated nor properly connected.

Rule 26b A **run-on sentence** is two or more sentences that are written as one sentence and are separated by a comma or no mark of punctuation at all.

Run-on sentences usually take two forms.

WITH A COMMA	Laurie arrived on time, everyone else came 15 minutes later.
WITH NO PUNCTUATION	The sofa was too large for the room it had to be returned.

EXERCISE 5 *Finding Run-on Sentences*

Number your paper 1 to 10. Label each group of words *sentence* or *run-on*.

1. The longest day of each year preceding a leap year is June 22, of other years it is June 21.
2. Dr. Grenfell brought a herd of 250 Lapland reindeer to Alaska in the first year, 150 fawns were born.
3. Although the snow wasn't very deep, skiing was surprisingly good.
4. The bear cubs followed their mother, traveling as fast as their legs could carry them.
5. Chinese navigators probably used compasses first, these were made of magnetic iron.
6. In its natural state, the cocoa bean does not taste good it is very bitter.
7. Our lawn does best in wet weather, its roots do not go deep enough to tap underground water supplies.
8. For my first experience with horseback riding, I picked a big dappled mare.
9. May I borrow your camera I want to take pictures during my vacation in Washington, D.C.
10. Spring is the season of the year that I like best.

Ways to Correct Run-on Sentences

One way to correct a run-on sentence is by dividing it into two separate sentences. This solution should be used if the sentences are not closely related. A run-on sentence can also be corrected by changing it into a compound sentence or into a complex sentence.

RUN-ON SENTENCE	Aaron hurt his arm Hank went in to pitch for him.
SEPARATE SENTENCES	Aaron hurt his arm. Hank went in to pitch for him. [separated with a period and a capital letter]

COMPOUND SENTENCE — Aaron hurt his arm, and Hank went in to pitch for him. [combined with a comma and a conjunction]

Aaron hurt his arm; Hank went in to pitch for him. [combined with a semicolon]

COMPLEX SENTENCE — When Aaron hurt his arm, Hank went in to pitch for him. [combined by changing one independent clause into a subordinate clause]

EXERCISE 6 *Correcting Run-on Sentences*

Number your paper 1 to 20. Using different ways, correct the following run-on sentences. Add capital letters and punctuation where needed.

1. There's no school on Friday I'm going to the lake.
2. An octopus has eight legs a squid has ten legs.
3. Jenny lost the election, we tried to cheer her up.
4. Gophers have pouches in their cheeks they use them as sacks to carry food.
5. The reverse rockets fired, the capsule slowed down.
6. Onyx is a kind of striped agate, it consists of white and black layers.
7. Avoid ragweed it is a major cause of hay fever.
8. The ancient Egyptians had no money, trade was carried on by bartering.
9. June Barbato came in first, Caroline Rosen was second.
10. In 1833, there were 25,000 patents on file in the United States Patent Office today there are over one million.
11. The large claw of the fiddler crab looks frightening, it is used mainly for bluff.
12. I just roasted my first turkey it turned out very dry.
13. Flying squirrels don't fly, they just glide from tree to tree.
14. Put the dishes in the dishwasher then you can go out.
15. Leaves manufacture plant food, other parts of the plant store the food.
16. Jed dribbled the ball a basket would win the game.
17. Amber didn't win the science contest, she had worked very hard on her project.
18. The movie got worse and worse finally I left.
19. The Plains Indians wandered from place to place the Pueblo Indians built permanent settlements.
20. Come to my house at noon Dad will drive us to the game.

EXERCISE 7 Cumulative Review

Number your paper 1 to 15. Then write the following sentences, correcting each sentence fragment or run-on sentence. Add capital letters and punctuation where needed.

Facts and Figures

1. The voters elected John F. Kennedy in 1960. By a narrow margin.
2. There are many pictures of Abraham Lincoln, he is not smiling in a single one of them.
3. Louis XIV had 40 wigmakers. And owned nearly 1,000 wigs.
4. Fleas can jump 100 times their height. Even though they don't have any wings.
5. The slowest animal in the world is the snail. Moving at only three hundredths of a mile per hour.
6. The most common noncontagious disease is tooth decay, almost no one can avoid it.
7. *Uncle Tom's Cabin* was the first American novel. To sell one million copies.
8. A Packard was the first car to cross the American continent the trip took 52 days in 1903.
9. Many famous people were left-handed. Including Babe Ruth, Charlie Chaplin, and Leonardo da Vinci.
10. Eskimos have always been hearty eaters their diet consists almost entirely of meat and fish.
11. Hummingbirds can hover and they can fly straight up.
12. Pirates put holes in their ears and wore earrings. Because they thought it would help them see better.
13. The largest tree in Sequoia National Park is as high as a 20-story building. And weighs more than 2,000 pounds.
14. Only two words in English contain all the vowels in the proper order, they are *facetious* and *abstemious*.
15. There are 602 rooms in Buckingham Palace. The home of the queen of England.

Application to Writing

Think of something that you do not like to do, such as ironing clothes or making your bed. Then invent a device that would do that chore for you. In a paragraph describe your invention as specifically and clearly as possible. When you have finished, find and correct any sentence fragments or run-on sentences.

USING YOUR TEXT

Commas with Compound or Complex Sentences (777, 786)

Grammar: Editing for Sentence Errors

Your first step in editing should be to look for sentence fragments and run-on sentences. If you read aloud what you have written, you will find these errors easily.

Checking Your Understanding Rewrite the following paragraph, correcting all sentence fragments and run-on sentences. Make sure that you correct the errors in a variety of ways. Add capital letters and punctuation where needed.

> In 1891, William Wrigley moved to Chicago. And set up the Wrigley Company. With just $32 of his own money and a $5,000 loan. His company first sold only soap. And then branched out into baking powder. Wrigley looked for a clever way. To increase his sales. He decided on chewing gum, two packs were given with each ten-cent package of baking powder. His sales force soon came back with their reports, the gum was easier to sell than the baking powder. Wrigley was quick, To see the enormous possibilities. By the turn of the century. Wrigley's gum was a huge success. Selling in stores and vending machines from coast to coast.

Writing a Letter As part of a student exchange program, you have been given the name of a teenager in Mexico. You are supposed to write to that student, introducing yourself and inviting him or her to stay with your family for two weeks this coming summer.

Write freely for several minutes, jotting down everything you might say in the letter. Look over your notes and choose the four or five most important things to include. Then write the first draft of your letter, using a friendly, conversational tone and following the correct form for a personal letter. As you revise your letter, ask yourself if you have included enough specific details to give the student in Mexico a feeling of knowing you through your letter. ***Application:*** When you edit what you have written, correct any sentence errors. Then make a final copy of your letter.

Chapter 26

Review

A **Correcting Sentence Errors** Write the following sentences, correcting each sentence fragment or run-on sentence. Add capital letters and punctuation where needed.

1. The swallow flew too fast. To capture with my camera.
2. Tammy hit a home run in the last inning. And sent the game into extra innings.
3. The connection is very bad I can hardly hear you.
4. For the interior of the car, we had our choice of several colors. Tan, white, and black.
5. The door opened everyone yelled, "Surprise!"
6. You must fill in an application form. Before you can have an interview.
7. I skipped dessert, there are so many calories in fruitcake.
8. My new computer uses 3½-inch disks. Replacing the old 5¼-inch disks.
9. Eric just got a Russian blue. A rare breed of cat.
10. Your research papers are due this coming Friday. At the beginning of class.
11. The bite of the black widow is painful. But is seldom fatal.
12. The island of Bermuda is made of coral. A rocklike substance consisting of the skeletons of tiny sea animals.
13. In our woodpile we found three garter snakes. Which slithered out as we moved the wood.
14. In Colonial villages people got their daily news from a town crier by 1760, 11 of the 13 colonies had newspapers.
15. Whenever Dr. Jekyll changed his form. He called himself Mr. Hyde.
16. Have you ever ridden on a roller coaster it provides a thrill a second.
17. Andrew Jackson was born in a log cabin, at age thirteen he fought in the American Revolution.
18. A typical beef cow has a deep, wide body. With thick muscles, a broad neck, and short legs.

19. The *Logo* staff met yesterday afternoon. To discuss the assignments for the next issue.
20. Appearing fearless. The penguins approached the two explorers.

B **Correcting Sentence Errors** Rewrite the following paragraphs, correcting all sentence fragments and run-on sentences. Make sure that you correct the errors in a variety of ways. Add capital letters and punctuation where needed.

Hiccups occur when the muscles in your chest and throat suddenly tighten. If you eat or drink too much or too fast. You might find yourself with a bad case of hiccups. Usually hiccups last for only a few minutes they can be serious—even fatal—if they last too long.

Everyone, of course, has a cure for hiccups the cures run from the familiar to the strange. A common cure is a sudden surprise. Made by a loud noise, for example. Less common is drinking water backwards. Out of the far side of a cup.

Hiccups were once believed to be caused by a person. Who had spoken your name. You would have to say the name of everyone you knew. Until you got the right person. Only then would the hiccups stop. Most hiccups, however, would probably have gone away on their own. Without any cure at all.

Mastery Test

Number your paper 1 to 10. Then label each group of words *sentence, fragment,* or *run-on.*

1. Watching the Super Bowl at home with friends.
2. Mr. Sims asked a question no one could answer it.
3. We don't have another light bulb.
4. The cap fell off the toothpaste, now the medicine chest is a mess.
5. Set the table for dinner.
6. When Nancy calls from the library.
7. A pound of apples, a dozen oranges, and a pint of strawberries.
8. Practice begins at three o'clock.
9. As a result of the commission's report on clean air.
10. The ride to the airport took an hour, we got into rush-hour traffic.

Chapter 27

Using Verbs

Diagnostic Test

Number your paper 1 to 10. Then write the past or the past participle of each verb in parentheses.

EXAMPLE The captain (bring) the ship safely into the harbor.
ANSWER brought

1. Yesterday Brad and I (swim) ten laps in our neighbor's swimming pool.
2. Have you ever (ride) a surfboard off the California coast?
3. The rain (begin) just as we sat down outside to eat.
4. Jorge has (know) about the assignment for a week.
5. I (eat) the last apple in the refrigerator.
6. Last summer we (freeze) these strawberries.
7. Ryan carelessly (leave) his notebook and his wallet in the cafeteria.
8. Lani (drive) to the stadium by herself.
9. Have you (sell) your compact disk player yet?
10. Has Emma (write) to the manufacturer for a refund for the defective camera?

Principal Parts of Verbs

In the preceding section of this book, you learned the various elements of grammar. In this section on usage, you will see how to use those elements properly in your writing and speaking. This chapter will review the many forms of verbs and the uses of those forms.

The four basic forms of a verb are called its *principal parts.* Knowing the principal parts of a verb is important because all the tenses of a verb are formed from them.

Rule 27a The **principal parts** of a verb are the *present,* the *present participle,* the *past,* and the *past participle.*

Notice in the following examples that the present participle and the past participle have helping verbs when used as the main verb of a sentence.

PRESENT	I **study** each night.
PRESENT PARTICIPLE	I *am* **studying** now.
PAST	I **studied** last night.
PAST PARTICIPLE	I *have* **studied** every night this week.

Regular Verbs

Most verbs are *regular verbs.* They form their past and past participle the same way.

Rule 27b A **regular verb** forms its past and past participle by adding *-ed* or *-d* to the present.

When certain endings are added to the present, a spelling change sometimes occurs. Check a dictionary if you are unsure of a particular spelling.

PRESENT	PRESENT PARTICIPLE	PAST	PAST PARTICIPLE
sail	sailing	sailed	(have) sailed
smile	smiling	smiled	(have) smiled
bat	batting	batted	(have) batted
drip	dripping	dripped	(have) dripped

USAGE

Note: Dropping the *-ed* or *-d* ending from the past or the past participle of a verb is a common error. Do not make this mistake with such verbs as *asked, hoped, supposed,* and *used.*

INCORRECT We **use** to have picnics here in the summer.
CORRECT We **used** to have picnics here in the summer.

EXERCISE 1 *Principal Parts of Verbs*

Make four columns on your paper. Label them *present, present participle, past,* and *past participle.* Then write the four principal parts of the following regular verbs.

1. wait
2. cook
3. stop
4. bake
5. paint
6. dream
7. open
8. climb
9. plan
10. play

Irregular Verbs

A smaller group of verbs is called *irregular verbs.* Irregular verbs form their past and past participle in different ways.

Rule 27c **An irregular verb does not form its past and past participle by adding *-ed* or *-d* to the present.**

The following irregular verbs have been divided into groups according to the way they form their past and past participle.

Note: *Have* is not part of the past participle. It is being shown here to remind you that a past participle must have a helping verb when it is used as a verb.

Group 1

These irregular verbs have the same form for the present, the past, and the past participle.

PRESENT	PRESENT PARTICIPLE	PAST	PAST PARTICIPLE
burst	bursting	burst	(have) burst
cost	costing	cost	(have) cost
hit	hitting	hit	(have) hit
hurt	hurting	hurt	(have) hurt
let	letting	let	(have) let
put	putting	put	(have) put
set	setting	set	(have) set

Group 2

These irregular verbs have the same form for the past and the past participle.

PRESENT	PRESENT PARTICIPLE	PAST	PAST PARTICIPLE
bring	bringing	brought	(have) brought
buy	buying	bought	(have) bought
catch	catching	caught	(have) caught
feel	feeling	felt	(have) felt
find	finding	found	(have) found
get	getting	got	(have) got or gotten
hold	holding	held	(have) held
keep	keeping	kept	(have) kept
lay	laying	laid	(have) laid
lead	leading	led	(have) led
leave	leaving	left	(have) left
lose	losing	lost	(have) lost
make	making	made	(have) made
say	saying	said	(have) said
sell	selling	sold	(have) sold
send	sending	sent	(have) sent
sit	sitting	sat	(have) sat
teach	teaching	taught	(have) taught
tell	telling	told	(have) told
win	winning	won	(have) won

EXERCISE 2 *Using the Correct Verb Form*

Write the past or the past participle of each verb in parentheses. Then read each sentence aloud to check your answer.

1. Have you (make) the decorations for the party yet?
2. The general (lay) a wreath at the Tomb of the Unknown Soldier.
3. Hank (put) the scissors in the toolbox.
4. I (sit) beside your mother at the meeting last night.
5. The drum major (lead) the band across the football field.
6. The Davidsons have (win) a free trip to Hawaii.
7. Tad has (hit) more home runs than any other player.
8. The last skyrocket has just (burst).
9. They (leave) shortly after dinner.
10. Have you (sell) your tape deck yet?

11. I've looked everywhere, but I haven't (find) my knapsack.
12. Teresa (feel) extremely happy after winning the award.
13. Who (say) you shouldn't apply for the job?
14. Jesse (lose) his new catcher's mitt.
15. I have (keep) the beautiful card you sent me.
16. Have you (let) the cat out?
17. Yesterday I (send) the package parcel post.
18. Last weekend Bart (teach) his brother how to ride a bicycle.
19. Who (bring) an extra pencil?
20. Have I already (tell) you this story?
21. I think I (catch) my sister's cold.
22. Raymond (buy) a filing program for his computer.
23. She (get) a book from the library.
24. The Robinsons have (hold) on to that property for a hundred years.
25. Have you (set) the table for dinner?

Group 3

These irregular verbs form the past participle by adding *-n* to the past.

PRESENT	PRESENT PARTICIPLE	PAST	PAST PARTICIPLE
break	breaking	broke	(have) broken
choose	choosing	chose	(have) chosen
freeze	freezing	froze	(have) frozen
speak	speaking	spoke	(have) spoken
steal	stealing	stole	(have) stolen

Group 4

These irregular verbs form the past participle by adding *-n* to the present.

PRESENT	PRESENT PARTICIPLE	PAST	PAST PARTICIPLE
blow	blowing	blew	(have) blown
draw	drawing	drew	(have) drawn
drive	driving	drove	(have) driven
give	giving	gave	(have) given
grow	growing	grew	(have) grown
know	knowing	knew	(have) known
rise	rising	rose	(have) risen
see	seeing	saw	(have) seen
take	taking	took	(have) taken
throw	throwing	threw	(have) thrown

EXERCISE 3 *Determining the Correct Verb Form*

Number your paper 1 to 10. Then write the correct verb form for each sentence.

1. Have you ever (drove, driven) across the country?
2. Last week's storm (blew, blown) the roof off the barn.
3. I haven't (spoke, spoken) with Jamie since yesterday.
4. Lai Kin just (stole, stolen) third base!
5. Our new TV has been (broke, broken) for a week.
6. Have you (chose, chosen) the topic for your next history report?
7. I (saw, seen) a hilarious movie last night.
8. We have (took, taken) enough supplies to last a month.
9. Have you (gave, given) your speech yet?
10. I should have (knew, known) her name.

EXERCISE 4 *Using the Correct Verb Form*

Number your paper 1 to 20. Then write the past or the past participle of each verb in parentheses.

1. Lou caught the ball and (throw) it to first base.
2. Timmy must have (grow) three inches since May.
3. Our tulips (freeze) during the last spring frost.
4. I haven't (see) the movie at the Plaza yet.
5. Dr. Rosen (speak) at the assembly yesterday.
6. Everyone (rise) when the national anthem was played.
7. Have you ever (draw) portraits of your family?
8. Seth (give) a great talk about fads of the 1980's.
9. No one (know) how to record with the new VCR.
10. I should have (take) Spanish II this year.
11. Who (break) the clock in the living room?
12. Maria (choose) to ride Buddy, an older horse.
13. That is the sixth base Stephen has (steal) so far in this game.
14. Who (drive) you to choir practice?
15. Someone has (throw) out my old sneakers!
16. We have (freeze) some fresh strawberries in plastic bags.
17. I have (blow) up so many party balloons that I'm out of breath.
18. Cindy (draw) us a map of the way to her house.
19. Dad (grow) carrots in his garden last year, but the rabbits ate most of them.
20. The bread has (rise) above the top of the pan.

Group 5

These irregular verbs form the past and past participle by changing a vowel.

PRESENT	PRESENT PARTICIPLE	PAST	PAST PARTICIPLE
begin	beginning	began	(have) begun
drink	drinking	drank	(have) drunk
ring	ringing	rang	(have) rung
shrink	shrinking	shrank	(have) shrunk
sing	singing	sang	(have) sung
sink	sinking	sank	(have) sunk
swim	swimming	swam	(have) swum

Group 6

These irregular verbs form the past and past participle in other ways.

PRESENT	PRESENT PARTICIPLE	PAST	PAST PARTICIPLE
come	coming	came	(have) come
do	doing	did	(have) done
eat	eating	ate	(have) eaten
fall	falling	fell	(have) fallen
go	going	went	(have) gone
lie	lying	lay	(have) lain
ride	riding	rode	(have) ridden
run	running	ran	(have) run
tear	tearing	tore	(have) torn
wear	wearing	wore	(have) worn
write	writing	wrote	(have) written

EXERCISE 5 *Determining the Correct Verb Form*

Number your paper 1 to 10. Then write the correct verb form for each sentence.

1. I haven't (wrote, written) my science report yet.
2. Roy (ran, run) around the track ten times.
3. Have you (begun, began) to make dinner yet?
4. My best T-shirt has (shrank, shrunk) in the wash.
5. The twelve o'clock chimes have already (rang, rung).
6. Your pen must have (fell, fallen) out of your notebook.
7. They (ate, eaten) at a Thai restaurant last night.

8. Willis (came, come) to the meeting an hour late.
9. I have (did, done) this jigsaw puzzle before.
10. Luella (swam, swum) in the county swim meet.

EXERCISE 6 *Using the Correct Verb Form*

Number your paper 1 to 15. Then write the past or the past participle of each verb in parentheses.

1. Lionel has (go) to the store for a quart of milk.
2. Who (drink) the last bowl of homemade chicken soup?
3. I have never (ride) in a helicopter.
4. Their tent has (lie) on the ground all day.
5. The story (begin) with a flashback.
6. Who (sing) the solo during last night's concert?
7. The Beckermans (go) to Alaska for their vacation.
8. I should have (wear) gloves and a scarf.
9. His box of bait (sink) to the bottom of the pond.
10. The fullback (tear) through the line of scrimmage.
11. You (do) a great job!
12. He (lie) down and took a short nap before dinner.
13. You should have (come) to the game with us.
14. Kenneth (write) his report on a word processor.
15. We (ride) to the restaurant in Diana's new car.

EXERCISE 7 *Supplying the Correct Verb Form*

Number your paper 1 to 10. Then complete each pair of sentences by supplying the correct form of the verb in parentheses at the beginning of the sentence. (This exercise includes verbs from all six groups.)

1. *(write)* I _______ for an application. Have you _______ for one yet?
2. *(burst)* The dam _______ last April. Has it _______ again?
3. *(give)* Have you _______ your speech yet? I _______ mine yesterday.
4. *(throw)* Today at practice Tom _______ a fastball. Has he _______ many curveballs?
5. *(swim)* Last week I _______ across the lake. I have often _______ greater distances.
6. *(come)* Has the mail _______ yet? It _______ an hour ago.
7. *(see)* Have you _______ Andrew? I just _______ him in the library.

8. *(make)* Have you ______ your bed yet? I ______ mine as soon as I woke up.
9. *(choose)* Have you ______ your courses for next year? I ______ them a week ago.
10. *(begin)* Has the concert ______? It ______ an hour ago.

EXERCISE 8 *Using the Correct Verb Form*

Number your paper 1 to 15. Then write the correct verb form of each underlined word. If the verb is correct, write *C* after the number. (This exercise includes verbs from all six groups.)

1. Everyone has <u>went</u> swimming at Lake Omega.
2. Last night he <u>takes</u> the wrong turn at the intersection.
3. When the balloon <u>bursted</u>, the child began to cry.
4. Two hours ago I <u>seen</u> my sister at the ball game.
5. Have you ever <u>taught</u> him how to water-ski?
6. The committee <u>come</u> to a unanimous decision.
7. You should have <u>wrote</u> him a thank-you note.
8. I don't believe that you <u>drank</u> the whole quart of milk!
9. Jerry <u>drived</u> down the narrow street too fast.
10. I have never <u>ran</u> so fast in my whole life!
11. He has <u>threw</u> the newspaper into the bushes every day!
12. The Civil War <u>begun</u> in South Carolina in 1861.
13. Jennifer <u>leaved</u> the party without saying good-bye.
14. I have already <u>sended</u> out the party invitations.
15. The small meteorite <u>fell</u> to Earth and landed in a field.

EXERCISE 9 *Cumulative Review*

Number your paper 1 to 15. Then write the past or the past participle of each verb in parentheses.

Good Eating

1. In 1960, American scientists (face) a serious problem.
2. Spacecraft (weigh) too much.
3. No solution was (find) until a dried, compressed material was (invent).
4. It could be (use) for cabinets and panels.
5. The exciting aspect of the discovery was that it also could be (eat)!
6. The early version of this material, however, would have (break) the astronauts' teeth if it had been (eat).

7. Another version was eventually (make) from powdered milk, cornstarch, flour, banana flakes, and grits.
8. The grits were extremely important because they (hold) the mixture together.
9. The mixture was (call) Edible Structural Material.
10. Once it was (bake), it was hard enough to drill holes in.
11. Before it could be (consume), it first had to be soaked.
12. That (bring) back its edible consistency.
13. The material (taste) like banana-flavored cereal.
14. The scientists, however, were (refuse) a patent because an edible structure had already been (patent).
15. That honor had (go) to the ice-cream cone.

Verb Tense

The principal parts of a verb are used to form the tenses of a verb. *Tense* is the form a verb takes to express a particular time. The six tenses are *present, past, future, present perfect, past perfect,* and *future perfect.* In the following examples, the six tenses of the verb *see* are used to express action at different times.

PRESENT	I **see** at least one movie a week.
PAST	I **saw** a movie last night.
FUTURE	I **will see** another movie this weekend.
PRESENT PERFECT	I **have seen** three movies so far this month.
PAST PERFECT	I **had** not **seen** many movies before last year.
FUTURE PERFECT	By the end of this year, I **will have seen** almost 100 movies.

Conjugation of a Verb

One of the best ways to study the tenses of a verb is to look at the conjugation of that verb. A *conjugation* is a list of all the singular and plural forms of a verb in its various tenses. Following is a conjugation of the verb *swim.*

Note: The present participle is used to conjugate only the progressive forms of a verb. *(See page 669.)*

Conjugation of *Swim*

PRINCIPAL PARTS

PRESENT	PRESENT PARTICIPLE	PAST	PAST PARTICIPLE
swim	swimming	swam	swum

Present

This tense expresses action (or state of being) that is taking place at the present time.

SINGULAR	PLURAL
I swim	we swim
you swim	you swim
he, she, it swims	they swim

Past

This tense expresses action (or state of being) that occurred at a definite time in the past.

SINGULAR	PLURAL
I swam	we swam
you swam	you swam
he, she, it swam	they swam

Future

This tense expresses action (or state of being) that will take place in the future. The future tense is formed by adding *shall* or *will* to the present.

SINGULAR	PLURAL
I shall/will swim	we shall/will swim
you will swim	you will swim
he, she, it will swim	they will swim

Present Perfect

This tense expresses action (or state of being) that was completed at some indefinite time in the past. It is also used to express action that started in the past and is still going on. The present perfect tense is formed by adding *has* or *have* to the past participle.

SINGULAR	PLURAL
I have swum	we have swum
you have swum	you have swum
he, she, it has swum	they have swum

Past Perfect

This tense expresses action (or state of being) that took place before another past action. It is formed by adding *had* to the past participle.

SINGULAR	PLURAL
I had swum	we had swum
you had swum	you had swum
he, she, it had swum	they had swum

Future Perfect

This tense expresses action (or state of being) that will be completed by some given time in the future. It is formed by adding *shall have* or *will have* to the past participle.

SINGULAR	PLURAL
I shall/will have swum	we shall/will have swum
you will have swum	you will have swum
he, she, it will have swum	they will have swum

EXERCISE 10 *Conjugating a Verb*

Using the conjugation of the verb *swim* as a model, write the conjugation of the following two verbs.

1. work, working, worked, worked
2. go, going, went, gone

Progressive Forms Each of the six tenses has an additional form that is used to express continuing action. This form, called the *progressive form,* consists of a form of the verb *be* plus the present participle of the verb. Following are the progressive forms of *swim.*

PRESENT PROGRESSIVE	am, is, are swimming
PAST PROGRESSIVE	was, were swimming
FUTURE PROGRESSIVE	shall/will be swimming
PRESENT PERFECT PROGRESSIVE	has, have been swimming
PAST PERFECT PROGRESSIVE	had been swimming
FUTURE PERFECT PROGRESSIVE	shall/will have been swimming

Conjugation of the Irregular Verb *Be* The principal parts of *be* are *am, being, was,* and *been.* Since the principal parts of the verb *be* are highly irregular, the conjugation of that verb is very different from other irregular verbs.

Conjugation of *Be*

PRINCIPAL PARTS

PRESENT	PRESENT PARTICIPLE	PAST	PAST PARTICIPLE
am	being	was	been

Present

SINGULAR	PLURAL
I am	we are
you are	you are
he, she, it is	they are

Past

SINGULAR	PLURAL
I was	we were
you were	you were
he, she, it was	they were

Future

SINGULAR	PLURAL
I shall/will be	we shall/will be
you will be	you will be
he, she, it will be	they will be

Present Perfect

SINGULAR	PLURAL
I have been	we have been
you have been	you have been
he, she, it has been	they have been

Past Perfect

SINGULAR	PLURAL
I had been	we had been
you had been	you had been
he, she, it had been	they had been

Future Perfect

SINGULAR	PLURAL
I shall/will have been	we shall/will have been
you will have been	you will have been
he, she, it will have been	they will have been

Application to Writing

Write several paragraphs in which you explain any past working experience. Use at least three different tenses of the verb *work,* including some progressive forms.

EXERCISE 11 *Identifying Verb Tenses*

Number your paper 1 to 20. Then write the tense of each underlined verb.

EXAMPLE Pat was here just a moment ago.
ANSWER past

1. In 1790, the first United States census showed a population of 3,929,214 persons in the 13 states.
2. Everyone in the library was studying hard.
3. In Amsterdam, Holland, more than one third of the people own bicycles.
4. Kevin will be going to college next fall.
5. The first United States coin to bear the portrait of an actual person was the Lincoln penny of 1909.
6. Buck told us that he had seen that movie three times.
7. The team has been practicing for two weeks now.
8. This book has been extremely helpful to me.
9. Tom will have arrived by the time we get to the gate at the airport.
10. I am taking an advanced course in Spanish.
11. Wendy will be in our homeroom.
12. The blue sweater is my first choice.
13. A horse will eat about 15 pounds of hay and 9 pounds of fodder each day.
14. Before you called, I had been worrying.
15. Last night we were planning our trip to Arizona.
16. Earthquakes and volcanoes have caused cities to sink beneath the sea.
17. By next March we will have known each other for five years.
18. Lee has been working at Hayley's Hardware Store every other weekend.
19. The dog has been a friend to humans longer than the cat.
20. There are over twice as many chickens in the United States as there are people.

Uses of the Tenses

Each tense expresses a particular time. Some tenses show the time relationship between events. To communicate clearly and accurately, you need to know the uses of the various tenses.

The Present Tense This tense is used mainly to express action (or state of being) that is taking place at the present time. The present tense also has two other uses: to express customary or habitual action and to express a general truth.

PRESENT ACTION	Pamela **skates** very well.
HABITUAL ACTION	Every Saturday we **meet** at the gym.
A GENERAL TRUTH	Honesty **is** the best policy.

The Past Tense This tense expresses action (or state of being) that occurred at a definite time in the past.

Last week I **won** a handball match against Ron Nevins.

The Future Tense This tense expresses action (or state of being) that will take place in the future.

Bill **will arrive** on the 9:37 flight from Atlanta.

The Present Perfect Tense This tense expresses action (or state of being) that occurred at some indefinite time in the past. It is also used to express action that started in the past and is still going on.

Peggy **has called** Mr. Miller about a summer job. [You do not know exactly when she called.]

Ray Jones **has been** the team manager for two seasons. [He is still the manager.]

The Past Perfect Tense This tense expresses action (or state of being) that took place before some other event in the past.

Jan **had lived** in New York for two years before she moved to Florida. [The *living* came before the *moving*.]

The Future Perfect Tense This tense expresses action (or state of being) that will be completed at some future time before some other future event. This tense is seldom used.

I **will have left** for Texas by the time you receive this letter.

Note: Remember that the progressive forms of the tenses are used to express continuing action.

Terry **is talking** on the phone now.

EXERCISE 12 *Choosing the Correct Tense*

Number your paper 1 to 20. Then write the correct form of the verb in parentheses.

EXAMPLE Sirens (blew, have blown) for an hour last night.
ANSWER blew

1. The Cardinals (won, have won) every game to date.
2. I discovered that Frank (broke, had broken) the stereo.
3. Marie (work, worked) at the hospital last year.
4. In September our new gymnasium (opened, has opened).
5. I (practice, will practice) my serve all next week.
6. Since last summer I (wanted, have wanted) to own a car.
7. We (lived, had lived) in Oklahoma for three years before we moved to Texas.
8. It was late, and Lamar (forgot, had forgotten) to study.
9. Yesterday I learned that I (won, had won) the contest.
10. The umpire insisted that the second baseman (dropped, had dropped) the ball.
11. Last week I (learned, have learned) to use a computer.
12. Tomorrow Timothy (begins, will begin) his new job.
13. My uncle (owned, has owned) a boat for ten years.
14. When the bell rang, we (finished, had finished) making the posters.
15. Elena (is, has been) at our school since November.
16. So far my family (visited, has visited) 40 states.
17. I hope we (hear, will hear) from him by tomorrow.
18. When I got there, I realized I (take, had taken) my sister's book.
19. Barbara (played, has played) the piano since age ten.
20. Last week I (read, had read) a mystery story.

Shifts in Tense

Writers use the past tense most often when they write a story. Whatever tense you choose to write in, use it consistently throughout your story or report. A shift in tense can often cause confusion and misunderstanding.

Rule 27d **Avoid shifting tenses when relating a sequence of events.**

A shift in tense can occur incorrectly within a sentence or between related sentences.

INCORRECT The engine of the old car **began** [past] to sputter and then suddenly **stalls.** [present]

CORRECT The engine of the old car **began** [past] to sputter and then suddenly **stalled.** [past]

INCORRECT After everyone **had seen** [past perfect] the movie about car accidents, three people **told** [past] their personal experiences. The audience **listens** [present] carefully.

CORRECT After everyone **had seen** [past perfect] the movie about car accidents, three people **told** [past] their personal experiences. The audience **listened** [past] carefully.

EXERCISE 13 *Correcting Shifts in Tense*

Number your paper 1 to 10. If the sentence or pair of sentences contains a shift in tense, write the second verb in the correct tense. If a sentence or pair of sentences is correct, write *C.*

1. The beagle saw the Siamese and runs after it.
2. When Ed hooked the bass, he has a hard time landing it.
3. Stewart sprinted the last 30 yards. Then he collapses.
4. Once Jen became club president, she forms many committees.
5. Denny jumped overboard. His oar had fallen into the water.
6. When Nathan reaches the cabin, he always built a fire.
7. The temperature is so high that the flowers are wilting.
8. Although Dan had known the combination, he never told anyone.
9. The search party went back to the camp. Martin continues to look for the lost campers by himself.
10. When Carmen got a *D* in history, she vows to do better.

EXERCISE 14 *Correcting Shifts in Tense*

Rewrite the following paragraph, correcting any shifts in tense.

A Lasting Change

William Hoy was an outfielder on six teams between 1888 and 1902. He compiles a .288 lifetime batting average and an impressive record as an outfielder and as a base stealer. There is, however, something extra special about Hoy. He is completely deaf as a result of a childhood illness. "I found it no handicap," Hoy says of his deafness. Initially there was one problem. Hoy couldn't hear the umpire call balls and strikes when he is at bat. Then Hoy has an idea. He asks an umpire to signal a strike with his right arm. Soon all umpires follow suit. This practice has continued ever since.

Active and Passive Voice

In addition to tense, a verb has voice. There is the *active voice* and the *passive voice.*

Rule 27e The **active voice** indicates that the subject is performing the action.

Rule 27f The **passive voice** indicates that the action of the verb is being performed upon the subject.

In the following examples, the same verb is used both in the active voice and the passive voice. The verb in the active voice has a direct object. The verb in the passive voice has no direct object.

ACTIVE VOICE Cal **pilots** the WGBH helicopter. (d.o.: helicopter)

PASSIVE VOICE The WGBH helicopter **is piloted** by Cal. (subj.: helicopter)

Only transitive verbs can be used in the passive voice. *(See page 554.)* When an active verb is changed to passive, the direct object of the active verb becomes the subject of the passive verb. The subject of the active verb is then included in a prepositional phrase.

ACTIVE VOICE The flood **destroyed** many homes. (d.o.: homes)

PASSIVE VOICE Many homes **were destroyed** by the flood. (subj.: homes)

EXERCISE 15 *Recognizing Active and Passive Voice*

Number your paper 1 to 10. Write the verb in each sentence. Then label it *active* or *passive*.

1. The Gulf Stream warms the west coast of Europe.
2. Only female mosquitoes bite people.
3. Crickets are kept as pets in China.
4. Do not lift a rabbit by its ears.
5. Nearly all horses are mounted from the left side.
6. *Two Years before the Mast* was written by Richard Dana.
7. The giraffe has excellent vision.
8. A single fly may carry a million bacteria.
9. Rock music is enjoyed by many young people.
10. In the film the space invaders are attacked by the army.

Use of Voice

When you write, use the active voice as much as possible. The active voice adds directness and impact to your writing. Use the passive voice, however, when the doer of the action is unknown or unimportant or when you want to emphasize the receiver of the action.

Main Street **has** just **been resurfaced.** [doers unknown]
Adam **was given** the prize. [emphasis on the receiver]

EXERCISE 16 *Using the Active Voice*

Number your paper 1 to 10. Then write each sentence, changing the passive voice to the active voice if appropriate. If a sentence is better in the passive voice, write *C* after the number.

1. Two arguments against a class dance were given by Alan.
2. The Blue Grotto is located on the Italian island of Capri.
3. Her campaign speech will never be forgotten by Russ.
4. Honeybees were introduced to our country from Europe.
5. Copper weathervanes were made by early American metalworkers.
6. Recently great interest in acid rain has been shown by many.
7. The new rules were posted on the bulletin board.
8. For hours the blaze was fought by the fire fighters.
9. Many acres of forest are needlessly destroyed each year.
10. An excellent speech about Picasso was given by Kate.

Integrating Language Skills

USING YOUR TEXT
Verbs (552–561)
Journal Writing (13 and 36)

Usage: Editing for Verb Errors

When editing your written work, look for errors in the use of verbs. You should check specifically for the following problems.

- Use of incorrect verb forms. Watch especially for irregular verbs.
- Incorrect shifts in tense.
- Inappropriate use of the passive voice. Use the active voice whenever possible.

You are likely to find errors in verb usage easily if you read your work aloud.

Checking Your Understanding Edit the following paragraph for all verb errors. Then rewrite the paragraph to include your changes.

> The world's best violins were made by Antonius Stradivarius. After he play the violin, he become interested in making these instruments. At first he perform many experiments with the shape of the violin. He want his violins to sound as lovely as the human voice. Success was achieved by him early in his career. Since his death in 1737, no one had been able to duplicate the sound of his violins. Unfortunately his secret was never shared by him, not even with his sons.

Writing a Journal Entry A journal is a personal history. It is an excellent way to keep a record of major events in your life. To create a journal entry, make three lists on your paper and label them *Past, Present,* and *Future.* Then jot down at least three things that you have already done today, three things that are presently happening, and three more that you expect to be doing during the rest of the day. Record your thoughts about the day.

Write a first draft of a personal essay for today. Using your notes, include the events that have already taken place, those that are presently taking place, and those that are still going to take place. Next, as you revise your first draft, make sure that you have used colorful, fresh verbs to portray your experiences. ***Application:*** Looking specifically for verb errors, edit your first draft. Then write the final draft.

Chapter 27

Review

A Using the Correct Verb Form Number your paper 1 to 15. Then write the past or the past participle of each verb in parentheses.

1. Roman soldiers (eat) onions, believing the vegetable would make them brave.
2. The coaches (choose) Otis as the most valuable player.
3. You should have (give) him a second chance.
4. Tina (see) the artist sketch an ocean scene.
5. The singer (shrink) back from the group of eager admirers.
6. The central water main (burst) yesterday.
7. Francis Scott Key (write) the lyrics to our national anthem.
8. Where have you (lay) the hammer?
9. By finding my ring, Georgia (do) me an enormous favor.
10. In the legends, King Arthur (hold) his court in Camelot.
11. My father has (wear) the same after-shave lotion for years.
12. We (find) some old records in my grandmother's attic.
13. How long have you (know) about this?
14. The school has (buy) six more computers.
15. In 1215, King John (put) his seal to the Magna Carta.

B Choosing the Correct Tense Number your paper 1 to 10. Then write the correct form of the verb in parentheses.

1. By the time the clouds disappeared, the sun already (set, had set).
2. Two months ago I (ordered, have ordered) a bicycle.
3. Pam (beats, beat) me at tennis whenever we play.
4. I (look, will look) for you on the news tonight.
5. Our team (played, has played) very well so far this season.
6. Yesterday Greg (run, ran) the 100-yard dash.
7. By last summer Ann (earned, had earned) enough money for a ten-speed bicycle.
8. When the storm broke, we wondered if we (closed, had closed) the car windows.
9. Lee (ask, asked) for directions to the new stadium.
10. Sharon (began, has begun) playing the drums in May.

C Determining Active and Passive Voice Number your paper 1 to 15. Write the verb in each sentence. Then label it *active* or *passive*.

1. The car wash was sponsored by the sophomore class.
2. The Southern Hemisphere has only one species of bear.
3. Our ripe corn was harvested by a hungry raccoon.
4. All of the flowers in our garden were planted by my dad.
5. Jules Verne wrote *From the Earth to the Moon*.
6. I am taking driver's education this semester.
7. Do you want an apple or a peach?
8. The awards were announced over the intercom.
9. The SAT's are taken by many juniors.
10. I need a new pair of boots for winter.
11. Most of the tourists took the tour to the castle.
12. The audience applause was measured by a sound monitor.
13. The telephone has been ringing all day.
14. Jimmy raised the window without any problem.
15. By mistake your letter was opened by Aunt Louise.

Mastery Test

Number your paper 1 to 10. Then write the past or the past participle of each verb in parentheses.

1. The play had already (begin) by the time we arrived at the theater.
2. Have you ever (write) a 20-page term paper before?
3. Marguerite (sing) a solo in the spring concert.
4. The birds have (eat) all the sunflower seeds.
5. Clyde (go) in to replace the left forward.
6. Mom's string of pearls (break) last night.
7. The gale has (tear) our awnings to pieces.
8. Paula has been (choose) president of our class.
9. Within ten minutes another bus (come) along.
10. Have you (see) the headline in the newspaper this morning?

C h a p t e r

28 Using Pronouns

Diagnostic Test

Number your paper 1 to 10. Then write the correct form of the pronoun in parentheses.

EXAMPLE Brian showed Ramon and (I, me) the new dance step.
ANSWER me

1. Mom knits sweaters for Concetta and (I, me).
2. Is that (she, her) in the plaid dress?
3. Alberto drove (their, they're) car to the mall.
4. To (who, whom) did you give the camera?
5. Otis and (he, him) climbed Black Gum Mountain for the first time last weekend.
6. Gary can type as fast as (she, her).
7. One of the men was late for (his, their) appointment.
8. Take the advice of (we, us) computer experts.
9. The police questioned a suspect (who, whom) they thought had a motive for the crime.
10. Each of the girls should bring (her, their) own diving equipment to the lesson.

The Cases of Personal Pronouns

At one time nouns in the English language had special endings to show how they were used within a sentence. Several hundred years ago, however, English nouns began to drop those endings. Now the word *boy,* for example, is the same whether it is a subject or an object. The only time the form changes is when a noun is used to show possession. Then *boy* becomes *boy's.*

Pronouns did not follow suit. Therefore, you must use *he* for a subject, *him* for an object, and *his* to show possession. These changes occur because all nouns and pronouns have *case.*

Rule 28a **Case** is the form of a noun or a pronoun that indicates its use in a sentence.

Nouns and pronouns in English have three cases: the *nominative case,* the *objective case,* and the *possessive case.* Pronouns usually change form for each of the cases.

Nominative Case

(Used for subjects and predicate nominatives)

SINGULAR	I, you, he, she, it
PLURAL	we, you, they

Objective Case

(Used for direct objects, indirect objects, and objects of prepositions)

SINGULAR	me, you, him, her, it
PLURAL	us, you, them

Possessive Case

(Used to show ownership or possession)

SINGULAR	my, mine, your, yours, his, her, hers, its
PLURAL	our, ours, your, yours, their, theirs

Note: *You* and *it* are the same in both the nominative and the objective cases.

EXERCISE 1 *Determining Case*

Number your paper 1 to 10. Write the personal pronouns in each sentence. Then write the case of each one: *nominative, objective,* or *possessive.*

1. My sister and I will take the skates with us.
2. Did your brother see him at the game on Friday?
3. They haven't made up their minds yet.
4. He told me that her car was being repaired.
5. Did she tell them that the desk lamp is his?
6. Take ours or theirs.
7. We want a kitten from this litter of hers.
8. I gave the magazine to her yesterday.
9. Our team won the state championship.
10. We spoke to him briefly after his trip.

The Nominative Case

The nominative case pronouns are *I, you, he, she, it, we,* and *they.*

Rule 28b The **nominative case** is used for subjects and predicate nominatives.

Pronouns as Subjects A pronoun can be the subject of either an independent clause or a subordinate clause. *(See pages 625–645 for a review of subordinate clauses.)*

INDEPENDENT CLAUSE	**He** is my best friend.
	We arrived at seven, but **they** came even later.
SUBORDINATE CLAUSE	Jane said that **she** called you last night. [*That she called you last night* is the subordinate clause.]
	After **we** eat, let's go to the movies. [*After we eat* is the subordinate clause.]

Because selecting the correct pronoun in a compound subject can sometimes present a problem, you should follow two steps. First, check to make sure that you have selected a nominative case pronoun. Second, test your selection by saying each pronoun separately.

Matt and (he, him) are taking trumpet lessons.
He is taking trumpet lessons.
Him is taking trumpet lessons.

The nominative case *he* is the correct form to use.

Matt and **he** are taking trumpet lessons.

This test also works if both subjects are pronouns.

She and **I** are now living in New York.

Pronouns as Predicate Nominatives A predicate nominative follows a linking verb and identifies or renames the subject. *(See page 556* and *557 for lists of common linking verbs.)*

That was **she** on the phone.

The winner was **he.**

Each pronoun in a compound predicate nominative should be carefully checked to make sure it is in the nominative case.

The award winners were Tracy and **they.**
The members not voting were Paulo and **she.**

Nominative case pronouns are not always used for predicate nominatives in casual conversation. You often hear people say, "It's me" instead of "It is I," or "That's him" instead of "That is he." As common as this usage is in conversation, it is not correct and should be avoided in written work.

Appositives with Nominative Case Pronouns Sometimes a pronoun that is used as a subject or a predicate nominative will have a noun appositive. An appositive identifies or explains the noun or pronoun in front of it. *(See pages 603–605.)* An appositive never affects the case of a pronoun. In fact, you can easily check whether you have used the correct pronoun by dropping the appositive from the sentence.

We *members* will hold a fund-raising drive. [*We* will hold a fund-raising drive.]

The highest scorers in basketball were **we** *sophomores.* [The highest scorers in basketball were *we.*]

EXERCISE 2 *Using Pronouns in the Nominative Case*

Number your paper 1 to 10. Then write the correct form of the pronoun in parentheses.

1. Nat Gardner and (I, me) will be ushers at the play.
2. The best singers in the school musical were Lloyd and (she, her).
3. Were Marie and (he, him) surprised to see you?
4. Is that (she, her) and Marsha at the concession stand?
5. (He, Him) and (I, me) were friends in grammar school.
6. The Jensons or (they, them) will hold a clambake.
7. The students with the highest grade point average are (he, him) and (she, her).
8. (They, Them) and the guides were lost in the woods for over five hours.
9. I think the most talented people in our class are Lea and (he, him).
10. (They, Them) and (I, me) will be attending the meeting.

EXERCISE 3 *Supplying Pronouns in the Nominative Case*

Number your paper 1 to 10. Complete each sentence by writing an appropriate pronoun in the nominative case. (Do not use *you* or *it*.) Then write how the pronoun is used—*subject* or *predicate nominative*.

EXAMPLE The class president should be ______.
POSSIBLE ANSWER she—predicate nominative

1. ______ are my best friends this year.
2. Will you and ______ do your juggling act?
3. The new swimming champion is ______.
4. Mr. Handley promised that ______ would speak with you after school.
5. ______ bird-watchers will meet in the park at five in the morning.
6. The entertainers at the assembly will be ______ actors.
7. If ______ doesn't answer the phone, ______ should go over to the house.
8. The last one up in the morning is usually ______.
9. The best runners on the team are Rayma and ______.
10. The only ones who are qualified for the job are ______ and ______.

EXERCISE 4 *Finding Nominative Case Errors*

Number your paper 1 to 10. If an underlined pronoun is in the wrong case, write it correctly. If it is in the correct case, write *C* after the number.

EXAMPLE You and <u>me</u> should wash the car today.
ANSWER I

1. The master of ceremonies will be <u>him</u>.
2. The O'Rileys and <u>them</u> went fishing over the weekend.
3. <u>Us</u> inexperienced travelers got lost twice in Denver.
4. The featured reporters were Lynn and <u>she</u>.
5. We'll hang the posters after Rosalie and <u>her</u> finish them.
6. Janina and <u>I</u> cataloged the new library books.
7. Do you really think <u>them</u> are the right ones to buy?
8. It was <u>he</u> who called you last night.
9. Neither Conrad nor <u>him</u> attended practice today.
10. The outstanding performers were the Jeffersons and <u>them</u>.

EXERCISE 5 *Writing Sentences*

Write two sentences for each of the following groups of words. In the first sentence, use the words as subjects. In the second sentence, use them as predicate nominatives.

1. you and I **2.** he and she **3.** we runners

The Objective Case

The objective case pronouns are *me, you, him, her, it, us,* and *them.*

Rule 28c The **objective case** is used for direct objects, indirect objects, and objects of a preposition.

Pronouns as Direct and Indirect Objects If a pronoun answers the question *Whom?* after an action verb, it will be a direct object. A sentence that has a direct object can also have an indirect object. A pronoun used as an indirect object will come before the direct object and will answer the question *To whom?* or *For whom?* A pronoun used as a direct object or an indirect object is in the objective case.

DIRECT OBJECTS	Carlos wants **them** to visit. Show **her** through the house.
INDIRECT OBJECTS	Claire told **us** the details. [*Details* is the direct object.] Please pour **me** a glass of milk. [*Glass* is the direct object.]

Always check to see if the pronouns in a compound direct object are in the objective case. You can use the test you used to check compound subjects. Say each pronoun separately.

Did you see Joel and (he, him) last night?
Did you see **he** last night?
Did you see **him** last night?

The objective case *him* is the correct form to use.

Did you see Joel and **him** last night?

You can also use the same test to check the pronouns used in a compound indirect object.

Show Jessica and (I, me) the new schedule.
Show **I** the new schedule.
Show **me** the new schedule.

The objective case *me* is the correct form to use.

Show Jessica and **me** the new schedule.

Pronouns as Objects of a Preposition A prepositional phrase begins with a preposition and ends with a noun or a pronoun called the *object of a preposition.* *(See page 575 for a list of common prepositions.)* A pronoun used as the object of a preposition is in the objective case.

I hope Al goes with **us.** [*With us* is the prepositional phrase.]

The lifeguard shouted to **them.** [*To them* is the prepositional phrase.]

A pronoun used as part of a compound object of a preposition can also be checked by saying each pronoun separately.

The Chases' dog always barks at Inés and (I, me).
The Chases' dog always barks at **I.**
The Chases' dog always barks at **me.**

The objective case *me* is the correct form to use.

The Chases' dog always barks at Inés and **me.**

Appositives with Objective Case Pronouns A pronoun used as a direct object, an indirect object, or an object of a preposition can have a noun appositive. An appositive never affects the case of a pronoun.

The principal thanked **us** *volunteers.* [The principal thanked *us.*]

Peter gave **us** *hikers* a cool drink. [Peter gave *us* a cool drink.]

Smile for **us** *photographers.* [Smile for *us.*]

EXERCISE 6 *Using Pronouns in the Objective Case*

Number your paper 1 to 20. Then write the correct form of the pronoun in parentheses.

1. My uncle took my cousin and (I, me) to the state fair.
2. Give Todd and (she, her) some orange juice.
3. Who is sitting between Pilar and (she, her)?
4. Dad warned my sister and (I, me) about careless driving.
5. The sailboat belongs to the Levins and (they, them).
6. The package should be sent to (they, them) or (we, us).
7. Yoko told Justin and (he, him) about Japan.
8. Will you take a picture of (he, him) and (I, me)?
9. Paula showed Martin, Ellen, and (they, them) her slides of Maine.
10. Dues should be given to Pat or (we, us).
11. Leave some of the salad for Ralph and (I, me).
12. Did you give Lola and (she, her) directions to your house?
13. We're expecting the Danielsons and (they, them) any minute now.
14. Do you want to go to the basketball game with Claudia and (we, us)?
15. Tonia sent Félix and (I, me) some oranges from Florida.
16. The referee called a double foul on Max and (he, him).
17. The audience gave (we, us) actors a standing ovation.
18. Mr. Antell loaned Norman and (she, her) fishing poles.
19. Horses like (they, them) are called thoroughbreds.
20. The votes were divided between Ginny and (I, me).

EXERCISE 7 *Supplying Pronouns in the Objective Case*

Complete each sentence by writing a pronoun in the objective case. (Do not use *you* or *it*.) Then write how the pronoun is used—*direct object, indirect object,* or *object of a preposition.*

1. Will you call Tim and _______ when dinner is ready?
2. Please teach Angela and _______ the rules of that game.
3. During the assembly the coach praised _______ athletes.
4. Those tapes belong to Charlotte and _______.
5. Steven drove Brewster and _______ to the horse show.
6. Landlubbers like _______ shouldn't go in the water.
7. Give _______ your ideas about the school newspaper.
8. Mr. Lee called Chad and _______ into the yard.
9. Mr. Tobias will take Kena and _______ to the rink.
10. This matter should be discussed among _______ members.

EXERCISE 8 *Finding Objective Case Errors*

Number your paper 1 to 10. If an underlined pronoun is in the wrong case, write it correctly. If it is correct, write *C* after the number.

1. The lifeguard warned Ellen and <u>me</u> about the undertow.
2. Just between you and <u>I</u>, his plan will never work.
3. Please notify <u>we</u> committee members of the next meeting.
4. There's an extra piece of pizza for you or <u>him</u>.
5. Mr. Dobson showed Rosa and <u>I</u> a beautiful wood carving.
6. My sister bought tickets for Kevin and <u>them</u>.
7. There were no other volunteers except Carlos and <u>she</u>.
8. Joyce found Warren and <u>he</u> studying in the library.
9. Beginners like you and <u>they</u> should jog only a mile.
10. The store manager gave Dan and <u>I</u> a nice raise.

EXERCISE 9 *Writing Sentences*

Write five sentences that follow the directions below.

1. Use *Kate* and *me* as a compound direct object.
2. Use *Roger* and *him* as a compound indirect object.
3. Use *Greg* and *her* as a compound object of a preposition.
4. Use *us joggers* as a direct object with an appositive.
5. Use *them* and *us* as a compound object of a preposition.

The Possessive Case

The possessive case pronouns are *my, mine, your, yours, his, her, hers, its, our, ours, their,* and *theirs.*

Rule 28d The **possessive case** is used to show ownership or possession.

Some possessive case pronouns can be used to show possession before a noun or before a gerund. Others can be used by themselves.

BEFORE A NOUN	I enjoyed **her** story very much.
BEFORE A GERUND	**His** practicing has helped.
BY THEMSELVES	Is this notebook **yours** or **mine**?

Unlike the possessive noun, the possessive personal pronoun does not take an apostrophe.

POSSESSIVE PRONOUN	**Her** piano is out of tune.
POSSESSIVE NOUN	**Martha's** piano is out of tune.

Note: Do not confuse certain possessive pronouns with contractions. *Its, your, their,* and *theirs* are possessive pronouns. *It's, you're, they're,* and *there's* are contractions.

EXERCISE 10 *Using Pronouns in the Possessive Case*

Number your paper 1 to 15. Then write the correct word in parentheses.

1. Did your dad object to (your, you're) taking up the oboe?
2. The blue sweater is (hers, her's).
3. (Their, They're) having a block party this weekend.
4. I've found my ticket, but where are (their's, theirs)?
5. They say (its, it's) speed is incredible.
6. Could these keys be (theirs, there's)?
7. (Your, You're) sitting on my notebook!
8. The ranger objected to (their, them) swimming in the lake.
9. Those old bicycles are (ours, our's).
10. The coach thinks (me, my) exercising is too strenuous.
11. (His, His's) temperature is finally down.
12. I think (its, it's) time to leave.
13. (Their, They're) shouts warned us of the fire.
14. I think (your, you're) report is excellent.
15. (Their's, There's) a special bulletin on TV.

EXERCISE 11 Cumulative Review

Number your paper 1 to 20. Find and write each pronoun that is in the wrong case. Then write it correctly. If a sentence is correct, write *C* after the number.

EXAMPLE Was that him pitching during the third inning?
ANSWER him—he

1. Us hikers froze like statues when we saw the snake.
2. There's some cold chicken in the refrigerator for both Carrie and her.
3. The prize money will be split between them and we.
4. People like Arlene and he should be veterinarians.
5. We were proud of them winning the scholarships.
6. The captains of the soccer team are Hans and him.
7. What can you do to stop them running across your lawn?
8. The meal pleased even we gourmets.
9. Ask them or us anything you want to know about the computerized filing system.
10. Ernie and him gave up their weekend jobs.
11. My parents squeezed my brother, my sister, the dog, and I into the car, and we headed west.
12. He mailed Lupe and I a box of pecans from Austin, Texas.
13. Everybody ate a second helping except Otis and me.
14. Finally they found seats in the bleachers beside Maureen and he.
15. That's him going into the auditorium right now.
16. He was pleased with me trying out for the varsity soccer team.
17. Ruth and me are taking tennis lessons on Saturdays.
18. Us photographers shot pictures of them on the field.
19. Fortunately Philip and her didn't drop any glasses on the floor.
20. It's them, all right.

Application to Writing

Write a short essay in which you describe the unique traits or characteristics of each member of a family. You may, if you wish, include relatives beyond the immediate family or describe a family member's favorite friends. Be sure that all of the pronouns in your essay are used correctly.

Pronoun Problems

People answering the phone often say, "Whom should I say is calling?" They really should say, "Who should I say is calling?" Choosing between *who* and *whom* can be a problem. Another pronoun problem arises with an incomplete construction called an *elliptical clause.* Should you say, "Carl is more alert than I" or "Carl is more alert than me"? Both of these problems will be explained in the following section.

Who or *Whom*

Who is a pronoun that changes its form depending on how it is used in a sentence. The singular and plural forms of *who* and its related pronouns, however, are the same.

NOMINATIVE CASE	who, whoever
OBJECTIVE CASE	whom, whomever
POSSESSIVE CASE	whose

Who and its related pronouns are used mainly in questions and subordinate clauses.

Rule 28e **The correct case of *who* is determined by how the pronoun is used in a question or a clause.**

In Questions *Who* or one of its related pronouns is often used to ask a question. The form of *who* you choose will depend upon how the pronoun is used in a question.

NOMINATIVE CASE	**Who** will drive me to school? [subject]
OBJECTIVE CASE	**Whom** did you invite? [direct object] To **whom** were you speaking? [object of the preposition *to*]

EXERCISE 12 *Using Forms of* Who *in Questions*

Number your paper 1 to 10. Write the correct form of the pronoun in parentheses. Then write how each pronoun is used—*subject, direct object,* or *object of a preposition.*

1. (Who, Whom) won the award for best athlete after the game?
2. For (who, whom) should I ask?
3. (Who, Whom) did you nominate for best float in the parade?

4. With (who, whom) are you going?
5. (Who, Whom) did the principal decide to send to the conference?
6. (Who, Whom) should be introduced first, the mayor or the president of the senate?
7. To (who, whom) was the package sent?
8. (Who, Whom) will present the award?
9. About (who, whom) were you speaking?
10. (Who, Whom) did they take to the benefit concert?

In Clauses Forms of *who* are also used in both adjective and noun clauses. The way in which *who* or one of its related pronouns is used in a clause determines its case. The following examples show how forms of *who* are used in adjective clauses.

NOMINATIVE CASE	He is the man **who fixed the roof.** [*Who* is the subject of *fixed.*]
OBJECTIVE CASE	A woman **whom we met in Maine** is visiting us. [*Whom* is the direct object of *met.* We met whom in Maine.]
	This is Mrs. Brooks, **with whom I work.** [*Whom* is the object of the preposition *with.*]

The following examples show how *who* is used in noun clauses.

NOMINATIVE CASE	Show your pass to **whoever stops you.** [*Whoever* is the subject of *stops.*]
	I don't know **who my guidance counselor is.** [*Who* is a predicate nominative.]
OBJECTIVE CASE	Take **whomever you want.** [*Whomever* is the direct object of *want.*]
	Gary usually agrees with **whomever he is speaking to.** [*Whomever* is the object of *to.*]

A parenthetical expression, such as *I believe,* may interrupt a clause. To decide on a nominative case pronoun or an objective case pronoun, say the sentence without the parenthetical expression.

John Foster, (who, whom) I believe gave the best speech, didn't win the debate.

John Foster, **who gave the best speech,** didn't win the debate. [With the parenthetical expression *I believe* removed, it is easy to see that *who* is the subject of *gave.*]

EXERCISE 13 *Using Forms of* Who *in Clauses*

Number your paper 1 to 20. Write the correct form of the pronoun in parentheses. Then, using the following abbreviations, write how each pronoun is used in the clause.

subject = *subj.*	object of a preposition = *o.p.*
predicate nominative = *p.n.*	direct object = *d.o.*

1. Mr. Fletcher has not said (who, whom) the committee will choose to go to Washington, D.C.
2. Give the ticket to (whoever, whomever) you like.
3. The coach has not said (who, whom) tomorrow's pitcher will be.
4. Isaac is the student (who, whom) Miss Crompton thinks should play the leading role.
5. At the football game, free noisemakers were given to (whoever, whomever) asked for them.
6. She is the salesperson from (who, whom) we bought our television set.
7. Alicia is the person (who, whom) we chose as the most valuable player on the team.
8. About (who, whom) are you speaking?
9. Those are the skaters (who, whom) will represent the United States in the next Olympics.
10. She is complimentary to (whoever, whomever) she is with.
11. Speak to the Jacksons, with (who, whom) we will be going to the dance.
12. Is there any question about (who, whom) should receive the trophy?
13. Ms. Nichols, from (who, whom) I learned Spanish, is once again living in Mexico.
14. A person (who, whom) we all admire is Ben Cameron.
15. Anyone (who, whom) plans to compete in the mixed doubles must sign up by Monday.
16. Ask (whoever, whomever) you want to the party.
17. Senator Murphy submitted the names of two seniors (who, whom) he hopes will be accepted at Annapolis.
18. I wish I knew (who, whom) the judges are.
19. Mr. Randall, (who, whom) I believe is the director of the camp, hired Ned as a counselor.
20. John Steinbeck was a writer (who, whom) wrote novels about farm workers in the Southwest.

Elliptical Clauses

An *elliptical clause* is a subordinate clause that begins with *than* or *as*. Although words are omitted from an elliptical clause, they are understood to be there.

Peg spends more time with Jeff **than I.**
Peg spends more time with Jeff **than me.**

Your choice of *I* or *me* in the preceding examples depends upon the meaning you wish to convey.

Peg spends more time with Jeff **than *I* spend with Jeff.**
Peg spends more time with Jeff **than she spends with *me*.**

I is correct in the first example because it is the subject of the clause. *Me* is correct in the second example because it is the object of the preposition *with.*

Rule 28f **In an elliptical clause, use the form of the pronoun you would use if the clause were completed.**

The best way to decide the case of a pronoun in an elliptical clause is to complete the clause mentally. Then choose the form of the pronoun that expresses the meaning you want. Some elliptical clauses, of course, will express only one meaning.

EXERCISE 14 *Using Pronouns in Elliptical Clauses*

Number your paper 1 to 20. Write each sentence, completing the elliptical clause. Be sure to choose the pronoun that is correct for each clause. Then underline the pronoun you chose.

EXAMPLE I think I dance as well as (he, him).
ANSWER I think I dance as well as <u>he</u> dances.

1. Peg is almost as tall as (she, her).
2. Chuck plays a better game of chess than (I, me).
3. My aunt spends more time with them than (we, us).
4. Willis is better than (he, him) in the high jump.
5. My brothers are stronger than (they, them).
6. They spent more money on Kenneth than (I, me).
7. I think Mia is smarter than (she, her).
8. Joe's two brothers are both older than (he, him).

9. Terry runs faster than (I, me).
10. I wish everyone were as friendly as (she, her).
11. No one works harder than (he, him).
12. I think Glen likes her more than (I, me).
13. I know that I am a better player than (he, him).
14. They seemed to spend more time together than (we, us).
15. Did you collect as many signatures as (she, her)?
16. He can run much faster than (I, me).
17. Jason studied for the test longer than (she, her).
18. Mary conducts the orchestra better than (he, him).
19. The governor spoke longer with Mr. Hayes than (I, me).
20. I think we were more frightened than (they, them).

EXERCISE 15 *Cumulative Review*

Number your paper 1 to 20. Find and write each pronoun that is in the wrong case. Then write it correctly. If a sentence is correct, write *C* after the number.

1. Between Bruce and I, we ate a dozen pancakes.
2. Wasn't it him who fumbled the ball?
3. The two teenagers who took part in the rescue received an award.
4. Do you think you can punt the ball farther than me?
5. We campers are used to the rugged life.
6. Aren't you and I on the entertainment committee?
7. Whom do you suppose will be elected class president?
8. I saw them at the skating rink with Margaret and he.
9. Is Larry going to the game with Lee and they?
10. A man who I knew in Knoxville started a software company.
11. Is Carrie younger than her?
12. Many of we sophomores are tutoring students at the middle school.
13. Erica and me helped him fix up his old Plymouth.
14. That's them riding the bumper cars.
15. Did you hear whom the new athletic director will be?
16. The mayor thanked we volunteers for our help.
17. She thinks that we should be leaving now.
18. For whom is she planning this party?
19. Sheila plays hockey much better than me.
20. At the time I thought that them meeting you at the airport was a good idea.

Pronouns and Their Antecedents

A pronoun and its *antecedent,* the word that the pronoun replaces or refers to, must agree in number and gender. *Number* is the term used to indicate whether a noun or a pronoun is singular or plural. The term *singular* indicates one; the term *plural* indicates more than one. *Gender* is the term used to indicate whether a noun or a pronoun is *masculine, feminine,* or *neuter.*

Masculine	Feminine	Neuter
he, him, his	she, her, hers	it, its

Rule 28g **A pronoun must agree in number and gender with its antecedent.**

Agreement between a single-word antecedent and a pronoun usually does not present a problem.

If Dan makes a dinner, **he** doesn't have to do the dishes.

The hikers lost **their** way on the mountain trail.

If an antecedent is more than one word, however, you need to remember two rules.

Rule 28h **If two or more singular antecedents are joined by *or, nor, either/or,* or *neither/nor,* use a singular pronoun to refer to them.**

All the conjunctions listed in the previous rule indicate one *or* the other. Since *one* or *the other* is singular, the pronoun must be singular.

Either Bart or Claude will sell us **his** drums.

In this example Bart *or* Claude will sell his drums—not both Bart and Claude. The pronoun, therefore, is singular.

Rule 28i **If two or more singular antecedents are joined by *and* or *both/and,* use a plural pronoun to refer to them.**

The conjunctions listed in the preceding rule always indicate more than one. Since *more than one* is plural, the pronoun must be plural.

Both Faye and Donna signed **their** names to the petition.

In this example both Faye and Donna—two people—signed their names. The pronoun, therefore, is plural.

The gender of most antecedents is clear. *John,* for example, is masculine; *Louise* is feminine. Sometimes the gender of an antecedent is unknown. Standard English solves this agreement problem by using *his* or *his or her* to refer to such antecedents.

Every student must turn in **his** report on Friday.

Every student must turn in **his or her** report on Friday.

This problem can be eliminated totally by rewriting such sentences, using the plural form.

All students must turn in **their** reports on Friday.

EXERCISE 16 *Making Pronouns Agree with Their Antecedents*

Number your paper 1 to 20. Then write the pronoun that correctly completes each sentence.

1. Neither Stanley nor Chris has paid ______ dues.
2. Has your cat had ______ litter yet?
3. Sift the dry ingredients and add ______ to the batter.
4. Either Maureen or Yvonne will lend you ______ skis.
5. Since both Karen and Jane got jobs, ______ won't be able to go with us.
6. Will Fidel or Ralph give ______ report tomorrow?
7. Deer shed ______ horns once a year.
8. Franklin said that ______ would be late.
9. All the candidates must submit ______ applications by Monday.
10. Mary and Beth displayed the paintings ______ had finished in art class.
11. Neither of the girls has found ______ skates.
12. Many travelers carry ______ own luggage onto a plane.

13. After the students read the magazines in the library, _______ put them away.
14. Either Roger or David will loan you _______ stereo.
15. When Nancy saw the fire, _______ called the fire department.
16. After skiing all afternoon, Paula and Leslie warmed _______ hands in front of the fireplace in the lodge.
17. It's easy to teach a puppy to hold out _______ paw and shake hands.
18. Goldfish, which belong to the carp family, change _______ color readily.
19. Neither Thomas nor Martin brought _______ guitar to the party Saturday night.
20. Either the Coxes or the Cases will loan us _______ mower.

Indefinite Pronouns as Antecedents

The antecedent of a personal pronoun can be an indefinite pronoun. Agreement can be confusing because some singular indefinite pronouns suggest a plural meaning. Other indefinite pronouns can be either singular or plural.

The following list divides the common indefinite pronouns into three groups. A personal pronoun must be singular if its antecedent is a singular indefinite pronoun or plural if its antecedent is a plural indefinite pronoun. If the antecedent of a personal pronoun is one of the indefinite pronouns in the last group, the personal pronoun should agree in number and gender with the object of the preposition that follows the indefinite pronoun.

Common Indefinite Pronouns	
SINGULAR	anybody, anyone, each, either, everybody, everyone, neither, nobody, no one, one, somebody, someone
PLURAL	both, few, many, several
SINGULAR/PLURAL	all, any, most, none, some

Each of the women was given **her** own office. [singular]

Both of the Scouts were praised for **their** bravery. [plural]

Some of the bacon was burned on **its** edges. [singular]

Some of the apples have bruises on **them.** [plural]

Sometimes the gender of a singular indefinite pronoun is not indicated in a sentence. Standard English solves the problem of agreement by using *his* or *his or her.*

Everyone must have **his** hearing checked.

Everyone must have **his or her** hearing checked.

EXERCISE 17 *Making Personal Pronouns Agree with Indefinite Pronouns*

Number your paper 1 to 20. Then write the pronoun that correctly completes each sentence.

1. One of your sisters found _______ ring.
2. All of the pine trees have shed _______ needles.
3. One of the men found a parking ticket on _______ car.
4. Someone on the girls' softball team forgot _______ glove.
5. Most of the ice sculpture has lost _______ shape.
6. Several of the guests complained about _______ rooms.
7. Few of my friends have _______ own cars.
8. Neither of the girls has finished _______ science project.
9. Some of the teachers have brought _______ grade books.
10. Everyone at the boys' military academy will receive _______ new uniform on Friday.
11. Many of the houses lost _______ shutters in the storm.
12. Any of the managers could have _______ names submitted as the next vice president.
13. Everyone in the men's tennis tournament will be assigned _______ starting time this afternoon.
14. Neither of the boys will tell _______ side of the story.
15. Most of the workers will receive _______ pensions at age sixty-five.
16. Each of my brothers has to make _______ bed every day.
17. Both of the cans were missing _______ labels.
18. All of the cheerleaders can pick up _______ pompoms.
19. None of the balloons have lost _______ air yet.
20. Either of the girls might have a chance to sing _______ song on television.

Integrating Language Skills

USING YOUR TEXT
Descriptive Paragraphs (144–153)

Usage: Editing for Pronoun Errors

When you edit something you have written, you should check to see if the pronouns are in the correct case and if there is agreement between pronouns and their antecedents. You should also check for pronoun shifts and vague or missing antecedents.

PRONOUN SHIFT	I like winter because **you** can go skiing then.
CORRECT	I like winter because **I** can go skiing then.
VAGUE ANTECEDENT	Before you give the lamb its bottle, shake **it.** [Is *lamb* or *bottle* the antecedent of *it*?]
CORRECT	Before you give the lamb its bottle, shake **the bottle.**
	Shake the bottle before giving **it** to the lamb.
MISSING ANTECEDENT	We went fishing in Nauset and caught five of **them.** [There is no antecedent for *them.*]
CORRECT	We went fishing in Nauset and caught five **bass.**

Checking Your Understanding Number your paper 1 to 20. Then rewrite each sentence to fix the pronoun error and make the meaning of the sentence clear.

1. John's father was elected mayor when he was only six years old.
2. Walter looked outside and knew it would be impossible without snow tires.
3. I enjoy playing hockey because you're always getting plenty of exercise.
4. After the doctor had set Jim's leg, he went home.
5. I like mowing lawns and trimming hedges because you are your own boss.
6. Although I had never flown in an airplane before, I liked it.
7. Before you give that meat to the dog to eat, cut it into pieces.
8. We like to climb Blue Hill because you get a perfect view of the city from there.

9. After the mechanic at George's Service Station fixed the flat tire, we drove it home.

10. When Joshua and Scott were at the beach on Saturday, he got very sunburned.

11. My sister is studying to be a lawyer, and she expects to like it very much.

12. Laura told Janet that it was her turn to chair the meeting of the dance committee.

13. I enjoy ice-skating because it gives you a chance to be outside in the winter.

14. In San Francisco we visited an aircraft carrier and saw where they eat.

15. About an hour before the game started, Paul asked his father where his car keys were.

16. We have a woodburning stove in our living room so that you can reduce your fuel bills.

17. Anne casually strolled to the plate and knocked it into right field for a home run.

18. Harriet visited Martha before she left for New Orleans for spring vacation.

19. I prefer to do my homework early in the evening because you are not tired then.

20. José took his brother to the swimming pool, but he didn't go into the water.

Describing a Person Imagine that you have just read about a contest in which the winner gets a new desktop computer. To enter the contest, you have to write a long paragraph titled "The Most Interesting Person I Know." Choose a friend or a relative about whom you can write an amusing or informative character sketch. Write freely about that person for several minutes—jotting down everything that comes to mind. Then organize your notes in spatial order or order of importance. (*See pages 106, 107, and 148.*)

As you write your first draft, make sure that you include specific details or examples from your prewriting notes. Revise your character sketch, making sure you have used fresh, picture-making adjectives. Next reread your paragraph to see if it flows smoothly and is easy to follow. ***Application:*** As you edit, pay particular attention to any pronoun shifts, vague antecedents, or missing antecedents. Then write your final draft.

Chapter 28

Review

A Using Pronouns in the Correct Case

Number your paper 1 to 20. Then write the correct form of the pronoun in parentheses.

1. The contest now is only between you and (she, her).
2. Carl, Van, and (I, me) went bobsledding for the first time last winter.
3. That was (he, him) on the high diving board.
4. Don't forget (we, us) hard workers.
5. Is that new car the Milligans' or (theirs, there's)?
6. (Who, Whom) do you believe will be the team's most improved player?
7. My younger brother Chan is almost as tall as (I, me).
8. I will take Roger and (they, them) in the car with me.
9. The cheerleaders think (them, their) shouting sometimes causes laryngitis.
10. The candidate (who, whom) the experts thought did not have a chance won by a landslide.
11. Will you take a picture of Amanda and (I, me) as we finish the race?
12. Maggie admitted that it was (she, her) behind the large dragon mask.
13. Steve prefers to play tennis with partners who are better than (he, him).
14. The statue memorialized six original settlers, each of (who, whom) gave a great deal to the city.
15. (Him, His) singing that song brought back memories to many of us.
16. After Andrew bought the farm, life for both (he, him) and his grandfather became more pleasant.
17. Heather is the tennis player (who, whom) you remember won the trophy two years in a row.
18. It's (I, me) who should speak to her.
19. (Who, Whom) will be our new principal next year?
20. You must always remember that (we, us) friends are here if you need us.

B **Making Pronouns Agree with Antecedents** Number your paper 1 to 10. Then write the personal pronoun that correctly completes each sentence.

1. Neither Alex nor Edgar has had ______ physical yet.
2. All of the candidates promised ______ support.
3. Both the blue jay and the cardinal get most of ______ food from our bird feeder.
4. If Lisa answers the phone, tell ______ to take a message.
5. Some of the cheese has lost ______ sharpness.
6. Either Mom or Aunt Francesca will give ______ travel alarm clock to you.
7. While our neighbors were away on vacation, ______ newspapers stacked up on the doorstep.
8. One of the women left ______ briefcase in the conference room.
9. Several of the drivers stopped ______ cars during the heavy downpour.
10. Dennis or Rico will loan you ______ tape recorder.

Mastery Test

Number your paper 1 to 10. Then write the correct form of the pronoun in parentheses.

1. A free sample was sent to (whoever, whomever) answered the ad.
2. Both of the players did (his, their) share of blocking.
3. (Who, Whom) do you think will win the race?
4. There was no room on the bus for Larry and (I, me).
5. When making a decision, no one can take as long as (he, him).
6. Sherry and (I, me) are now working on Saturdays.
7. (We, Us) members of the Ecology Club are cleaning up the woods near the high school.
8. Every squirrel in our yard seems to have had (its, their) fill of acorns.
9. Could that be (their, they're) dog in our yard?
10. I think that's (they, them) getting off the plane now.

Chapter

29 Subject and Verb Agreement

Diagnostic Test

Number your paper 1 to 10. Write the subject in each sentence. Then next to each one, write the form of the verb in parentheses that agrees with the subject.

EXAMPLE Each of the films (is, are) considered a classic.
ANSWER each—is

1. Exploration of outer space (has, have) made many scientific advances possible.
2. There (is, are) many reasons for the special meeting.
3. The two buildings next to the Plaza (was, were) torn down.
4. (Doesn't, Don't) he know the way to the lake?
5. Fifty cents (is, are) not too much for that pen!
6. Deer (was, were) often seen browsing along that stretch of road.
7. The mustard and the ketchup (has, have) caused a terrible stain on the tablecloth.
8. One of the fire fighters (was, were) hurt.
9. Why (hasn't, haven't) the magazines on the table been put away?
10. Either Yvonne or her brother (is, are) at home.

Agreement of Subjects and Verbs

When certain keys on a piano are played together, they create a pleasant, harmonious sound. Other keys played together cause people to wrinkle their foreheads and hold their ears. In this way language is similar to music. Some subjects and verbs go together. Others do not. When a subject and a verb fit together, a sentence is said to have *agreement.* This chapter will show how to make subjects and verbs agree.

Keep in mind one basic rule as you go through this chapter.

Rule 29a **A verb must agree with its subject in number.**

The term *number* indicates whether a noun or pronoun is singular or plural. The term is also applied to verbs. *Singular* indicates one; *plural* indicates more than one.

Most nouns form their plural by adding *-s* or *-es* to the singular form, but a few nouns form their plural irregularly. Pronouns form their plural by changing form.

Nouns		Pronouns	
SINGULAR	**PLURAL**	**SINGULAR**	**PLURAL**
boy	boys	I	we
lunch	lunches	he, she, it	they
goose	geese		

Present tense verbs also have singular and plural forms. The third person singular form ends in *-s* or *-es.* Most verb forms that do not end in *-s* or *-es* are plural.

THIRD PERSON SINGULAR he, she, it **eats**
OTHERS I, you, we, they **eat**

The verbs *be, have,* and *do* have irregular singular and plural forms for the present tense. *Be* also has irregular forms for the past tense.

Present Tense

SINGULAR	PLURAL
I **am, have, do**	we **are, have, do**
you **are, have, do**	you **are, have, do**
he, she, it **is, has, does**	they **are, have, do**

Past Tense

SINGULAR	PLURAL
I **was**	we **were**
you **were**	you **were**
he, she, it **was**	they **were**

Since a subject and a verb both have number, they must agree.

Rule 29b A singular subject takes a singular verb.

Rule 29c A plural subject takes a plural verb.

The **boy lends.**	The **boys lend.**
The **lunch was** good.	The **lunches were** good.
The **goose flies.**	The **geese fly.**
He is here.	**They are** here.

Be, have, and *do* are often used as helping verbs. When they are, they must agree in number with the subject.

Rule 29d The helping verb must agree in number with the subject.

Kim is going. **They have** gone.

EXERCISE 1 *Making Subjects and Verbs Agree*

Number your paper 1 to 10. Then write the form of the verb in parentheses that agrees with the subject.

1. The floor (shines, shine).
2. The curtain (rises, rise).
3. Rabbits (jumps, jump).
4. Grace (does, do) work.
5. They (is, are) dancing.
6. The car (does, do) rattle.
7. The teams (is, are) tied.
8. The athlete (jogs, jog).
9. It (has, have) dropped.
10. I (answers, answer).

EXERCISE 2 *Making Subjects and Verbs Agree*

Number your paper 1 to 10. Find and write the verbs that do not agree with their subjects. Then write them correctly. If a sentence is correct, write *C* after the number.

Facts and Figures

1. Seven United States presidents was born in Ohio.
2. Insects have three pairs of legs.
3. The sewing machine were invented by Elias Howe in 1846.
4. California is known as the Golden State.
5. Your hair grow faster during the day than during the night.
6. Ocean tides is caused by the moon.
7. Napoleon were exiled to St. Helena in 1815.
8. A 25th wedding anniversary is observed with gifts of silver.
9. The first bifocal lenses was made by Benjamin Franklin.
10. Jupiter have the shortest day of all the planets.

Interrupting Words

A verb always agrees with its subject—whether the verb comes right next to the subject or is separated from it by other words. If a phrase or a clause separates a subject and a verb, a mistake in agreement is sometimes made. The verb may be incorrectly made to agree with the object of a preposition or some other word that is closer to the verb.

Rule 29e **The agreement of a verb with its subject is not changed by any interrupting words.**

The subjects and the verbs in the following examples are in heavy type. Notice that they agree in number—regardless of the words that separate them.

The **dogs** in the kennel **were** howling. [The plural verb *were* agrees with the plural subject *dogs,* even though *kennel* is closer to the verb.]

The **dish** filled with peaches **was** put on the table. [*Was* agrees with the subject *dish*—not *peaches.*]

David, not one of his brothers, **is** getting the job. [*Is* agrees with the subject *David*—not *brothers.*]

The **satellites** that are orbiting in the sky **shine** like planets. [*Shine* agrees with the subject *satellites*—not *sky.*]

EXERCISE 3 *Making Interrupted Subjects and Verbs Agree*

Number your paper 1 to 20. Write the subject in each sentence. Then next to each one, write the form of the verb in parentheses that agrees with the subject.

1. Excessive salt in foods (makes, make) people thirsty.
2. Earl, together with his two cousins, (is, are) joining us.
3. Hawaii, not the Philippines, (was, were) discovered by Captain James Cook.
4. The cottage, partly hidden by huge pine trees, (was, were) standing at the park entrance.
5. The knots in a wooden board (is, are) harder than the rest of the wood.
6. The coach, not the players, (decides, decide) when to change pitchers.
7. The brilliance of the moon's rays (blots, blot) out all but the brightest stars.
8. Many students who attended the class meeting (has, have) volunteered to help on the car wash.
9. The wood of poison ivy, as well as its leaves, (is, are) poisonous.
10. The two boys on the raft (was, were) rescued in 14 hours.
11. The pine, as well as other evergreens, (grows, grow) new needles before the old ones fall off.
12. Television, not newspapers, (is, are) my major source of news.
13. Translations of the Bible (has, have) appeared in nearly every living tongue or dialect.
14. Dad's toolbox, which is filled with many expensive tools, (has, have) been misplaced.
15. The quarterback, together with his teammates, (was, were) practicing on the field.
16. Approximately ten million people in the world (has, have) the same birthday as you.
17. Sir Arthur Conan Doyle, who wrote all of the Sherlock Holmes stories, (was, were) a doctor.
18. On average, every person in the United States (eats, eat) eight pounds of pickles a year.
19. Equipment once used only by professional divers (is, are) now available to anyone.
20. Many roads along the Gulf of Mexico (is, are) paved with crushed oyster shells.

EXERCISE 4 *Making Interrupted Subjects and Verbs Agree*

Number your paper 1 to 10. Find and write the verbs that do not agree with their subjects. Then write them correctly. If a sentence is correct, write *C* after the number.

1. Senator Parks, along with his staff, have arrived at the airport.
2. The first newspaper to appear in the American colonies was published in Boston in 1704.
3. The pictures that Nancy took on her trip is in that album.
4. Two rolls for the player piano is torn.
5. Most accidents in the home is a result of carelessness.
6. The juice of lemons and limes were mixed to create a very refreshing drink.
7. The collie, as well as many other dogs, were originally raised as a work animal.
8. On a warm day, the roots of a single corn plant draws several pounds of water from the soil.
9. A schedule of community events have been posted on the school bulletin board.
10. Two cats that belong to my neighbor were howling all night.

Application to Writing

Write ten original tongue twisters, such as *The big brown boat is bobbing boisterously.* Write them all in the present tense. Then make sure that the subject and verb in each one agree.

Compound Subjects

There are two rules to remember when a verb must agree with a compound subject.

Rule 29f **When subjects are joined by *or, nor, either/or,* or *neither/nor,* the verb agrees with the closer subject.**

This rule applies to any combination of compound subjects: two or more singular subjects, two or more plural subjects, or one singular and one plural subject. The verb always agrees with the subject closer to it. *(See the examples on the next page.)*

Beth or **Craig is** going to buy a word processor. [*Is* agrees with *Craig,* the subject closer to the verb.]

Either the roads or the **sidewalks have** been slated for repaving. [*Have* agrees with *sidewalks,* the subject closer to the verb.]

Neither Art nor his **brothers have** ever owned a car. [*Have* agrees with *brothers,* the subject closer to the verb—even though *Art* is singular.]

Different conjunctions are the basis of the second rule.

Rule 29g **When subjects are joined by *and* or *both/and*, the verb is plural.**

These conjunctions always suggest more than one. As a result, the verb is always plural—regardless of whether the individual subjects are singular, plural, or a combination of singular and plural.

Ted's **pen** and **pencil were** missing from his notebook. [Two things—the pen and the pencil—were missing. The verb must be plural to agree with them.]

A **truck** and two **cars were** involved in the accident. [Even though *truck* is singular, the verb is still plural because the truck and the two cars—together—were involved in the accident.]

There are exceptions to the second rule. On a few rare occasions, subjects joined by *and* refer to only one person or one thing. When this is the case, the verb must be singular.

The artist and inventor **was** given a standing ovation. [The artist and inventor are the same person.]

Cheese and crackers **is** my favorite after-school snack. [*Cheese and crackers* is considered one item of food.]

Another exception to the second rule involves the words *every* and *each* when they come before a compound subject that is joined by *and.* In situations such as this, each subject is being considered separately. As a result, a singular verb is needed.

Every man and woman **is** asked to vote.
Each tree and bush **was** infested with bugs.

EXERCISE 5 *Making Verbs Agree with Compound Subjects*

Number your paper 1 to 10. Then write the correct form of the verb in parentheses.

1. Sleet or snow (is, are) predicted for tomorrow.
2. Seals and sea lions (is, are) often confused by circus goers.
3. The captain and quarterback (is, are) Ryan Anderson.
4. Neither the lilac nor the apple (does, do) well in a subtropical climate.
5. Every bird and animal in the forest (heeds, heed) the blue jay's warning cry.
6. Both grades and attendance (was, were) considerations in the committee's selection of the scholarship winner.
7. Peaches or watermelon (needs, need) to be added to the fruit salad.
8. Strawberries and cream (is, are) my favorite dessert.
9. Either Rebecca or her sister (is, are) going to drive you to the airport.
10. Each orange and grapefruit (was, were) inspected for bruises.

EXERCISE 6 *Making Verbs Agree with Compound Subjects*

Number your paper 1 to 10. Find and write the verbs that do not agree with their subjects. Then write them correctly. If a sentence is correct, write *C* after the number.

1. Both St. Petersburg and Sarasota are on the west coast of Florida.
2. Each cup and saucer were used at the reception.
3. Neither the violinists nor the harpist have arrived yet.
4. Fish and chips are a favorite meal in England.
5. Either peppercorns or garlic are needed in the spaghetti sauce.
6. Every horse and colt on the Thompson ranch are white.
7. Five hundred and twenty-five songs and instrumental pieces have been written about Abraham Lincoln.
8. The coach and art teacher are Ms. O'Reilly.
9. Sandwiches and a fruit salad was served for lunch.
10. Neither the high winds nor the ice on the runway were responsible for the accident.

EXERCISE 7 Cumulative Review

Number your paper 1 to 25. Find and write the verbs that do not agree with their subjects. Then write them correctly. If a sentence is correct, write *C* after the number.

1. The wedding cake of the ancient Greeks was almost always cheesecake.
2. Each local painter and sculptor were honored at the museum's opening.
3. Bacon and eggs are my normal Sunday breakfast.
4. The largest crabs in the world stands three feet high.
5. Both sheets and a blanket was needed for his bunk.
6. Neither Martha nor her brother sing very well.
7. Iceland and Costa Rica has no armed forces.
8. Pills or a shot are recommended by the doctor.
9. The average pulse of adults is 70 or 80 beats per minute.
10. The gorillas shown in the National Geographic film is very gentle creatures.
11. Every man, woman, and child in the United States is guaranteed certain rights.
12. Scrabble, one of the most popular board games, was invented in 1948.
13. People in the United States consumes over one billion tubes of toothpaste each year.
14. My grandparents and all my cousins are attending the family reunion.
15. Coffee, like many other beverages, acts like a stimulant.
16. The first shots of the American Revolution was fired in Lexington, Massachusetts.
17. Neither the tomatoes nor the corn are ripe.
18. A complete, normal adult set of teeth contain 32 teeth.
19. Both a quarter and a dime was found under the cushion of the couch.
20. The first astronomer who used a telescope to observe the heavens was Galileo.
21. Either a pen or a pencil are acceptable for the test.
22. Every glass and dish were packed in the boxes.
23. The traditional dress worn by Japanese women are called a kimono.
24. Bacon, lettuce, and tomato is the sandwich I like best.
25. A certificate of bravery and an award were presented to Mr. Dowd by the chief of police.

Special Agreement Problems

Certain kinds of subjects and the position of subjects sometimes cause special agreement problems.

Indefinite Pronouns as Subjects In the previous chapter, you learned that some indefinite pronouns are singular, some are plural, and some can be either singular or plural.

Rule 29h **A verb must agree in number with an indefinite pronoun used as a subject.**

Common Indefinite Pronouns	
SINGULAR	anybody, anyone, each, either, everybody, everyone, neither, no one, one, somebody, someone
PLURAL	both, few, many, several
SINGULAR/PLURAL	all, any, most, none, some

SINGULAR **One** of the class workers **was** asked to be a member of the school board.

PLURAL **Few** of my friends **are** going to the dance.

SINGULAR OR PLURAL **Some** of the milk **was** spilled.

Some of the pages **were** torn.

EXERCISE 8 *Making Verbs Agree with Indefinite Pronoun Subjects*

Number your paper 1 to 20. Write the subject in each sentence. Then next to each one, write the form of the verb in parentheses that agrees with the subject.

1. Neither of the climbers (was, were) able to reach the summit of the mountain.
2. Each of the billions of brain cells (sends, send) out fibers to the spinal cord.

3. Most of the mushrooms grown in the United States (comes, come) from Pennsylvania.
4. All of the arms of an octopus (has, have) suction cups on their undersides.
5. Many of the old records (was, were) warped.
6. One of the runners (was, were) too exhausted to continue.
7. Any of these posters (is, are) for sale.
8. Somebody at my school (is, are) responsible for saving a boy's life.
9. Several of the boxes in the attic (was, were) filled with old coins.
10. Both of my brothers (is, are) working at the post office.
11. Some of the extra bread (was, were) frozen.
12. No one in the chorus (was, were) absent today.
13. None of the spaghetti (is, are) for us.
14. Everybody in my house (is, are) starting to exercise.
15. Few of the new magazines (has, have) been read yet.
16. Most of today's newspaper (is, are) wet from the snow.
17. (Has, Have) anyone seen my sneakers?
18. Either of the books (is, are) a good source of information.
19. Some of the apples (has, have) been imported.
20. None of the tests (has, have) been graded.

Subjects in Inverted Order Most sentences are in natural order with the subject coming before the verb. Some sentences, though, are in inverted order with the subject following the verb or part of a verb phrase. Regardless of where a subject is in a sentence, the verb must agree with it.

Rule 29i **The subject and the verb of an inverted sentence must agree in number.**

There are several types of inverted sentences. To find the subject in an inverted sentence, turn the sentence around to its natural order. In the following examples, each subject is underlined once, and each verb is underlined twice.

INVERTED ORDER Hidden in the back of the closet was Kevin's birthday present. [Kevin's birthday present was hidden in the back of the closet.]

QUESTIONS	Was the dog fed today? [The dog was fed today.]
SENTENCES BEGINNING WITH *HERE* OR *THERE*	Here is your clean laundry. [Your clean laundry is here.]
	There were too many people crowded into the auditorium. [Occasionally you must drop *here* or *there* before putting the sentence into its natural order. Too many people were crowded into the auditorium.]

EXERCISE 9 *Making Verbs Agree with Subjects in Inverted Order*

Number your paper 1 to 20. Write the subject in each sentence. Then next to each one, write the form of the verb in parentheses that agrees with the subject.

1. There (is, are) about 100 poems included in this book.
2. In the tall grass near the riverbank (is, are) some cattails.
3. Why (was, were) Nelson absent from school today?
4. In a nest in the old stone wall (is, are) five baby weasels.
5. There (is, are) only 12 letters in the Hawaiian alphabet.
6. (Was, Were) they able to get tickets to the concert?
7. Hanging from the ceiling (was, were) a colorful mobile.
8. There (is, are) at least 450 active volcanoes in the world.
9. Why (has, have) she signed up for that course?
10. There (is, are) an empty seat by the aisle.
11. In a shop window in the mall (was, were) many yellow silk flowers.
12. (Was, Were) you in the class play last year?
13. On the other side of a buffalo nickel, there (is, are) a picture of an American Indian.
14. Here (is, are) the two letters you asked me to mail.
15. On the grassy slopes of the lake (was, were) 18 deer.
16. (Does, Do) they know when the plane will arrive?
17. There (is, are) enough leaves to mulch the tulip beds.
18. Why (is, are) the boys still at the skating rink?
19. On the mantle (was, were) four bowling trophies.
20. Here (is, are) the perfect picture for your room.

Collective Nouns *Team, herd, committee,* and *class* are all *collective nouns.* They all name a group of people or things.

Rule 29j **Use a singular verb with a collective-noun subject that is thought of as a unit. Use a plural verb with a collective-noun subject that is thought of as individuals.**

The **jury has** been out for ten hours. [The jury is acting together as a whole unit. Therefore, the verb is singular.]

The **jury have** not been able to come to an agreement. [Members of the jury are acting as individuals—each with a separate opinion. Therefore, the verb is plural.]

Words Expressing an Amount Words that express quantities usually are considered singular.

Rule 29k **A subject that expresses an amount, a measurement, or a weight is usually singular and takes a singular verb.**

Even though most quantities are plural in form, they are thought of as a single unit.

Ten miles is too far to walk. [one unit of distance]

Use a singular verb when an amount tells *how much.* Use a plural verb when an amount tells *how many.*

Half of the meeting **was** devoted to questions. [How much of the meeting?]

Half of the members **were** not present. [How many members?]

The Number Of, A Number Of These two expressions present different problems in agreement.

Rule 29l **Use a singular verb with *the number of* and a plural verb with *a number of.***

The number of girls taking mechanical drawing **has** doubled this year.

A number of girls **are** taking mechanical drawing this year.

Singular Nouns That Have a Plural Form Words such as *molasses, measles, economics, physics,* and *social studies* look plural because they end in *-s.* However, they name single things, such as one type of food, one disease, or one area of knowledge.

Rule 29m **Use a singular verb with certain subjects that are plural in form but singular in meaning.**

Mumps is a dangerous disease for adults to contract.

Physics is his major in college.

EXERCISE 10 *Making Subjects and Verbs Agree*

Number your paper 1 to 25. Then write the correct form of the verb in parentheses.

1. Mathematics (has, have) been made easier by the use of pocket calculators.
2. A number of parents (has, have) requested more homework for their teenagers.
3. One third of the year (is, are) over already.
4. The faculty (meets, meet) every Tuesday afternoon.
5. Four gallons of gas (was, were) all the tank would hold.
6. The number of six-lane highways (is, are) increasing.
7. Only three fourths of the seats in the new stadium (was, were) occupied.
8. Twenty-five pounds (is, are) too much to carry on the hike.
9. Television news (is, are) too condensed for me.
10. The final two days (was, were) devoted to dress rehearsals.
11. Fifty dollars (was, were) all he could afford for a new jacket.
12. The fleet of ships (was, were) heading for the open seas.
13. At the battles of Lexington and Concord, the total number of British casualties (was, were) close to 200.
14. Half of Chico's spare time (is, are) spent working with his computer.
15. The male quartet from our school (is, are) singing at the civic auditorium tonight.
16. Gymnastics (is, are) the featured event of the program.
17. The Florida State University football team (is, are) known as the Seminoles.
18. A number of hurricane warnings (has, have) been posted.

19. Two thirds of the winning contestants (has, have) already been selected.
20. Four miles (is, are) the distance from my house to the junior high school.
21. In downtown Lima, Peru, there (is, are) a large brass statue dedicated to Winnie-the-Pooh.
22. (Does, Do) most cars get better mileage when driven at 45 or 55 miles per hour?
23. In the murky water of the inlet (is, are) several scuba divers looking for the missing sailboat.
24. (Has, Have) anyone locked the front door?
25. There (is, are) more insects in one square mile of rural land than there are human beings on the entire earth.

Doesn't* and *Don't When you write a contraction, always say the two words that make up the contraction. Then check for agreement with the subject.

Rule 29n **The verb part of a contraction must agree in number with the subject.**

Doesn't, isn't, wasn't, and *hasn't* are singular and agree with singular subjects. *Don't, aren't, weren't,* and *haven't* are plural and agree with plural subjects.

The **game does**n't start until four o'clock.
Don't **plants** give off oxygen?

Subjects with Linking Verbs A verb always agrees with its subject—regardless of any other word in the sentence.

Rule 29o **A verb agrees with the subject of a sentence, not with the predicate nominative.**

Peanuts are a good source of protein. [The plural verb *are* agrees with the plural subject *peanuts*—even though the predicate nominative *source* is singular.]

The major cleanup **problem is** bottles and paper. [*Is* agrees with the subject *problem*—not with the compound predicate nominative, *bottles* and *paper*.]

Titles Although a title may have many words in it, it is considered singular because it is the name of one book or one work of art. Most multiword names of businesses and organizations are also considered singular.

Rule 29p **A title is singular and takes a singular verb.**

***Seven Gothic Tales* was** written by Isak Dinesen.

The Home Owners Association is holding a block party.

EXERCISE 11 *Making Subjects and Verbs Agree*

Number your paper 1 to 20. Then write the correct form of the verb in parentheses.

1. (Doesn't, Don't) the citizens of Monaco have to pay taxes?
2. *My Life and Hard Times* (tells, tell) about amusing incidents in James Thurber's childhood.
3. He (wasn't, weren't) able to find the dictionary.
4. Mark's major interest (is, are) tennis.
5. The League of Women Voters (is, are) sponsoring a debate among the candidates.
6. (Doesn't, Don't) the oak keep some of its leaves until the following spring?
7. Politics (was, were) the main issue at the meeting.
8. (Isn't, Aren't) the economics class being held in the auditorium today?
9. *The Last of the Mohicans* (is, are) full of excitement.
10. He (wasn't, weren't) ready when the bus came.
11. Sapphires (is, are) her first choice for the necklace.
12. F. E. Finley and Sons (is, are) the best department store in town.
13. The oranges (hasn't, haven't) been squeezed yet.
14. "Stars and Stripes Forever" (was, were) composed by John Philip Sousa.
15. Why (wasn't, weren't) the lights turned off?
16. The dessert (was, were) fresh strawberries.
17. The commuter train (doesn't, don't) stop in Pottsville.
18. Why (wasn't, weren't) the jury ready with its verdict?
19. *Cat People* (is, are) a book of photographs of people and their cats.
20. (Isn't, Aren't) two pieces of the puzzle missing?

EXERCISE 12 Cumulative Review

Number your paper 1 to 20. Find and write the verbs that do not agree with their subjects. Then write them correctly. If a sentence is correct, write *C* after the number.

The Old and the New

1. Probably everyone throughout the world has heard of the Olympic Games.
2. The people in Greece was the originators of these games in 776 B.C.
3. In those days every boy were trained in running, jumping, and wrestling.
4. The ideal of all Greeks was to have a sound mind in a healthy body.
5. The modern Olympic Games are patterned after those held in ancient Greece.
6. There is, however, many important differences.
7. The games in the original competition was always held in Olympia, Greece.
8. Each of the modern events are held in a different city of the world.
9. In the early days, only young men of Greek descent was able to participate in the games.
10. A modern change in the games are events for women.
11. Now female winners in an event receive the same honors as men.
12. In the ancient games, there was honors for cultural achievements.
13. So far, competition in the modern games are entirely athletic.
14. Many of the contests held in the modern Olympics was unknown in early times.
15. Soccer, basketball, and judo are some modern additions.
16. One of the most popular events of the modern games are the marathon.
17. This 26-mile footrace wasn't part of the ancient games—even though the marathon originated in Greece.
18. A more recent development in the Olympics are the winter games.
19. Skiing and ice hockey is some of the featured events.
20. Not one of the cold-weather sports were developed in the warm climate of southern Greece.

USING YOUR TEXT
Chronological Order (139)
Narrative Paragraphs (137–143)

Usage: Editing for Errors in Subject-Verb Agreement

Always edit your writing to be sure that the subjects in your sentences agree with the verbs.

Checking Your Understanding Find and write the verbs that do not agree with their subjects in the following paragraph. Then write those verbs correctly.

> The average life of dollar bills are less than a year. Where does all the money go when it gets too old to use? Banks in the Federal Reserve system sends the old money to the Treasury Department. There is four to five tons of money received each day. The old money, which comes in from the banks, are canceled in a machine called a *macerator.* A million dollars in bills of various denominations is destroyed every minute! Damaged paper money don't mean it's worthless. If three fifths of a note are preserved, you can send it to the Treasury and redeem its full value. Don't expect anything, however, if you has only two fifths of a bill or less.

Writing a Commentary Brainstorm for a list of events your school has held during the past couple of months. Possible events include a homecoming parade or an important basketball game. Choose one and re-create it clearly in your mind. As you do so, list the main features of that event and put them in chronological order.

Now imagine that the event is still taking place and that a local radio station has asked you to comment during it. Write the first draft of your commentary—in the present tense. For a sports event, for example, you might say something like "As the Weaver High team runs onto the court, the noisy crowd in the stands goes wild." ***Application:*** As you revise and edit your commentary, look carefully for mistakes in agreement between subjects and verbs. Then write the final draft of your commentary.

Chapter 29

Review

A **Making Subjects and Verbs Agree** Number your paper 1 to 25. Then write the correct form of the verb in parentheses.

1. The number of solar houses (is, are) steadily increasing.
2. (Doesn't, Don't) the red cedar have blueberries?
3. The main feature of the auto show (is, are) new camper vehicles.
4. The tent and the sleeping bag (was, were) borrowed for us.
5. Here (is, are) the wood for the bookcase.
6. Macaroni and cheese (is, are) my favorite dish.
7. None of the tires (was, were) in good shape.
8. One of those lifeguards (is, are) my cousin.
9. In the 1950's, twenty-five cents (was, were) the price of a gallon of gasoline.
10. Neither Ari nor Pedro (is, are) willing to run for class office.
11. The cloud layers that surround Venus (is, are) much like the smog layers that afflict many large cities.
12. *Little Women* (was, were) written by Louisa May Alcott.
13. Five dollars (seems, seem) like a fair price for the lamp.
14. In the stream (was, were) two beautiful rainbow trout.
15. A case of measles (renders, render) the victim immune to the disease.
16. Many of our early television programs (was, were) produced live.
17. Each quarter of a football game (is, are) 15 minutes of play.
18. The choir (has, have) been measured for their new robes.
19. A painter famous for his paintings of sunflowers (was, were) Vincent van Gogh.
20. After the first snowstorm, every mountain and hill in Vermont (was, were) alive with skiers.
21. Neither milk nor juice (was, were) needed from the store.
22. The American Professional Football Association, the forerunner of the NFL, (was, were) formed in 1920.
23. Most of the houses on our street (has, have) no garage.
24. Either daisies or roses (is, are) needed for the bouquet.
25. There (is, are) approximately 125 million licensed drivers in the United States.

B **Making Subjects and Verbs Agree** Number your paper 1 to 10. Find and write the verbs that do not agree with their subjects. Then write them correctly. If a sentence is correct, write *C* after the number.

1. The furnishings of a Pilgrim home was very simple.
2. The tomato plants in the field was thriving.
3. There is approximately 100,000 species of butterflies.
4. Five hundred dollars was raised by the students for the victims of the flood.
5. Information about summer job opportunities was posted on the bulletin board this morning.
6. Hot dogs and beans are my first choice for dinner.
7. A number of two-family houses has recently been built in this city.
8. That hotel don't allow dogs or cats in the rooms.
9. Neither Marty nor his friends have ever performed in public before.
10. There is many kinds of migratory birds.

Mastery Test

Number your paper 1 to 10. Write the subject in each sentence. Then, next to each one, write the form of the verb in parentheses that agrees with the subject.

1. (Haven't, Hasn't) you ever gone scuba diving?
2. Neither Aaron nor Oliver (was, were) ready to leave at six o'clock.
3. The twigs of the sassafras tree (produces, produce) a spicy oil.
4. Three days (was, were) all Amanda had before she started her new job.
5. Covering the bed (was, were) a colorful old patchwork quilt.
6. The ship's crew (was, were) given a two-day leave.
7. Neither of his friends (has, have) found a job.
8. Some of my homework (is, are) already finished.
9. There (is, are) more than 300 kinds of hummingbirds on the North American continent.
10. You and Leslie (has, have) been very helpful.

Chapter

30 Using Adjectives and Adverbs

Diagnostic Test

Number your paper 1 to 10. Then write the correct form of the modifier in parentheses.

EXAMPLE Amy is the (shorter, shortest) of my three sisters.
ANSWER shortest

1. Which of the two cars is (more, most) expensive?
2. Kenneth arrived (later, latest) than his brother.
3. You will be credited with ten points for every question you answer (correct, correctly).
4. Rick is a better runner than (any, any other) contestant in today's race.
5. Of the two courses, I like this one (better, best).
6. After the tennis match, I (could hardly, couldn't hardly) catch my breath.
7. Which do you think tastes (better, best), cantaloupe or honeydew melon?
8. Her Chihuahua is the (smallest, most smallest) I have ever seen.
9. Lucía always does (good, well) in math.
10. Who is (stronger, strongest), Bart or Carlos?

Comparison of Adjectives and Adverbs

When you go to a restaurant, the first thing you probably do is look at the menu. You then might say to yourself, "Chicken would taste *good,* but some fish would taste *better.*" Then, after looking further, you might make your selection by saying, "Beef, however, would taste the *best* tonight." While making your selection, you would have used the modifier *good* and both of its forms of comparison. The different forms of comparison will be reviewed in this chapter, as well as some problems with comparisons.

To show degrees of comparison, most modifiers have three forms: the *positive,* the *comparative,* and the *superlative.*

Rule 30a **Most modifiers show degrees of comparison by changing form.**

The *positive* degree is the basic form of an adjective or an adverb. It is used when no comparison is being made.

George is **strong.**

The *comparative* degree is used when two people, things, or actions are being compared.

George is **stronger** than Kent.

The *superlative* form is used when more than two people, things, or actions are being compared.

George is the **strongest** member of the wrestling team at our high school.

Following are some additional examples of the three degrees of comparison.

POSITIVE	Today is a **nice** day. [adjective] Teddy works **fast.** [adverb]
COMPARATIVE	Today is **nicer** than yesterday. Teddy works **faster** than Brian.
SUPERLATIVE	Today is the **nicest** day so far this spring. Teddy works the **fastest** of all.

EXERCISE 1 *Determining Degrees of Comparison*

Number your paper 1 to 10. Write the underlined modifier in each sentence. Then label its degree of comparison—*positive, comparative,* or *superlative.*

EXAMPLE This is the most delicious peach I have ever eaten.
ANSWER most delicious—superlative

1. Those apples are very shiny.
2. This is the driest summer in 50 years.
3. Joanne talks even more softly than Rebecca.
4. Which of the two pillows is softer?
5. When the rain started, everyone quickly ran for cover.
6. Loren did the puzzle more slowly than Alan.
7. That was the highest the horse had ever jumped.
8. The wind is more fierce now than it was an hour ago.
9. I think Meg is taller than her older sister.
10. This is the most exciting day of my life!

Regular and Irregular Comparison

Most modifiers form the comparative and the superlative degrees regularly, but a few modifiers form their comparisons irregularly.

Regular Comparisons The majority of modifiers follow one of three rules to form their comparisons. The rules are based on the number of syllables in a modifier.

Rule 30b **Add *-er* to form the comparative degree and *-est* to form the superlative degree of one-syllable modifiers.**

POSITIVE	COMPARATIVE	SUPERLATIVE
old	older	oldest
clean	cleaner	cleanest
soon	sooner	soonest

Most two-syllable words form their comparative and superlative degrees the same way. Some two-syllable words, however, sound awkward when *-er* or *-est* is added. For these modifiers, *more* or *most* should be added instead.

Rule 30c **Use *-er* or *more* to form the comparative degree and *-est* or *most* to form the superlative degree of two-syllable modifiers.**

More and *most* are always used with adverbs that end in *-ly.*

POSITIVE	COMPARATIVE	SUPERLATIVE
easy	easier	easiest
fragrant	more fragrant	most fragrant
sweetly	more sweetly	most sweetly

Let your ear be your guide when deciding between *er/est* and *more/most* with two-syllable modifiers. If adding *-er* or *-est* makes a word difficult to pronounce, use *more* or *most* instead. It is obvious, for example, that you would never say "gracefuler" or "aimlesser."

Modifiers with three or more syllables always form their comparative and superlative degrees by adding *more* and *most.*

Rule 30d **Use *more* to form the comparative degree and *most* to form the superlative degree of modifiers with three or more syllables.**

POSITIVE	COMPARATIVE	SUPERLATIVE
considerate	more considerate	most considerate
accurately	more accurately	most accurately

Use *less* and *least* to form the negative comparisons of adjectives and adverbs.

considerate	less considerate	least considerate
accurately	less accurately	least accurately

Irregular Comparisons The comparative and superlative degrees of a few modifiers are formed irregularly.

POSITIVE	COMPARATIVE	SUPERLATIVE
bad/badly/ill	worse	worst
good/well	better	best
little	less	least
many/much	more	most

Be sure that you do not add the regular-comparison endings to the comparative and the superlative degrees of these irregular modifiers. For example, *worse* is the comparative form of *bad*. You should never use "worser."

EXERCISE 2 *Forming the Comparison of Modifiers*

Number your paper 1 to 20. Copy each modifier. Then write its comparative and superlative forms.

1. low
2. good
3. rapidly
4. bad
5. rough
6. fast
7. calmly
8. many
9. clever
10. well
11. eager
12. beautiful
13. lean
14. little
15. different
16. thin
17. tasty
18. slowly
19. tough
20. dramatic

EXERCISE 3 *Using the Correct Form of Comparison*

Number your paper 1 to 15. Then write the correct form of the modifier in parentheses.

1. Is the *Concorde* the (faster, fastest) commercial airplane?
2. Of the two books, I enjoyed this one (more, most).
3. Who ran the mile (faster, fastest), Mavis or Janet?
4. Of the two dogs, Cider is the (friendlier, friendliest).
5. Liver is my (less, least) favorite food.
6. Between marketing and public relations, I think marketing is the (better, best) profession.
7. Which is (fresher, freshest), the whole-wheat or the white bread?
8. Of the three songs, which is played the (more, most) on the radio?
9. Anne received the (higher, highest) number of points of all the contestants.
10. Was the (smoother, smoothest) ride in the blue or the green car?
11. Which is (taller, tallest), the Eiffel Tower or the Empire State Building?
12. Which of the two suggestions did you like (better, best)?
13. Cleaning out the basement is (worse, worst) than cleaning out the garage.
14. That is absolutely the (more, most) humorous movie that I've seen all year.
15. Which do you think are (more, most) fragrant, apple blossoms or orange blossoms?

Problems with Modifiers

A few problems that can cause confusion in your writing or speaking may arise when you use modifiers.

Double Comparisons Use only one method of forming the comparative or superlative form of a modifier. Never use both at the same time.

Rule 30e **Do not use both -*er* and *more* to form the comparative degree, or both -*est* and *most* to form the superlative degree.**

DOUBLE COMPARISON	I've never seen a **more funnier** movie.
CORRECT	I've never seen a **funnier** movie.
DOUBLE COMPARISON	Which is the **most highest** mountain?
CORRECT	Which is the **highest** mountain?

***Other* and *Else* in Comparisons** When a comparison is made, the similarities or differences between people or things are pointed out. Sometimes, however, a comparison is incorrectly made. This happens when people or things are compared with themselves as well as with other people or things. Using the word *other* or *else* will help you avoid this problem.

Rule 30f **Add *other* or *else* when comparing a member of a group with the rest of the group.**

INCORRECT	That jet is faster than any plane. [Since the jet is an airplane, it is being incorrectly compared with itself.]
CORRECT	That jet is faster than any **other** plane. [When the word *other* is added, the jet is being compared only with other planes—not with itself.]
INCORRECT	Edgar has won more races than anyone on the team. [Since Edgar is on the team, he is being incorrectly compared with himself.]
CORRECT	Edgar has won more races than anyone **else** on the team. [When the word *else* is added, Edgar is being compared only with others on the team—not with himself.]

EXERCISE 4 *Correcting Mistakes in Comparisons*

Number your paper 1 to 20. Then write the following sentences, correcting each mistake.

1. I think the rhinoceros is the most ugliest animal in the whole world.
2. Jerry is faster than anyone on his relay team.
3. Which is pitched more higher, the piccolo or the flute?
4. The unabridged dictionary is larger than any book in the library.
5. The most greatest number of swallows fly to California.
6. The weather couldn't be worser than it has been this past week.
7. My brother Richard is taller than anyone on either side of the family.
8. Yosemite Falls in California is the most highest falls in the country.
9. High blood pressure is the most commonest disease in the United States today.
10. Milk contains more of the elements essential to growth than any beverage.
11. The restaurant gets more wider in the back.
12. The thighbone is longer and stronger than any bone in the body.
13. In the mile race, Derek seems to run more faster during the last quarter.
14. This clock is the most oldest antique that we own.
15. Mary sings better than anyone I know.
16. Occasionally there have been tales of a mountain more higher than Mount Everest.
17. Which is more fiercer, the leopard or the lion?
18. The Snake River cuts a deeper gash in the surface of the United States than any river in the country.
19. That was the most sweetest honey I have ever eaten!
20. There are more beetles on Earth than any living creature.

Illogical Comparisons When you write a comparison, be sure you compare two or more similar things. When you compare different things, the comparison is illogical.

Rule 30g Compare only items of a similar kind.

ILLOGICAL COMPARISON	These **tomatoes** are tastier than the **Hamiltons.** [Tomatoes are being compared with people.]

LOGICAL COMPARISON	These **tomatoes** are tastier than the Hamiltons' **tomatoes.** [Now tomatoes are being compared with tomatoes.]
ILLOGICAL COMPARISON	The boys' **gym** in our school is larger than the **girls.** [A gym is being compared to girls.]
LOGICAL COMPARISON	The boys' **gym** in our school is larger than the girls' **gym.** [Now two gyms are being compared.]

Note: See page 809 for the use of an apostrophe with possessive nouns.

Double Negatives The following words are all considered to be negatives.

Common Negatives	
but (meaning "only")	none
hardly	not (and its contraction *n't*)
never	nothing
no	only
nobody	scarcely

Rule 30h Avoid using a double negative.

A double negative often cancels itself out, leaving you with a positive statement. For example, if you say, "We didn't meet nobody on the trail," you are actually saying, "We did meet somebody on the trail."

DOUBLE NEGATIVE	Dad says he does**n't** need **no** more ties for his birthday.
CORRECT	Dad says he does**n't** need any more ties for his birthday.
DOUBLE NEGATIVE	There is**n't hardly** any air in the tire.
CORRECT	There is **hardly** any air in the tire.
DOUBLE NEGATIVE	We did**n't** find **nothing** in the box.
CORRECT	We did**n't** find anything in the box.
CORRECT	We found **nothing** in the box.

EXERCISE 5 Correcting Mistakes with Modifiers

Number your paper 1 to 20. Then write the following sentences, correcting each mistake.

1. Sometimes strangers' criticisms are more helpful than your friends.
2. The Florida Everglades haven't never been completely explored.
3. This year's team is better than last year.
4. We couldn't hardly stand the heat in Death Valley.
5. We wanted to go skiing, but there wasn't no snow at Mount Killington.
6. Our cat is older than the Kennedys.
7. Accident figures for our town are worse than Hartford.
8. Jack didn't give us none of the prize money.
9. I haven't scarcely had time to read a magazine.
10. Aren't there no seats left?
11. The governor can't hardly expect the citizens to be happy about the tax increase.
12. My gas mileage is better than your car.
13. I can't find my jacket nowhere.
14. There wasn't no one who knew the combination to the lock.
15. After pulling a muscle, Greg couldn't run no farther.
16. Hadn't you never seen an eclipse before?
17. Our school's pool is larger than Jefferson High.
18. There wasn't hardly any reason for Philip to lose his temper.
19. The prices at the discount store are lower than the department store.
20. I was so sleepy I couldn't hardly keep my eyes open.

Adjective or Adverb? An adjective modifies a noun or a pronoun. An adverb modifies a verb, an adjective, or another adverb. An adverb follows an action verb, but an adjective follows a linking verb. *(See pages 556 and 557 for lists of linking verbs.)*

ADVERB This week passed **quickly.** [*Passed* is an action verb.]

ADJECTIVE The auditorium became **silent** when the curtain went up. [*Became* is a linking verb.]

ADVERB She looked **sadly** at the broken lamp. [*Looked* is used as an action verb.]

ADJECTIVE She looked **sad** yesterday. [*Looked* is used as a linking verb.]

Good is always used as an adjective. *Well* is usually used as an adverb. However, when *well* means "in good health" or "attractive," it is an adjective.

ADJECTIVE Your report was very **good.**
ADVERB The car is running **well.**
ADJECTIVE I don't feel **well** today, so I will have to miss practice. [in good health]

EXERCISE 6 *Choosing an Adjective or an Adverb*

Number your paper 1 to 15. Then write the correct form of the modifier in parentheses.

1. Although Mr. Harris spoke (calm, calmly), we all knew he was upset.
2. How (good, well) can you play chess?
3. Our tomato plants grew unusually (good, well) because of frequent rains.
4. I don't think I answered two of the questions on the geometry test (correct, correctly).
5. Grapefruit juice tastes too (tart, tartly) for me early in the morning.
6. Ted's idea sounds (good, well) to me.
7. Katherine hasn't felt (good, well) for over a week.
8. After Jake had a tooth pulled, his lower jaw was swollen (bad, badly).
9. From where we sat, we could see and hear everything quite (good, well).
10. Doesn't the turkey smell (good, well)?
11. Although we all thought the biscuits looked (peculiar, peculiarly), none of us said anything.
12. I can't study (effective, effectively) if the radio is on.
13. After being ill for two weeks, Lucas is finally feeling (good, well) again.
14. Barbecued steaks taste (delicious, deliciously) if they aren't overcooked.
15. Jeanne plays the French horn unusually (good, well).

EXERCISE 7 Cumulative Review

Number your paper 1 to 20. Rewrite the following sentences, correcting each mistake. If a sentence is correct, write *C* after the number.

1. The magnifying glass is more older than either eyeglasses or the telescope.
2. Which is farther north—Point Barrow, Alaska, or Bangor, Maine?
3. Lake Green in Montana has the purest water of any lake in North America.
4. The parade hadn't scarcely begun when the downpour started.
5. During her speech Maura spoke too rapid.
6. Vatican City is the most smallest country in the world.
7. The elephant has more muscles in its trunk than any animal has in its entire body.
8. Whatever Beth cooks, she cooks good.
9. Of all animals the cheetah is the fastest.
10. I think Spanish is the bestest language in existence.
11. The hurricane that struck Texas was worse than the one that struck Florida.
12. Weighing 802 pounds, William Cobb was the most heaviest wrestler in the world.
13. More books and articles have been written about chess than about any game.
14. The apples from your tree tasted very good.
15. Of those three Lincoln biographies, I think Carl Sandburg's is the better.
16. Which has been tamed longest, the cat or the dog?
17. The United States is now the world's largest producer of cheese.
18. Even with a ladder, I couldn't hardly reach the kitten in the tree.
19. In heavy traffic I always drive cautious.
20. Chico always gets along good with everyone.

Application to Writing

When you were younger, monsters and other scary things in movies were more frightening to you than they are now. Write a paragraph that gives an example from your early life and explains the reason why you felt that way. Be sure to use the correct forms of all modifiers.

Integrating Language Skills

USING YOUR TEXT

Brainstorming (20–21)
Persuasive Essays (234–269)

Usage: Editing for Errors with Modifiers

Facts and statistics in a report often become more relevant if they are compared with facts and statistics about something else. If you use this technique, be sure to use the correct form of comparison and to avoid the common problems with comparisons.

Checking Your Understanding Write the following paragraphs, correcting each mistake.

Because Mars doesn't have no cloud cover, it can be seen easy from Earth with the aid of great telescopes. More was learned about Mars, however, when *Viking 1* and *Viking 2* landed there in 1976.

Mars is more like Earth than any planet. Both have an iron core, a layer of rock, and a rocky crust. Both have four seasons, although those on Mars are twice as long.

There are, of course, many differences. Mars's year is almost twice as long as Earth. Being more farther from the sun, Mars is more colder than Earth. Afternoon temperatures range from 0°C to 27°C. At night the temperature drops sharp to a low of nearly −125°C.

Is there life on Mars? Experiments conducted by *Viking 1* and *Viking 2* showed some strangely chemical processes on the surface of Mars. None of these experiments, however, showed no signs of life.

Persuading Others Think of something you do that is unusual or unique. Perhaps, for example, you play a cello or work in a bakery on weekends. Brainstorm for reasons why what you do might sound appealing to your friends. Then organize your reasons in order of importance. *(See pages 256–257.)*

Write the first draft of an essay that tries to convince others that what you do is very special. ***Application:*** Revise and edit your persuasive essay, looking particularly for errors with modifiers. Then write a final copy.

Chapter 30

Review

Correcting Errors with Modifiers Number your paper 1 to 30. Then write the following sentences, correcting each mistake. If a sentence is correct, write *C* after the number.

1. Niagara Falls has a steadier flow of water than any waterfall in the world.
2. Who is the best diver, Jessie or Mark?
3. Tara learned the new signals easy.
4. Of all the runners on the team, Phyllis wins races most consistently.
5. We hadn't but one hour to tour the entire truck-assembly plant.
6. Our house isn't as large as the McDonalds.
7. I like Isaac Asimov's science-fiction novels better than any books.
8. Don't you think Cora dances extremely well?
9. The youngest of the two Fletcher girls is going to college in the fall.
10. Luis didn't have no time to make his bed or eat breakfast this morning.
11. The grass is always greener on the other side.
12. I received an answer more quickly than I had expected.
13. One of the most busiest spots in the world is the intersection of State and Madison in downtown Chicago.
14. Manuel couldn't decide which of the six horses was the tamest.
15. The United States has more telephones than any country in the world.
16. Of the two jobs I have had, I like this one best.
17. The fans groaned as Andrew, who usually plays good, fumbled the ball.
18. Is there an animal more smarter than the porpoise?
19. Who do you think has more computer training, Miguel or Maria?
20. By the time Tim and I got to Kate's house, there wasn't no food left.
21. After a whole summer in Quebec, Jonathan speaks French quite good.

22. I have painted many pictures, but I think this one of the owl is better.
23. This computer works faster than any computer in this store.
24. I don't know which is worst, packing when I go away or unpacking when I return.
25. I can't figure out none of the clues in this mystery story.
26. A cool shower would feel good on such a hot day.
27. I looked at six cameras because I wanted the best for my money.
28. Donald just got the most cutest kitten you have ever seen.
29. This pen writes darker than Kathy.
30. Which do you like best, polyester or cotton?

Mastery Test

Number your paper 1 to 10. Then write the correct form of the modifier in parentheses.

1. Of the two pumpkins, there was no doubt that Juan's was (larger, largest).
2. Of all these vegetables, I like Brussels sprouts the (less, least).
3. I (could hardly, couldn't hardly) find the light switch in the dark.
4. Which did you like (more, most) in the play, the singing or the dancing?
5. My uncle's old car still runs (good, well).
6. Hawk is larger than (any, any other) dog you have had before.
7. Which is (worse, worst), cleaning your room or defrosting the refrigerator?
8. Of the two candidates, which one do you think will make the (better, best) mayor?
9. This lotion feels (good, well) on my sunburn.
10. Which are (larger, largest), your feet or mine?

A Writer's Glossary of Usage

Although you have covered the fundamental aspects of usage, there are some specific elements that will be reviewed in this last section of the usage unit. Since the 70 entries in this section have been arranged alphabetically, you can use it as an easy reference tool.

Throughout this section you will see examples of standard English and nonstandard English. *Standard English* refers to the rules and conventions of usage that are accepted and used most widely by English-speaking people throughout the world. *Nonstandard English* has many variations because it is influenced by regional differences in dialects, as well as by current slang. Since nonstandard English lacks uniformity, always use standard English when you write.

a, an Use *a* before words beginning with consonant sounds and *an* before words beginning with vowel sounds. Always keep in mind that this rule applies to sounds, not letters. For example, *an hourglass* is correct because the *h* is silent.

Today was **a** humid day.
Mr. Reynolds is **an** honorable man.

accept, except *Accept* is a verb that means "to receive with consent." *Except* is usually a preposition that means "but" or "other than."

Everyone **accepted** the award **except** Tony.

advice, advise *Advice* is a noun that means "a recommendation." *Advise* is a verb that means "to recommend."

Your **advice** saved me time and money.
I **advise** you to go to bed early tonight.

affect, effect *Affect* is a verb that means "to influence." *Effect* is usually a noun that means "a result" or "influence." As a verb, *effect* means "to accomplish" or "to produce."

The devastating **effects** of the hurricane **affected** the lives of everyone in the small coastal town. [*effect* as a noun]

New taxes **effected** a change in our budget. [*effect* as a verb]

ain't This contraction is nonstandard English. It should be avoided.

NONSTANDARD That **ain't** my notebook.
STANDARD That **isn't** my notebook.

all ready, already *All ready* means "completely ready." *Already* means "previously."

The actors are **all ready** for the curtain call.
I have **already** eaten dinner.

all together, altogether *All together* means "in a group." *Altogether* means "wholly" or "thoroughly."

Is the camping equipment **all together** in the garage?
The fund-raising drive was **altogether** successful.

a lot These two words are often written incorrectly as one. There is no such word as "alot." *A lot* should be avoided in formal writing. (Do not confuse *a lot* with *allot,* which is a verb that means "to distribute by shares.")

INFORMAL I like him **a lot.**
FORMAL I like him **very much.**
Were the chores **allotted** evenly?

among, between Both of these words are prepositions. *Among* is used when referring to three or more people or things. *Between* is usually used when referring to two people or things.

I divided my lunch **among** three of my friends.
Please keep this conversation just **between** you and me.

amount, number *Amount* refers to a singular word. *Number* refers to a plural word.

A large **number** of town merchants contributed a substantial **amount** of money to the scholarship fund.

anymore Do not use *anymore* for *now* or *nowadays*. *Anymore* is usually used in a negative statement.

NONSTANDARD	Most automobile manufacturers are interested in fuel efficiency **anymore.**
STANDARD	Most automobile manufacturers are interested in fuel efficiency **nowadays.**
STANDARD	I don't collect stamps **anymore.**

anywhere, everywhere, nowhere, somewhere Do not add *-s* to any of these words.

NONSTANDARD	I can't go **anywheres** tonight.
STANDARD	I can't go **anywhere** tonight.

as far as This expression is sometimes confused with "all the farther," which is nonstandard English.

NONSTANDARD	This is **all the farther** the hose will go.
STANDARD	This is **as far as** the hose will go.

at Do not use *at* after *where*.

NONSTANDARD	Do you know **where** he's **at?**
STANDARD	Do you know **where** he is?

EXERCISE 1 *Determining the Correct Word*

Number your paper 1 to 20. Then write each word in parentheses that correctly completes the following sentences.

1. Would you (accept, except) an invitation to dinner?
2. The possibility of bad weather could (affect, effect) their plans to drive to Toledo.
3. Divide the apple (among, between) the three of you.
4. The family were (all ready, already) to go except Brian.
5. What did he (advice, advise) you to do to get rid of the dog's fleas?

6. Governor, we appreciate (a lot, very much) the time you have spent on this interview.
7. I looked (everywhere, everywheres) for my notebook.
8. Driver, is Blue Hills Avenue (all the farther, as far as) this bus goes?
9. A large (amount, number) of accidents occur on the road.
10. The freezing temperatures seemed to have little (affect, effect) on the skiers.
11. I don't (all together, altogether) understand the directions to the test.
12. Polly sat (among, between) the two contestants as the program began.
13. I hate to admit it, but Mariella usually gives excellent (advice, advise).
14. Have you (all ready, already) seen that movie?
15. (All together, Altogether) they sang "Happy Birthday" as she blew out the candles.
16. Smaller cars seem to be the trend in this country (anymore, nowadays).
17. The new graduation requirements will (affect, effect) the entering class but will have no (affect, effect) on the students presently enrolled.
18. I (accept, except) all your suggestions (accept, except) the last one.
19. We tried to (affect, effect) a change in the bylaws of the club.
20. Just (among, between) you and me, sharing one part (among, between) four actors will never work.

awhile, a while *Awhile* is an adverb that stands alone and means "for a short period of time." *A while* is an expression made up of an article and a noun. It is used mainly after the preposition *for.*

After watching TV **awhile,** I fell asleep.
Did you have to wait for **a while** in the doctor's office?

bad, badly *Bad* is an adjective and often follows a linking verb. *Badly* is used as an adverb. In the first two examples, *feels* is a linking verb.

NONSTANDARD	Henry feels **badly** today.
STANDARD	Henry feels **bad** today.
STANDARD	He hung the wallpaper **badly.**

because Do not use *because* after *the reason.* Use one or the other in a sentence.

NONSTANDARD The **reason** he left is **because** he had an important appointment this afternoon.

STANDARD He left **because** he had an important appointment this afternoon.

STANDARD The **reason** he left is **that** he had an important appointment this afternoon.

being as, being that These expressions should be replaced with *because* or *since.*

NONSTANDARD **Being that** the air was cold, we went inside.

STANDARD **Because** the air was cold, we went inside.

beside, besides *Beside* is always a preposition that means "by the side of." As a preposition, *besides* means "in addition to." As an adverb, *besides* means "also" or "moreover."

Come sit **beside** me. [by the side of]

Besides the students the faculty will also participate in the paper drive. [in addition to]

Their plane was late, and some of their luggage was lost **besides.** [also]

both Never use *the* before *both.*

NONSTANDARD **The both** of them went to the concert.

STANDARD **Both** of them went to the concert.

bring, take *Bring* indicates motion toward the speaker. *Take* indicates motion away from the speaker.

Please **bring** me an apple.
Take the trash out.

can, may *Can* expresses ability. *May* expresses possibility or permission.

Tammy **can** drive you to the airport.
May I have another helping of green beans?

can't help but Use a gerund instead of *but.*

NONSTANDARD I **can't help but miss** them.
STANDARD I **can't help missing** them.

different from Use this form instead of *different than.*

NONSTANDARD Her pea soup tastes **different than** yours.
STANDARD Her pea soup tastes **different from** yours.

doesn't, don't *Doesn't* is singular and should be used only with singular nouns and the pronouns *he, she,* and *it. Don't* is plural and should be used with plural nouns and all the other personal pronouns.

NONSTANDARD He **don't** come here anymore.
STANDARD He **doesn't** come here anymore.

NONSTANDARD Geometry **don't** come easily to me.
STANDARD Geometry **doesn't** come easily to me.

double negative Words such as *hardly, never, no, not,* and *nobody* are considered negatives. Do not use two negatives to express one negative meaning. *(See page 731 for a list of negative words.)*

NONSTANDARD I did**n't hardly** know what to say.
STANDARD I did**n't** know what to say.
STANDARD I **hardly** knew what to say.

emigrate, immigrate These words are both verbs. *Emigrate* means "to leave a country to settle elsewhere." *Immigrate* means "to enter a foreign country to live there." One emigrates *from* a country and immigrates *to* another country. *Emigrant* and *immigrant* are the noun forms.

Edward Bok *emigrated* from Holland.
He *immigrated* to the United States.

etc. *Etc.* is an abbreviation for a Latin phrase, *et cetera,* that means "and other things." Never use the word *and* with *etc.* If you do, what you are really saying is "and and other things." It is best, however, not to use this abbreviation at all in formal writing.

INFORMAL Remember to take tents, sleeping bags, **etc.**
FORMAL Remember to take tents, sleeping bags, **and other necessities.**

EXERCISE 2 *Determining the Correct Word*

Number your paper 1 to 20. Then write each word in parentheses that correctly completes the following sentences.

1. I think Virginia took the news (bad, badly).
2. Why (doesn't, don't) they understand these simple rules?
3. I like to sit (beside, besides) the window in a plane.
4. She (emigrated, immigrated) to the United States in 1903.
5. I stayed at the party for (a while, awhile).
6. He didn't have (any, no) answers to my questions.
7. (Because, Being that) you're here already, you can help us.
8. I can't help (but be, being) proud.
9. (Beside, Besides) a history test, I have a geometry test.
10. (Can, May) I carry those packages for you?
11. The weather forecast for tomorrow looks (bad, badly).
12. I found the life-style in California (different from, different than) the life-style in New England.
13. I can't go with you (because, being as) I have to take my brother to karate practice.
14. (Both, The both) twins joined the track team.
15. He can't (ever, never) sleep on a feather pillow.
16. Let's work (a while, awhile) longer, and then we can rest.
17. (Being as, Because) you're sick, you (can, may) stay home.
18. Most of the people who (emigrated, immigrated) to the United States between 1840 and 1850 had (emigrated, immigrated) from Germany and Ireland.
19. It (doesn't, don't) matter if they (doesn't, don't) wish to go.
20. (Bring, Take) me your excuse and then please (bring, take) the attendance report to the office.

farther, further *Farther* refers to distance. *Further* means "additional" or "to a greater degree or extent."

How much **farther** do we have to go before we get there?
Further details will not be known until later.

fewer, less *Fewer* is plural and refers to things that can be counted. *Less* is singular and refers to quantities and qualities that cannot be counted.

Fewer dollars were spent on education this year.
There is **less** milk than I need for the recipe.

good, well *Good* is an adjective and often follows a linking verb. *Well* is an adverb and often follows an action verb. However, when *well* means "in good health" or "attractive," it is used as an adjective.

> You report was very **good.** [adjective]
> Heidi dances quite **well.** [adverb]
> I don't feel **well** at all. [adjective—"in good health"]

have, of Never substitute *of* for the verb *have.* When speaking, many people make a contraction of *have.* For example, someone might say, "We should've gone." Because *'ve* sounds like *of, of* is often mistakenly substituted for *have* in writing.

NONSTANDARD We couldn't **of** known that at the time.
STANDARD We couldn't **have** known that at the time.

hear, here *Hear* is a verb that means "to perceive by listening." *Here* is an adverb that means "in this place."

> We can **hear** the music well from the bandstand **here** on the lawn.

hole, whole A *hole* is an opening. *Whole* means "complete."

> Has this **hole** in the wall been here the **whole** time?

imply, infer Both of these words are verbs. *Imply* means "to suggest" or "to hint." *Infer* means "to draw a conclusion by reasoning or evidence." A speaker implies; a listener infers. *Implication* and *inference* are the noun forms.

> Kent **implied** that he agreed with us.
> We **inferred** from Kent's remarks that he agrees with us.

in, into Use *into* when you want to express motion from one place to another.

> After going **into** the stadium, we found people sitting **in** our seats.

its, it's *Its* is a possessive pronoun and means "belonging to it." *It's* is a contraction for *it is.*

> The committee will report **its** findings next week.
> **It's** too late now to go to the lecture.

kind of, sort of Never substitute these expressions for *rather* or *somewhat.*

NONSTANDARD	Your sister is **kind of** smart.
STANDARD	Your sister is **rather** smart.
NONSTANDARD	I feel **sort of** tired right now.
STANDARD	I feel **somewhat** tired right now.

knew, new *Knew,* the past tense of the verb *know,* means "was acquainted with." *New* is an adjective that means "recently made" or "just found."

From the beginning he **knew** which of the **new** bicycles he wanted for his birthday.

learn, teach Both of these words are verbs. *Learn* means "to gain knowledge." *Teach* means "to instruct."

NONSTANDARD	Leonard **learned** me how to speak German.
STANDARD	Leonard **taught** me how to speak German.
STANDARD	I have **learned** to speak German.

leave, let Both of these words are verbs. *Leave* means "to depart" or "to go away from." *Let* means "to allow" or "to permit."

NONSTANDARD	**Leave** me help you with the dishes.
STANDARD	**Let** me help you with the dishes.
STANDARD	We should **leave** for the airport soon, or you might miss your plane.

lie, lay *Lie* means "to rest or recline." *Lie* is never followed by a direct object. Its principal parts are *lie, lying, lay,* and *lain. Lay* means "to put or set (something) down." *Lay* is usually followed by a direct object. Its principal parts are *lay, laying, laid,* and *laid.*

LIE I'm so tired I must **lie** down for a few minutes.
The cats are **lying** in the sunny window.
Yesterday morning I **lay** in bed for ten extra minutes.
How long has the paper **lain** here in the puddle?

LAY **Lay** the packages on the counter.
They're **laying** our new carpet now.
Who **laid** that box on the glass table?
Have you **laid** out your clothes for tomorrow?

EXERCISE 3 *Determining the Correct Word*

Number your paper 1 to 20. Then write each word in parentheses that correctly completes the following sentences.

1. I have (fewer, less) classes this year than I had last year.
2. From his faltering steps, I (implied, inferred) that Pierre was tiring.
3. (Leave, Let) me drive you to the airport.
4. The (farther, further) I read, the more I like this book.
5. I think (its, it's) time for the TV special.
6. Everyone on the committee works (good, well) together.
7. You should (have, of) gone yourself!
8. My paycheck was (kind of, rather) small this week.
9. You will receive (farther, further) instructions.
10. We went (in, into) the auditorium to rehearse for the play.
11. He (learned, taught) me how to care for the kittens.
12. Please give me (fewer, less) dessert than you gave him.
13. The ride to Cape Cod was (sort of, somewhat) long.
14. Have you (learned, taught) your puppy to do any tricks?
15. Does the milk still taste (good, well) to you?
16. I (knew, new) you were wearing a (knew, new) jacket.
17. (Hear, Here) is the best place to (hear, here) the actors.
18. Did he (imply, infer) that he would leave the team?
19. The (hole, whole) time we watched, the (hole, whole) in the ground grew bigger and bigger.
20. Because we've had (fewer, less) rain this summer, we've been bothered by (fewer, less) mosquitoes.

EXERCISE 4 *Using* Lie *and* Lay *Correctly*

Number your paper 1 to 10. Then complete each sentence by writing the correct form of *lie* or *lay.*

1. My dog _______ down and sits up at my command.
2. Alfredo's kite crashed and _______ broken on the beach.
3. Please _______ those packages on the kitchen table.
4. If Pearl _______ down for a nap, she must have been sick.
5. Who _______ his wet coat on the couch?
6. Some birds _______ eggs in holes in the ground.
7. They are _______ the cornerstone of the building.
8. Gina's glove _______ in the driveway all night.
9. Your library book is _______ on top of the TV.
10. I have _______ my report card on the desk.

like, as *Like* is a preposition that introduces a prepositional phrase. *As* is usually a subordinating conjunction that introduces an adverb clause. In informal usage *like* is sometimes used as a conjunction. In formal usage avoid using *like* as a conjunction.

FORMAL It happened just **as** he said it would. [clause]
FORMAL Do you want the curtians hung **like** this? [prepositional phrase]

loose, lose *Loose* is usually an adjective that means "not tight." *Lose* is a verb that means "to misplace" or "not to have any longer."

Sew on that **loose** button, or you will **lose** it.

of Prepositions such as *inside, outside,* and *off* should not be followed by *of.*

NONSTANDARD Did you look **inside of** the box?
STANDARD Did you look **inside** the box?

ought Never use *have* or *had* with *ought.*

NONSTANDARD Melba **hadn't ought** to sit so long in the sun.
STANDARD Melba **ought** not to sit so long in the sun.

passed, past *Passed* is the past tense of the verb *pass.* As a noun *past* means "a time gone by." As an adjective *past* means "just gone" or "elapsed." As a preposition it means "beyond."

For the **past** three years, I have **passed** every subject I have taken in school. [*past* as an adjective]

In the **past** I never drove **past** the school on my way to the mall. [*past* as a noun and then as a preposition]

rise, raise *Rise* means "to move upward" or "to get up." *Rise* is never followed by a direct object. Its principal parts are *rise, rising, rose,* and *risen.* *Raise* means "to lift (something) up," "to increase," or "to grow something." *Raise* is usually followed by a direct object. Its principal parts are *raise, raising, raised,* and *raised.*

The balloon **rose** into the sky.
Raise your hand if you agree. [*Hand* is a direct object.]

-self, -selves A reflexive pronoun should not be used as a subject. (You should never use *hisself* or *theirselves.*)

NONSTANDARD	Jean and **myself** met at the museum.
STANDARD	Jean and **I** met at the museum.

shall, will Formal English uses *shall* with first person pronouns and *will* with second and third person pronouns. Today these words are used interchangeably with *I* and *we,* except that *shall* is usually used for questions.

Shall we eat at seven?
He **will** join us soon.

sit, set *Sit* means "to rest in an upright position." *Sit* is rarely followed by a direct object. Its principal parts are *sit, sitting, sat,* and *sat. Set* means "to put or place (something)." *Set* is usually followed by a direct object. Its principal parts are *set, setting, set,* and *set.*

Please **sit** down and stay awhile.
Set those boxes on the floor.

so *So* should not be used to begin a sentence.

NONSTANDARD	**So** how do you feel today?
STANDARD	The plane was late, **so** we missed our connection. [coordinating conjunction]
STANDARD	I'm **so** tired tonight. [adverb]

than, then *Than* is a subordinating conjunction and is used for comparisons. *Then* is an adverb and means "at that time" or "next."

Earth is larger **than** Mercury.
What do you want to do **then?**

that, which, who These words are often used as relative pronouns to introduce adjective clauses. *That* refers to people, animals, or things and always begins an essential clause. *Which* refers to animals and things. *Who* refers to people.

The man **that** just drove by is my math teacher.

A Midsummer Night's Dream, **which** you recommended, was very entertaining.

Mr. Jenkins, **who** is my next-door neighbor, just won the Chamber of Commerce award.

their, there, they're *Their* is a possessive pronoun. *There* is usually an adverb, but sometimes it also begins an inverted sentence. *They're* is a contraction for *they are.*

Have you seen **their** new uniforms?
There is a good reason why **they're** late.

theirs, there's *Theirs* is a possessive pronoun. *There's* is a contraction for *there is.*

Our invitation came a week ago; **theirs** came later.
There's a delicious turkey dinner waiting for us.

them, those Never use **them** as a subject or a modifier.

NONSTANDARD	**Them** are the ones to get. [subject]
STANDARD	**Those** are the ones to get.
NONSTANDARD	Do you like **them** shoes? [adjective]
STANDARD	Do you like **those** shoes?

EXERCISE 5 *Determining the Correct Word*

Number your paper 1 to 20. Then write each word in parentheses that correctly completes the following sentences.

1. (Shall, Will) we dance?
2. Be careful not to trip over your (loose, lose) shoelace.
3. (Theirs, There's) a good Italian restaurant that just opened on Tremont Street.
4. On the average, people were much shorter in the Middle Ages (than, then) they are today.
5. Please take (them, those) reports to the office for me.
6. Hold the racket (as, like) the instructor told you, and you will hit the ball correctly.
7. Members of the sophomore class produced the play (theirselves, themselves).
8. I never (loose, lose) my way around Houston.
9. (Their, They're) going to be half an hour late.
10. The player (which, who) shot the most baskets was only five feet.
11. We (passed, past) his car on the Meriden Turnpike.
12. (Them, Those) are the pictures I took.
13. Swing your golf club (as, like) I do.

14. (Their, There) new dog is a springer spaniel.
15. You (shall, will) be leaving on the seven o'clock flight.
16. If these keys are (theirs, there's), where are ours?
17. (There, They're) isn't a drop of milk in the house.
18. Brenda played the part (as, like) a professional.
19. Let's put the (passed, past) behind us.
20. (Them, Those) are the records for (them, those) students.

EXERCISE 6 *Using* Rise/Raise *and* Sit/Set *Correctly*

Number your paper 1 to 10. Then complete each sentence by writing the correct form of *rise/raise* or *sit/set.*

1. _______ the can of paint on the bench.
2. Mom _______ every morning at six o'clock.
3. Paul _______ next to me yesterday at the rally.
4. Who _______ the flag this morning?
5. The sun _______ brilliantly over the mountaintop.
6. After _______ in the reception room for an hour, I was shown into Dr. Rivera's office.
7. Don't you think we should _______ the temperature in the house by a few degrees?
8. Everyone _______ and saluted the flag.
9. Something is wrong; the bread isn't _______.
10. Fluffy always _______ on the windowsill in the afternoon.

this, that, these, those *This* and *that* are singular and modify singular nouns. *These* and *those* are plural and modify plural nouns.

NONSTANDARD I don't like **these** brand of sneakers.
STANDARD I don't like **this** brand of sneakers.

this here, that there Avoid using *here* or *there* in addition to *this* or *that.*

NONSTANDARD **This here** band is really good.
STANDARD **This** band is really good.

threw, through *Threw* is the past tense of the verb *throw. Through* is a preposition that means "in one side and out the other."

Roseanne swiftly **threw** the basketball right **through** the hoop.

to, too, two *To* is a preposition. *To* also begins an infinitive. *Too* is an adverb. *Two* is a number.

Adam went **to** the library **to** study.
Jogging **two** miles is **too** difficult for me.

try to Use *try to* instead of *try and,* which is nonstandard.

NONSTANDARD I will **try and** meet you at seven.
STANDARD I will **try to** meet you at seven.

way, ways Do not substitute *ways* for *way* when referring to a distance.

NONSTANDARD You live a long **ways** from school.
STANDARD You live a long **way** from school.

weak, week *Weak* is an adjective that means "not strong" or "likely to break." *Week* is a noun that means "a period of seven days."

I felt so **weak** I couldn't stand up.
A **week** is a long time to wait to hear if I got the job.

what Do not substitute *what* for *that.*

NONSTANDARD The car **what** we want is too expensive.
STANDARD The car **that** we want is too expensive.

when, where Do not use *when* or *where* directly after a linking verb in a definition.

NONSTANDARD A talus is **when** rock fragments accumulate at the base of a cliff.
STANDARD A talus is an accumulation of rock fragments at the base of a cliff.

NONSTANDARD Boulder is **where** there is low humidity.
STANDARD Boulder is a city **where** there is low humidity.

where Do not substitute *where* for *that.*

NONSTANDARD I read **where** there are going to be warmer winters.
STANDARD I read **that** there are going to be warmer winters.

who, whom *Who,* a pronoun in the nominative case, is used as a subject or a predicate nominative. *Whom,* a pronoun in the objective case, is mainly used as a direct object, an indirect object, or an object of a preposition. *(See pages 691–692.)*

Who sits behind you in English class? [subject]
Whom did you see at the museum? [direct object]

whose, who's *Whose* is a possessive pronoun. *Who's* is a contraction for *who is.*

Whose computer did you use?
Who's working in the lab?

your, you're *Your* is a possessive pronoun. *You're* is a contraction for *you are.*

You're sure this is **your** history book?

EXERCISE 7 *Determining the Correct Word*

Number your paper 1 to 20. Then write each word in parentheses that correctly completes the following sentences.

1. (These, This) cordless telephones are very practical.
2. The article stated (that, where) twins met for the first time after 30 years.
3. (Whose, Who's) driving us to the game?
4. We will try (and, to) meet you at the airport.
5. Why did you buy (that, those) pair of purple slacks?
6. The lilac bushes (that, what) shaded our front porch were uprooted.
7. (This, This here) apple juice is very tasty.
8. I've traveled a long (way, ways) to get here.
9. Who (threw, through) the ball into the punch bowl?
10. Do you want to try (these, this) make of tennis shoes?
11. (Your, You're) float was the best one in the parade.
12. I've been working on this project for a (weak, week).
13. Have you ever driven (threw, through) Yellowstone National Park?
14. For (who, whom) are you working now?
15. (That, That there) red convertible belongs to my uncle.
16. (Your, You're) the one they're looking for.
17. (That, Those) freshly baked muffins smell delicious.
18. He was very (weak, week) when he left the hospital.
19. (Whose, Who's) jacket are you wearing?
20. The trip (to, too, two) Seattle is (to, too, two) long, as it takes (to, too, two) hours.

Chapter

31 Capital Letters

Diagnostic Test

Number your paper 1 to 10. Then write each word that should be capitalized.

EXAMPLE are you going to the dance on saturday?
ANSWER Are, Saturday

1. is thanksgiving closer to the third or the fourth weekend in november?
2. next summer carrie will visit the grand canyon before heading west.
3. the courses i enjoy most are spanish, home economics II, european history, and chemistry.
4. did you read the article "computer mania in america" in the march issue of *newsweek*?
5. is boston or springfield the capital of massachusetts?
6. haverville high school, the newest school in marlin county, will open next year.
7. did you see senator rosen at the concert on monday?
8. dr. edwin t. hopper is the chief surgeon at carnegie hospital in southbury.
9. in her english class, my sister is reading *the house of the seven gables* by nathaniel hawthorne.
10. the jeffersons moved to the south last winter.

Rules for Capital Letters

A clear, detailed set of directions is extremely important if you are trying to find a friend's house for the first time. Capital letters and punctuation marks are like a good set of directions. As you read, they tell you when to go, when to slow down, and when to stop. They give you signals and clues that help you understand the meaning of sentences—just as directions give you signals and clues that help you find your way. Without directions you might not find your way to your friend's house. Without capital letters and punctuation, you might not find your way through even a short paragraph.

For many years you have been studying the rules for capital letters. Reviewing them in this chapter should help you use them correctly in any future written work.

First Words

A capital letter is like a green light. It indicates that you can begin to move through a new sentence or a new line of poetry.

Rule 31a **Capitalize the first word of a sentence or a line of poetry.**

SENTENCE **T**he mountain view was spectacular.

LINES OF POETRY
Time, you old gypsy man,
  Will you not stay,
Put up your caravan
  Just for one day?
      RALPH HODGSON

I and *O*

These single-letter words are always capitalized.

Rule 31b **Capitalize the pronoun *I*, both alone and in contractions. Also capitalize the interjection *O*.**

I If **I**'m going to be ready on time, **I** had better hurry.

O Monster! **O** prince, I went for Lancelot first.
      ALFRED, LORD TENNYSON

Note: *Oh* is capitalized only when it is the first word in a sentence.

MECHANICS

Proper Nouns and Proper Adjectives

A proper noun is the name of a particular person, place, or thing. A proper adjective is formed from a proper noun. *(See page 542 and page 563.)*

Rule 31c **Capitalize proper nouns and their abbreviations. Also capitalize most proper adjectives.**

PROPER NOUNS	**A**merica, **H**awaii, **D**enmark, **R**ome
PROPER ADJECTIVES	**A**merican cities, **H**awaiian pineapples, **D**anish accent, **R**oman citizen

Capitalize only the part of a compound adjective that is a proper noun or a proper adjective.

pro-**A**merican, **J**apanese-made, **M**exican-**A**merican

The following proper nouns have been divided into groups to help you remember them easily.

Names of Persons and Animals Capitalize the names of persons and animals.

PERSONS	**T**ad, **M**ary **L**ou **T**aylor, **C**arlos **T**. **R**ivera, **J**r.
ANIMALS	**D**usty, **D**uke, **M**ittens, **F**ang

Some surnames consist of two parts. You should usually capitalize the letter that follows *De, Mc, Mac, O', St.,* or *Von.* Since names do vary, however, it is always best to ask individual people how their names are capitalized.

Mac**D**onald, **O'R**eilly, **S**t. **J**ames, **V**on **H**ussen

Geographical Names Capitalize the names of places and bodies of water. Also capitalize the names of celestial bodies.

STREETS, HIGHWAYS	**S**tearns **H**ill **R**oad, **N**ew **Y**ork **F**reeway, **R**oute 36, **T**hirty-third **S**treet [The second part of a hyphenated numbered street is not capitalized.]
TOWNS, CITIES	**L**incoln, **T**erre **H**aute, **T**ampa, **W**aco
TOWNSHIPS, COUNTIES	**G**otland **T**ownship, **C**anby **C**ounty

STATES	**W**isconsin, **A**rizona, **W**est **V**irginia
COUNTRIES	**B**razil, **Z**aire, **E**gypt, **U**nited **S**tates
SECTIONS OF A COUNTRY	the **S**outheast, the **M**idwest, the **W**est [Compass directions do not begin with a capital letter. *Go **n**orth on Route 80.*]
CONTINENTS	**S**outh **A**merica, **A**sia, **A**ustralia
ISLANDS	**B**lock **I**sland, **C**anary **I**slands
MOUNTAINS	**M**ount **P**alomar, **R**ocky **M**ountains
PARKS	**G**lacier **N**ational **P**ark, **B**entley **P**ark
BODIES OF WATER	**G**ulf of **M**exico, **R**io **G**rande, **A**tlantic **O**cean, **C**hesapeake **B**ay, **L**ake **M**enken
STARS	**V**ega, **L**eo, **O**rion, **P**olaris, **A**ries
CONSTELLATIONS	the **L**ittle **D**ipper, **U**rsa **M**ajor
PLANETS	**J**upiter, **S**aturn, **M**ars, **N**eptune, **E**arth [Do not capitalize *sun* or *moon.* Also, do not capitalize *earth* if it is preceded by the word *the.*]

Note: Capitalize words such as *street, island, city, lake,* and *mountain* only when they are a part of a proper noun.

What **s**treet runs parallel to Ames **S**treet?

EXERCISE 1 *Using Capital Letters*

Number your paper 1 to 20. Then write the following items, using capital letters only where needed.

1. bangkok, thailand
2. the steens mountains
3. a chinese restaurant
4. the north star
5. a city in louisiana
6. grand rapids, michigan
7. dade county, florida
8. the mississippi river
9. the grand canyon
10. a nation in africa
11. the arctic ocean
12. sherwood island
13. forty-second street
14. south on route 66
15. the red bluff reservoir
16. african-american
17. a pier in tampa bay
18. the sun and mars
19. a highway in seattle
20. north of lake huron

EXERCISE 2 *Using Capital Letters*

Number your paper 1 to 25. Then write each word that should begin with a capital letter.

1. the river jordan daily pours six million tons of water into the dead sea.
2. recently in a letter from my aunt, i learned that the o'tooles have sold their ranch.
3. among the many flags that have flown over texas are those of spain, france, mexico, and the united states.
4. robert w. petersen of sacramento, california, set the marathon record for bowling.
5. second in distance from the sun, venus comes nearer to the earth than any other planet.
6. the black forest is located in germany.
7. the abacus is still widely used in china, japan, and parts of the middle east.
8. the name of ulysses s. grant's saddle horse was egypt.
9. did you know that the capital of the yukon is white horse?
10. we hand-carried a german-made clock on our flight home.
11. although some wheat is grown east of the mississippi, it is primarily a product of the midwest.
12. seventh avenue, forty-fourth street, and broadway cross each other at times square in new york city.
13. mexico city is the most populated city in latin america.
14. no north american country lies south of the equator.
15. the orbits of a few asteroids are highly irregular and reach close to mercury and as far out as saturn.
16. what river separates manhattan from the bronx?
17. the smallest of the scandinavian countries is denmark.
18. how many people in switzerland speak english?
19. port said is at the mediterranean end of the suez canal.
20. soon i'll be moving to carson city, the capital of nevada.
21. tim o'connell has two dogs named ruffy and gruffy.
22. a european country with a very high population density is monaco.
23. in 1609, galileo discovered 4 of jupiter's 14 moons.
24. we left the northeast and then headed south toward the smoky mountains.
25. of vapors, from whose solid atmosphere
    black rain, and fire, and hail will burst: o, hear!

    PERCY BYSSHE SHELLEY

Application to Writing

Choose a place named in an atlas. Then write a paragraph about its major geographical points of interest. Write the paragraph as if it were in a travel brochure published to lure tourists there. Begin by telling where the place is located. Be sure to capitalize all geographical names.

Names of Groups and Businesses Capitalize the names of organizations, businesses, institutions, government bodies, and political parties.

ORGANIZATIONS	**B**rentwood **C**ivic **A**ssociation, the **B**oston **C**eltics, the **U**nited **N**ations
BUSINESSES	**A**merican **M**otors, **M**etropolitan **L**ife **I**nsurance **C**ompany, **G**oodyear **T**ire
INSTITUTIONS	**W**est **V**irginia **I**nstitute of **T**echnology, **C**anton **H**igh **S**chool, **W**estwood **H**ospital [Words such as *college, school,* and *hospital* are not capitalized unless they are a part of a proper noun.]
GOVERNMENT BODIES	**H**ouse of **R**epresentatives, **D**epartment of **C**ommerce, the **S**upreme **C**ourt, the **H**ouse of **C**ommons, **P**arliament
POLITICAL PARTIES	the **D**emocratic **P**arty, a **R**epublican

Specific Time Periods, Events, and Documents Capitalize days of the week, months of the year, civil and religious holidays, and special events. Also capitalize the names of historical events, periods, and documents.

DAYS, MONTHS	**M**onday, **F**riday, **J**anuary, **D**ecember [Do not capitalize the seasons of the year.]
HOLIDAYS	**M**emorial **D**ay, the **F**ourth of **J**uly, **H**anukkah
SPECIAL EVENTS	the **R**ose **B**owl **P**arade, the **F**lower **S**how
HISTORICAL EVENTS	the **W**ar of 1812, the **B**attle of **B**unker **H**ill
PERIODS	the **R**enaissance, the **S**pace **A**ge
DOCUMENTS	the **D**eclaration of **I**ndependence, the **B**ill of **R**ights, the **T**reaty of **V**ersailles

Note: Prepositions are not capitalized.

Nationalities, Races, Languages, and Religions Capitalize the names of nationalities, races, languages, religions, and religious references.

NATIONALITIES	an **A**merican, a **R**ussian, a **P**ole
RACES	**C**aucasian, **O**riental, **M**ongoloid
LANGUAGES	**E**nglish, **F**rench, **G**erman, **S**panish
RELIGIONS	**R**oman **C**atholicism, **J**udaism
RELIGIOUS REFERENCES	**G**od, the **B**ible, the **K**oran, **G**enesis [Do not capitalize *god* when it refers to a mythological god.]

Other Proper Nouns Capitalize other nouns that name specific places and things.

VEHICLES	*Viking 1*, the *Orient Express*
AWARDS	**A**cademy **A**ward, **P**ulitzer **P**rize
BRAND NAMES	**A**pple computer, **D**ove soap [The product itself is *not* capitalized.]
MONUMENTS, MEMORIALS	**W**ashington **M**onument, **J**efferson **M**emorial, **V**ietnam **W**ar **M**emorial
BUILDINGS	**C**hrysler **B**uilding, **R**eunion **T**ower
SPECIFIC COURSE NAMES	**M**athematics II, **A**rt I, **E**nglish

Note: Unnumbered courses such as *history, woodworking,* and *science* are not capitalized. Also, do not capitalize class names such as *sophomore* and *senior* unless they are part of a proper noun, such as the *Junior Class.*

EXERCISE 3 *Using Capital Letters*

Number your paper 1 to 20. Then write the following items, using capital letters only where needed.

1. iowa state university
2. thursday, may 6
3. campbell soup
4. the united nations
5. equal rights amendment
6. delta airlines
7. the civil war
8. an oscar nomination
9. *spirit of st. louis*
10. tools of the stone age
11. members of the senate
12. winter and summer
13. palace of versailles
14. the republican party
15. a college in utah
16. a picnic on labor day
17. portuguese and italian
18. biology and shop II
19. the senior prom
20. psalms in the bible

EXERCISE 4 *Using Capital Letters*

Number your paper 1 to 25. Then write each word that should begin with a capital letter.

1. in 1981, sandra day o'connor became the first woman member of the united states supreme court.
2. last year we drove to rhode island and spent the summer in the east.
3. in 1960, the submarine *triton* circumnavigated the globe.
4. the speedy office supply company on ashburton drive carries acme copiers.
5. sargent shriver was the first director of the peace corps.
6. the national council of jewish women held its annual meeting last fall in hartford, connecticut.
7. george custer was badly defeated at the battle of the little big horn.
8. over labor day weekend, our family is going to camp out in red oak park.
9. in 1981, the united states roundly defeated argentina to win the davis cup.
10. the monroe doctrine warned european countries not to interfere in the americas.
11. last spring i studied french, but now i wish i had taken spanish instead.
12. everyone voted for laurie as treasurer of the sophomore class because she's a genius in mathematics.
13. in 1913, the sixteenth amendment to the united states constitution introduced the income tax.
14. on monday, may 25, 1981, daniel goodwin climbed the 110-story sears tower in chicago—on the outside!
15. john f. kennedy was the first roman catholic president.
16. yesterday i bought a pair of nike tennis shoes at bob's bootery on chestnut street.
17. the enormous sculptures on mount rushmore in the black hills of south dakota can be seen from 60 miles away.
18. if you are taking european history, algebra, chemistry, english composition, and art II, you're going to be busy!
19. the space age began with the launching of *sputnik I.*
20. franklin pierce was a member of the democratic party, but millard fillmore was a whig.
21. brigham young, who was leader of the mormons after joseph smith, led the group from illinois to utah in 1846.

22. in 1886, grover cleveland dedicated the statue of liberty.
23. no freshman was allowed to go to the sophomore swing, the class's annual dance.
24. the horse that won the first triple crown was sir barton.
25. in 1664, the english forced the dutch to surrender what is now new york.

Application to Writing

Write an essay that describes some historical event. Mention the people and the places associated with that event. Be sure to capitalize all proper nouns.

EXERCISE 5 *Cumulative Review*

Number your paper 1 to 25. Then write each word that should begin with a capital letter.

Facts and Figures

1. abraham lincoln signed the emancipation proclamation on january 1, 1863.
2. the american revolution began in lexington, massachusetts, on april 19, 1775.
3. stone was rarely used in the construction of the earliest buildings of the egyptians, babylonians, and assyrians.
4. the washington redskins played the los angeles raiders in the 1984 super bowl; the raiders won.
5. in 1903, the steinway company presented its 100,000th piano to the white house.
6. the largest collection of baseball cards belongs to the metropolitan museum of art in new york.
7. many of the cheese-making advances of the middle ages were made by catholic monks.
8. the sides of *old ironsides* are actually made of wood.
9. the earliest kodak cameras were preloaded at the factory with rolls of film containing 100 exposures.
10. the chicken was a common fowl in europe by the time of the roman empire.
11. rockefeller center in new york city extends from forty-eighth street to fifty-second street.

12. according to parker brothers, almost 70 million monopoly games had been sold throughout the world by the mid-1970's.
13. the gulf of bothnia separates sweden and finland.
14. three major airports serve washington, d.c.: national, dulles, and baltimore-washington.
15. unlike earth, jupiter radiates more heat back into space than it gets from the sun.
16. the empire state building exceeds the height of the eiffel tower by only 265.5 feet.
17. the city of hamilton, in ontario, canada, is closer to the equator than it is to the north pole.
18. in 1929, the general foods corporation revolutionized american eating when it introduced birds eye frozen foods.
19. george VI became the first british monarch to set foot on american soil when he visited the world's fair in 1939.
20. each year the most outstanding college football player in the united states is awarded the heisman trophy.
21. in the middle ages, merchants and craftspeople in europe organized guilds to guarantee fair business practices.
22. the first united states satellite was *explorer I.*
23. the united states department of agriculture inspects food-processing plants to ensure the quality of food.
24. san francisco bay is the drowned valley of the lower sacramento river.
25. in one night the world trade center in new york city uses more electricity than the entire city of troy, new york.

Titles

Capital letters indicate the importance of titles of people, written works, and other works of art.

Rule 31d **Capitalize titles of people and works of art.**

Titles Used with Names of People Capitalize a title showing office, rank, or profession when the title comes directly before a person's name. The same title is usually not capitalized when it follows a name.

BEFORE A NAME Have you met **S**enator Ames?
AFTER A NAME Harold Ames is our new **s**enator.

Titles Used Alone Capitalize a title that is used alone when it is being substituted for a person's name in direct address. The titles *President, Vice President, Chief Justice,* and *Queen of England* are almost always capitalized when they stand alone.

USED AS A NAME	I disagree with you, **G**overnor.
NOT USED AS A NAME	Who will our next **g**overnor be?
HIGH GOVERNMENT OFFICIAL	Has the **P**resident arrived yet?

Note: *President* and *vice president* are capitalized when they stand alone only if they refer to the current president and vice president.

Titles Showing Family Relationships Capitalize a title showing family relationship when it comes directly before a person's name, when it is used as a name, or when it is being substituted for a person's name.

BEFORE A NAME	Did you call **U**ncle David?
USED AS A NAME	Is **D**ad going too?
DIRECT ADDRESS	May I go with you, **M**om?

Do *not* capitalize titles showing family relationships when they are preceded by a possessive noun or pronoun—unless they are considered a part of a person's name.

Jenny's **a**unt is visiting from Oklahoma.
Jenny's **A**unt Mildred is visiting from Oklahoma. [*Aunt* is part of the name.]

Titles of Works of Art Capitalize the first word, the last word, and all other important words in the titles of books, newspapers, magazines, stories, poems, movies, plays, television productions, musical compositions, and other works of art. Do *not* capitalize a preposition, a conjunction, or an article—unless it is the first word in a title.

Did you read "**A H**arvest for the **H**ungry" in ***Time***?

My favorite movement from Grofé's ***Grand Canyon Suite*** is "**T**he **P**ainted **D**esert."

Usually you should *not* capitalize *the* as the first word of the name of a newspaper or a periodical—the ***Boston Globe.***

Note: For capitalization within letters, see Chapter 12, page 425.

EXERCISE 6 *Capitalizing Titles*

Number your paper 1 to 25. Then write each word that should begin with a capital letter.

1. have you ever read *the last of the mohicans*?
2. george gershwin wrote the music for the broadway musical *porgy and bess*.
3. i'm sure i wasn't speeding, officer.
4. the president has just spent the weekend at camp david.
5. franklin r. marsh has run for mayor three times.
6. when general lee surrendered, president lincoln asked the band to play "dixie."
7. call mom and tell her that grandmother gibson and i will be late.
8. *the mouse trap,* by agatha christie, holds the world's record for the longest-running play.
9. soon we will have to call my aunt jean "senator mason."
10. irving berlin donated all of his profits from the song "god bless america" to the boy scouts of america.
11. are you driving or flying to cincinnati, dad?
12. rodin's statue *the thinker* was not meant to be a man in thought; it represents the poet dante.
13. tim's cousin michelle is a reporter for the *miami herald*.
14. do you know dr. milio roberto, our state representative?
15. felix mendelssohn wrote his most famous overture, *a midsummer night's dream,* when he was seventeen.
16. yes, senator, our group will meet with you at the state house on wednesday, november 6.
17. both of the movies, *the wizard of oz* and *the secret garden,* have black-and-white and color sequences.
18. my uncle from monroe, louisiana, will visit us this spring.
19. verdi wrote the opera *aida* to commemorate the opening of the suez canal.
20. who was the tenth president of the united states?
21. the senior senator from our state held a fund-raising dinner at the biltmore hotel.
22. today the president vetoed a bill passed by congress.
23. the theme song from the movie *butch cassidy and the sundance kid* was "raindrops keep falling on my head."
24. did uncle joseph take you to the rodeo at palmer ranch?
25. the review in the *springfield gazette* unfavorably criticized the movie at showtime cinema.

EXERCISE 7 Cumulative Review

Number your paper 1 to 20. Then write each word that should begin with a capital letter.

What's the Answer?

1. is the grand coulee dam in washington or oregon?
2. what time is it in london, england, when it is noon in sioux city, iowa?
3. who was the famous general from the south who led the confederate forces?
4. arizona, new mexico, utah, and what other state meet at the same point?
5. was dr. mccoy or dr. zorba the doctor aboard the *u.s.s. enterprise*?
6. who was the author of *the old man and the sea,* which won the nobel prize in 1954?
7. what are the first five words of abraham lincoln's gettysburg address?
8. are the headquarters for the defense department in the pentagon or the united states capitol?
9. does the winner of the play-offs of the national hockey league win the stanley cup or the davis cup?
10. where can you see charles lindbergh's plane the *spirit of st. louis*?
11. who was the first man to sign the declaration of independence?
12. was the first permanent english colony on the american mainland in massachusetts or virginia?
13. does the book *the red badge of courage* take place during the american revolution or the civil war?
14. who was lewis and clark's interpreter as they explored from the mississippi to the pacific ocean between 1804 and 1806?
15. which planet is closer to the sun, earth or venus?
16. who was vice president during george washington's terms in office?
17. what did the thirteenth amendment to the united states constitution abolish?
18. who founded the red cross during the civil war?
19. do you know if there are 22 or 32 teams in the 4 divisions of the national basketball association?
20. is the annual kentucky derby held at churchill downs or epsom downs?

Language Integrating Skills

USING YOUR TEXT

Descriptive Writing (144–153)
Letters (422–437)

Mechanics: Editing for Capitalization Errors

Always edit your written work for correct capitalization.

Checking Your Understanding Number your paper 1 to 25. Then write all the words in the following paragraphs that should have a capital letter. You do not need to include words that are already capitalized.

> The alamo, the old spanish mission founded in 1718 at san antonio, texas, was the site of one of the most famous sieges in all of american history. The army of general santa anna was made up of poorly trained and poorly equipped mexicans, plus some mayan indians who could not understand spanish. Such factors, however, had little effect on the outcome of the battle. The texans were too greatly outnumbered—fewer than 200 americans to 6,000 mexican troops.
>
> The historic old church that stands at the alamo today looked quite different in 1836, when the battle took place. It is only one ninth the size of the building that such famous men as davy crockett and jim bowie defended so many years ago. The old mission originally included not only the church but also the alamo plaza city park and several surrounding streets.

Creating Background for a Character Develop a character for a short story. Make this person seem real by giving him or her a past. For example, write down where and when the person was born, a description of his or her family and early friends, languages he or she can speak, places the character has visited, companies he or she has worked for, and even books that the fictional character has read. Also provide a conflict the character has to struggle with. Then write the first draft of a letter to a fiction editor at a magazine. Describe the character you have developed and ask for the editor's reactions. ***Application:*** As you edit your letter, pay particular attention to your use of capital letters. Then write your final copy.

Chapter 31

Review

A **Using Capital Letters** Number your paper 1 to 20. Then write the following items, using capital letters only where needed.

1. lake michigan
2. queen elizabeth
3. a tour of the south
4. the lincoln park zoo
5. my uncle from iowa
6. typing and english
7. a lieutenant
8. the fourth of july
9. the moons of jupiter
10. south of portland
11. a senator from montana
12. spring and fall
13. the pure food and drug act
14. peter pan peanut butter
15. the french and indian war
16. a high school in elwood
17. the sophomore class
18. the bank on main street
19. my brother clifford
20. *columbia*'s orbit

B **Using Capital Letters** Number your paper 1 to 20. Then write each word that should begin with a capital letter.

1. the surface of mercury is similar to that of the moon.
2. the movie *law and order* is about wyatt earp.
3. the area drained by the amazon river in south america would cover three fourths of the united states.
4. the president, along with senator parks, had a meeting yesterday with the british ambassador.
5. the largest french-speaking population in the united states lives in louisiana.
6. the republican party is represented by an elephant.
7. did i tell you, mom, that robert r. majors, jr., my french teacher, called you today?
8. during most of the pre-civil war period in the united states, james buchanan was president.
9. by looking in the *reader's guide to periodical literature*, i was able to locate an article called "exercising for fitness."
10. the bulova watch company sold the first quartz crystal watch in america.
11. on the morning of may 20, 1927, charles lindbergh took off for paris from roosevelt field in new york.
12. the first battle of world war I was the battle of the marne.

13. polaris, also called the north star, is the end star in the handle of the little dipper.

14. the theme song for the long-running television series *all in the family* was "those were the days."

15. the invention of the steam-driven press produced a flood of printed material during the victorian period.

16. my brother jason became a baptist and joined the park street church.

17. last fall i started to do volunteer work for the united way.

18. the name of the first dog to orbit the earth was laika.

19. besides russian, aunt bertha is taking accounting and english composition at the high school on weekends.

20. hattie wyatt caraway was the first woman to be elected to the united states senate.

Mastery Test

Number your paper 1 to 10. Then write each word that should be capitalized.

1. did you read the column "the changing styles and fads in america" in yesterday's *chicago tribune*?

2. in american history we recently studied the treaty of versailles, which was signed after world war I.

3. next semester i will enroll in geometry II, french, gym, english literature, history, art, and study hall.

4. on the fourth of july, the macbrides are going to larkin park for a picnic.

5. when did jessie transfer from larchmont high school in pottersville to our school?

6. if you want to vote for senator jensen in the democratic primary, you must register at city hall.

7. professor mark w. wilson, jeffrey's father, will be the guest speaker at the assembly.

8. my cat fluffy will eat only purina cat food.

9. the 555-foot washington monument was completed in 1884.

10. we got lost when we went south on the freeway.

Chapter

32 End Marks and Commas

Diagnostic Test

Number your paper 1 to 10. Write each sentence, adding a comma or commas where needed. Then add an appropriate end mark.

EXAMPLE Did you hear Bill that we will visit Indianapolis Indiana this spring

ANSWER Did you hear, Bill, that we will visit Indianapolis, Indiana, this spring?

1. Whiskers my gray tabby is strictly an indoor cat
2. While we were in Colorado we visited Boulder Denver and Vale
3. After trying for three years we finally won the soccer championship
4. Do you want this picture hung Dad or should I put it in the attic
5. Many places in the United States according to the experts are subject to earthquakes
6. You can send her a card at Memorial Hospital 190 Lake Drive Albuquerque New Mexico 87112 before Friday
7. Why was she given a long slim rosebud
8. Take biology not chemistry next year
9. Oh no I can't believe this is happening to me
10. Inside the statue of Thomas Jefferson rose above us

Kinds of Sentences and End Marks

There are four basic kinds of sentences: *declarative, imperative, interrogative,* and *exclamatory.* Each of these kinds of sentences has a different purpose or function. The end mark you use at the end of a particular sentence is determined by that sentence's purpose or function.

One purpose of a sentence is to make a statement or to express an opinion.

Rule 32a **A declarative sentence makes a statement or expresses an opinion and ends with a period.**

The following two examples are both declarative sentences. Although the second example includes an indirect question, it is still a statement.

The secretary bird can run as fast as a horse**.**
Mom asked what time the meeting starts**.** [The direct question would be *What time does the meeting start?*]

The second purpose of a sentence is to give directions, make requests, or give commands. *You* is usually the understood subject of these sentences.

Rule 32b **An imperative sentence gives a direction, makes a request, or gives a command. It ends with either a period or an exclamation point.**

If a command is spoken in a normal voice, it is followed by a period when written. However, if emotion is expressed, an exclamation point follows the command.

Take your time**.** [normal voice]
Look out for the falling tree**!** [emotional voice]

Note: Sometimes an imperative sentence is expressed as a question, but no reply is expected. Since the purpose of the sentence still remains a request or a command, the sentence is followed by a period or an exclamation point—not by a question mark.

Will you please open the window**.**
May I make my position clear**.**

The third purpose of a sentence is to ask a question.

Rule 32c **An interrogative sentence asks a question and ends with a question mark.**

The following examples are both interrogative sentences. Although the second example is phrased as a statement, it is intended as a question. Even questions that are incompletely expressed, like the third example, should be followed by a question mark.

Which is the largest of the Great Lakes**?**
You want me to believe that**?**
You left after dinner. Why**?**

The fourth purpose of a sentence is to express a feeling such as joy, anger, or fear.

Rule 32d **An exclamatory sentence expresses strong feeling or emotion and ends with an exclamation point.**

The first sentence in the following examples is an exclamatory sentence. The second sentence includes an interjection that is followed by an exclamation point. *(See page 579.)*

Our hard work has all been worth it**!**
Oh**!** I forgot to return your call.

EXERCISE 1 *Classifying Sentences*

Number your paper 1 to 10. Write an appropriate end mark for each sentence. Then label each sentence *declarative, imperative, interrogative,* or *exclamatory*.

1. Feed the dog after you take her for a walk
2. She wants to know what is in the paper bag
3. I thought the movie was rather boring
4. Will you please listen
5. Stand at attention when I speak to you
6. Which state grows the most cotton
7. Open the package carefully
8. I just found your missing watch
9. Paper money was invented by the Chinese
10. Did Karen go to the library

Periods with Abbreviations

Abbreviations can be a personal form of shorthand. Using them can help you take notes in class more quickly. Most abbreviations, however, should be avoided in formal writing.

Rule 32e **Use a period after most abbreviations.**

The following list contains some abbreviations that are acceptable in formal writing. For other abbreviations look in the dictionary.

TITLES WITH NAMES	**Mr.**	**Ms.**	**Rev.**	**Sgt.**	**Jr.**
	Mrs.	**Dr.**	**Gen.**	**Lt.**	**Sr.**
TIMES WITH NUMBERS	**A.M.**	**P.M.**	**B.C.**	**A.D.**	

The Rev**.** Martin Luther King, Jr**.**, was awarded the Nobel Peace Prize in 1964.

The Battle of Hastings was fought in A**.**D**.** 1066.

A statement that ends with an abbreviation needs only one period. An interrogative or an exclamatory sentence that ends with an abbreviation needs both marks of punctuation.

The play begins at 8:30 P**.**M**.**
Does the play begin at 8:30 P**.**M**.**?

Note: Certain special types of abbreviations are used without periods. Following are several examples.

ABC	American Broadcasting Company	TX	Texas
mph	miles per hour	km	kilometer

EXERCISE 2 *Writing Abbreviations*

Number your paper 1 to 10. Then write the abbreviations that stand for the following items. Be sure to include periods where needed. If you are unsure of the spelling or the punctuation of a particular abbreviation, look it up in the dictionary.

1. before Christ
2. junior
3. United States
4. Rhode Island
5. October
6. milliliter
7. association
8. miles per hour
9. avenue
10. dozen

Commas

Basically a comma has two purposes. Commas are used to separate items, and commas are used to enclose items.

Commas That Separate

Without commas, some items in a sentence would run into one another, causing confusion. Following are some situations in which commas should be used to separate items.

Items in a Series Three or more similar items together form a series. Words, phrases, or clauses can be written as a series.

Rule 32f **Use commas to separate items in a series.**

WORDS I need to buy paper, pencils, and pens. [nouns]
Today I washed the car, mowed the lawn, and cleaned out the basement. [verbs]

PHRASES Did you look in the closet, behind the sofa, and under the bed? [prepositional phrases]

CLAUSES I don't know what time the meeting is, where it is, or what its purpose is. [noun clauses]

If a conjunction connects the last two items in a series, a comma is optional. However, if that comma is omitted, some sentences could be misread. That is why it is always better to include the comma before a conjunction.

CONFUSING The restaurant had banana, bran, blueberry and raisin muffins.

CLEAR The restaurant had banana, bran, blueberry, and raisin muffins.

If conjunctions connect all the items in a series, no commas are needed.

The tickets can be used on Friday **or** Saturday **or** Sunday.

Note: Some words, such as *macaroni and cheese,* are thought of as a single item. If one of these pairs of words appears in a series, consider it one item.

For breakfast I ordered juice, ham and eggs, and a muffin.

Adjectives before a Noun Sometimes a comma should separate two adjectives that are not connected by a conjunction.

We followed the steep, winding road to their house.

Rule 32g **Use a comma sometimes to separate two adjectives that precede a noun and are not joined by a conjunction.**

There is a test that can help you decide if a comma is needed between two adjectives. If a sentence reads sensibly with *and* between the adjectives, a comma is needed.

COMMA	Don't lean on that old, rickety table. [*Old* ***and*** *rickety table* reads well.]
NO COMMA	Don't lean on that old picnic table. [*Old* ***and*** *picnic table* does not read well.]

EXERCISE 3 *Using Commas to Separate*

Number your paper 1 to 25. Then write each sentence, adding a comma or commas where needed. If a sentence does not need any commas, write *C* after the number.

1. Billy Joe can hit well run fast and play left field like a professional.
2. Yellow poppies forget-me-nots and even some kinds of orchids grow on the Arctic plains.
3. Bananas are an inexpensive versatile fruit.
4. The cabin cruiser rolled and pitched and tossed in the stormy waters.
5. I don't know whether I should stay whether I should go or whether I should wait another ten minutes.
6. From the cliff we viewed the dark blue sea.
7. The directions said to go down Maple Avenue turn right at the firehouse and continue straight for a mile.
8. Over the centuries ketchup has been made from such substances as oysters green walnuts and mushrooms.
9. Young growing spiders can regenerate missing legs.
10. The snow fell throughout the night into the morning and until three o'clock the following afternoon.
11. Famous left-handed people include Paul McCartney Harry Truman and Gerald Ford.

12. Hot humid weather doesn't bother me at all.
13. The air you breathe is composed of nitrogen and oxygen and other elements.
14. Tell me what you have planned what I can bring and when you need it.
15. Before dinner should we offer nuts cheese and crackers or fresh fruit?
16. We spent the hot July weekends at the beach.
17. New York is America's largest city its richest port and its leader in art and music.
18. Carrots or potatoes or almost anything would grow in that rich dark earth.
19. Thomas Jefferson was an architect a farmer an inventor and a president.
20. No one knows the new school cheer.
21. Bob described threshing corn feeding livestock harvesting and other farm jobs.
22. I think the town my uncle lives in must be the dirtiest noisiest place on Earth.
23. Do you want meat loaf franks and beans or meatballs and spaghetti for dinner?
24. The class members have to decide if they want a dance when they want it and where it should be held.
25. The long muscular legs of the Russian wolfhound make it an excellent runner.

EXERCISE 4 *Writing Sentences*

Write sentences that follow each set of directions. Add commas where needed.

1. Include a series of verbs that describe the actions of someone diving off a high board.
2. Include a series of nouns that name what you ate for lunch yesterday.
3. Include a series of prepositional phrases that tell where you might look for a missing Ping-Pong ball.
4. Include two adjectives before a noun that are separated by a comma.
5. Include two adjectives before a noun that are *not* separated by a comma.

Compound Sentences A compound sentence becomes a run-on sentence when independent clauses are not separated.

Rule 32h **Use a comma to separate the independent clauses of a compound sentence if the clauses are joined by a coordinating conjunction.**

A comma is usually placed before the conjunctions *and, but, or, nor, for,* and *yet* in a compound sentence.

> Come to my house, and we'll study for the test.
> The octopus swims forward, but it walks backward.

A comma is not needed in a very short compound sentence—unless the conjunction separating the independent clauses is *yet* or *for.*

NO COMMA	He left but I stayed.
COMMA	I waited, for I was curious.

Note: Be careful that you do not confuse a compound sentence with a simple sentence that has a compound verb. No comma comes before the parts of a compound verb unless there are three or more verbs.

COMPOUND SENTENCE	Jill pitched the tent, and I built a fire. [A comma is needed.]
COMPOUND VERB	Jill pitched the tent and built a fire. [No comma is needed.]

Note: A compound sentence can also be joined by a semicolon. *(See page 816.)*

EXERCISE 5 *Using Commas with Compound Sentences*

Number your paper 1 to 25. Then write each sentence, adding a comma where needed. If a sentence does not need a comma, write *C* after the number.

1. I made a fire for it was very chilly.
2. I was late and the bus left without me.
3. Japanese cherry trees are beautiful but they bear no fruit.
4. Squirrels bury acorns and help reseed the forests.
5. The Venus's-flytrap is misnamed for it feeds primarily on ants.

6. My throat was sore and my head was hot.
7. Each day many birds eat more than half their weight and young birds can eat even more.
8. A counterfeit coin usually has uneven edges and often feels greasy.
9. Slow down for we have time.
10. Woodchucks belong to the squirrel family but they live in burrows in the ground.
11. George Washington was six feet two inches tall but Abraham Lincoln topped him by two inches.
12. Meet me at the gym or I will see you in study hall during the last period.
13. The climbers were close to the summit but turned back because of the strong wind.
14. The curtain rose and the play began.
15. Almost any wood will fuel a fire but oak and maple burn the longest.
16. It's warm outside yet I feel cold.
17. The hikers plowed through the underbrush and made their way to a clearing.
18. Mats and ropes are manufactured from the bark of the lime tree and baskets are made from its wood.
19. The earth was once entirely liquid but the surface has cooled into a hard crust.
20. Nantucket has no major industry and depends entirely upon the tourist trade for its prosperity.
21. A sweet potato is a root but a white potato is just a swollen stem.
22. Hurry or you will be late!
23. Most gold mining is done by machine but Alaska still has a few hopeful prospectors with picks and sieves.
24. Sign these papers now for they must be mailed by tomorrow morning.
25. The right side of the body is controlled by the left side of the brain and the left is controlled by the right.

EXERCISE 6 *Writing Sentences*

Write one compound sentence for each of the following subjects. Make sure that the clauses in each compound sentence are related. Add commas where needed.

1. telephones **2.** basketball **3.** sunlight **4.** cooking **5.** clocks

Introductory Elements Certain words, phrases, and clauses that come at the beginning of a sentence need to be separated from the rest of the sentence by a comma.

Rule 32i **Use a comma after certain introductory elements.**

Following are examples of introductory elements that should be followed by a comma.

WORDS	**Why,** sure you're invited. [*No, now, oh, well,* and *yes* are other introductory words—unless they are a part of the sentence. *Why didn't you go?*]
PREPOSITIONAL PHRASE	**After five hours on the plane,** I never wanted to sit down again. [A comma comes after a prepositional phrase of four or more words. (Punctuation of shorter phrases varies. See the last set of examples below.) Never place a comma after a phrase or phrases followed by a verb. *Into the center of the target landed the arrow.*]
PARTICIPIAL PHRASE	**Opening my grammar book,** I found my missing class notes.
ADVERB CLAUSE	**Since the day was overcast,** I took an umbrella to school with me.
OTHERS	**In Room 151,** 100 persons were gathered. **In front of Ben,** Stanley paced back and forth. [Commas are used in these sentences to prevent confusion.]

EXERCISE 7 *Using Commas with Introductory Elements*

Number your paper 1 to 25. Then write each sentence, adding a comma where needed. If a sentence does not need a comma, write *C* after the number.

1. Now this is your last chance.
2. Without heat and light from the sun there would be no life on Earth.
3. Since the invention of Coca-Cola only seven people have known its formula.
4. Climbing the steep mountain trail we often had to stop and rest.

5. From here you can see five other states.
6. In 1978 41,216 new books were published in the United States.
7. After flourishing for 140 million years the dinosaur suddenly died out some 65 million years ago.
8. Now is the time to register to vote.
9. In the early years of the industry France led the world in automobile production.
10. Dating back to the thirteenth century Denmark's flag is the oldest unchanged national flag in existence.
11. During its lifetime the average human heart beats 100,000 times per day.
12. Among India's 700 million people 880 languages and dialects are spoken.
13. After Brazil Colombia is the world's second largest coffee exporter.
14. Since their formation 10,000 years ago the Niagara Falls have eaten their way seven miles upstream.
15. No I don't know the words to that song.
16. Found in every state of the Union the skunk is truly an all-American animal.
17. Under the sofa scampered the frightened kitten.
18. According to one scientific hypothesis the moon split off from the earth.
19. Although the piano is less than 300 years old it is the most popular instrument in the Western world.
20. Yes city dogs usually live longer than country dogs.
21. On the floor lamps of all sizes and shapes were on sale.
22. When a person looks at something pleasing the pupil of the eye expands as much as 45 percent.
23. Without clouds and other elements the earth would reach 176°F at the equator by day and 220°F by night.
24. While dunking the ball into the basket David heard the referee's whistle.
25. Away from the raging fire ran the frightened dog.

EXERCISE 8 *Writing Sentences*

Write sentences that follow each set of directions. Add commas where needed.

1. Begin a sentence with the introductory word *why.*
2. Begin a sentence with a three-word prepositional phrase.

3. Begin a sentence with a prepositional phrase of four or more words.
4. Begin a sentence with a participial phrase.
5. Begin a sentence with an adverb clause.

Commonly Used Commas Commas are most commonly used to separate the elements in dates and addresses. They are also used to separate the salutation and the closing from the body of a letter.

Rule 32j **Use commas to separate the elements in dates and addresses.**

Notice in the following examples that a comma is also used to separate a date or an address from the rest of the sentence. No comma, however, separates the state and the ZIP code.

DATE	On Monday, March 9, 1969, my parents were married.
ADDRESS	Order the envelopes from Paper Products, 1330 West 11th Street, Cleveland, Ohio 44113, today.

Note: Commas may be omitted when just the month and the year are given.

A world's fair began in Brussels in April 1958.

Rule 32k **Use a comma after the salutation of a friendly letter and after the closing of all letters.**

SALUTATIONS	Dear Mom,	Dear Kathy,
CLOSINGS	Love,	Sincerely yours,

EXERCISE 9 *Using Commas with Dates and Addresses*

Number your paper 1 to 10. Then write each sentence, adding commas where needed. If a sentence does not need any commas, write *C* after the number.

1. On March 12 1888 a terrible blizzard struck New York City.
2. Belfast Ireland is the largest linen manufacturer in the world.
3. Send all inquiries to Martha Witt 3297 Princeton Drive Mobile Alabama 36618 before May.
4. The temperature near Death Valley reached a record high of 134°F in July 1913.
5. On October 1 1908 Henry Ford introduced his famous Model T Ford.

6. All reports are due on Friday February 6.
7. On May 14 1948 the new state of Israel was proclaimed in Tel Aviv.
8. The first professional football game was played on September 3 1895 in Latrobe Pennsylvania.
9. On Sunday May 18 1980 Mount St. Helens erupted.
10. We met in Little Rock Arkansas on July 4 1990 for a huge family reunion.

EXERCISE 10 *Using Commas Correctly*

Number your paper 1 to 20. Then write each sentence, adding a comma or commas where needed. If a sentence does not need any commas, write *C* after the number.

1. Since the electricity is still off we'll have to cook on the outdoor grill.
2. The battle between the *Monitor* and the *Merrimac* on March 9 1862 ushered in the age of armored warships.
3. Take a good strong pair of binoculars with you to the football game.
4. The rhododendron flourishes in the Appalachian highlands along the Atlantic seacoast and throughout New England.
5. After bathing the small child went straight to bed.
6. Well I can't see any reason for your not going.
7. Your warm cheerful smile always brightens my day and makes me feel good.
8. Like the spaniel and the poodle the beagle is a good pet.
9. Malaria was a chief cause of the failure of the Jamestown Colony the fall of Rome and the decline of Greece.
10. *Well* and *fit* can best describe him now.
11. Old ghost towns in the Rocky Mountains are reminders of the colorful gold-rush days.
12. Adam didn't care for swimming nor was he interested in any other water sport.
13. The first mail-order house was established by Montgomery Ward 825 North Clark Street Chicago Illinois in 1872.
14. Although the blue whale is the largest animal in the world it lives almost entirely upon tiny shellfish.
15. Terns and sandpipers and gulls busily combed the beach for food.
16. Finding a gap in the pack the cyclist sped ahead of his competitors.

17. Have you heard Willie Nelson's version of this popular country-western song?
18. Anchored at the dock in Belmont Harbor were several new cabin cruisers.
19. In filling out Form 1212 107 students failed to sign their full names.
20. What important event in the history of the United States took place on December 11 1620 at Plymouth Massachusetts?

EXERCISE 11 *Cumulative Review*

Write the paragraph that follows, adding commas where they are needed.

A Winner at Sixty

On May 6 1929 a group of athletes lined up at City Hall in New York City. They were waiting for the start of a footrace across the country to San Francisco California. Among the eager group of participants was 60-year-old Abraham Lincoln Monteverde. Although he was older than the other contestants he was a competitor to be reckoned with. Monteverde had been running for years and he had completed more than 100 marathons.

During the 3,145 miles of the course Monteverde's younger competitors dropped out one by one. When Monteverde neared San Francisco he found that he had no company at all. Everyone else had quit the race. By reaching San Francisco's City Hall at 7:10 P.M. on July 24 Monteverde had crossed the country in 79 days 10 hours and 10 minutes. Monteverde's experience and determination had paid off!

Application to Writing

Think about a character from history or a person living today who interests you. Write the first four or five paragraphs of a biography of this person. Include significant dates and places and mention other interesting facts about your subject. When you have finished writing your introductory paragraphs, check your work for the correct use of commas. Then put your work in your writing folder to be continued at a later date.

Commas That Enclose

One or two commas are used to set off or enclose some expressions that interrupt the flow of a sentence. These expressions generally add information that is not needed to understand the main idea of a sentence. If one of these interrupters comes in the middle of a sentence, two commas are needed to set it off from the rest of the sentence. If an interrupter comes at the beginning or at the end of a sentence, only one comma is needed to set it off.

Direct Address Names, titles, or other words used to address someone directly are set off by commas. These expressions are called nouns of *direct address.*

Rule 32l Use commas to set off nouns of direct address.

Randy, do you know who won the game?
The statistics**, Senator,** are all in this report.
Thanks for the surprise party**, my friends.**

Parenthetical Expressions A parenthetical expression provides additional information that could easily be removed without changing the meaning of a sentence.

Rule 32m Use commas to set off parenthetical expressions.

Consequently, they were two hours late.
Labor Day**, like Thanksgiving,** is a legal holiday.
Meals are extra**, according to the brochure.**

Following is a list of some common parenthetical expressions.

Common Parenthetical Expressions

after all	for instance	of course
at any rate	generally speaking	on the contrary
by the way	I believe (guess, hope, know, think)	on the other hand
consequently	in fact	moreover
however	in my opinion	nevertheless
for example		to tell the truth

Note: The parenthetical expressions listed in the box are set off by commas only when they interrupt a sentence.

COMMAS	The spaghetti sauce**, I believe,** is too spicy.
NO COMMAS	I believe everything you said.

Contrasting expressions, which usually begin with *not,* are also considered parenthetical expressions.

Violets**, not roses,** are her favorite flower.

Appositives An appositive with its modifiers identifies or explains a noun or a pronoun in the sentence. *(See page 603–605.)*

Rule 32n **Use commas to set off most appositives and their modifiers.**

Mr. Roberts**, our track coach,** just got married.
We just returned from Albany**, the capital of New York.**

Commas are *not* used with an appositive if it identifies a person or thing by telling which one or ones. Usually these appositives are names and have no modifiers.

I enjoyed the book ***Robinson Crusoe.*** [Which book?]
The color **blue** has many shades. [Which color?]

Note: Titles and degrees that follow a name are also set off by commas.

Lawrence T. Mahoney**, Jr.,** was elected treasurer.
Jennifer Morgan**, Ph.D.,** will be the speaker.

EXERCISE 12 *Using Commas with Interrupters*

Number your paper 1 to 20. Then write each sentence, adding a comma or commas where needed. If a sentence does not need any commas, write *C* after the number.

1. Death Valley the lowest point in North America is 280 feet below sea level.
2. The elephant seal by the way is the largest animal in America.
3. Randy not Stewart won the 100-meter race in the track meet.
4. Have you seen my baseball cap Mom?
5. The screech owl unlike other birds may occupy the same nest for life.

6. Our school just put on the musical *Camelot.*
7. The bagpipe the national instrument of Scotland did not originate in Scotland.
8. Maria is Dr. Angelo S. DeVito Jr. your physician or your dentist?
9. Derek has had many years of mountain-climbing experience moreover.
10. The temperature of the inner core of the earth a ball of solid iron and nickel is about 9,000°F.
11. The water moccasin unlike the rattlesnake strikes without warning.
12. My brother Joey works at Mac's Garage on State Road 7 and MacDade Boulevard.
13. One type of spider for example can jump 40 times its own length.
14. Her report was on Benjamin Harrison the 23rd president of the United States.
15. Kodak a popular make of camera was named by its inventor George Eastman an American scientist.
16. The anableps a fish that inhabits the waters of the Amazon has four eyes.
17. Despite popular belief only one lightning bolt out of a hundred actually strikes the earth.
18. The word *receipt* is often misspelled.
19. Mordecai Brown one of baseball's greatest pitchers had only three fingers on his pitching hand.
20. The Panama Canal the link between the Atlantic Ocean and the Pacific Ocean was opened in 1914.

Nonessential Elements Sometimes a participial phrase or a clause is not essential to the meaning of a sentence.

Rule 32o **Use commas to set off nonessential participial phrases and nonessential clauses.**

A participial phrase or a clause is nonessential if it provides extra, unnecessary information. As a test, read the sentence without the phrase or the clause. If the phrase or the clause could be removed without changing the basic meaning of the sentence, it is nonessential. A phrase or a clause that modifies a proper noun is almost always nonessential.

NONESSENTIAL PARTICIPIAL PHRASE — Roy Pierce**, standing by the door,** is a transfer student. [Roy Pierce is a transfer student.]

NONESSENTIAL ADJECTIVE CLAUSE — In July we visited Oxnard**, which is north of Los Angeles.** [In July we visited Oxnard.]

No commas are used if a participial phrase or a clause is essential to the meaning of a sentence. An essential phrase or clause usually identifies a person or thing and answers the question *Which one?* Adjective clauses that begin with *that* are always essential.

ESSENTIAL PARTICIPIAL PHRASE — The student **standing by the door** is Roy Pierce. [*Standing by the door* is essential because it is needed to tell which student is Roy Pierce.]

ESSENTIAL ADJECTIVE CLAUSE — The muffins **that you baked** were delicious. [*That you baked* is essential because it is needed to tell which muffins were delicious.]

Note: Nonessential and essential elements are also called *nonrestrictive* and *restrictive.*

EXERCISE 13 *Using Commas with Nonessential Elements*

Number your paper 1 to 25. Then write each sentence, adding a comma or commas where needed. If a sentence does not need any commas, write *C* after the number.

1. The world's tallest tree which is taller than a football field is long is a California redwood.
2. The words engraved inside my grandmother's wedding ring are no longer readable.
3. A ruby that is flawless is more valuable than a flawless diamond of equal size.
4. The old Harrison house on Turner Street deserted for years has finally been sold.
5. Roller skates which originally consisted of four wheels on rubber pads were invented about 1860.
6. A huge snowflake measuring 15 inches in diameter fell in Montana in 1887.
7. The icicles hanging down from the roof of the barn are almost two feet long.
8. Pierre Fauchard who practiced in Paris around 1715 is considered the founder of modern dentistry.

9. The first wristwatch made by a man in Switzerland appeared in 1790.
10. Our new telephone which we bought on sale is in the shape of a frog.
11. The car that was parked in our driveway last week belongs to my grandparents.
12. The first Europeans to land in Australia were the Dutch who arrived in 1606.
13. The photographs found at the bottom of the trunk were of my great-grandparents.
14. Twenty-pound crabs of the South Pacific climb trees in search of coconuts which they love to eat.
15. The first coin officially issued by the United States bore the motto "Mind your business."
16. The largest prehistoric bird was the elephant bird which laid eggs more than a foot long.
17. The 30-foot 2-ton *Stegosaurus* dinosaur had a brain that weighed only about 2.5 ounces.
18. Did you notice the sign that was posted on the gymnasium door?
19. Edward VIII of England abdicated his throne in 1936 to marry a woman who was not of royal blood.
20. The temperature which has been rising all day is now 98 degrees.
21. Honey that has been found in Egyptian tombs tastes very good after thousands of years.
22. The box wrapped in silver paper and a red ribbon has no name on it.
23. Abraham Lincoln standing at six feet four inches was taller than any other president before him.
24. My three brothers shooting baskets in the driveway get along well together.
25. The chance that two fingerprints will be identical is one in about 64 billion.

EXERCISE 14 *Editing for Commas with Nonessential Elements*

Write the following paragraphs, adding commas where needed.

True or False?

Was Captain John Smith who was the leader of the English settlement in Jamestown, Virginia, in 1607 rescued from death by Pocahontas? Smith's first book covering his experiences at

Jamestown does not include Pocahontas who was the daughter of Chief Powhatan. Actually Smith never mentioned her until 16 years later. Smith, however, had a reputation for being a great storyteller who loved to entertain his friends. Did he make up the story of Pocahontas? It's possible.

Just before the Declaration of Independence was signed, three men visited a woman named Betsy Ross. She was a seamstress in Philadelphia. These men were members of the flag committee of the Continental Congress commissioned in 1776. The men asked her to sew the first flag which was sketched on a piece of paper. In fact, there was no official flag committee in 1776, and this event never happened. Almost one hundred years later, William J. Canby who was Betsy Ross's grandson first told the story about his grandmother's making the flag. However, there is no written proof, and none of Betsy's other relatives ever remembered seeing her make the first Stars and Stripes!

EXERCISE 15 *Using Commas Correctly*

Write each sentence, adding commas where needed. If a sentence does not need any commas, write *C* after the number.

1. The umbrella was invented as a sunshade not as protection from the rain.
2. The computers at school much to my surprise are easy to use.
3. Of the 25 highest mountains on the earth 19 are in the Himalayas.
4. The metal lithium floats in water.
5. Please Terry find today's newspaper for me.
6. Andean Indians who live at altitudes of up to 17,000 feet have larger lungs and hearts than other people have.
7. The Grand Canal in China is 20 times as long as the Panama Canal yet it was built 1,300 years ago!
8. Sandra moved from 89 Southard Avenue Rockville New York to 47 Main Street Clearwater Florida on July 6 1984.
9. The winning entry a still life of a bowl of fruit was painted by Maureen Hanover.
10. Tomorrow by the way is Uncle Herman's birthday.
11. The poisonous Portuguese man-of-war has tentacles that may trail as long as 40 feet.
12. John James Audubon the famous artist of birds and wildlife was born in Haiti.

13. For their anniversary we gave them a cuckoo clock made in Germany.
14. Good evening ladies and gentlemen and welcome to the Shubert Theater.
15. At the first sign of danger young Egyptian mouthbreeder fish dart into their mother's mouth for protection.
16. During his lifetime Samuel Morse the inventor of the telegraph was better known as a painter than as a scientist.
17. The heaviest organ in the human body is the liver which weighs an average of three and a half pounds.
18. Until it is full-grown a blue whale gains about 200 pounds each day.
19. The tallest oldest tree in the yard was hit by lightning.
20. Almost half the kinds of food that Americans eat today were first discovered by the American Indians.

EXERCISE 16 *Writing Sentences*

Write sentences that follow each set of directions. Use commas where needed.

1. Include direct address at the beginning of a sentence.
2. Include a parenthetical expression in the middle of a sentence.
3. Include an appositive that needs commas.
4. Include an essential participial phrase.
5. Include a nonessential adjective clause.

EXERCISE 17 *Cumulative Review*

Write the following paragraph, adding commas where needed.

Flying Low

Where can a plane fly farther below sea level than some submarines can dive? The answer of course is the Dead Sea. The shore of the Dead Sea the deepest land depression on Earth lies about 1,300 feet below sea level on the border of Israel and Jordan. The Dead Sea which receives some six million tons of water each day from the Jordan River should be constantly increasing in size. The surface level of the salt lake however remains almost constant. The high rate of evaporation that occurs in this desert area is the reason. Nevertheless climatic changes scientists report have caused the lake to rise. As a matter of fact it has risen 20 feet since the 1880's.

Integrating Language Skills

USING YOUR TEXT

Descriptive Writing (144–153)
Persuasive Writing (154–161)

Mechanics: Editing for Comma Errors

As you edit your work, always read it through for the proper use of commas and end marks.

Checking Your Understanding Write the following paragraph, adding commas where needed.

At the closing ceremony of the 1912 Olympic Games in Stockholm the King of Sweden spoke with Jim Thorpe a young American Indian. The king praised Thorpe for being the greatest athlete in the world and the American certainly was. Thorpe who had studied at Carlisle Institute excelled in boxing wrestling lacrosse gymnastics swimming hockey handball football track and baseball. Indeed many authorities rate Thorpe as the finest football player who ever lived. Playing on his college team Thorpe scored 25 touchdowns and made 198 points in a single season. When Thorpe was thirty-two he got into professional football and pro football's Hall of Fame eventually made him a member.

Writing a Film Review Jot down the names of the movies you have seen during the past month. Which one did you like most? Brainstorm a list of reasons for recommending that film to others. Beside each reason give an example to prove or illustrate that point. Then arrange your reasons in order of importance, putting the most important first.

As you begin the first draft of your review, get the attention of your readers. You can do this by briefly describing an interesting scene in the movie or by including a catchy phrase from or about the film. Then, after you tell the major strengths of the movie, write a summary and a strong recommendation of the film. Next, let a friend read your review. Ask him or her how convincing it is. Rework any weak parts to make your recommendation more convincing. ***Application:*** As you edit your work, pay particular attention to the correct use of commas. Have you omitted any needed commas? Have you included any commas that are unnecessary? When you have finished your editing, write a final draft.

Chapter 32

Review

A Understanding Sentence Structure

Number your paper 1 to 10. Write an appropriate end mark for each sentence. Then label each sentence *declarative, imperative, interrogative,* or *exclamatory.*

1. Did you go to the dance on Saturday
2. Leave your muddy shoes outside
3. My toothache is killing me
4. Don't touch the wet paint
5. Only twelve people attended the meeting
6. Fred wants to know what you want to do tonight
7. Nearly everyone has read the assignment
8. How much rainfall did we have this month
9. Please buy a newspaper on your way home
10. I've never been happier

B Using Commas Correctly

Number your paper 1 to 20. Then write each sentence, adding a comma or commas where needed. If a sentence does not need any commas, write *C* after the number.

1. The blue whale not the sperm whale is the largest creature on land or sea.
2. My neighbor Ed Masters has a purebred Eskimo dog.
3. On October 17 1770 General Burgoyne surrendered at Saratoga New York.
4. Jon do you want to see a movie or should we go skating?
5. As Bryan waited for the starting gun his heart beat rapidly.
6. The movie that I told you about is on cable TV tonight.
7. An orangutan may reach a height of only four feet but its outstretched arms sometimes span seven feet.
8. The lead husky on a sled team is chosen for speed willingness and intelligence but not for strength.
9. The opera *La Traviata* was written by Giuseppe Verdi.
10. Terry Rosoff now swimming the freestyle teaches swimming.
11. Throughout the night we could hear loud howling winds.

12. If you like jazz you'll love this record.
13. In Rome for instance one can visit the Coliseum St. Peter's and the Vatican Museum in a single day.
14. The railroads pushed the frontier westward and the cattle trails shifted their courses accordingly.
15. On December 14 1911 Roald Amundsen a Norwegian explorer discovered the South Pole.
16. In the woods behind our house are many rabbits and squirrels.
17. It will be impossible to replace that old wooden bookcase.
18. After defrosting frozen foods should be used immediately.
19. A full-grown lion can jump a 12-foot fence and dash 100 yards at 60 miles per hour.
20. The tiny Yorkshire terrier was sleeping between the paws of the friendly protective Great Dane.

Mastery Test

Number your paper 1 to 10. Write each sentence, adding a comma or commas where needed. Then add an appropriate end mark.

1. After the end of World War I who proposed the League of Nations
2. Running as hard as I could I crossed the finish line two seconds before anyone else
3. Dan would you like scrambled eggs cereal and milk or a cheese omelet for breakfast
4. My brother graduated from a college in Chicago Illinois on Friday May 15 1985
5. The short interesting documentary was about lions tigers and other large members of the cat family
6. Why that's a spectacular idea
7. Ronald Reagan a Republican from California became president in 1981
8. To tell the truth I said I liked broccoli not asparagus
9. If you want to go to the skating rink with us call me before seven o'clock
10. Make your bed clean up your room and pack your lunch before you leave for school

Chapter

33 Underlining and Quotation Marks

Diagnostic Test

Number your paper 1 to 10. Then write each sentence, adding underlining, quotation marks, and other punctuation marks needed with direct quotations. Only a sentence with a speaker tag *(he said, she asked)* should be considered a direct quotation.

EXAMPLE Some of Georgia O'Keeffe's paintings appear in the book Art Today, he said.

ANSWER "Some of Georgia O'Keeffe's paintings appear in the book <u>Art Today</u>," he said.

1. Is a black widow spider dangerous Kenneth asked.
2. Daniel Webster said There is always room at the top.
3. The poem Pennsylvania Station by Langston Hughes appears in the anthology Our World Today.
4. The reports of my death Mark Twain said are greatly exaggerated.
5. Do you think we'll win Mark asked the coach.
6. The Gift of the Magi appears in the book Best Loved Short Stories.
7. Rehearsal has been canceled for tonight Meg stated. There will be practice as usual tomorrow night.
8. Did you know that a violin has four strings Tony asked.
9. My favorite song from the folk opera Porgy and Bess is Summertime.
10. Don't go near that hornets' nest Lani shouted.

Underlining

A novel without any conversation would probably be rather dull. Conversation, or dialogue, adds realism to characters in stories and books. A report without references to factual evidence could be questioned or not taken seriously. Stating what authorities say can add support and verification to a report. Since both of these situations involve quotations, learning to punctuate quotations properly is an important skill to master.

This chapter will cover the uses of quotation marks with direct quotations, as well as with titles. First, however, the uses of underlining will be reviewed.

Italics is a type of print that slants to the right. Unless you are using a word processor that allows you to use italic type, you cannot produce letters in italics. When you write by hand or type on a typewriter, substitute underlining for italics.

ITALICS	I have read *The Odyssey* by Homer.
UNDERLINING	I have read The Odyssey by Homer.

Certain letters, numbers, words, titles, and names should be underlined.

Rule 33a **Underline letters, numbers, and words when they are used to represent themselves. Also underline foreign words that are not generally used in English.**

LETTERS, NUMBERS	You never cross your t's or write your 2's correctly.
WORDS, PHRASES	I often get chose and choose mixed up.
FOREIGN WORDS	What does merci beaucoup mean?

Note: Only the *t* and the *2* in the first example above are underlined—not the *'s*.

Rule 33b **Underline the titles of long written or musical works that are published as a single unit. Also underline the titles of paintings and sculptures and the names of vehicles.**

Long written works include books, magazines, newspapers, full-length plays, and long poems. Long musical compositions include operas, symphonies, ballets, and albums. Vehicles include airplanes, ships, trains, and spacecraft. Titles of movies and of radio and TV series should also be underlined.

We read Steinbeck's novel The Pearl in English class.

In an issue of Yachting, I read that Australia II was the first foreign yacht to win the America's Cup in 132 years.

Only on the weekend is the Hartford Courant delivered to our house. [*The* is generally not considered a part of the title of a newspaper or a periodical.]

EXERCISE 1 *Using Underlining*

Number your paper 1 to 10. Write each sentence. Then underline each letter, number, word, or group of words that should be italicized.

1. Drums along the Mohawk is a novel that describes frontier life in what is now New York State.
2. The Mona Lisa is probably the most recognized painting in the world.
3. Founded in 1919, the New York Daily News is the largest newspaper in the United States.
4. The film Quo Vadis, a spectacle set in ancient Rome, employed some 30,000 extras.
5. On July 25, 1956, an Italian luxury liner, the Andrea Doria, sank off the coast of Massachusetts.
6. Strength is the only eight-letter word in the English language with just one vowel.
7. Charles Dickens's A Tale of Two Cities gives a vivid picture of Paris during the French Revolution.
8. What does the expression sic transit gloria mundi mean?
9. The Reader's Digest has one of the largest circulations of any magazine today.
10. The French dish ratatouille is made from eggplant, tomatoes, peppers, onions, and zucchini.

Quotation Marks

Quotation marks come in pairs. They are placed at the beginning and at the end of uninterrupted quotations and certain titles.

Quotation Marks with Titles

Titles of long works of art and of publications such as newspapers or magazines are underlined. Most of these long works, however, are made up of smaller parts. The titles of these smaller parts should be enclosed in quotation marks.

Rule 33c **Use quotation marks to enclose the titles of chapters, articles, stories, one-act plays, short poems, and songs.**

Smaller parts of long works include episodes from a TV series and movements from long musical compositions. Titles of essays and compositions should also be enclosed in quotation marks.

Did you read the article "The Art of Winning" in U.S. News and World Report?

In your textbook Earth Science, read the chapter "Atoms to Minerals" for homework.

EXERCISE 2 *Using Quotation Marks with Titles*

Number your paper 1 to 10. Then write each sentence, adding quotation marks and underlining where needed.

1. The Allure of Fiber Optics was an interesting article in a recent issue of Time.
2. Home, Sweet Home is the only song that John Howard Payne ever wrote.
3. Origins of American Folk Songs was the title of the winning essay in the writing contest.
4. The Nature of Dreams is the best chapter in the book The Forgotten Language.
5. The Bear is probably William Faulkner's most famous story.
6. The one-act play To the Chicago Abyss is by Ray Bradbury.
7. The chapter The Changing City in our textbook World Geography took me less than an hour to read.
8. On the Trail is the best-known movement from the Grand Canyon Suite.
9. The Yellow Rose of Texas and My Wild Irish Rose are among the many song titles that refer to roses.
10. The poem Richard Cory by Edwin Arlington Robinson can be found in the book Modern American Poetry.

Application to Writing

Write a note to a friend. Recommend possible sources of information for a report your friend is working on. Include titles of a book, a magazine article, and a newspaper article, along with the titles of the magazine and the newspaper. Punctuate titles correctly.

Quotation Marks with Direct Quotations

Only a *direct quotation*—the exact words of a person—is enclosed in quotation marks.

Rule 33d **Use quotation marks to enclose a person's exact words.**

Amber said, "I will be late for the meeting."

Quotation marks are not used, however, with an *indirect quotation*—a paraphrase of someone's words.

Amber said that she will be late for the meeting.

Note: The word *that* often signals an indirect quotation.

A one-sentence direct quotation can be written in several ways. It can be placed before or after a speaker tag, such as *she said* or *Bob asked.* When the quotation comes before or after a speaker tag, quotation marks enclose the person's exact words from beginning to end.

April commented, "The ocean is unusually rough."
"The ocean is unusually rough," April commented.

A speaker tag can interrupt a one-sentence quotation. Two pairs of quotation marks are needed in such a situation because quotation marks enclose only a person's exact words—not the speaker tag.

"The ocean," April commented, "is unusually rough."

If you are quoting more than one sentence, place quotation marks at the beginning and at the end of the entire quotation. It is not necessary to put quotation marks around each sentence within a quotation—unless a speaker tag interrupts.

"The ocean is unusually rough," April commented. "That normally means that a storm is offshore. It could rain."

EXERCISE 3 *Using Quotation Marks with Direct Quotations*

Number your paper 1 to 10. Write each sentence, adding quotation marks where needed. In this exercise place the comma or end mark that follows a quotation *inside* the closing quotation marks.

1. Martin Luther King, Jr., once said, Injustice anywhere is a threat to justice everywhere.
2. Why did we take this route to the airport? Wendy asked.
3. The temperature, Edmund stated, has been below freezing for a whole week now!
4. Ruth Renkel said, Never fear shadows. They simply mean there's a light shining somewhere nearby.
5. Education, George Lorimer said, is about the only thing a person can have as much of as he's willing to haul away.
6. The other team was leading through the third quarter. Then we made two touchdowns, Bart explained.
7. Truth crushed to the earth shall rise again, said William Cullen Bryant.
8. Beware of little expenses, mused Benjamin Franklin. A small leak will sink a ship.
9. Ralph Waldo Emerson commented, Fear always springs from ignorance.
10. I don't think this hamburger was cooked. It was incinerated! the angry customer complained.

Commas with Direct Quotation Your voice naturally pauses between a direct quotation and a speaker tag when you speak. In written material these pauses are indicated by commas.

Rule 33e **Use a comma to separate a direct quotation from a speaker tag. Place the comma inside the closing quotation marks.**

"The groceries are still in the car**,**" Mom said. [The comma goes *inside* the closing quotation marks.]

Mom said**,** "The groceries are still in the car."

"The groceries**,**" Mom said**,** "are still in the car." [The first comma goes *inside* the closing quotation marks.]

Notice in the last example that two commas are needed because the one-sentence quotation is interrupted.

EXERCISE 4 *Using Commas with Direct Quotations*

Number your paper 1 to 10. Write each sentence, adding quotation marks and commas where needed. In this exercise, place the comma or end mark that follows a quotation *inside* the closing quotation marks.

Thought-Provoking Quotes

1. Casey Stengel joked Ability is the art of getting credit for all the home runs somebody else hits.
2. Words are the most powerful drug used by mankind said Rudyard Kipling.
3. Do what you can Theodore Roosevelt stated with what you have, where you are.
4. The price of greatness is responsibility said Winston Churchill.
5. People who say they sleep like a baby Leo Burke joked don't have one.
6. Ours is the only country deliberately founded on a good idea John Gunther stated.
7. An old Vermont proverb says Don't talk unless you can improve the silence.
8. Sir Richard Steele announced Reading is to the mind what exercise is to the body.
9. Paul Signac said about Monet He paints as a bird sings.
10. Double—no, triple—our troubles Ronald Reagan stated and we'd still be better off than any other people on Earth.

End Marks with Direct Quotations When a direct quotation comes at the end of a sentence, it must have an end mark. A period follows a quotation that is a statement or an opinion.

Rule 33f **Place a period inside the closing quotation marks when the end of the quotation comes at the end of a sentence.**

Susan said, "The flowers are for you**.**" [The period goes *inside* the closing quotation marks.]

A one-sentence quotation that is interrupted by a speaker tag is still one sentence. Therefore, the period comes at the end of the sentence—inside the closing quotation marks.

"The flowers," Susan said, "are for you**.**"

If a quotation comes at the beginning of a sentence, the period follows the speaker tag.

"The flowers are for you," Susan said**.**

If a quotation has more than one sentence, a period comes at the end of each sentence.

"The flowers are for you," Susan said**.** "They just arrived**.** I wonder who sent them**."** [The last period goes *inside* the closing quotation marks.]

Rule 33g **Place a question mark or an exclamation point inside the closing quotation marks when it is part of the quotation.**

Mary asked, "Did the weather forecaster predict rain or sunshine for tomorrow**?"**

"Did the weather forecaster predict rain," Mary asked, "or sunshine for tomorrow**?"**

"Did the weather forecaster predict rain or sunshine for tomorrow**?"** Mary asked.

Leon shouted, "Don't touch that poison ivy**!"**

"Don't touch that poison ivy**!"** Leon shouted.

A question mark and an exclamation point are placed *inside* the closing quotation marks when they are part of the quotation. On a rare occasion, a question or an exclamatory statement may include a direct quotation. When such situations occur, the question mark or the exclamation point goes *outside* the closing quotation marks. Placing the end mark outside the quotation marks shows that the whole sentence—not just the quotation—is a question or an exclamatory statement.

Who said, "Give me liberty or give me death**"?** [The whole sentence, not just the quotation, is the question.]

I'll never forget the day that the president looked at me and said, "Hello**"!** [The whole sentence, not just the quotation, is exclamatory.]

In the two examples above, notice that the end marks for the quotations are omitted.

EXERCISE 5 *Using End Marks with Direct Quotations*

Number your paper 1 to 10. Then write each sentence, adding commas and end marks where needed.

EXAMPLE Karen asked "What important event in American history took place on July 20, 1969"

ANSWER Karen asked, "What important event in American history took place on July 20, 1969?"

1. Pamela said "I just learned that Sydney is the largest city in Australia"
2. "Your reports are due on Friday" Mr. David stated
3. Rachel asked "Is the Missouri River the second longest river in the United States"
4. "Are there really palm trees in Dublin" Sean asked
5. "Stand back" the officer shouted
6. "The wet floor is very slippery" she shouted
7. Did Miss Ramirez say "Read the next chapter in your textbook"
8. "The busiest airport in the world" Anton stated "is O'Hare Airport in Chicago"
9. "Where is the cat" Maxine asked "I haven't seen him all day"
10. I was shocked when Mr. Landis said "Class will be dismissed early today"

Capital Letters with Direct Quotations A capital letter begins each sentence of a quotation—just as one begins a regular sentence.

Rule 33h **Begin each sentence of a direct quotation with a capital letter.**

"**J**ogging regularly has changed my life," she said.

If a quotation follows a speaker tag, two capital letters are needed—one for the first word of the sentence and one for the first word of the quotation.

She said, "**J**ogging regularly has changed my life."

If a single-sentence quotation is interrupted by a speaker tag, only one capital letter is needed—at the beginning of the sentence. In the following example, it would not make sense to capitalize *has,* since it comes in the middle of the sentence.

"**J**ogging regularly," she said, "has changed my life."

EXERCISE 6 Using Capital Letters with Direct Quotations

Number your paper 1 to 10. Then write each sentence, adding capital letters and end marks where needed.

1. "is the Sears Tower the highest building in the world" Edward asked
2. she said, "a deciduous tree sheds its leaves in winter
3. "the smallest of the Great Lakes is Lake Ontario," Terry reported
4. then she asked, "which is the largest of the Great Lakes"
5. "Lake Michigan," she stated, "is the answer"
6. "which is the windiest city in the United States" Melba asked
7. "most people think it's Chicago," Lucy said, "but it's really Great Falls, Montana"
8. "I really was surprised" Devon exclaimed "seventy percent of the earth's surface is covered with water"
9. "do you know who is on the twenty-dollar bill" Pete asked
10. Ann answered hesitantly, "it's a president could it be Andrew Jackson"

EXERCISE 7 Cumulative Review

Number your paper 1 to 10. Write each sentence, adding capital letters, quotation marks, and other punctuation marks where needed. Check your sentences carefully.

Famous Quotes

1. Shakespeare wrote shall I compare thee to a summer's day
2. genius is 10 percent inspiration and 90 percent perspiration said Thomas Edison
3. I have nothing to offer Winston Churchill declared but blood, toil, tears, and sweat
4. don't give up the ship Captain Lawrence shouted
5. Ben Franklin said nothing is certain but death and taxes
6. love doesn't make the world go 'round Franklin Jones said love is what makes the world worthwhile
7. these are the times Thomas Paine warned that try men's souls
8. when did Commodore Perry say we have met the enemy and they are ours
9. Elizabeth Barrett Browning wrote how do I love thee let me count the ways
10. did Gertrude Stein write a rose is a rose is a rose

Other Uses of Quotation Marks

Before you write a story with dialogue or a report in which you quote long passages from a book or a periodical, you should be aware of some special applications of quotation marks.

Quoting Long Passages Reports sometimes include quotations of more than one paragraph to support a particular point.

Rule 33i **When quoting a passage of more than one paragraph, place quotation marks at the beginning of each paragraph—but at the end of only the last paragraph.**

Closing quotation marks are omitted at the end of each paragraph, except the last one, to indicate to a reader that the quotation is continuing.

> "In the 1950's and 1960's, rock and roll music blasted its way across the United States. Teenagers loved it; adults hated it. Today people are collecting those early records. [no quotation marks]
>
> "The big names in those days were Chuck Berry, Little Richard, Fats Domino, and Buddy Holly. The early records of these singers are worth the most money. They might sell for two to twenty-five dollars each. [no quotation marks]
>
> "Prices for old 45-rpm records and albums change a great deal. A book called *Collectible Rock Records* by Randal C. Hill gives today's prices, as well as a big list of people and stores that buy and sell records. This book can be found in most libraries." [closing quotation marks]

Quotations within Quotations A direct quotation sometimes contains a title or another quotation.

Rule 33j **Use single quotation marks to enclose a quotation or certain titles within a quotation.**

> Tim stated, "I heard the coach say, 'That was the best game of the season.'"
>
> Mr. Ray said, "Ed, read the poem 'The Raven' to us."

Notice in the first example that the closing single quotation mark and the closing double quotation marks come together.

Integrating Language Skills

USING YOUR TEXT

Creative Writing (380–419)

Mechanics: Punctuating Dialogue Correctly

Stories often include dialogue—a conversation between two or more people. Dialogue is written in a special way so that readers know who is speaking.

Rule 33k **When writing dialogue, begin a new paragraph each time the speaker changes.**

The following conversation takes place between a husband and wife. Each quotation follows the rules you have just studied, but each time the speaker changes, a new paragraph begins.

> She turned to him wildly. "I have—I have—I've lost Mme. Forestier's necklace."
>
> He stood up appalled. "What! . . . How? . . . Impossible! You're sure you had it on when you left the ball?"
>
> "Yes, I felt it in the vestibule of the Ministry."
>
> GUY DE MAUPASSANT, "The Necklace"

Checking Your Understanding Correctly rewrite the following dialogue between Sherlock Holmes and John Clay, a criminal whom Holmes has just captured. Add punctuation and indentation where needed.

> It's no use, John Clay said Holmes blandly. You have no chance at all. So I see Clay answered with the utmost coolness. I fancy that my pal is all right. There are three men waiting for him at the door said Holmes.
>
> SIR ARTHUR CONAN DOYLE, *The Hound of the Baskervilles*

Writing a Story Write freely for about five minutes about the future. Then choose the best idea from your notes and use it to develop a brief outline of the plot. ***Application:*** As you write the first draft of your story, be sure to include dialogue. Then, as you edit, check for the correct punctuation of the dialogue.

Chapter 33

Review

A Punctuating Titles Correctly Number your paper 1 to 10. Then write each sentence, adding quotation marks and underlining where needed. (None of the following sentences should be considered direct quotations.)

1. In the Shakespearean play Julius Caesar, I played the part of Cassius.
2. Clickety-clack, Toy Trains Are Back was an interesting article in this issue of the magazine called Smithsonian.
3. For homework I have to read the chapter Human Heredity in my science book Biology for Today.
4. When You Wish upon a Star is the Oscar-winning song from the 1940 movie Pinocchio.
5. I wrote an essay about the poem The Centaur by May Swenson.
6. Have you seen The Starry Night, a painting by Vincent van Gogh?
7. Ski Season Has Rocky Start was the lead story in the Manchester Daily News today.
8. I recently heard a recording of Invasion from Mars, the one-act radio play that made people believe Martians had landed.
9. Read the definition of the word differential from the American Heritage Dictionary.
10. Columbus's ships were the Santa Maria, the Pinta, and the Niña.

B Punctuating Direct Quotations Number your paper 1 to 20. Then write each sentence, adding underlining, capital letters, and punctuation marks where needed.

1. is the giant panda a native of China Erwin asked
2. hold the bus Karen yelled
3. Novia Scotia was colonized by the Scottish Kim said
4. Wanda asked how many keys does a standard piano have
5. that's easy Jake replied a piano has 88 keys
6. when you're ready Al said meet me outside
7. Mrs. Cranston asked who wrote the poem Kubla Khan
8. fruit stains can be removed with boiling water she told me
9. is the Constitution moored in Boston Lee asked
10. Susan Mr. Hobbs asked did Nathan Hale or Patrick Henry say give me liberty or give me death

11. an old proverb states a bad peace is better than a good war
12. who wrote the operetta The Student Prince Marie asked
13. the word tam-o'-shanter Peggy explained is the name for a Scottish woolen cap with a wide crown and a pom-pom
14. Danny asked did our volleyball team win
15. Ulysses S. Grant once said I know only two tunes one of them is Yankee Doodle, and the other isn't
16. that snake must have been two feet long Steve exclaimed
17. my grandparents are celebrating their golden wedding anniversary Jan said they have been married for 50 years
18. in Dickens's story A Christmas Carol, Ebenezer Scrooge is famous for saying bah, humbug
19. tomorrow is the song that was made famous in the Broadway musical Annie Mom reminded us
20. who has read Edgar Allan Poe's short story The Pit and the Pendulum Mrs. Hafeller asked

Mastery Test

Number your paper 1 to 10. Then write each sentence, adding underlining, quotation marks, and other punctuation marks needed with direct quotations. Only a sentence with a speaker tag should be considered a direct quotation.

1. Tony, is that your camera Jennifer asked.
2. We seldom see a mountain lion in this valley said the forest ranger.
3. Ticket sales Sandy announced will be handled by Barry this year.
4. Last night I read The Monkey's Paw in the anthology Famous American Short Stories.
5. The game was very disappointing Frieda said We lost by three touchdowns.
6. Don't leave without me Janet yelled.
7. Ira Gershwin wrote the lyrics for the musical An American in Paris as well as for the song Strike Up the Band.
8. Did Winston Churchill or Franklin Roosevelt say We have nothing to fear but fear itself
9. Ask not what your country can do for you; ask what you can do for your country said John F. Kennedy.
10. I saw Rembrandt's painting The Night Watch when I was in Europe last summer.

Chapter

34 Other Punctuation

Diagnostic Test

Number your paper 1 to 10. Then write each sentence, adding apostrophes, semicolons, colons, and hyphens where needed.

EXAMPLE The computer had been carefully checked nevertheless, it failed to operate properly.

ANSWER The computer had been carefully checked; nevertheless, it failed to operate properly.

1. You trim the sails Ill take the wheel.
2. I cant tell the difference between your 7s and your 9s.
3. Please give me a dollars worth of those nails.
4. Didnt you realize that the meeting started at 730 P.M.?
5. The lamp was delivered on time however, it had been damaged.
6. Everyones speech will be delivered at the assembly.
7. George Mason, an ex senator, gives lectures at the university.
8. Twenty five pages was all I read.
9. Barry is an expert in three sports tennis, basketball, and soccer.
10. The Petersons dogs bark all the time ours are quiet.

Apostrophes

Punctuation marks are a fairly modern invention. The colon is said to have first been introduced about 1485, but the semicolon did not appear until almost a century later. Without these and other marks of punctuation, imagine how difficult it must have been to decipher written material. Likewise, imagine how difficult it would be for people to decipher your written work if needed punctuation was missing! This chapter will cover apostrophes, semicolons, colons, hyphens, and two less commonly used marks of punctuation, dashes and parentheses.

The first section of the chapter will show the uses of apostrophes. Apostrophes are used most frequently with contractions, but they are also commonly used with nouns and some pronouns to show ownership or relationship.

Apostrophes to Show Possession

Nouns and pronouns have a special form to show possession or relationship. An apostrophe is used to form the possessive of nouns and some pronouns.

The Possessive Forms of Nouns The first step in forming the possessive of any noun is to decide whether the noun is singular or plural.

Rule 34a **Add 's to form the possessive of a singular noun.**

Write a singular noun—without adding or omitting any letter. Then just add *'s* at the end.

man + 's = man's	Is this a man**'s** shirt?
Carla + 's = Carla's	I think you have Carla**'s** notebook.
month + 's = month's	What are your month**'s** earnings?

Singular compound nouns and the names of most businesses and organizations form their possessive the way other singular nouns do.

A two-year-old**'s** vocabulary is limited.
I enjoy looking at J.C. Penney**'s** catalog.
McLaughlin and Reilly**'s** business published sheet music.

The possessive form of a plural noun is formed differently.

Rule 34b **Add only an apostrophe to form the possessive of a plural noun that ends in s.**

books + ' = books'	All the **books'** covers are wet.
tenants + ' = tenants'	The **tenants'** rights were spelled out in the contract.

A few plural nouns do not end in *s*. The possessive of these nouns should be formed the way singular nouns are—by adding *'s*.

men + 's = men's	This is the **men's** department.
mice + 's = mice's	Those **mice's** teeth are sharp.

Note: Do not confuse a plural possessive with the simple plural form of a noun.

POSSESSIVE	The two **hours'** hike was exhausting.
PLURAL	The movie will last two hours.

EXERCISE 1 *Forming the Possessive of Nouns*

Number your paper 1 to 20. Write the possessive form of each noun. Then use five of the forms in sentences of your own.

1. committee
2. Graves
3. women
4. Cohen
5. governors
6. tomatoes
7. teachers
8. children
9. sister
10. boys
11. monkeys
12. year
13. Sarah
14. dogs
15. Boise
16. city
17. brother
18. hour
19. pen
20. boxes

EXERCISE 2 *Using the Possessive of Nouns*

Number your paper 1 to 20. Then write the possessive form of each underlined word or words.

1. After a year practice, Susan joined the high school tennis team.
2. The cats bowls are being kept in the pantry.
3. Dancing is Eric main interest right now.
4. Have you ever gone fishing in the St. John River?
5. The Smiths generosity was overwhelming.
6. Ralph bowling average is 150.

7. The coach office is located next to the gym.
8. The sailors leave lasted a week.
9. Where can I find women shoes?
10. At halftime the game score was 3–2.
11. I value my best friend opinion very much.
12. Roberta will stay at her sister-in-law house in Clearwater, Florida.
13. Have you seen Susan new springer spaniel?
14. Last week newspapers should be thrown out.
15. The twins beds were moved into the other room.
16. All the committees recommendations were accepted by the town council.
17. Have you signed up for the town softball team?
18. Mr. Graham is out of the office on a years leave of absence.
19. Rudolph Sporting Goods is having a sale on sweaters.
20. The attorney-at-law office opens at nine o'clock.

The Possessive Forms of Pronouns Unlike a noun a personal pronoun does not use an apostrophe to show possession. Instead, it changes form. Notice that none of the following possessive pronouns include apostrophes.

Possessive Pronouns			
my, mine	his	its	their, theirs
your, yours	her, hers	our, ours	

Rule 34c **Do not add an apostrophe to form the possessive of personal pronouns.**

Her bicycle is in the garage; **yours** is next door.

Instead of changing form the way a personal pronoun does, an indefinite pronoun forms the possessive the same way a singular noun does—by adding *'s*. *(See page 547 for a list of common indefinite pronouns.)*

Rule 34d **Add 's to form the possessive of indefinite pronouns.**

Anyone**'s** guess is as good as mine.
Has everyone**'s** vote been counted?

EXERCISE 3 *Using the Possessive of Pronouns*

Number your paper 1 to 10. Then rewrite any incorrect possessive form of a pronoun. If the possessive form is correct, write *C* after the number.

1. Someone's tennis racket was left in my car.
2. These are my notes, but which are your's?
3. If this enormous venture is going to succeed, we need everyones cooperation.
4. Have you finished you're history assignment yet?
5. My used bicycle cost fifty dollars, but hers cost less.
6. Nobodys lines were forgotten on opening night.
7. That station wagon is their's.
8. A family of mockingbirds has built its nest in our cherry tree.
9. No ones house on Jordan Street was damaged by the terrible windstorm.
10. Our's were the only poems that were read aloud.

Other Uses of Apostrophes

In addition to showing possession, an apostrophe has several other uses.

Apostrophes with Contractions A contraction combines two words into one. An apostrophe is added to take the place of the missing letter or letters.

Rule 34e **Use an apostrophe in a contraction to show where one or more letters have been omitted.**

we ~~a~~re = we're	there ~~i~~s = there's
let ~~u~~s = let's	it ~~i~~s = it's
can~~no~~t = can't	of ~~th~~~~e~~ clock = o'clock

Usually no letters are added and no letters are moved around in a contraction. There is, however, one exception: *will not* = *won't.*

Note: Do not confuse a contraction with a possessive pronoun. *It's, you're, they're, there's,* and *who's* are contractions. *Its, your, their, theirs,* and *whose* are possessive pronouns.

EXERCISE 4 *Writing Contractions*

Write the contraction for each pair of words.

1. you are
2. will not
3. has not
4. that is
5. we have
6. is not
7. I have
8. they are
9. do not
10. have not
11. I would
12. I am
13. who is
14. let us
15. does not
16. it is
17. there is
18. we will
19. did not
20. were not

EXERCISE 5 *Distinguishing between Contractions and Possessive Pronouns*

Write the word in the parentheses that correctly fills each blank.

1. (who's, whose) _______ pitching? _______ mitt is she using?
2. (it's, its) Don't let _______ looks deceive you; _______ a gem under the hood.
3. (you're, your) _______ judging the fruit only with _______ eyes.
4. (they're, their) Because _______ experienced mechanics, I asked for _______ advice.
5. (their, there's) _______ a present for _______ dog too.
6. (it's, its) _______ called a secretary bird because _______ crest of long feathers looks like a clerk's quill pens.
7. (who's, whose) _______ house are we looking for, and _______ going to be there?
8. (there's, theirs) _______ a camera. Is it _______?
9. (you're, your) If _______ wise, you'll have _______ teeth checked.
10. (they're, their) _______ going to bring _______ new baby.

Apostrophes Used to Show Joint or Separate Ownership

Apostrophes distinguish between joint and separate ownership.

Rule 34f Add 's to only the last name to show joint ownership.

These are Lenny and Harold**'s** test tubes. [The test tubes belong to both Lenny and Harold.]

If one of the words in a phrase showing joint ownership is a possessive pronoun, the noun must also show possession.

These are Lenny**'s** and **his** test tubes.

Separate ownership is indicated in a different way.

Rule 34g **Add 's to each name to show separate ownership.**

These are Lenny**'s** and Harold**'s** test tubes. [Both Lenny and Harold have their own test tubes.]

Apostrophes to Form Certain Plurals Certain items form their plural by adding *'s*.

Rule 34h **Add 's to form the plural of numbers, letters, symbols, and words that are used to represent themselves.**

Your *k***'s** and *h***'s** look exactly the same.
There are too many *and***'s** and *or***'s** in that paragraph.

Note: The items themselves should be underlined (italicized). *(See page 795.)* The *'s*, however, should not be underlined.

EXERCISE 6 *Using Apostrophes in Special Situations*

Number your paper 1 to 10. Then correctly write each letter, symbol, or word that needs an apostrophe or an apostrophe and an *s*.

1. You shouldnt use so many *and* and *well* when you speak.
2. Rhonda and Kenneth cakes were both sold at the fair.
3. Well meet at six oclock at the school.
4. Bart never crosses his *t* or dots his *i*.
5. The ¶ indicate where new paragraphs should begin.
6. Kent and Martha daughter is in college now.
7. Lets go to the concert if they dont cancel it.
8. A hyphen is only one –, but a dash is two –.
9. If theres no more milk, Ill go out and buy some.
10. Troy and Jon skills contribute much to the team success.

EXERCISE 7 *Using Apostrophes*

Number your paper 1 to 10. Then correctly write each word that needs an apostrophe or an apostrophe and an *s*.

1. A chameleon tongue is as long as its body.
2. Isnt this notebook yours?

3. At Mount Rushmore, Abraham Lincoln mouth is 22 feet wide.
4. Place a comma before all the *and* in those compound sentences.
5. Can you be ready at six o clock?
6. In September 1908, the United States Army arranged for a special demonstration of the Wright brothers plane.
7. Are these gloves Ray or Gerald?
8. Contrary to almost everyone belief, the Pilgrims did not land at Plymouth Rock when they first arrived.
9. The hikers camp was located in a clearing in the woods.
10. About 10 percent of the earth land surface is still covered by glaciers.

EXERCISE 8 Cumulative Review

Number your paper 1 to 15. Then correctly write each letter or word that needs an apostrophe or an apostrophe and an *s*.

1. The team picture was in this morning *Herald*.
2. I think Ive read somewhere that the mud in beavers dams is held together by leaves, roots, and grasses.
3. I told my parents that Im going to try to make straight *A* next term.
4. No one claim to the man fortune held up in court.
5. Greg house is just around the corner from Jean store.
6. Mandy and her stories were read aloud in class.
7. In most tennis tournaments, the women play-offs are held before the men.
8. During March everyone eyesight will be checked in the nurse office.
9. Due to budget cuts, the fire fighters salaries havent been raised for two years.
10. Is that striped shirt your father or your brother?
11. Arent there three *r* in the word *preferred?*
12. The MacGregors poodle and the Goldens collie have impressive pedigrees.
13. Mom and Dad station wagon needs new tires before the vacation trip starts.
14. Sybilla Masters device for reducing corn into meal and Margaret E. Knight machine for cutting shoes are two important American inventions.
15. In your report change some of those *and* and *but* to *although, when, because,* or *since.*

Semicolons and Colons

The most common use for a semicolon (;) is to separate the independent clauses of a compound sentence. A colon (:), on the other hand, is used mainly to introduce a list of items.

Semicolons

The independent clauses of a compound sentence can be joined in several ways. You have already learned that a comma and a conjunction can join the clauses. *(See page 777.)*

Our cat had six kittens**, and** two of them are black.

Clauses in a compound sentence can also be joined by a semicolon.

Our cat had six kittens**;** two of them are black.

Rule 34i **Use a semicolon between the clauses of a compound sentence that are not joined by a conjunction.**

Rhode Island is the smallest state**;** Alaska is the largest.

Semicolons with Transitional Words Clauses in a compound sentence can also be joined by a semicolon and certain transitional words.

Rule 34j **Use a semicolon between the clauses of a compound sentence that are joined by certain transitional words.**

We waited in line for an hour**; however,** the tickets were sold out before we could buy ours.

Following is a list of common transitional words.

Common Transitional Words		
accordingly	furthermore	moreover
consequently	hence	nevertheless
for example	however	otherwise
for instance	instead	therefore

Notice in the following examples that the transitional word is preceded by a semicolon and followed by a comma.

> The history assignment is difficult**; furthermore,** it has to be completed by tomorrow.
>
> Come to the house by seven o'clock**; otherwise,** I'll meet you at the library.

Note: Some of the transitional words listed on the preceding page can also be used as a parenthetical expression within a single clause. *(See page 784.)*

JOINING CLAUSES	The lights in the theater were very dim**; consequently,** I couldn't read the program.
WITHIN A CLAUSE	The lights**, consequently,** were very dim.

Semicolons to Avoid Confusion A semicolon is substituted for a comma in two situations.

Rule 34k **Use a semicolon instead of a comma between the clauses of a compound sentence if there are commas within a clause.**

> Don't make tacos**,** pizza**,** or chili**;** for Robert hates tomatoes.

Rule 34l **Use semicolons instead of commas between items in a series if the items themselves contain commas.**

> Next week the President will visit Norfolk**,** Virginia**;** Cincinnati**,** Ohio**;** and San Antonio**,** Texas.

Note: See Chapter 32 for rules for commas.

EXERCISE 9 *Using Semicolons*

Number your paper 1 to 10. Then write each sentence, adding a semicolon where needed. If a sentence does not need a semicolon, write *C* after the number.

1. Ice skates did not originate in Holland roller skates did.
2. Ice balls will not form if the ground temperature is below freezing consequently, hail rarely falls in winter.
3. The Statue of Liberty was paid for by the French Americans paid only for the concrete pedestal.

4. Peanuts can be used to make oil, cheese, ink, and soap but they have over 300 other uses as well.
5. Men have walked on the moon nevertheless, parts of Greenland have never been explored.
6. A giant tortoise can crawl five yards a minute a rabbit can cover the same distance in less than a half second.
7. The gym is available for the dance on Saturday, May 7 Friday, May 13 or Saturday, May 21.
8. The people on the planning committee, however, could not agree on a location for the arts festival.
9. I need white poster board, red paint, and two paintbrushes and then I can construct the posters for the play.
10. Human life expectancy in Hawaii is 73 years moreover, that figure is higher than that of any other state.

EXERCISE 10 *Using Semicolons*

Number your paper 1 to 10. Then write the following sentences, adding semicolons and commas where needed.

Facts and Figures

1. The smallest fish in the world is the *Pandaka pygmea* it is no larger than an ant.
2. The iguana has one of the most rugged bodies of any living creature nevertheless it is very timid.
3. A jogger burns up 100 calories per mile a person playing checkers burns up the same amount in an hour.
4. Michelangelo was a painter sculptor and architect and he was also a poet.
5. A housefly beats its wings 190 times a second however a honeybee beats its wings 250 times a second.
6. The French people nevertheless are the world's greatest cheese eaters.
7. An elephant has 40,000 muscles in its trunk alone an entire human body has only 656 muscles.
8. The four state capitals that have been named after presidents are Jackson, Mississippi Lincoln, Nebraska Jefferson City, Missouri and Madison, Wisconsin.
9. Sunglasses are nothing new for example tinted lenses were common during the sixteenth century.
10. Panama hats are not made in Panama they are made in Peru and Ecuador.

Colons

A colon points ahead—usually to a list of items that is about to follow.

Rule 34m **Use a colon before most lists of items, especially when a list comes after an expression like *the following*.**

You can respond by using one of the following**:** telephone, letter, or personal interview.

There are four principal forms of clouds**:** cumulus, stratus, cirrus, and nimbus.

Notice that commas separate the items in the series. *(See page 774.)*

When you write a list, do not place a colon after a verb or a preposition.

NO COLON	Our school colors are red, white, and blue.
COLON	Our school has three colors**:** red, white, and blue.

Colons are also used in a few other common situations.

Rule 34n **Use a colon in certain special situations.**

BETWEEN HOURS AND MINUTES	3**:**30 P.M.
BETWEEN BIBLICAL CHAPTERS AND VERSES	Psalms 62**:**5
AFTER SALUTATIONS IN BUSINESS LETTERS	Dear Sir or Madam**:**

EXERCISE 11 *Using Colons*

Write each sentence, adding a colon where needed. If a sentence does not need a colon, write *C* after the number.

1. Common breeds of cats include the following Siamese, Persian, Angora, and Manx.
2. The term *precious stones* actually applies only to diamonds, rubies, sapphires, and emeralds.
3. The nine English words most often used are *and, be, it, of, the, will, I, have,* and *you.*
4. There are two basic ways to produce musical tones with wind or with vibrating strings.
5. Water may appear in three forms solid, liquid, and gas.
6. I have lived in Texas, Louisiana, and Alabama.

7. The concert was supposed to begin at 8 00 P.M., but the musicians didn't arrive until 8 30.
8. Three kinds of fish popular with hobbyists are the angelfish, the guppy, and the gourami.
9. The costume committee still needs to find the following items a top hat, a pair of gloves, and a red cape.
10. Four states have been admitted to the United States since 1912 New Mexico, Arizona, Alaska, and Hawaii.

EXERCISE 12 *Cumulative Review*

Number your paper 1 to 15. Then write the following sentences, adding semicolons, colons, and commas where needed.

1. We heard Katherine sing last night furthermore we thought she was fantastic!
2. Arlene is not a junior she's a sophomore.
3. I must find the cooler the beach towels and my sunglasses and then I will be ready to go.
4. All living things need the following five nutrients proteins fats carbohydrates minerals and vitamins.
5. There are no penguins in the Northern Hemisphere they live only in the Southern Hemisphere.
6. The committee members are Tran Lo a senior Carla Totaro a junior Jeff Higgins a sophomore and Ryan Travers a freshman.
7. Television can be very informative for instance last night I watched an interesting program about space exploration.
8. Long ago ingredients for London pie included the following 12 eggs 1 pound of potatoes 40 chestnuts and 18 sparrows.
9. Baby sea lions do not know how to swim they have to be taught by their mothers.
10. On our vacation we wanted to go to Maine instead we decided to go to Wisconsin.
11. At the end of the first half, we were losing by 21 points nevertheless we weren't discouraged.
12. Pollen never deteriorates it is one of the few naturally secreted substances that lasts indefinitely.
13. My dentist appointment was for 4 15 P.M.
14. Among the many words invented by Americans in the past 125 years are the following *blizzard gangster* and *realtor*.
15. The earthworm has no lungs it breathes through its skin.

Other Marks of Punctuation

Although you use hyphens, dashes, and parentheses less often than other marks of punctuation, you should know the rules for using them.

Hyphens

A hyphen has several uses in addition to dividing words at the end of a line.

Hyphens with Numbers and Words Certain numbers and fractions are written with a hyphen.

Rule 34o **Use a hyphen when writing out the numbers *twenty-one* through *ninety-nine*. Also use a hyphen when writing out a fraction that is used as an adjective.**

Sixty-two people attended the town meeting.
Each partner received a one-third share of the profits.

No hyphen is used when a fraction is used as a noun.

I've typed two thirds of my report.

Hyphens with Compound Nouns and Adjectives Some compound nouns and compound adjectives are written as one word or as two separate words. Other compound nouns and compound adjectives are written with a hyphen. Since compound nouns and compound adjectives can take several forms, it is always best to check the dictionary for the correct spelling.

Rule 34p **Use a hyphen to separate the parts of some compound nouns and adjectives.**

COMPOUND NOUNS	father-in-law, stand-in, pom-pom
COMPOUND ADJECTIVES	far-off, fast-food, do-it-yourself

Note: Compound adjectives are usually hyphenated when they come before a noun. You should *never* hyphenate a compound adjective, however, that includes a word ending in the suffix *-ly.*

Hyphens with Certain Prefixes Certain prefixes and the suffix *-elect* are separated from their root words by a hyphen.

Rule 34q **Use a hyphen after the prefixes *ex-*, *self-*, and *all-* and before the suffix *-elect***

ex-convict, self-addressed, all-out, president-elect

Also use a hyphen with all prefixes before a proper noun or a proper adjective.

pre-Civil War, pro-American, mid-October, pre-Christmas

EXERCISE 13 *Using Hyphens*

Number your paper 1 to 10. Then correctly write each word that should be hyphenated. If no word in the sentence needs a hyphen, write *C* after the number.

1. Last night Alex and Allie attended the pre Olympic trials for figure skating.
2. Three fourths of the proceeds went toward new equipment for the gym.
3. Twenty five years from now I'll be thirty five years old.
4. Greg, the ex captain of the Valley High School football team, is an all around athlete.
5. The mayor elect will take office in January.
6. The members could not vote, since a two thirds majority was not present.
7. It is important that you learn to be self sufficient.
8. My cousin, an attorney at law, has set up an office in the new building on Main Street.
9. Twenty one days in Hawaii is the prize.
10. The all Indian council will meet with the President.

Hyphens to Divide Words Although you should avoid dividing words when possible, sometimes it is necessary to divide words in your writing.

Rule 34r **Use a hyphen to divide a word at the end of a line.**

The following guidelines will help you divide words correctly.

Guidelines for Dividing Words

1. Divide words only between syllables.

   production: pro-duction or produc-tion

2. Never divide a one-syllable word.
   strap pour match joint

3. Never separate a one-letter syllable from the rest of the word; for example, the following words should never be divided.

   DO NOT BREAK a-mong e-ven u-nite

4. Two-letter divisions are permissible at the end of a line, but two-letter word endings should not be carried over to the next line.

   BREAK in-fant de-fense en-dear
   DO NOT BREAK loss-es ful-ly mon-ey

5. Usually divide words containing double consonants between the double consonants.
   tomor-row shim-mer run-ning oc-cur
6. Divide hyphenated words only after the hyphens.
   mother-in-law double-decker flip-flop
7. Do not divide a proper noun or a proper adjective.
   Henderson Pacific Detroit American

EXERCISE 14 *Using Hyphens to Divide Words*

Write each word, adding a hyphen or hyphens to show where the word can be divided. If a word should not be divided, write *no* after the number. Then check your answers in the dictionary.

1. enthrone
2. envelop
3. even
4. heather
5. midway
6. might
7. necessary
8. negative
9. prince
10. printer
11. proxy
12. rapport
13. recommend
14. Rogers
15. secret
16. serious
17. stretch
18. three-ring
19. tropical
20. well-wisher

Dashes and Parentheses

In some situations dashes and parentheses are used like commas. They separate certain words or groups of words from the rest of a sentence. There are, however, slight distinctions among the uses of the three marks of punctuation.

Dashes Dashes indicate a greater separation between words than commas do. They can be used in the following situations.

Rule 34s **Use dashes to set off an abrupt change in thought.**

The Caspian Sea—the name *sea* is misleading—is by far the largest lake in the world.

Rule 34t **Use dashes to set off an appositive that is introduced by words such as *that is, for example,* or *for instance.***

Some family names —for example, Baker, Butler, and Gardner—come from occupations.

Some plants—for instance, the pitcher, the sidesaddle, and the sundew—devour insects.

Rule 34u **Use dashes to set off a parenthetical expression or an appositive that includes commas.**

Thomas Jefferson—scientist, architect, philosopher—was truly a great person.

Three scientists—Finlay, Reed, and Theiler—are responsible for conquering yellow fever.

Note: You can write or type a dash by placing two hyphens together. Do not leave space before or after the hyphens.

Parentheses When using parentheses, remember that they come in pairs.

Rule 34v **Use parentheses to enclose additional information that is not needed in a sentence.**

The ostrich (usually pictured with its head in the sand) can run faster than any other bird.

EXERCISE 15 *Using Dashes and Parentheses*

Number your paper 1 to 10. Then write the following sentences, adding dashes and parentheses where needed.

1. Clara Weick Schumann composer, pianist, and music teacher was married to composer Robert Schumann.
2. Our school supports many sports for example, soccer, tennis, field hockey, and lacrosse.
3. We saw 24 yes, we counted them bluebirds.
4. Is it true that some African animals for instance, the camel and the tiger once roamed the American continent?
5. We had quite a time at our house the week my cousins I have five of them stayed with us.
6. The newspaper *Pravda* which means "truth" in Russian was begun in 1912.
7. Six men Balboa, Ponce de León, Cortés, de Soto, Pizarro, and Coronado explored the interior of America.
8. Pound for pound, the peanut dieters beware has more calories than sugar!
9. Some reptiles for example, the toad and the alligator may live 25 years or more.
10. Over 100 million Americans that is more than half of the population read one or more comic strips regularly.

EXERCISE 16 Cumulative Review

Number your paper 1 to 25. Then write each sentence, adding punctuation marks where needed. If a sentence does not need any punctuation, write *C* after the number.

1. Throughout history legal tender has included all of the following hides glass beads and pigs jawbones.
2. Florida produces about 70 percent of the worlds grapefruit.
3. Three presidents Thomas Jefferson John Adams and James Monroe died on the Fourth of July.
4. Eyeglasses once commanded respect they suggested learning and importance.
5. I think this is everyones favorite song.
6. There are three types of tea black green and oolong.

7. Bulls can see no colors at all consequently they do not react to red.
8. The wingspread of a Boeing 747 195.7 feet from tip to tip is longer than the distance covered by the Wright brothers initial flight.
9. Over one fifth of the population of the United States lived in Virginia at the beginning of the nineteenth century.
10. The average American three year old spends more time watching television than participating in any other single activity.
11. Eskimos wear sunglasses theyve been wearing them for 2,000 years to ward off snow blindness.
12. Some English words that are derived from Indian words are *skunk woodchuck* and *toboggan.*
13. The Roller Derby is not an all womens sport.
14. Several birds for example the cassowary and the kiwi have lost the ability to fly.
15. Wade McGee however owns a one sixth share in his fathers manufacturing company.
16. The earth is not perfectly round it is flattened at the poles.
17. Many animals the cow the goat the reindeer the yak the llama and the buffalo give milk for human consumption.
18. Havent you received your first weeks salary yet?
19. I suggested the names Marvin, Harry, and George for the new cat but my sister chose the name Tiger.
20. Last summer we camped out in three national parks Glacier Yellowstone and Yosemite.
21. This pocket sized calculator runs by solar power.
22. Some cities that have been the capital of the United States are Philadelphia Pennsylvania New York New York Baltimore Maryland and Trenton New Jersey.
23. Well drive if the weather permits otherwise well fly.
24. Putting two *c*s in *recommend* is a common error.
25. The gestation period the time from conception to birth is almost two years for an elephant.

Application to Writing

If you had to live out your life as an animal, what animal would you be? Write a paragraph that tells the reasons for your choice. Be sure to punctuate the paragraph correctly.

Integrating Language Skills

USING YOUR TEXT

Personal Essays (270–297)

Mechanics: Editing for Correct Punctuation

Incorrect punctuation or missing punctuation can cause confusion for your reader. Therefore it is always important to edit your writing for correct punctuation.

Checking Your Understanding Read the following paragraphs aloud. Then write the two paragraphs adding whatever punctuation marks may be needed.

Earthquakes

If the crust of the earth werent mostly solid, it would be shaking constantly. There are places they are technically called faults in the rocks of the earths crust where it isnt held together. Sometimes, along one of these breaks in the crust, one rock mass will rub against another with tremendous force. The energy of this rubbing is then changed to vibration in the rocks consequently an earthquake is formed.

There are two ways in which an earthquake is described in terms of size one is by noting the force of the earthquake itself, and the other is by reporting the amount of damage it does. The greatest earthquake in North American history occurred in San Francisco, California, in 1906. Seven hundred people died property damage amounted to about $425 million. More recently earthquakes in the Los Angeles and San Francisco areas caused more than a billion dollars worth of damage. Other great earthquakes have occurred in Lisbon Portugal Sicily Italy and Tokyo Japan.

Writing a Personal Essay Think about the saying "No guts, no glory." Then write freely for several minutes, jotting down everything that comes to mind as you think of that saying. You may want to write your personal definition of this saying, examples of what it means, or your reaction to the saying. Then organize your notes in a short outline and write the first draft of your essay. ***Application:*** As you edit your essay, double-check for correct punctuation. Then write a final draft.

Chapter 34 Review

A **Using Correct Punctuation** Number your paper 1 to 20. Then write each sentence, adding punctuation where needed.

1. We will be taking our vacation in mid August.
2. Seventy five dollars was the original cost for speaking on the telephone for three minutes between London and New York.
3. A number of chickens I estimated at least 16 have escaped through a hole in the fence.
4. Egg-drop soup is made from the following ingredients eggs chicken broth and noodles.
5. That rabbits foot is Mikes good luck charm.
6. A lobster has five pairs of legs four pairs are used for walking.
7. Horse shows will be held in Pittsburgh Pennsylvania Dayton Ohio and Richmond Virginia.
8. Its an hours drive from Concord, New Hampshire, to my grandparents house.
9. The four fastest growing products in the United States are computers air conditioners video recorders and boats.
10. Garlic probably first grew in southern Siberia however it is now found in Asia and the Mediterranean area.
11. For our new apartment, we had to buy new curtains bedspreads and towels but we bought them all on sale.
12. Sharks teeth replace themselves as they wear out.
13. A two thirds majority voted for passage of the amendment.
14. Have you seen Dan and his fathers new boat?
15. Many languages for example, English German Swedish French and Italian come from a common source.
16. Isnt your appointment at 930 A.M.?
17. I need my lucky catchers mitt for the all star game today.
18. A quarter has 119 grooves along its circumference a dime has 118.
19. Dogs have been known to have very large litters for example one dog had a litter of 23 puppies.
20. Five states were admitted to the Union after 1900 New Mexico Oklahoma Arizona Alaska and Hawaii.

B Editing for Correct Punctuation Write the following paragraphs, adding punctuation where needed.

Charles Hatfield, modern historys greatest rainmaker, built his reputation by doing the following filling lakes, saving crops, and ending droughts. His greatest feat occurred in 1916 in San Diego, California. He promised to fill the citys reservoir for ten thousand dollars; however, he wouldnt accept payment if no rain fell. Hatfields offer was instantly accepted. After all, the reservoir had never been more than one third full since it was built.

Five days after Hatfield had prepared his special mixture it worked through a process of chemical evaporation, rain began to fall. Twenty one days later the rain stopped all but five inches of the reservoir had been filled. His all out effort had been enormously successful! The members of the City Council, however, were not pleased in fact, they refused to pay Hatfield. The rain had caused enormous damage such as 200 destroyed bridges, thousands of demolished houses, and miles of ruined railroad tracks.

Mastery Test

Number your paper 1 to 10. Then write each sentence, adding apostrophes, semicolons, colons, and hyphens where needed.

1. Tryouts will be held in the towns auditorium on the following days Monday, Wednesday, and Friday.
2. Have you ever seen a wolfs den?
3. Thirty six members were present only 22 voted.
4. The first half of the movie was good however, I slept through the second half.
5. Someones jacket was left in the cafeteria.
6. Too many *and*s and *or*s connect your sentences.
7. We will have dinner at my sister in laws house.
8. We need to buy several things for the party paper plates, refreshments, and decorations.
9. The mayor elect will make a speech on television tonight.
10. I earned twenty dollars for five hours work.

Appendix

Using a Word Processor

Word processors have features that will help you in all stages of the writing process. When using a word processor (or a computer, a keyboard, and a word-processing program), you can open and name documents, create and store files, and input drafts on the monitor. After drafting compositions, you can then revise, edit, and even publish them. If you take the time to master word-processing skills, you will be able to accomplish writing assignments more easily and quickly than by writing in longhand or using a typewriter.

The conveniences of word processing are available through *word-processing programs* of which there are several. Some programs offer more special features than others. Once you learn the program available to you, though, you can easily convert to another.

Even though they recognize the advantages of word processing, many students are reluctant to meet the challenge because they do not type. While learning typewriting skills early in your schooling is to your advantage, you can still pick up those skills as you learn word processing. In fact, many find it easier to learn to type this way because of the capabilities of most word-processing programs.

Prewriting

Almost any prewriting activity that you complete with paper and pencil can be done on a word processor. For example, you can input journal entries, freewrite, brainstorm, and use computer conferencing to explore subjects. You can create files listing ideas for possible writing subjects and then add to those lists any time you have a new idea. You could even have separate subject files for each of the different writing purposes and list "Things I Could *Explain*," "Things I Would Like to *Describe*," "Things I Would Like to *Persuade* Others to Think or Do," "Thoughts and Feelings I Would Like to *Express*," and "Ideas to *Create* Stories, Poems, and Plays." Once you have named and stored your subject files, you can read them at any time at the touch of a key. Following are some other strategies for using the word processor when prewriting.

Prewriting on a Word Processor

1. Create a subject file by inputting your answers to questions for exploring your interests and knowledge. *(See page 10.)*
2. Create a reader's response file in which you record your responses to literature. *(See pages 305–315.)*
3. Store your Learning Log in the computer or on a disk and update it by logging in interesting information that you learn in other subject areas. *(See page 13.)*
4. Explore a subject by listing elements or aspects of it, possible main ideas for a composition about it, possible working thesis statements, and supporting details. *(See pages 203–210.)*
5. Freewrite about your observations, experimenting with descriptive and sensory details. *(See pages 19 and 146–147.)*
6. List questions for developing a subject through inquiring. *(See page 23.)*
7. Input audience profiles or freewrite letters to real or imaginary members of your audience to help clarify your ideas. *(See pages 17, 206, 251, and 281.)*
8. If you are working on computers that are interconnected, use computer conferencing to explore a subject through dialogue with a partner. For group brainstorming, you and your classmates can keyboard questions and responses directly onto one another's monitors.

Collecting and Organizing Information When you are writing expository essays or reports, you can use the word processor to help you gather and organize the information you need. If your computer is linked to an information network, for instance, you can use electronic bulletin boards to access data bases—computerized reference materials. You may even be able to communicate by electronic mail with experts on your subject. Then, as you gather information, you can maintain a computer file listing all your sources. Some programs will automatically generate footnotes or entries in the correct form for a works cited page. *(See pages 368–370.)*

Whatever your writing purpose is, take advantage of any software available to you that lets you create clusters, diagrams, outlines, and charts for classifying, comparing, or contrasting. Even without special software, grouping and ordering ideas and information are easy on a word processor because a keyboard command lets you copy and move, or cut and paste, blocks of text. *(See pages 20–22 and 211–217.)*

Drafting

On a word processor, drafting is a simple procedure. You can keyboard freely—type and enter commands—without worrying about the ends of lines, the beginnings of paragraphs, or any mechanical errors. By scrolling back and forth, you can read your document on the monitor and work on any part of it at any time. Keyboard functions let you move back and forth between drafting and revising as you rearrange, delete, or insert words, sentences, and paragraphs. Because you can delete any unwanted writing at the touch of a key, you are free to include alternative ways of expressing an idea or alternative versions of an introduction or of a conclusion. Following are a few tips for using a word processor effectively when drafting.

Drafting with a Word Processor

1. Start by setting the format so that all your writing will automatically be in standard manuscript form. Double- or triple-space for easy marking on printed copies.
2. With your outline on the monitor, expand your outline into a composition by inserting writing after each heading.
3. Save your work often—about every 20 minutes—and print copies often to work on when you are not at the computer.

Revising

When you are ready to revise, you will find that working on a word processor really saves time. Furthermore, writers are far more likely to revise when they can eliminate the dreary task of hand-copying several versions of a corrected draft. Once you have completed your draft, you can use networking, or electronic conferencing, to help evaluate your work. After reading your composition on their monitors, for example, your classmates or other readers can directly input their reactions, questions, and suggestions for improving your draft. Another timesaving strategy is to store revision checklists in the computer or on a disk for easy reference. You can also use software that includes a dictionary and a thesaurus to help you check your spelling and improve your word choices. The following examples suggest ways to use the word processor when you revise.

Revising on the Word Processor

1. Use the INSERT command to add ideas, details, transitions between sentences and paragraphs, and parenthetical citations.
2. Use the MOVE or CUT and PASTE command to rearrange the order of words, sentences, and paragraphs.
3. DELETE unnecessary words and details and any sentences or paragraphs that detract from the unity of your composition.
4. Use the FIND or SEARCH and REPLACE feature to substitute words and phrases.

Editing and Publishing

The same keyboarding functions that help in revising also help in editing. For instance, you can use the SEARCH and REPLACE command to correct automatically a particular kind of error in all the places where it occurs. In addition, most word-processing programs have a SPELL feature that automatically checks your spelling.

Before you edit your revised draft, mark final corrections on a copy—or printout—using proofreading marks. To guide you in marking your copy, you could store your Personalized Editing Checklist and other editing checklists in the computer or on a disk for quick reference.

Word processors make publishing your work a creative challenge. You can experiment with the design features of the computer program to enhance the layout and appearance of your composition before the final printout. Design features include different sizes, styles, and decorative treatments of type, called fonts. Many programs also let you use files of ready-made graphics, or even let you create graphics of your own.

Printing out a manuscript that you have designed yourself and giving it to your readers to enjoy can give you great satisfaction. Remember, however, that you can publish electronically too. In electronic publishing you share your work with readers through electronic mail or on a network bulletin board.

From prewriting to publishing, word processing simplifies many aspects of the writing process and saves time. It also gives you convenient new ways to keep records and to express your creativity. Although using a word processor cannot automatically make you a good writer, it can help you in many ways to do your best.

Useful Conventions in Writing

In addition to using standard manuscript form, you should always proofread your completed work carefully. Also keep in mind the following guidelines—as well as the usage, mechanics, and spelling chapters in this book.

Dividing Words Although you should avoid dividing words whenever possible, sometimes doing so is necessary to keep the right-hand margin of your paper fairly even. Follow the rules on page 823 for dividing words.

Writing Numbers In general, spell out the numbers one through ten. Use numerals for numbers above ten.

two ten 11 46 238 7,145 2,980,124

To avoid six or more zeros, a combination of numerals and words should be used.

three million 42 million 85 billion 6.7 billion

Always spell out a number at the beginning of a sentence or revise the sentence if you prefer to use numerals.

Two hundred forty-three fans saw the season opener.
The season opener drew **243** fans.

Use numerals for dates, street and room numbers, page numbers, percents, decimals, and times with A.M. and P.M.

March 7, 1850 room 7 page 9 8 percent 6:45 A.M.

Using Abbreviations Most abbreviations should be avoided in formal writing. Do not abbreviate names of states, countries, days of the week, months, weights, or measurements. See page 773 for examples of abbreviations that are acceptable in formal writing.

Quoting Long Passages When you write a report, you might want to support a point by quoting a passage from a book or some other source. When quoting a passage of more than one paragraph, place quotation marks at the beginning of each paragraph—but at the end of only the last paragraph. *(See page 804.)* Remember to give credit to the author for the quoted material. *(see pages 366–370.)*

Glossary of Terms

A

Abbreviation An abbreviation is a shortened form of a word. A period is used after most abbreviations. *(See page 773.)*

Action verb An action verb tells what action a subject is performing. *(See page 553.)*

Active voice The active voice indicates that the subject is performing the action. *(See pages 121 and 675.)*

Adjective An adjective is a word that modifies a noun or a pronoun. *(See page 563.)*

Adjective clause An adjective clause is a subordinate clause that is used like an adjective to modify a noun or a pronoun. *(See page 630.)*

Adjective phrase An adjective phrase is a prepositional phrase that is used to modify a noun or a pronoun. *(See page 600.)*

Adverb An adverb is a word that modifies a verb, an adjective, or another adverb. *(See page 568.)*

Adverb clause An adverb clause is a subordinate clause used like an adverb to modify a verb, an adjective, or an adverb. *(See page 627.)*

Adverb phrase An adverb phrase is a prepositional phrase that is used like an adverb to modify a verb, an adjective, or an adverb. *(See page 601.)*

Alliteration Alliteration is the repetition of a consonant sound at the beginning of a series of words. *(See page 311.)*

Analogies Analogies show the logical relationships between pairs of words. *(See pages 466 and 506–507.)*

Antecedent An antecedent is the word or group of words that a pronoun replaces or refers to. *(See page 696.)*

Antonym An antonym is a word that means the opposite of another word. *(See page 465.)*

Appositive An appositive is a noun or a pronoun that identifies or explains another noun or pronoun in a sentence. *(See page 603.)*

Audience Audience is the person or persons who will read your work or hear your speech. *(See pages 17 and 439.)*

Autobiography An autobiography is a person's written account of his or her life. *(See page 192.)*

B

Brainstorming Brainstorming means writing down everything that comes to mind about a subject. *(See pages 20–21.)*

Business letter A business letter has six parts: the heading, inside address, salutation, body, closing, and signature. *(See pages 422–424.)*

C

Card catalog The card catalog is a cabinet of drawers containing author, title, and subject cards for all materials in a library. *(See pages 483–485.)*

Case Case is the form of a noun or a pronoun that indicates its use in a sentence. In English there are three cases: the *nominative case,* the *objective case,* and the *possessive case.* *(See page 681.)*

Characterization Characterization is a variety of techniques used by writers to show the personality of a character. *(See page 312.)*

Chronological order Chronological order arranges events in the order in which they happened. *(See page 139.)*

Classification Classification involves grouping similar types of information together into categories. *(See pages 101–102.)*

Clause A clause is a group of words that has a subject and a predicate. *(See page 625.)*

Cliché A cliché is a worn out, overused expression that has lost its power to call any clear images to a reader's mind. *(See page 55.)*

Clustering Clustering is a brainstorming technique in which the writer writes a subject at the center of a page, writes supporting details, and connects those details to the subject with lines. *(See page 22.)*

Coherence A paragraph or an essay has coherence if the ideas in it are presented in logical order with clear transitions. *(See pages 117, 118, and 185.)*

Colloquialism A colloquialism is an informal phrase or expression appropriate for conversation but not for formal writing. *(See page 458.)*

Comparative degree The comparative degree of a modifier is used when two people, things, or actions are compared. *(See page 725.)*

Comparison and contrast Comparison and contrast is a method of development in which the writer examines similarities and differences between two subjects. *(See pages 213–215.)*

Complement A complement is a word that completes the meaning of an action verb. *(See page 585.)*

Complete predicate A complete predicate includes all the words that tell what the subject is doing or that tell something about the subject. *(See page 528.)*

Complete subject A complete subject includes all the words used to identify the person, place, thing, or idea that the sentence is about. *(See page 526.)*

Complex sentence A complex sentence consists of one independent clause and one or more subordinate clauses. *(See page 638.)*

Compound-complex sentence A compound-complex sentence consists of two or more independent clauses and one or more subordinate clauses. *(See pages 638–639.)*

Compound noun A compound noun is a common noun with more than one word. *(See page 541.)*

Compound sentence A compound sentence consists of two or more independent clauses. *(See page 638.)*

Compound subject A compound subject is two or more subjects in one sentence that have the same verb and are joined by a conjunction. *(See page 531.)*

Compound verb A compound verb is two or more verbs that have the same subject and are joined by a conjunction. *(See page 531.)*

Concluding paragraph A concluding paragraph completes an essay and reinforces its main idea. *(See page 187.)*

Concluding sentence A concluding sentence adds a strong ending to a paragraph by summarizing, referring to the main idea, or adding an insight. *(See page 93.)*

Conjugation of a verb A conjugation of a verb lists all the singular and plural forms of a verb in its six tenses. *(See pages 667–670.)*

Conjunction A conjunction connects words or groups of words. *(See page 578.)*

Connotation The connotation of a word is the emotional meaning a word suggests. *(See page 54.)*

Context clue A context clue is the clue to a word's meaning provided by the sentence or passage in which the word is used. *(See page 460.)*

Contraction A contraction is a word that combines two words into one. It uses an apostrophe to replace any missing letters. *(See page 812.)*

Cooperative learning Cooperative learning occurs when a group works together to achieve a goal or accomplish a task. *(See pages 451–452.)*

Coordinating conjunction A coordinating conjunction is a single connecting word used to connect compound subjects, compound verbs, and compound sentences. *(See page 578.)*

Correlative conjunction Correlative conjunctions are pairs of conjunctions used to connect compound subjects, compound verbs, and compound sentences. *(See page 578.)*

D

Dangling modifier A dangling modifier is a phrase that has nothing to modify in a sentence. *(See page 616.)*

Declarative sentence A declarative sentence makes a statement or expresses an opinion and ends with a period. *(See page 771.)*

Demonstrative pronoun A demonstrative pronoun points out a person, a place, or a thing. *(See page 547.)*

Denotation The denotation of a word is the dictionary definition of a word. *(See page 54.)*

Descriptive paragraph A descriptive paragraph creates in words a vivid picture of a person, an object, or a scene. *(See page 144.)*

Developmental order In developmental order, information is organized so that one idea grows out of the preceding idea. *(See page 106.)*

Dewey decimal system The Dewey decimal system is used by libraries to arrange nonfiction books on shelves in numerical order. This order uses ten subject categories. *(See pages 481–483.)*

Dialogue A dialogue is a conversation between two or more persons. In writing, a new paragraph begins each time the speaker changes. *(See page 311.)*

Direct object A direct object is a noun or a pronoun that receives the action of a verb. *(See page 585.)*

Direct quotation A person's exact words are quoted in a direct quotation. Quotation marks are used before and after a direct quotation. *(See page 798.)*

Double negative A double negative is the use of two negative words to express an idea when only one is needed. *(See page 731.)*

E

Editing Editing is the stage of the writing process that follows revising. In this stage, writers polish their work by correcting errors and making a neat copy. *(See page 35.)*

Elliptical clause An elliptical clause is a subordinate clause in which words are omitted but understood to be there. *(See page 694.)*

Encyclopedia An encyclopedia contains general information about a variety of subjects. The information is arranged alphabetically by subject. A specialized encyclopedia focuses on one subject. *(See page 486.)*

Essay An essay is a composition that presents and develops one main idea in three or more paragraphs. *(See page 172.)*

Essential phrase or clause An essential phrase or clause is essential to the meaning of a sentence and is therefore not set off with commas. *(See page 787.)*

Etymology An etymology of a word is the history of a word from its earliest recorded use to its present use. *(See page 456.)*

Exclamatory sentence An exclamatory sentence expresses strong feeling and ends with an exclamation point. *(See page 772.)*

Expository paragraph An expository paragraph explains or informs with facts and examples or gives directions. *(See page 88.)*

F

Fact A fact is a statement that can be proved. *(See pages 246 and 447.)*

Fiction Fiction refers to prose works of literature, such as short stories and novels, that are partly or totally imaginary. *(See page 312.)*

Figurative language Figurative language is the imaginative, nonliteral use of language. *(See pages 55 and 147.)*

First draft Writing the first draft is the second stage of the writing process. At this stage writers use their prewriting notes to get their ideas on paper as quickly as possible. *(See page 28.)*

Freewriting Freewriting is a prewriting technique of nonstop writing that encourages the flow of ideas. *(See page 12.)*

G

Gerund A gerund is a verb form ending in *-ing* that is used as a noun. *(See page 610.)*

H

Helping verb A helping, or auxiliary, verb and the main verb make up a verb phrase. *(See page 529.)*

I

Idiom An idiom is a phrase or expression that has a meaning different from what the words suggest in their usual meanings. *(See page 458.)*

Imperative sentence An imperative sentence makes a request or gives a command and ends with either a period or an exclamation point. *(See page 771.)*

Indefinite pronoun An indefinite pronoun refers to an unnamed person or thing. *(See page 547.)*

Independent clause An independent (or main) clause can stand alone as a sentence because it expresses a complete thought. *(See page 625.)*

Indirect object An indirect object is a noun or a pronoun that answers the question *to or for whom?* or *to or for what?* after an action verb. *(See page 586.)*

Infinitive An infinitive is a verb form that usually begins with *to* and is used as a noun, an adjective, or an adverb. *(See page 613.)*

Inquiring Inquiring is a common prewriting technique in which the writer asks questions such as *Who? What? Where? When?* and *Why? (See page 23.)*

Interjection An interjection is a word that expresses strong feeling. *(See page 579.)*

Interrogative pronoun An interrogative pronoun is used to ask a question. *(See page 547.)*

Interrogative sentence An interrogative sentence asks a question and ends with a question mark. *(See page 772.)*

Intransitive verb An intransitive verb is an action verb that does not have an object. *(See pages 554–555.)*

Introduction An introduction to an essay introduces a subject, states or implies a purpose, and presents a main idea. *(See page 176.)*

Irregular verb An irregular verb does not form its past and past participle by adding *-ed* or *-d* to the present. *(See page 660.)*

J

Jargon Jargon is the specialized vocabulary used in particular professions. *(See page 458.)*

Journal A journal is a daily notebook in which a writer records thoughts and feelings. *(See page 13.)*

L

Linking verb A linking verb links the subject with another word in the sentence. This other word either renames or describes the subject. *(See page 555.)*

M

Metaphor A metaphor implies a comparison by saying that one thing *is* another. *(See pages 55 and 147.)*

Meter Meter is the rhythm of stressed and unstressed syllables in each line of a poem. *(See page 311.)*

Misplaced modifier A misplaced modifier is a phrase or a clause that is placed too far away from the word it modifies, thus creating an unclear sentence. *(See pages 616 and 634.)*

Mood Mood is the atmosphere or feeling created by a work of literature. *(See pages 164 and 389.)*

N

Narrative paragraph A narrative paragraph tells a real or an imaginary story. *(See page 137.)*

Nominative case The nominative case of a pronoun is used for subjects and predicate nominatives. *(See page 682.)*

Nonessential phrase or clause A nonessential phrase or clause is not essential to the meaning of a sentence and is therefore set off with commas. *(See page 786.)*

Nonfiction Nonfiction is prose writing that contains facts about real people and real events. *(See page 303.)*

Noun A noun is a word that names a person, a place, a thing, or an idea. A common noun gives a general name. A proper noun names a specific person, place, or thing and always begins with a capital letter. *(See pages 541–542.)*

Noun clause A noun clause is a subordinate clause that is used like a noun. *(See page 635.)*

Novel A novel is a long work of narrative fiction. *(See pages 303 and 312.)*

O

Objective case The objective case of a pronoun is used for direct objects, indirect objects, and objects of a preposition. *(See page 685.)*

Onomatopoeia Onomatopoeia is the use of words whose sounds suggest their meaning. *(See page 311.)*

Opinion An opinion is a judgment that varies from person to person. *(See pages 246 and 447.)*

Order of importance, interest, size, or degree Order of importance, interest, size, or degree is a way of organizing information by arranging details in the order of *least to most* or *most to least*. *(See pages 106 and 158.)*

Outline An outline organizes information about a subject into main topics and subtopics. *(See pages 216–217.)*

P

Paragraph A paragraph is a group of related sentences that present and develop one main idea. *(See page 88.)*

Parenthetical citation A parenthetical citation is a brief reference in the body of a research paper to the source of borrowed information. *(See page 368.)*

Participial phrase A participial phrase is a participle with its modifiers and complements—all working together as an adjective. *(See page 608.)*

Participle A participle is a verb form that is used as an adjective. *(See page 607.)*

Passive voice The passive voice indicates that the action of a verb is being performed upon its subject. *(See pages 121 and 675.)*

Peer conference A peer conference is a meeting with one's peers, such as other students, to share information and ideas. Peer conferences are commonly used as a prewriting and revising strategy. *(See pages 21, 33 and 34.)*

Personal pronoun A personal pronoun refers to a particular person, place, thing, or idea. *(See page 545.)*

Persuasive paragraph A persuasive paragraph states an opinion and uses facts, examples, and reasons to convince readers. *(See page 154.)*

Phrase A phrase is a group of related words that function as a single part of speech and do not have a subject and a verb. *(See page 599.)*

Play A play is a composition written for dramatic performance on the stage. *(See page 311.)*

Plot Plot consists of the events in a story or a play. *(See page 311.)*

Poem A poem is a highly structured composition with condensed, vivid language, figures of speech, and often the use of meter and rhyme. *(See page 311.)*

Point of view In first person point of view, the narrator takes part in the story. In third person point of view, the narrator tells what happens to others and is not a character in the story. *(See pages 140 and 311.)*

Possessive pronoun A possessive pronoun is used to show ownership or possession. *(See page 689.)*

Predicate adjective A predicate adjective is an adjective that follows a linking verb and modifies the subject. *(See page 589.)*

Predicate nominative A predicate nominative is a noun or a pronoun that follows a linking verb and identifies, renames, or explains the subject. *(See page 588.)*

Prefix A prefix is a word part that is added to the beginning of a word and changes its basic, or root, meaning. *(See page 462.)*

Preposition A preposition is a word that shows the relationship between a noun or a pronoun and another word in the sentence. *(See page 575.)*

Prepositional phrase A prepositional phrase is a group of words that begins with a preposition, ends with a noun or a pronoun, and is used as an adjective or an adverb. *(See pages 576 and 599.)*

Prewriting Prewriting is the first stage of the writing process. It includes all the planning steps that come before writing the first draft. *(See page 10.)*

Principal parts of a verb The principal parts of a verb are the *present*, the *past*, and the *past participle*. The principal parts help form the tenses of verbs. *(See page 659.)*

Pronoun A pronoun is a word that takes the place of one or more nouns. *(See page 545.)*

Proofreading symbols Proofreading symbols are a kind of shorthand that writers use to correct their mistakes while editing. *(See pages 36–37.)*

Propaganda Propaganda is the effort to persuade by distorting and misrepresenting information or by disguising opinions as facts. *(See page 447.)*

Protagonist A protagonist is the principal character in a story. *(See page 418.)*

Publishing Publishing is the final stage of the writing process. At this stage, writers present their work to an audience in final correct form. *(See page 40.)*

Purpose In writing, purpose is the reason for writing. *(See pages 16–17.)* The purpose of a speech is the reason for speaking *(See page 439.)*

R

Readers' Guide to Periodical Literature The *Readers' Guide* is an index of magazine and journal articles. *(See pages 487– 488.)*

Regular verb A regular verb forms its past and past participle by adding *-ed* or *-d* to the present. *(See page 659.)*

Relative pronoun A relative pronoun relates an adjective clause to the modified noun or pronoun. *(See page 630.)*

Research paper A research paper is a composition of three or more paragraphs that uses information from books, magazines, and other sources. *(See page 346.)*

Revising Revising is the third stage of the writing process. At this stage a writer changes a draft as often as needed to improve it. *(See page 30.)*

Rhyme scheme Rhyme scheme is a pattern of rhymed sounds at the end of lines in a poem. *(See page 311.)*

Root A root is the part of a word that carries the basic meaning. *(See page 462.)*

Run-on sentence A run-on sentence is two or more sentences that are written as one sentence. They are separated by a comma or have no mark of punctuation at all. *(See pages 651 and 652.)*

S

Sensory word A sensory word appeals to one of the five senses: seeing, hearing, touching, tasting, and smelling. *(See page 146.)*

Sentence A sentence is a group of words that expresses a complete thought. *(See page 525.)*

Sentence combining Sentence combining is the method of combining short sentences into longer, more fluent sentences by using phrases and clauses. *(See pages 62–66.)*

Sentence fragment A sentence fragment is a group of words that does not express a complete thought. *(See pages 38 and 647.)*

Sequential order In a paragraph that gives directions or steps in a process, sequential order presents the details in the proper sequence. *(See page 107.)*

Setting The setting is the location and time of a story. *(See page 311.)*

Short story A short story is a short work of narrative fiction. *(See page 386.)*

Simile A simile states a comparison by using the word *like* or *as*. *(See pages 46, 55 and 147.)*

Simple predicate A simple predicate, or verb, is the main word or phrase in a complete predicate. *(See page 528.)*

Simple sentence A simple sentence consists of one independent clause. *(See page 638.)*

Simple subject A simple subject is the main word in the complete subject. *(See page 526.)*

Slang Slang expressions are nonstandard expressions developed and used by particular groups. *(See page 458.)*

Sound devices Sound devices are ways to use sounds in poetry to achieve certain effects. *(See page 311.)*

Spatial order Spatial order arranges details according to their location. *(See page 148.)*

Speech A speech is an oral composition presented by a speaker to an audience. *(See page 438.)*

Subordinate clause A subordinate (or dependent) clause cannot stand alone because it does not express a complete thought. *(See page 625.)*

Subordinating conjunction A subordinating conjunction is used in a complex sentence to introduce an adverb clause. *(See pages 627–628.)*

Suffix A suffix is a word part that is added to the end of a word and changes its basic, or root, meaning. *(See page 462.)*

Superlative degree The superlative degree of a modifier is used when more than two people, things, or actions are compared. *(See page 725.)*

Supporting sentences Supporting sentences explain or prove a topic sentence with specific details, facts, examples, or reasons. *(See page 92.)*

Synonym A synonym is a word that has nearly the same meaning as another word. *(See page 465.)*

T

Tense Tense is the form a verb takes to show time. The six tenses are the *present, past, future, present perfect, past perfect,* and *future perfect. (See page 667.)*

Theme Theme is the underlying idea, message, or meaning of a work of literature. *(See pages 124 and 311.)*

Thesaurus A thesaurus is a special dictionary that gives several synonyms for one word. *(See page 465.)*

Thesis statement A thesis statement states the main idea and makes the purpose of an essay clear. *(See pages 178 and 218.)*

Timed writing Timed writing is an essay test that must be written in a prescribed amount of time. *(See page 519.)*

Tone Tone is the attitude of a writer toward the subject of a composition. *(See pages 176 and 311.)*

Topic sentence A topic sentence states the main idea of a paragraph. *(See page 89.)*

Transitions Transitions are words and phrases that show how ideas are related. *(See pages 139, 148, and 158.)*

Transitive verb A transitive verb is an action verb that has an object. *(See pages 554–555.)*

U

Understood subject An understood subject of a sentence is a subject that is understood rather than stated. *(See page 533.)*

Unity A paragraph or an essay has unity if all the supporting sentences relate to the main idea expressed in the topic sentence. *(See pages 116 and 185.)*

V

Verbal A verbal is a verb form used as some other part of speech. *(See page 607.)*

Verb phrase A verb phrase is a main verb plus one or more helping verbs. *(See pages 529 and 553.)*

W

Working thesis A working thesis is a preliminary thesis statement that is refined in the process of writing. *(See page 210.)*

Works cited page A works cited page comes at the end of a research paper and lists all the sources cited in the paper. *(See page 370.)*

Index

A

Q

R

U

V

W

Acknowledgments

The authors and editors have made every effort to trace the ownership of all copyrighted selections found in this book and to make full acknowledgment of their use. Grateful acknowledgment is made to the following authors, publishers, agents, and individuals for their permission to reprint copyrighted material.

Page 3: "Identity," by Julio Naboa Polanco, from *The Rican, Journal of Contemporary Thought,* copyright © 1973, reprinted by permission of the author. **4:** "Theme for English B," from *Montage of a Dream Deferred,* by Langston Hughes, copyright © 1951 by Langston Hughes; renewed © 1979 by George H. Bass, an Executor for the Estate of Langston Hughes. **6:** "I'm Nobody! Who Are You?" by Emily Dickinson. Reprinted by permission of the publishers and the Trustees of Amherst College, from *The Poems of Emily Dickinson,* Thomas H. Johnson, ed., Cambridge, MA: by the Belknap Press of Harvard University Press, copyright 1951, © 1955, 1979, 1983 by the President and Fellows of Harvard College. **6:** "Mirror," by John Updike, from *The Carpentered Hen,* by John Updike, copyright © 1957 by John Updike. By permission of Harper & Row, Publishers, Inc. **49:** "No Problem, but It Needs a Solution," from *Fatherhood,* by Bill Cosby, copyright © 1986 by William H. Cosby, Jr. Used by permission of Doubleday, a division of Bantam Doubleday Dell Publishing Group, Inc. **51:** "Primer Lesson," from *Slabs of the Sunburnt West,* by Carl Sandburg. Copyright © 1922 by Harcourt Brace Jovanovich, Inc., copyright 1950 by Carl Sandburg. Reprinted by permission of the publisher. **83:** "The Sounds of Richard Rodgers," from *At Large,* by Ellen Goodman. Copyright © 1981 by The Washington Post Company. Reprinted by permission of Summit Books, a division of Simon & Schuster, Inc. **124:** From *Opposites,* by Richard Wilbur, copyright © 1973 by Richard Wilbur. By permission of Harcourt Brace Jovanovich, Inc. **127:** From *West with the Night,* by Beryl Markham, copyright © 1983 by Beryl Markham. Published by North Point Press. Reprinted by permission. **167:** From "Fifth Chinese Daughter," abridged "Puritans of the Orient," by Jade Snow Wong, from *The Immigrant Experience.* Edited by Thomas C. Wheeler and used by permission. Copyright © 1971 by The Dial Press. **197:** "Dial versus Digital," by Isaac Asimov. Reprinted by permission of *American Way,* inflight magazine of American Airlines, copyright © 1985 by American Airlines. **235:** "The Obligation to Endure," by Rachel Carson, copyright © 1962 by Rachel Carson. Reprinted by permission of Houghton Mifflin Company. **271:** "The Jacket," from *Small Faces,* by Gary Soto, copyright © 1986 by Gary Soto. Reprinted by permission of Arte Publico Press, University of Houston. **299:** "Courage," from *The Awful Rowing toward God,* by Anne Sexton. Copyright © 1975 by Loring Conant, Jr., Executor of Estate of Anne Sexton. By permission of Harcourt Brace Jovanovich, Inc. **300:** "The Courage That My Mother Had," by Edna St. Vincent Millay, from *Collected Poems,* Harper & Row. Copyright 1954 by Norma Millay Ellis. **307:** "The Explorer," from *BLACKS,* by Gwendolyn Brooks. Copyright © 1987, The David Company, Chicago, Publishers. Used by permission of the author. **308:** "The Road Not Taken," from *The Poetry of Robert Frost,* edited by Edward Connery Lathem. Copyright 1916. © 1969 by Holt, Rinehart and Winston. Copyright 1936, 1942, 1944 by Robert Frost. Copyright © 1964, 1970 by Lesley Frost Ballantine. Reprinted by permission of Holt, Rinehart and Winston, Publishers, and Jonathan Cape Ltd., for the Estate of Robert Frost. **336:** "The Coach of Life," translated by Babette Deutsch, from *The Works of Alexander Pushkin,* by Alexander Pushkin, edited by Avram Yarmolinsky. Copyright 1936 and renewed © 1964 by Random House, Inc. Reprinted by permission of Random House, Inc. **339:** "The Pedestrian," by Ray Bradbury, copyright 1951, © renewed 1979 by Ray Bradbury. Reprinted by permission of the Harold Matson Company, Inc. **381:** From "Ghost Town," from *The Collected Stories of Jack Schaefer.* Copyright 1954. Copyright © renewed 1982 by Jack Schaefer. Reprinted by permission of Harold Matson Company, Inc.

Cover Design: Studio Goodwin-Sturges. Illustration: Mahler Ryder. Calligraphy: Colleen

Unit Openers Design: Studio Goodwin-Sturges. Photography by Ken O'Donoghue © D.C. Heath. Calligraphy: Colleen

Interior Calligraphy Lisa Tarca

Illustrations **2–7:** Debra Strick. **8:** *b,* Patrice Rossi. **18:** Margery Mintz. **21:** Zita Asbaghi. **26:** Fran O'Neill. **44:** Amy L. Wasserman. **48–51:** Robert de Michiell. **72:** Catherine Bennett. **82–87:** Thomas Gonzalez. **94:** Fran O'Neill. **98:** William Cone.

105: Joan Hall. **126–135:** Winslow Pinney Pells. **159, 166–171:** Amy L. Wasserman. **175:** Diane Jaquith. **205:** Tom Norton. **222–223:** Margery Mintz. **234–239:** Linda Scharf. **252:** Chris Pinkerton. **256:** William Cone. **266:** Kevin Hawkes. **270–275:** Daniel Moreton. **294:** Amy L. Wasserman. **302:** *b*, Patrice Rossi. **304–305:** Tom Norton. **318:** Scott Webber. **334:** Joan Paley. **338–346:** Kevin Hawkes. **380–385:** Vince Capudo. **388–389:** William Cone. **398:** Joyce Tremain. **411:** Cynthia Carrozza.

Photography **8:** *Mirror and Plastic,* © Michael de Camp. **9:** Ralph Mercer, © D.C. Heath. **19:** *Hand with Reflecting Globe,* M.C. Escher, 1935. © 1990 M.C. Escher Heirs/Cordon Art, Baarn, Holland. **23:** Michael Moseley/Anthro-Photo. **27:** *Four Corrugated Cubes from One,* 1980. Original 20″ × 24″ Polaroid © Robert Cumming. Photo by Stephen Petegorsky. **30:** Library of Congress. **34:** David Jeffrey/The Image Bank. **52:** *The Scrabble Game, Jan. 1, 1983.* Photographic collage, 39″ × 58″. © David Hockney. **60:** © Audrey Gibson. **63:** © Jordan Coonrad. **65:** *l*, The University of Pennsylvania Archives; *r*, Mark Gottlieb/FPG International. **67:** Peter Veit/DRK Photo. **78:** *l&r*, Photofest. **88:** © Francine Zaslow. **122:** © Jon Goell. **136:** UPI/Bettmann. **138:** *Italy,* Francesco Clemente, 1983. Pastel on paper, 28″ × 18″. Philadelphia Museum of Art: Hunt Manufacturing Company, Arts Collection Program. **149:** Pete Turner/The Image Bank. **150:** J. Taposchaner/FPG International. **162:** Kevin Horan/Stock Boston. **172:** Joe Viesti/Viesti Associates, Inc. **174:** Michael Holford. **183:** Globus Brothers/The Stock Market. **185:** Joe Viesti/Viesti Associates, Inc. **190:** © Jerome F. Shaw. **196–201:** Ralph Mercer, (197*c*, 199*l* © D.C. Heath). **202:** Ron Lowery/Tony Stone Worldwide, Chicago. **206:** *Unfruitful Search for the Planet Leverrier,* Honore Daumier. Lithograph. Delteil 1531. Armand Hammer Foundation, Los Angeles, CA. **208:** Julian Baum, Science Photo Library/Photo Researchers, Inc. **212:** N. Ross/FPG International. **215:** John P. Kelly/The Image Bank. **230:** Jim Heemstra/Picture Group. **233:** Ralph Mercer, © D.C. Heath. **242:** Herbert S. Terrace/Anthro-Photo. **245:** Yerkes Regional Primate Research Center of Emory University. **254:** Robert Brenner/PhotoEdit. **276:** *Coathangers,* © Sandy Skoglund. **279:** Mike Yamashita / Woodfin Camp & Associates, New York. **286:** *Beach Umbrella,* 1971. Acrylic on Canvas, 48″ x 35¾″. © David Hockney. **288:** © D.C. Heath. **298–301:** Scott Kuckler, © D.C. Heath. **302:** *tl*, Bettmann Archive; *tr*, UPI/Bettmann; *bl*, Burt Glinn/Magnum Photos, Inc.; *br*, UPI/Bettmann. **305:** *overprint*, Jerry Howard, © D.C. Heath. **307:** *The Subway,* George Tooker, 1950. Egg tempera on composition board, 18″ × 36″. Collection of Whitney Museum of American Art. Juliana Force Purchase 50.23. **308:** *The Puddle,* M.C. Escher, 1952. Woodcut. © 1990 M.C. Escher Heirs/Cordon Art, Baarn, Holland. **313:** *Photo-Transformation,* Lucas Samaras, 11/1/73. Los Angeles County Museum of Art. Ralph M. Parsons Fund. **327:** Joe Palmieri/AFI Photo Illustrations. **347:** Doug Mindell, © D.C. Heath. **351:** Ken Biggs/Photo Researchers, Inc. **355:** National Archives. **357:** *The Bicycle Race,* Lyonel Feininger, 1912. Oil on canvas, 31⅝″ × 39½″. National Gallery of Art, Washington, D.C.; collection of Mr. and Mrs. Paul Mellon. **360:** *The Builders No. 1,* Jacob Armstead Lawrence, 1970. Gouache on paper, 22″ × 30″. Henry Art Gallery, University of Washington, Seattle. Gift of the artist. **367:** © Alan & Sandy Carey. **370:** Public domain. **376:** *Statue of Liberty Crying,* © Cosimo. **378:** The Bettmann Archive. **386:** *Beancils,* © Bruno Photography. **395:** Steve Dunwell/The Image Bank. **398:** *Witness,* Joyce Treiman, 1988. Collection of ARA Services, Inc., Philadelphia, PA. **403:** *Gregory Walking, Venice, California,* February, 1983. Photographic collage, 12″ × 23″. © David Hockney. **407:** *The Artist and His Mother,* Arshile Gorky, circa 1926–36. Oil on canvas, 60″ × 50″. Collection of Whitney Museum of American Art. Gift of Julien Levy for Maro and Natasha Gorky in memory of their father. Purchase 50.17. **416:** © Doug Mindell. **440:** Photofest. **446:** Photofest. **452:** Photofest. **471:** Diane Lowe/Stock Boston. **475:** John Coletti/Stock Boston. **478:** Steven Gottlieb/FPG International. **482, 484, 485, 487, 488, 491, 493, 494, 495, 497:** Doug Mindell & Margery Mintz, © D.C. Heath.

Cartoons **96:** Drawing by Booth; © 1976 The New Yorker Magazine, Inc. **232:** The Far Side © 1987 Universal Press Syndicate. Reprinted with permission. **240:** The Far Side, © 1990 Universal Press Syndicate. Reprinted with permission. **260:** Elivia Savadier © 1990. **328:** Drawing by Ziegler; © 1979 The New Yorker Magazine, Inc. **408:** Tamar Haber-Schaim. **459, 462:** Elivia Savadier © 1990. **500:** Peanuts by Charles M. Schulz. Reprinted with permission of United Feature Syndicate, Inc. **508:** The Far Side, © 1986 Universal Press Syndicate. Reprinted with permission. **512:** Calvin & Hobbes, © 1990 Universal Press Syndicate. Reprinted with permission. **515:** *Shoe,* by Jeff MacNelly. Reprinted by permission, Tribune Media Services © 1990. **518:** The Far Side, © 1986 Universal Press Syndicate. Reprinted with permission. ***Picture Research*** Connie Komack/Pictures and Words